WILLIAM BECKFORD
A Bibliography

WILLIAM BECKFORD

A Bibliography

——

JON MILLINGTON

THE BECKFORD SOCIETY
2008

© Jon Millington 2008

First published in Great Britain 2008
by The Beckford Society
The Timber Cottage, Crockerton, Warminster BA12 8AX

Typeset in Sabon
by Waveney Typesetters, Wymondham, Norfolk

Printed and bound in Great Britain
by Biddles Ltd, King's Lynn, Norfolk

Designed by Humphrey Stone

ISBN 978-0-9537836-3-2

Contents

Introduction

Beckford studies were greatly enriched by the publication in 1930 of Guy Chapman and John Hodgkin's *Bibliography of William Beckford of Fonthill*. It was a beautifully produced account of all known editions of Beckford's works published in his lifetime, with collotype facsimiles of the title pages. Since then the need to bring it up to date and extend its range has often been felt, in particular to track the many posthumous editions of Beckford's works, and to record the vast body of writing about him. It is for this reason that the present work has been prepared. Because of Beckford's contribution to a number of diverse fields apart from literature, such as architecture, landscape gardening and collecting, it seemed worthwhile to try to cover all these aspects in separate sections. In this way Beckford's influence from his lifetime onwards can begin to be appreciated.

Eight biographies, as well as a number of full-length studies, demonstrate the fascination that Beckford has exerted over the years. Perhaps the last half-century has seen the greatest expansion in academic and popular works, with a turning point being the bicentenary of his birth in 1960 which was marked by an exhibition at Yale and a smaller one at the British Museum. At the same time the Middle East's homage was a valuable collection of essays from the University of Cairo. Further exhibitions of ever-increasing size were to follow, beginning with a well-chosen group of objects at the Holburne Museum in Bath in 1966, enhanced by a finely printed and most informative catalogue that is prized by collectors today. Then, in 1976, came the wide-ranging William Beckford Exhibition which opened in Salisbury before transferring to Bath. Great attention was paid to creating suitable settings for the exhibits, including an inner sanctum containing some wonderful objects. In the 1980s and 1990s smaller exhibitions attracted visitors to Beckford's Tower in the summer months.

After many years of planning and extensive research the third, and most recent, major exhibition was staged in New York at the Bard Graduate Center for Studies in the Decorative Arts, Design and Culture in the autumn of 2001. Early in the following year it came to the Dulwich Picture Gallery in London. Accompanying the exhibition was a monumental catalogue that provides a reminder of the works of art shown, and is also of permanent value as a source of reference for future scholars and enthusiasts, containing as it does sixteen well-illustrated essays on many aspects of

Beckford. Selections from this bibliography previously appeared in that catalogue, *William Beckford 1760–1844: An Eye for the Magnificent*, published by the Bard Graduate Center for Studies in the Decorative Arts, Design and Culture in collaboration with Yale University Press.

Two other events stimulated a wide interest in Beckford. One was the formation of the Beckford Tower Trust by Dr and Mrs Hilliard in 1977. As a result the Tower became a focal point for those who were already interested in Beckford, or were prepared to be persuaded. Then, encouraged by the success of the Trust both under the Hilliards and, from 1993, under the more ample wing of Bath Preservation Trust, the Beckford Society was formed in 1995. Through lectures, visits and publications, the Society has sought to promote an understanding of the life and works of William Beckford. This aim is reflected in the present bibliography which is divided into two main sections: his life and his literature.

This bibliography covers works published up to the end of 2005 and concentrates on those printed in English and other European languages. For additional foreign sources, two studies are particularly valuable: André Parreaux, *William Beckford, Auteur de Vathek* (1960), and Maria Laura Bettencourt Pires, *William Beckford e Portugal* (1987). Several institutions hold manuscript material of the greatest interest and importance, and principal among these is the Bodleian Library, Oxford, where a vast archive of letters, literary drafts and other papers is held in the Department of Western Manuscripts. Another important collection is in the Beinecke Library at Yale University. Some information on these sources can be found on the Internet. Indeed there are many relevant websites offering information of varying degrees of reliability. Actual website addresses are not given in this work because they change or go out of date so rapidly.

Generally only the first edition of a work mentioning Beckford is cited, except when he does not appear until a later one. On the whole, reprints are not noted. Heights, where given, are to the nearest half centimetre and include the binding. For some early works the figure may be on the low side, depending on the binder's plough.

Most entries are in alphabetical order although in places chronological order seemed more informative. Cross-references have been kept to a minimum, partly by repeating an entry, for example, John Britton's two-volume *Auto-biography*, which is virtually two distinct works. In most cases an author's name is spelt as in the work cited. For instance, Gavin de Beer also appears as Sir Gavin de Beer and Gavin R. De. Beer.

When a periodical article subsequently appeared in book form it is only entered under 'articles', although this is followed by the title of the book, if known. However, any slight revisions are not noted. Volume numbers are given in Arabic numerals throughout, even if they are in Roman numerals in the original. Sometimes publishers confused matters by alternating between the two forms. No volume numbers have been given for some common periodicals such as *Country Life* and the *Times Literary Supplement*, while *The Athenæum* is one of the few not to have used volume numbers at all. The title of a review is not mentioned if it is the same as the work under review. Where possible the page numbers relevant to Beckford are given, as well as those for the whole chapter or article.

Whilst this bibliography is the most comprehensive listing of Beckford's works and references to him so far produced, there will inevitably be many omissions, especially of articles scattered in newspapers and elsewhere; in any case there are so many that it would be almost impossible to include all of them. Moreover, contemporary newspapers and periodicals copied widely from one another. Articles in most general encyclopaedias tend to cover the same ground and are omitted for this reason.

On the whole entries have been put where you would expect to find them, but there are instances where the title is misleading. For example, 'Fonthill Abbey' in Burke's *Anecdotes of the Aristocracy* (1850) is a general account of Beckford's life; on the other hand Peach, in his *Historic Houses in Bath* (1883), wrote primarily about Fonthill. A few references are incomplete and so might possibly appear in the wrong section if I had only a title to guide me; this seemed better than leaving them out.

Some entries involved a surprising amount of detection. For example, Ida Kingsbury, in her *Castles, Caliphs and Christians . . . Monserrate* (Lisbon, 1994), quoted Francis Thompson's remark that Beckford was 'that Atlas among enchanters'. I searched in vain through Thompson's collected poems, but then came across it in André Parreaux's *William Beckford* (Paris, 1960); luckily he had noted the source, Francis Thompson's *Shelley*. That was sufficient for me to trace the quotation to the *Dublin Review*, after reading the article in book form published the following year, 1909.

Similarly, in November 1844 an article on Beckford by a writer who claimed to be 'almost a daily observer of the deceased for years' appeared in the *Bath and Cheltenham Gazette*. At the end was the source, *Sam Sly's African Journal*, and a few e-mails to the central library in Cape Town elicited the information that there was indeed such a journal. Following this, they kindly sent me a copy of the original article.

In compiling this bibliography I broadly followed the *Chicago Manual of Style* (15th ed., 2003) with two main deviations. One is that inclusive page numbers are given in full, so 104–107, not 104–7. The other is that single quotes are used in preference to double ones. There were times when the word processor I was using, Word 2000, thought it knew better. One was when it changed 'secretaires' to 'secretaries', but fortunately I noticed. There may well be other occasions when I have missed a well-meaning correction.

Many people have generously provided information for this bibliography, which was much appreciated. I would specially like to thank Phil Baker,

Edward Bayntun-Coward, Wolfram Benda, Graham Cave, Laurent Châtel, Dick Claésson, Tony Coombes, Carlos Enrich, Amy Frost, Robert Gemmett, Simon Gikandi, Kenneth Graham, Jan Gross, George Haggerty, Elke Heinemann, Anthony Hobson, Keith Honess, Bet McLeod, Elizabeth Moore, Steve Moore, Rictor Norton, Naji Oueijan, Laura Pires, Tony Robinson, Christopher Thacker and Trevor Winkfield. I gratefully acknowledge the help willingly give by the staff of the Arts and Social Sciences Library at the University of Bristol, the Reference Libraries at Bath, Bristol, Trowbridge and Salisbury, and the British Library at St. Pancras, London. I would particularly like to express my gratitude to Jerry Nolan for his helpful research and to the members of the Beckford Society Committee for their support: Richard Allen and Stephen Clarke for many important suggestions and proof reading, Philip Hewat-Jaboor, Malcolm Jack, Jane Wainwright and John Wilton-Ely, and principally Sidney Blackmore for invaluable help at every stage. Above all, I would like to thank my wife for endless advice and encouragement.

Chronology

1760   September 29. William Beckford born at Fonthill, Wiltshire.

1764   Later claimed to have been pupil of Mozart during his London visit.

c.1766 Portrait painted by Andrea Casali. (Now in Lennoxlove, Scotland.)

1768   October. Robert Drysdale appointed his first tutor, until 1771.

1770   June 21. Death of his father, Alderman Beckford. Buried at Fonthill.

1773   Alexander Cozens appointed his drawing master.

1777   June. First visit abroad, to Geneva with his tutor, Rev. John Lettice.

1778   Met Voltaire at Ferney early in the year. Returned November.
      December. Wrote *The Long Story*, published as *The Vision* in 1930.

1779   June. Met William 'Kitty' Courtenay at Powderham Castle, Devon, during English tour with John Lettice.
      Winter. Met Louisa, wife of his first cousin Peter Beckford, at Fonthill.

1780   Spring. *Biographical Memoirs of Extraordinary Painters* published.
      June. Embarked with John Lettice on the Grand Tour until April 1781.
      November. Met Lady Hamilton, first wife of Sir William, in Naples.

1781   February. In Paris for two months on his way back from Italy.
      June. Portrait painted by George Romney. (Now in Upton House, Banbury.)
      Coming-of-age and Christmas parties at Fonthill Splendens.
      Or 1782. His overture to the ballet *Phæton* published in Paris.

1782   January–August. Wrote *Vathek* in French.
      February–May. Portrait painted by Joshua Reynolds. (Now in National Portrait Gallery.)
      April. Performance of his score for Lady Craven's operetta *Arcadian Pastoral*.
      May–November. Second tour to Italy, with retinue including John Robert Cozens and John Lettice.
      August. Death of the first Lady Hamilton.

1783   April. *Dreams, Waking Thoughts and Incidents* suppressed on publication.
      May 5. Married Lady Margaret Gordon in London. Honeymoon in Switzerland.

1784   January–March. In Paris. At sale of Duc de la Vallière's library.
      April. MP for Wells until June 1790.

May. Their first child stillborn.

September. Scandal at Powderham Castle.

October. His name in list of those to be raised to the peerage.

1785 April 9. Birth of elder daughter, Maria Margaret Elizabeth, at Fonthill.

July. In Switzerland, with his wife. He stayed until the end of 1786.

1786 May 14. Birth of younger daughter, Susan Euphemia.

May 26. Death at Vevey of his wife, aged 23.

June 7. Unauthorised publication by Henley of *Vathek* in English.

December. Lausanne edition of *Vathek* in French.

1787 March. First visit to Portugal, until November.

May 28. Met Gregorio Franchi in Lisbon.

July. Paris edition of *Vathek* in French.

November. In Spain until June 1788.

1788 July. In Paris, mostly at rue de Varenne, until August 1789.

Alterations at Fonthill Splendens including designs by John Soane.

1789 August. In Switzerland.

1790 Spring. Commissioned Gothick ruin from James Wyatt.

June. MP for Hindon until December 1794.

October. In Paris until June 1791 with (until Dec) Robert Drysdale

1791 April 30. Death at Florence of Louisa Beckford, aged 35.

November. In Paris at rue de Grenelle until June 1792.

1792 June–October. In Switzerland.

October–December. In Italy.

1793 January–July. In France and Switzerland.

Autumn. Ordered barrier wall to be built round the Fonthill estate.

November. Second visit to Portugal until October 1795.

1794 June 2–13. Visited monasteries of Alcobaça and Batalha in Portugal.

1795 October–December. In Spain.

December. In Portugal until March 1796.

Winter. *Modern Novel Writing* published.

1796 Summer. Building of Fonthill Abbey began.

Bought Gibbon's library for £950. Later gave it to Dr Schöll.

1797 Grand fête at Fonthill on Twelfth Night for tenants and workmen.

Azemia published.

1798 July 22. Death at Hampstead of his mother, the 'Begum'. Buried at Fonthill.

October. Third visit to Portugal until about July 1799.

1799 Autumn. Watercolours of Fonthill Abbey commissioned from J. M. W. Turner.

c.1800 Portrait painted by John Hoppner. (Now in Salford Art Gallery.)

1800 December 20–24. Lord Nelson, Sir William and the second Lady Hamilton (Emma) at Fonthill for Christmas.

1801   May. In Paris at rue St Dominique until May 1803.
        Summer. Colonnades and east pavilion of Splendens demolished.
1802   Excursion to Lausanne.
1806   November. MP for Hindon until February 1820.
1807   Summer. Moved to Fonthill Abbey and demolished Splendens.
1810   April 26. Susan married the Marquess of Douglas, later 10th Duke
        of Hamilton.
1811   February 18. Birth to Susan of the first of his five grandchildren,
        William, later 11th Duke.
        May 15. Margaret eloped with Colonel (later Lieut-General) James
        Orde.
1812   Building of the Eastern Transept of Fonthill Abbey began.
1814   October–December. In Paris.
1818   September 7. Death at Bath of Margaret, aged 33.
1819   February 16. His son-in-law became 10th Duke of Hamilton on
        father's death.
        May–June. Last visit to Paris.
        End of building at Fonthill Abbey.
1822   October. Abbey sold to John Farquhar and Christie's sale cancelled.
        Moved to 66 Great Pulteney Street, and then Lansdown Crescent,
        Bath.
1823   September 9–October 29. Phillips's thirty-seven day sale at Fonthill
        Abbey.
c.1824 Remodelled interiors of 19 & 20 Lansdown Crescent.
1825   December 21. Fall of the Abbey's central tower.
1827   Exterior of Beckford's Tower and Embattled Gateway completed.
1828   Early August. Death in London of Gregorio Franchi, his friend for
        forty years.
1834   January 27. Birth of Henry, first of seven great-grandchildren born
        in his lifetime.
        June. *Italy; with Sketches of Spain and Portugal* published.
1835   June. *Recollections of an Excursion to the Monasteries of Alcobaça
        and Batalha* published.
1844   February. Intended publication date of *Views of Lansdown Tower,
        Bath*, illus. by Willes Maddox.
        May 2. Died at Lansdown Crescent, Bath.
        May 18. Funeral and burial at Bath Abbey Cemetery.
1848   April 28. Consecration of Lansdown Cemetery. Beckford reburied
        there.

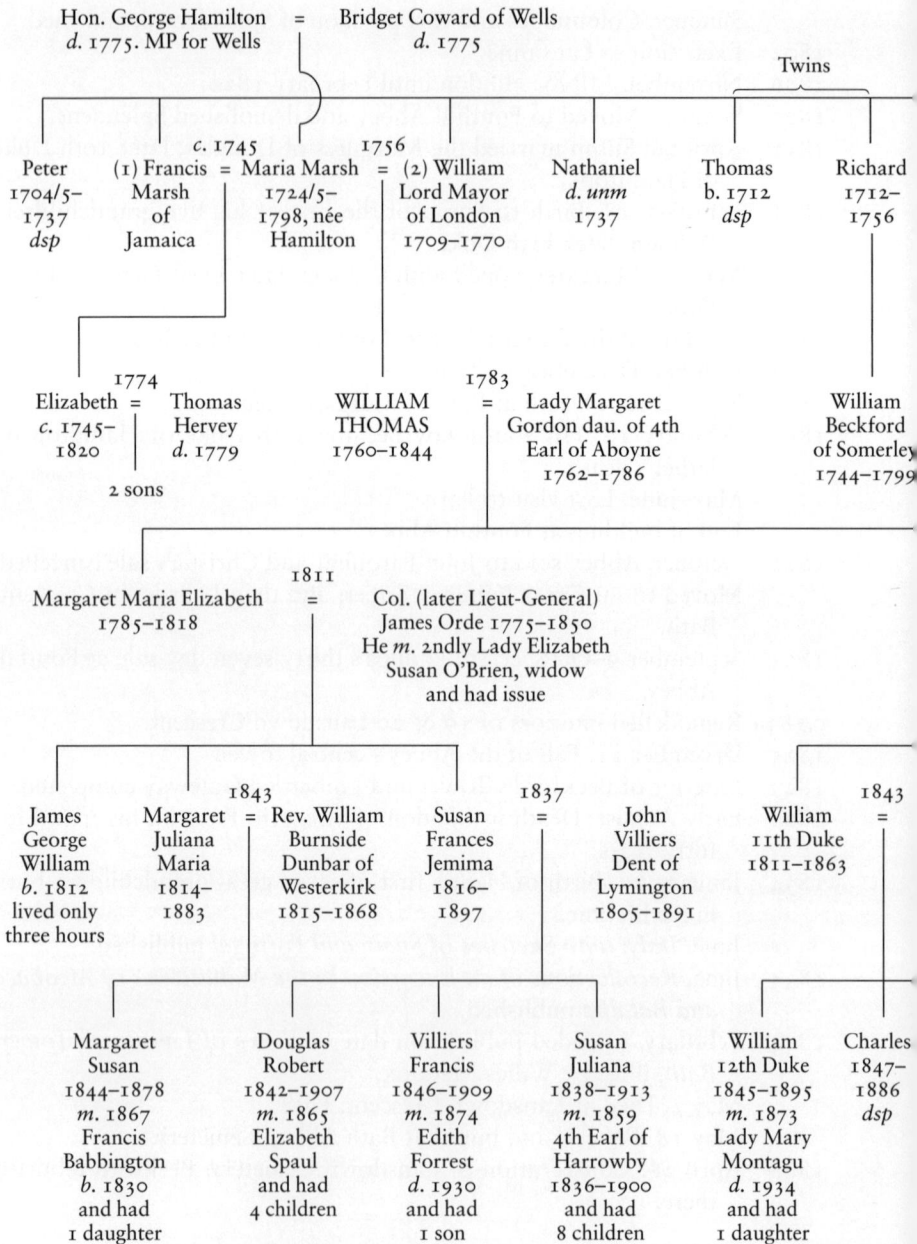

Family Tree

Hon. George Hamilton = Bridget Coward of Wells
d. 1775. MP for Wells   d. 1775

Twins

Peter	(1) Francis	*c.* 1745	Maria Marsh	1756	(2) William	Nathaniel	Thomas	Richard
1704/5–	Marsh	=	1724/5–	=	Lord Mayor	*d. unm*	b. 1712	1712–
1737	of		1798, née		of London	1737	*dsp*	1756
dsp	Jamaica		Hamilton		1709–1770			

1774
Elizabeth = Thomas   WILLIAM   1783   Lady Margaret   William
c. 1745– Hervey   THOMAS   =   Gordon dau. of 4th   Beckford
1820   d. 1779   1760–1844   Earl of Aboyne   of Somerley
                                         1762–1786   1744–1799
2 sons

1811
Margaret Maria Elizabeth   =   Col. (later Lieut-General)
1785–1818   James Orde 1775–1850
                               He *m.* 2ndly Lady Elizabeth
                               Susan O'Brien, widow
                               and had issue

James	1843		Susan	1837			1843
George	Margaret	= Rev. William	Frances	=	John	William	=
William	Juliana	Burnside	Jemima		Villiers	11th Duke	
b. 1812	Maria	Dunbar of	1816–		Dent of	1811–1863	
lived only	1814–	Westerkirk	1897		Lymington		
three hours	1883	1815–1868			1805–1891		

Margaret	Douglas	Villiers	Susan	William	Charles
Susan	Robert	Francis	Juliana	12th Duke	1847–
1844–1878	1842–1907	1846–1909	1838–1913	1845–1895	1886
m. 1867	*m.* 1865	*m.* 1874	*m.* 1859	*m.* 1873	*dsp*
Francis	Elizabeth	Edith	4th Earl of	Lady Mary	
Babbington	Spaul	Forrest	Harrowby	Montagu	
b. 1830	and had	*d.* 1930	1836–1900	*d.* 1934	
and had	4 children	and had	and had	and had	
1 daughter		1 son	8 children	1 daughter	

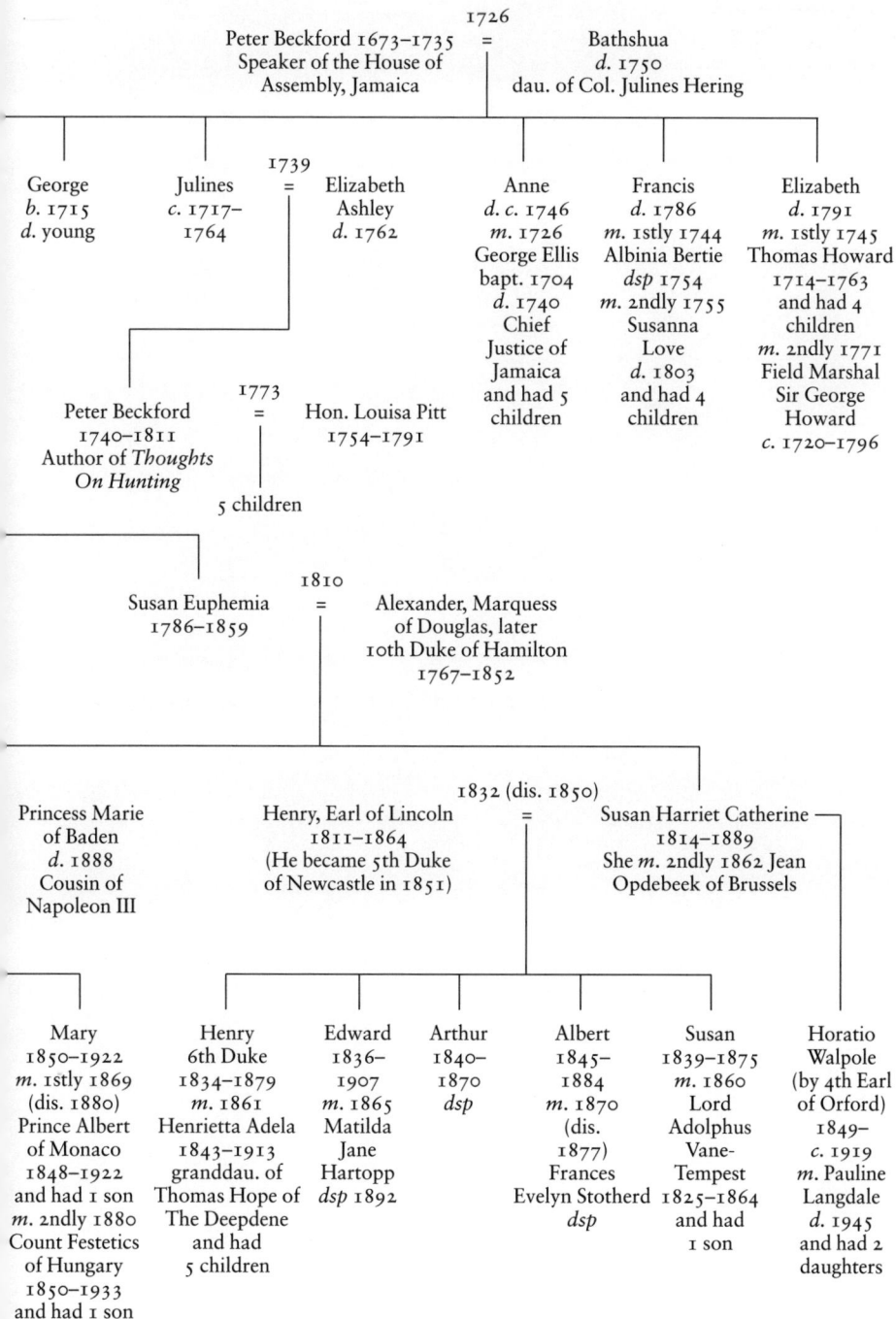

1726

Peter Beckford 1673–1735 = Bathshua
Speaker of the House of   d. 1750
Assembly, Jamaica   dau. of Col. Julines Hering

George	Julines	1739	Elizabeth	Anne	Francis	Elizabeth
b. 1715	c. 1717–	=	Ashley	d. c. 1746	d. 1786	d. 1791
d. young	1764		d. 1762	m. 1726	m. 1stly 1744	m. 1stly 1745
				George Ellis	Albinia Bertie	Thomas Howard
				bapt. 1704	dsp 1754	1714–1763
				d. 1740	m. 2ndly 1755	and had 4
				Chief	Susanna	children
				Justice of	Love	m. 2ndly 1771
				Jamaica	d. 1803	Field Marshal
				and had 5	and had 4	Sir George
				children	children	Howard
						c. 1720–1796

1773

Peter Beckford = Hon. Louisa Pitt
1740–1811   1754–1791
Author of *Thoughts
On Hunting*

5 children

1810

Susan Euphemia = Alexander, Marquess
1786–1859   of Douglas, later
                       10th Duke of Hamilton
                       1767–1852

1832 (dis. 1850)

Princess Marie   Henry, Earl of Lincoln = Susan Harriet Catherine ———
of Baden   1811–1864   1814–1889
d. 1888   (He became 5th Duke   She m. 2ndly 1862 Jean
Cousin of   of Newcastle in 1851)   Opdebeek of Brussels
Napoleon III

Mary	Henry	Edward	Arthur	Albert	Susan	Horatio
1850–1922	6th Duke	1836–	1840–	1845–	1839–1875	Walpole
m. 1stly 1869	1834–1879	1907	1870	1884	m. 1860	(by 4th Earl
(dis. 1880)	m. 1861	m. 1865	dsp	m. 1870	Lord	of Orford)
Prince Albert	Henrietta Adela	Matilda		(dis.	Adolphus	1849–
of Monaco	1843–1913	Jane		1877)	Vane-	c. 1919
1848–1922	granddau. of	Hartopp		Frances	Tempest	m. Pauline
and had 1 son	Thomas Hope of	dsp 1892		Evelyn Stotherd	1825–1864	Langdale
m. 2ndly 1880	The Deepdene			dsp	and had	d. 1945
Count Festetics	and had				1 son	and had 2
of Hungary	5 children					daughters
1850–1933						
and had 1 son						

PART ONE
BECKFORD'S LIFE

PART ONE

BECKFORD'S LIFE

1. Accounts of Beckford's Life

BIOGRAPHIES

Redding, Cyrus. *Memoirs of William Beckford of Fonthill, Author of "Vathek"*. 2 vols. London: Charles J. Skeet, 1859 [1858]. Portrait frontis. after Sauvage. iv, 352 & iv, 402 pp. 20½ cm. Vol. 1: ancestors & 1760–1787. Vol. 2: 1787–1844. A revised version of his 1846 manuscript, now in the Bodleian Library, MS. Beckford c.85–86.

> REVIEWS. *Athenæum*, 11 Dec 1858, 749–752. (Also a letter by J. S. correcting a quotation from Beckford's tomb, 18 Dec, 800.) Reprinted in *Littell's Living Age* 60 (Jan, Feb, March 1859): 406–413 (? + more). Mostly reprinted in *Bath Chronicle*, 16 Dec 1858, 6b–d. *Idem*, 30 Dec, 3d, Nelson's visit & other anecdotes.
> *Gentleman's Magazine* n.s. 6 (March 1859): 255–260.
> *Illustrated London News* 33 (18 Dec 1858): 581. Scathing dismissal. *Idem* 34 (8 Jan 1859): 31. Fonthill tower fell owing to sandy foundations.
> 'A Literary Millionaire.' *Chambers's Journal* 31 (5 Feb 1859): 93–95.
> 'Memoirs of Beckford.' *Saturday Review* 6 (18 Dec 1858): 618–619.
> *Tait's Edinburgh Magazine* n.s. 26 (Feb 1859): 76–80.
> [Tiffany, Osmond.] *North American Review* 90 (April 1860): 297–321. Reprinted in *The Knickerbocker Magazine; or New York Monthly Magazine* 55 (June 1860): 640–642.

Melville, Lewis. [Lewis S. Benjamin, pseud.] *The Life and Letters of William Beckford of Fonthill (Author of "Vathek")*. London: Heinemann, 1910. xv, 391 pp. 13 pl. 26 cm. Mostly letters to and from Beckford.

> REVIEWS. *Athenæum*, 11 June 1910, 695–696.
> 'The Author of "Vathek."' *Times Literary Supplement*, 5 May 1910, 161.
> 'Beckford. The Builder of Lansdown Tower. His Life and Letters.' *Bath Chronicle*, 2, 16 June 1910, 6a–b, 6a.
> ?Bettany, G. T. *Sunday Times*.
> 'Book of the Week.' *Country Life*, 27 Aug 1910, 308–309.
> Chesson, W. H. *Daily Chronicle*.

Jung, Fritz. *Englische Studien* (Leipzig) 45 no. 2 (Sept 1912): 318–321.

Lane-Poole, Stanley. "The Author of 'Vathek'." *Quarterly Review* 213 (Oct 1910): 377–401. Melville not a much better writer than Redding.

More, Paul Elmer. 'William Beckford.' In *The Drift of Romanticism*, 3–36. Boston, MA: Houghton Mifflin, 1913. Shelburne Essays VIII.

[Strachey, James.] *Spectator*, 25 June 1910, 1076.

Wiltshire Archæological and Natural History Magazine 36 (Dec 1910): 631–632.

Also untraced reviews in *The Bookman, Daily Telegraph, Nation, New York Times,* and *Scotsman.*

Oliver, J. W. *The Life of William Beckford*. London: Oxford University Press, 1932. xi, 343 pp. 2 pl. 21½ cm. Reissued with a cancel title page in Oxford Bookshelf Series, 1937.

REVIEWS. 'The Author of Vathek.' *The Periodical* (O.U.P. house magazine) 17 (Oct 1932): 145–148.

Birrell, A. *Observer*, 19 Nov 1932.

Brandl, A. *Deutsche Literaturzeitung* (Berlin) 59 (1938): 880–882.

'The Caliph of Fonthill.' *Times Literary Supplement*, 3 Nov 1932, 797–798. The leading article. Letter from Oliver praising review and explaining why Beckford was not an ideal traveller, 17 Nov, 859.

Garnett, David. 'Our Great Extravagant.' *New Statesman and Nation*, 10 Dec 1932, 734, 736.

H., J. [Hayward, John.] *The Criterion* 12 (1933): 535–536, reprinted 1967.

Lewis, W. S. *Saturday Review of Literature*, 31 Dec 1932, 352.

Saturday Review, 19 Nov 1932, 537.

Tompkins, J. M. S. *Review of English Studies* 10 (July 1934): 362–365.

Watt, Sholto. 'The Author of "Vathek".' *Sunday Times*, 12 Jan 1933.

Wiltshire Archæological and Natural History Magazine 46 (June 1933): 288–289.

Chapman, Guy. *Beckford*. London: Jonathan Cape & New York: Charles Scribner's Sons, 1937. 365 pp. 8 pl. 20½ cm. Reissued 1940 in the Life and Letters Series No. 98 with cancel title page. Reissued again c.1944; as 1940 but without illus. or free endpapers. 2nd ed., 1952, with a new preface, but no illus. or folding family tree.

REVIEWS. 'The Abbot of Fonthill. Beckford's work and fantasies.' *Times Literary Supplement*, 13 March 1937, 185.

'Books of the Day . . . Beckford. A New Biography.' *The Times*, 30 March 1937, 16c.

Church, R. *London Mercury* 36 (1937): 86.

Cowie, A. *Saturday Review of Literature*, 29 May 1937, 6.

Evans, B. Ifor. 'The Author of "Vathek". Ups and downs of the Beckford family.' *Observer*, 28 March 1937.

Geismar, M. *Nation*, 15 May 1937, 568.

Grierson, Flora. 'The Bulpington of Fonthill.' *New Statesman and Nation*, 20 March 1937, 486, 488.

Hayward, John. 'The Life and Legend of William Beckford.' *Spectator*, 12 March 1937, 478.

Johnson, E. *New Republic*, 18 Aug 1937, 55.

King, William. *The Criterion* 17 (Jan 1938): 367–369, reprinted 1967.

Kronenberger, L. *New York Times Book Review*, 25 July 1937, 2.

Stillman, C. G. *New York Herald Tribune Books*, 9 May 1937, 32.

Wilson, Mona. 'Strange Life of William Beckford.' *Sunday Times*, 4 April 1937.

Wiltshire Archæological and Natural History Magazine 48 (June 1938): 257–258.

Brockman, H. A. N. *The Caliph of Fonthill*. London: Werner Laurie, 1956. 219 pp. 13 pl. 22 cm. Grey cloth, gilt. Remainder binding: light blue linson with dark blue lettering. Largely about Fonthill Abbey.

REVIEWS. 'Beckford at Fonthill.' *The Times*, 9 Aug 1956, 9e.

Church, Richard. *Country Life*, 23 Aug 1956, 399, 401.

Gillett, Eric. *National and English Review* 147 (1956): 156.

P., A. M. 'William Beckford – Eccentric from the Past.' *Bath & Wilts Chronicle & Herald*, 4 Aug 1956, 4a–e, 5c. *Idem*, Letters: Harold J. Collett, 8 Aug, 4e; E. J. Ford, 10 Aug, 4e; O. G. Sargent, 14 Aug, 4d; H. J. Collett, 16 Aug, 4d. Review also in *Bath Weekly Chronicle & Herald*, 11 Aug, 7a–e.

Parreaux, André. *Études Anglaises* 10 no. 1 (1957): 62.

'Romantic Beckford.' *Times Literary Supplement*, 7 Sept 1956, 526.

Wentworth-Shields, F. W. *Contemporary Review* 190 (1956): 314–315.

Lees-Milne, James. *William Beckford*. Tisbury, Wilts: Compton Russell, 1976 & Montclair, New Jersey: Allanheld & Schram, 1979. 128 pp. 104 illus. 26 cm. Reprinted, London: Century, 1990. 146 pp. 10 pl. 21¼ cm. National Trust Classics.

REVIEWS. Alexander, Boyd. 'Shades of Beckford.' *Apollo* 104 (Aug 1976): 146–147. With a review of *William Beckford Exhibition* 1976.

'Books.' *House & Garden*, July–Aug 1976, 108.

Buckle, Richard. *Books and Bookmen*, July 1976, 77.

Daniels, Jeffery. 'The recluse of Fonthill Abbey.' *The Times*, 10 May 1976, 12d–f. With a review of *William Beckford Exhibition*, 1976.

Fox, Celina. 'The exclusive possessor.' *Times Literary Supplement*, 9 July 1976, 847.

Goring, Edward. 'Beckford, the man Bath never understood.' *Bath & Wilts Evening Chronicle*, 22 April 1976, 4.

Marter, Shirley Van. *The Eighteenth Century: A Current Bibliography* n.s. 3 for 1977 (1981): 167. Review of the American ed.

Quennell, Peter. 'At Fonthill Abbey.' *History Today* 26 (July 1976): 480–481.

Sunday Telegraph, 25 April 1976. Portrait of Beckford in Vandyke costume.

Wells, John. 'Facing both ways.' *Spectator*, 22 May 1976, 22.

Western Daily Press, 24 April 1976. Account of the launch.

Fothergill, Brian. *Beckford of Fonthill*. London: Faber, 1979. 387 pp. 12 pl. 22 cm. A highly readable biography. Reprinted, Stroud, Glos: Nonsuch, 2005 with a new introduction by Sidney Blackmore.

REVIEWS. *Church Times*, 16 March 1979.

Forster, Margaret. 'Choked by a silver spoon.' *Evening Standard*, 20 Feb 1979.

Graham, Kenneth W. *Eighteenth-Century Studies* 15 no. 4 (Summer 1982): 480–482. Biography is 'eloquent, sensitive, coherent and balanced'.

Grigson, Geoffrey. 'The ogre of Fonthill.' *Guardian*, 22 Feb 1979.

Jack, Malcolm. 'Brian Fothergill's Beckford.' *Beckford Tower Trust Newsletter*, Spring 1991, 3.

Keates, Jonathan. 'Who Active?' *New Statesman*, 27 April 1979, 599–600.

Lees-Milne, James. 'Aristocratic Malcontent.' *Books and Bookmen*, April 1979, 18–19.

MacAndrews, Elizabeth. *The Eighteenth Century: A Current Bibliography* n.s. 5 for 1979 (1983): 340–343. 'Clearly written', but with missing pieces.

Norton, Rictor. 'Through the fumes.' *Gay News* 163 (1979): 29.

Powell, Anthony. 'Flamboyant eccentric.' *Daily Telegraph*, 8 March 1979.

Raven, Simon. 'Gothic folly.' *Spectator*, 24 Feb 1979, 22.

'A sage and his folly.' *Economist*, 24 Feb 1979, 105–106.

Toynbee, Philip. 'Follies and fantasies.' *Observer*, 18 Feb 1979, 36.

Mowl, Timothy. *William Beckford: Composing for Mozart*. London: John Murray, 1998. xii, 324 pp. 31 illus. 24 cm.

REVIEWS. Adamson, John. 'Buildings and bottoms.' *Sunday Telegraph Review*, 7 June 1998.

Ballantyne, Andrew. 'The view from Lansdown Tower.' *Times Literary Supplement*, 18 Sept 1998, 20–21.

Berland, Kevin. *Eighteenth-Century Studies* 33 no. 3 (2000): 457–460. With a review of Malcolm Jack, *William Beckford: An English Fidalgo*.

Brindley, Brian. *Catholic Herald*, 12 June 1998.

Carpenter, Humphrey. 'Getting the abbey habit.' *Sunday Times*, 2 Aug 1998, 5.

Claésson, Dick. *Eighteenth-Century Novel* 1 (2001): 1–7.

Clarke, Roger. *Evening Standard*, 15 June 1998.

Darton, Eric. '*William Beckford: Composing for Mozart* by Timothy Mowl.' *Beckford Journal* 7 (2001): 30–33.

Edmonds, Richard. *Birmingham Post*, 4 July 1998.

Elliott, Kirsten. 'The English Muenchhausen.' *Bath and West Life*, Late Summer 1998, 31.

Hall, Michael. 'Not Chaste, but Tasteful.' *Country Life*, 11 June 1998, 190.

Hensher, Philip. 'Poor little rich boy.' *Spectator*, 6 June 1998, 27, 30. Beckford an extremely difficult subject as he falsified his own past.

Hillier, Bevis. 'Do Not Despise the Dilettante.' *Literary Review*, June 1998, 4–5.

Hughes, Kathryn. 'The monstrous fictions of a boy-fancier.' *Daily Telegraph Arts & Books*, 20 June 1998, A2.

Jack, Malcolm. 'Composing for Mozart.' *Beckford Journal* 5 (1999): 2–3.

Jeffreys, Sophie. 'Unravelling the Beckford Files.' *The Times*, 30 July 1998, 39a–e.

Lewis, Peter. 'The eccentric, his wife and a dangerous liaison.' *Daily Mail*, 6 June 1998, 39.

Miller, Lucasta. 'Doomed voluptuary.' *New Statesman*, 26 June 1998, 54–55.

Mortimer, John. 'Book of the Week.' *Mail on Sunday*, 14 June 1998.

Reid, Helen. 'Incredible life of man who was mates with Mozart.' *Western Daily Press*, 3 July 1998, 7.

Roose-Evans, James. *Hampstead and Highgate Express*, 19 June 1998.

Thicknesse, Robert. *The Tablet*, 11 July 1998.

White, Roger. *House & Garden*, September 1998.

Wiltshire Archæological and Natural History Magazine 92 (1999): 149.

FULL-LENGTH STUDIES

See also 'Full-length Studies' in Sections 2 and 15

Alexander, Boyd. *England's Wealthiest Son. A Study of William Beckford*. London: Centaur, 1962. ix, 308 pp. 10 pl. 22 cm. An invaluable account of aspects of Beckford's life, including his finances.

REVIEWS. 'Baffling Beckford.' *Times Literary Supplement*, 2 March 1962, 134.

Fleming, John. *Apollo* 76 (July 1962): 415.

Grigson, Geoffrey. 'Road to Reading Goal.' *Spectator*, 9 March 1962, 312.
'Mystery Man of Fonthill.' *The Times*, 1 March 1962, 15d–e.
Nicholson, Harold. 'The romantic egoist.' *Observer*, 18 Feb 1962, 30.
Pritchett, V. S. 'Vile Body.' *New Statesman*, 23 Feb 1962, 265–266.
Spring, Howard. *Country Life*, 1 March 1962, 477.

Bertfield, Harvey. *Sugar, Slavery and Sex: The Beckfords and Fonthill Abbey*.
BA thesis for Manchester University, June 2001. ii, 48 pp. incl. 14 illus. In
Bristol Reference Library.

Chadourne, Marc. *Eblis ou l'Enfer de William Beckford*. Paris: Pauvert,
1967. 343 pp. 21½ cm. 'L'homme', 17–155. 'L'œuvre en ses meilleures
pages': 'Le cycle d'Eblis' – extracts from *Vathek* & *The Episodes*,
159–281; *Alcobaça and Batalha*, 285–328.

REVIEWS. Kanters, Robert. 'Le voyage de William Beckford au-delà de
l'enfer.' *Figaro Littéraire*, 3–9 July 1967, 19.
Pia, Pascal. 'Un Anglais perverti, William Beckford.' *Magazine littéraire*
No. 8 (June 1967).

Claésson, Dick. *William Beckford av Fonthill, Wilts., 1760–1844. En
forskningsöversikt*. Gothenburg: Göteborgs universitet, 1995. iv, 34 pp.
20½ cm. Meddelanden No. 17. A chronicle of Beckford's life with bibliography. In Swedish.

Girard, Didier. *William Beckford: Terroriste au Palais de la Raison*. Paris:
José Corti, 1993. 225 pp. 18½ cm. 'Petit système des mélancolies', 9–27;
'Vertige des solitudes', 29–73; Rebellions sybarites, tentations exquises',
75–146; 'De l'art de s'emmurer avec élégance', 147–202; 'Détours sans
retour', 203–221.

REVIEWS. Braudeau, Michel. 'Quelques entrées dans le décor.' *Le
Monde*, 12 March 1993, 24. With a review of *Histoire du Prince
Ahmed*, ed. Didier Girard (1993).
Hilliard, Elizabeth. *Beckford Tower Trust Newsletter*, Spring 1993, 3–4.
Jack, Malcolm. 'Terrorist in the Palace of Reason.' *Beckford Tower Trust
Newsletter*, Spring 1994, 4–5.

Gregory, William, ed. *The Beckford Family. Reminiscences of Fonthill
Abbey and Lansdown Tower*. Bath: Queen Square Library, 1887. [iii], 91
pp. 15½ cm. Portrait frontis. Limited to 100 copies. Engravings of Fonthill
Abbey, Lansdown Crescent and Beckford's Tower were bound into a few
copies. 2nd ed. London: Simpkin, Marshall, etc., 1898. [ix], 171 pp. 20
pl. Portrait frontis. 19 cm. Limited to 250 copies, price 10s. 6d. A useful
anthology of articles with five new chapters, handsomely bound.

REVIEWS. *Bath Chronicle*, 24 Feb 1898, 6a.

Bath Weekly Argus, cited in *Wiltshire Archæological and Natural History Magazine* 30 (June 1898): 73.

'The Beckfords.' *Keene's Bath Journal*, 5 March 1898, 8e.

Millington, Jon. 'William Gregory's *The Beckford Family*.' *Beckford Journal* 9 (2003): 45–51. Gives sources for the new chapters not in 1st ed. (1887).

'Our Library Table.' *Athenæum*, 13 Aug 1898, 225.

W., C. 'Written in a library.' *Bristol Times and Mirror*, 22 July 1905, 22c.

Heinemann, Elke. *Babylonische Spiele: William Beckford und das Erwachen der modernen Imagination* (Babylonian Games: William Beckford and the Awakening of the Modern Imagination). Munich: Wilhelm Fink, 2000. 240 pp. Based on her doctoral thesis for Freie Universität, Berlin, 1997.

Lansdown, Henry Venn. *Recollections of the Late William Beckford of Fonthill, Wilts and Lansdown, Bath*. Bath: Privately printed, 1893. 48 pp. 18½ cm. Limited to 100 copies, price 4s. 6d. Pale blue cloth. Five letters to his sister Charlotte, publ. by his daughter, also Charlotte: 21 Aug 1838, pictures and works of art at Lansdown Crescent & the Tower, 5–30; Oct 1838, visit to Tower, 30–32; 3 Nov 1838, conversations, 32–33; 10 Nov 1838, reminiscences, 33–38; ?Nov 1844, visit to Fonthill Abbey ruins & grounds, 38–48 (reprinted in Gemmett, *Beckford's Fonthill* (2003), 372–381). Facsimile reprint, Bath: Kingsmead, [1969]. 19 cm. Limited to 750 copies. (Dust jacket on early copies depicted Alderman Beckford.) Reprinted again, Whitefish, Montana: Kessinger Publishing, n.d.

REVIEW. 'William Beckford Memories.' *Observer*, 14 June 1931, 11.

May, Marcel. *La Jeunesse de William Beckford et la Genèse de son «Vathek»*. Paris: Presses Universitaires de France, 1928. 439 pp. 21 illus. 22½ cm. Part 1: 'Beckford. – De l'enfance à la majorité', 7–172. Part 2: '«Vathek»', 173–419. Bibliography, 431–437.

REVIEWS. Baker, Ernest A. *Review of English Studies* 5 (April 1929): 235–241.
Cazamian, L. *Revue Anglo-Américaine* 6 (1928): 69–70.
Douady, J. *Revue Critique* 63 (1929): 133–135.
English Studies (Amsterdam) 12 (April 1930): 74.
Lemonnier, Léon. *Les langues modernes* 26 (1928): 457–458.
Philological Quarterly 8 no. 2 (April 1929): 181.
Richter, Helene. *Englische Studien* (Leipzig) 63 no. 3 (May 1929): 431–434.

Parreaux, André. *William Beckford, Auteur de Vathek*. Paris: Nizet, 1960. 577 pp. 25 cm. 'Introduction: La personnalité', 19–93. Book 1: 'L'imagination Beckfordienne et ses premières tentatives d'expression', 95–197.

Book 2: 'Vathek et les Épisodes', 199–475. Appendices, 479–540. Bibliography, 543–563.

REVIEWS. Carter, John. *Book Collector* 9 no. 4 (Winter 1960): 473–474, 477–478.
[Lonsdale, R. H.] 'The Mask of Beckford.' *Times Literary Supplement*, 10 Feb 1961, 81–82.
Mayo, Robert. *Philological Quarterly* 41 no. 3 (July 1962): 567–569.
Mayoux, Jean-Jacques. 'La Damnation de Beckford.' *English Miscellany* 12 (1961): 41–77. Reprinted with revisions in his *Sous de vastes portiques: études de littérature et d'art anglais*, 73–110. Paris: Nadeau, 1981.
Milner, Max. *Revue d'histoire littéraire de la France* 52 (1962): 427–429.
Moussa-Mahmoud, Fatma. *Cairo Studies in English*, 1961–1962, 249–251.
Moussa-Mahmoud, Fatma. 'A Monument to the Author of *Vathek*.' *Études Anglaises* 15 (April–June 1962): 138–147.

Rogal, Keith H. *Of Dreams and Towers: William Beckford and the Practice of Associationism*. AB thesis for Harvard University, 1984. 72 pp. + 7 pp. bibliography + 22 pp. Plates.

Sitwell, Sacheverell. *Beckford and Beckfordism*. London: Duckworth, 1930. 39 pp. 22½ cm. Limited to 265 copies numbered and signed by the author. Originally announced as *William Beckford: A Footnote to the Study of Baroque Art* in *Times Literary Supplement*, 14 Aug 1930, 650.

REVIEWS. MacCarthy, Desmond. 'Beckfordism.' *Sunday Times*, 18 Jan 1931. Reprinted in his *Criticism*, 103–114, London: Putnam, 1932.
'William Beckford, Romantic.' *Times Literary Supplement*, 4 Dec 1930, 1034. With brief reviews of *Vathek* in Philip Henderson, ed., *The Shorter Novels of the Eighteenth Century*. Vol. III, & (very briefly) Chapman's *Bibliography*.

CONTEMPORARY ACCOUNTS

'Beckford (William).' In *Public Characters of All Nations; Consisting of Biographical Accounts of Nearly Three Thousand Eminent Contemporaries*, 1:122. 3 vols. London: Sir Richard Phillips & Co., 1823.
'Biography of Eccentric Characters. William Beckford.' *The Ladies' Monthly Museum* n.s. 19 (Feb 1824): 67–71. For its time, a highly critical account.
Birth. *Gentleman's Magazine* 30 (Oct 1760): 489.
Birth. *Salisbury Journal*, 6 Oct 1760, 3c. On 29 Sept 'at Fonthill'.
Christmas Fête, 6 Jan 1797. [Lettice, John.] *Salisbury and Winchester Journal*, 9 Jan 1797, 4c. Fête on Twelfth Night. *Idem*, 16 Jan, 1b–c. (Quoted

in Colt Hoare's, *Modern Wiltshire* (1829), 25.) Reprinted as 'Account of the magnificent Fete given by William Beckford, Esq. at his Seat at Fonthill, in Wiltshire, on the 6th of January, 1797' in *Weekly Entertainer* (Sherborne, Dorset) 29 (23 Jan 1797): 71–75. Almost identical version: 'Account of the Christmas Festivities at Fonthill. (By a Correspondent who was present.)' *European Magazine* 31 (Jan 1797): 4–6, reprinted in Gemmett, *Beckford's Fonthill* (2003), 211–214.

Christmas Fête. 'Fonthill in 1797.' *Devizes & Wiltshire Gazette*, 28 Aug 1823, 4c. The Fête on 6 Jan was attended by 'several of the first artists in the kingdom'. ¼ column. Also reported in *Morning Chronicle*, 16 Jan 1797, *The Times*, 20 Jan, 4a & *Bath Journal* 23 Jan, 2d–e.

Coming-of-age. *Il Tributo*. 'A Pastoral Cantata, From the Original Italian of Sig. Girolamo Tonioli. Set to Music by Sig. Venanzio Rauzzini. And Performed September the 29th, 1781, at Fonthill, In the County of Wilts, on the Celebration of the Birth-Day of William Beckford, Esq. Salisbury: Printed by Collins and Johnson, on the Canal. 1781.' 9 pp. Title, [1]; 'Dialogue between Philenus, Sig. Pachiarotti [and] Thirsis, Sig. Tenducci [with] Chorus of Shepherds', [2]; text f cantata, [3]–9. 'Thirsis: I know, my dear *Philenus*, that this is the happy day, which puts our amiable Youth WILLIAM, into the full Possession of his ample Inheritance'. 4.

Coming-of-age. *Salisbury and Winchester Journal*, 1 Oct 1781, 3b. 'A grand entertainment' on Saturday last. 6 paragraphs.

'Conversations with the late W. Beckford, Esq. Contributed by Various Friends. No. III.' *New Monthly Magazine* 72 (Sept 1844): 18–24. Signed 'H'. For Conversations I & II see Redding, below.

'Conversations with the late W. Beckford, Esq. Contributed by Various Friends. No. IV.' *New Monthly Magazine* 72 (Oct 1844): 212–221.

'Conversations with the late W. Beckford, Esq. No. V.' *New Monthly Magazine* 72 (Nov 1844): 418–427. Nos. III, IV & V are by the same author.

Delicate health. *Bath Chronicle*, 2 May 1844, 3c. Duchess of Hamilton visited her father, 'the venerable Mr. Beckford, who is still in delicate health'. 'During the past week he gave directions' for placing three Maddox lunettes in the Tower. 21 lines. Also in *Sherborne and Yeovil Mercury*, 4 May 1844, 4b.

H., W. H. [Harrison, William Henry.] 'Conversations with the late W. Beckford, Esq. with various friends. No. VI.' *New Monthly Magazine* 72 (Dec 1844): 516–522.

[Lettice, John.] 'William Beckford, Esq. of Fonthill.' *European Magazine* 32 (Sept 1797): *147–*150 & portrait roundel engraved by Singleton after Sauvage. Beckford's efforts to negotiate peace with France. Reprinted as 'Sketch of the Life and Character of William Beckford, Esq. of Fonthill.' *Weekly Entertainer* (Sherborne, Dorset) 30 (16 Oct 1797): 306–311. Article in *European Magazine* noted in *The Times*, 11 Oct

1797, 4a, hoping that his talents will be 'employed in the service of the country'. 15 lines.

Marriage. *Gentleman's Magazine* 53 pt. 1 (May 1783): 451.

Marriage. *Salisbury and Winchester Journal*, 12 May 1783, 3b. By special licence on 6th at Lady Iphigenia Steuart's in Cleveland-court, St. James.

Member of Parliament. *Salisbury and Winchester Journal*, 18 May 1807, 4c. Elected MP for Hindon, with Benjamin Hobhouse.

Peerage. *Salisbury and Winchester Journal*, 11 Oct 1784, 2a. Twelve more commoners, including Beckford, to be created peers during the winter. Also in *Morning Intelligencer*, 1 Oct & *Morning Chronicle*, 9 Oct.

[Redding, Cyrus.] 'Recollections of the Author of "Vathek".' ['Conversations' I and II.] *New Monthly Magazine* 71 (June, July 1844): 143–158 & portrait roundel, 302–319. Most of 155–156 & 156–157 reprinted as 'Anecdotes of Mr. Beckford' in *Bath and Cheltenham Gazette*, 12 June 1844, 4b.

Redding, Cyrus. 'Notes of the Week.' *The Critic: Journal of British and Foreign Literature and the Arts* 23 (1861): 69–70 at 70. Letter of 13 July 1860. He had not put his name on his *Memoirs* as he did not want the Duchess to know he had used Lettice's now lost diary when writing about Beckford's early life.

Smeeton, George, publ. 'William Beckford, Esq.' *The Unique* No. 18 (4 Oct 1823). Portrait & 6 pp. London: George Smeeton. Item 243 in the Beckford Exhibition at Yale, 1960: '*Portraits and biography of public characters*', Gotlieb, *William Beckford of Fonthill* (1960), 79. Altogether there were 87 weekly numbers and they were reissued in book form with revised biographies in 1825.

Vincent. *Salisbury and Winchester Journal*, 21 Nov 1796, 4d. William Vincent, one of Beckford's workmen, drowned in pond near Splendens.

Welcomed home. *Salisbury and Winchester Journal*, 4 July 1796, 4c. Beckford's return to Fonthill from Lisbon welcomed by villagers.

OBITUARIES AND FUNERAL

Bath and Cheltenham Gazette, 8 May 1844, 3b. ' . . . vigorous energy and intellectual power'. 62 lines. Reprinted as 'The late Mr. Beckford' in *Salisbury and Winchester Journal*, 11 May 1844, 4d.

'Mr Beckford and Fonthill.' *Chambers's Edinburgh Journal* n.s. 2 (17 Aug 1844): 101–103. 'At length, after upwards of sixty years of mature life spent in unlimited indulgence of the highest intellectual tastes, this singular man meets the common fate', 103.

'Death of Mr. Beckford of Bath.' *Bristol Times and Bath Advocate*, 4 May 1844, 3e. 31 lines.

'Death of the Author of "Vathek." – Fonthill Abbey.' *Pictorial Times* 3 (18

May 1844): 308. Three woodcuts: Abbey copied from Storer (1812); Beckford's Tower from N copied from Goodridge's lithograph, c.1827; portrait roundel.

'Death of W. Beckford, Esq.' *Littell's Living Age* 1 (15 June 1844): 269.

'Deaths.' *Bath Chronicle*, 9 May 1844, 3a. 52 lines. *Idem*, 3c. Beckford's portrait painted by Maddox.

Devizes & Wiltshire Gazette, 9 May 1844, 3b. Death of 'the originator of the once gorgeous palace of Fonthill', 7 lines. 'Mr. Beckford and Fonthill Abbey.' *Idem*, 16 May, 3c: 'The late Mr. Beckford was desirous of realizing in life what he had only imagined in literature.' ¼ column. 'Funeral of the late William Beckford, esq.' *Idem*, 23 May, 3c. ¼ column.

Embalming by English & Hiscox. *The Times*, 11 May 1844, 7a. *Bath Chronicle*, 16 May 1844, 3c. 41 lines, including description of the coffin. *Bristol Times and Bath Advocate*, 18 May 1844, 4e. 3 lines.

'Funeral of the late William Beckford, Esq.' *Bath and Cheltenham Gazette*, 22 May 1844, 2b–c. Two columns.

'Funeral of the late Wm. Beckford, Esq.' *Bath Chronicle*, 23 May 1844, 3c. ½ column.

'Funeral of the late Wm. Beckford, Esq.' *Bath Herald*, 25 May 1844, 3c.

'The Funeral of the Late Mr. Beckford Leaving His House in Lansdowne Crescent, Bath.' *Pictorial Times* 3 (25 May 1844): 332. Woodcut of scene. ADVERT for article. *Bath Chronicle*, 23 May 1844, 2f.

Keene's Bath Journal, 6 May 1844.

[Lansdown, Henry Venn.] 'Wm. Beckford, Esq.' *Bath Herald*, 18 May 1844, 3e. Reprinted in Gregory, *The Beckford Family* (2nd ed., 1898), 138–142 and, with omissions, in *The Times*, 23 May 1844, 6a.

'The Late William Beckford.' *Mirror of Literature* n.s. 5 (11 May 1844): 294–296.

'The Late William Beckford, Esq.' *Salisbury and Wiltshire Herald*, 11 May 1844, 2c. 'Funeral of the late William Beckford.' *Idem*, 25 May, 3d–e.

'The Late William Beckford, Esq. of Bath.' *Sam Sly's African Journal* (8 August 1844). Reprinted (without the death announcement at the end from *Keene's Bath Journal*) in *Bath and Cheltenham Gazette*, 27 Nov 1844, 4.

Literary Gazette 28 (11 May 1844): 308. A few lines.

'Monthly Literary Bulletin.' *United States Magazine and Democratic Review* 15 (July 1844): 109.

The Record (London), 4 May 1844, 4d. 7 lines.

Sherborne and Yeovil Mercury, 11 May 1844, 4d. Report of Beckford's death.

Smith, George. 'Reminiscences.' *Keene's Bath Journal*, 5 March 1898, 2d. Beckford's coffin made by Mr Tucker, cabinet maker, off Guinea Lane, Bath.

'W. Beckford, Esq.' *Athenæum*, 11 May 1844, 430. Reprinted in *[Cleave's] Gazette of Variety* 1 (25 May 1844): 287 and in *Littell's Living Age* 1 (29 June 1844): 396–397.

W., I. 'The Late William Beckford, Esq.' *Athenæum*, 18 May 1844, 455–456. Followed by paragraph on Alderman Beckford in 'Our Weekly Gossip.' Reprinted in *[Cleave's] Gazette of Variety* 1 (1 June 1844): 302–303 and in *Littell's Living Age* 1 (29 June 1844): 397.

Will proved at under £80,000. *The Times*, 9 Oct 1844, 5f and *Gentleman's Magazine* n.s. 22 (Dec 1844): 659.

'William Beckford, Esq.' *The Art-Union* 6 (June 1844): 144.

'William Beckford, Esq.' *Gentleman's Magazine* n.s. 22 (Aug 1844): 209–213. Written, at least in part, by Henry Venn Lansdown. Reprinted, with omissions, in *Annual Register, or a view of the History and Politics of the Year 1844*, 86 (1845), 'Appendix to Chronicle': 236–238.

GENERAL ACCOUNTS

Books

Anderson, Patrick & Alistair Sutherland. *Eros: An Anthology of Friendship*. London: Anthony Blond, 1961. Short account of William Beckford, 201–203. Extracts from *Vathek*: 'The Sacrifice of the Boys', 204–206; 'The Charming Gulchenrouz', 206–209; 'A Bliss of Childhood', 209–210.

Anster, John. 'Beckford, William.' In *The Imperial Dictionary of Universal Biography* . . ., ed. J. F. Waller et al., 1:454–455. 3 vols. Glasgow: Mackenzie, [1857–1863]. Originally issued in Division 3 (Bar–Bic, *c*.1858) of 16 divs.

Arthaud, Claude. *Les Palais du Rêve*. Paris: Paris-Match, 1970. Trans. as *Enchanted visions: Fantastic Houses and Their Treasures*. New York: Putnam, 1972. London ed.: 'Beckford and Fonthill Abbey.' In *Dream Palaces: Fantastic Houses and Their Treasures*, 117–132 & 14 illus. on pp. 116, 133–135. London: Thames & Hudson, 1973.

Ashley, Mike. 'William Beckford.' In *Who's Who in Horror and Fantasy Literature*, 29–30. London: Elm Tree Books, 1977.

Beeton, S. O. & John Sherer. 'Beckford, William.' In *Beeton's Dictionary of Universal Information*, 186. London: Beeton, [1859]. In vol. A–D.

Blackie, publ. 'Beckford, William.' In *Popular Encyclopedia or Conversations Lexicon*, half-vol. 2:476–477. London: Blackie, 1875.

Boutet de Monvel, Roger. 'Beckford.' In *Grands seigneurs et bourgeois d'Angleterre*, 201–262 & 2 pl. Paris: Plon, 1918. With essays on George Selwyn, Fanny Burney & Romeo Coates. Reprinted in 1930 without Coates.

Britton, John. *Auto-biography*. Part 1. 8vo. ed. London: Printed for the Author, 1850 [?1857]. Favourable memoir of Beckford, 226–233. For

Part 2 see '5. Fonthill Abbey. Contemporary Accounts after 1823'. There was also a 4to. ed.

Burke, J. Bernard. 'Fonthill Abbey.' In *Anecdotes of the Aristocracy, Second Series*, 2:1–28. 2 vols. London: E. Churton, 1850. Reprinted with slight alterations and paragraph on Hadlow Castle in his *The Romance of the Aristocracy*, 3:141–161, 3 vols., London: Hurst & Blackett, 1855.

Bushell, Peter. 'Brollies, Bowlers and Builders.' In *Great Eccentrics*, 37–43. London: George Allen & Unwin, 1984.

Cardwell, Rev. John Henry. *Men and Women of Soho*. London: Truslove & Hanson, [1904]. Pp. 57–59. Portrait roundel, 58.

Caufield, Catherine. 'Beckford. William.' In *The Emperor of the United States of America & Other Magnificent British Eccentrics*, 21–24. London: Routledge & Kegan Paul, 1981. Paperback, London: Corgi, 1982, 26–29.

Clayden, P. W. *Rogers and his Contemporaries*. 2 vols. London: Smith Elder, 1889. 1:23–25, 273–274.

Colegate, Isabel. *A Pelican in the Wilderness: Hermits, Solitaries and Recluses*. London: HarperCollins, 2002. William Beckford, 191–195 & drawing of Beckford's Tower, 194.

Cousin, John W. 'Beckford, William (*c*.1760–1844).' In *A Short Biographical Dictionary of English Literature*, 31. London: Dent, 1910.

Craven, Baroness Elizabeth, afterwards Elizabeth, Margravine of Brandenburg-Anspach and Bayreuth. *Memoirs of the Margravine of Anspach*. 2 vols. London: Colburn, 1826. 2:103–106. Reprinted as *The Beautiful Lady Craven. The Original Memoirs of Elizabeth Baroness Craven afterwards Margravine of Anspach . . . 1750–1828*, ed. A. M. Broadley & Lewis Melville, 2 vols., London: John Lane, 1914.

Donaldson, William. 'Beckford, William.' In *Brewer's Rogues, Villains Eccentrics: An A–Z of Roguish Britons Through the Ages*, 54–56. London: Cassell, 2002. Romney's portrait between pp. 118 & 119.

Fitzgerald, Percy H. 'Beckford and Fonthill Abbey.' In *Kings and Queens of an Hour. Records of Love, Romance, Oddity*, 2:191–217. 2 vols. London: Tinsley Bros, 1883.

Fyvie, John. "The Splendid Author of 'Vathek'." In *Literary Eccentrics*, 65–95. London: Constable, 1906. General account with portrait.

Garnett, Richard. 'Beckford, William.' In *Dictionary of National Biography*, ed. Leslie Stephen, 4:82–85. London: Smith, Elder, 1885.

George, Daniel. 'Caliph.' In *A Book of Characters*, 43–45. London: Edward Hulton, 1959. Extracts from Redding's *Fifty Years' Recollections* (1858).

Gray, Jennie. *Horace Walpole & William Beckford. Pioneers of the Gothic Revival*. Chislehurst, Kent: The Gothic Society, 1994. Beckford's scandals, with quotations from *Life at Fonthill* (1957), 20–32 with eight illus.

Hall Caine, T. 'Beckford, William of Fonthill Abbey.' In *Celebrities of the Century*, ed. Lloyd Charles Sanders, 109. London: Cassell, 1887.

Hammerton, J. A., ed. 'Beckford, William.' In *Concise Universal Biography*, 1:219. 2 vols. London: Amalgamated Press, 1934–1935. Originally in part 8 (of 52) issued 3 April 1934.

Harper, Charles G. 'Fonthill Abbey.' In *Mansions of Old Romance*, 48–55. London: Cecil Palmer, 1930. Frontis., SW view of Abbey from Storer (1812). South view of Beckford's Tower, 53. A superficial account.

Hearn, Lafcadio. 'William Beckford.' In *Some Strange Literary Figures of the Eighteenth and Nineteenth Centuries*, ed. R. Tanabé, 40–51. Tokyo: Hokuseido Press, 1927. A lecture delivered to the students of English Literature, Graduate Class of 1899, Imperial University of Tokyo. Reprinted, Freeport, NY: Books for Libraries, [1965].

Jeaffreson, J. Cordy. 'William Beckford.' In *Novels and Novelists from Elizabeth to Victoria*, 1:389–405. 2 vols. London: Hurst & Blackett, 1858.

Jenner, Michael. *A Traveller's Companion to the West Country*. London: Michael Joseph, 1990. Pp. 168, 169.

Jolliffe, John. 'William Beckford (1759–1844).' In *Eccentrics: The Great and the Good*, 53–65. London: Duckworth, 2001.

Jourdain, Margaret. 'William Beckford of Fonthill.' In *Memorials of Old Wiltshire*, ed. Alice Dryden, 116–127. London: Bemrose & Sons, 1906. A rather hostile account. Noted in *Wiltshire Archæological and Natural History Magazine* 34 (Dec 1906): 442.

    REVIEW. Kite, Edward. *Wiltshire Notes and Queries* 5 (Sept 1906): 330–334 at 333.

Knight, Derrick. 'An Eighteenth Century Godfather [Alderman Beckford].' & 'Xanadu on a Wiltshire Hilltop.' In *Gentlemen of Fortune*, 36–52 & 113–126. London: Muller, 1978.

Lees-Milne, James. 'Biographical Introduction.' In *William Beckford Exhibition 1976*, [ed. Julian Berry], 7–10. Tisbury, Wilts: Compton Press, 1976.

Marshall, George W. 'Beckford.' In *The Genealogist's Guide*, 49. Guildford: Privately Printed, 1893. Eight sources listed.

Mayne, Ethel Colburn. *A Regency Life. Lady Bessborough and her Friendships*. London: Macmillan, 1939. Samuel Rogers at Fonthill in 1817, 256–257. 'Remember me' on title page of the *Vathek* given to Byron by Caroline Lamb, 270.

McConnell, Anita. 'Beckford, William (1760–1844).' In *Oxford Dictionary of National Biography*, ed. H. C. G. Matthew & Brian Harrison, 4:731–737. Oxford: Oxford University Press, 2004. Not wholly reliable.

[Miller, William Haig.] 'The Man of Wealth.' In *The Mirage of Life*, 20–30. London: Religious Tract Society, [1850]. Emma Hamilton at Fonthill, 97–98. Beckford in Portugal, 103. Reprinted, [1857]. New ed., [1867], 'The Man of Wealth.' 39–55, with two illus. by John Tenniel (Abbey under scaffolding & Sale works of art) engraved by Butterworth & Heath.

REVIEW. Millington, Jon. *Beckford Tower Trust Newsletter*, Spring 1982, 8.

Millington, Jon. 'William Beckford, une biographie sommaire.' In *Argenteries. Le Trésor du National Trust for Scotland*, 16–22. Brussels: National Trust for Scotland, 1992. Exhibition catalogue in French and Flemish. Pp. 4–6 in English trans.

Millington, Jon. 'William Beckford.' In his *Souvenirs of Fonthill Abbey*, 4–6. Bath: Bath Preservation Trust, 1994. Exhibition catalogue.

Monkland, George. *The Literature and Literati of Bath*. Bath: R. E. Peach, 1854. Beckford's retirement at Lansdown, 68.

Mowl, Timothy. 'William Beckford: A Biographical Perspective.' In *William Beckford, 1760–1844: An Eye for the Magnificent*, ed. Derek E. Ostergard, 16–31. New Haven & London: Yale University Press for the Bard Graduate Center, 2001. Exhibition catalogue.

Neale, Rev. Erskine. 'The Man of Taste. Beckford of Fonthill.' In *The Closing Scene; or, Christianity and Infidelity contrasted in the Last Hours of Remarkable Persons*, 1–30. 2nd Series. London: Longman, etc., 1849. 2nd ed., 1850, 1–25. An illuminating and, at times, rather censorious account.

REVIEW. *The Britannia* (London, weekly). Reprinted in *Littell's Living Age* 21 (21 April 1849): 99–101 at 100.

Nicholas, Margaret. 'Ups and Downs of Beckford's Towers.' In *The World's Greatest Cranks and Crackpots*, 44–47. London: Octopus, 1982.

Ostergard, Derek E. 'Introduction.' In *William Beckford, 1760–1844: An Eye for the Magnificent*, ed. Derek E. Ostergard, 11–15. New Haven & London: Yale University Press for the Bard Graduate Center, 2001. Exhibition catalogue.

Praz, Mario. 'Il Califfo Beckford.' In *Studi e svaghi inglesi*, 281–289. Florence: Sansoni, 1937. Biblioteca Italiana IV.

Quennell, Peter. *Romantic England. Writing and Painting 1717–1851*. London: Weidenfeld & Nicolson, 1970. Well-illus. biographical account, 21–35. Also 14, 36, 37, 44, 45, 224, 258.

Quinn, Tom. *Tales of the Country Eccentrics*. Newton Abbot: David & Charles, 1996. Beckford, 109–114. Modern artist's portrait of Beckford & dwarf, 68.

Redding, Cyrus. 'Chapter V.' In *Fifty Years' Recollections, Literary and Personal, with Observations on Men and Things*, 3:87–128 at 3:87–124. 3 vols. London: Charles J. Skeet, 1858. Beckford gardening, 3:152–153. Also 3:5, 190. 2nd ed. rev. 1858. 3rd ed. London: Saunders & Otley, 1867.

REVIEWS. *Athenæum*, 9 Jan 1858, 46–47. Reprinted in *Littell's Living Age* 56 (13 March 1858): 686–688.

Gentleman's Magazine n.s. 4 (May 1858): 494–495.

New Monthly Magazine 136 (April 1866): 484–485.

Redding, Cyrus. 'Beckford's Life.' In *Yesterday and To-day*, 3:33–35. 3 vols. London: T Cautley Newby, 1863. The fate of his 1846 MS. life of Beckford.

Redding, Cyrus. 'William Beckford.' In *Past Celebrities whom I Have Known*, 1:292–347. 2 vols. London: Charles J. Skeet, 1866. Dr Wolcot at Fonthill for Nelson's visit, 1:249, 263.

Reynolds, Frederic. *The Life and Times of Frederick Reynolds written by himself.* 2 vols. London: Colburn, 1826. 1:295–296.

Riches, Ann. 'William Beckford of Fonthill Abbey.' In *The British Eccentric*, ed. Harriet Bridgeman & Elizabeth Drury, 114–126. London: Michael Joseph, 1975. Eleven illus. including drawing of Beckford on horseback by Lucius Gahagan, 117.

Russell, W. Clark. 'William Beckford 1760–1844.' In *The Book of Authors: A Collection of Criticisms*, 356–358. New. Ed. London: Warne, [1871]. Entry based on other author's quotations about Beckford.

Sewell, Gordon A. 'Beckford of Fonthill.' In *A Wessex Notebook*, 94–98. Southampton: G. F. Wilson, 1956. SW view by Storer (1812), facing 100. James Wyatt & Fonthill, 18, 23.

Spalding, William. 'Beckford.' In *Cyclopaedia of Biography*, ed. Elihu Rich, 72. 2nd ed. London: Richard Griffin, 1858. (1st ed. 1854.)

Timbs, John. 'The Beckfords and Fonthill.' In *English Eccentrics and Eccentricities*, 1–19. New ed. (?3rd). London: Chatto & Windus, 1877. (1st ed. 1866.) Also 'Alderman Beckford's Monument Speech, in Guildhall', 19–21. Portrait of William Beckford, 1. Caricature of Farquhar, 21.

Timpson, John. 'Colossucentrics.' In *Timpson's English Eccentrics*, 161–165. Norwich, Norfolk: Jarrold, 1991. Text based on Caufield (1981), see above. Five colour photos.

Treasure, Geoffrey. 'William Beckford 1759–1844.' In *Who's Who in Late Hanoverian Britain 1789–1837*, 99–101. London: Shepheard-Walwyn, 1997. First publ. as *Who's Who in History.* Vol. 5. Oxford: Blackwell, 1974.

Vapereau, G. *Dictionnaire universel des littératures* . . . Paris: Hachette, 1876. P. 223.

Villena, Luis Antonio de. 'Beau satan. Sobre William Beckford of Fonthill.' In *Corsarios de Guante Amarillo: Sobre el Dandysmo*, 43–74. Barcelona: Tusquets, 1983. On dandyism, including essays on Byron and Oscar Wilde.

Vincent, Leon H. "Fonthill, 'Vathek,' and Beckford." In *Dandies and Men of Letters*, 172–191. Boston, MA: Houghton Mifflin, 1913.

Wade, G. J. & J. H. *Rambles in Somerset.* 2nd rev. ed. London: Methuen, 1923. (1st ed. 1912.) Brief outline of life, 37–38.

'Walpole and Beckford.' In *Great British Eccentrics*, 20–22. London: Reader's Digest, 1982. Also 'The [10th] Duke of Hamilton', 19–20.

Walters, Cuming. 'The Lansdown Bagdad and its Caliph.' In *Bygone Somerset*, ed. Cuming Walters. 136–148. London: Andrews, 1897. 'He was an intellectual giant'.

Watts, Alaric Alexander. *Alaric Watts. A Narrative of his Life.* 2 vols. London: Bentley, 1884. Met Beckford, who had just bought a picture, at the British Institution in 1833, 2:110–116.

Watts, Kenneth. 'William Beckford: the Caliph of Fonthill.' In *Figures in a Wiltshire Scene*, 159–172. East Knoyle, Wiltshire: Hobnob Press, 2002.

Weeks, David & Jamie James. *Eccentrics.* London: Phoenix, 1996. (1st ed. 1995). Pp. 34–35.

Young, Rev. Julian Charles. *A Memoir of Charles Mayne Young, Tragedian, with Extracts from his Son's Journal.* 2 vols. London: Macmillan, 1871. Anecdotes in the son's diary entry for 2 Feb 1838, 2:6–26. Reprinted in *Personal Reminiscences by Chorley, Planché and Young*, 282–292, ed. Richard Henry Stoddard, New York: Scribner, Armstrong, 1874.

REVIEWS. [Doran, John.] 'Charles Young and His Times.' *Temple Bar* 32 (June 1871): 321–334. 'It is very well said of Beckford that there has seldom existed a man who, inheriting so much, did so little for his fellow-creatures.' Reprinted in *Littell's Living Age* 110 (29 July 1871): 298–305 at 304.

'Literature. A Memoir of Charles Mayne Young.' *Galaxy* (New York) 12 (Aug 1871): 274–282 at 277. 'Considerable space is given to one of the most singular men England has produced, the famous "Sybarite," Beckford, the builder of Fonthill Abbey'.

Articles

Alexander, Boyd. 'William Beckford: Do We Do Him Justice?' *Folio*, Jan–March 1958, 7–10. Essay to promote the Folio Society selection for February 1958, *Vathek*, with Edward Bawden's lithographs.

Alexander, Boyd. 'William Beckford. Man of Taste.' *History Today* 10 (Oct 1960): 686–694. Valuable account with seven illus.

Alexander, Boyd. 'William Beckford of Fonthill.' *Yale University Library Gazette* 35 no. 4 (April 1961): 161–169. Inaugural lecture for Beckford Exhibition at Yale (1960).

American Traveller. 'Gore House.' *New Monthly Magazine* 86 (June 1849): 135–151. Anecdotes. Reprinted in *Littell's Living Age* 22 (28 July 1849): 145–154 at 145–146.

Anton, P. 'The Author of Vathek: The Story of a Magnificent Idler.' *The People's Friend*, 16–17 Jan 1898.

Armour, Richard W. 'The Caliph of Fonthill.' *Reading and Collecting* (Chicago) 1 (Nov 1937): 9–10.

Atthill, Robin. 'The Folly.' *West Country Magazine* 2 no. 3 (Autumn 1947): 183–188 at 187. Reprinted in his *The Curious Past. West Country Studies*, 36–45 at 42. Taunton, The Wessex Press, 1955. Also reprinted in J. C. Trewin, ed. *West Country Book Number One*, 27. London: Westaway Books, 1949.

Babb, James T. 'William Beckford of Fonthill.' *Yale University Library Gazette* 41 no. 2 (Oct 1966): 60–67. Revised version of his lecture in Beckford's Library at 19 Lansdown Crescent on 16 June 1966 as part of Bath Festival. *Idem*, 'Note', 67–69. Lists 23 books from Beckford's library sold at the Clements sale, Sotheby's, 4–5 July 1966, and bought by Yale.

Baker, H. Barton. 'A Modern Sybarite.' *Gentleman's Magazine* 252 (March 1882): 342–352. Fair survey reflecting the attitude to Beckford at that time.

'The Beckford Scandal.' *Wiltshire & Somerset Courier* 1 no. 12 (Sept/Oct 1963): 18–19, 31. Popular account with two photos of Fonthill Abbey remains.

Behm, Harald. 'William Beckford – Kunstsammler, Romancier und Romantiker. Englands reichster Sohn (WB – art collector, novelist and romantic. England's wealthiest son).' *Weltkunst* 51 (15 June 1982): 1764–1767. Seven illus.

Chamberlain, V. C. 'The strange story of William Beckford.' *Wiltshire and Wessex Life*, Feb 1974, 36–37. A popular general account with three photos.

[Chapman, Guy.] 'Beckford the Caliph. A Traveller in Two Worlds.' *Times Literary Supplement*, 6 May 1944, 222. Letters from C. F. Bell partly about the state of the Beckford Papers in 1922, 13 May, 235 & [Guy Chapman] denying Bell's suggestion that he had mistaken Alexander Cozens for his son, 20 May, 247.

Cheke, Marcus. 'William Beckford of Fonthill.' *Historical Association of Lisbon. Eighth Annual Report & Review*, 495–513. Lisbon, 1944. Centenary Lecture given on 2 May 1944. Three illus.

Codd, Joanna. 'A lasting monument to Beckford's folly.' *Bath and West Evening Chronicle*, 26 June 1986, 18.

'An Eccentric Tale. Who Was William Beckford?' *Leisureline* (Welsh Borders), Dec 1991–Jan 1992, 18.

Edmonson, Roger. 'William Beckford.' *Playguy* (New York), Oct 1998, 81–82.

Fothergill, Brian. 'William Beckford, Prince of Amateurs.' *Essays by Divers Hands* n.s. 38 (1975): 33–47. A perceptive and sympathetic study.

Gardner, Albert Ten Eyck. 'Beckford's Gothic Wests.' *The Metropolitan Museum of Art Bulletin* 13 no. 2 (Oct 1954): 41–49. Seven illus. of objects from the Museum's collection.

'Gothic Revival's Grand Showman.' *The Times*, 24 Sept 1960, 7f–g. Celebrating the bicentenary of Beckford's birth on 29 Sept 1760.

Harcourt-Smith, Simon. *The Tatler and Bystander*, c.Feb 1946. Little-known biographical details. Noted by 'Sul' in 'New light on Beckford', *Bath & Wilts Chronicle & Herald*, 22 Feb 1946, 3. (Also in weekly ed., 23 Feb, 11.)

'Hobbies and their Riders.' *The Overland Monthly* (San Francisco) 7 no. 3 (Sept 1871): 258–267 at 261. Anecdotes about this 'Prince of Dilettanti'.

James, Jamie. 'The Caliph of Fonthill.' *American Scholar* (Washington) 72 no. 1 (Winter 2003): 67–79. A general account inspired by the author's collection of Beckford's literary works.

Jeffreys, Sophie. 'The Caliph of Fonthill. The Enigma of William Beckford.' *Wiltshire Life* 2 no. 10 (April 1997): 24–26. A popular account.

Jordan, R. Furneaux. 'Beckford's Folly.' ?*Sunday Times*, 1953.

Jullian, Philippe. 'William Beckford.' *Revue des Deux Mondes*, 15 May 1956, 329–340.

Lawrence, Richard. 'William Beckford.' *Book and Magazine Collector* No. 172 (July 1998): 58–71. Bibliography with guide to values, 70–71.

Melville, Lewis. [Lewis S. Benjamin, pseud.] 'William Beckford, of Fonthill Abbey.' *Fortnightly Review* n.s. 86 (1 Dec 1909): 1011–1023. An essay to promote his 1910 biography. Reprinted in his *Some Eccentrics & a Woman*, 189–215, London: Martin Secker, [1911]. Portrait facing 192. Noted in *Wiltshire Archæological and Natural History Magazine* 36 (June 1910): 500.

Meredith, F. D. 'The Old Man of the Mountain. A story of a Wessex Eccentric.' *Somerset and Wessex Life*, May 1970, 32–33. Brief general account with photo of Tower & portrait by C. F. Tayler wrongly identified as Beckford.

Mooney, Bel. 'The folly of William Beckford.' *Weekend Telegraph*, 23 May 1998, 19. Publicising the Beckford Tower Appeal.

Myer, Val, 'The Eccentric Millionaire.' *The Listener* 35 (24 Jan 1946): 118–119 with Romney & Rutter illus. A talk broadcast on the BBC's Eastern Service by the architect of Broadcasting House.

North, W. 'William Beckford.' *Literature. An Illustrated Weekly Magazine* (Alden, publ., New York) 2 no. 45 (29 Dec 1888): 50–53. Slightly abridged from Slater's ed. of *Vathek* (1849). Followed by an extract from *Vathek* (see '11. *Vathek* and *The Episodes*: Editions'). Reprinted in *Literary Portraits*, 2 vols., New York: Alden, 1888–1889, 2:50–53.

Pendle, George. 'The Ruined Man.' *Cabinet* (New York) Issue 20 (Winter 2005): 61–63. General article emphasising Beckford's isolation. Lithograph of Buckler's drawing of the ruins of Fonthill Abbey (1825 [1826]), 63.

Penley, Belville S. 'Random Papers. A Man of Mystery. Beckford and his Eccentricities.' *Wiltshire Times & Trowbridge Advertiser*, 13 Aug 1927,

7b–c. General account – stories of orgies groundless. Noted in *Wiltshire Archæological and Natural History Magazine* 44 (Dec 1927): 88.

Pitman, Ben. 'Bekford, Vathek, Fonthil.' *Phonetic Journal* 34 (1875): 9–11. Reprinted in standard English as 'Beckford, "Vathek," Fonthill' in Gregory, *The Beckford Family* (2nd ed., 1898), 144–153.

Pryce-Jones, Alan. 'William Beckford, Dilettante.' *New York Times Book Review*, 16 Feb 1969, 2, 40. Author of a famous but 'almost universally unread novel'.

Reid, R. D. 'The Gothic Revival.' *Somerset Archæological and Natural History Society. Proceedings of the Bath & District Branch* 8 (1939–1947): 399–409 at 401–402. In Part 9. Paper read on 9 Jan 1947.

'The Scandalous William Beckford.' *Parade* (Melbourne, Australia) No. 288 (Nov 1974): 38–39. A lively popular account with two fuzzy illus.

Schiff, Gert. 'Über William Beckford' *Du, Kulturelle Monatsschrift* (Zurich) No. 249 (Nov 1961): 21–22, 24–25 & 4 illus. «Ich bin reich und entschlossen Türme zu bauen» (I grow rich and mean to build towers).

Smith, George Barnett. 'The Author of "Vathek".' *Time* n.s. 8 (April 1883): 454–471. Monument to Alderman Beckford in St George's, Botolph Lane, 455.

Spring, Philip. 'Croesus in Queer Street.' *Courier* 23 no. 4 (Oct 1954): 57–59. A lively general account with Romney's portrait and SW view of Fonthill Abbey almost identical to that in Rutter's *New Descriptive Guide* ... (1823).

Stollar, Derek. 'Beckford – a towering figure in Regency life.' *[Bath] Evening Chronicle*, 21 June 1993, 8. With reproduction of woodcut from *Pictorial Times*, 25 May 1844, of funeral procession leaving Lansdown Crescent.

'Strange Freaks of a Millionaire.' *Exeter News-Letter* (New Hampshire), 28 Feb 1859, 1f–g. 'One of the most remarkable men of modern times'.

'Sul'. 'Beckford of Fonthill.' *Bath & Wilts Chronicle & Herald*, 14 Nov 1945, 3. (Also in *Bath Weekly Chronicle and Herald*, 17 Nov, 12.) Geoffrey Grigson to give a talk on Beckford on the BBC West of England Home Service.

Summers, Montague. 'The Abbot of Fonthill.' *Everybody's Weekly*, 23 Nov 1946, 13. Popular account by the author of *A Gothic Bibliography* (1940).

Sumner, Ian. 'A stylish eccentric.' *Fosse Way Magazine* (Stalbridge, Dorset), 13 April 2001, 45 & two photos. Also photo of Tower staircase, 1.

Walmsley, Thomas A. 'William Beckford of Fonthill.' *Paisley Daily Express*, 17, 31 Oct, 14, 28 Nov, 26 Dec 1958, 6, 6, 3, 6, 5. Five general articles beginning with his relationship to the Abercorns of Paisley.

Whibley, Charles. 'The Caliph of Fonthill.' *The New Review* 16 (Jan 1897): 59–70. Reprinted in his *The Pageantry of Life*, 199–218, London:

Heinemann, 1900. An excellent, well-written essay. Article noted in *Wiltshire Archæological and Natural History Magazine* 30 (Dec 1898): 158.

'The Writer of "Vathek".' *The Bookman*, June 1910, 133–134.

Wyatt, Robin. 'The Man with a Passion for Towers.' *House & Garden*, Dec 1973/Jan 1974, 78–79. Concise article & fine photo of Beckford's Tower.

CHILDREN'S BOOKS

[Marson, Richard & Anne Dixon.] 'The Fool of Fonthill.' In *Blue Peter BBC Annual 2005*, 76–79. Exeter: Pedigree, [2004]. Twelve colour illus. by Bob Broomfield. Book No. 34. Based on a *Blue Peter* television programme transmitted on BBC1 on Monday, 30 June 2003.

'These Men Had Queer Habits . . . William Beckford – The millionaire eccentric.' In *Every Boy's Annual*, 26. London: Juvenile Productions, [1954]. With illus. by G. E. Lang of Fonthill's tower collapsing.

2. Aspects of Beckford

Beckford Society Publications

Blackmore, Sidney, ed. *The Beckford Newsletter. An Occasional Newsletter of the Beckford Society*. Privately printed, 1996 to date.

Millington, Jon, compiler. *Beckford and His Circle in the Gentleman's Magazine*. London: *The Beckford Society*, 2001. 61 pp. An annotated index of entries from 1731 to 1882 relating to Beckford.

Millington, Jon, ed. *The Beckford Journal*. Publ. annually. Vols. 1–11 (1995–2005). See separate entries throughout this bibliography. Successor to the *Beckford Tower Trust Newsletter*, publ. annually from 1980 to 1994.

Millington, Jon, ed. *The Beckford Society Annual Lectures 1996–1999*. London: *The Beckford Society*, 2000. 80 pp. See separate entries (author, section): John Wilton-Ely, 5; João de Almeida Flor, 15; William Hauptman, 8; Michel Baridon, 2.

Millington, Jon, ed. *The Beckford Society Annual Lectures 2000–2003*. London: *The Beckford Society*, 2004. 88 pp. See separate entries (author, section): Kevin Cope, 2; Edward Chaney, 13; Kenneth W. Graham, 12; Mirella Billi, 15.

Full-length Studies
See also 'Full-length Studies' in Sections 1 and 15

Graham, Kenneth W. & Kevin Berland, eds. *William Beckford and the New Millennium*. New York: AMS Press, 2004 [2005]. xiv, 313 pp. 34 illus. 23½ cm. Intro. & twelve essays (see separate entries: author, section) in five parts: 'Thresholds' (John Beynon, 2; Mirella Billi, 15; Dick Claésson, 15), 'Mature Fiction' (John Garrett, 15; Didier Girard, 12; Kenneth Graham, 12), 'Beckford in Portugal' (Laura Pires, 13; Paulo Kühl, 13), 'Fonthill Abbey and Bath' (Stephen Clarke, 5; Laurent Châtel, 7; George Haggerty, 6) & 'Afterword on the Millennium' (Kevin Cope, 2).

Moussa-Mahmoud, Fatma, ed. *William Beckford of Fonthill, 1760–1844. Bicentenary Essays*. Suppl. to *Cairo Studies in English*, 1960. 159 pp. 1 pl. 24 cm. Seven essays (see separate entries: author, section): André Parreaux, 14; Boyd Alexander, 2; Geoffrey Bullough, 13; Magdi Wahba, 13; Fatma Moussa-Mahmoud, 9 & 12; Mahmoud Manzalaoui, 12. Reprinted, Port Washington, NY: Kennikat Press, 1972.

REVIEWS. 'Eccentric writer.' *Times Literary Supplement*, 28 July 1961, 462.

Frykman, Erik. *Studia Neophilologica* 33 (1961): 343–345.

Philological Quarterly 41 no. 3 (July 1962): 567. Contents list.

Rawson, C. J. *Notes and Queries* 207 (May 1962): 196–198.

Thompson, Karl F. *Modern Language Quarterly* 23 no. 2 (June 1962): 181–182.

Books

Acton, Eliza. 'Rice à la Vathek, or Rice Pudding à la Vathek. (Extremely Good.)' In *Modern Cookery, for Private Families . . .*, 440. Enlarged ed. London: Longman, etc, 1855. Not in the earlier eds.

Alexander, Boyd. 'The Decay of Beckford's Genius.' In *William Beckford of Fonthill, 1760–1844. Bicentenary Essays*, ed. Fatma Moussa-Mahmoud, 17–29. Suppl. to *Cairo Studies in English*, 1960.

Alger, John Goldworth. *Englishmen in the French Revolution*. London: Sampson Low, 1889. Beckford's arrest, 350.

Blackmore, Sidney. 'William Beckford in London.' & 'The Bath Years: 1822–44.' In *William Beckford, 1760–1844: An Eye for the Magnificent*, ed. Derek E. Ostergard, 250–261 & 262–277. New Haven & London: Yale University Press for the Bard Graduate Center, 2001. Exhibition catalogue.

Borrow, George. *Lavengro*. London: John Murray, 1902. (1st ed. 1851.) Editorial note explaining that the Stranger crossing Salisbury Plain in 1825 (pp. 330 et seq.) could not have been Beckford because the topographical details are not consistent with a meeting near Fonthill, which he sold in 1822, 566.

Brunel. Rolt, L. T. C. *Brunel*. London: Longmans, Green, 1957. Beckford approved design of Clifton Suspension Bridge & footnote by Sacheverell Sitwell about painting by Bellini found later in Beckford's house, 57. Telford's rejected design unfavourably compared with Fonthill, 54.

Buckle, Richard. *The Most Upsetting Woman. Autobiography 1*. London: Collins, 1981. Fonthill, 29. Beckford, 215, 225. Called 'Arab' when young by Lady Craven who remained his friend after 1784, 217.

Burke, John. 'Beckford of Fonthill.' In *A Genealogical and Heraldic History of the Commoners of Great Britain and Ireland*, 1:678–682. 4 vols. London: Henry Colburn, 1833–1837. 'Beckford of Basing Park', vol. 2 (1835), 599–601. In 1837 '*Landed Gentry: or*' was added to the title before '*Commoners*'.

Burke, John & John Bernard Burke. 'Beckford of Fonthill.' In *A Genealogical and Heraldic Dictionary of the Landed Gentry of Great Britain and Ireland*. 1:77–78. 2 vols. + suppl. London: Henry Colburn, 1849.

Cope, Kevin L. 'The Millennium Continues to be an Incident: Occasional Reflections on the Renewability of Beckford's Reputation.' In *William Beckford and the New Millennium*, ed. Kenneth W. Graham & Kevin Berland, 283–307. New York: AMS Press, 2004 [2005].

Davenport-Hines, Richard. 'William Beckford.' In *Gothic: 400 Years of Excess, Horror, Evil and Ruin*, 202–212. London: Fourth Estate, 1998. Also 4, 8, 25, 146.

Fermor, Patrick Leigh. *Words of Mercury*, ed. Artemis Cooper. London: John Murray, 2003. The background to a Greek archbishop's portrait is likened to 'a soaring Beckfordian complex of lancets, triforia, clerestories and crocketed finials', 152–153.

Forgues, Paul Emile Daurand. *Originaux et Beaux-Esprits de l'Angleterre contemporaine*. 2 vols. Paris: Charpentier, 1860. 1:46–47.

Gallet, Michel. 'Promenade étrange de Sir William Beckford en compagnie de Ledoux.' In *Claude-Nicolas Ledoux 1736–1806*, 269–271. Paris: Picard, 1980. Letter to Louisa about Beckford's occult experience in Paris in 1784, trans. from Oliver (1932, 172–181). Also 24, 26, 254.

Goodden, Angelica. *Miss Angel: The Art and World of Angelica Kauffman*. London: Pimlico, 2005. Beckford on Ferdinand IV of Naples, 193 & 252 n42, and praising Kauffmann to Sir Wm. Hamilton, 229–230 & 354 nn57–61.

Gore-Browne, Robert. *Chancellor Thurlow. The Life and Times of an XVIIIth Century Lawyer*. London: Hamish Hamilton, 1953. Alderman Beckford, 38, 41. Beckford was Thurlow's ward in Chancery, 131. Lady Craven's *Arcadian Pastoral*, 209. Thurlow urged Beckford to retire to Switzerland with his wife after 1784 scandal, & reluctantly supported his peerage application, 223–224.

Huxley, Aldous. *Prisons. With the 'Carceri' etchings by G. B. Piranesi. Critical study by Jean Adhémar*. London: Trianon Press, [1949]. P. 16.

Le Brun, Annie. *Les châteaux de la subversion*. Paris: Pauvert, 1982. Walpole's 'Gothic mousetrap', 163. Abbey in ruins (illus. wrong way round), 285. Also 283, 286, 291 n89.

Nicolson, Benedict. *Joseph Wright of Derby: Painter of Light*. 2 vols. London: Paul Mellon Foundation, 1968. Quote from *England's Wealthiest Son* (1962, 73–74) about Beckford visiting an ironworks, 1:121–122.

Quennell, Peter. *The Marble Foot*. London: Collins, 1968. Attacked by Harold Acton for making derogatory remarks about Beckford, 167–168.

Schama, Simon. *Landscape & Memory*. London: HarperCollins, 1995. 61,800 Scotch firs planted at Fonthill, 168. John Robert Cozens in the Alps and Italy with Beckford, 475, 477.

Scott, Jonathan. *The Arabian Nights Entertainments*. 6 vols. London: Longman, etc., 1811. Beckford owned part of Arabian manuscript for *1001 Nights*, 6:456–457.

Strachey, Lytton. *The Letters of Lytton Strachey.* Ed. Paul Levy. London: Viking, 2005. To Virginia Woolf on 23 Aug 1921 recommending Beckford's *Memoirs of Painters*, 495. To Roger Senhouse on 19 Dec 1930 about Lord Courtenay, 636.

Sweetman, John. *The Oriental Obsession. Islamic Inspiration in British and American Art and Architecture 1500–1920.* Cambridge: Cambridge University Press, 1988. Beckford a romantic, 3. His preoccupation with the Orient, 83–85 & 272–273 nn25–28, 31. Fonthill compared to the palace of Yuan Ming Yuan, Peking, 113. Turkish carpet in *Biographical Memoirs* (1780), 274 n39. Three paintings in 1807 Fonthill sale, 276 n56. Colour pl. III, 'Beckford Cup' by James Aldridge (1814). 'Moorish summer-house . . . mid 1820s', fig. 41.

Sykes, Christoper Simon. *Private Palaces. Life in the Great London Houses.* London: Chatto & Windus, 1985. Beckford described the gardens of Chesterfield House as the finest in London, 118. Party at Home House in 1782, 215, 218. Richard Beckford at 1 Greek Street, 144 & two illus., 145.

Symonds, John Addington. *The Letters of John Addington Symonds.* Ed. Herbert M. Schueller & Robert L. Peters. 3 vols. Detroit: Wayne State University Press, 1967–1969. Vol. 2 (1968). To Mrs Arthur Hugh Clough on 12 Dec 1871, 'like Beckford I shall keep my compositions to myself', 186 & n.

Turner, Paul Venable. *Joseph Ramée.* Cambridge: Cambridge University Press, 1996. 'Oriental' tent constructed for Beckford by Ramée, 36–38.

Vidler, Anthony. *Claude-Nicolas Ledoux: Architecture and Social Reform at the End of the Ancien Régime.* Cambridge, MA: M.I.T. Press, 1990. 'The Ideal City of Chaux, 1780–1804', 337–340 & 442 nn105–107. *Vathek*, 343, 346 & 443 n12. Also 356, 379.

Westland, Peter. *The Romantic Revival, 1780–1830.* Based on the original work of Arthur Compton-Rickett. London: English Universities Press, 1950. Pp. 163–164. Teach Yourself History of English Literature.

Williams, E. N. *Life in Georgian England.* London: Batsford, 1962. *Vathek*, 'oriental romance', 159. Fonthill Abbey, with SW view from *Gentleman's Magazine* (Sept 1822), 162.

Wilstach, Paul. *Fifty Games of Solitaire With Cards.* Indianapolis: Carlon & Hollenbeck, Printers, 1891. One of the games is 'Vathek'.

Articles

[Allen, Grant.] 'Lyme Regis; a Splinter of Petrified History.' *Cornhill Magazine* 42 (Dec 1880): 709–720 at 718. 'Beckford Bridge . . ., by the way, gives rise to another famous surname, which all of us know through the brilliant author of "Vathek," and the owner of Fonthill Abbey'. Reprinted in *Littell's Living Age* 148 (1 Jan 1881): 57.

Baridon, Michel. 'From Beckford to Mallarmé: The tradition of *L'Art pour l'Art*.' In *The Beckford Society Annual Lectures 1996–1999*, ed. Jon Millington, 55–80. London: *The Beckford Society*, 2000. The 1999 lecture.

Beer, Gavin de, ed. 'Voltaire's British Visitors.' *Studies on Voltaire and the Eighteenth Century* 4 (1957): 130–132. On tour with John Lettice in 1777 & 1778. Reprinted, jointly ed. with André-Michel Rousseau, and new final paragraph, *Idem* 49 (1967): 193–196.

Bishop, Franklin. 'Masonic Rites and Architecture.' *The Goth*, Dec 1992, 3–7 at 5–7. Claude-Nicolas Ledoux and his ideal city of Chaux.

Brion, Marcel. "Le secret du 'Calife' Beckford." *Revue des Deux Mondes*, 1 July 1949, 156–165.

Britton, John. 'The late Wm. Beckford, Esq.' *Bath Herald*, 25 May 1844, 3b. Comments in his *Fonthill Abbey* (1823) on genealogical tables of Beckford.

Brunel. Buchanan, R. Angus. 'Brunel in Bath.' *Bath History* 10 (2005): 158–186 at 162–163 & 185 n6. Brunel's diary entry of his visit to Beckford at Lansdown Crescent with his friend Acraman on 17 Sept 1830.

Calcuttensis. 'Hannah Lightfoot.' *Notes and Queries* 3rd Series 11 (5 Jan 1867): 11. Querying the statement in 'Conversations with Mr. Beckford' in the *New Monthly Magazine* 72 (Oct 1844): 216 that George III had secretly married Hannah Lightfoot. William J. Thoms, *Idem* (16 Feb 1867): 131–132, said Beckford had never mentioned her to a friend of his. R. K., *Idem* (1 June 1867): 446, thought it odd that no one had heard about Beckford's opinion.

Carter, Angela. 'Bathed in Englishness.' *New Society* 33 (18 Sept 1975): 648. Beckford in a group of 'famous madmen'. Reprinted as 'Bath, Heritage City' in *Nothing Sacred: Collected Writings*, 72, 74. London: Virago, 1982.

Cave, Graham. 'Beckford at the Salisbury Festival.' *Beckford Tower Trust Newsletter*, Spring 1992, 8. Lecture by James Malpas of Sotheby's.

Chadourne, Marc. "L'incroyable William Beckford." *Revue de Paris* 69 (Jan 1962): 43–58.

Claésson, Dick. 'Författarskap och biografi. En diskussion kring det biografiska problemet "Beckford".' (Authorship and Biography. A Discussion about the Biographical Problems of Beckford.) *Tidskrift för litteraturvetenskap* (Magazine of Literature) (1999.3–4): 109–128. In Swedish.

Cope, Kevin. 'How Beckford Keeps Making Himself Relevant: Or, Is the Millennium an 'Incident'?' In *The Beckford Society Annual Lectures 2000–2003*, ed. Jon Millington, 3–24. London: *The Beckford Society*, 2004. The 2000 lecture.

Didimus, H. *United States Magazine and Democratic Review* 16 (May 1845): 429–433 at 430. Review of *New Orleans as I found it* by Henry Didimus (New York: Harper & Brothers, 1845) mentioning a strange gentleman, shrouded in mystery, who invites Mr. Didimus to his house 'where he lives after the manner of Beckford of Fonthill'.

Dixon, Anne Campbell. 'It's your turn in the dome of pleasure.' *[Daily] Telegraph Travel*, 26 Oct 2002, 5. George IV, while Prince Regent, briefly compared with Beckford.

Durrant, Digby. 'A Random Harvest.' *Spectator*, 5 July 2003, 32–34 at 32. Expressing surprise that the *Spectator* should have reviewed Beckford's *Recollections* in 1835 in view of his 'openly scandalous' life.

Gamekeeper. 'Queries . . . Green and Gilbert.' *Wiltshire Notes and Queries* 4 (March 1903): 233. G. F. T. Sherwood noted that Joseph Green of Fonthill Gifford or Tisbury was said to have been Beckford's gamekeeper at Fonthill Abbey.

Gemmett, Robert J. 'The Birth Date of William Beckford.' *American Notes and Queries* 6 no. 10 (June 1968): 149–150. Explains why Beckford's date of birth was 29 Sept 1760 and not, as Redding stated, 1759.

Girard, Didier. 'William Beckford and the Gothic Charivari.' *Beckford Journal* 8 (2002): 50–65. Beckford's special brand of Gothicism.

Grigson, Geoffrey. 'Kubla Khan in Wales.' *Conhill Magazine* 162 (Spring 1947): 275–283 at 276, 281. Beckfod and Hafod. Reprinted in his *Places of the Mind*, London: Routledge, 1949, 8–15 at 9, 13.

Hazen, A. T. 'Booksellers' "Ring" at Strawberry Hill in 1842.' *Studies in Bibliography* 7 (1955): 196. Lord Derby, Beckford and W. H. Miller [?author of *Mirage of Life* (1850), see '1. Beckford's Life'] bought heavily, 196.

Hillier, Bevis. 'House Style. Case Study.' *The Times Magazine*, 29 April 1995, 42–43. James Lees-Milne in Beckford's Library, with three colour photos.

Jackman, Margaret. 'Beckford's bread.' *Bath & Wilts Chronicle & Herald*, 18 Sept 1956, 5. Note in Sul's 'Day by Day' diary about 1847 advert by Brooks, baker, 28 Broad St, Bath, who supplied Beckford with bread for twenty years.

Jackson, H. J. *Marginalia. Readers Writing in Books.* New Haven: Yale University Press, 2001. Beckford's annotations, 38–41. Also 73, 88, 246–247, 265, 273 n48.

Lees-Milne, James. 'Blake and Beckford: A Television Script.' *Beckford Journal* 4 (1998): 5–17. Transmitted on 9 August 1967. 'Beckford was an enthusiastic admirer of Blake's illuminated books. He was one of the very few people to attend the exhibition of Blake's drawings in 1809.', 12.

Magny, Olivier de. "L'esthétique de l'ennui." *Les lettres nouvelles* 5 (March 1957): 403–411.

Millington, Pat. 'Rice Pudding à la Vathek.' *Beckford Journal* 3 (1997): 36–39. Eliza Acton's recipe from her *Modern Cookery, for Private Families ...* (1855).

Nisbett, Jean. 'A Gothic Folly.' & 'Going Gothic. Interiors.' *Dolls' House Magazine* Nos. 77 & 78 (Oct & Nov 2004): 46, 47–48 & 64–65. 'My tower is an amalgam of features taken from both Fonthill and Lansdown'.

Parreaux, André. 'William Beckford (Principaux Problèmes Chronologiques).' *Bulletin des Etudes Portugaises* 1 (1931): 47–57. Beckford's date of birth, Mozart, stays in Paris & Portugal, Beckford and Bocage.

Rousseau, André-Michel. "L'Angleterre et Voltaire (1718–1789)." *Studies on Voltaire and the Eighteenth Century* 146 (1976): 287–288, 291, 321–322 and *Idem* 147 (1976): 606, 608, 626–628, 691, 787, 867.

Turner, Paul V. 'Joseph-Jacques Ramée's first career.' *Art Bulletin* 67 (June 1985): 259–276. Ramée's work for Beckford.

Vidler, Anthony. 'The Architecture of the Lodges: Ritual Form and Associational Life in the Late Enlightenment.' *Oppositions* (New York) No. 5 (Summer 1976): 75–97 at 89–90, 97 nn56–58 & fig. 10. Rev. reprint in his *The Writings of the Walls*, 100–101, 210–211 nn73–75 & fig. 91. Princeton: Princeton Architectural Press, 1987. A study of the spatial forms of freemasonry.

Weston, Peter. 'Inspired by the spirit of Beckford.' *Bath Chronicle*, 1 November 2004, 24. James Lees-Milne, 'distinguished biographer of William Beckford', in Beckford's library.

MEMOIRS AND DIARIES

See also '4. Contemporaries' & '13. Travel', especially Whaley (France), Hawcroft (Italy), Bombelles, Gordon, Quillinan (Portugal) and Lawless (Switzerland)

Books

Acton, Harold. *More Memoirs of an Aesthete*. London: Methuen, 1970. Lectured on Beckford at Grenoble University, 284. In 1956 went to a ball in Paris as Beckford, 340, 341, 344.

Angelo, Henry. *The Reminiscences of Henry Angelo*. 2 vols. London: Kegan Paul, etc., 1904. (1st ed. 1828–1830.) 1:174–175.

Beaton, Cecil. *Ashcombe: The Story of a Fifteen-Year Lease*. London: Batsford, 1949. Bathing in a lake at Fonthill and visit to tower there, 35–36.

Delaney, Mary. *The Autobiography and Correspondence of Mary Granville, Mrs Delaney*. Ed. Lady Llanover. 2nd series. 3 vols. London: Richard Bentley, 1862. Criticism of how Beckford hung his paintings, 3:139–142.

Durrell, Lawrence. *Bitter Lemons*. London: Faber, 1957. Thoughts of Beckford in Cyprus, 98.

Green, Martin. *Children of the Sun*. London: Constable, 1976. Dandy, 40. Admired by Evelyn Waugh, 230.

Lees-Milne, James. *Ancient as the Hills. Diaries 1973–1974*. London: John Murray, 1997. Pp. 72, 94, 135, 151, 199–200.

Lees-Milne, James. *Through Wood and Dale. Diaries 1975–1978*. London: John Murray, 1998. Passim.

Lees-Milne, James. *Deep Romantic Chasm. Diaries 1979–1981*. London: John Murray, 2000. Portraits of Beckford, 31, 107, 118, 187.

Lees-Milne, James. *Holy Dread. Diaries 1982–1984*. London: John Murray, 2001. Fonthill Lake, 167 & n. Gave a copy of his *Beckford* to a friend, 209.

Lees-Milne, James. *Beneath a Waning Moon. Diaries 1985–1987*. London: John Murray, 2003. Beckford, 65 & n. Beckford & W. J. Bankes, 71–72. 'Millionaire homosexual snob', 78, 88. Lees-Milne acquires relics of Beckford, 126–127, 165, 194, 221, 244.

Lees-Milne, James. *Ceaseless Turmoil. Diaries 1988–1992*. London: John Murray, 2004. 'How Beckford attracts the loonies', 16. Lady Fforde a descendant of Beckford, 154. Beckford mentioned, 222. Visit from four members of 1991 Beckford Round Table, 241. Boathouse to be repaired, 301.

Lees-Milne, James. *The Milk of Paradise. Diaries 1993–1997*. London: John Murray, 2005. Visited by Philippa Bishop on 17 Feb 1995, 155 & n, and by Sidney Blackmore on 12 Oct 1997, 297 & n.

Lockhart, John Gibson. *Memoirs of Sir Walter Scott*. 5 vols. London: Macmillan, 1900. Letter of 1815 to Byron, 2:511. *Vathek* in 1826 diary, 5:69.

Parreaux, André. *The Publication of The Monk, a Literary Event, 1796–1798*. Paris: Marcel Didier, 1960. In 1796 'Monk' Lewis succeeded Beckford as MP for Hindon, 43, 136. Character in *The Episodes*, 140–141. Links between Beckford and Matthew Gregory Lewis, 141–142. *Vathek*, 158. Lewis hid his homosexuality better than Beckford, 160.

[Pückler-Muskau, Prince Hermann Ludwig Heinrich von.] *Briefe eines Verstorbenen* (Letters of a Dead Man), *Ein fragmentarisches Tagebuch aus England, Wales, Irland und Frankreich . . .* 2 vols. Stuttgart: Hallberger, 1831. 2:276–279. Trans. by Sarah Austin as *Tour in England, Ireland and France in the years 1828 and 1829*. 2 vols. London: Effingham Wilson, 1832. 2:210–213. Anecdotes in a letter from Bath dated 23 Dec 1828, noting that the Tower was unfinished. (New & rev. ed. of *Tour*, Zurich: Massie, 1940.)

REVIEW. *Gentleman's Magazine* 101 pt. 2 (Suppl. 1831): 609–610 at 610.

Sadleir [Sadler], Michael. *Things Past*. London: Constable, 1944. P. 193.

Salaman, Malcolm C. 'The Fonthill fever.' *The Times*, 26 Sept 1925, 8d. Letter about Salaman's father visiting Beckford in 1841 and noting that he would eat alone but with the table set for a number of guests.

CHARACTER

Books

'Beckford, William.' In *The Book of Days. A Miscellany of Popular Antiquities in Connection with the Calendar*, ed. R Chambers, 1:585–586. 2 vols. London: W. & R. Chambers, 1869. (1st ed. 1863–1864.) 'May 2', an anecdote about Duchess of Gordon from *New Monthly Magazine* 71 (July 1844): 310–311.

Chard, Chloe. 'Effeminacy, pleasure and the classical body.' In *Femininity and Masculinity in Eighteenth-century Art and Culture*, ed. Gill Perry & Michael Rossington, 142–161 at 151, 159 n24. Manchester: Manchester University Press, 1994. Letter from Thun (1777) about horses and visiting.

Grigson, Geoffrey. *The Harp of Aeolus*. London: Routledge, 1947. Beckford as a romantic, 45, 49–50, 51–52, 68.

Hudson, W. H. *The Illustrated Shepherd's Life*. London: The Bodley Head, 1987. Cat injured by trap after poaching in "Squire Beckford's" woods, 121–122. *A Shepherd's Life* was first publ. by Methuen in 1910.

Jullian, Philippe & John Phillips. *Violet Trefusis: Life and Letters*. London: Hamish Hamilton, 1976. Both Beckford and Trefusis were 'precociously gifted' and 'could write effortlessly in flawless French', 143. Also 77.

Langford, Paul. *Englishness Identified: Manners and Character 1650–1850*. Oxford: Oxford University Press, 2000. 'Author of the bizarre *Vathek*', 50, 331 n117. Beckford humiliated the Duchess of Gordon (1748/9–1812), 309. Alderman Beckford, 123, 209.

Marlow, Louis. *Seven Friends*. London: Richards Press, 1953. Beckford more ostentatious than Aleister Crowley, 51–52.

Tyte, William. *Tales and Sketches*. Bath: S. W. Simms, 1917. Beckford insulted lodge keeper at Prior Park, then gave her a guinea, 26–27.

White, R, J. *Life in Regency England*. London: Batsford, 1963. Beckford would have liked to have lived in London, 104–105. Also 143.

Articles

'Anecdote of Mr. Beckford of Fonthill.' *Devizes & Wiltshire Gazette*, 5 Sept 1822, 4b. Clandestine visit to Fonthill Abbey by a young man. ½ column. 'Anecdote of Fonthill.' *Idem*, 30 May 1844, 3b, similar version involving a surveyor. 'Anecdotes of Mr. Beckford.' *Idem*, 25 Sept 1823, 4e. ¼ column.

Anecdotes 'from a local paper'. *Courier*, 22 Sept 1823, 4.

'Anecdotes of Mr. Beckford.' *Morning Post*, 20, 22 Sept 1823, 2, 3 & *The Observer*, 21 Sept, 2, 4.

'Mr. Beckford – Several anecdotes illustrative of this gentleman's character, are in circulation.' *Bath and Cheltenham Gazette*, 23 Sept 1823, 2c–d.

'Beckford, His Daughter, and the Cry of the Peacock.' *Bath and County Graphic* 7 no. 5 (Sept 1902): 53. Beckford imitating peacocks.

B[oyd], Andrew K. H. 'Concerning Disappointment and Success.' *Fraser's Magazine* 61 (Jan 1860): 1–20. The author did not want to think of 'grand disappointments . . . the satiety of Vathek, turning sickly away from his earthly Cintra'. Reprinted in *Littell's Living Age* 64 (17 Aug 1860): 451–466 at 463. Reprinted again in *The Recreations of a Country Parson. 2nd Series*. London: Parker Son & Bourn, 1861.

Ehrhart. *Salisbury and Winchester Journal*, 10 Oct 1798, 4c. Dr Ehrhart treats 30 or 40 patients a day at Fonthill at Beckford's expense. ⅓ column.

Ferrets. 'Porter's *Cruize in the Pacific Ocean.*' *Quarterly Review* 13 (July 1815): 352–383 at 354. Review article mentioning Beckford objecting to cruel treatment of ferrets.

'Galton on Hereditary Genius.' *Edinburgh Review* 132 (July 1870): 100–125 at 122. Beckford 'was a man of real genius', and in his writings 'there are passages of the very highest imaginative order, a sense of the picturesque approaching to sublimity'. Reprinted in *Littell's Living Age* 106 (10 Sept 1870): 679–680.

Generosity. *Salisbury and Winchester Journal*, 3 Feb 1823, 4c. Beckford sent £50 to his 'late neighbourhood' for blankets for the poor inhabitants.

Generosity on his birthday. *Courier*, 1 Oct 1823, 2. Beckford gave money to villagers to remember his birthday even after he had left for Bath.

Hilliard, Elizabeth. 'Annuities for Beckford's Servants.' *Beckford Tower Trust Newsletter*, Spring 1985, 2–3. Deeds from William Naile and others.

Hitchings, Henry. 'Sadistic Longings.' *New Statesman*, 17 May 1999, 46–47 at 47. Review of two books on the Marquis de Sade. Beckford: 'Gothic oddball'.

Jung, Fritz 'Beckfords Persönlichkeit (Personality).' *Englische Studien* (Leipzig) 46 no. 2 (June 1913): 252–268.

Massingham, Hugh. 'The Lost Eccentrics.' *Lilliput* 23 (Dec 1948). Anecdote about Beckford vowing to have Christmas dinner in his new mansion when the kitchen burst into flames, as it was not ready. Noted by 'Sul' in 'Beckford anecdote' & 'A rash vow', *Bath & Wilts Chronicle & Herald*, 12 Jan 1949, 3. (Also in *Bath Weekly Chronicle and Herald*, 15 Jan, 12.)

Thompson, Francis. 'Shelley.' *Dublin Review* 143 (July 1908): 25–49 at 45n. '. . . that Atlas among enchanters, Beckford'. Reprinted, London: Burns &

Oates, 1909, 74n. Also reprinted in *The Works of Francis Thompson*, 3 vols., London: Burns & Oates, 1913, 3 (Prose): 1–37 at 35n.

POLITICS

Christie, Ian R. 'Private Patronage versus Government Influence: John Buller and the Contest for Control of Parliamentary Elections at Saltash.' *English Historical Review* 71 (April 1956): 249–255 at 254, 255. Beckford's role in helping John Buller during the disputed election at Saltash from 1783.

Corruption. 'What is Corruption?' *Mirror of Literature* 1 (2 Nov 1822): 10–11. Beckford's bill for preventing bribery and corruption at elections.

Evans, Godfrey. 'The Acquisition of Stuart Silver by the Dukes of Hamilton.' In *The Stuart Court in Rome. The Legacy of Exile*, ed. Edward Corp. Aldershot, Hants: Ashgate, 2003. Beckford's lack of interest in Jacobinism, 138.

Ginter, Donald E. *Voting Records of the British House of Commons 1761–1820.* 6 vols. London: Hambledon Press, 1995. *Vol. 2. Biographical Listings A–F.* MP for Wells 5 April 1784 to 11 June 1790, for Hindon 19 June 1790 to Dec 1794 & 3 Nov 1806 to 29 Feb 1820, 104. Alderman Beckford (19 Dec 1709–21 June 1770) & Richard Beckford (*d.*12 Aug 1796), 104. Julines Beckford (?1717–27 Nov 1764) & Peter Beckford (?1739–18 Feb 1811), 103.

'Hindon, Wilts.' In *The Universal British Directory of Trade, Commerce, and Manufacture . . .*, 3 (*c.*1794): 269–275. 5 vols. London: Printed at the British Directory Office, 1793–1798. Prosecution of sitting members in 1775–1776, 270–274. William Beckford, present member, 274. Alderman Beckford, 274–275. Facsimile reprint, 1993.

Oldfield, T. H. B. 'Hindon.' In *The Representative History of Great Britain and Ireland: Being a History of the House of Commons . . .*, 5:119–140 at 140. 6 vols. London: Baldwin, Cradock & Jay, 1816. Hindon, 110 voters, Lord Calthorpe & William Beckford, Proprietors, 5:119–140. Also Richard Beckford and the corrupt 1773 election, 5:126–140.

Port, M. H. 'Beckford, William.' In *The House of Commons 1754–1790*, ed. Sir Lewis Namier & John Brooke, 2:78–79. 3 vols. London: HMSO for the History of Parliament Trust, 1964. Beckford MP for Wells [until 1790] with Clement Tudway, 5 April 1784, 1:373. Also Alderman Beckford by Lucy S. Sutherland, 2:75–78.

Port, M. H. & R. G. Thorne. 'Beckford, William.' In *The House of Commons 1790–1820*, ed. R. G. Thorne, 3:170–171. 5 vols. London: Secker & Warburg for the History of Parliament Trust, 1986. MP for Hindon (1790–Dec 1794 & 1806–1820).

Report from the Select Committee appointed to try and determine the Merits of the Petition of James Calthorpe, Esquire, and Richard Beckford, Esquire, complaining of An undue Election and Return for the Borough of Hindon, in the County of Wilts. 1775. 98 pp. The Report found these two, together with Mrs Beckford's candidate, General Richard Smith, and Thomas Brand Hollis, were all guilty of gross bribery. Election was declared void.

PORTRAITS

Alexander, Boyd. 'Fonthill and Portraits of William Beckford (1760–1844).' *Register of the Museum of Art. University of Kansas* 3 (Winter 1967): 2–13.

'Bearsted Collection.' *Country Life,* 31 March 1955, 871. Romney's portrait.

Beckett, Sister Wendy. *Sister Wendy's 1000 Masterpieces.* London: Dorling Kindersley, 1999. Romney's portrait, 396.

Ch., G. [Chapman, Guy.] 'Un portrait inconnu de William Beckford.' *Revue de Littérature Comparée* 27 (1953): 113–114. Portrait by Richard Cosway.

Chapman, Guy. 'A Portrait of Beckford.' *Times Literary Supplement,* 4 July 1929, 538. Enquiry about the whereabouts of Romney's portrait.

Cross, David A. *A Striking Likeness. The Life of George Romney.* Aldershot, Hants: Ashgate, 2000. Beckford was one of Chancellor Thurlow's wards, and both were painted by Romney, as were Beckford's daughters, 107. Beckford had a house at Hampstead, 194. Also 234 n91. Beckford's portrait: influenced by Batoni, 55; neo-classicism, 93; Sawrey Gilpin may have painted the deer, 99; Sexual ambiguity, 112; Colour pl. VII.

Davis, Frank. 'Talking about Salerooms.' *Country Life,* 14 Feb 1972, 296–297. Portrait of a member of the Beckford family by Thomas Hudson (1701–1779) sold at Sotheby's.

Doyle, John. *Equestrian Sketches.* London: T. McLean, 1842. Lithograph of Beckford on horseback, aged about 78, pl. 42.

Gemmett, Robert J. "The Behnes' Portrait of William Beckford." *Études Anglaises* 19 no. 3 (July–Sept 1966): 261–262. Not a faithful portrait.

Ingamells, John. *National Portrait Gallery, Mid-Georgian Portraits 1760–1790.* London: National Portrait Gallery, 2004. Alderman Beckford, 43–44. William Beckford, 45–46.

Kidson, Alex. *George Romney 1734–1802.* London: National Portrait Gallery, 2002. The Beckford Children, 204–205. Catalogue of a travelling exhibition.

Laing, Alastair. *In Trust for the Nation. Paintings from National Trust Houses.* London: National Trust & National Gallery, 1995. No. 9: Romney portrait: text, 34, 198 nn1–9. Whole-page colour illus., 35.

Lees-Milne, James, intro. *Upton House. The Bearsted Collection: Pictures.* London: The National Trust, 1964. No. 68: Portrait of William Beckford by George Romney (1734–1802). Canvas, 93 × 57 in., pp. 25–26 & pl. 1a.

Leslie, Charles Robert. *Life and Times of Sir Joshua Reynolds.* 2 vols. London: John Murray, 1865. 'The list . . . includes some interesting and curiously contrasted personages', 2:343–344. 'First sitting to Sir Joshua on February the 15th [1782]', 348–350. Exhibited at the Royal Academy, 25 April 1782, 361. List of sitters for 1782, Beckford (Feb) & Louisa (April), 387.

Lloyd, Stephen. *Cosway, Richard & Maria: Regency Artists of Taste and Fashion*. London: National Portrait Gallery, 17 Nov 1995–18 Feb 1996. William, 3rd Viscount Courtenay, no. 93. 9th Duke of Hamilton, no. 150. Susan Beckford, *c*.1800–1805, no. 155. Western Entrance of Fonthill Abbey in 1807, pen & ink, no. 166. Exhibition catalogue.

National Portrait Gallery. Report of the Trustees 1980–81. London: National Portrait Gallery, 1982. Acquisition No. 5340: portrait by Joshua Reynolds (1782), 21; illus., pl. 8. Also 18. Noted in Jon Millington, Editorial, *Beckford Tower Trust Newsletter*, Spring 1984, 1.

O'Donoghue, Freeman. *Catalogue of Engraved British Portraits preserved in the Department of Prints and Drawings in the British Museum*. 6 vols. London: Printed for the Trustees, 1908–1925. Vol. 1, A–C. Lists six portraits of Beckford, 152, and twelve of Alderman Beckford, 151–152. Henry M. Hake. *Idem*, Vol. 6, Suppl. and Indexes, 1925. Lists one portrait of Beckford, 34, and two of Alderman Beckford, 34.

Piper, David. *The English Face*. London: Thames & Hudson, 1957. Lost portrait of Beckford by Mengs, 339 n129.

Saywell, David & Jacob Simon. *Complete Illustrated Catalogue. National Portrait Gallery, London*. London: Unicorn, 2004. Reynolds portrait (No. 5340) and Kirk's medal of Alderman Beckford (No. 5758), 44.

RELIGION

Darton, Eric. 'William Beckford and Religion.' *Beckford Journal* 4 (1998): 33–38. 'Beckford devotedly accepted the Christian religion'.

Godwin, Joscelyn. *The Theosophical Enlightenment*. Albany: State University of New York Press, 1994. 1781 Christmas party stage-managed by de Loutherbourg & Beckford's visit in 1784 to an apartment near Paris designed by Claude-Nicolas Ledoux, 111–114. Also 1, 115.

[Hillier, Bevis.] 'William Beckford and Islam.' *Connoisseur* 191 (April 1976): 250–253. Editorial linking Beckford with the World of Islam Festival.

Luff, S. G. A. 'The Romantick Abbey. A Consideration of Beckford's Folly.' *The Aylesford Review* 6 (Winter 1963–1964): 26–32.

Nolan, J. C. M. 'The Devotee Glances at the Glorious One.' *Beckford Journal* 4 (1998): 39–47. Beckford's veneration of St Anthony of Padua.

Quæsitor. 'William Beckford. The English Shaberon?' *Theosophical Quarterly* 31 no. 1 (July 1933): 14–30. Shaberon – Tibetan term meaning adept. Article prompted by letter of 20 June 1882 from Baroda in: Helena Petrovna Blavatsky, *The Letters of H. P. Blavatsky to A. P. Sinnett*, London: Unwin, 1925, p. 20.

Rector of Fonthill Gifford. Obituary of John Still, Rector from 1797, *Gentleman's Magazine* n.s. 11 (June 1839): 664.

Rope, H. E. G. 'William Beckford and the [Roman Catholic] Faith.' *The Month*, 176 (Sept 1940): 155–163. A pilgrim to the Grande Chartreuse.

Jay, William (1769–1853)

Boase, G. C., rev. Anne Plimlott Baker. 'Jay, William (1769–1853).' In *Oxford Dictionary of National Biography*, ed. H. C. G. Matthew & Brian Harrison, 29:824. Oxford: Oxford University Press, 2004. Worked with his father on building of Fonthill Abbey.

C., T. S. 'William Jay.' *Bath and County Graphic* 4 no. 6 (Oct 1899): 75. Jay's oratory praised by Beckford. Photo of Argyle Chapel.

Gamble, Thomas. 'Romance of Wm Jay, Savannah Architect . . .' *Savannah Morning News*, 8 May 1932. Jay and Fonthill Abbey mentioned in article about his son, also William, who was in Savannah from 1818 to *c.*1825.

Jay, William. *The Autobiography of the Rev. William Jay*. London: Hamilton, Adams, 1854. Ed. George Redford & John Angell James. 'Mr. Beckford and Fonthill Abbey', 23–30, 580. Letter from Goodridge in an Appendix to the 2nd ed. defending Beckford against remarks by Rev. Erskine Neale in *The Closing Scene* (1849), 581–584.

REVIEWS. 'Editorial Notes. English Literature.' *Putnam's Monthly Magazine* (New York) 4 (Dec 1854): 672.

Gentleman's Magazine n.s. 43 (Feb 1855): 171–172 at 172.

Obituary. *Gentleman's Magazine* n.s. 41 (March 1854): 324–325.

Silvester, Rev. James. 'Two Famous Bath Preachers.' *Bath Chronicle*, 12, 26 Jan, 2 Feb 1899, 3, 3, 6. William Jay worked at Fonthill, Beckford's praise for his preaching, and his *The Christian Contemplated* (12 lectures, 1826). Reprinted as *Two Famous Preachers of Bath*, London: C. J. Thynne, [1900], 2–3, 18, 22. William Connor Magee was the other preacher.

SEXUALITY

Books

Aldrich, Robert. *Colonialism and Homosexuality*. London: Routledge, 2003. The *Episodes* are 'suffused with sexual ambiguity', 110 & 146 n12.

Betsky, Aaron. *Queer Space: Architecture and Same-Sex Desire*. New York: William Morrow, 1997. Beckford created 'fantasy interior landscapes', 11. Quotation from *Vathek* about the palace named 'The Delight of the Eyes', 56 & 201 n1. 'The greatest builder of queer spaces', 67–71 & 201–202 nn15–21. Clough Williams-Ellis built a fantasy village in the manner of Beckford, 106.

Beynon, John. ' "Mr. Beckford's Favourite Propensity": The Erotics of

Boyhood and the Emergence of a Sexual Self in Late-Eighteenth-Century England.' In *William Beckford and the New Millennium*, ed. Kenneth W. Graham & Kevin Berland, 7–35. New York: AMS Press, 2004 [2005].

Blumberg, Jane. *Byron and the Shelleys. The Story of a Friendship*. London: Collins & Brown, 1992. Letter to Francis Hodgson on 25 June 1809: Byron's comments on Beckford when changing horses at an inn, 25.

Boynton, Lindsay. 'Scandal and Society.' In *Squanderous and Lavish Profusion: George IV, his image and patronage of the arts*, ed. Dana Arnold, 44–50 at 47–48 & 50 nn26–31. London: The Georgian Group, 1995.

Carter, Elizabeth. *Letters from Mrs. Carter to Mrs. Montagu . . . upon Literary and Moral Subjects*. 3 vols. London: Rivington, 1817. From Deal, 19 Dec 1784, condemning 'B—'s horrid behaviour' and pitying 'poor Lady —', 3:233–234. Quoted in Alexander, *England's Wealthiest Son* (1962, 110–111).

Courtis, Jason. *Just Williams: a study of the influence of medical speculation and discourse on the public perception of homosexuality as deduced through the literature on William Beckford*. 67 leaves. BSc dissertation. Wellcome Institute for the History of Medicine, London, 1995. Chapters on 'The Man', 'The Scandal', 'The [Eight] Biographers' & 'The Analysis'.

Crompton, Louis. *Byron and Greek Love: Homophobia in 19th-Century England*. Berkeley: University of California Press, 1985. Beckford's wealth & talent, 64–65. His attraction for Byron, 118–121. Veiled homosexuality in *Vathek*, 122–123. Ostracism, 232, 233–234. Also passim.

Davis, Whitney. 'The Site of Sexuality: William Beckford's Fonthill Abbey 1780–1824.' In *Archaeologies of Sexuality*, ed. Robert A. Schmidt & Barbara L. Voss, 104–116. London & New York: Routledge, 2000.

Dellamora, Richard. 'Constituting the National Subject: Benjamin Disraeli, Judaism, and the Legacy of William Beckford.' In *Mapping Male Sexuality: Nineteenth-Century England*, ed. Jay Losey & William D. Brewer, 145–177, incl. 128 notes. Rutherford, NJ: Fairleigh Dickinson University Press, 2000, and revised in Richard Dellamora, *Friendship's Bonds: Democracy and the Novel in Victorian England*, 47–69 & 61 notes, Philadelphia: University of Pennsylvania Press, 2004.

Elfenbein, Andrew. 'William Beckford and the Genius of Consumption.' In *Romantic Genius: The Prehistory of a Homosexual Role*, 39–62, 224–228 nn1–71. New York: Columbia University Press, 1999. Appendix: 'Idyllium of Hylas', from Bodleian Library, MS. Beckford d.21, 60–62. Also 14, 63, 80, 86, 91, 92, 95, 105, 125.

Emens, Elizabeth. *William Beckford: Sexuality and Reputation*. PhD thesis for Cambridge University, 2001. Abstract in *Index to Theses* 52 pt. 1 (April 2003): 36.

Haggerty, George E. 'William Beckford.' In *The Gay and Lesbian Literary Heritage: A Reader's Companion to the Writers and Their Works from*

Antiquity to the Present, ed. Claude J. Summers, 85. London: Blooms-bury, 1995. 'Travel in Literature' by G. S. Rousseau, 701–705. Also 91, 128, 234, 235, 237, 238, 239, 241, 242, 248, 249, 334, 519, 556.

Haggerty, George E. 'Beckford's Pæderasty.' In *Illicit Sex: Identity Politics in Early Modern Culture*, ed. Thomas DiPiero & Pat Gill, 123–142. Athens, GA: University of Georgia Press, 1997. Revised in his *Men in Love: Masculinity and Sexuality in the Eighteenth Century*, 136–151, 194–199 nn1–43. New York: Columbia University Press, 1999.

REVIEW. Jack, Malcolm. 'The Professor of Paederasty.' *Beckford Journal* 7 (2001): 45–46.

Heicker, Dino. *Gespenster und Geschlechter. Homoerotik in der europäis-chen Schauerliteratur* (Ghosts and Sex. Homoeroticism in European horror literature). Hamburg: MännerschwarmSkript, 2004. Bibliothek rosa Winkel.

Norton, Rictor. 'Beckford of Fonthill.' & 'Beckford's Scrap Books.' In *Mother Clap's Molly House: The Gay Subculture in England 1700–1830*, 221–231. London: Gay Men's Press, 1992.

Norton, Rictor. 'William Beckford.' In *Who's Who in Gay and Lesbian History, From Antiquity to World War II*, ed. Robert Aldrich & Garry Wotherspoon, 45–50. London and New York: Routledge, 2001.

Pepys, Lady Paulina. *Powderham Castle [Devon]*. Derby, 1972. 'Notorious William Beckford', 12. New ed. N.p., c.1985. P. [7]. Guide books.

Porter, Roy. *English Society in the Eighteenth Century*. London: Penguin, 1982. Alderman Beckford, 74. 'Beckford, the rich and strange son of the City alderman', 247. 'Notorious homosexual', 264. Rev. ed., 1990, pp. 74, 247, 264. Reprinted, London: Folio Society, 1998, pp. 72, 229, 245 with SW view of Abbey by Storer (1812), 229.

Saslow, James M. *Pictures and Passions. A History of Homosexuality in the Visual Arts*. New York: Viking, 1999. Beckford, 165–166, 178.

Spencer, Colin. *Homosexuality: a History*. London: Fourth Estate, 1995. William Beckford, 199–200.

Sykes, Christopher Simon. 'Apostles of Pederasty.' In *Black Sheep*, 241–248. London: Chatto & Windus, 1982. The Powderham scandal.

Tinker, John. *William Beckford: The First English Homosexual*. 186 pp. PhD thesis for Stanford University, 1996. *Dissertation Abstracts Interna-tional* 57 no. 5 (Nov 1996): 2053-A.

Wilson, A. N. *Iris Murdoch as I Knew Her*. London: Hutchinson, 2003. Conversation about Beckford and bisexuality in car journey to Fonthill in 1977, 192–194. Beckford's 'faux-Gothic abbey', 191.

Articles

Haggerty, George E. 'Literature and Homosexuality in the Late Eighteenth Century: Walpole, Beckford, and Lewis.' *Studies in the Novel* 18 (Winter

1986): 341–352. Reprinted in *Homosexual Themes in Literary Studies*, ed. Wayne R. Dynes & Stephen Donaldson, 167–178. New York: Garland, 1992.

Heicker, Dino. "Der Kult des Kindlichen: William Beckford und seine 'childish errors'." *Forum Homosexualität und Literatur* 43 (2003): 99–119.

Morning Herald, 27 Nov 1784, 'the rumour concerning a *Grammatical mistake of Mr. B*— and the *Hon. Mr. C*— in regard to the genders . . .' *Idem*, 29 Nov, '. . . was to have had an *English Peerage*.' *Idem*, 8 Dec, '. . . a pair of fashionable *male lovers*'. *Idem*, 30 Dec, 'The Fonthill fool is ere this in Italy'.

Norton, Rictor. 'The Fool of Fonthill.' *The Advocate* (Los Angeles) 23 (1973). Revised reprint, 'The Fool of Fonthill: Rich, Gay, and Merrie in Perilous Times.' *Gay News* 41 (28 Feb–13 March 1973): 9 & cover portrait.

Picano, Felice. 'Forever Florence . . . the Forbidden Passion . . . of Tuscany . . .' *The Advocate* (Los Angeles), Issue 920, 17 Aug 2004. 'Byron satisfied Beckford and all of his live-in boys.'

Potkay, Adam. 'Beckford's Heaven of Boys.' *Raritan* (Rutgers University) 13 no. 1 (Summer 1993): 73–86. Reprinted in *Three Oriental Tales*, ed. Alan Richardson, Boston, MA: Houghton Mifflin, 2002, 296–305. Byron, boys, *Vathek*.

Public Advertiser, 1 Dec 1784. Beckford 'gone post haste to *Italy!*' *Idem*, 10 Dec 'The Lady of Mr. B— . . . had scarcely any provision of a separate maintenance'.

Robertson, P. J. 'Beckford past.' *Bath Chronicle*, 20 Sept 2000, 10. Letter about William Courtenay.

Sage, Lorna. 'Violet Cream.' *New Statesman*, 19 Aug 1977, 250–251. Beckford mentioned in review of Ronald Firbank's works.

'Thoughts on a Late Biography.' *Monthly Visitor and Entertaining Pocket Companion* 2 (Oct 1797): 343.

SLAVERY

For William Beckford of Somerley (1744–1799) see '3. Family'
For the Channel 4 programme 'Sugar Dynasty' see '16. Works influenced by Beckford. Dramatisations & Events'

Books

Aykroyd, W. R. *Sweet Malefactor. Sugar, Slavery and Human Society*. London: Heinemann, 1967. Alderman & William Beckford mentioned, 46.

Hall, Douglas. *In Miserable Slavery. Thomas Thistlewood in Jamaica, 1750–86*. London: Macmillan, 1989. Diary entries in the 1770s mentioning William Beckford of Somerley, 21, 63, 237, 256.

'King Sugar's Bitter Bequest.' *The British Empire* (BBC TV Time-Life Books), No. 91 (1973), 2521–2523. Picture of Fonthill Abbey, 'built from sugar profits amassed by William Beckford'.

Thomas, Hugh. *The Slave Trade. The History of the Atlantic Slave Trade: 1440–1870.* London: Papermac, 1998. (1st ed. 1997.) Peter Beckford (*d.*1735), 230 & 834 n24, 245, 248. Alderman Beckford: son of Peter, 245; slave-owning family, 248; friend of Pitt, 272n; needed slaves, 367 & 839 n15; mocked by Dr Johnson, 476 & 845 n23.

Articles

Crawshaw, Andrew. 'Beckford's Hand?' *Georgian Jamaica* (Newsletter of the Friends of the Georgian Society of Jamaica) 6 no. 2 (June 1998): 3. Ruins of Auchindown linked to Fonthill. *Idem* 6 no. 3 (Sept 1998): 2. Letter from Sheila Bennett about two Font Hills in Jamaica. *Idem* 6 no. 4 (Dec 1998): 2. Letter from Andrew Crawshaw about reference to Auchindown in *England's Wealthiest Son* (1962, 204 & 290 n15).

Gikandi, Simon. 'Aesthetic Reflection and the Colonial Event: The Work of Art in the Age of Slavery.' *The Journal of the International Institute* (Michigan) 4 no. 3 (Spring/Summer 1997): 12–14. Beckford wealth founded on sugar and slavery in the Jamaican plantations.

Hackmann, W. K. '[Alderman] William Beckford's Profit from Three Jamaican Offices.' *Historical Research* 63 (Feb 1990): 107–109. 'One person held the offices collectively as the Secretary.'

Smith, Stephanie. 'Ill-favoured by the Sun: The Orientation of Slavery in William Beckford's Imagination.' *Beckford Journal* 9 (2003): 62–69.

Wheatcroft, Geoffrey. 'Oh, to be in Antigua: This Caribbean island makes an Englishman feel right at home.' *Atlantic Monthly* 274 (Oct 1994). Georgian terraces and crescents of Bath were built with sugar money. Overlooking the city is Beckford's Tower, 'a strange edifice put up by William Beckford . . .'.

WEALTH

Books

Carter, Barbara J. *Location of Documents for Wiltshire Parishes. Part 3. Ditteridge to Hilperton.* Swindon: The Author, 1981. 'Fonthill Bishop', [42]–[43], 'Fonthill Gifford', [43]–[44]. Parish registers, tax returns and other records.

Gray, Robert. *Letters During the Course of a Tour through Germany, Switzerland, and Italy, in the Years MDCCXCI and MDCCXCII.* London: Rivington, 1794. Letter of 12 Sept 1791 from Geneva, presumably referring to Beckford, condemning both his 'Erreur du Moment' and any admiration of his wealth, 209–210.

Sizer, Theodore. 'William Beckford and his American Property.' *Yale University Library Gazette* 39 no. 1 (July 1964): 42–45. See also *The Autobiography of Colonel John Trumbull, patriot-artist, 1756–1843*, ed. Theodore Sizer, New Haven: Yale University Press, 1953, 307.

Timbs, John. *Things to be Remembered in Daily Life*. London: W. Kent, 1863. 'Large fortunes', 189–191.

Articles

Brassey. 'Culture and Progress. New English Books.' *Scribner's Monthly* 16 (June 1878): 294–299 at 298. 'Thomas Brassey, the elder, who better deserved than Beckford Lord Byron's epithet of "England's Wealthiest Son" . . .'.

'How We Spend Our Money.' *Harper's New Monthly Magazine* 63 (Aug 1881): 505–509 at 506. Compared to his father, 'Beckford could so shake off the golden shackles of commerce and free himself from the dark, restricted prison-house of the counting room, as to rise with a bold flight into the ethereal regions of fancy and imagination.'

'Human Peacocks.' *Spectator*. Possibly the rich, like Beckford, showed 'over-refinement of culture and fastidiousness'. Reprinted in *Littell's Living Age* 92 (23 March 1867): 766–768 at 767.

Jack, Malcolm. "How Wealthy Was 'England's Wealthiest Son'?" *Beckford Tower Trust Newsletter*, Spring 1987, 4.

'A Philosophic Bankrupt.' *Continental Monthly* (New York) 1 (May 1862): 496–502 at 501. WB's 'too lavish gifts of fortune' perverted his talent.

Want of money. *Salisbury and Winchester Journal*, 1 Sept 1823, 3b. Reports from the *Morning Chronicle* that Beckford needed money were false.

PUBLISHING BECKFORD

Chapman, Guy. *A Kind of Survivor*. London: Gollancz, 1975. Abbey Classics [1922], 95. Proposed complete edition of Beckford's works, 109. His *Beckford*, 119–123, 124, 151. Beckford and Portugal, 272–273.

Goodman, Jonathan, ed. *The Master Eccentric. Journals of Rayner Heppenstall, 1969–1981*. London: Allison & Busby, 1986. Buying the Marzials ed. of the *Episodes* (1912), 96.

Harrison, Brian. 'Comparative biography and the DNB.' *Comparative Criticism* 25 (2003): 3–26 at 10 & 24 n33. Lewis Namier said in 1950 that there were many biographies of Beckford but few of his father because 'it was so much easier to write about someone who has written.'

Hart-Davis, Rupert, ed. *The Lyttelton Hart-Davis Letters 1955–6*. London: John Murray, 1978. Beckford's letters, 106–107. *Vathek*, 110, 112.

Disparaging remarks about Herbert Grimsditch, 62. Noted in Jon Millington, *Beckford Tower Trust Newsletter*, Spring 1986, 9.

Tanselle, G. Thomas. 'Copyright Records and the Bibliographer.' *Studies in Bibliography* 22 (1969): 114. The case of Beckford v. Hood (1798) showed that it was advisable to register a title at the Stationer's Company.

Tyson, Gerald P. 'Joseph Johnson. Eighteenth-Century Bookseller.' *Studies in Bibliography* 28 (1975): 1, 2. Joseph Johnson, publisher of the first ed. of *Vathek*, 'discovered' Beckford.

Wilde, Oscar. *The Complete Letters of Oscar Wilde*. Ed. Rupert Hart-Davis. London: Hart-Davis, 1962. To Leonard Smithers on 22 Aug 1897: 'Would an edition of Beckford [illus. by Louis Anquetin] be any use?', 927.

Wynne-Tyson, Jon. *Finding the Words. A Publishing Life*. Wilby, Norfolk: Michael Russell, 2004. Boyd Alexander's study of Beckford in 1961 Centaur Press cat., 62. Brief account of Alexander, 80–81. *Recollections* (1835) publ. by Centaur in 1972, 117–118, with quotes from glowing reviews in *TLS, Church Times & British Book News*, 203–204.

REVIEW. McKitterick, David. *Times Literary Supplement*, 27 May 2005, 27.

Ziegler, Philip. *Rupert Hart-Davis. Man of Letters*. London: Chatto & Windus, 2004. Guy Chapman's *Beckford* (1937) publ. by Jonathan Cape, 95.

BECKFORD IN LISTS OF SUBSCRIBERS

Britton, John. *The History and Antiquities of the Abbey, and Cathedral Church of Bristol*. London: Longman, etc., 1830. 'William Beckford, Esq.' one of four subscribers to 'Imperial quarto with proofs and etchings.'

Cornwall, Peter Monamy. *A Sermon, preached before the Glocestershire Society, at St. James's in Bristol, on Thursday October 11, 1781*. Bristol: Hill & Blagden, 1782. 22 pp. 2nd ed. Sarum: E. Easton, 1783. 19 pp.

Cozens, Alexander. *Principles of Beauty, relative to the Human Head*. London: James Dixwell, 1778. vi, 15 pp. Trans. from *Principes de beauté, considerés relativement à la tête humaine*. Londres: Jacques Dixwell, 1777. iv, 15 pp. 17 plates engraved by Francesco Bartolozzi. Folio.

Dallas, R. C. *Miscellaneous Writings: consisting of Poems: Lucretia a Tragedy: and Moral Essays. With a Vocabulary Of The Passions in which their sources are pointed out, their regular currents traced, and their deviations delineated*. London: Longmans, 1797. The first work of Dallas, a friend of Byron. Francis Love Beckford was the next name in the list of subscribers.

English, Edmund. *Views of Lansdown Tower, Bath*. Illus. by Willes Maddox. Bath: Edmund English Junʳ, & London: Thomas McLean, 1844. Beckford was one of 109 subscribers. Among the others were the Duke of Hamilton, Edmund Lansdown (probably a cousin of Henry Venn

Lansdown), James Morrison (who bought Fonthill Pavilion) and John Vaughan (builder of Tower).

Murphy, James. *Plans, Elevations, Sections and Views of the Church of Batalha, in the Province of Estremadura in Portugal . . .* London: Printed for I. & J. Taylor, 1795. Originally publ. in five parts.

Richardson, George. *The New Vitruvius Britannicus.* 2 vols. London: Printed by W. Bulmer & Co. for the Author, 1802 & 1808. 'William Beckford, Esq.'

Soane, John. *Plans, Elevations and Sections of Buildings Executed in the Counties of Norfolk, Suffolk, Yorkshire, Staffordshire, Warwickshire, Hertfordshire etc.* London: Taylor, 1788. 'William Beckford, Esq. Fonthill'. List headed by 'The King'.

Tatham, Charles Heathcote. *Etchings, representing the best examples of Ancient Ornamental Architecture; drawn from the originals in Rome, and other parts of Italy, during the years 1794, 1795, and 1796.* London: T. Gardiner, 1799.

COLLECTIONS OF BECKFORDIANA ON PAPER

Bath: Bath Central Library. See '6. Beckford's Tower and Bath. General Accounts.'

Bath: Bath Preservation Trust. Various Beckford archives including albums of press cuttings compiled by Dr and Mrs Leslie Hilliard.

Devizes: Wiltshire Archaeological and Natural History Society Library. See '5. Fonthill. General Accounts'.

Farmington, CT: The Lewis Walpole Library. Babb-Beckford Collection. Many engraved portraits, and views of Fonthill & Beckford's Tower.

London: Society of Antiquaries Library. Jackson Wiltshire Collection. See '5. Fonthill. General Accounts.' Updated typescript of Goddard's *A Wiltshire Bibliography* (1929). See '17. Bibliographies'.

London: Victoria & Albert Museum. Drawings Collection of the Royal Institute of British Architects. *J. M. Lockyer & D. Mocatta,* ed. Jill Lever; *The Wyatt Family,* ed. Derek Linstrum; *The Pugin Family,* Alexandra Wedgwood. See '5. Fonthill Abbey. Other Images'. *J. B. Papworth,* George McHardy, see '5. Fonthill Pavilion'. *Burn, W.,* ed. Margaret Richardson, see '5. Fonthill New Abbey'. *Henry Edmund Goodridge,* ed. Jill Lever, see '6. Beckford's Tower and Bath. Henry Edmund Goodridge'. *Samuel Sanders Teulon,* ed. Jill Lever, see '6. Beckford's Tower and Bath. Architecture and History'.

New Haven, CT: Beinecke Rare Book and Manuscript Library, Yale University. William Beckford Collection. GEN MSS 102. 281 folders in 13 boxes. The collection is divided into four series: *Correspondence, Writings, Family Papers* and *Other Papers.* Also Papers of James Lees-Milne (1908–1997).

GEN MSS 476. 1124 folders in 30 boxes. The papers are organized into four series: *Correspondence, Writings, Other Papers* and *Photographs*.

Oxford: Bodleian Library. See '14. Beckford's Other Works. The Beckford Papers & Other Beckford Papers'.

INTERNATIONAL CONGRESSES

Clarke, Stephen. 'Beckford in Los Angeles.' *Beckford Journal* 10 (2004): 11–13. Report on the 2003 Beckford Round Table.

'Eighth International Congress on the Enlightenment. Beckford Round Table. Introductory notes by the participants.' *Beckford Tower Trust Newsletter*, Spring 1991, 12–18. Summaries of six papers for 25 July and six for 26th.

Graham, Kenneth W., Chair. 'Seminars on William Beckford [in Bristol & Bath].' *Beckford Tower Trust Newsletter*, Spring 1991, 11. Lists twelve papers.

Graham, Kenneth W. 'Beckford Round Table: William Beckford and Avant-gardisme.' *Beckford Journal* 1 (1995): 9–11. Participants and their papers at Münster.

Jack, Malcolm. 'Beckford would have been amused by our ponderings.' *Anglo-Portuguese News*, 5 Nov 1987, 13, and 'Recollections of a Congress at Sintra.' *Beckford Tower Trust Newsletter*, Spring 1988, 3–4. Reports of the 2nd International Congress on Romanticism at Sintra.

Jack, Malcolm. 'More Than a Transient Gleam.' *Beckford Tower Trust Newsletter*, Spring 1992, 13–14. Report on the 1991 Beckford Round Table in Bristol & Bath on 25 & 26 July.

Jack, Malcolm. 'Westphalian Delights.' *Beckford Journal* 2 (1996): 33–35. Report on the 1995 Beckford Round Table in Münster. Call for papers in *Beckford Tower Trust Newsletter*, Spring 1994, 2.

Jack, Malcolm. 'Portuguese Pilgrims and Irish Seminarians.' *Beckford Journal* 6 (2000): 6–7. (Beckford Society visit and) 1999 Round Table in Dublin.

OBITUARIES IN THE *BECKFORD JOURNAL*

Bishop, Philippa. 'Leslie Theodore Hilliard (1905–1997).' *Beckford Journal* 3 (1997): 2–5. Also: 'City doctor dies at 91.' *Bath Chronicle*, 25 Jan 1997, 13. Leslie Hilliard, with colour photo. Announcement of death, *Idem*, 21 Jan 1997, 13.

Bishop, Philippa. 'Doris Elizabeth Hilliard (1903–2001).' *Beckford Journal* 8 (2002): 2–5. Edited version in *The Independent Review*, 14 June 2001, 6. Also: Pearce, James. 'Former Beckford Tower owner dies.' *Bath Chronicle*, 13 June 2001, 12.

Blackmore, Sidney. 'James Lees-Milne 1908–1997.' *Beckford Journal* 4 (1998): 2–5.
Clifford, Helen. 'Clive Wainwright (1942–1999).' *Beckford Journal* 6 (2000): 2–4.
Kenneth W. Graham. 'Devendra Varma.' *Beckford Journal* 1 (1995): 12–13. Also: *The Independent*, 5 Jan 1995, by Harvey Peter Sucksmith.
Lee, Brian North. 'Peter Summers.' *Beckford Journal* 1 (1995): 13–14.

LETTERS SEEKING OR GIVING INFORMATION

Alexander, Boyd. 'William Beckford.' *Times Literary Supplement*, 25 Sept 1948, 541. Appeal for information for forthcoming biography.
Blackmore, Sidney. 'William Beckford.' *Times Literary Supplement*, 31 March 1995, 15. Proposal to form an international Beckford Society.
Blackmore, Sidney. 'New society is formed.' *Bath Chronicle*, 28 Nov 1995, 10. Letter. Also letters in *Perspectives on Architecture*, Oct 1995, 4; *Apollo* 143 (Feb 1996): 77; *The Art Newspaper*, April 1996; and *Furniture History Society Newsletter*, May 1996, 6.
Chapman, Guy. 'William Beckford.' *Times Literary Supplement*, 25 Jan 1936, 75. Five queries for forthcoming biography, one asking for whereabouts of Beckford-Clarke letters of 1830–1834.
'Desiderata Bodleiana.' *Bodleian Quarterly Record* 6 no. 68 (4th quarter 1930): 187. List of 34 works by Beckford wanted by the library. *Idem*, no. 69 (1st quarter 1931): 220, 222. Twenty-four of these bequeathed by John Hodgkin.
Hamilton Palace. *Country Life*, 11 July 1996, 73. Query about a watercolour of Hamilton Palace. *Idem*, 25 July, 84, reply from John Harris saying view was by Goodridge, probably exhibited at the Royal Academy in 1842, & a letter from Edward Bulmer.
Hobson, A. R. A. 'Query 120. Beckfordiana.' *Book Collector* 8 no. 4 (Winter 1959): 432. About seven volumes of transcripts of Beckford's notes, handwritten by George Beltz. They were bought by Quaritch at the Beckford Library Sale, 30 June 1882, Part 1, lot 735, and have since disappeared. Also a similar letter to the ?*Times Literary Supplement*. (Letter saying that all Beckford's notes were removed by his agent, *Courier*, 22 Sept 1823, 2.)
'Look at Beckford.' *Bath Chronicle*, 16 June 2000, 9. Announcement of Beckford Society AGM.
Moussa-Mahmoud, Fatma, ed. 'Cairo Studies in English.' *Notes and Queries* 205 (March 1960): 82. Call for contributions.

3. Family

ALDERMAN WILLIAM BECKFORD (1709–1770), FATHER

Baddeley, John James, compiler. *The Guildhall of the City of London*. 7th ed. London: Corporation of London, 1939. Remonstrance to George III, 13–14. Monument, 43, 46 (illus.), 50, 53, 60–62, 61 (illus.), 125 (distant view).

Beaven, Alfred B. *Aldermen of the City of London*. 2 vols. London: Corporation of the City of London, 1908–1913. 1:198.

'Beckford, William.' In *Encyclopædia Londinensis, or Universal Dictionary of Arts, Sciences and Literature*, 2 (1810): 842–843. Portrait of Alderman Beckford, publ. 'April 19. 1798 by J. Wilkes', J. Chapman, sculp.

'Beckford's Election.' In *Twenty Four Country Dances, for the Year 1770. With proper Directions to each Dance, as they are perform'd at Court & Almacks, Bath, Scarborough, Tunbridge & all other Publick Assemblys*. London: Printed for Longman & Co., [1770].

Bourne, Henry Richard Fox. 'William Beckford. (1708–1770.)' In *Famous London Merchants. A Book for Boys*, 198–220. London: James Hogg, 1869. One of thirteen merchants portrayed.

Chatterton. Groom, Nick. 'Chatterton, Thomas (1752–1770).' In *Oxford Dictionary of National Biography*, ed. H. C. G. Matthew & Brian Harrison, 11:240. Oxford: Oxford University Press, 2004. Upset by Alderman Beckford's death.

Chatterton. Ingram, John H. *The True Chatterton*. London: Fisher Unwin, 1910. Pp. 226, 229, 242–244. Illus. of engraving of Moore's statue.

Chatterton. Kelly, Linda. *The Marvellous Boy. The Life and Myth of Thomas Chatterton*. London: Weidenfeld & Nicolson, 1971. Upset by Alderman Beckford's death, 33. Remonstrance, 34. Depicted in Alfred de Vigny's play *Chatterton* (1835), 109.

Chatterton. *Quarterly Review* 8 (Sept 1812): 94. Chatterton's memorandum on Alderman Beckford's death in a review of D'Israeli's *Calamities of Authors*.

[Chatterton, Thomas.] *An Elegy on the Much Lamented Death of William Beckford, Esq. Late Lord-Mayor of, and Representative in Parliament for, the City of London*. London: G. Kearsley, 1770. 14 pp. Also as 'Elegy. On W. Beckford, Esq.' in *The Works of the English Poets, from Chaucer to Cowper*, ed. Samuel Johnson, 15:454–455. 21 vols. London: 1810. 12 four-line stanzas.

Church, Richard. 'Where Beckford Lived.' *The Times*, 25 Nov 1963, 11e. Preservation order on No. 1, Greek Street, on corner of Soho Square. Thought to be the London residence of Alderman Beckford and then his son.

City Biography, containing anecdotes and memoirs of the Rise, Progress, Situation, & Character, of the Aldermen and other conspicuous Personages of the Corporation and City of London. London: West & Chapple, 1799. Pp. 63–80.

Cowper, William. *The Letters and Prose Writings of William Cowper*. Ed. James King & Charles Ryskamp. 5 vols. Oxford: Clarendon Press, 1979–1986. Letter to the Rev. William Unwin on 13 Feb 1780 about Alderman Beckford's poor command of English, 1:314 & nn4, 5.

Dewes, Simon. 'Greek Street – Alderman Beckford.' In *Soho*, 57–72. London: Rich & Cowan, 1952. Popular account of the Alderman's defiance of George III and treatment of Chatterton. Illus. of the Alderman & the House of Charity. Mentioned, 16, 20, 83, 135, 136, 175, 191.

Fiske, John. 'Beginnings of the American Revolution.' *Atlantic Monthly* 61 (March 1888): 398–416 at 411. 'Alderman Beckford, father of the illustrious author of Vathek' gave advice on a dispute in New York.

Glover, E. *A History of the Ironmongers' Company*. London: The Worshipful Company of Ironmongers, 1991. John Francis Moore's statue of Alderman Beckford donated by his son in 1833. Also passim.

Grenville, Richard Temple, Earl Temple. *The Grenville Papers. Being the correspondence of Richard Grenville Earl Temple, K. G., and The Right Hon. George Grenville . . .* Ed. William James Smith. 4 vols. London: John Murray, 1852–1853. Vol. 2, 1762–1764 (1852): 8, 133, 158, 195, 202, 214, 217, 495. Vol. 3, 1765–1766 (1853): 341, 386, 389, 396. Vol. 4, 1767–1777 (1853): 213, 517, 520 (died intestate, 14 natural children). *Additional Grenville Papers 1763–1765*. Ed. John R. G. Tomlinson. Manchester: Manchester University Press, 1965. Pp. 105, 321.

Hughes, George Bernard. *English and Scottish Earthenware 1660–1860*. London: Lutterworth Press, 1961. Figurine of Alderman Beckford.

Kent, Charles. 'Beckford, William.' In *Dictionary of National Biography*, ed. Leslie Stephen, 4:80–82. London: Smith, Elder, 1885.

Kielmansegge, Friederick. *Diary of a Journey to England in the Years 1761–1762*. Trans. Countess Philippa Kielmansegg. London: Longmans, 1902. Alderman Beckford's 'vigorous speech in favour of the German war', 162–163.

Knill, Lady Lucy. *The Mansion House*. London: Stanley Paul, 1937. Alderman Beckford, 116–117, 175.

Lea, R. S. 'Beckford, William.' In *The House of Commons 1715–1754*, ed. Romney Sedgwick, 1:451–452. 2 vols. London: HMSO for the History of Parliament Trust, 1970.

Low, S. J. M. & F. S. Pulling. 'Beckford, Alderman.' In *Dictionary of English History*, 144. London: Cassell, 1896. (1st ed. 1884.) New ed., rev. & enl. F. J. C. Hearnshaw et al., 1928, p. 130.

Millington, Jon. 'Commemorative Medals of Alderman Beckford.' *Beckford Journal* 10 (2004): 50–53. Two crown-size medals from 1770 and a much smaller one issued with the *Sentimental Magazine* for July 1773.

Moore, J. F. Kenworthy-Browne, John. 'Moore, John Francis (*d*.1809).' In *Oxford Dictionary of National Biography*, ed. H. C. G. Matthew & Brian Harrison, 38:981. Oxford: Oxford University Press, 2004. Patronised by Alderman Beckford. Chimneypieces for Splendens, 1765. Statue in Ironmongers' Hall (since 1833), 1767. Guildhall statue, 1772.

O'Connell, Sheila. *London 1753*. London: British Museum Press, 2003. Alderman Beckford, 47, 64, 68–69, 101, 184, 198. Exhibition catalogue.

Phillips, Hugh. *Mid-Georgian London*. London: Collins, 1964. Alderman Beckford lived at 23 Soho Square, 297. Account of 1 Greek St & Richard Beckford, 235, 298.

Pickford, John. Great bell of St Paul's tolled at Alderman Beckford's death. *Notes and Queries* 6th Series 3 (12 March 1881): 215.

Pickford, John. 'Is there a biography of Alderman Beckford?' *Notes and Queries* 6th Series 11 (30 May 1885): 424. Replies by Constance Russell, (27 June 1885): 514 & Algernon Graves, 6th Series 12 (11 July 1885): 36.

Rule, John. *Albion's People. English Society, 1714–1815*. London: Longman, 1992. Alderman Beckford, 53, 55. William Beckford's visit to a Cornish mine in 1787, 155.

Samuel, Arthur Michael, Lord Mancroft. 'Lord Mayor Beckford.' *The Saturday Review*, 10 July 1920, 30–31. Reprinted in his *The Mancroft Essays*, 243–248. London: Cape, 1923. New ed., 1937, 262–265.

Sheppard, F. H.W. *Survey of London. Vol. 33. The Parish of St. Anne Soho*. London: Athlone Press, University of London, 1966. Alderman Beckford lived at 22 Soho Square, 1751–1770, & died there, 81b. Richard Beckford lived at 1 Greek Street, The House of St. Barnabas-in-Soho, 1754–1755, 89, 96.

Sheridan, Richard B. 'Beckford, William (*bap*.1709. *d*.1770).' In *Oxford Dictionary of National Biography*, ed. H. C. G. Matthew & Brian Harrison, 4:728–730. Oxford: Oxford University Press, 2004.

Speech to George III. *Literary Gazette* 6 (24 Aug 1822): 540. Editor's reply to a query as to whether Alderman Beckford addressed George III *extempore*.

Speech to George III. Denial by L. S. that Alderman Beckford made the speech. *Notes and Queries* 1st Series 2 (21 Sept 1850): 262. Note by John Hebb to say that he did write it, 8th Series 11 (15 May 1897): 386–387. Confirmation by Edward H. Marshall, (5 June 1897): 454, & by H. J. B.

Clements, Richard Hemming, John Pickford, 8th Series 12 (17 July 1897): 56.

Summers, Judith. *Soho. A History of London's Most Colourful Neighbourhood.* London: Bloomsbury, 1989. Pp. 47, 48–50, 117.

Thornbury, Walter (Vol. 1) & Walford, Edward (Vols. 3 & 4). *Old and New London.* 6 vols. London: Cassell, Petter, Galpin, n.d. Monument, 1:387. Speech to George III, 1:407. House in Soho Square, 3:185. William Beckford, 1:408, 4:340, 374, 412, 424.

Valentine, Alan. 'Beckford, William 1709–1770.' In *The British Establishment 1760–1784. An Eighteenth-Century Biographical Dictionary,* 67–68. 2 vols. Oklahoma: University of Oklahoma Press, 1970. MP for Shaftesbury, 1747–1754, & London, 1754–1770. Also: Julines (c.1718–1764), 66; Peter (1740–1811), 66–67; Richard (d.1796), 67.

Vizetelly, Branston, publ. *The Georgian Era.* 4 vols. London: Vizetelly, Branston, 1832–1834. 1:537.

W., A. C. 'Who was responsible for the monument to Beckford erected in the Guildhall?' *Notes and Queries* 7th Series 11 (4 April 1891): 269. Replies from Corrie Leonard Thompson & J. F. Mansergh saying it was Moore, (18 April 1891): 317–318 & 318.

W., W. C. Alderman Beckford's marriage, 8 June 1756, in parish register, Loughton, Essex. *Notes and Queries* 8th Series 2 (15 Oct 1892): 304.

Ward-Jackson, Philip. 'Guildhall. Monument to William Beckford.' In *Public Sculpture of the City of London,* 163–166. Liverpool: Liverpool University Press, 2003. Also xvii–xviii & xxx n11, xx. Monument by J. F. Moore, with brief biography of him, 471. Public Sculpture of Britain, vol. 7.

Waylen, James. 'The Wiltshire Compounders.' *Wiltshire Archæological and Natural History Magazine* 23 (1887): 337–339. The Cottington Family.

Wyld, Helen. *John Francis Moore's Monument to William Beckford.* MA thesis for University of London (Courtauld Institute of Art), 2004.

Obituaries and Funeral

Death & Funeral. *Salisbury Journal,* 18 June 1770, 3a. Lord Mayor now out of danger. *Idem,* 25 June, 2c–d, 3a, 3b. Death (from *L. E. Post*), election of new mayor, account of Alderman. *Idem,* 2 July, 3b. Funeral at Fonthill. *Idem,* 9 July, 1b–c, 2c. Character of Alderman, proposal for statue of him.

Death on 21 June, & Obituary. *Universal Magazine* 46 (June 1770): 331 & 334.

Poem. 'To the Memory of William Beckford, Esq; who died the 21st June 1770, aged 65.' *Universal Magazine* 46 (Suppl. June 1770): 375. 32 lines.

Will of 19 June 1765. 'Substance of the Will of the Right Honourable William Beckford, late Lord Mayor of the City of London.' *Universal*

Magazine 47 (July 1770): 46–47. Burial at Fonthill & proposal for statue, 49–50.

Witham

Collinson, Rev. John. 'Witham-Friary.' In *The History and Antiquities of the County of Somerset* . . . 2:232–236. 3 vols. Bath: Cruttwell, 1791. Fonthill Gifford, 233. William Beckford present owner of manor, 234. In 'List of Justices', 1:xlii.

Hammond, Norman. "Monastery gives up two 'lost' country mansions." *The Times*, 29 July 1996, 20c–f. House designed by Robert Adam rediscovered by archaeologists, with an engraving from *Vitruvius Britannicus* (1771).

Harris, Eileen. *The Genius of Robert Adam. His Interiors*. New Haven: Yale University Press, 2001. Witham Priory begun 1762 and abandoned 1770, 3, 185–186, 243. Quote from Oliver (1932, 106–107) about meeting the Countess of Home, 303–304.

Jeffries, I. I. 'Branch and Affiliated Societies.' *Somerset Archæological & Natural History Society* 110 (1965–1966): 7–10 at 8. Witham Priory. Mansion destroyed by 'the notorious William Beckford'.

McGarvie, Michael. *Witham Friary. Church and Parish*. Frome: Frome Society for Local Study, 1981. (1st ed. 1970.) Bought Witham in 1762 for £40,000, sold by his son in 1812 for £145,000, 14. Began new house designed by Robert Adam, 34. Beckford Arms at Druley, closed 1864, 39.

McGarvie, Michael. 'The Beckford Family and Witham Friary.' *Beckford Tower Trust Newsletter*, Spring 1982, 2–4.

McGarvie, Michael. 'A Seal with the Beckford Arms.' *Beckford Tower Trust Newsletter*, Spring 1985, 8. Presented by William Beckford in 1787 to the Ecclesiastical Court of Witham Friary.

Meade, Canon De Courcy. 'President's Inaugural Address.' *Somerset Archæological & Natural History Society* 24 (1878): 8–18 at 10–11. Mansion unfinished and materials removed to Wiltshire.

Wilson-North, Robert. 'Witham. From Carthusian monastery to Country House.' *Current Archaeology* No. 148 (June 1996): 151–156.

Wilson-North, Robert & Stephen Porter. 'Witham, Somerset: From Carthusian Monastery to Country House to Gothic Folly.' *Architectural History* 40 (1997): 81–98.

Woolfe, John & James Gandon. *Vitruvius Britannicus*. Vol. 5. London, 1771. 'Whitham Park' in English and French, 5–6. 'Plan of the principal Floor of Witham in Sommersetshire', pl. 38; 'Principal Front of Witham in Somersetshire. A Seat of W. Beckford Esq.', pl. 39–40; 'North East Front of Witham', pl. 41–42. Reprinted, New York: Blom, 1967. See also Breman & Addis in '5. Fonthill Splendens'.

MRS MARIA BECKFORD, 'THE BEGUM' (1724/5–1798), MOTHER

Birdwood, Vere, ed. 'Letters [to Lady Chatham] from Mrs William Beckford, 1758–1773.' In *So Dearly Loved, So Much Admired*, 225–229. London: HMSO, 1994. Nine fascinating letters, all but one from Fonthill, largely about Beckford's education.

Death & Funeral. *Salisbury and Winchester Journal*, 30 July 1798, 4c. Death on 22 July. *Idem*, 6 Aug, 4c–d. Body brought to Fonthill from Hampstead.

Obituary. *Gentleman's Magazine* 68 pt. 2 (July 1798): 637–639.

Weindling, Dick. 'West End House and the Beckford scandal.' *Camden History Review* 20 (1996): 19–23. Mrs Beckford's home (demolished 1871) from 1775 until her death in 1798.

ELIZABETH HERVEY (*c.*1745–1820), HALF-SISTER

Hervey, Elizabeth. Four novels: *Melissa and Marcia* (2 vols., 1788); *Louisa* (3 vols., 1790); *The Mourtray Family* (4 vols., 1800); *Amabel* (4 vols., 1814).

Hervey, Hon. William. *Journals of the Hon. William Hervey, In North America and Europe, From 1755 to 1814; with Order Books at Montreal, 1760–1763. With Memoir and Notes.* Ed. & intro. S. H. A. H. [Sydenham H. A. Hervey.] Bury St. Edmund's: Paul & Mathew, 1906. Brief account of Elizabeth Hervey, xliii–xliv. Family tree showing her two sons, xlvii. William Hervey rode through Fonthill grounds to Wardour Castle on 24 Oct 1792, 392. Suffolk Green Books No. XIV.

Melville, Lewis. [Lewis S. Benjamin, pseud.] Several queries, *Notes and Queries* 10th Series 11 (15 May 1909): 386. S. H. A. H. [Sydenham H. A. Hervey] replied that Elizabeth March married Thomas Hervey on 5 May 1774, (29 May 1909): 438.

Obituary. *Gentleman's Magazine* 90 pt. 1 (March 1820): 284. 'Deaths . . . Feb . . . 27 . . . At Acton Lodge, aged 70, Mrs. Hervey.'

Ponsonby, D. A. *Call a dog Hervey*. London: Hutchinson, [1949]. In 1774, Elizabeth married Thomas, who in that year was granted permission to drop the name of Hanmer and take the name and arms of Hervey, 101.

Sadleir [Sadler], Michael. 'Elizabeth Hervey and some anonymous novels.' *Notes and Queries* 153 (12 Nov 1927): 350. List of four novels attributed to Elizabeth Hervey and query about two others publ. in 1796 and 1797.

LADY MARGARET BECKFORD (1762–1786), WIFE

Anglesey, Marquess of, (George Paget), ed. *The Capel Letters . . .* 1814–1817. London: Jonathan Cape, 1955. Letter from Georgiana Capel in July 1816 about Lady Margaret Beckford at the Château de la Tour, Vevey, 167. Noted in Sidney Blackmore, ' "One More Triste" – A Memory of Lady Margaret Beckford.' *Beckford Tower Trust Newsletter*, Spring 1993, 15.

Death & Funeral. *Salisbury and Winchester Journal*, 5 June, 1786, 3b. Death 'a few days since, at the Castle of La Tour', 4 lines. *Idem*, 26 June, 3b. Remains landed at Margate. 6 lines. *Idem*, 3 July, 3b. Corpse laid in family vault at Stop, near Fonthill, plate on coffin read 'Lady Margaret Beckford died May 27, 1786, aged 23 years.' 23 lines.

MARGARET MARIA BECKFORD (1785–1818), DAUGHTER

Birth. *Salisbury and Winchester Journal*, 11 April 1785, 3b. Born at Fonthill on Saturday, 9th.

Elopement. *The Times*, 23 May 1811, 3e. 'Miss Beckford . . . eloped a few days since with a Military Officer. Her father is said to be inexorable.'

Marriage. *Gentleman's Magazine* 81 pt. 1 (May 1811): 490.

Obituary. *Gentleman's Magazine* 88 pt. 2 (Nov 1818): 470. She died at Bath.

SUSAN EUPHEMIA BECKFORD (1786–1859), DAUGHTER

Beckford's younger daughter cut off with a 'pittance of one hundred thousand pounds' & barrier wall built. *Bell's Weekly Messenger*, 6 Jan 1799.

Birth of Susan, and death of Lady Margaret. *Gentleman's Magazine* 56 pt. 1 (June 1786): 528.

Bulloch, J. M. 'The Gay Gordons. A Study in Inherited Privilege.' *Blackwood's Edinburgh Magazine* 163 (Feb 1898): 254–261 at 260. 'Lord Aboyne's cousin . . . daughter of the author of "Vathek," had previously married the Duke of Hamilton.' Reprinted in *Littell's Living Age* 216 (26 March 1898): 894.

Egmont, Count. *Salisbury and Winchester Journal*, 18 June 1804, 3c. Count Egmont of Spain had landed at Falmouth with the intention of proposing to Susan Beckford. On the way to Fonthill via Salisbury. 10 lines.

Marriage. *Gentleman's Magazine* 80 pt. 1 (April, 1810): 384. '*Marriage of Marquis of* Douglas *with Miss* Beckford'. *Idem* (May): 484–485, 1¼ pp.

Morton, H. V. *In Search of Scotland*. 15th ed. London: Methuen, 1931. (1st ed. 1929.) Duke of Hamilton's wife, Susan, daughter of Beckford, 266.

Obituary. *Gentleman's Magazine* n.s. 7 (July 1859): 91.

'Projected Union between Comte d'Egmont and Miss [Susan] Beckford.' *Lady's Monthly Museum* 14 (March 1805): 167–168.

ALEXANDER, 10TH DUKE OF HAMILTON (1767–1852), SON-IN-LAW

Hobson, A. R. A. 'L'abate e il marchese.' *La Bibliofilia* (Florence) Anno CII (2000): 105–108. About the Marquess of Douglas. Beckford mentioned, 105, 107.

Obituaries. 'Death of the Duke of Hamilton.' *The Times*, 20 Aug 1852, 6a. *Gentleman's Magazine* n.s. 38 (Oct 1852): 424–425.

Sanders, Lloyd C., rev. K. D. Reynolds. 'Hamilton, Alexander Douglas-, tenth duke of Hamilton and seventh duke of Brandon (1767–1852).' In *Oxford Dictionary of National Biography*, ed. H. C. G. Matthew & Brian Harrison, 24:761, 762. Oxford: Oxford University Press, 2004. Added to Beckford's collection and married his daughter, Susan Euphemia.

WILLIAM, 11TH DUKE OF HAMILTON (1811–1863), GRANDSON

Birth, 'In Grosvenor-place'. *Gentleman's Magazine* 81 pt. 1 (Feb 1811): 181.

Hamilton Palace. *Some Brief Particulars regarding the Arrival of the Marquis of Douglas and his Illustrious Bride, Her Highness the Princess Marie of Baden, at Hamilton Palace, on Thursday, September 14, 1843.* Glasgow: James McNab, 1844. 33 pp. & 5 lithographs.

Obituary. *Gentleman's Magazine* n.s. 15 (Aug 1863): 237–239.

Sanders, Lloyd C., rev. K. D. Reynolds. 'Hamilton, William Alexander Anthony Archibald Douglas-, eleventh duke of Hamilton and eighth duke of Brandon (1811–1863).' In *Oxford Dictionary of National Biography*, ed. H. C. G. Matthew & Brian Harrison, 24:929. Oxford: Oxford University Press, 2004. Son of Susan Euphemia Beckford.

PETER BECKFORD (1740–1811), COUSIN

Beckford, Peter. *Familiar Letters from Italy to a Friend in England.* 2 vols. Salisbury: J. Easton, 1805.

[Beckford, Peter.] *Letters and Observations written in a Short Tour through France and Italy.* Salisbury: E. Easton, 1786.

[Beckford, Peter.] *Thoughts upon Hare and Fox Hunting. In a Series of Familiar Letters to a Friend.* Salisbury: E. Easton, 1781. Many subsequent editions.

Darton, Eric. 'William Beckford's Cousin.' *Beckford Tower Trust Newsletter*, Spring 1989, 9–11.

Death, 'At Stepleton'. *Gentleman's Magazine* 81 pt. 1 (March 1811): 294.

Harrison, Robert. 'Beckford, Peter.' (1740–1811.) In *Dictionary of National Biography*, ed. Leslie Stephen, 4:79–80. London: Smith, Elder, 1885.

Harvey, Adrian N. 'Beckford, Peter (1739/40–1811).' In *Oxford Dictionary of National Biography*, ed. H. C. G. Matthew & Brian Harrison, 4:726–728. Oxford: Oxford University Press, 2004.

Higginson, A. Henry. *Peter Beckford*. London: Collins, 1937. 307 pp. Frontis. & nine illus. William Beckford & Louisa, 129–142 & passim.
  REVIEWS. Firth, J. B. 'A Sporting Squire. Cultivated Peter Beckford.' *Sunday Times*, ? Jan 1938.
  The Times, 21 Dec 1937, 20b.
  Times Literary Supplement, 6 Nov 1937, 821.

I., J. H. Who was 'Peter Beckford' (1740–1811)? *Notes and Queries* 6th Series 4 (1 Oct 1881): 267–268. Replies from Edward Solly, 15 Oct, 311–312 & J. Ingle Dredge, 5 Nov, 374.

Miller, Alan J. 'Peter Beckford of Stepleton.' *Dorset Life* No. 284 (Nov 2002): 18–20 with colour illus.

Robinson, John Martin. 'Stepleton House, Dorset.' *Country Life*, 29 May 2003, 110–115. Fine colour photos.

Thormanby. [W. Willmott Dixon.] *Kings of the Hunting-Field. Memoirs and Anecdotes* . . . London: Hutchinson, 1899. Peter Beckford, 9–16.

White, T. H. *The Scandalmonger*. London: Jonathan Cape, 1952. Peter Beckford (1740–1811) and hunting.

WILLIAM BECKFORD OF SOMERLEY (1744–1799), COUSIN

Beckford, William. *A Descriptive Account of the Island of Jamaica* . . . 2 vols. London: T & J. Egerton, 1790. French trans. by J. S. P. 2 vols. Lausanne: Durand l'aîné, 1793.

Beckford, William (author of the ancient part). *The History of France, from the most Early Records, to the Death of Louis XVI.* 4 vols. London: Jordan, 1794.

Beckford, William. *Remarks upon the Situation of Negroes in Jamaica* . . . London: T & J. Egerton, 1788.

Burney, Fanny. *The Journals and Letters of Frances Burney (Madame d'Arblay)*. Ed. Joyce Hemlow. 12 vols. Oxford: Clarendon Press, 1972–1984. Vol. 11 (1984) 'Mayfair 1818–1824'. Fanny Burney was a great friend of William's wife Charlotte, and mentioned her in a Journal entry (winter 1818), 33n.

Death, 'in Wimpole-street'. *Gentleman's Magazine* 69 pt. 1 (Feb 1799): 172.

Goodwin, Alfred. 'Beckford, William.' In *Dictionary of National Biography*, ed. Leslie Stephen, 4:82. London: Smith, Elder, 1885. Writer on Jamaica.

Pares, Richard. *A West-India Fortune*. London: Longmans, Green, 1950. William Beckford of Somerley, 105, 109, 111, 138, 139, 353 n17.

Sandiford, Keith A. *The Cultural Politics of Sugar: Caribbean Slavery and Narratives of Colonialism*. Cambridge: Cambridge University Press,

2000. William Beckford of Somerley, 2, 7, 9, 11, 13, 17. Alderman Beckford, 14, 15. William Beckford, 118.

Sheridan, Richard B. 'William Beckford (1744–1799), Patron of Painters in Jamaica.' *Register of the Museum of Art. University of Kansas* 3 (Winter 1967): 14–22.

Sheridan, Richard B. 'Beckford, William (1744–1799).' In *Oxford Dictionary of National Biography*, ed. H. C. G. Matthew & Brian Harrison, 4:730–731. Oxford: Oxford University Press, 2004.

SUSAN, COUNTESS OF LINCOLN (1814–1889), GRANDDAUGHTER

Gilliland, J. 'Opdebeck, Lady Susan Harriet Catherine (1814–1889).' In *Oxford Dictionary of National Biography*, ed. H. C. G. Matthew & Brian Harrison, 41:887. Oxford: Oxford University Press, 2004.

Surtees, Virginia. *A Beckford Inheritance: the Lady Lincoln Scandal.* Wilton, Wilts: Michael Russell, 1977. About the disastrous marriage of Susan, 10th Duke of Hamilton's daughter, to Lord Lincoln, heir to Duke of Newcastle.

REVIEWS. Annan, Gabriele. 'Mr Gladstone and the case of the pregnant heiress.' *Sunday Times*, 3 July 1977.

Fulford, Roger. 'Love in a blizzard.' *Times Literary Supplement*, 2 Sept 1977, 1054.

Hillier, Bevis. 'Faithless Suzie.' *The Times*, 15 Sept 1977, 19a–b.

Magnus, Sir Philip. 'Gladstone the rescuer.' *Daily Telegraph*, 23 June 1977, 15.

OTHER MEMBERS OF BECKFORD'S FAMILY

Books

C., G. E. [Cokayne, George Edward.] 'Hamilton.' In *The Complete Peerage of England . . .*, ed. H. A. Doubleday et al., 6:273–274. New ed. London: St Catherine Press, 1926. Beckford, 274 n(d).

D., M. J. M. [Dunbar, Margaret Juliana Maria.] *Art and Nature under an Italian Sky.* Edinburgh: Thomas Constable, 1852. Frontis., viii, 301 pp. List of subscribers headed by Queen Victoria, 16 pp. 27 cm. A journey in 1845 with her husband, the Rev. William Dunbar (author of *From London to Nice*, Edinburgh: Edmonston & Douglas, 1861). By Beckford's granddaughter and dedicated to her aunt, Susan, Duchess of Hamilton. Reprinted, London: Thomas Nelson, 1860, 5 extra pl. 22½ cm.

REVIEWS. 'Our Library Table.' *Athenæum*, 15 May 1852, 541.

Gentleman's Magazine n.s. 38 (Dec 1852): 610–611.

Hartley, Christopher. 'Le Chateau de Brodick sur l'isle d'Arran.' In *Argenteries. Le Trésor du National Trust for Scotland*, 12–15. Brussels:

National Trust for Scotland, 1992. Exhibition catalogue in French and Flemish. Pp. 2–3 in English trans.

Louisa Beckford. Mannings, David. *Reynolds*. Ed. Nicholas Penny. London: Royal Academy of Arts, 1986. '131. Master Hamilton', the future 10th Duke, 302–303. 'Mrs. Peter Beckford', 303–305. Both painted for Beckford in 1782. Exhibition catalogue.

Low, D. M., ed. *Gibbon's Journal*. London: Chatto & Windus, 1929. Beckford family, xlv. At Julines Beckford's house, 50, 65.

Sheridan, Richard B. 'Beckford, Peter (*bap*.1643. *d*.1710).' In *Oxford Dictionary of National Biography*, ed. H. C. G. Matthew & Brian Harrison, 4:724–726. Oxford: Oxford University Press, 2004. Beckford's grandfather.

Sheridan, Richard B. 'Beckford, Peter (1672/7–1735).' In *Oxford Dictionary of National Biography*, ed. H. C. G. Matthew & Brian Harrison, 4:726. Oxford: Oxford University Press, 2004. Beckford's uncle.

Thorold, Peter. *The London Rich. The Creation of a Great City, from 1666 to the Present*. London: Viking, 1999. Beckford family, 144, 145. Richard Beckford, 132. Alderman Beckford, 119, 130–132. William Beckford, 142, 144.

Wilson, Harriette. *Memoirs of Harriette Wilson [1746–1830]*. 8 vols. London: J. J. Stockdale, 1831. Horace Beckford, 1:55, 57, 222. New ed., *The Game of Hearts*, ed., Lesley Blanch, London: Gryphon, 1957.

Articles

Fraser, Mike C., Danaë E. Beckford Stanton & John W. Fox. 'William Beckford's Paternal Half-siblings and Their Descendants.' *Beckford Journal* 10 (2004): 14–29. Includes a family tree.

Gollin, G. J. 'The Beckford Family and Ashtead.' *Proceedings of the Leatherhead and District Local History Society* 4 no. 5 (1981): 135–140. Reprinted in *Bygone Ashtead*, 50–57. Leatherhead, Surrey, 1987. William Beckford (1657–1731) & Thomas Beckford (1685–1757).

Grimaldi family. Bedells, J. H. B. & D. G. Williamson. 'The House of Grimaldi. Part 1.' *The Coat of Arms. An Heraldic Quarterly Magazine* 4 nos. 29 & 30 (Jan & April 1957): 185–188 & 228–232 at 232. 'In 1869 he [Albert 1 of Monaco, grandfather of Prince Rainier] married Lady Mary Douglas-Hamilton, daughter of the 11th Duke of Hamilton.' Also noted in: *Almanach de Gotha. Annuaire Généalogique, Diplomatique et Statistique*, 1882; Gwen Robyns, *Princess Grace 1929–1982*, London: Allen, 1976, 132; Maria Kroll & Jason Lindsey, *The Country Life Book of Europe's Royal Families*, Feltham, Middlesex: Country Life Books, 1979, 58.

Grimaldi family. 'Surprise for Prince Rainier's sister at Bath.' *Bath & Wilts Chronicle & Herald*, 10 June 1966, 1, 32. Princess Antoinette of Monaco told she was descended from Beckford. Also in *Bath Weekly Chronicle*, 11 June, 1.

Harrison, Mrs Burton. 'Colonel William Byrd of Westover, Virginia.' *Century* 42 (June 1891): 163–178 at 174. Another ally of the Colonel was Peter Beckford (1643–1710) whose grandson was 'the author of "Vathek" and the builder of Fonthill Abbey, that new wonder of the world.' Letter from Peter Beckford, 175.

Hilliard, Elizabeth. 'Charles Hamilton, the Creator of Pains Hill Park.' *Beckford Tower Trust Newsletter*, Spring 1981, 3–4.

'The House of Hamilton.' *Illustrated London News* 81 (15 July 1882): 70. History of the Hamiltons publ. to coincide with the Hamilton Palace sale.

J., G. F. Early history of the Beckford family. *Notes and Queries* 8th Series 11 (3 April 1897): 262–263.

Mannings, David. 'Reynolds, Hogarth and Van Dyck.' *Burlington Magazine* 126 (Nov 1984): 689–690 & nn1–9. Reynolds 1756 portrait of Susanah Love, Mrs Francis Beckford, in the Tate Gallery was closely based on Van Dyck's portrait of Lord Russell. Companion portrait of Francis Beckford (Alderman Beckford's brother) mentioned. Both illus., figs 28, 29.

Millington, Jon. 'Keszthely.' *Beckford Journal* 3 (1997): 34–35. The Hungarian home of 11th Duke of Hamilton's daughter, Mary, one of Beckford's great granddaughters. Prince Rainier of Monaco was descended from her.

Miscellanea Genealogica et Heraldica n.s. 3 (1880). Marriage of eldest daughter of George & Elizabeth Beckford, 94*. *Idem* n.s. 4 (1884), Portrait of Alderman Beckford et al., 130. Alderman Beckford in will about property and slaves in Jamaica, 397. *Idem* 5, 2nd Series (1894), Alderman Beckford mentioned in Sir Peter Floyer's will, 138. Lady Beckford in pedigree of Evelyn of Wotton, 203. *Idem* 2, 3rd Series (1898), Louisa Beckford inscription of 1788 in Protestant Cemetery at Leghorn, 150. *Idem* 3, 3rd Series (1900), sale of Witham to Alderman Beckford & mansion (Fonthill Splendens) taken down by his son *c.*1790, 86.

Pine, W. D. 'Who was Richard Beckford?' *Notes and Queries* 8th Series 9 (8 Feb 1896): 108. Replies from A. H. & H. J. B. Clements, (7 March): 193.

4. Contemporaries

Austen, Jane (1775–1817)

Adams, Oscar Fay. 'In the Footsteps of Jane Austen.' *New England Magazine* (Boston) 14 (July 1893): 598. Beckford among writers who came to Bath.

Austen-Leigh, William & Richard Arthur Austen-Leigh. *Jane Austen. Her Life and Letters. A Family Record*. London: Smith, Elder, 1913. 29 May 1811, 251–252. Also 18 April 1811, 245; 25 April 1811, 248.

Austen-Leigh, William & Richard Arthur Austen-Leigh. *Jane Austen. A Family Record*. Rev. & enl. Deirdre Le Faye. London: British Library, 1989. Miss Maria Beckford (Beckford's cousin & sister of Francis Love Beckford), 155. Miss Beckford, frequently called at the Cottage, usually with her niece Charlotte-Maria Middleton (who married her cousin Charles Douglas Beckford, son of Francis Love Beckford), 177. Poem about Miss Beckford's pain in her head, Feb 1811, 177–178.

Brabourne, Lord Edward, ed. *Letters of Jane Austen*. 2 vols. London: Bentley, 1884. Vol. 2. Doubting that Jane Austen was the Beckfords' cousin, 80. Letters: 29 May 1811, 101. Also 18 April 1811, 82; 25 April 1811, 92.

Chapman, R. W., ed. *Jane Austen's Letters to her sister Cassandra and others*. 2nd ed. London: Oxford University Press, 1969. (1st ed. 1932.) 29 May 1811, 280. Also 18 April 1811, 267; 25 April 1811, 274; 4 Feb 1813, 301.

Chapman, R. W., ed. *Jane Austen. Selected Letters 1796–1817*. Intro. Marilyn Butler. Oxford: Oxford University Press, 1985. (1st ed. 1955.) 29 May 1811, 119, 213n. Also 18 April 1811, 109; 25 April 1811, 115; 4 Feb 1813, 135.

Halperin, John. *The Life of Jane Austen*. Brighton: Harvester Press, 1984. Jane Austen knew Beckford's daughters, 169–170. Elopement in *Pride and Prejudice* possibly suggested by Margaret Beckford's, 198. Also 196, 214.

Honan, Park. *Jane Austen. Her Life*. London: Weidenfeld & Nicolson, 1987. Charlotte-Maria Beckford (née Middleton), 265, 269–270. Maria Beckford, 269, 323.

Johnson, R. Brimley. *Jane Austen: Her Life, Her Work, Her Family, and Her Critics*. London: Dent, 1930. Mrs. Radcliffe burlesqued by Beckford in *Modern Novel Writing* and *Azemia*, 67–68.

Le Faye, Deirdre, ed. *Jane Austen's Letters*. 3rd ed. Oxford: Oxford University Press, 1995. 'Col. Orde has married our cousin, Marg^t Beckford', 29 May 1811, 187. Maria Beckford, cousin (?1766–?1854), mentioned, 18 April 1811, 179; 25 April 1811, 183; 4 Feb 1813, 203–204; 29 Nov 1814, 283.

Beltz, George Frederick (1774–1841). See '5. Fonthill Abbey. Heraldry'

Bentham, Jeremy (1748–1832)

Bowring, John, ed. *The Works of Jeremy Bentham*. 11 vols. Edinburgh: William Tait, 1843. Coming-of-age, 10:91, 97, 107. At Wilton, Beckford 'sat down at the harpsichord and played delightfully', 122. Beckford would pay £10 to paper the room he was about to sleep in, 285.

Christie, Ian R., ed. *The Correspondence of Jeremy Bentham. Volume 3. January 1781 to October 1788*. London: University of London, The Athlone Press, 1971. To George Wilson on 24 Aug 1781, Beckford 'comes of age and gives a grand fête to all the world', 55 & n2. To Jeremiah Bentham on 31 Aug, again mentioning the fête, 68. To George Wilson on 24 Sept 1781, Lord Camden and his daughter, Miss Pratt, were going to Fonthill from Wilton, 97.

Bohn, Henry George (1796–1884). See '8. The Collection. Beckford's Library'

Britton, John (1771–1857). See '1. Accounts of Beckford's Life' and '5. Fonthill Abbey'

Byron, Lord George Gordon, (1788–1824)

Byron, Lord George Gordon. *The Works of Lord Byron: with His Letters and Journals, and His Life*. Ed. Thomas Moore. 17 vols. London: John Murray, 1832–1833. *Childe Harold's Pilgrimage*, Canto 1, stanzas 22–23 & note about Beckford, 8:25–26 & n1. 'Eblis' in *The Giaour* from Herbelot: 'Eblis, the Oriental Prince of Darkness', 9:178 n2. Influence of *Vathek* in *The Siege of Corinth*, 10:131 & n1. 'To Dives. A Fragment', 17:241. Also letter to John Murray on 15 May 1819 about Mrs. Hervey fainting on seeing Byron, 4:150.

Byron, Lord George Gordon. *The Complete Works of Lord Byron . . .* Ed. John Galt. Paris: Baudry's European Library, 1835. *Childe Harold's Pilgrimage*, Canto 1, stanzas 22–23, and footnote about Beckford at Cintra & *Vathek*, 88. 'To Dives', 175. Influence of *Vathek* on *The Giaour*, 231, & *The Siege of Corinth*, 296.

Byron, Lord George Gordon. *Byron's Letters & Journals*. Ed. Leslie A. Marchand. London: John Murray. Vol. 1, *1798–1810* (1973): To Francis

Hodgson on 25 June 1809, telling him he had changed horses at inn where Beckford had stayed, 210 & n2. Vol. 2, *1810–1812* (1973): To Robert Charles Dallas on 26 Sept 1811, asking him whether he should change his stanzas on 'Vathek' in *Childe Harold* (1, 22–23), 107 & n2. Vol. 6, *1818–1819* (1976): To Samuel Rogers on 3 March 1818, asking him to obtain the *Episodes of Vathek*, 17–18 & n2. Vol. 11, *1823–1824* (1981): To Charles F. Barry on 11 Oct 1823, about a copy of 'Calyph Vathek', 76 & n.

Byron, Lord George Gordon. *Lord Byron. The Complete Poetical Works.* 7 vols. Ed. Jerome J. McGann. Oxford: Clarendon Press, 1980–1986. Vol. 2 (1980), *Childe Harold's Pilgrimage* (1812), stanzas 22–23 & variant for stanza 23, 'To Dives', 18–19, & 'Commentary', 276 (lines 270–278 var, 279–287). Also 274 (l. 260). Byron's debt to *Vathek* noted in the 'Commentary' to the poems in vols. 3–6: vol. 3 (1981), *The Giaour* (1813), 415–421 passim, 423, 424 (Poem 207), *The Bride of Abydos* (1813), 436, *The Corsair* (1814), 449, *The Siege of Corinth* (1816), 486; vol. 4 (1986), 'Darkness' (1816), 460 (l. 65–66), *Manfred* (1816), 465, 472 (l. 105–107), 473 (l. 14–15), 474 (l. 1–10), *The Prophecy of Dante* (1819), Byron mentioned *Vathek* in his Preface, 214 & note on 501: '*Vathek*, one of Byron's favourite books'; vol. 5 (1986), *Don Juan* (1819–1824), 707 (l. 201), 722 (l. 688), Byron's dwarfs perhaps a recollection of Beckford's, 709; vol. 6 (1991), *Cain* (1821), 650, 655 (l. 61–62). *Werner* (1822), 720 (l. 381–382).

Cheetham, Simon. *Byron in Europe. In Childe Harold's Footsteps.* Wellingborough, Northants: Equation, 1988. 'Flamboyant' Beckford at Monserrate, 26. His fate, 48, *Vathek*, 108, 150.

Court Journal, 6 Oct 1832, 662. Byron plagiarising *Vathek*.

Garber, Frederick. 'Beckford, Delacroix and Byronic Orientalism.' *Comparative Literature Studies* 18 (Sept 1981): 321–332.

Garber, Frederick. 'An Oriental Twist.' In *Self, Text, and Romantic Irony: The Example of Byron*, 69–101 at 70–79, 81, 83–84, 89–90, 91, 98, 100–101. Princeton: Princeton University Press, 1988.

Giddey, Ernest. 'Byron and Beckford.' *Byron Journal* 6 (1978), 38–47. Discusses the relationship between the two men.

Grosskurth, Phyllis. *Byron: The Flawed Angel.* London: Hodder & Stoughton, 1997. Falmouth, 81. 'To Dives', 86. Elizabeth Hervey at dinner, 286 n.

Joseph, M. K. *Byron the Poet.* London: Victor Gollancz, 1964. '. . . Beckford's *Vathek*, on which he drew far more than local colour', 44–45 & 66 nn41–48. *Vathek*, 86 & 101 n64, 103 & 127 n6, 120 & 130 n88, 121.

Longford, Elizabeth. *Byron.* London: Hutchinson / Weidenfeld & Nicolson, 1976. Pp. 21, 59, 87, 113, 184.

McGann, Jerome. 'Childe Harold's Pilgrimage I – II: A Collation and Analysis.' *Keats-Shelley Memorial Bulletin* 17 (1966): 37–54 at 41 & nn11, 12. Deletion of the 'To Dives' stanza. *Vathek* mentioned, 46, 53.

Medwin, Thomas. *Journal of the Conversations of Lord Byron noted during a Residence with his Lordship at Pisa in the years 1821 and 1822.* London: Colburn, 1824. Byron borrowed from *Vathek* for *Siege of Corinth*, 265–266.

Millington, Jon. 'Beckford and Byron.' *Beckford Journal* 1 (1995): 41–46. The suppressed stanza 'To Dives' and Byron's attitude to Beckford.

Parreaux, André. 'Beckford et Byron: I. L'Influence de «Vathek».' *Études Anglaises* 8 no. 1 (Jan–March 1955): 11–31.

Parreaux, André. 'Beckford et Byron: II. Deux Destins.' *Études Anglaises* 8 no. 2 (April–June 1955): 113–132.

Stauffer, Andrew M. 'Byron, Medwin, and The False Fiend: Remembering "Remember Thee".' *Studies in Bibliography* 53 (2000): 265–276 at 276. Inscription 'To Bd.' on a manuscript, possibly referred to Beckford.

Thompson, A. Hamilton, ed. *Childe Harold's Pilgrimage.* Cambridge: Cambridge University Press, 1913. *Vathek*, 195 n275.

Thompson, Karl F. 'Beckford, Byron, and Henley.' *Études Anglaises* 14 (1961): 225–228.

Wiener, Harold. 'Byron and the East: Literary Sources of the "Turkish Tales".' In *Nineteenth-Century Studies*, ed. Herbert Davis et al., 89–129. Ithaca, NY: Cornell University Press, 1940.

Clarke, William (c.1752–1830) & George (his son). See '10. Beckford's Works. First Editions. Letters'

Constable, John (1776–1837). See '5. Fonthill. 1822 and Christie's Sale'

Courtenay, William (1768–1835)

Barker, Nicolas. 'Mismanaging Mother: Was William Beckford really a forger?' *Times Literary Supplement*, 2 Oct 1998, 17. Refuting Timothy Mowl's suggestion in *William Beckford* (1998) that Beckford suppressed evidence of his relationship with Courtenay. *Idem*, 9 Oct, 19. Reply by Mowl: 'William Beckford, fact, myth and forgery.' *Idem*, 6 Nov, 21. Letter from Stephen Lloyd supporting Barker, correcting caption to Cosway portrait and denying that Courtenay was a victim. Barker's article reprinted in his *Form and Meaning in the History of the Book: Selected Essays*, London: British Library, 2003, 390–392.

Courtenay, Sir Christopher. *The Courtenay Family.* Privately printed, 1967.

Lees-Milne, James. 'The Powderham Castle Affair.' In *Society Scandals*, ed. Harriet Bridgeman & Elizabeth Drury, 36–50. Newton Abbot, Devon: David & Charles, 1977.

[Nichols, John Gough.] *Gentleman's Magazine* n.s. 4 (July 1835): 89. Obituary, ¾ page. *Idem* n.s. 4 (Dec 1835): 670. Will.

Cozens, Alexander (c.1717–1786) & John Robert (1752–1797). See '8. The Collection. Paintings'

Danby, Francis (1793–1861). See '8. The Collection. Paintings'

Disraeli, Benjamin. 1st Earl of Beaconsfield (1804–1881). See also '16. Works influenced by Beckford'

Barker, Nicolas. *Treasures from the Libraries of National Trust Country Houses*. New York: Royal Oak Foundation & Grolier Club, 1999. Cat. No. 100: *Vathek* (1815) presented to Benjamin Disraeli, p. 154, illus., p. 153.

Gunn, J. A. W. et al., eds. *Benjamin Disraeli Letters*. 6 vols. Toronto: University of Toronto Press, 1982–1997. References are to letter numbers. To Beckford: Vol. 1, *1815–1834* (1982): 13 June? 1834, sending him a piece of marble, 327 & nn1, 2; 16 June 1834?, ?sending him a copy of *Contarini Fleming*, 330; 3 July 1834, about 'The Infernal Marriage' in *New Monthly Magazine*, 335 & n1. Vol. 2, *1835–1837* (1982): 17 May 1837, sending him a copy of *Venetia*, 612 & n2. Vol. 3, *1838–1841* (1987): 6 Jan 1840?, praise for *Alcobaça and Batalha*, 1026 & nn1, 2; 19 Dec 1835, ? met Westmacott, 453x (p. 371). To Sarah, his sister: Vol. 1: 26 May 1832, received courteous letter praising *Contarini Fleming*, 193 & n1; 2 March 1833, received large paper *Vathek* from Beckford, 242; 16 June 1834, 'Beckford's feeling for the fine arts is beyond all conception', 329 & n3; 26? July 1834, 'found a scene worthy of Caliph Vathek', 341. Vol. 4, *1842–1847* (1989): 16 Jan 1843, ref. to an Eblisian scene, 1272 & n6. To Sarah Austen: Vol. 1: 16? March 1833, received letter from Beckford 'in which you will rejoice', 253 & n2. To [Helen Selina Blackwood.]: Vol. 1. 18? March 1833, letters on *Alroy* from Caliph Vathek himself, 255 & nn6, 7. To Lord Londonderry: Vol. 5, *1848–1851* (1993): 22 Nov 1848, ref. to Caliph Vathek's tower, 1748. To Lord Derby: Vol. 6, *1852–1856* (1997): 4 June 1852, Prince Albert's plans 'worthy of Caliph Vathek', 2300 & n1. Also 281 & n13, 332 & n4, 337 n8.

Hibbert, Christopher. *Disraeli. A Personal History*. London: HarperCollins, 2004. Beckford's enthusiasm for *Contarini Fleming*, 59. Encounter at opera, 61, 75. Reluctance to meet Disraeli, a heavy smoker, 161n.

[Layard, Austen Henry.] 'The Early Life of Lord Beaconsfield.' *Quarterly Review* 168 (Jan 1889): 28. Beckford's praise for *Alroy* (1833). Reprinted in *Littell's Living Age* 180 (2 March 1889): 529–530.

Monypenny, William Flavelle. *The Life of Benjamin Disraeli, Earl of Beaconsfield*. 6 vols. London: John Murray, 1910. Vol. 1 (1804–1837).

Beckford, 'that fantastical genius', 199. Letters to Sarah Disraeli: Beckford's admiration for *Contarini Fleming*, 26 May, 5 July 1832, 191, 191–192; met Beckford at opera, 4 June 1834, 248; Beckford, the man 'of the greatest taste', 4 Aug 1834, 253–254.

Mowl, Tim. 'Disraeli's Novels and the Beckford Connection.' In *Benjamin Disraeli, Earl of Beaconsfield: Scenes from an Extraordinary Life*, ed. Helen Langley, 29–34. Oxford: Bodleian Library, 2003. Exhibition catalogue. Illus. by C. F. Tayler's portrait (not of Beckford) & Maddox's exterior of Beckford's Tower.

Nolan, Jerry. "Brief Encounter of Beckford and Disraeli, or The Radical Pair of 'Oriental Voluptuaries'." *Beckford Journal* 8 (2002): 66–78.

Stephen, Leslie. 'Luxury.' *National Review* 23 (March 1894): 29–48. The hero in one of Disraeli's novels proposed to copy Beckford's tower at Fonthill and build one just for the sake of doing so. Reprinted in *Littell's Living Age* 201 (14 April 1894): 67–80 at 72.

Willis, Nathaniel Parker. 'Pencillings by the Way.' *New York Mirror* (weekly), 1830s. Disraeli's extraordinary language in describing Beckford. Reprinted in *Littell's Living Age* 35 (23 Oct 1852): 183. Reprinted again in 'Editor's Easy Chair.' *Harper's New Monthly Magazine* 59 (Aug 1879): 462, and repeated 62 (Feb 1881): 466–467.

Drysdale, Robert (c.1747–1823 or later)

'County Notes . . . The Young Man from Scotland.' *Wiltshire Gazette*, 13 March 1924, 5a. Paragraph commenting on the articles reprinting Drysdale's letters.

Paul, Sir James Balfour, ed. Robert Drysdale's letters to his old university friend, Rev. James Nairne (*d.*1819) – both at St Andrew's University, 1765–1768. [Part 1] 'A Scots Tutor and William Beckford: Interesting unpublished letters come to light. Beckford's boyhood home described from inside.' *Wiltshire Gazette*, 14 Feb 1924, 3a–b. Dated 13 Oct 1768: Drysdale describes his new position. [Part 2] 'The Young Scots Tutor of William Beckford. His description of Alderman Beckford's mansion.' *Idem*, 21 Feb, 3b. Two letters, the second of 9 Dec 1769 being a report on Beckford's academic progress. [Part 3] 'William Beckford's First Tutor. A fashionable watering place 150 years ago.' *Idem*, 28 Feb, 3c. Dated 3 Aug 1775: Drysdale at Brighton (he had left the Beckfords in 1771). In 1776 he was tutor to the family of William Burt, one of Beckford's guardians. [Part 4] 'Robert Drysdale, Scotch Tutor. Another tutorship in South Wilts.' *Idem*, 6 March, 3b. Tutor to four sons of Richard Dawkins of Standlynch. [Part 5] 'Beckford's First Tutor. Last of the Edinburgh letters.' *Idem*, 13 March, 3c–b. At Weymouth in 1783. From May 1790 stayed with Beckford at Fonthill. Went with him to London in Oct, and accompanied him to Paris. Letter dated 18 Nov 1791: back at Fonthill. Noted in *Wiltshire*

Archæological and Natural History Magazine 43 (June 1924): 525. See Oliver, *Life of Beckford* (1932) for Drysdale and extracts from letters.

Eginton, Francis (1736/7–1805). See '8. The Collection. Stained Glass'

Farington, Joseph (1747–1821)

The Diary of Joseph Farington. 16 vols. New Haven: Yale University Press for the Paul Mellon Centre for Studies in British Art, 1978–1984. Passim. New ed. prepared from the MS. in the Royal Library at Windsor Castle. Vols. 1–6 (1978–1979) covering July 1793 to Dec 1804, ed. Kenneth Garlick & Angus Macintyre. Vols. 7–16 (1982–1984) covering Jan 1805 to Dec 1821, ed. Kathryn Cave. Evelyn Newby. *The Diary of Joseph Farington. Index.* 1998. Beckford, 68–69. Fonthill, 336.
REVIEW of vols. 1 & 2. Powell, Anthony. 'A war-artist at the Academy.' *Daily Telegraph*, 18 Jan 1979, 6.
Farington, Joseph. 'William Beckford in Farington's Diary.' *Beckford Journal* 11 (2005): 50–75. Compilation by Jon Millington of all references to Beckford in the *Diary*.
Greig, James, ed. *The Farington Diary.* 8 vols. London: Hutchinson, 1922–1928. Vol. 1, 1793–1802. 'Peerage', 51–52. Beckford's character, 51n, 187–188, 214, 217, 218, 233, 237. Fonthill, 18n, 213, 251, 308. 'Beckford as Peacemaker', 219–220, 225. Buys two Claudes, 269. Turner's seven drawings of Fonthill, 289. Nelson at Fonthill, 307. Vol. 2, 1802–1804. His motive for gothic design of Abbey & disgusted with Wyatt, 217. Saw in Paris small marble figure for Beckford by Moitte, 45. At sales, Beckford looked like a dealer, 118. Vol. 3, 1804–1806. His finances & daughters, 95 & n. His elder daughter taller and handsomer, 248 & n. Mentioned, 34n, 127. Vol. 4, 1806–1808. 'Colt Hoare at Fonthill', 33. Fonthill sale (1807), 197. 'Beckford and his Fortune', 'Beckford and Persecution' & 'In Love with Beckford', 242–243 & portrait. Vol. 5, 1808–1809. He sold his 'Altieri' Claudes, 84. Vol. 6, 1810–1811. Saw Beckford at B. West's, 35. Only Beckford and clergyman present when Susan married M. of Douglas, 51. Vol. 7, 1811–1814. Bought a Poussin, 192. Death of Wyatt who, said West, had caused Beckford much trouble, 204.

Farquhar, John (1751–1826). See '5. Fonthill Abbey'

Franchi, Gregorio (1770–1828). See also '8. The Collection'

Alexander, Boyd. *From Lisbon to Baker Street: The Story of the Chevalier Franchi, Beckford's Friend.* Lisbon: The British Historical Society of Portugal, 1977. 32 pp. Passim.
Blackmore, Sidney. 'Chevalier Franchi's Tomb.' *Beckford Tower Trust Newsletter*, Part 2, Spring 1980, [4]. Cemetery of St John's Wood Chapel.

Darton, Eric. 'Franchi's Last Days.' *Beckford Tower Trust Newsletter*, Spring 1982, 5.

Darton, Eric. 'The Enigma of Chevalier Gregorio Franchi.' *Beckford Tower Trust Newsletter*, Spring 1993, 12–14. Account of his life.

Shaffer, Elinor. 'Franchi, Gregorio (1769/70–1828).' In *Oxford Dictionary of National Biography*, ed. H. C. G. Matthew & Brian Harrison, 20:731–731. Oxford: Oxford University Press, 2004.

Gibbon, Edward (1737–1794). See '8. The Collection. Beckford's Library'

Goodridge, Henry Edmund (bap.1797. d.1864). See '6. Beckford's Tower and Bath'

Gore, Mrs Catherine (1799–1861). See also Poe in '12. *Vathek* and *The Episodes*: Criticism' and '16. Works influenced by Beckford'

Adburgham, Alison. *Silver Fork Society. Fashionable life and literature from 1814–1840*. London: Constable, 1983. Beckford helped Mrs Gore with *Cecil, or the Adventures of a Coxcomb* (1841), 317.

B., S. *Notes and Queries* 1st Series 10 (1 July 1854): 19. Beckford's help with her novels.

'Mrs. Gore.' *Illustrated London News* 38 (16 Feb 1861): 147. Long obituary with portrait.

Horne, Richard. H., ed. *A New Spirit of the Age*. 2 vols. 2nd ed. London: Smith, Elder, 1844. 1:234–235. Concerning *Cecil* (1841), 'She wrote the story, and Mr. Beckford helped her to the learning.'

[Jacox, Francis.] 'Female Novelists (No. II): Mrs Gore.' *New Monthly Magazine* 95 (June 1852): 157–168. Beckford admired Mrs Gore's novels. Reprinted in *Littell's Living Age* 34 (18 Sept 1852): 545–550 at 548.

Gregory, William (c.1818–1898)

Library sale. *Bath Chronicle*, 16 Nov 1899, 4b. Extra-illustrated works relating to Beckford from Gregory's library to be sold by Powell & Powell on 17th.

Obituaries. *Bath Chronicle*, 31 March 1898, 3d, and *Bath and County Graphic* 2 no. 12 (April 1898): 149.

Hamilton, Emma (1761–1815)

Bowen, Marjorie. *Patriotic Lady: a study of Emma, Lady Hamilton . . .* London: John Lane, 1935. Beckford, 69–70, 99, 283, 291, 313. The Christmas visit to Fonthill, 278–282.

D'Auvergne, Edmund B. *To Dear Emma: The Story of Emma Lady Hamilton, her Husband and her Lovers*. London: George G. Harrap, 1936. Beckford, 22, 101, 130, 142, 148, 223, 224, 232, 238, 245–246.

Death in Calais & Refused Christian burial. *Gentleman's Magazine* 85 pt. 1 (Feb 1815): 183 & 190.

Fraser, Flora. *Beloved Emma. The Life of Emma Lady Hamilton.* London: Weidenfeld & Nicolson, 1986. Pp. 36–37, 162, 170, 198–199, 211, 236, 275, 280, 344, 355.

Hardwick, Mollie. *Emma, Lady Hamilton: a study.* London: Cassell, 1969. The Christmas visit to Fonthill, 73–75. Beckford, 191, 271.

Lofts, Norah. *Emma Hamilton.* London: Michael Joseph, 1978. Nelson's visit to Fonthill, 54, 95.

Moorhouse, E. Hallam. *Nelson's Lady Hamilton.* London: Methuen, 1906. Beckford, 93, 281–282, 295.

Sherrard, O. A. *A Life of Emma Hamilton.* London: Sidgwick and Jackson, 1927. Beckford, 136, 286, 311.

Sichel, Walter Sydney. *Emma, Lady Hamilton.* London: Constable, 1905. Feted at Fonthill (1791), 133–135. Beckford in Paris (1792), 144, 148. Emma's second invitation to Fonthill (1801), 230 & n1. Beckford put his London house at the Hamiltons' disposal (1800), 335, 338. Beckford offered Hamilton a large annuity in 1802 for a peerage to revert to him, 389–390. Also 5, 14, 16.

Simpson, Colin. *Emma: the life of Lady Hamilton.* London: The Bodley Head, 1983. Beckford, 157, 162–167.

Tours, Hugh. *The Life and Letters of Emma Hamilton.* London: Victor Gollancz, 1963. Beckford, 162. The Christmas visit to Fonthill, 166–170.

Warner, Oliver. *Emma Hamilton and Sir William.* London: Chatto & Windus, 1960. Pp. 42–43, 113, 125, 161, 189–190, 201.

Hamilton, Lady Catherine (d.1782)

Death in Naples. *Gentleman's Magazine* 52 (Sept 1782): 455.

Deutsch, Otto Erich. 'The First Lady Hamilton.' *Notes and Queries* 197 (6 & 20 Dec 1952): 540–543 & 560–565. William Beckford, passim.

Hamilton, Sir William (1730–1803)

Constantine, David. *Fields of Fire: A Life of Sir William Hamilton.* London: Weidenfeld & Nicolson, 2001. At Naples in 1780, 103–108. Beckford's reaction to Catherine Hamilton's death in 1782, 115–118. Also passim.

Death in Piccadilly. *Gentleman's Magazine* 73 pt. 1 (April 1803): 390.

Fothergill, Brian. *Sir William Hamilton. Envoy Extraordinary.* London: Faber & Faber, 1969. Catherine Hamilton, 32–33, 177. At Palazzo Sessa, 59–60. Beckford at Naples in 1780, 166–171. Powderham scandal, 202–203. Peerage, 393–394, 412. Nelson at Fonthill, 394–396. Also 101, 248, 391.

Jenkins, Ian & Kim Sloan. *Vases and Volcanoes: Sir William Hamilton and his Collection.* London: Trustees of the British Museum, 1996. Pp. 17, 44,

58 & 64 n164, 134–137, 176, 223, 262, 264, 276, 280–281, 294–295. Exhibition catalogue.

Knight, Carlo. *Hamilton a Napoli. Cultura, svaghi, civita una grande capitale europea.* Naples: Electa Napoli, 1990. Pp. 42, 54, 92, 101, 105, 106, 135.

Mayer, Dorothy Moulton. *Angelica Kauffmann.* Gerrards Cross: Colin Smythe, 1972. Hamilton commissioned a picture from Kauffmann which pleased him so much that he wrote to Beckford about it, 109.

Wroth, Warwick. 'Hamilton, Sir William.' In *Dictionary of National Biography*, ed. Leslie Stephen, 24:226. London: Smith, Elder, 1890. Beckford not mentioned in the *ODNB* (2004) article on Hamilton.

Hamilton, William (1751–1801). See '8. The Collection. Stained Glass'

Hazlitt, William (1778–1830). See also '5. Fonthill Abbey' and '8. The Collection. Paintings and Drawings'

Hazlitt, W. Carew. *Memoirs of William Hazlitt.* 2 vols. London: Richard Bentley, 1867. 'In the Winter of 1823 Mr. Hazlitt, in company with Mr. Patmore, visited some of our principal picture-galleries – Stafford House, Dulwich, Stourhead, Burleigh, and last, *and least*, Fonthill.', 2:97.

Howe, P. P. *The Life of William Hazlitt.* Harmondsworth, Middlesex: Penguin, 1949. (1st ed. 1922). Article on the pictures at Fonthill in *London Magazine* in Nov 1822, 350. At Fonthill in Sept 1823 with P. G. Patmore, 358–360.

Howe, P. P., ed. *The Complete Works of William Hazlitt.* 21 vols. London: Dent, 1930–1934. 'Pictures at Wilton, Stourhead, &c' (*London Magazine*, Oct 1823 & *Sketches of the Principal Picture-Galleries in England*, 1824), 10:55, 56, 58–61, 315–316 nn[2, 12–20]. 'On the Pleasure of Hating' (*The Plain Speaker*, 1826), 12:135, 401 n. 'On a Portrait of an English Lady, by Vandyke' (*The Plain Speaker*, 1826), 12:292. 'The Main Chance' (*New Monthly Magazine*, Feb 1828), 17:279–280, 417 n[3]. 'Travelling Abroad' (*New Monthly Magazine*, June 1828), 17:335. 'Fonthill Abbey' (*London Magazine*, Nov 1822), 18:173–180, 441–442 nn[1–7]. 'Mr. Beckford's Vathek' (*Morning Chronicle*, 10 Oct 1823), reprinted for the first time, 19:98–104, 104 n1, 343–344 nn[1–4]. 'Queries Addressed to Political Economists' (*The Examiner*, 9 April 1826), 19:335.

Waller, A. R. & Arnold Glover, eds. *The Collected Works of William Hazlitt.* 12 vols. London: Dent, 1902–1904. 'On a Portrait of an English Lady, by Vandyke' (*The Plain Speaker*, 1826), 7:292, 507 n[12]. 'Pictures at Wilton, Stourhead, &c' (*London Magazine*, Oct 1823), 9:55, 56, 58–61, 445 nn[1, 8–13]. 'Fonthill Abbey' (*London Magazine*, Nov 1822), 9:348–355, 468–469 nn[1–24]. 'The Main Chance' (*New Monthly Magazine*, Feb 1828), 12:83, 479 n[3].

Wu, Duncan, ed. *The Selected Writings of William Hazlitt*. 9 vols. London: Pickering & Chatto, 1998. 'On the Pleasure of Hating' (*The Plain Speaker*, 1826), 8:124, 378 n31. 'On a Portrait of an English Lady, by Vandyke' (*The Plain Speaker*, 1826), 8:272. 'The Main Chance' (*New Monthly Magazine*, Feb 1828), 9:165, 249 n2. 'The History of the Caliph Vathek' (*Morning Chronicle*, 10 Oct 1823), 9:115–120, 238–239 nn1–17.

Heard, Sir Isaac (1730–1822). See '5. Fonthill Abbey. Heraldry'

Henley, Samuel (1740–1815)

Chamberlain, Mellen. 'Sketch of the Life of the Rev. Samuel Henley.' *Proceedings of the Massachusetts Historical Society* 15 (1876–1877): 230–241.

Mayer, S. R. Townshend. 'Who was Henley?' *Notes and Queries* 4th Series 7 (14 Jan 1871): 35. Replies by Thomas E. Winnington, (4 Feb): 113. W. P. Courtney, (25 Feb): 174. W. H. P., (18 March): 244.

'Memoir of the Rev. Samuel Henley, D.D.' *Gentleman's Magazine* 86 pt. 1 (Feb 1816): 182.

Moriarty, G. P. 'Henley, Samuel.' In *Dictionary of National Biography*, ed. Leslie Stephen & Sidney Lee, 25:420. London: Smith, Elder, 1891.

Moriarty, G. P., rev. John D. Haigh. 'Henley, Samuel (1740–1815).' In *Oxford Dictionary of National Biography*, ed. H. C. G. Matthew & Brian Harrison, 26:364. Oxford: Oxford University Press, 2004.

Herbert, Henry. 10th Earl of Pembroke (1734–1794)

Herbert, Henry, 10th Earl of Pembroke. *Henry, Elizabeth and George (1734–80). Letters and Diaries of Henry, Tenth Earl of Pembroke and his Circle*. Ed. Lord Herbert. London: Cape, 1939. Reissued 1942 as *The Pembroke Papers (1734–1780)* . . . Dr Eyre to Lord Herbert, 1 Jan 1779, Beckford's State Bed lent to Wilton 'To accommodate their Majesties with a good Bed', 139. Idem. *The Pembroke Papers (1780–1794)* . . ., 1950. Lord Pembroke to Lord Carmarthen: 28 Sept 1781, 'Beckford, just come of age, is giving force fêtes', 156. Pembroke to Herbert: 2 Oct, 'Beckford's Fêtes were really magnificent dans tous les genres', 158. Lady Pembroke to Herbert: 10 Oct, sent Duchess of Buccleuch 'some account of Fête at Fonthill' & Beckford at Wilton, 161–162 & n1. Pembroke to Carmarthen: 3 Jan 1782, sorry C. hadn't seen Beckford who had 'amused & astonished every body here yesterday exceedingly', 189. Pembroke to Herbert: 23 Feb 1785, asking about 'Bd of F's cursed affair', 268; 16 March, 'is it true Beckford's wife will not leave him?' & 'what was the exact business? ', 269; 10 May, 'Is Beckford at Fonthill, & is he chassé or still recd in company?', 274; 24 Nov, the Beckfords at Wilton, 292; 1 Jan

1787, met Beckford at Palais Royal, 324; 24 Jan, met him again at Palais Royal, Beckford has gone 'to England in order to embark immediately for Jamaica', 329–330.

Hoare, Sir Richard Colt (1758–1838). See '5. Fonthill. General Accounts'

Huber, Jean (1721–1786)

Jean-Aubry, G. 'Un original du XVIIIe siècle: Jean Huber ou le démon de Genève.' *Revue de Paris* 3 (1, 15 June 1936): 593–626, 807–821.

Jay, William (1769–1853). See '2. Aspects of Beckford. Religion'

Lansdown, Henry Venn (1804–1860). See also '1. Accounts of Beckford's Life'

Millington, Jon. 'Henry Venn Lansdown, 1804–1860.' *Beckford Journal* 11 (2005): 20–29. Illus. by Lansdown's drawings of Abbey, Tower & Tomb.

Obituary. *Gentleman's Magazine* n.s. 8 (March 1860): 303–304.

Lettice, John (1737–1832)

Barber, M. J. *The Vicar's Tin Box. The Life of John Lettice. Vicar of Peasmarsh 1785–1832.* Rye, Sussex: Neame, 2002. Lettice as Beckford's tutor, then companion and, finally, friend. 'A New Pupil' in 1770, 6. 'Life at Fonthill', 7. 'To Switzerland' in 1777, 8–9. 'The English Tour' in 1779, 10. 'Lettice as Bear-leader' in 1780–1781, 11–12. 'The Pupil comes of age' in 1781, 13. 'To Europe again' in 1782, 14. 'The Beckford Connection', tutor to Beckford's daughters in the 1790s, 23–25. 'The Vicar's Tin Box', containing an MS. of Lettice's autobiography which disappeared on his death in 1832, including his recollections of Beckford, 35–37. Also 19, 27, 31, 38, 39, 40, 41. Illus. include Beckford by Romney, John Lettice and Fonthill Splendens.

Burney, Frances. *The Early Diary of Frances Burney, 1768–1778.* Ed. Annie Raine Ellis. 2 vols. London: George Bell, 1907. Comments on Lettice's reticence and old-fashioned piano playing made in Feb 1772, 1:151, 155–157, 155n. Also her observations in Sept 1783 on the mixture of good and bad pictures at Fonthill Splendens, 2:323.

Obituary. *Gentleman's Magazine* 102 pt. 2 (Nov 1832): 477–480 at 478.

Shaw, W. A. 'Lettice, John.' In *Dictionary of National Biography*, ed. Sidney Lee, 33:133. London: Smith, Elder, 1893.

Shaw, W. A., rev. William Gibson. 'Lettice, John (1737–1832).' In *Oxford Dictionary of National Biography*, ed. H. C. G. Matthew & Brian Harrison, 33:511. Oxford: Oxford University Press, 2004. Tutor to the Beckford family.

Loutherbourg, Philippe-Jacques de (1740–1812)

Baugh, Christopher. 'Loutherbourg, Philippe-Jacques de (1740–1812).' In *Oxford Dictionary of National Biography*, ed. H. C. G. Matthew & Brian Harrison, 34:490. Oxford: Oxford University Press, 2004. Transformed rooms at Splendens for Christmas party in 1781.

Loutherbourg. *Philippe Jacques de Loutherbourg, RA 1740–1812*. London: Greater London Council, 1973. Christmas at Fonthill in 1781, [7]. Exhibition at Kenwood.

'That Strange Adventurer de Loutherbourg.' *The Times*, 9 Dec 1958, 13d–e. A general account by 'A Correspondent'.

Ziter, Edward. *The Orient on the Victorian Stage*. Cambridge: Cambridge University Press, 2003. Influence of de Loutherbourg on Beckford, 19–20. Byron and Beckford, 66. Royal Coburg production of *The Caliph Vathek* (1823), 77.

Macquin, Abbé Ange Denis (1756–1823). See '5. Fonthill Abbey. Heraldry'

Maddox, Willes (1813–1853). See '8. The Collection. Paintings'

Marialva, 5th Marquis (1739–1803). See '13. Travel. Portugal'

Moore, John Francis (d.1809). See '3. Family. Alderman Beckford'

Moore, Thomas (1779–1852)

Dowden, Wilfred S., ed. *The Journal of Thomas Moore*. 6 vols. Newark: University of Delaware Press, 1983–1991. Numbers in brackets refer to *Memoirs, Journal, and Correspondence of Thomas Moore*, ed. Lord John Russell, 8 vols, London: Longman, etc., 1853–1856. 18 Oct 1818, Beckford delighted with *Lalla Rookh* & wanted Moore to go with Samuel Rogers to Fonthill to look over his 'Travels', 1:67 & 118 n7 (2:193). 19 Oct 1818, Moore mentioned his invitation at a dinner but was advised to be careful because of what happened to Colt Hoare, who had been 'called to account', 1:69 & 118 n3 (2:196). 21 Oct 1818, talked about *Azemia* and the *Elegant Enthusiast*, written to ridicule the novels of Beckford's half-sister, Mrs Hervey, 1:70 & 119 n2 (2:197–198). 8 Sept 1821, Duchess of Hamilton member of Polymnia Caledonia Society in Rome, 2:484 (3:274). 31 Oct 1821, passed Abbey on the way to John Benett, 2:500 (3:296). 12 May 1822, 'What would I take to be doomed to live with the Duke of Hamilton? aye – or even with the Duchess?', 2:562 (3:352, quote omitted from reference to the Duchess). 24 Sept 1823, at Bowood, Lord Lansdowne bidding for *A Journey to the Moon* at the Fonthill sale, 2:677 & 707 n1 (4:131). 1 Oct 1823, Beckford's passion for spending money,

2:678 (4:133). 19 Oct 1823, *Vathek* based on 'some Persian manuscripts', 2:684 & 708 n1 (4:143). 20 Oct 1823, went to top of tower at Fonthill, lunch in servant's hall converted into a coffee-room, 2:684–685 (4:143–144). 21 Oct 1823, saw Abbey illuminated after dinner, 2:685–686 (4:145). 13 March 1824, found the Duchess of Hamilton at the opera, 2:718 (4:167). 21 Aug 1824, M. Durazzo's 'astonishment at the oddity of Fonthill', 2:761–762 (4:234–235). 30 Dec 1826, saw Mrs Hervey at a dinner (in July 1816), 3:988–989. 19 Aug 1827, visited ruins of Fonthill, 3:1048. 17 Sept 1832, at Bowood talked of Beckford's French in *Vathek*, 4:1486 (6:283). 20 Oct 1838, reminiscing about party in 1805 or 1806 where Thomas Hope was 'making assiduous love' to Susan Beckford, 5:2011 (7:241). 13 June 1839, 'My old friend, the Duchess of Hamilton', 5:2070 (7:261). 'Glossary of Proper Names . . . Beckford', 6:2447.

Jeffrey, Francis. 'An Editor's Letters.' *Cornhill Magazine* n.s. 24 (Jan 1895): 21–28 at 24–25. Letter of 23 May 1816 from Thomas Moore to Francis Jeffrey, ed. of the *Edinburgh Review*, agreeing to review *Vathek*. Reprinted in *Littell's Living Age* 204 (26 Jan 1895): 254–255.

The Poetical Works of Thomas Moore. 10 vols. London: Longman, 1840–1841. 'To Miss Susan B–CKF–D.* On Her Singing.' *The present Duchess of Hamilton, 2:157–158. A juvenile poem of eight 4-line stanzas, *c*.1805.

Quennell, Peter, ed. *The Journal of Thomas Moore*. London: Batsford, 1964. 18 Oct 1818, Beckford delighted with *Lalla Rookh* & wanted Moore to go with Samuel Rogers to Fonthill to look over his 'Travels', 10. 30 Dec 1826, saw Mrs Hervey at a dinner (in July 1816), 145. 19 Aug 1827, visited ruins of Fonthill, 157.

Russell, Lord John, ed. *Memoirs, Journal, and Correspondence of Thomas Moore*. 8 vols. London: Longman, etc., 1853–1856. Letters: from Samuel Rogers on 21 Oct 1810, 'The Marchioness of Douglas (Miss Beckford) is still in or near town. The Prince has heard her sing. He admired her song, but not her beauty' 8:89; on 28 May 1816 Francis Jeffrey, ed. of the *Edinburgh Review*, sent Moore *Vathek* to review, 'I commit Vathek to you with the greatest pleasure, though I have not an idea what you will do with him', 2:100. For entries in Moore's *Journal* see Dowden, above.

Nelson, Horatio (1758–1805). See also '5. Fonthill Abbey'

Beresford, Charles & H. W. Wilson. *Nelson and His Times*. London: Harmsworth, [1897]. Visit to Fonthill with three views from Rutter (1823), 134–135.

Hodgkin, Louis. *Nelson and Bath*. Rev. ed. Billingshurst, Sussex: The Nelson Society, 2004. (1st ed. 1991.) Four oval paintings by Casali from 'William Beckford's Fonthill Abbey', 44. Nelson's contemporaries in Bath: 'Beckford, Sir William', 47–48. Christmas visit to Fonthill in 1800, 61.

Jeaffreson, John Cordy. *Lady Hamilton and Lord Nelson.* 2 vols. London: Hurst & Blackett, 1888. Beckford, 1:246–248. His hoped-for peerage, 2:196, 199–205, 231, 246. At Fonthill, 206–210. Beckford's house in Grosvenor Square, 221, 227.

Mahan, Alfred Thayer. *The Life of Nelson.* 2 vols. London: Sampson Low, 1897. Beckford's opinion of Lady Emma Hamilton, 1:381. Fonthill visit, 2:51–53.

Oman, Carola. *Nelson.* London: Hodder & Stoughton, 1947. Hamiltons given open invitation by Beckford to his London house at 22 Grosvenor Square, 408. Fonthill visit, 412–413, 688 n24. Hardy's easy-chairs by Foxhall & Fryer who worked for Beckford, 418. Beckford's suggestion of peerage for Sir William Hamilton with reversion to him, 494, 501 & 705 nn35–36, 507. Nelson declined invitation to Fonthill in 1805, 593. Beckford playing the harpsichord at Merton, 600. Nelson's letters bought by Alfred Morrison, 675–676, 712 n42.

Pettigrew, Thomas Joseph. *Memoirs of the Life of Vice-Admiral Lord Viscount Nelson, K.B.* 2 vols. London: T. & W. Boone, 1849. Letters about Beckford's hoped-for peerage, 1:402–406.

Walder, David. *Nelson.* London: Hamish Hamilton, 1978. Beckford's house in Grosvenor Square and his hopes for a peerage, 359. Nelson at Fonthill in 1800, 362. At Merton where George Matcham, Nelson's nephew, did not take to Beckford, 447.

Piozzi (formerly Thrale), Hester Lynch (1741–1821)

Balderston, Katharine, ed. *Thraliana. The Diary of Mrs Hester Lynch Thrale (Later Mrs. Piozzi) 1776–1809.* 2 vols. Oxford: Clarendon Press, 1942. 2 Jan 1782, Fonthill mentioned in poem about Pacchierotti, 1:526. 27 June 1784, visit to Wilton & Fonthill, 1:598. 27 June 1786, Beckford accused of unnatural vice, 2:640. 27 Jan 1791, Vathek 'a mad Book to be sure, and written by a mad Author . . . Mr Beckford's *favourite Propensity* is all along visible', 2:799 & nn1–3. Nov 1796, 'Vathek a Romance written by Beckford with much Invention', 2:969 n2. Also Aug–Sept 1777, Alderman Beckford: Political Alphabet (1771), 'A was an Alderman factious and proud', 1:122 & n6, 1:123 n5. 18 March 1790, about Mrs Hervey, 2:762.

Bloom, Edward A. & Lillian D., eds. *The Piozzi Letters. Correspondence of Hester Lynch Piozzi 1784–1821, formerly Mrs. Thrale.* 6 vols. Newark: University of Delaware Press, 1989–1999. Vol. 1 (1989), 1784–1791: To Hester Maria Thrale, 27 June 1784, about a visit to Fonthill, 66 n3. Vol. 2 (1991), 1792–1798: To Hester Maria Thrale, 21 Dec 1796, found *Vathek* 'a strange thing and a wicked Thing in my Mind', 411, 413 n12. Vol. 4 (1996), 1805–1810: To Lady Keith, 22 March 1810, believing that Beckford wasn't dead, and seeing Casali paintings in Bath's Theatre Royal from the 'beautiful Fonthill *we saw* together 26 years ago', 281–284 at 282, 283, 284 nn5, 9 & 89 n6. Vol. 5 (1999), 1811–1816: To Sir James Fellowes, 30 Oct 1815, Portrait by Hogarth seen at Fonthill in Beckford's absence, 421.

McCarthy, William. *Hester Thrale Piozzi: Portrait of a Literary Woman.* Chapel Hill, NC & London: University of North Carolina Press, 1985. *Vathek* one of only seven novels in her library in 1806, 65. Reading 'Beckford's camp Oriental thriller *Vathek*', 66.

Pitt, William. *1st Earl of Chatham (1708–1778)*

Taylor, W. S. & J. H. Pringle, eds. *Correspondence of William Pitt, Earl of Chatham.* 4 vols. London: John Murray, 1838–1840. Vol. 2 (1838): From Alderman Beckford, thanking Pitt for agreeing to be godfather to William, 11–12. Vol. 4 (1840): From several friends to Mrs. Beckford, praising William on 1 Sept 1772, 240. William disappointed at not seeing Pitt, 290–291. From John Lettice on 11 Dec 1773, on William's good educational progress, 313–316.

Redding, Cyrus (1785–1870)

Millington, Jon. 'Beckford's First Biographer.' *Beckford Tower Trust Newsletter*, Spring 1984, 6–8. Revised version: 'Cyrus Redding: Beckford's First Biographer', *Beckford Journal* 2 (1996): 26–32.

Nolan, Jerry. 'Redding's Alps and Beckford's Pencillings.' *Beckford Journal* 10 (2004): 61–70. Beckford attracted to Redding's poem, *Gabrielle* (1829).

Seccombe, Thomas. 'Redding, Cyrus.' In *Dictionary of National Biography*, ed. Sidney Lee, 47:370–371. London: Smith, Elder, 1896.

Seccombe, Thomas, rev. Ray Boston. 'Redding, Cyrus (1785–1870).' In *Oxford Dictionary of National Biography*, ed. H. C. G. Matthew & Brian Harrison, 46:250. Oxford: Oxford University Press, 2004. Friend of Beckford who wrote memoir of him.

Rogers, Samuel (1763–1855)

Barbier, Carl Paul, ed. *Samuel Rogers and William Gilpin: Their Friendship and Correspondence.* London: Oxford University Press, 1959. Rogers read *Vathek* in Dec 1799, 52.

Gower, Granville Leveson (1st Earl Granville). *Private Correspondence 1781–1821.* Ed. by Castalia, Countess Granville. 2 vols. London: John Murray, 1916. Samuel Rogers at Fonthill in 1817, 2:544–545. Susan (referred to as 'the sapphire') to be married to Douglas, 317. Horace Beckford [son of cousin Peter] & Miss Rigby, 287–288.

Roberts, R. Ellis. *Samuel Rogers and His Circle.* London: Methuen, 1910. Letter of 17 Oct 1817 inviting Rogers to Fonthill, and Beckford reading two unfinished *Episodes of Vathek* to him, 102–104.

Rogers, Samuel. *Italy, a Poem*. London: Moxon, 1839. (1st ed. in 2 parts, 1822, 1828.) Beckford's unpubl. travels acknowledged, 78.

Rogers, Samuel. *Recollections of the Table-Talk of Samuel Rogers*. London: Edward Moxon, 1856. *Vathek* & the two burlesque novels, 214–217.

Rutter, John (1796–1851). See '5. Fonthill Abbey'

Santa Cruz, Marquise de (1763–1808)

Kann, Roger, ed. 'Marquise de Santa Cruz. Lettres d'amour à William Beckford.' *Studies on Voltaire and the Eighteenth Century* 341 (1996): 239–332. 45 letters written in French between May 1788 and Feb 1789. REVIEW. Hilliard, Elizabeth. 'Marquise de Santa Cruz: Love-Letters to William Beckford. Transcribed and Annotated by Roger Kann.' *Beckford Journal* 2 (1996): 3–6.

Soane, Sir John (1753–1837). See '5. Fonthill Splendens'

Southey, Robert (1774–1843)

[Anster, John, attrib.] 'Southey's *Life and Correspondence*.' *North British Review* 12 (Feb 1850): 371–410. Thalaba (1801) "compares more fairly with 'Vathek' than with any existing work". Reprinted in *Littell's Living Age* 25 (20 April 1850): 103–114 at 111.

Bernhardt-Kabisch, Ernest. *Robert Southey*. Boston, MA: Twayne, 1977. Southey's *Thalaba* was to poetry what *Vathek* was to prose, 85. Eblis, 91, 94.

Cabral, Adolfo. *Southey e Portugal 1774–1801. Aspectos de Uma Biografia Literária*. Lisbon: P. Fernandes, 1960. Southey's encounter with Beckford, 353.

Curry, Kenneth, ed. *New Letters of Robert Southey*. 2 vols. New York: Columbia University Press, 1965. To Grosvenor Charles Bedford on 20 Feb 1796, 'Beckford is at Lisbon . . . "he has many pence".', 1:105 & n2.

Dowden, Edward, ed. *The Correspondence of Robert Southey with Caroline Bowles*. Dublin: Hodges, Figgis, 1881. To Southey on 23 July 1834, 'Beckford's book [*Italy*] greatly offends me', 307. His reply on 20 Aug agreeing with her and mentioning Beckford's house at Monserrate.

Haller, William. *The Early Life of Robert Southey, 1774–1803*. New York: Columbia University Press, 1917. *Vathek's* affinities with moral purpose of *Thalaba the Destroyer* (2 vols., 1801), 254–255.

Luedtke, Luther S. *Nathaniel Hawthorne and the Romance of the Orient*. Bloomington: University of Indiana Press, 1989. Influence of *Vathek*: on Southey's *Thalaba* (1801) and *The Curse of Kehama* (1810), 60; on *The Scarlet Letter* and *Fanshawe*, 58–59, *Fanshawe*, 77–78. Also 127, 155.

Pratt, Lynda, ed. *Robert Southey: Poetical Works 1793–1810*. 5 vols.

London: Pickering & Chatto, 2004. Southey took *Vathek* as his model when writing *Thalaba* (1801), 3:viii–ix, and was proud of his notes, comparing them to Henley's in *Vathek*, xxi. Beckford read *The Curse of Kehama* (1810) and was attracted by its oriental imagery, 4:xviii.

Robberds, John. W. *A Memoir of the Life and Writings of the late William Taylor of Norwich.* 2 vols. London: John Murray, 1843. Southey's letter to Taylor of 27 July 1801 comparing one of his poems to *Vathek*, 1:371.

Warter, John W., ed. *Selections from the Letters of Robert Southey.* 4 vols. London: Longmans, etc., 1856. To Miss Barker on 24 Dec 1804, telling her about *Vathek* and admiring Henley's notes, 1:303. To Rt. Hon. C. W. W. Wynn on 7 July 1834, saying he had often met Beckford in Portugal and had not seen his *Italy*, 4:378.

[Willmott, Robert Aris.] 'Southey's Life and Correspondence.' *Fraser's Magazine* 41 (Feb 1850): 200–217. Beckford's description of Cintra in review of Southey's *Life and Correspondence*, Longman, 1849. Reprinted in *Littell's Living Age* 24 (30 March 1850): 577–589 at 586.

Turner, Joseph Mallord William (1775–1851). See '5. Fonthill. Images of the Abbey'

Walpole Horace (1717–1797)

'Character and Writings of Horace Walpole.' *New Monthly Magazine* 38 (Aug 1833): 424. Beckford and Walpole compared.

[Donne, William Bodham.] 'Horace Walpole.' *Bentley's Quarterly Review* 1 (March 1859): 227–258. Review of Horace Walpole's Letters, 9 vols. He 'did not possess the glowing pencil of Beckford or Byron'. Reprinted in *Littell's Living Age* 61 (7 May 1859): 326–344 at 335.

Fothergill, Brian. *The Strawberry Hill Set. Horace Walpole and His Circle.* London: Faber, 1983. Strawberry Hill has outlived Fonthill, 65, 117. Unlike Beckford, Walpole could not outbid kings in the saleroom, 224.

Hazen, Allen T. *A Catalogue of Horace Walpole's Library.* 3 vols. London: Oxford University Press, 1969. #1609:54, letter from Pitt with reply by ?Alderman Beckford, 2:38. #3803, *The Arno Miscellany* (Florence, 1784), Walpole at first thought the poems were by Beckford, 3:218. #3943, *Vathek* (1786) now at Harvard not found in Strawberry Hill records 3:269. Numerous references to Beckford as bidder for lots at the Strawberry Hill Sale, with quotations from his correspondence.

Lewis, Wilmarth Sheldon, ed. *The Yale Edition of Horace Walpole's Correspondence.* 48 vols. London or Oxford: Oxford University Press, 1944–1983. To Mary Berry, 9 July 1789, head of Jupiter Serapis in basaltes later in Beckford collection (Hamilton Palace sale 1882, lot 469), 11:29 n33. To Mary Berry, 8 Nov 1790, Elizabeth Hervey his half sister, 11:132 n18. To Sir Horace Mann, 8 July 1784, wrongly attributing the

Arno Miscellany to Beckford, 25:507–508 & nn12–13, 517 n8. To Rev. William Mason, 14 April 1782, 'I was at a kind of pastoral opera written by Lady Craven', 29:235 n7. To Lady Ossory, 26 Dec 1789, Elizabeth Hervey's novels satirised by Beckford, 34:89 n8. Beckford's MS. note in his copy of Isaac D'Israeli's *Calamities of Authors* (Beckford Library sale, 1882, pt. 1, lot 2548 & Christie's, Margadale sale, 2 April 1975, lot 226), 1812, 43:195. Also many references to Alderman Beckford.

Lewis, Wilmarth Sheldon. *Horace Walpole's Library*. Cambridge: Cambridge University Press, 1958. Poor cataloguing at 1842 sale, 49n. William Smith buying for Beckford, 50. Bohn bid for Anderson's *Yvery* (1742) for Beckford, 51n. Robins a good auctioneer, 52. Bohn protested at 5% Queen's duty on purchases, 53n. Lord Rosebery bought many of Beckford's Strawberry Hill sale books at the Hamilton Palace sale, 55, 63.

Mowl, Timothy. *Horace Walpole*. London: John Murray, 1996. 'Beckford was to relive Horace's life', 253.

West, Benjamin (1738–1820). See '8. The Collection. Paintings'

Wildman family, lawyers: Thomas (1740–1795), Henry (d. Jan 1816), James (1747–1816) & Col. Thomas.

Beckett, John. *Byron and Newstead. The Aristocrat and the Abbey*. Newark: University of Delaware Press, 2001. Col. Thomas Wildman bought Newstead in 1817, deriving his fortune from his father and two uncles who grew rich by swindling Beckford, 293.

Coope, Rosalys. 'The Wildman Family and Colonel Thomas Wildman of Newstead Abbey, Nottinghamshire.' *Transactions of the Thoroton Society* 95 (1991): 50–66.

Wyatt, James (1746–1813). See '5. Fonthill Abbey'

5. Fonthill

Books

Channer, Nick. 'Around the Fonthills.' In *Wiltshire: from Salisbury to the Kennet*, 72–75. Norwich: Jarrold, 2004. Area map, 73. Fonthill Arch, 74.

Chettle, H. F. 'The Background to the Beckfords.' In *Two Centuries at Fonthill Gifford*, 1–15. N.p.: Privately printed, [1953]. 45 pp. typescript. A clear account of working conditions, especially on farms.

Colvin, Howard M. *A Biographical Dictionary of English Architects 1660–1840*. 3rd ed. New Haven & London: Yale University Press, 1995. (1st ed. 1954.) Splendens (*c*.1757–1770) attributed to William Hoare, 499. Soane's Picture Gallery, 909. Work by Wyatt, 1120. Fonthill (1796–1812) by Wyatt, 1118. Lodges, etc., at Fonthill (1829–1842) by J. B. Papworth, 733. Lansdown Tower (1824–1827), remodelled interiors in 19 Lansdown Crescent (1837), drawing of Hamilton Palace Library (exhibited at the Royal Academy, 1842), unexecuted design for Hamilton Mausoleum (1846) & Lansdown Cemetery Entrance (1848) by Goodridge, 415–416.

Crowley, D. A., ed. *A History of Wiltshire*. Victoria County Histories. Oxford: Oxford University Press, *Vol. 11, Downton Hundred. Elstub and Everleigh Hundred*, 1980. Fonthill Bishop, 77–82, East Knoyle, 82–83, Hindon, 98–103 at 99, Hawking Down House said to have been built for Beckford's valet, *c*.1822. *Vol. 13, Chalke and Dunworth Hundred*, 1987. Chilmark, 114–125. Fonthill Gifford: History, 155–161; Abbey & House, 161–163; Economic History, 163–166; Church, 166–169; and passim. Tisbury, 214, 236. Illus.

REVIEWS. Millington, Jon. 'Victoria County History of Wiltshire. Vol. XIII.' *Beckford Tower Trust Newsletter*, Spring 1988, 9.

Rogers, K. H. *Wiltshire Archaeological and Natural History Magazine* 74/75 (1979/1980): 209 for Vol. 11 & *Idem* 82 (1988): 188–189 for Vol. 13.

Devizes. Wiltshire Archaeological and Natural History Society Library. Extensive collection of material relating to Fonthill, including Buckler Collection of Wiltshire Drawings: Fonthill Gifford Church, 2:16; Fonthill House in 1806, 10:44. Buckler Collection was noted in *Wiltshire Archæological and Natural History Magazine* 40 (June 1918): 166. Fonthill Abbey: volume of correspondence.

Dewhurst, Richard. *Crosstracks to Hindon*. East Knoyle, Wiltshire: Hobnob Press, 2005. Beckford as an MP, 40, 54–56. Nelson's visit, 79–80. Endowed free school in 1783, 110. Fonthill, 10, 83, 95, 99, 102, 103, 108. Alderman Beckford, 50, 51, 53–54.

Dunning, Robert W. *Somerset & Avon*. Edinburgh, Bartholomew, 1980. Stained glass in Lord Mayor's Chapel, Bristol, 49. Staircase ironwork [and stone treads] from Fonthill Splendens at Dodington, 72.

Edwards, Ralph & L. G. G. Ramsey, eds. *The Connoisseur's Complete Period Guides to the Houses, Decoration, Furnishing and Chattels of the Classic Periods*. London: The Connoisseur, 1968. Fonthill Abbey, 815. William Burn's Fonthill New Abbey, 1277, 1314 & illus. of his drawing in R.I.B.A. collection, 1290. Originally publ. in separate vols., 1956–1958.

Hoare, Richard Colt & James Everard, Baron Arundell. *The History of Modern Wiltshire. Hundred of Dunworth and Vale of Noddre*. London: Nichols, 1829. 'Fountel, or Fonthill Giffard': Early history, 12–23; 1755–1828, 23–27; Farquhar, 27–28. Patrons & Clergy, 195–196. Records, 210–211. Family tree facing 20. Farquhar's will, 230–233. Portrait of Alderman Beckford & 5 pl. of Fonthill: Antiquus; Redivivus A⁰ 1755; Splendens A⁰ 1805; Eheu! Dilapsus A⁰ 1825; Resurgens A.D. 1828. Folding map of Dunworth Hundred.

    ADVERTS. *Gentleman's Magazine* 96 pt. 1 (May 1826): 438. The next vol. 'will include Fonthill, Wardour, &c. &c. and be very rich in engravings'. 'Ready for Publication.' *Idem* 99 pt. 2 (July 1829): 67.

    REVIEW. *Idem* 99 pt. 2 (Sept 1829): 226–228 at 226, 'this magnificent work'.

Jackson Wiltshire Collection compiled by John Edward Jackson. 14 folio vols., MS. 817, in the Society of Antiquaries Library, London. In 'Eddington–Knoyle' vol.: four pages of press cuttings & engravings, 40v–42r.

Lewis, Samuel. *A Topographical Dictionary of England* ... 4 vols. London: Lewis, 1831. 'Fonthill (Bishop's)' & 'Fonthill (Gifford)', 2:191.

Moody, Robert. *John Benett of Pythouse. His life and ancestors at Norton Bavant and Pythouse c.1450–1852*. East Harptree, Somerset: The Author. 2003. Pp. 144, 177, 180, 181, 184, 193, 198.

Sawyer, Rex. 'The Fonthills.' In *The Nadder Valley in Old Photographs*, 33–42. Stroud, Glos: Alan Sutton, 1994. Photos & postcards with captions.

Sawyer, Rex. 'The Fonthills – Beckford's Glittering Folly.' In *Tales of a Wiltshire Valley. The Nadder*, 24–29. Stroud, Glos: Alan Sutton, 1995.

Sheard, Norah. *The History of Hindon*. N.p.: The Author, 1979. Alderman Beckford helped pay for recasting bells in 1754, 16. Alderman Beckford, 18. Beckford's reluctance to become an MP and his expenses during 1812 election, decided to build Abbey in 1796, Nelson's visit, fragments of

Abbey in three Hindon buildings, 30. Morrison's land purchases and house at Hawking Down for Beckford's valet, 31–32. Lease of Dene House from Beckford in 1807, 34. School endowed by Beckford, 35. Water supply from Abbey grounds, 38–39. MP in 1790–1795, 1806–1807, 1807–1809, 1812–1818 & 1818–1820, 49. Other refs., passim. A much enlarged reissue of the author's *A Short History of Hindon*. N.p.: Privately duplicated, 1970.

Whiffen, Marcus. *Stuart and Georgian Churches: The Architecture of the Church of England outside London, 1603–1837*. London: Batsford, 1947. Fonthill Gifford Church diminutive version of St Paul's, Covent Garden, 62.

Articles

Chandler, John, ed. *Printed Maps of Wiltshire 1787–1844*. Vol. 52 for the year 1996. Trowbridge: Wiltshire Record Society, 1998. Fonthill House: Cary (1787), 4; Tunnicliff (1791), 11; Cary (1801), 27; Smith (1801), 36. Fonthill Abbey: Greenwood (1820), 132; Crocker (c.1821–1824) for Hoare's *Modern Wiltshire*, 179.

Chettle, Lt.-Col. H. F. 'The Successive Houses at Fonthill.' *Wiltshire Archæological and Natural History Magazine* 49 (June 1942): 505–512. Discusses the fate of seven Fonthill houses.

'Fonthill Abbey. The Estate, and the Successive Mansions.' *Wiltshire Gazette*, 6 Dec 1923, 3a–c. Photo of remains from NE. For previous week's article, 'The Fall of Fonthill Abbey Tower' see below.

Hussey, Christopher. 'A Country House Conversion . . .' *Country Life*, 22 July 1949, 269, 271. Berwick House, near 'Beckford's celebrated folly'.

Millington, Jon. 'Fonthill after Beckford.' *Beckford Journal* 2 (1996): 46–59. Outlines the fate of the Abbey and subsequent buildings on the estate.

T., W. 'Ill-Fated Fonthill and its Owners.' *Bath and County Graphic* 8 no. 10 (Feb 1904): 116–117.

FONTHILL HOUSE, UP TO THE FIRE IN 1755

Einberg, Elizabeth. *Catalogue Raisonné of the works of George Lambert*. [1700–1765.] London: Walpole Society, 2001. 'Fonthill Antiquus, Wiltshire', c.1736–1740, 142–143 & fig. 52. 'Fonthill Redivivus, Wiltshire', c.1740, 143 & fig. 53. The Society's 63rd vol.

Fire. *Salisbury Journal*, 17 Feb 1755, 3b–c. Fire last Thursday, ¼ column. *Idem* 24 Feb, 3b. Fire consumed the whole building, 2 paragraphs.

Harris, John. *The Artist and the Country House: A History of Country House and Garden View Painting in Britain 1540–1870*. London: Sotheby Parke Bernet, 1979. Fonthill House by George Lambert, 1740, 247, 262 (pl. 278). Hendrik de Cort's view of Fonthill Splendens, *c.*1791, 333. Turner's view of Abbey with spire, 1798, 346, 349 (pl. 395).

Pococke, Richard. *The Travels through England of Dr. Richard Pococke*. Ed. James Joel Cartwright. London: Camden Society, 1888–1889. Visit to Fonthill on 3 July 1754, 'Mr Beckford has built a Church', 2:47.

Sudden fire. *Gentleman's Magazine* 25 (Feb 1755): 90. Whole loss £30,000. *Western Gazette*, Feb 1755.

FONTHILL SPLENDENS (C.1755–1768, MOSTLY DEMOLISHED 1807)

Books

Angus, William. *The Seats of the Nobility and Gentry in Great Britain and Wales*. London: W. Angus, *c.*1800. 'Fonthill House in Wiltshire', pl. 50.

Beamon, Sylvia P. & Susan Roaf. *The Ice-Houses of Britain*. London: Routledge, 1990. Large domed chamber in grounds of Fonthill House, 449.

Beard, Geoffrey. *Craftsmen and Interior Decoration in England 1660–1820*. London: Bloomsbury, 1986. (1st ed. 1981.) Staircase from Splendens at Dodington, 77. Wyatt's 'Gothic pile' of Fonthill, 218.

Breman, Paul & Denise Addis. *Guide to Vitruvius Britannicus: Annotated and Analytic Index to the Plates*. New York: Blom, 1972. Splendens attributed to [George?] Hoare, 39. Witham Park, designed by Robert Adam for Alderman Beckford but never built, 4.

Britton, John. *The Beauties of Wiltshire*. 2 vols. London: Vernor & Hood, etc., 1801. 1:208–249 & 2 pl. Beckford donated the second plate, a view of s front. Description of contents of the house, especially paintings, and grounds. For vol. 3 (1825) see Fonthill Abbey, below.

[Brydges, Sir Samuel Egerton & Stebbing Shaw, eds.] *The Topographer*. 4 vols. London: Robson & Clarke; J. Walker, 1789–1791. Vol. 4, p. 237.

Climenson, Emily J., ed. *Passages from the Diaries of Mrs Philip Lybbe Powys . . . 1756 to 1808*. London: Longmans, 1899. Comments after a visit in 1776 about the principal rooms being above the rustic and further from the garden, 166–167. Partly quoted in Mark Girouard, *Life in the English Country House*, New Haven: Yale University Press, 1978, p. 214.

Dyott, William. *Dyott's Diary 1781–1845. A Selection from the Journal of William Dyott, sometime General in the British Army and Aide-de-Camp to His Majesty King George III*. Ed. Reginald W. Jeffery. 2 vols. London: Constable, 1907. Visited Splendens in Dec 1779, house uncomfortable but grounds pretty, 'Mr. Beckford is building a curious tower' two miles away, 1:134–135 & nn1, 2.

Easton, James. *The Salisbury Guide . . .* 3rd ed. Salisbury: Easton, 1774. 'Mr. Beckford's seat at Fonthill . . .', 58–59. 11 lines. *Idem*, 14th ed., 1790 & 19th ed., 1797, text similar to 3rd ed.: 'Fonthill House. The Seat of W.

Beckford, Esq.', 75 & 76. *Idem*, 21st ed., 1800, 22nd ed., 1801 & [new ed.] 1806, text now extended: 'Fonthill House. The Seat of W. Beckford, Esq. Fourteen miles west of Salisbury.', 74–75, 73–75 & 76–78. For later editions see Fonthill Abbey, below.

Espie, Félix François, Comte d' (1708–1792). *The Manner of Securing all Sorts of Buildings from Fire . . .* Trans. Louis Dutens. London: H. Piers, [1756.] Extract of letter from Alderman Beckford, Soho-Square, 12 May 1755, to Peter Wyche FRS about rebuilding Fonthill using Espie's methods, 61–62.

Espie. Harris, Eileen. *British Architectural Books and Writers 1556–1785*. Cambridge: Cambridge University Press, 1990. Peter Wyche presented a copy of the French ed. of Espie's work to Alderman Beckford after the Splendens fire and had instigated the English trans. which he dedicated to the Alderman, 191.

Godber, Joyce, ed. 'The Travel Journal of her husband, Philip Yorke [2nd Earl of Hardwicke], 1744–63.' In *The Marchioness Grey of Wrest Park*, 159. Bedford: Bedfordshire Historical Record Society, vol. 47, 1968. The entry for 1 Aug 1760 reads: 'Took a view of Mr. Beckford's new house at Fonthill (the shell of which is finished but no part of the inside fitted up).'

Goede, Christian August Gottlieb. *England, Wales, Irland und Schottland*. 5 vols. Dresden, 1804–1805. Description of the Turkish room, 5:116.

Grosley, Pierre Jean. *Londres*, 3 vols. Lausanne, 1770. Notes on almost-finished chimneypiece (1765), 3:22–23. Now in Manor House, Beaminster, Dorset.

Hague, William. *William Pitt the Younger*. London: HarperCollins, 2004. Letter from Pitt to his mother, 7 Oct 1781, mentioning 'that stupid Fête at Fonthill', 75 & n.

Harris, John. *The Artist and the Country House, from the Fifteenth Century to the Present Day*. London: Sotheby, ?1996. No. 91, Fonthill Splendens seen from the east across the lake by Hendrik de Cort, *c*.1791, 120. Sotheby's exhibition.
  REVIEW. Hall, Michael. 'Only a Picture of a House.' *Country Life*, 11 Jan 1996, 26–29 at 28, 29. Henrik de Cort's painting illus.

Hewat-Jaboor, Philip. 'Fonthill House: "One of the Most Princely Edifices in the Kingdom".' In *William Beckford, 1760–1844: An Eye for the Magnificent*, ed. Derek E. Ostergard, 50–71. New Haven & London: Yale University Press for the Bard Graduate Center, 2001. Exhibition catalogue.

Holbrook, Mary & Sidney Blackmore. *The True Style*. Holburne Museum, Bath, September 1972. Dodington: two Wyatt drawings of staircase from Splendens, no. 36. Splendens: photo of Soane's design for chimneypiece, no. 97. Lansdown Tower: nos. 81–84, 227–229. Exhibition catalogue.

Inglis-Jones, Elisabeth. *Peacocks in Paradise*. London: Faber, 1950. Thomas Johnes of Hafod bought items at Phillips's 1807 sale at Fonthill, 208–209.

Hafod acquired by 4th Duke of Newcastle, whose eldest son married the daughter of Susan, Duchess of Hamilton, 244. Reissued 1960.

Kenworthy-Browne, John A. *Dodington [Gloucestershire]*. Derby, *c*.1970. Staircase (stone treads and ironwork, except the handrail) from Fonthill Splendens, 12, illus. on 13, 15, 16 & 18. Guide Book.

Meister, Jacques Henri. *Letters Written during a Residence in England*. London: T. N. Longman & O. Rees, 1799. Letter XIX, 'Fonthill': 'The author, under the similitude of a dream, gives the Countess de V— a description of the magnificent country seat of William Beckford, Esq in Wiltshire', 295–314. About the grounds, visited by Meister probably in the summer of 1793, and Beckford's character. (Letter XX, 'The Countess de V— 's answer to the foregoing letter': 'In return, she relates her dream, in which she thought the shade of her deceased father appeared to her, and gave her a relation of the enjoyments and occupations of departed souls, in the region of bliss', 315–324.) Trans. of *Souvenirs de mes voyages en Angleterre*, 2 vols., (Expanded from 1791 ed. which contained only letters I–X), Zurich: Orell, Gessner & Fussli, 1795, 2:235–257. All but the first twelve lines of Letter XIX reprinted in Gregory, *The Beckford Family* (2nd ed., 1898), 26–33.

Mowl, Tim & Brian Earnshaw. *Trumpet at a Distant Gate: The Lodge as Prelude to the Country House*. London: Waterstone, 1985. Bishop's Fonthill gateway, 89–91, with photos of pillar, 90, and gateway, colour pl. x. Goodridge's Lansdown Cemetery gateway, 158, with photo, 157. Hugh Grosvenor, third Marquess of Westminster, inherited the Fonthill estate in 1869, 194, 195.

Shelburne, Sophia, Countess of. Unpubl. diary. Vol. 5, 14 July 1769 to 15 September 1770. At Fonthill House from 25–30 July 1769, with her husband, Lord Lyttelton, and others, 4–9.

Soane. Watkin, David. 'Soane, Sir John (1753–1837).' In *Oxford Dictionary of National Biography*, ed. H. C. G. Matthew & Brian Harrison, 51:514. Oxford: Oxford University Press, 2004. Picture gallery at Splendens.

Stroud, Dorothy. *Sir John Soane, Architect*. London: Faber, 1984. Visit by Soane in 1787 to draw up plans for proposed gallery, 59–60, 61 & nn20–21.

Stutchbury, Howard E. *The Architecture of Colen Campbell*. Manchester: Manchester University Press, 1967. Splendens attributed to James Paine, 109. Also 86 n8.

[Sulivan, Sir Richard Joseph.] *Observations made during a Tour through Parts of England, Scotland, and Wales* . . . London: T. Becket, 1780. Splendens, 50–51. *Idem*. 2nd ed. 1785. Paintings, 126–128. Edited reprint in *The British Tourists, or Traveller's Pocket Companion* . . . ed. William Mavor, 3rd ed., 6 vols., London: Phillips, 1809–1814, 3 (1809): 27–28.

Summerson, John. *The Unromantic Castle and Other Essays*. London: Thames & Hudson, 1990. Beckford oppressed by his father's house, 11.

Warner, Richard. *Excursions from Bath*. Bath: R. Cruttwell, 1801. Letter dated 5 Sept 1800 mentioning 'the stupendous building which Mr. Beckford is erecting upon a high hill', 119–127.

REVIEW. [Gough, Richard.] *Gentleman's Magazine* 71 pt. 2 (Oct 1801): 913–919 at 915.

Woodforde. *The Diary of a Country Parson: The Reverend James Woodforde*. Ed. John Beresford. 5 vols. London: Oxford University Press, 1924–1931. Vol. 3 (1927): On 15 June 1789 paid housekeeper 2/6d to see Fonthill, 'very handsome, complete', 114 & n1. Vol. 4 (1929): Editor's note to entry of 16 Oct 1793 about Wyatt 'rebuilding' Fonthill Abbey, 70 n2.

Woolfe, John & James Gandon. *Vitruvius Britannicus*. Vol. 4. London, 1767. Text in English and French, p. 9. 'Ground Plan of Fonthill', pl. 82. 'Plan of the Attic Floor' & 'Plan of the Principal Floor of Fonthill', pl. 83. 'Elevation of the Principal Front of Fonthill in Wiltshire, the Seat of Willm Beckford Esqr', pl. 84/85. 'South Front of Fonthill', pl. 86/87. Reprinted, New York: Blom, 1967.

Articles

Brulé, André. 'Une Visite à Fonthill en 1792.' *Revue Anglo-Américaine* 10 no. 1 (Oct 1933): 33–42.

Elderton, John. 'Tour into the lower parts of Somersetshire.' *Gentleman's Magazine* 61 pt. 1 (March 1791): 229–231 at 231. Account of house and grounds. Reprinted in George Laurence Gomme, ed., *Topographical History of Shropshire and Somersetshire. A Classified Collection of the Chief Contents of "The Gentleman's Magazine" from 1731 to 1868*, London: Elliot Stock, 1898, p. 195.

Fonthill House. *Universal Magazine* 47 (Sept 1770): 113. Twenty lines to accompany the facing plate: 'The principal Front of Fonthill in Wiltshire, the Seat of the late Wm Beckford, Esqre.'

'Fonthill Volunteers'. Colours presented to them by Miss Beckford on lawn in front of Fonthill House. *The Times*, 7 Oct 1799, 4a. 1 column.

Hardy, John. 'Fonthill Splendens: An Iconographic Chimneypiece Rediscovered.' *Apollo* 130 (July 1989): 40–42, 69n. Chimneypiece by John Francis Moore, now in a private collection.

Harris, John. 'Fonthill, Wiltshire I – Alderman Beckford's Houses.' *Country Life*, 24 Nov 1966, 1370–1374. For Part II: Abbey, see Alexander, below.

Hussey, Christopher. 'Dodington Park, Gloucestershire – II.' *Country Life*, 29 Nov 1956, 1230, 1231 (pl. 4, 5), 1232. Wrought ironwork from Splendens staircase installed in 1812.

Kitching, Carol. 'A bed for a king.' *Hampshire View* No. 14 (June 2005): 77. Bed lent to Wilton House in 1778 for state visit by George III.

Opened to the public again. *The Times*, 13 Aug 1802, 2b.

Thacker, Christopher et al. 'Twin Towers.' *Journal of the Georgian Group* [5] (1995): 115–118. Alderman Beckford's tower on Stop Beacon. 4 illus.

Wirtemberg. *European Magazine* 31 (May 1797): 363. Fonthill visited in West Country tour by Duke of Wirtemberg before he married the Princess Royal.

Wittkower, Rudolf. 'Pseudo-Palladian Elements in Neo-Classical Architecture.' *Journal of the Warburg and Courtauld Institutes* 6 (1943). Splendens an almost exact copy of Houghton Hall, Norfolk, 157 & n8, 160.

Woodbridge, Kenneth. 'Bélanger en Angleterre: son carnet de voyage.' *Architectural History* 25 (1982): 8–19 at 10, 11, 19 & pl. 18c. Three sketches of Splendens, possibly 1772–1774: 'M. Beckfort', fol. 134 (pl. 18c); 'Plan de la Maison de M. Bekfort', block plan of house and one wing, fol. 136; 'M. Bekfort', elevation of Fonthill, fol. 138.

Woodward, Christopher. 'William Beckford and Fonthill Splendens. Early works by Soane and Goodridge.' *Apollo* 147 (Feb 1998): 31–40 at 31–38. For the end of the article see '6. Beckford's Tower and Bath'.

NELSON'S VISIT, 20–24 DEC 1800

An Architect. [John Carter.] 'The Pursuits of Architectural Innovation. No. XXXV. Gothic.' *Gentleman's Magazine* 71 pt. 1 (May 1801): 417–418. Scathing comments on Nelson's visit.

Salisbury and Winchester Journal, 22 Dec 1800, 4c–d. Nelson & party left Salisbury for Fonthill on 20th. *Idem*, 29 Dec, 4c. Left Fonthill on 24th.

The Times, 24 Dec 1800, 3d. Reception at Salisbury & arrival at Fonthill.

[Tresham, Henry.] *Gentleman's Magazine* 71 pt. 1 (March, April 1801): 206–208, 297–298. '*Letter from a Gentleman, present at the Festivities at* Fonthill, *to a Correspondent in Town*.' Dated 28 Dec 1800. 3½ pp. Plate (supplied by Beckford): 'Lord Nelson's Reception at Fonthill.' facing 289. Account reprinted in *Wilts County Mirror*, 30 Sept 1907, and Gemmett, *Beckford's Fonthill* (2003), 222–228.

Modern commentaries

Admiral Nelson's visit. *Wiltshire Gazette*, 20 Sept 1923.

Cruikshank, Dan. 'Ghost of Christmas Past.' *The Guardian*, 22 Dec 1997, 12–13. Celebrations during Nelson's 1800 visit predated the rediscovery of the old English Christmas by Walter Scott and Charles Dickens.

Girouard, Mark, compiler. 'Lord Nelson and Emma visit Fonthill Abbey 1801.' In *A Country House Companion*, 101–103. New Haven: Yale

University Press, 1987. From the *Gentleman's Magazine*, with engraving, 93. Also engraving of the dwarf at Fonthill, 121. Sketch of Beckford's dog, 'Lord Foppington' [Viscount Fartleberry], 147. 'Faithful dogs at Fonthill 1812', 150. These three from *Life at Fonthill* (1957, facing 214, facing 147, 120).

Hudson, Roger. *Nelson and Emma*. London: Folio Society, 1994. The Hamiltons and Nelson visit to Fonthill, 168–170. Based on account in *Gentleman's Magazine* 71 pt. 1 (March, April 1801): 206–208, 297–298.

Millington, Jon. 'Where Nelson went in Fonthill Abbey.' *Beckford Journal* 8 (2002): 43–49. With a plan of the Abbey in 1800.

1801 Phillips Furniture Sale

For all sale catalogues, see '8. The Collection. Sales'

Adverts. 'Magnificent and Valuable Effects – Fonthill'. *The Times*, 23, 27, 29 July 1801; 3, 5, 10, 11, 12, 13, 14, 15, 17, 18, 19, 20, 21 Aug. All on page 4.

Bamford, Francis, ed. *Dear Miss Heber. An Eighteenth Century Correspondence*. London: Constable, 1936. Letters to Mary Heber (sister of Richard Heber) of Weston, Northants, from Elizabeth Iremonger of Wherwell, Hants; on 27 June 1799, asking whether Miss Heber had seen Beckford's Claudes, 190 & 268 n247; on 1 Sept 1801 about visiting the Fonthill sale where the Prince of Wales bought the organ, and Beckford being told last year some home truths by Lady Hamilton's mother (Mary Lyon), 209–210 & 270–271 nn265–266.

'Fonthill Auction. Aug 21.' *The Times*, 26 Aug 1801, 3c–d. ½ column. Reprinted in 'Country News.' *Gentleman's Magazine* 71 pt. 2 (Sept 1801): 853–854.

Furniture. *The Times*, 24 July 1801, 3b. Sale 'has caused much surprize'. 7 lines.

'Magnificent and Valuable Effects, Fonthill to be sold by auction.' *The Sun*, 27 July 1801.

Sale report. *Bell's Weekly Messenger*, 30 Aug 1801.

Sale report. *The Times*, 21 Aug, 2b. 'At Mr. Beckford's sale at Fonthill'. 13 lines.

1802 Christie's Picture Sales

Adverts. 'Most Superb, Capital and Valuable . . . Pictures.' *The Times*, 16, 17, 20, 22, 23, 24, 25, 26, 27 ('This Day') Feb 1802, 4a, 4d, 3d, 4a, 4c, 4b, 4a, 3c, 4a.

Pictures sold 'much below their value'. *The Times*, 1 March 1802, 3d.

Pictures 'merely common furniture pieces'. *The Times*, 2 March 1802, 2d. 10 lines.

Advert. 'Small, Capital . . . Collection of pictures.' *The Times*, 23 March 1802, 4d.

1807 Phillips Furniture & Pictures, and Building Materials Sales

'Fonthill Mansion, Wilts, to be sold.' *Courier*, 11 Aug 1807.
Adverts. 'The Building Materials of Fonthill House.' *The Times*, 10, 11, 16
    Sept 1807, 4c, 4b, 4c.
Pictures and porcelain. *The Times*, 29 Aug 1807, 3d; 29 Sept, 3a, mansion
    about to be pulled down. *Bell's Weekly Messenger*, 30 Aug 1807.
Furniture & picture sale ended. 'Country News.' *Gentleman's Magazine* 77
    pt. 2 (Sept 1807): 880.

1808 & 1817 Leigh, Sotheby Book Sales

Adverts. Books & prints. *The Times*, 7, 8 June 1808, 4c, 4c.
Adverts. Books & drawings. *The Times*, 5, 6 May 1817, 4b, 4b.

Casali Ceilings (see also '6. Beckford's Tower and Bath')

[Brushfield, Jean.] *The Casali Paintings*. Bath: Bath Royal Literary and
    Scientific Institution, [2003]. Eight-page booklet describing the restora-
    tion of four Casali paintings, with colour photos.
Egan, Pierce. *Walks through Bath*. Bath: Meyler, 1819. Ceiling paintings by
    Casali from Fonthill presented to Theatre Royal by [Paul] Methuen, 143.
K-B, J. [Kenworthy-Browne, John.] *Dyrham Park. Gloucestershire*. London:
    The National Trust, 1961. Three Casali ceiling paintings in the Great Hall
    & two over the staircases, 22. *Idem*, 1975, 7–8. *Idem*, 1981, 2. Garnett,
    Oliver. *Dyrham Park*. London: The National Trust, 2000. Three Casali
    ceiling paintings from Fonthill Splendens in the Great Hall, 4. Guide
    books.
Lowndes, William. *The Theatre Royal at Bath*. Bristol: Redcliffe, 1982. Five
    Casali ceiling paintings removed from Theatre in 1839, sold to Col. Blath-
    wayt in 1845 to avoid further damage from gas lighting installed in 1827
    and taken to Dyrham [and so not lost in the 1862 Theatre fire], 37.

FONTHILL ABBEY (1796–1818, MOSTLY DEMOLISHED 1846)

Guide Books

Storer, James. *A Description of Fonthill Abbey, Wiltshire*. London: W.
    Clarke, etc., 1812. ii, 24 pp. 7 pl. 24 cm. Also large paper. Grounds, 1–6.
    'Abbey', 6–24, including 'Brown Parlour', 9–12; 'Yellow Damask Room',
    13–14; 'Japan Room', 15; 'Gallery', 15–16; 'Octagon', 17–18; 'Oratory',
    23–24. Storer's text reprinted in Melville's *Life and Letters of William
    Beckford* (1910), 355–366, and elsewhere.

ADVERTS. *Edinburgh Review* 20 (Nov 1812): 505.
Quarterly Review 8 (Dec 1812): 514–515.

Salisbury and Winchester Journal, 15 July, 1a; 12, 26 Aug, 4e, 4e; 2, 9, 16, 23, 30 Sept, 4f, 4e, 4f, 4f, 4e; 7 Oct, 4e.

Storer's *A Description* reissued with a cancel title page dated 1817 and bound with the catalogue of Beckford's library extracted from *Repertorium Bibliographicum* (1819), London: William Clarke, 1817. 25½ cm.

REVIEW. Millington, Jon. 'A Reissue of Storer's *Fonthill*.' *Beckford Journal* 4 (1998): 71–75.

Rutter, John. *A Description of Fonthill Abbey and Demesne*. Shaftesbury: J. Rutter, 1822. 1st ed. Frontis., v, 66 pp. 21 cm. 2nd–6th eds. Frontis., xii, 74 pp. Poem by W. L. Bowles. All editions: 'Historical Sketch of Fonthill Gifford and its Possessors', 1–15; 'A Descriptive Guide through the Abbey Grounds', 17–24; 'General Description of Fonthill Abbey, with its Collection . . .', 25–68 (60 in 1st ed.); 'A brief Notice of the outer Grounds and of the former Mansion', 69–74 (61–66 in 1st ed.). Partly culled from Storer's *Description of Fonthill Abbey* (1812).

ADVERTS. *Gentleman's Magazine* 92 pt. 2 (Aug 1822): 157. 'Ready for Publication'.
Literary Gazette 6 (31 Aug 1822): 558. 2nd ed. Price 3/6d.
New Monthly Magazine 6 (1 Oct 1822): 463.
Salisbury and Winchester Journal, 15, 22, 29 July 1822, 1a ('in a few days will be published'), 1a ('Just published'), 1a; 26 Aug, 4e (2nd ed. just publ.); 2, 9 Sept, 4f, 4e (3rd ed. just publ.).
REVIEW. [Nichols, John Bowyer.] *Gentleman's Magazine* 92 pt. 2 (Sept 1822): 258.

Whittaker, publ. *A New Guide to Fonthill Abbey*. London: G. & W. B. Whittaker, 1822. xii, 60 pp. Frontis., west view of Abbey. 19½ cm. Introduction from *The Times* (30 Sept 1822, 3a), vii–xii. Part 1, 'Historical and topographical . . .', 1–11. Part 2, 'Description of the Grounds', 12–17. Part 3, 'A description of the Abbey . . .', 19–32. Parts 1–3 culled from Rutter's *Description* (1822), with poem from *Literary Gazette* 6 (21 Sept 1822). Part 4, 'Articles for Sale', from Christie's *Catalogue* (1822), 33–60.

ADVERTS. *Edinburgh Review* 37 (Nov 1822): 541.
Monthly Magazine; or, British Register 54 (1 Nov 1822): 361.
Quarterly Review 28 (Oct 1822): 270.
REVIEW. *Gentleman's Magazine* 92 pt. 2 (Oct 1822): 351. A 'hasty compilation'.

Storer, James. *Description of Fonthill Abbey*. Salisbury: Brodie, 1823. 14 pp. 8 pl. 17 cm. Price 2/6d. Also large paper, 22 cm, with proofs of the plates. Price 4s. Pp. 2–3 (exterior), 3–12 (interior), 13–14 (grounds) reprinted from pp. 7–9, 9–24, 2–6 of Storer (1812). Offprint from No. 1 (Oct 1822) of *The Port-Folio*. 4 vols. London: Nornaville & Fell, 1823–1824. Pp. 1–6, 6–11, 11–14 reprinted as 'Fonthill Abbey' with woodcuts in *The Gleaner* 1 nos. 23, 24, 25 (1, 8, 15 Oct 1823): 353–355 & 'South West View', 369–371 & 'The Oratory, or North-end of the Gallery', 385–387 & 'The Hall and part of the Octagon'.

ADVERTS. *Bath Chronicle*, 3 Oct 1822, 1b.

Gentleman's Magazine 92 pt. 2 (Sept 1822): 259. 'Preparing for Publication . . . The Port-folio . . . first number contains interior Views of Fonthill Abbey'.

Literary Gazette 7 (22 March 1823): 191. Advert for *The Port-Folio*. *Idem* (28 June): 415. Advert for Storer's *Description*.

Salisbury and Winchester Journal, 30 Sept ('published this day'), 7 Oct 1822, 4e, 4e. 23, 30 June 1823, 4e, 1b, 7, 14 July, 4e, 1b, 1 Sept, 1b. All adverts for No. 1 of *The Port-Folio*.

The Times, 3 Oct 1822, 1b.

REVIEW. *Gentleman's Magazine* 93 pt. 2 (July 1823): 57–58. Fonthill not mentioned.

Rutter, John. *A New Descriptive Guide to Fonthill Abbey and Demesne.* Shaftesbury: J. Rutter, 1823. Frontis., engraved title page, viii, 98 pp. 19½ cm. 'General Description of Fonthill Abbey . . .', 1–8. 'Interior of the Abbey, and its Collection . . .', 9–68. '. . . Abbey Grounds', 69–86. 'An Historical Sketch of Fonthill and its Possessors . . .', 87–98. A totally revised edition.

ADVERTS. *Edinburgh Review* 39 (Oct 1823): 278.

New Monthly Magazine 9 (1 Sept 1823): 412.

Quarterly Review 29 (April 1823): 282.

Salisbury and Winchester Journal, 4, 11 Aug 1823, 4e, 1b.

Britton, John. *Graphical and Literary Illustrations of Fonthill Abbey, Wiltshire.* London: The Author, 1823. viii, 68, 4 pp. 11 pl. 29 cm. Limited to 500 copies. Also large paper, 34 cm. Limited to 270 copies and a further 30 copies with 'Proofs and Etchings'. Fonthill Abbey, 23–36. Abbey and Collection, 37–59. Beckford family. 61–64. Eight genealogical tables.

ADVERTS. *Edinburgh Review* 37 (Nov [publ. Dec] 1822): 540.

Gentleman's Magazine 93 pt. 1 (Feb 1823): 160. Ready 'early in April'. *Idem* 93 pt. 2 (July 1823): 58. 'Ready for Publication'.

Literary Gazette 7 (8 March 1823): 158. 'Will be published early in the following Month'. *Idem* (4 Sept): 575. Works publ., price 21s & £2 2s.

Monthly Magazine; or, British Register 54 (1 Oct 1822): 259.

New Monthly Magazine 6 (1 Nov 1822): 511. *Idem* 9 (1 March 1823): 129. Ready 'early in April'.

Quarterly Review 27 (July [publ. Oct] 1822): 561. 'A Description of Fonthill Abbey, with Eight engraved Views. Folio, large paper, 21s.'

Salisbury and Winchester Journal, 30 Sept 1822, 4e. In preparation. ¼ column. Publ., 8 Sept 1823, 4c. 15 lines.

REVIEWS. *Country Literary Chronicle and Weekly Review*, 13, 20 Sept 1823, 577–578, 605–607.

Gentleman's Magazine 93 pt. 2 (Sept 1823): 242–243. *Idem* 94 pt. 2 (Suppl. 1824): 582. Letter from Britton about the increasing value of his *Fonthill*.

Ladies' Monthly Museum n.s. 18 (Oct 1823): 215–217.

Literary Gazette 7 (30 Aug 1823): 555.

New Monthly Magazine 9 (1 Oct 1823): 458.

Rutter, John. *Delineations of Fonthill and its Abbey*. Shaftesbury: The Author, 1823. xxiv or xxvi, 127 pp. 14 pl. Folding map of Domain. 29½ cm. Approaches, 1–6. Interior, 7–65. Exterior, 66–81. Walks within and without the Barrier, 82–91, 92–96. Ride through the Domain, 97–100. Fonthill Gifford & former mansions, 103–107. Origin and Progress of Fonthill Abbey, 108–112. Three genealogical tables, 113–118. An extremely comprehensive guide, beautifully printed. Also large paper, 37 cm. Reprinted, Farnborough, Hants: Gregg, 1972. Reprinted again, Llanfapley, Abergavenny: Monmouth House Books, 2000.

ADVERTS. *Literary Gazette* 6 (26 Oct 1822): 686 & 7 (4, 25 Oct, 6, 13 Dec 1823): 639 ('will be published on the 1st of October'), 687, 783, 798.

Monthly Magazine; or, British Register 54 (1 Nov 1822): 349.

New Monthly Magazine 6 (1 Nov 1822): 511.

ADVERTS & NEWS. *Salisbury and Winchester Journal*, 30 Sept 1822, 4e. In preparation. ¼ column. *Idem*, 7 Oct, 4e. Delayed by new research, 2 June 1823, 4c. 14 lines. Nearly ready, 9 June, 4c. Publ. soon, 8 Sept, 4e. Delayed by discovery of Wyatt's plans, ready on Wed (1 Oct), 29 Sept, 4c. Dinner given in Salisbury on 24 Oct for Rutter by those involved in the work to congratulate him on his excellent publication, 3 Nov, 2b. ½ col.

REVIEWS. *Country Literary Chronicle and Weekly Review*, 8, 15 Nov 1823, 715–716, 732–734.

Gentleman's Magazine 93 pt. 2 (Oct 1823): 345–346.

Neale, John Preston. *Graphical Illustrations of Fonthill Abbey, The Seat of John Farquhar, Esq*. London: Sherwood, Jones, etc., 1824. iv, 16 pp. 5 pl. 24½ cm. Also large paper, 31½ cm. Dedicated to Farquhar. 'A List of the

most celebrated Pictures and other splendid effects at Fonthill Abbey',
13–16. Offprint from vol. 1 of Neale's *Views of the Seats of Noblemen
and Gentlemen.* 5 vols. 2nd series. London: Sherwood, Jones,
1824–1829.

REVIEW. 'Neale's Seats, Second Series. – No. 1. Fonthill.' *Literary Chronicle and Weekly Review*, 7 Feb 1824, 93–94.

Nichols, John Bowyer, ed. *Historical Notices of Fonthill Abbey, Wiltshire.*
London: Nichols & Son, 1836. 52 pp. 11 pl., including 10 from Rutter's
Delineations (1823). 29 cm. Also large paper, 38 cm. Nine chapters culled
from previous guide books, Colt Hoare's *Modern Wiltshire* (1829),
Gentleman's Magazine and Christie's sale catalogue, *Magnificent Effects*
(1822).

REVIEWS. [Carlos, Edward John.] *Gentleman's Magazine* n.s. 6 (July
1836): 58–59.
Millington, Jon. "Nichols' *Historical Notices of Fonthill Abbey.*" *Beckford Journal* 6 (2000): 75–78. Contains an analysis of the contents.

Anthology

Charlesworth, Michael, ed. & intro. *The Gothic Revival 1720–1870. Literary Sources and Documents.* 3 vols. Robertsbridge, Sussex: Helm, 2002.
Vol. 2, *Living the Gothic Revival.* 'Fonthill Abbey', 2 pl., 116, 130. Intro.,
117–118. No. 54: James Storer, 'A Description of Fonthill Abbey, Wiltshire', 119–129. No. 55: John Rutter, 'The Abbey is no *Frankenstein*',
intro., 131–132. Ch. 2, 3, 4 & Appendix B from *Delineations* (1823),
132–144. No. 56: J. C. Loudon, 'The Landscape of Fonthill' from *Gardener's Magazine* 11 (Sept 1835), 145–148. No. 58: 'An Excursion to the
Grande Chartreuse in the year 1778', from *Dreams* (1783), 172–189. No.
59: 'Alcobaça and Batalha', from *Recollections* (1835), 6th–9th Day,
190–226. No. 60: John Britton and Henry Tresham, 'Lord Nelson's entertainment at Fonthill Abbey', from Britton's *Fonthill* (1823), 227–231. No.
61: *Life at Fonthill 1807–1822* (1957), 18 extracts, 232–239. No. 69: E. J.
Willson, 'Remarks on Gothic Architecture', from Augustus Pugin, *Speci-
mens of Gothic Architecture* (1826), fall of the tower, 723 n14.

CONTEMPORARY ACCOUNTS BEFORE 1822

Books

Blease, H. J. *A System of British Geography, for the Use of Schools.* London:
Darton, etc., 1820. Fonthill Mansion and Abbey noted, 82–83.
Britton, John. *The Beauties of England and Wales. [Wiltshire] . . . Vol. XV.*
London: Vernor & Hood, 1814. Exteriors of Abbey & Splendens,

265–268. Beckford's interest in Hindon borough, and note about 1775 election, 263.

Cary, John. *New Itinerary; or, an Accurate Delineation of the Great Roads* ... 6th ed. London: J. Cary, 1815. (1st ed. 1798.) Eight lines on Fonthill, column 124.

Cooke, George Alexander. *Topographical and Statistical Description of the County of Wilts.* London: Sherwood, Neely & Jones, c.1820. Double-page frontis., 'Fonthill' one of four views. Description of the Abbey, copied from Storer (1812), 97–113. Previously publ., London: C. Cooke, c.1805, 117–121.

Dugdale, James. *The New British Traveller.* 4 vols. London: J. Robins, 1819. Fonthill, 4:464–465.

Easton, James. *The Salisbury Guide* ... 25th, 27th & new eds. Salisbury: Easton, 1810, 1814 & 1818. 'Fonthill Abbey. The Seat of W. Beckford, Esq. Sixteen miles west of Salisbury.', 73–76, 76–79 & 75–78. *Idem,* new ed. 1822. Same text except last two paragraphs replaced by new one, 75–78. *Idem,* 30th ed., 1825. Same text as 1822 except last paragraph omitted & tipped-in note facing p. 76 about fall of Tower, 75–77. *Idem,* 31st ed., 1830. Same text as 1825 except note about Tower (with new second paragraph) now at end, 76–78. For earlier editions see Fonthill Splendens, above.

Elmes, James. *Lectures on Architecture.* London: Ollier, 1821. Abbey 'among the most convenient, splendid and tasteful [buildings] in the country', 399.

[Fenton, Richard.] under pseud. 'A Barrister'. *A Tour in Quest of Genealogy.* London: Sherwood, Neely & Jones, 1811. Denied admittance in 1807, 225.

Frith, William Powell. 'The Fonthill Story.' In *My Autobiography and Reminiscences,* 2:131–137. London: Richard Bentley, 1887. Anecdotes about Beckford in Phillips's auction rooms & clandestine visitor to the Abbey. 7th ed. in one vol., 1889, pp. 349–354. Mostly reprinted in *A Victorian Canvas,* London: Bles, 1957, 140–145 and partly quoted in W. H. S., 'Beckford and his Uninvited Guest', *Bath and County Graphic* 8 no. 9 (Jan 1904): 103. Also reprinted in Philip Gooden, ed., *The Mammoth Book of Literary Anecdotes.* London: Robinson, 2002, 416–421.

REVIEW of 1st ed. Archdale, George. 'William Powell Frith, R.A.' *Temple Bar* 82 (Jan 1888): 65–81. Reprinted in *Littell's Living Age* 176 (4 Feb 1888): 292–300 at 298–299.

Gilpin, William. *Observations on the Western Parts of England Relative chiefly to Picturesque Beauty to which are added a few remarks on the picturesque beauty of the Isle of Wight.* London: T. Cadell & W. Davies, 1798. Pp. 116–117.

Mitford, Mary Russell. *The Friendships of Mary Russell Mitford, as recorded in letters from her literary correspondents*. Ed. Alfred Guy Kingham L'Estrange. 2 vols. London: Hurst & Blackett, 1882. Letter from William Cobbett to Dr Mitford on 29 Aug 1808 highly praising Fonthill, 1:41–42.

Mogg, Edward. *A Survey of the High Roads of England and Wales, with part of Scotland, planned on a scale of one inch to a mile*. London: Mogg, 1817. 'London to Exeter', Hindon & 'The Magnificent Seat of W. Beckford Esqr', pl. 163. 'Fonthill Abbey' in 'Index to the Country Seats', [9b–10a]. 'Fonthill Down, Wilts' and 'Fonthill Giffard, Wilts' in 'Index to the Direct and Cross Roads', [52a].

Watkin, David. *Sir John Soane: Enlightenment Thought and the Royal Academy Lectures*. Cambridge: Cambridge University Press, 1966. Lecture V, first delivered in 1813: 'the rich abbey at Fonthill', 336; pictures from Splendens 'too large, and unsuitable to the decoration of a modern Gothic abbey', 556.

Articles

'Buildings at Fonthill.' *Salisbury and Winchester Journal*, 24 Dec 1798, 4c. Dimensions of the Abbey. See Gemmett, *Beckford's Fonthill* (2003), 79.

Collecting materials. *Salisbury and Winchester Journal*, 12 Sept 1796, 4c. Beckford 'collecting the materials for a building of wonderful grandeur and utility', a tower on Stops' Beacon. Reprinted as 'Mr. Beckford's New Mansion' in *The Times*, 15 Sept 1796, 3a, & in 'Country News', *Gentleman's Magazine* 66 pt. 2 (Sept 1796): 784.

Compo-cement. *Gentleman's Magazine* 76 pt. 2 & 77 pt. 1 (Dec 1806 & April 1807): 1128 & 326. Letters by Observator & Albion about poor state of cement.

Gothic improvements at Fonthill. *Bell's Weekly Messenger*, 23 May 1802.

A Passer By. *Gentleman's Magazine* 91 pt. 2 (Dec 1821): 495–496. Critical one-page account of exterior of the Abbey.

Prince Regent. *Morning Chronicle*, 20 Sept 1823. Beckford refused the Prince Regent admittance to Fonthill Abbey (at an unknown date).

[?Reed, Isaac.] 'Account of the Works Now Executing at Fonthill.' *European Magazine* 31 (Feb 1797): 104–107. Reprinted in Gemmett, *Beckford's Fonthill* (2003), 215–221.

Storm damage. *The Times*, 20 May 1800, 3b. Fall of Tower.

Storm damage. *The Times*, 27 May 1800, 3b. Only timber frame damaged. Similar account in *Gentleman's Magazine* 70 pt. 1 (May 1800): 476. Tower not demolished.

'William Bankes' Account of his Surreptitious Visit to Fonthill.' *Beckford Journal* 1 (1995): 47–50. Letter of 23 December 1811.

JAMES WYATT (1746–1813)

A., R. 'Short Memoirs of the Life of James Wyatt, Esq.' *Gentleman's Magazine* 83 pt. 2 (Sept 1813): 296–297 at 297. Obituary in which Abbey is noted.

Briggs, Martin S. *Goths and Vandals*. London: Constable, 1952. Wyatt, 144–145, 146. The 'whimsies of Strawberry Hill and Fonthill', 150.

Crook, J. Mordaunt & M. H. Port. *The History of the King's Works. Vol. VI 1782–1851*. London: HMSO, 1973. General ed. H. M. Colvin. Beckford's comments on Wyatt's poor state of health, 54 & nn8, 11, 12.

Curl, James Stevens. *A Dictionary of Architecture*. Oxford: Oxford University Press, 1999. Wyatt and Fonthill, 747.

Dale, Antony. *James Wyatt*. Oxford: Basil Blackwell, 1936. Fonthill, 76–81, 82, 86, 91, 103, 107, 117, 121, 124. John Martin's NW view of Abbey facing 76. Romney's portrait of Beckford facing 78. Revised ed., 1956. 'Fonthill Abbey', 143–158 & pl. 55, 56. Also 166, 170, 172, 177, 197, 199–200, 214, 216.

Fletcher, Banister & Banister F. Fletcher. *A History of Architecture on the Comparative Method*. 5th ed. London: Batsford, 1905. (1st ed. 1896.) Wyatt, 582, 591. Choragic Monument of Lysicrates, 86 (photo), 87–88.

[Mitford, John.] *Gentleman's Magazine* n.s. 16 (Dec 1841): 622–627 at 626. Review of Britton's *Toddington*: Wyatt 'disgraced himself' over Abbey.

[Nichols, John Gough.] 'Toddington, Gloucestershire.' *Gentleman's Magazine* n.s. 7 (March 1837): 256–259 at 257. Wyatt criticised for 'poor and even trifling designs' at Fonthill, Windsor and other seats.

Nicholson, Albert. 'Wyatt, James.' In *Dictionary of National Biography*, ed. Sidney Lee, 63:179, 180. London: Smith, Elder, 1900.

Peckham, Morse. 'James Wyatt (1746–1813).' In *The Birth of Romanticism 1790–1815*, 46–48. Greenwood, Florida: Penkevill, 1986. Fonthill 'was the perfection of the Picturesque', 46. In 1800 Beckford bought Turner's 'The Fifth Plague of Egypt', 228. Sold 'Altieri' Claudes in 1807, 229.

Richards, J. M., ed. *Who's Who in Architecture*. London: Weidenfeld & Nicolson, 1977. Wyatt's 'sensational and unwieldy' Fonthill Abbey, 355.

Robinson, John Martin. *The Wyatts: An Architectural Dynasty*. Oxford: Oxford University Press, 1979. Beckford, 77–78, 80. Fonthill Abbey, 63, 77, 78, 85, 177, 191, 241 & pl. 50, 51. Splendens, 241, 263. Fonthill Gifford Church (1866, by T. H. Wyatt), 225, 263 & pl. 137.

Robinson, John Martin. 'Wyatt, James (1746–1813).' In *Oxford Dictionary of National Biography*, ed. H. C. G. Matthew & Brian Harrison, 60:574, 576. Oxford: Oxford University Press, 2004. Beckford's irritation with Wyatt, and the Batalha-inspired Fonthill Abbey.

Turnor, Reginald. *James Wyatt*. London: Art and Technics, 1950. Beckford, 9, 13, 15, 23. Fonthill, 33, 39, 40–42. Illus.: frontis., title page, 41, 43, 45 & 4 pl.

Wedgwood, Alexandra. 'Architecture.' In *The Cambridge Guide to the Arts in Britain. Vol. 6 Romantics to Early Victorians*, ed. Boris Ford, 184–225 at 189, 190. Cambridge: Cambridge University Press, 1990. Abbey, with SW view, from Britton (1823). *Vathek*, 9. Reissued in 1992 as *The Cambridge Cultural History of Britain. Vol. 6 The Romantic Age in Britain*.

Worsley, Giles. 'Masterbuilder. James Wyatt 1746–1813.' *[Daily] Telegraph Property*, 18 Aug 2001, 8. SW view of Abbey.

HERALDRY

Beltz. Woodcock, Thomas. 'Beltz, George Frederick (1774–1841).' In *Oxford Dictionary of National Biography*, ed. H. C. G. Matthew & Brian Harrison, 5:47. Oxford: Oxford University Press, 2004. Friend of Beckford and frequent visitor at Abbey.

Burke, Bernard. 'Beckford.' In *The General Armory of England, Scotland, Ireland and Wales*, 65. London: Harrison, 1884. (1st ed. 1842.)

G., F. H. 'Beckford: Hastings.' *Notes and Queries* 4th Series 1 (1868): 99. Beckford quartered the arms of the Catesbys of Northants through his great grandmother, Mary Hastings.

Heard. White, D. V. 'Heard, Sir Isaac (1730–1822).' In *Oxford Dictionary of National Biography*, ed. H. C. G. Matthew & Brian Harrison, 26:150. Oxford: Oxford University Press, 2004. Correspondence with Beckford.

L. [Beltz, Sir George.] 'Armorial Decorations at Fonthill Abbey.' *Gentleman's Magazine* 92 pt. 2 (Sept, Oct, Nov 1822): 201–204, 317–320, 409–414. Engraving of SW view of Abbey drawn by J. C. Buckler facing 201. *Idem* n.s. 17 (Jan 1842): 107. Obituary of Beltz noting these articles.

Macquin. Bellenger, Dominic Aidan. 'Macquin, Ange-Denis (1756–1823).' In *Oxford Dictionary of National Biography*, ed. H. C. G. Matthew & Brian Harrison, 36:7. Oxford: Oxford University Press, 2004. Beckford's librarian, secretary and heraldic adviser.

Millington, Jon. 'Beckford's Quarterings.' *Beckford Tower Trust Newsletter*, Spring 1992, 9. Scheme of 30 quarterings registered in 1808.

Woodcock, Thomas & John Martin Robinson. *The Oxford Guide to Heraldry*. Oxford: Oxford University Press, 1988. Scheme of thirty quarterings, 134 & colour pl. 24. The Abbey 'was bedecked with all the heraldry he [Beckford] could command or imagine in plaster, stone, and stained glass', 182.

1822 AND CHRISTIE'S SALE

For Christie's sale catalogue, 1822, see '8. The Collection. Sales'

Books

Cholmondeley, Richard Hugh, ed. *The Heber Letters, 1783–1832*. London: Batchworth Press, 1950. Letter from Richard Heber to his sister Mrs Charles Cholmondeley on 20 Oct 1822 asking her, 'Were you among the disappointed visitors at Fonthill?' and quoting Edward Stanley's comparison of 'the fine Gothic building . . . to a Cathedral fitted up by a Lunatic Bishop', 302 & nn2, 3.

Constable, John. Leslie, C. R. *Memoirs of the life of John Constable. Composed chiefly of his letters*. London: Phaidon, 1951. (1st ed. 1843.) Letter of 29 Aug 1823 to his wife about visiting Fonthill the previous day, 105. This letter, and another of 24 Aug in: Jon Millington, 'John Constable's Visits to Fonthill Abbey in 1823', *Beckford Tower Trust Newsletter*, Spring 1983, 8–9.

Constable. *John Constable's Correspondence*. Ed. R. B. Beckett. Ipswich: Suffolk Records Society. Vols. 6, 1964; 10, 1966 & 12, 1968. Vol. 18, ed. Ian Fleming-Williams, Tate Gallery & SRS, 1975. From Archdeacon John Fisher on 14 Sept 1822, suggesting that they go to the Fonthill sale, 12:95; on 6 Oct, Fonthill 'a strange mad place . . . collection of pictures is small', 12:97. To Fisher on 7 Oct, 'I do not regret not seeing Fonthill . . . nothing fine in the picture way', 12:98 & n2. From Fisher on 11 Oct, commenting on Farquhar and, when he visited Fonthill, on Beckford's 'propensities' and searching the shelves for 'stimulating' books, 18:120 & nn1, 2; on 30 Nov, mentioning 'a beautiful Woovermans at Fonthill', 12:105. To his wife on 24 Aug 1823, passing Fonthill Gate, 'so fairy like', 6:283 & n2; on 29 Aug, about visiting Fonthill the previous day, 6:284–285 (extract, 12:129–130 & 129 n2); on 5 Sept, again mentioning the visit to Fonthill, 6:287. To Fisher on 30 Sept, having heard he was at the sale with his wife, 12:133; on 2 Oct, confirming that he was at Fonthill where he spoke to Phillips, 12:135 (extract, 10:219). From Fisher on *c.*16 Oct about the sale of the 'Fonthill treasures', 12:138. To Fisher on 19 Oct, commenting on the Fonthill sale, 12:140. From Fisher on 27 Jan 1825, 'Beckford is here playing with bricks & mortar on the top of Lansdown', 12:194 & n1.

[Defauconpret, Auguste Jean Baptiste.] *Londres en Mil Huit Cent Vingt-Deux*. Paris: Gide Fils, 1823. Lettre XX. 'Fonthill Abbey. Londres, le 1ᵉʳ octobre 1822', 221–229.

Dudley, Earl of (John William Ward, 1781–1833). *Letters of the Earl of Dudley to the Bishop of Llandaff*. London: John Murray, 1840. 3 Aug 1822: the Bishop's account of Fonthill made Dudley want to see it, 345.

8 Sept 1822: 'It is certainly worth seeing . . . a *sham* abbey is absurd . . .', 354.

Dudley, Earl of. Romilly, S. H. *Letters to 'Ivy' from the first Earl of Dudley*. London: Longmans, 1905. 4 Sept 1822, dismissive remarks on Abbey, 312.

[?Harley, James.] *The Press, or Literary Chit-chat. A Satire*. London: Lupton Relfe, 1822. A three-part satire in verse, with scathing comments on the sale by 'Jocus' and 'Hocus' in Part 2, 63–64 & 101–102 nn17, 18.

Hawker, Peter. *The Diary of Col. P. Hawker 1802–1853*. 2 vols. London: Longmans, 1893. In 1811, Beckford's house at Cintra a ruin, 1:26–27. A day at Fonthill on 26 Aug 1822, view from tower 'one of the finest', grounds 'monotonous', 1:247–249. Reprinted, 1988. Letter quoting Fonthill visit in *Country Life*, 13 Dec 1956, 1412.

Heber, Amelia. *The Life of Reginald Heber, D.D . . .* 2 vols. London: John Murray, 1830. Letter to Stow on 21 Oct 1822, 'All the world in England have been running crazy to get a sight of Fonthill and its rarities . . .', 2:65.

Jerdan, William. *The Autobiography of W. J.* 4 vols. London: A. Hall. Virtue, 1853. The Abbé Macquin 'contributed a series of papers' on the Abbey to the *Literary Gazette* in 1822, 3:103–110.

Whalley, Thomas Sedgewick. *Journals and Correspondence of Thomas Sedgewick Whalley*. Ed. Rev. Hill Wickham. 2 vols. London: Bentley, 1863. Letter from Sir Walter Jones in July 1822 asking Whalley not to go to Fonthill without him, 2:485. Editorial note about Beckford and Fonthill, 2:485–486.

Wordsworth, William. *The Letters of William and Dorothy Wordsworth*. Ed. Ernest de Selincourt. Oxford: Clarendon Press, 1939. 'The Later Years, Vol. 1, 1821–1830.' In a letter to Richard Sharp (businessman, critic, traveller & MP for Ilchester, 1826) in mid-Oct 1822, 'How singular is the fate of Fonthill! The Papers give a sentimental and silly account of the Place, but one cannot help longing to see it, with all its wonders.', 91–92 & 91n. 2nd ed., 1978, ed. Alan G. Hill. 'Vol. 3. The Later Years, Part 1, 1821–1828', 157 & n4.

Articles

E., J. [Elderton, John?] *Gentleman's Magazine* 92 pt. 1 (April 1822): 325–327. Letter to the editor, 'Mr. Urban'. Account of interior from Storer (1812).

'Fonthill Abbey.' *Salisbury and Winchester Journal*, 24 June 1822, 4c. Announcement of Christie's sale. 23 lines. Reprinted in *Gentleman's Magazine* 92 pt. 1 (Suppl. 1822): 628.

Abbey open. *Salisbury and Winchester Journal*, 8 July 1822, 4c. 21 lines.

Rutter. *Salisbury and Winchester Journal*, 15 July 1822, 4c. 52-line extract from pp. 13–15 of the 1st ed. of Rutter's *Description of Fonthill Abbey*. *Idem*, 15 July, 1a, refreshments provided at Abbey for servants and horses.

A Tourist. 'Fonthill Abbey.' *Morning Herald*, 10 Aug 1822. 'A desire to see so interesting structure as Fonthill . . .' 76 lines. *Idem*, 15 Aug. Abbey described as 'the most delightful fairy tale'.

Britton, John. 'Fonthill Abbey.' *The Museum* No. 17 (17 Aug 1822): 264–265. Account of exterior based on that in his *Wiltshire* (1814), 265–268. Reprinted in *Gentleman's Magazine* 92 pt. 2 (Aug 1822): 100–102 and Gemmett, *Beckford's Fonthill* (2003), 229–233.

[Macquin, Abbé Ange Denis.] 'Sketches of Society. A Visit to Fonthill Abbey.' *Literary Gazette* 6 (17 Aug 1822): 520–521. 'Visit to Fonthill. [Second Paper].' 24 Aug, 527–528 & woodcut SW view. 'Visit to Fonthill. [Third Paper].' 31 Aug, 555–556. 'Visit to Fonthill. [Fourth Paper].' 14 Sept, 585. Papers 1–3 reprinted in *Weekly Entertainer; and West of England Miscellany* (Sherborne, Dorset) n.s. 6 (2, 16, 23 Sept 1822): 150–153, 177–178, 193–196. Papers 1–4 reprinted in Gemmett, *Beckford's Fonthill* (2003), 240–245, 246–248, 249–252, 253–255. For 'Fonthill Abbey. [Fifth Paper]' see Poems, below.

'Fonthill Abbey.' *Salisbury and Winchester Journal*, 19 Aug 1822, 4b. 'The curiosity excited to see this vast structure . . .' 37 lines. Similar account in *Devizes & Wiltshire Gazette*, 29 Aug, 3a.

'Fonthill Abbey.' *Bath Chronicle*, 22 Aug 1822, 4c. General account, ⅔ column.

'A Visit to Fonthill Abbey.' *Devizes & Wiltshire Gazette*, 22 Aug 1822, 4b–c. Continuing 'interest attached to the sale of effects'.

'Fonthill Abbey.' *Gazette of Fashion* Part 3 no. 4, 24 Aug 1822, etching of Abbey by J. Clark facing 49. *Idem* Part 3 no. 5, 31 Aug, 65–67, 79 (Earl Grosvenor is said to have bought Abbey). 'Fonthill.' *Idem* Part 3 no. 12, 19 Oct, 181–182. *Idem* Part 4 no. 7, 14 Dec, Farquhar remaining at Abbey, 110. Pp. 65–67 reprinted in Gemmett, *Beckford's Fonthill* (2003), 234–239.

[Knight, Charles.] 'Fonthill Abbey.' *Guardian*, 25 Aug, 8, 15, 22, 29 Sept, 13 Oct 1822, 269, 287, 294, 301, 309, 325. Reprinted in Gemmett, *Beckford's Fonthill* (2003), 256–273.

'Fonthill Abbey.' *Salisbury and Winchester Journal*, 26 Aug 1822, 4b–c. An experience 'not to be excelled by any in the kingdom'. 44 lines.

Earl Grosvenor. *Bath Chronicle*, 29 Aug 1822, 3a. Rumour that Earl Grosvenor had bought Abbey.

Abbey open for inspection. *New Monthly Magazine* 6 (1 Aug 1822): 383.

'Sale Effects at Fonthill Abbey.' *Observer*, 1, 2 Sept 1822, 3, 2.

'Fonthill Abbey.' *Sherborne and Yeovil Mercury*, 2 Sept 1822, 4b. Sale postponed until October. ¼ column.

Visits by nobility. *Salisbury and Winchester Journal*, 2 Sept 1822, 4d. Visits by 'several noble families', listing some of them. 33 lines.

An Artist. 'Fonthill Abbey.' *Morning Chronicle*, 2, 5 Sept 1822, 3, 5.

'Fonthill Abbey.' *Devizes & Wiltshire Gazette*, 5 Sept 1822, 3a. Abbey 'is literally crammed with articles of the Vertu'. ¼ column.

'Fonthill Abbey.' *Sherborne and Yeovil Mercury*, 9 Sept 1822, 4a. This 'enchanting spot' was attracting a greater number of visitors.

Duke of Gloucester. *Salisbury and Winchester Journal*, 9 Sept 1822, 4b–c. The Duke 'honoured Fonthill with a visit'. 47 lines. *Idem*, 4e. New ed. of James Easton's *Salisbury Guide* 'published this day', price 2s. 6d.

Sale Anecdotes. *The Times*, 14 Sept 1822, 2e, bustle on roads. *Idem*, 17 Sept, 2d, lady broke £40 piece of china. *Idem*, 20 Sept 2d, anecdotes from *Southampton Chronicle*. *Idem*, 23 Sept, 2d, curiosities of Eastern manufacture. *Idem*, 30 Sept, 3a, property on view. Sale 'deferred from the 1st to the 8th of October'.

'Fonthill Abbey.' *Salisbury and Winchester Journal*, 16 Sept 1822, 4c. The need to allow enough time 'for viewing this superb edifice'. 48 lines. *Idem*, 4f. Christie's viewing will close on Saturday 28 Sept.

Abbey still attracting visitors. *Bath Chronicle*, 19 Sept 1822, 3c. 15 lines.

'Fonthill Abbey.' *Devizes & Wiltshire Gazette*, 19 Sept 1822, 3c. Report on contents for sale. ½ column.

Abbey still frequented. *Salisbury and Winchester Journal*, 23 Sept 1822, 4c. 69 lines.

'From the Beacon-cliffe at Fonthill.' *Devizes & Wiltshire Gazette*, 26 Sept 1822, 3c. Comments on the view from high ground.

'Fonthill Abbey.' *Salisbury and Winchester Journal*, 30 Sept 1822, 4b. Sale postponed until 8 Oct. 11 lines. Similar account in *Sherborne and Yeovil Mercury*, 30 Sept 1822, 4b. 29 lines.

'The Fonthill Property.' *The Times*, 1 Oct 1822, 2e.

'The Fonthill Property.' *Morning Herald*, 1 Oct 1822, 1.

'The Fonthill Effects.' *The Times*, 2 Oct 1822, 3a. ½ column. 'Fonthill Abbey.' *Idem*, 3 Oct, 2e. 'Fonthill Property.' *Idem*, 4 Oct, 3a, description of the grounds. ⅔ column. 'Fonthill Abbey.' *Idem*, 5 Oct, 2e, ¼ column. 'The Fonthill Property.' *Idem*, 7 Oct, 3a. ⅓ column.

'The Fonthill Property.' *Devizes & Wiltshire Gazette*, 3 Oct 1822, 3a. Great variety of visitors.

Tonstall, Cuthbert. [Thomas Frognall Dibdin, pseud.] 'The Fonthill Fever.' *The Museum* Nos. 24–29 (5, 12, 19, 26 Oct, 2, 9 Nov 1822): 379–380, 393–395, 410–412, 428–430, 441–442, 455–456. A series of six articles reprinted in Gemmett, *Beckford's Fonthill* (2003), 274–287.

Sale on 8 Oct. *Salisbury and Winchester Journal*, 7 Oct 1822, 4b. Sale will begin tomorrow, as advertised.

'Fonthill Abbey.' *Morning Herald*, 7 Oct 1822, 2–3. Grounds compared with the Happy Valley of *Rasselas*. *Idem*, 8, 16 Oct 1822, 2–3, 3.

'Fonthill Grand Disappointment' *Morning Post*, 8 Oct 1822, 3.

'Fonthill Abbey.' *The Times*, 9 Oct 1822, 3d. Sale cancelled. Abbey closed. Rumour that Farquhar was the buyer.

Fonthill Abbey and Farquhar. *Courier*, 9 & 10 Oct 1822.

'The Fonthill Property.' *Devizes & Wiltshire Gazette*, 10 Oct 1822, 3c. Exhibition of articles for sale closed on 5 Oct. ½ column. Abbey sold for £330,000. Account of Beckford, with source of his wealth. ¾ column.

Fonthill. *Morning Herald*, 11 Oct 1822, 3.

'Fonthill Abbey.' *Literary Gazette* 6 (12 Oct 1822): 653. Christie's sale cancelled.

'Sale of the Whole of the Fonthill estate.' *Observer*, 13 Oct 1822, 4.

Sale of Abbey. *Examiner*, 14 Oct 1822. Sale on 7 Oct. Also *The News*, 13 Oct.

'Fonthill Abbey.' *Salisbury and Winchester Journal*, 14 Oct 1822, 4c. Sale cancelled. Purchase by Farquhar. Phillips at Abbey. 29 lines. From *Morning Herald*, Friday 9 Oct.

'Fonthill Abbey.' *Sherborne and Yeovil Mercury*, 14 Oct 1822, 4b. Abbey had 'changed proprietors' since the last report. 39 lines.

'A Wiltshire Ciceron.' *Devizes & Wiltshire Gazette*, 17 Oct 1822, 3b. Reaction of victim of the 'Fonthill epidemic' to statue of Marcus Aurelius at Wilton. 'Mr. Fonthill. Oct. 9.' Reprinted in *Mirror of Literature* 1 (9 Nov 1822): 31.

Abbey sold. *Devizes & Wiltshire Gazette*, 17 Oct 1822, 4b. Phillips concluded sale of Abbey to Farquhar.

J., M. 'Fonthill Abbey.' *County Literary Chronicle and Weekly Review*, 19 Oct 1822, 665–667. Letter dated 9 Oct from a Kensington writer with remarks about the Abbey in the years before the 1822 sale view.

'Fonthill Abbey and Domain.' *Evans and Ruffy's Farmer's Journal*, 21 Oct 1822.

'Fonthill Abbey and Domain.' *Devizes & Wiltshire Gazette*, 24 Oct 1822, 3b. Mystery about Farquhar's purchase of the Abbey. 12 lines.

'The Editor's Excursion to Fonthill Abbey.' *New European Magazine* 1 (Oct 1822): 364–370.

Viator. [Richard Colt Hoare.] 'Fonthill Abbey. On its close.' *Gentleman's Magazine* 92 pt. 2 (Oct 1822): 291–292. Abbey 'doomed to greet a second Abbot'.

Abbey described. *New Monthly Magazine* 6 (1 Oct 1822): 479–480.

'Survey of Font-Hill Abbey.' *Lady's Magazine* n.s. 3 (Oct, Nov 1822): 474–477 & woodcut SW view, 554–557. 'Additional Particulars respecting Font-Hill Abbey; with two views of different parts of that edifice', *Idem* (Dec): 621 & W and SE views above Beckford's facsimile signature.

Mostly culled from *Literary Gazette* 6 (17, 24 Aug (woodcut), 31 Aug, 14 Sept 1822), Britton (*Museum* 1822), Storer (1812) & Rutter (1822).

ADVERT for Oct & Dec issues in *Literary Gazette* 6 (21, 28 Sept, 30 Nov 1822): 606, 622, 765.

Fonthill. *New Times*, 5 Nov 1822, 3.

'Fonthill Abbey.' *Mirror of Literature* 1 (23 Nov 1822): 49–52 & woodcut w view. Copied verbatim from Whittaker's *A New Guide to Fonthill Abbey* (1822), itself mostly culled from Rutter's *Description* (1822). Most of *Mirror* article reprinted in Thomas Dugdale, *Curiosities of Great Britain. England & Wales*, London: Tallis, *c*.1843, 'Fonthill Gifford', 790–792 (in Div.2 of 9).

Monthly Magazine; or, British Register 54 (1 Nov 1822): 347. Brief account of Abbey mentioning Britton's *Fonthill* and sale to Farquhar, 22 lines.

'Epitome of Public Affairs for October 1822.' *Ladies' Monthly Museum* n.s. 16 (Nov 1822): 284–285. One-page account of the sale 'now passed away'.

Tonstall, Cuthbert. [Thomas Frognall Dibdin, pseud.] *Gentleman's Magazine* 92 pt. 2 (Nov 1822): 388–391 at 388. Extract about a visit to Stourhead 'from "A Trip to the Abbey; or, the Fonthill Fever.," printed in the *London Museum*.'

G., W. [Garbett, William.] 'Candid Critique on the Architecture of Fonthill Abbey.' *Gentleman's Magazine* 92 pt. 2 (Dec 1822): 491–494. Reprinted in Gemmett, *Beckford's Fonthill* (2003), 288–293.

'Varieties from the London Magazines, Nov. and Dec [1822]. Fonthill Abbey.' *The Athenæum, or Spirit of the English Magazines* (Boston, MA) 12 (15 Feb 1823): 406. Farquhar at Fonthill to prepare for auction sale.

Gomme, George Laurence, ed. *Topographical History of Warwickshire, Westmoreland, and Wiltshire. A Classified Collection of the Chief Contents of "The Gentleman's Magazine" from 1731 to 1868.* London: Elliot Stock, 1901. Fonthill, 184, 233–258. Being extracts from *Gentleman's Magazine*: 1821 pt. 2, 495–496; 1822 pt. 1, 326–327; 1822 pt. 2, 100–102, 201–204, 291–292, 317–320, 409–414.

Christie's Advertisements

Bath Chronicle. 'Fonthill Abbey, Wilts.', 29 Aug 1822, 5, 12 Sept, 1d, 1c, 1c; 19 Sept (sale postponed until 1 Oct), 1b; 26 Sept, 1c; 3 Oct, 3b (Sale postponed until next Tuesday, the 8th).

Literary Gazette 6 (1822). Pictures on 24 Sept and silver & gilt plate to begin on 17 Sept, (10 Aug): 509. Furniture to begin on 17 Sept, (17 Aug): 525. Sale postponed until 1 Oct, and pictures to begin on 8 Oct, (31 Aug): 558. Silver & gilt plate to begin on 1 Oct, (7 Sept): 573.

Salisbury and Winchester Journal. 'Fonthill Abbey, Wilts.', 1, 15, 22, 29 July

1822, 4d, 1a, 1a, 1a; 5, 12, 19, 26 Aug, 1a, 4e, 4e, 4e; 2, 9, 16, 23, 30 Sept, 4f (Sale postponed until 1 Oct), 4e, 4f, 4f, 4e; 7 Oct, 4e.

The Times. 'Fonthill Abbey, Wilts.', 12, 19, 25 July 1822, 1e, 1d, 4e (× 2); 2, 8, 15, 22, 29 (Sale postponed until 1 Oct) Aug, 4c (× 2), 4e, 4e, 4d, 4c; 13, 19 Sept, 4b, 4e; 1 (Sale deferred to 8 Oct), 7 (Sale on Tuesday next, ie. 8th), 8, 9 (rumoured purchase of Abbey by Farquhar) Oct, 4c, 4b, 2e, 2e.

Other Advertisements

Salisbury and Winchester Journal. John Snelgrove, Beckford Arms, 5, 12 Aug 1822, 1a, 4e. T[homas]. Harrison, Lamb Inn, Hindon, 2 Sept, 4f. Wm. Harris, Swan Inn, Hindon, 2, 9 Sept 4f, 4e. Elizabeth Cross, Boot Inn, Tisbury, 2, 9 Sept, 4f, 4e. T. Roberts, Ship Inn, Mere, 9 Sept, 4e. James Stride, Crown Inn, Hindon, 16 Sept, 4f. Kendall & Richardson coach, 26 Aug, 2, 9, 16, 23 Sept, 4e, 4f, 4e, 4f, 4f. William Phelps trees & shrubs, Salisbury, 16 Sept, 4f. Eginton stained glass, 16, 23 Sept, 4f, 4f. C. Norton, auctioneer, 23 Sept, 4f. J. Elderton, auctioneer, 7 Oct 4e.

JOHN FARQUHAR (1751–1826)

Abbey acquired for £320,000. *The Times*, 21 Nov 1822, 2d. At Fonthill with auctioneer's son, preparing a catalogue.

Abbey and house in Portland place, London, bought. *The Times*, 16 Oct 1822, 2c.

Abbey bought as a speculation. *Literary Gazette* 6 (23 Nov 1822): 748.

Abbey bought by Farquhar. *New Monthly Magazine* 6 (1 Nov 1822): 527.

Abbey domain sold to John Benett. *New Monthly Magazine* 18 (Feb 1826): 80.

Darton, Eric. 'John Farquhar, Eccentric.' *Beckford Tower Trust Newsletter*, Spring 1986, 8–9.

Death & funeral. *The Times*, 8 July 1826, 3a & 17 July, 2e.

'Mr. Farquhar and Fonthill.' *The Times*, 11 Oct 1822, 3a. From a 'Morning Paper'. ½ column. Adapted with additions as 'Mr. Farquhar and Fonthill Abbey.' *Mirror of Literature* 1 (16 Nov 1822): 33–35.

'Mr. Farquhar & Fonthill Abbey.' In *The Wonders of the Universe; or, Curiosities of Nature and Art*, 111–113. London: Jones, 1825. Similar in part to *The Times* article above. New York: Solomon King, 1831, pp. 152–154.

'Mr. Farquhar and the Fonthill Estate.' *Observer*, 13 Oct 1822, 4.

'Mr. Farquhar and the Fonthill Property.' *Devizes & Wiltshire Gazette*, 17 Oct 1822, 4b. Farquhar 'is a man of an extraordinary character'.

Flattering account of Farquhar. *Salisbury and Winchester Journal*, 1 Sept 1823, 4b–c. 34 lines.

'Fonthill Abbey.' *Bath Chronicle*, 17 Oct 1822, 2c. Abbey sold to Farquhar. ½ column.

'Fonthill Abbey.' *Gentleman's Magazine* 93 pt. 1 (Jan 1823): 79. 'Mr. Farquhar has been residing at the Abbey ever since October'.

Henderson, T. F. 'Farquhar, John.' In *Dictionary of National Biography*, ed. Leslie Stephen, 18:1086–1087. London: Smith, Elder, 1889.

Henderson, T. F., rev. H. V. Bowen. 'Farquhar, John (1751–1826).' In *Oxford Dictionary of National Biography*, ed. H. C. G. Matthew & Brian Harrison, 19:89–90. Oxford: Oxford University Press, 2004.

Keith, Alexander. 'The Fantastic Millionaire, John Farquhar of Fonthill.' *Aberdeen Chamber of Commerce Journal*, March 1964, 84–87. Eminent Aberdonians No. 29. Reprinted as 'John Farquhar of Fonthill' in his *Eminent Aberdonians*, Aberdeen: Aberdeen University Press, 1984, 124–127.

[Loudon, John Claudius.] 'Domestic Notices. England.' *Gardener's Magazine* 1 (April 1826): 210. Farquhar sold Abbey to John Benett.

Obituary. *Morning Chronicle*, 15 July 1826.

Obituary. 'Mr Farquhar.' *New Monthly Magazine* 18 (Aug 1826): 342–344.

Obituary. *Gentleman's Magazine* 96 pt. 2 (Sept, Oct 1826): 278–280, 290. Abridged in *Annual Register . . . for the Year 1826*, 68 (1827): 266–267. Farquhar died on 6 July, aged 71.

Oblib. [pseud.] 'Extravaganza in Excelsus. Buchaner's £300,000 Sham Abbey.' *Buchan Observer and East Aberdeenshire Advertiser*, 9 Aug 1966.

Oblil. [pseud.] "A 'Fall Guy' who died rich." *Buchan Observer and East Aberdeenshire Advertiser*, 19 July 1966, 9. Also, anon, as 'The millionaire Brahman from Bilbo who played "Double Your Money" in 1822.' *Fraserburgh Herald*, 19 July 1966.

Parkins, J. W. 'Mr Farquhar.' *Morning Chronicle*, 5 Nov 1822, 3.

Salley, A. S., Jr., ed. 'Daniel Trezevant and some his Descendants. 25. Peter Trezevant.' *South Carolina Historical and Genealogical Magazine* 3 (1902): 38–41. Peter Trezevant married one of Farquhar's nieces.

Will. *The Times*, 12, 24, 25 Oct 1826, 2b, 2f, 3f; 15 Oct 1828, 3a; 24 March 1829, 3c. *Gentleman's Magazine* 96 pt. 2 (Suppl. 1826): 647–648. *Idem* 99 pt. 1 (June 1829): 555. Declared intestate. *Annual Register . . . for the Year 1829*, 71 (1830): 290–297. Lawsuit over will.

CONTEMPORARY POEMS

All reprinted in Gemmett, *Beckford's Fonthill* (2003),
and most in Varma, ed., *The Transient Gleam* (1991)

Bowles, William Lisle. 'On a First View of Fonthill Abbey, August 21st. 1822.' In John Rutter, *A Description of Fonthill Abbey and Demesne*, [ix]. 2nd ed. 1822. Reprinted in *Gentleman's Magazine* 92 pt. 2 (Aug 1822):

102; *Weekly Entertainer; and West of England Miscellany* (Sherborne, Dorset) n.s. 6 (9 Sept 1822): 176, and many times subsequently.

Cunningham, Alan, ed. 'Fonthill.' In *The Anniversary for 1829*, 214–216 & engraving after Turner's south view of Abbey (exhibited at Royal Academy, 1800). London: John Sharpe, 1828. Reprinted in *The Anniversary; an Elegant Literary Present*, ed. Horace Harvey, 280–282, London: R. A. Charlton, n.d.
REVIEW. *Gentleman's Magazine* 98 pt. 2 (Oct 1828): 353–354 at 353.

J., M. 'Fonthill, A Sonnet.' *County Literary Chronicle and Weekly Review*, 24 Aug 1822, 540. Reprinted in Jon Millington, 'A Transient Gleam', *Beckford Journal* 4 (1998): 64.

Jefferson, John. *Fonthill: A Poem*. Blandford, Dorset: T. Oakley, 1824. 41 pp. 25 cm. The glories of architecture, 5–19. Abbey exterior, 19–30. Abbey interior and contents, 30–36. Grounds, 36–39. Wiltshire, 39–41.

K., E. 'Fonthill Abbey, Wilts, Seat of W. Beckford, Esq., In July 1827.' Signed E. K. Jaulnah, Bombay, 1856. From a cutting (source unknown) in the Hunt Collection, 4:170–171, in Bath Central Library.

[Macquin, Abbé Ange Denis.] 'De Æde Fonthilliana.' *Literary Gazette* 6 (31 Aug 1822): 555. Four-line epigram in his 'Visit to Fonthill. [Third Paper].'

[Macquin, Abbé Ange Denis.] 'Fonthill Abbey. [Fifth Paper].' *Literary Gazette* 6 (21 Sept 1822): 602–603. Poem (with notes) from 'A Visitor', of which six lines were quoted in Boyd Alexander, *England's Wealthiest Son* (1962, 168).

[Pickering, Henry.] 'On the Alienation of Fonthill Abbey.' In *The Ruins of Pæstum: and Other Compositions in Verse*, 53–55. Salem, MA: Cushing & Appleton, 1822. Eleven four-line stanzas.

W., A. A. [Watts, Alaric Alexander.] 'The Sale at Fonthill – A Fragment.' *Literary Museum* No. 80 (1 Nov 1823): 701–702. He revised it for a broadside, 'Fonthill Sale. A Parody', which was reprinted in Melville, *Life and Letters of William Beckford* (1910), 315–319.

1823 AND PHILLIPS'S SALE

For Phillips's sale catalogue, 1823, see '8. The Collection. Sales'

Books

Brasbridge, Joseph. *The Fruits of Experience*. London: Printed for the Author, 1824. Comments on 1823 sale from a silversmith, 251.

Carlyle, Thomas. *Reminiscences*. Ed. K. J. Fielding & Ian Campbell. New ed. Oxford: Oxford University Press, 1997. Hazlitt at sale as a 'white-bonnet' to force up prices, 275 & 454n.

Constable, John. Correspondence. See 1822 and Christie's Sale, above.

[Defauconpret, Auguste Jean Baptiste.] *Londres en Mil Huit Cent Vingt-*

Trois. Paris: Gide Fils, 1824. Frontis.: 'Vue de Fonthill Abbey'. Lithograph. S. Baptiste delt. Lith: de G. Engelmann. Distant SW view. Lettre XVI. 'Voyage de Londres à Fonthill Abbey. Salisbury, le 14 aôut 1823', 147–151, 159. Lettre XVII. 'Suite du voyage à Fonthill Abbey. le 15 aôut 1823', 160–170. Lettre XVIII. 'Suite du voyage . . . le 16 aôut 1823', 171–184.

Fairfax-Lucy, Alice. *Charlecote and the Lucys*. London: Oxford University Press, 1958. George Lucy, as the new inheritor of Charlecote, at 1823 sale, 255–256.

Grove, Charlotte. *The Grove Diaries. The Rise and Fall of an English Family 1809–1925*. Ed. Desmond Hawkins. Wimborne, Dorset: Dovecote Press, 1995. On 12 Aug 1811 met Beckford's dwarf, 108. Went to 1823 sale on 11 Sept, books not selling well, 152. Comments on the fall of the Tower on 21 Dec 1825, 161–162. Peter Beckford, neighbour, 21–22, 85.

Havell, Robert. 'Fonthill Abbey, Wiltshire. View from the South.' In *A Series of Picturesque Views of Noblemen's and Gentlemen's Seats*, pl. [XX] & two unnumbered pages signed J. M. M. London: R. Havell & Son, 1823. Originally publ. in ten parts, 1814–1823.

Haydon, Benjamin Robert. *Benjamin Robert Haydon: Correspondence and Table-talk*. 2 vols. London: Chatto & Windus, 1876. Letter to Miss Mitford in Sept 1823: 'Hazlitt was up last week from Fonthill, where Phillips has fixed him to write up, for fifty guineas, what he wrote down from his conscience last year', 2:79.

Knight, Charles. *Passages of a Working Life during Half a Century*. 3 vols. London: Bradbury & Evans, 1864–1865. Extract from his 'An Unpublished Episode of Vathek' and publication by him of Rutter's *Delineations*, 1:309–312. See also '16. Works influenced by Beckford'.

Patmore, Peter George. *My Friends and Acquaintances*. 3 vols. London: Saunders & Otley, 1854. Hazlitt's stay at Fonthill Abbey, 3:60–61, 68–72. Partly quoted in Derek Patmore, *Portrait of My Family*, London: Cassell, 1935, 27–29.

Articles

Buckler, John. 'Preparing for Publication . . . Two large perspective views of Fonthill Abbey.' *Gentleman's Magazine* 93 pt. 1 (Jan 1823): 67. Advert: two large lithographic prints from drawings owned by Sir Richard Colt Hoare, 10s the pair, *Salisbury and Winchester Journal*, 4 Aug, 1 Sept 1823, 4e, 1b.

Octagonal Tower. *Gentleman's Magazine* 93 pt. 1 (Feb 1823): 98. Beauty of Fonthill's '*octagon* tower', and query about the date of such towers.

Abbey open in June. *Morning Herald*, 29 April 1823. Letter from near Fonthill saying the Abbey would be open to the public from

1 June. Quoted in *Salisbury and Winchester Journal*, 5 May 1823, 4d. 26 lines.

Coach to Fonthill. *Salisbury and Winchester Journal*, 19 May 1823, 4c. Coach would run from Salisbury if Abbey is shown in the summer.

'Fonthill Abbey.' *Salisbury and Winchester Journal*, 26 May 1823, 4c. Abbey being prepared for mid-June opening. Contents to be sold in Sept, probably by Phillips. London architect drawing up plans for Abbey after the sale. 22 lines.

'Fonthill Abbey.' *Devizes & Wiltshire Gazette*, 29 May 1823, 3c. Abbey soon to be opened. Britton's *Fonthill* delayed until the end of June. 9 lines.

'Fonthill Abbey.' *Salisbury and Winchester Journal*, 9 June 1823, 4c. Sale by Phillips now certain, incl. 20,000 volumes. 'The American Garden is now in the highest state of culture.' 39 lines.

'Fonthill Abbey.' *Salisbury and Winchester Journal*, 16 June 1823, 4b. Abbey 'open this day'. 25 lines.

'Fonthill Abbey.' *Salisbury and Winchester Journal*, 23 June 1823, 4b. Considerably more visitors last week than the week before. 3 lines.

'Fonthill.' *The Adventurer of the Nineteenth Century* No. 12, 28 June 1823, 177–181. Copied from Storer (1812), 1–6 & *Literary Gazette* 6 (17, 24 Aug 1822). Woodcut view of Abbey from w, copied from *Lady's Magazine*, 30 Nov 1822. *Adventurer* was a short-lived imitator of the *Mirror of Literature*.

ADVERT. *Salisbury and Winchester Journal*, 7 July 1823, 1b: 'Adorned with superior wood engravings . . . No. 12. Fonthill Abbey'.

Alpine Gardens. *Salisbury and Winchester Journal*, 30 June 1823, 4b. Visitors 'delighted with the Alpine Gardens'. 9 lines.

Coach overturned. *Salisbury and Winchester Journal*, 7 July 1823, 4c. Shaftesbury & Fonthill coach, near Beckford Arms, eight injured. 7 lines.

'Fonthill Abbey.' *Ackermann's Repository of Arts* 3rd series 2 no. 8 (1 Aug 1823): 103–105 & lithograph, 'The Pavilion (now used as a Dormitory for the Visitors) and the Lake, In the Old Park.'

Visitors. *Salisbury and Winchester Journal*, 4 Aug 1823, 4c. Increase in number of visitors in spite of bad weather, incl. Earl Grosvenor. Quote from *Ackermann's Repository of Arts*. ½ column.

'Fonthill Abbey.' *Devizes & Wiltshire Gazette*, 7 Aug 1823, 4a. Account of this 'Gothic pile'. ½ column.

'Fonthill Abbey.' *Examiner*, 10 Aug 1823, 514.

'Fonthill-Abbey.' *The Times*, 15 Aug 1823, 3d. Anecdotes about Abbey and sale. Quoted in *Salisbury and Winchester Journal*, 18 Aug, 3a. ¼ column.

Abbey crowded for sale view. *Courier* (Daily evening paper), 15 Aug 1823, 3.

Enthusiastic letter from visitor to Abbey. *Courier*, 21 Aug 1823, 3.

Watts, Alaric, ed. 'Humbug! Fonthill Abbey.' *Leeds Intelligencer*, 21 Aug 1823, 3e. Scathing article about objects in the Phillips sale. ¾ column.

'Fonthill Abbey.' *Morning Chronicle*, 21 Aug, 13, 17, 24, 25, 26 Sept, 1, 8 Oct 1823, 2, 3, 3, 2, 4, 3, 3, 4.

Distinguished visitors. *Salisbury and Winchester Journal*, 25 Aug 1823, 4c. Many visitors of high rank. Reports in *The Times* of overcharging at Beckford Arms denied. Moderate charges at all inns. 21 lines.

Littlebury, Isaac. [Thomas Frognall Dibdin, pseud.] 'Fonthill.' *Morning Chronicle* 26, 30 Aug 1823, 3, 3.

Fonthill. *New Times*, 27 Aug, 12, 13, 18 Sept 1823, 4, 3 & 4, 4, 4.

Warning about extra lots brought in. *Literary Gazette* 7 (30 Aug 1823): 555.

Harris, John. "C. R. Cockerell's 'Ichnographica Domestica'." *Architectural History* 14 (1971): 5–29 at 15–16 & fig. 13c. Diary entry of visit on 30 Aug 1823 & plan of Abbey (which he preferred to that at Blenheim or Woburn).

'Beauties of Wilts.' Increase in number of visitors. *Gentleman's Magazine* 93 pt. 2 (Aug 1823): 174. 'Fonthill Abbey.' *Idem* 93 pt. 2 (Oct): 364. Account of Phillips sale.

Templeton, A[rthur] M., Jr. [pseud.] 'A Second Visit to Fonthill.' *New European Magazine* 3 (Aug 1823): 135–142. For the first visit see *Idem* 1 (Oct 1822). Reprinted in Gemmett, *Beckford's Fonthill* (2003), 302–312.

Sale visitors. *Salisbury and Winchester Journal*, 1 Sept 1823, 4c. As sale nears, all ranks flocking to Abbey. 38 lines. Pavilion arranged for visitors. 9 lines.

Rumour about Duke of Hamilton buying back Abbey from Farquhar. *Courier*, 1 Sept 1823, 3. Origin of rumour, 8 Sept, 3.

Sale not postponed. *Salisbury and Winchester Journal*, 8 Sept 1823, 4b. Reports of postponement were false. 30 lines.

Fonthill. *Morning Herald*, 8, 11, 12, 13, 18, 22, 26, 27, 29 Sept, 1, 3, 15, 16 Oct, 1 Nov 1823, all p. 3. *Idem*, 10, 16, 17, 20, 24 Sept, all p. 2.

'Fonthill Abbey.' *Morning Post*, 8, 10, 17, 24, 25, 27 Sept, 1, Oct 1823, all 3.

Sale began yesterday, said Auctioneer. *Courier*, 10 Sept 1823, 3. 'Fonthill.' *Devizes & Wiltshire Gazette*, 11 Sept, 3b. Sale began Tuesday. 20 lines.

Accounts of sale. *Courier*, 11, 12, 18, 19 Sept 1823, 2, 2, 3, 4 (Borghese table).

'Sale at Fonthill.' *The Times*, 11 Sept 1823, 2b; 12 Sept, 2c, MS. by Beckford.

'Fonthill Abbey. A Familiar Letter from a Visitor, August 18, 1823.' *The Humorous Delineator; or Vehicle* 1 no. 10 (11 Sept 1823): 149–151. From the *British Traveller* (Evening Paper). A general description.

'Fonthill Abbey, Second Day's Sale.' & 'Further Particulars.' *Morning Post*, 12 Sept 1823, 3 & 4.

'Mr. Beckford.' *Morning Herald*, 17 Sept, 6, 10 Oct 1823, 1, 4, 3.

Beckford & the Abbey. *Courier*, 17 Sept 1823, 3.

'Fonthill Abbey.' & 'Mr. Beckford.' *Devizes & Wiltshire Gazette*, 18 Sept 1823, 3a. Sale report & Beckford's role in sale. ¼ column each.

Sale began on 8th Sept. *Bath Chronicle*, 18 Sept 1823, 3b. 4 lines.

Crockery, Jun. 'The Fonthill Mania.' *County Literary Chronicle and Weekly Review*, 20 Sept 1823, 603–604. Letter about too much publicity for the sale.

'Fonthill Sale.' *Literary Gazette* 7 (20 Sept 1823): 602. Dealers running up prices of books. *Idem* (27 Sept): 617–618. Extra lots brought in from elsewhere.

Riot. *Salisbury and Winchester Journal*, 22 Sept 1823, 4b. Farquhar let tenantry and neighbours view Abbey and grounds free on Sundays (closed to the general public), but on 14th a crowd from 'the lower orders' tried to force entry at the gate. 21 lines. Sale increases in importance daily. 47 lines. Similar accounts in *Bath Chronicle*, 25 Sept, 3c. 10 & 8 lines.

'Fonthill Sale.' *The Times*, 23 Sept 1823, 3b, article reprinted from *Literary Gazette* of 20 Sept. ⅓ column. *The Times*, 26 Sept, 3e. Letter from G. Lawford (who valued the books for Farquhar) refuting the allegations in that article.

Comments on the sale. *Bath and Cheltenham Gazette*, 23, 30 Sept, 28 Oct 1823, 3c, 3c, 3b–c.

'Fonthill.' *Devizes & Wiltshire Gazette*, 25 Sept 1823, 3b. Interest continues.

Watts, Alaric, ed. 'Literary Notices. Fonthill Abbey.' *Leeds Intelligencer*, 25 Sept 1823, 4a–d. Questioning Phillips's additions and quoting the *Literary Gazette*. 3 columns. First three-sevenths reprinted in *The Times*, 30 Sept 1823, 3d and Gemmett, *Beckford's Fonthill* (2003), 351–356.

'Mr. Beckford and the Fine Arts.' *Morning Herald*, 27 Sept 1823, 3.

Sale report. *Salisbury and Winchester Journal*, 29 Sept 1823, 4b. 17 lines.

Tickler, Timothy. [pseud.] 'Letters of Timothy Tickler, Esq to Eminent Literary Characters. No. X. To Christopher North, Esq.' *Blackwood's Edinburgh Magazine* 14 (Sept 1823): 313. 'Billy Hazlitt and Count Tims at Fonthill, busy writing puffs for Harry Phillips'.

'Serious Accident.' *The Times*, 2 Oct 1823, 2b. Salisbury coach upset near Abbey. Driver lost control of coach after hitting a tree while descending a hill in the park at speed. Injured taken to Hindon. 28 lines. Also 'Fonthill, Monday evening', *Devizes & Wiltshire Gazette*, 2 Oct, 3b. ¼ column. Also in *Courier*, 2 Oct, 2, & *Salisbury and Winchester Journal*, 6 Oct, 4c, 28 lines.

'Fonthill, 25 Sept.' *Devizes & Wiltshire Gazette*, 2 Oct 1823, 4b. Account of sale and people attending. ½ column.

Accounts of sale during Oct. *Courier*, 2, 3, 4, 8, 9, 11, 16, 18, 24 Oct 1823, 2, 3, 4, 4, 2, 4, 4, 4, 4.

Littlebury, Isaac. [Thomas Frognall Dibdin, pseud.] 'Fonthill Campaign. A slight Sketch.' *Literary Gazette* 7 (4 Oct 1823): 634–635. Reprinted in Gemmett, *Beckford's Fonthill* (2003), 357–359.

Pictures. *Salisbury and Winchester Journal*, 6 Oct 1823, 3b. ½ column report on picture sale. *Idem*, 4b. Important visitors and comments on *Vathek*. ¼ column.

Reports. *Devizes & Wiltshire Gazette*, 9 Oct 1823, 3a. Size of Fonthill domain. Suggestion that Beckford bought Pietre Commesse table. 'Fonthill Abbey, Oct. 1.' *Idem*, 4a–b. Violent storm & report of items sold. 5 & 7 lines.

Wyatt, M. *British Press; or, Morning Literary Advertiser*, 11 Oct 1823. Abbey inspired by Mafra and Batalha.

Paintings sale. *Salisbury and Winchester Journal*, 13 Oct 1823, 4c. 7 lines.

'Fonthill Abbey, Description . . .' *Morning Post*, 16 Oct 1823, 3.

'Fonthill Abbey . . .' *Devizes & Wiltshire Gazette*, 16, 23, 30 Oct 1823, 2d, 4b, 4b–c. Sale reports. ½, ¾, 1¼ columns.

'Valuable Pictures belonging to Mr. Beckford.' *The Times*, 17 Oct 1823, 2d. Sale prices of eleven paintings noted.

'Mr. Beckford. Fonthill Abbey.' *Gleaner* 1 no. 26 (22 Oct 1823): 407–409. Beckford 'has purchased *Lansdown Hill*'. For three previous articles in the *Gleaner*, see Storer, James, *Description of Fonthill Abbey* (1823), above.

'Illumination of the Abbey.' *Morning Chronicle*, 24 Oct 1823, 4.

Abbey open. *Salisbury and Winchester Journal*, 27 Oct 1823, 4c.

Topaz Cup. *Salisbury and Winchester Journal*, 27 Oct 1823, 4b. Lewis, a London silversmith, said cup was made of crystal, not topaz. Quoted in *The Times*, 28 Oct, 2e & *Courier*, 28 Oct, 2. Denial that Prof Buckland had seen cup, *The Times*, 30 Oct, 2c. Letter from Kensington Lewis defending his claim that cup was crystal, *The Times*, 5 Nov, 3e. Letter from J. Lacy, *The Times*, 6 Nov, 3d. Defensive letter from H. Phillips, subjoined by Wm Buckland's to him, *The Times*, 17 Nov, 3c & *Salisbury and Winchester Journal*, 17 Nov, 4c.

'Sale closes this day.' *Salisbury and Winchester Journal*, 17 Nov, 4c.

'A Day at Fonthill Abbey.' *New Monthly Magazine* 8 (Oct 1823): 368–380. Reprinted in Gemmett, *Beckford's Fonthill* (2003), 326–342.

ADVERTS. *Literary Gazette* 7 (27 Sept, 4 Oct 1823): 623, 640.

Attendance at sale. *Ladies' Monthly Museum* n.s. 18 (Oct 1823): 226. Crowds at sale smaller than expected.

Wyatt, Benjamin. 'Fonthill Abbey.' *Morning Post*, 1 Nov 1823, 2 & *Morning Herald*, 1 Nov 1823, 3.

Phillips, Harry. 'The Sale at Fonthill Abbey.' *Examiner*, 23 Nov 1823, 763.

Hazlitt, William. 'Queries Addressed to Political Economists.' *Examiner*, 9 April 1826. Pampered servants at Fonthill Abbey.

Hazlitt, William. 'On the Pleasure of Hating.' & 'On a Portrait of an English Lady, by Vandyke.' In *The Plain Speaker*. 2 vols. London: Colburn, 1826. 1:324 & 2:234. The 'heartless desolation' of the Abbey & 'I would not give twopence for the whole Gallery at Fonthill'.

Hazlitt, William. 'The Main-Chance.' *New Monthly Magazine* 22 (Feb

1828): 120. 'There was not a single room fit to sit, lie, or stand in'. Reprinted in *Literary Remains of the Late William Hazlitt*. 2 vols. London: Saunders & Otley, 1836, 2:290–292.

Hazlitt, William. 'Travelling Abroad.' *New Monthly Magazine* 22 (June 1828): 528. The 'ostentatious finery of Fonthill-Abbey'. Reprinted in *New Writings by William Hazlitt*, ed. P. P. Howe, 15, 205n. London: Secker, 1925.

Phillips's Advertisements

Bath and Cheltenham Gazette. 17, 24 June 1823, 2d, 2d; 1, 8, 15, 22, 29 July, 2e, 2d, 2f, 2f, 2f; 5, 19, 26 Aug, 2f, 2e, 2e; 2, 9, 16, 23, 30 Sept, 1c, 2d, 1b, 1b, 1c; 7, 14, 21, 28 Oct, 1c, 1d, 1c, 1d; 4, 11 Nov, 1d, 1d.

Bath Chronicle. 'Fonthill. The Abbey Grounds. And the Splendid Elegancies', 'The Extensive and Splendid Library of Fonthill' & 'Paintings at Fonthill Abbey', 4 (first advert), 11, 18, 25 (not Library) Sept 1823, 1b, 1c, 1b, 1c; 2 (not Library), 9 (not Library), 16 (only Abbey and Grounds), 23 Oct, 1b, 1b, 1c, 1c. 'Concluding Sale at Fonthill Abbey', 6 Nov, 1d. 'Cellars of Wine at Fonthill Abbey', 6, 13 Nov, 1d, 1c.

Devizes & Wiltshire Gazette. 26 June 1823, 3e; 17, 31 July, 1c, 1d; 14, 28 Aug, 1e, 1c; 4, 11 (4 adverts), 18 (3 adverts), 25 (2 adverts) Sept, 1c, 1c–d & 3a, 1c–d, 1c; 2, 9, 23 Oct, 1c, 1c, 1e; 6 Nov, 1d.

Salisbury and Winchester Journal. 9, 16, June 1823, 4e, 4d. Abbey on view from 16 June. Tickets for viewing, 1 guinea for two people on any two days. 30 June, 1b. Sale on Tue 9 Sept and about following 30 days. Ticket for three people for every day except Sundays and catalogue, 5 guineas. Complete catalogues 12s. First two parts 5s each. Third part 2/6d. 14, 21, 28 July, 4, 11, 18, 25 Aug, 1, 8, 15, ?22, 29 Sept, 6, 13, 20, 27 Oct, 3, 10 Nov (last two: 'concluding sale on 13 Nov'). All 1b except 4 Aug, 4e.

The Times. 'Fonthill Abbey.' All on page 4, date & column letter: 17b June 1823; 11c, 12d, 15b, 17c, 19d, 22c, 24c, 26c, 29e, 31c July; 2d, 5d, 8e, 9b, 12d, 14e × 2 (Property, Library), 16d, 19e × 2 (Prop, Lib), 21e, 23d, 26e × 2 (Prop, Lib), 28c, 31e Aug; 2e × 2 (Prop, Lib), 6e, 8e × 3 (Prop, Lib, Pictures), 11e × 3 (Prop, Lib, Pict), 13c × 4 (Open to public, Prop, Lib, Pict), 15e × 3 (Open, Lib, Pict), 22e × 3 (Open, Lib, Pict), 25d × 3 (Open, Prop, Pict), 29e × 3 (Open, Prop, Pict) Sept; 2d × 2 (Prop, Pict), 6c × 2 (Prop, Pict), 9e × 2 (Prop, Pict), 13c × 2 (Prop, Pict), 20c (Vertu), 21d (Vertu), 27c (Wine), 28d (Wine), 29d (Wine) Oct.

Other Advertisements

Bath and Cheltenham Gazette. W. Dore's coach from Bath to Fonthill on same dates and pages as Phillips adverts up to 16 Sept 1823, and Dore's table d'hôte menu at Abbey, 23, 30 Sept, 7 Oct.

Bath Chronicle. Accommodation, 2 Oct 1823, 3b. Coach trips by W. Dore of Bath to Fonthill, 19, 26 June, 3d, 1b; 17, 24, 31 July, 1e, 1d, 1e; 7, 14, 21, 28 Aug, 1c, 1c, 1d, 1c; 9, 16, 23 Oct, 1b, 1b, 1d.

Salisbury and Winchester Journal. Coaches: Kendal & Richardson, 9, 16, 23 June 1823, 4e, 4d, 4e. James Shrimpton, 'Salisbury & Fonthill Abbey Light Coach' (leaving Red Lion at 8.45 am, arriving at Abbey 10, returning at 7. Return fares: 'Inside 12s; Outside 9s.'), 9 June, 4e, 7 July, 4e, 8 Sept 4e. Joseph White of Salisbury lets out post horses to Fonthill, 8 Sept, 4e. Accommodation: Thomas Harrison, Lamb Inn, Hindon; Wm. Harris, Swan Inn, Hindon; William Shergold, Black Horse, Teffont; John Springford, Bath Arms, Warminster; all 16 June, 4d. Springford, 23 June, 4e. Elizabeth Cross, Boot Inn, Tisbury, 11 Aug, 1b. James Stride, Crown Inn, Hindon, 1 Sept, 1b. Catering: Wm Dore, 30 June, 1b, 28 July 1b. Mr Harrington (of Black Horse Inn, Salisbury) at Fonthill Pavilion, 1, 8 Sept, 4e, 4e.

FALL OF THE TOWER, 1825

Abbey has 'become a ruin'. *New Monthly Magazine* 18 (April 1826): 169.

Abbey 'uninhabited'. *Bath and Cheltenham Gazette*, 24 Jan 1826, 2d. Main windows removed. Also in *New Monthly Magazine* 18 (March 1826): 129.

[Adams, Thomas.] An evocation of the ruinous state of the Abbey by 'T. A. jun.' of Shaftesbury. *Gentleman's Magazine* 96 pt. 1 (May 1826): 424.

Destruction of Abbey. *Salisbury and Winchester Journal*, 23 Jan 1826, 4b. Building uninhabited. £9000 of glass broken. 6 lines. Reprinted in *The Times*, 24 Jan, 2b.

'Fall of Fonthill Tower.' *Bath and Cheltenham Gazette*, 27 Dec 1825, 2b–c. Description of fall, 25 lines. Similar account in *Bath Chronicle*, 29 Dec, 3b.

Fall of Tower expected. *Bath Chronicle*, 26 Jan 1826, 3c. 6 lines.

'Fonthill Abbey.' *Gentleman's Magazine* 95 pt. 2 (Dec 1825): 557.

'Fonthill Abbey.' *Mirror of Literature* 7 (28 Jan 1826): 54–55. ¼ page.

'Fonthill Abbey (from an Evening paper).' *The Times*, 24 Dec 1825, 3f, letter dated 21 Dec from J. F., Fonthill Gifford. 'Fonthill Abbey.' *Idem*, 28 Dec, 4b, reports reprinted from *Salisbury and Winchester Journal* (26 Dec), *Bath Journal* (25 Dec) & *Exeter Gazette*. ¼ column.

[Hoare, Richard Colt.] *Gentleman's Magazine* 96 pt. 1 (Feb 1826): 123.

Salisbury and Winchester Journal, 26 Dec 1825, 4c. 26 lines.

Wiltshire Gazette, 29 Dec 1825, 3b. 17 lines. *Idem*, 12 Jan 1826.

CONTEMPORARY ACCOUNTS AFTER 1823

Books

Britton, John. *The Beauties of Wiltshire.* Vol. 3. London: Longman & J. Britton, 1825. Rooms in Abbey briefly described, 328–331 & sw view. For Vols. 1 & 2 (1801) see Fonthill Splendens, above.

REVIEW. *Literary Gazette* 9 (15 Oct 1825): 657–658 at 657.

Britton, John. *Auto-Biography*. Part 2 & Appendix by T. E. Jones. 8vo. ed. London: Printed for the Author, 1849 & 1850 [?both 1857]. Fonthill, 6, 20–31, 181n, 206, 210–211 & Appendix, [189]. Beckford, 12, 59n. Two engravings from Britton's *Fonthill* (1823): 'View from the Western Avenue', 21 & 'Distant View from s.w.', facing 26. Also a 4to. ed. For Part 1 see '1. Accounts of Beckford's Life'.

REVIEW. [Mitford, John.] *Gentleman's Magazine* n.s. 34 (Dec 1850): 618–622 at 621. Beckford was 'gifted with great and various talents'.

Britton, John. *The History and Description, with Graphic Illustrations, of Cassiobury Park, Hertfordshire*. London: The Author, 1837. Footnote, 5.

Cobbett, William. *Rural Rides*. Ed. G. D. H. & Margaret Cole. 3 vols. London: Peter Davies, 1930. (1st ed. 1830, reprinted by his son, James Paul Cobbett with material omitted from that ed., 1853. Originally publ. from 1821 in the weekly *Political Register*.) Liked Highclere better than Fonthill, Blenheim & Stowe, 2 Nov 1821, 1:5. (*Pol. Reg.*, Nov 1821. Not in 1st ed. In first reprint, 1853.) Scathing remarks about Beckford and Fonthill Abbey prompted by a visit to Bowood on 5 Sept 1826, 2:406. (*Pol. Reg.*, Sept 1826.) Beckford in 'Index of Persons', 3:945–946. 'Singular' appearance of Mr May's house at Hadlow, 6 Sept 1823, 1:239. (*Pol. Reg.*, Sept 1823.)

Deacon, William Frederick. *Warreniana*. London: Longman, etc., 1824. Ostensibly endorsing Warren's blacking but really parodying contemporary writers. 'Fonthill fever.' mentioned in 'Annus Mirabilis' chapter, 116.

Goldsmith, Rev. J. [Sir Richard Phillips, pseud.] 'Fonthill Abbey.' In *The Natural and Artificial Wonders of the United Kingdom*, 2:321–326. 3 vols. London: G. B. Whittaker, 1825. Copied from Storer (1812), 2–5, 6, 7–8, 8–9. West view copied from Whittaker's *A New Guide to Fonthill Abbey* (1822).

Markham, Violet. *Paxton and the Bachelor Duke*. London: Hodder & Stoughton, 1935. Paxton's letter to his wife on seeing the ruined Abbey with the Duke of Devonshire in Dec 1835, 51–52. Also noted in Kate Colquhoun, *A Thing in Disguise: The Visionary Life of Joseph Paxton*, London: 4th Estate, 2003, 65.

Mogg, Edward. *Paterson's Roads; Being an Entirely Original and Accurate Description of all the Direct and Principal Cross Roads in England and Wales, with Part of the Roads of Scotland*. 17th ed. London: Longman, 1824. 'Fonthill Abbey, the superb seat of Wm. Beckford, Esq', 79.

Olivier, Edith. 'Mrs. Alfred Morrison.' In *Four Victorian Ladies of Wiltshire*, 45–72 at 46–47. London: Faber & Faber, 1945. Her husband Alfred saw Beckford on his last visit to Fonthill, c.1843. Reprinted by Semley Publishers, 1996.

Papworth, Wyatt. *J. B. Papworth, Architect to the King of Wurtemburg*. London: Privately printed, 1879. The Morrisons, 79–82. Letter to ?his wife in 1829 or 1830 about the ruinous state of the Abbey, 138–139.

Peniston, John. *The Letters of John Peniston, Salisbury Architect, Catholic, and Yeomanry Officer 1823–1830*. Vol. 50 for the year 1994. Ed. Michael Cowan. Trowbridge: Wiltshire Record Society, 1996. Brief letters on disposal of materials from the ruins of the Abbey, x, 57, 72, 76–77, 78, 82, 87, 89, 91, 92, 96, 97, 104, 105, 149. Peniston was acting for John Benett of Pythouse.

Townsend, Leonard. 'Fonthill Abbey.' In *An Alphabetical Chronology of Remarkable Events . . .*, 41. London: Tallis. *c.*1836. 12 lines.

Articles

d'Andrade, Mme C. 'L'abbaye de Fonthill.' *L'abeille* 2e année (1840), 250.

'A Day at Fonthill Abbey.' *Waldie's Select Circulating Library* (Philadelphia) 9 (1834). Followed by a series of letters by Beckford.

Earl Grosvenor. *Bath and Cheltenham Gazette*, 28 Feb 1826, 2c. Bought a large portion of Fonthill estate.

Estate sold by Farquhar to John Benett. *The Times*, 2 Jan 1826, 2d, and *Bath and Cheltenham Gazette*, 3 Jan, 2c. 8 lines.

Mr. Farquharson. [Farquhar.] *Bath and Cheltenham Gazette*, 31 Jan 1826, 2b. Has disposed of Abbey and interest in the Borough of Hindon.

'Fonthill Abbey, South East View.' *Mirror of Literature* 8 (15 July 1826): 25–26, account of Abbey & woodcut after Higham's sketch in Britton (1823).

Giles, John Allen. 'Diary and Memoirs of John Allen Giles.' *Somerset Record Society* 86 (2000): 41–42. Ed. David Bromwich. Visit to Fonthill as a boy, probably in 1822 or 1823, including five ascents of the tower.

Kempson, E. G. H. 'William Crowe.' *Wiltshire Archaeological and Natural History Magazine* 67 (1972): 165. On a walk, Crowe (1745–1829) noticed the absence of Fonthill's tower 'one day just before Christmas 1825'.

Le Fanu, Sheridan, ed. 'Exclusive Intelligence. Reminiscences of an Elderly Member of the Fourth Estate. Fonthill Abbey.' *Dublin University Magazine* 76 (Aug 1870): 196–199.

'Memoranda of the Origin and Progress of Fonthill Abbey.' *Bath Chronicle*, 9 May 1844, 3e–f. Contains an extract from the *Morning Herald*, 20 Dec 1824.

Repairs and Demolition. Public excluded owing to alterations at Abbey, *The Builder* 4 (2 May 1846): 213. Removal of Abbey remains and plans for a new building on the site, *Idem* 4 (14 Nov 1846): 551.

Sarisburiensis. 'Fonthill's Warning.' *The Crypt, or Receptacle for Things Past* 1 no. 5 (24 Oct 1827): 113–117. Letter dated 8 Oct pointing out defects at the Abbey, particularly the central tower.

Storm damage. *The Times*, 3 Dec 1824, 2c.

[Tymms, Samuel.] 'Compendium of County History. –Wiltshire.' *Gentleman's*

Magazine 95 pt. 2 (July 1825): 32–36 at 35. *Idem*, (Oct 1825): 321–324 at 321. The 'beauties of Fonthill'.

Woollen Mill

Darton, Eric. 'Fonthill: John Farquhar and After.' *Beckford Tower Trust Newsletter*, Spring 1987, 6–7. George Mortimer's cloth mill.

Farquhar lays foundation stone. *The Times*, 9 Oct 1824, 2b.

'Fonthill.' *Bath and Cheltenham Gazette*, 10 Oct 1826, 2c–d. Manufactory recently erected by Mortimer, nephew of Farquhar. 41 lines. From *Courier*.

Manufactory finished by Mortimer. *The Times*, 18 Oct 1827, 3c. 'The Abbey still remains in a state of ruin, but the natural beauties of the situation will always command the attention of travellers.' (from *World*.) Reprinted in *The Crypt, or Receptacle for Things Past* 1 no. 9 (19 Dec 1827): 220. Abridged reprint in 'Domestic Occurrences. Intelligence from various parts of the country', *Gentleman's Magazine* 97 pt. 2 (Oct 1827): 362.

Mill to be let. *Salisbury and Winchester Journal*, 8 June 1829. Advert.

Rogers, K. H. *Wiltshire and Somerset Woollen Mills*. Edington, Wilts: Pasold Research Fund, 1976. Mill near Fonthill lake to be run by Farquhar's nephew, George Mortimer, 251–252.

Sale of mill. *Devizes and Wiltshire Gazette*, 16 April 1829. Advert.

Willoughby, R. W. H. 'Water-Mills in West Wiltshire.' *Wiltshire Archaeological and Natural History Magazine* 64 (1969): 71–99 at 81 & nn44–48.

LATER ACCOUNTS – GENERAL

See also '16. Works influenced by Beckford. Dramatisations & Events'

Full-length Study

Gemmett, Robert J. *Beckford's Fonthill: The Rise of a Romantic Icon*. Norwich: Michael Russell, 2003. 473 pp. 30 pl. With two appendices: 'Contemporary Essays and Commentary on Fonthill 1797–1844', 211–381; 'Contemporary Verse Inspired by Fonthill 1800–1829', 385–430. 'A Fonthill Bibliography', 433–463.

REVIEWS. Hobson, Anthony. 'The pleasure dome in Wiltshire.' *Spectator*, 10 Jan 2004, 36.

Mowl, Timothy. *Country Life*, 23 Oct 2003, 93.

Wilton-Ely, John. 'A Mind of Fire.' *Beckford Journal* 10 (2004): 71–79.

Books

Barr, John. *Britain Portrayed: Colour-plate books and topographical illustration 1790–1840*. London: British Library, 1989. P. 88. Havell's 1823 aquatint, 89.

Blunt, Wilfred. *The Dream King. Ludwig II of Bavaria*. London: Hamish Hamilton, 1970. Comparison with Beckford & 'Interior of the Great Western Hall' from Rutter (1823), 215.

Boase, T. S. R. *English Art 1800–1870*. Oxford: Clarendon Press, 1959. 'Medievalism reached its climax in the building of Fonthill abbey', 22, 25–28. Plan of Abbey, 27. SW view of Abbey by Higham, pl. 12a.

Brewer, John. *The Pleasures of the Imagination. English Culture in the Eighteenth Century*. London: HarperCollins, 1997. Libertine followers of Beckford, 43. Abbey 'could be visited daily between twelve and four', 221.

Brode, Anthony. 'The South Country.' In *The Shell Book of English Villages*, ed. Miles Hadfield. London: Michael Joseph, 1980. 'Fonthill Gifford', 159.

Burton, Anthony. *The Shell Book of Curious Britain*. Newton Abbot: David & Charles, 1982. 'William Beckford installed a hermit in a fully furnished cave above the lake at Fonthill in Wiltshire', 76.

Burton, Elizabeth. *The Early Victorians at Home*. London: Longman, 1972. Fonthill in chapter on buildings, 55–57.

Byron, Robert, ed. 'Fonthill Gifford.' In *Shell Guide to Wiltshire*, 48–49. London: Architectural Press, 1935. Distant SW view from Britton (1823), title page. Fonthill arch, with photo, 26. Fonthill Park, 42. New ed. rev. by David Verey, 'Fonthill Gifford', 40–41. London: Faber & Faber, 1956. Distant SW view from Britton (1823), title page. Fonthill arch, 20, & photo, 40. 'Fonthill Bishop', 40. Fonthill Park, 28. 3rd ed., J. H. Cheetham & John Piper, Fonthill Gifford, 99–100. *Idem*, 1968. Fonthill Park, 29. Bishop's Fonthill, 64, 66.

Chandler, John. *The Prospect of Wiltshire*. Bradford-on-Avon: Ex Libris Press, 1995. 'Fonthill Lake', colour photo, 103.

Channer, Nick. *Pub Walks in Wiltshire*. Newbury, Berks: Countryside Books, 1993. '23. Fonthill Bishop. The King's Arms', 97–100 at 100. Area map, 99.

Charlesworth, Michael. 'The Ruined Abbey: Picturesque and Gothic Values.' In *The Politics of the Picturesque: Literature, landscape and aesthetics since 1770*, ed. Stephen Copley & Peter Garside, 62–80 at 75. Cambridge: Cambridge University Press, 1994.

Clarke, Stephen. 'The Ruin Of Fonthill: The Reputation And Influence Of Beckford's Abbey.' In *William Beckford and the New Millennium*, ed. Kenneth W. Graham & Kevin Berland, 181–203 & 9 illus. New York: AMS Press, 2004 [2005].

Conrad, Peter. *Shandyism. The Character of Romantic Irony*. Oxford: Blackwell, 1978. Abbey, 35–36, 37, 39–43, 46 & 48 n12. De Quincey's criticism of *Vathek*, 57 & 69 n4.

Crosland, Margaret, ed. *A Traveller's Guide to Literary Europe. Vol. II*.

Great Britain and Ireland. London: Hugh Evelyn, 1966. Bath, 11. Fonthill: 'You will not regret dodging lodge-keepers and exploring the vast park in the depths of which William Beckford lived alone in his jerry-built palace.', 24.

Drury, Jill & Peter. *A Tisbury History*. London: Element Books, 1980. Pp. 53–54, 57–59, 60. Painting of Fonthill Arch, 56.

Dunning, Alfred. 'The Fantastic Builder.' In *Some Curious Characters*, 38–49. London: Blackie, [1948]. Fanciful illus. of Abbey tower falling, 43. John Mytton & Charles Waterton were two of the other fifteen characters.

Dutton, Ralph. *The English Country House*. 3rd ed. London: Batsford, 1949. (1st ed. 1935.) General account of Fonthill Abbey, 88–89.

Dutton, Ralph. *Wessex. Dorset, Wiltshire, Hampshire* ... London: Batsford, 1950. Fonthill Park, 90–91. SW view of Abbey after J. C. Buckler (1822), pl. 87. Nelson's arch, pl. 88. Watercolour of Splendens by Buckler (1806), pl. 89.

Favret, Mary A. 'A Home for Art.' In *At the Limits of Romanticism. Essays in Cultural, Feminist and Materialist Criticism*, ed. Mary A. Favret & Nicola J. Watson, 59–82 at 79 n5. Bloomington: Indiana University Press, 1994. Abbey converted from 'living-space to showplace'.

Felmingham, Michael & Rigby Graham. *Ruins: A Personal Anthology*. London: Country Life, 1972. Abbey, 72, 74. Mentioned, 96, 97.

Fergusson, James. *History of the Modern Styles of Architecture*. London: John Murray, 1862. Pp. 314–316, with SW view, 315.

Finn, R. W. *Wiltshire*. London: Knopf, 1930. Borzoi County Histories.

'Fonthill Abbey.' In *Sober Truth*, compiled by Margaret Barton & Osbert Sitwell, 83–88. London: Duckworth, 1930. Extracts from *Gentleman's Magazine* obituary (1844), Redding's *Memoirs* (1859) & Timbs's *English Eccentrics* (1875). Reprinted, London: Macdonald, 1944. Most of the *Gentleman's Magazine* extract reprinted in the *Sunday Express*, 29 Aug 1943, 2.

Ford, Charles Bradley. 'A Note on Follies.' In Edmund Vale, *Curiosities of Town and Countryside*, 140–148 at 142, 146. London: Batsford, 1940. Fonthill, 142, with Eric Fraser's woodcut for *Radio Times* (1940), 146. Beckford's Tower: colour frontis. from English (1844) & photo, pl. 75 (facing p. 128), both inserted at the publisher's request but not mentioned in the text.

Foster, Richard. *Discovering English Churches*. London: British Broadcasting Corporation, 1981. Pp. 238–239. South view from Rutter (1823), 240.

Fraser, John Lloyd. *John Constable 1776–1837. The Man and his Mistress*. London: Hutchinson, 1976. At Fonthill in 1823, 131.

Grigson, Geoffrey. *Before the Romantics. An Anthology of the Enlightenment*. London: Routledge, 1946. 'Babel tower of Fonthill Abbey', vii.

Grigson, Geoffrey. *Wessex*. London: Collins, for the Festival of Britain

Office, 1951. Maligned genius, 48. Beckford's old domain, 79. Fonthill lake, 84. About Britain No. 2.

Grigson, Geoffrey. *The Wiltshire Book*. London: Thames & Hudson, 1957. A fragment of the Abbey, a 'portion of the cloisters', with photo, 81.

Hadfield, Miles, ed. *The Shell Guide to England*. London: Michael Joseph, 1970. 'Fonthill', 258–259.

Headley, Gwyn & Wim Meulenkamp. *Follies*. London: Jonathan Cape, 1986. Fonthill, 71–74 & pl. 43 (photo of remains), 44 (1823 admission ticket). Also 68, 69, 301, 521. Beckford's Tower, 31, 505. Beckford's protégé Goodridge, 51, 66. Hadlow, 105 & pl. 47. Charlecote Park, 327. Rev. ed., 1990. New ed., *Follies Grottoes & Garden Buildings*, London: Aurum, 1999. 'Lansdown (Avon). Lansdown Tower', 448–449. 'Fonthill Gifford. The Remains of Fonthill Abbey', 529–531. Both illus.

Heath, Frank R. 'Fonthill Abbey.' In *The Little Guides*. Wiltshire, 105–109. 7th ed., rev. by R. L. P. Jowitt. London: Methuen, 1949. (1st ed. 1911.) 'Fonthill Gifford', 109. Berwick St. Leonard, 52. Beckford, 31.

Herbert, Jane. *We Wander in Wessex*. London: Ward Lock, 1947. Fonthill Gateway with photo, 79, 81.

Hutton, Edward. *Highways and Byways in Wiltshire*. London: Macmillan, 1917. Fonthill, 187–191, with a drawing of Fonthill Arch by Nelly Erichsen, 188.

Jackson, Anna with Morna Hinton. *The V&A Guide to Period Styles: 400 Years of British Art and Design*. London: V&A Publications, 2002. Fonthill Abbey, 81.

Jaeger, Muriel. *Before Victoria*. London: Chatto & Windus, 1956. 'Beckford outdid Horace Walpole in fantastic architecture', 74.

Jenner, Michael. *A Traveller's Companion to the West Country*. London: Michael Joseph, 1990. Life at Fonthill, 168. Beckford, 169.

Jones, Sidney R. *England: South*. London: Studio Publ., 1950. Brief survey, 174.

Mais, S. P. B. *See England First*. London: Richards Press, 1927. General account, 286–287.

Michael, W., publ. 'History of Fonthill Abbey.' In *Important Spots in Wiltshire*. Westbury, Wilts: W. Michael, c.1880. 8 pp. Another ed., c.1886. Reissued as *Historic Spots in Wiltshire* [1901], but without Fonthill Abbey.

Millington, Jon. 'Fonthill Abbey in 1822 and 1823.' In his *Souvenirs of Fonthill Abbey*, 7–8. Bath: Bath Preservation Trust, 1994. Exhibition catalogue.

Morley, John. 'Beckford of Fonthill.' In *Regency Design 1790–1840*, 311–315 & pl. LXXXIX (p. 300). London: Zwemmer, 1993. Also 'Renaissance revival', on Beckford's Tower, 278–281 & pl. XXX, LXXVII, LXXVIII, CXXV (on pp. 96, 266, 266, 400). Noted in Jon Millington, *Beckford Tower Trust Newsletter*, Spring 1994, 3.

Murray, John. *A Handbook for Travellers in Wiltshire, Dorsetshire and Somersetshire*. 2nd ed. London: John Murray, 1859. (1st ed. 1856.) Fonthill, 86–88. Lansdown Crescent and Beckford's Tower, 168.

Nightingale, James E. *Objects of Interest in the Fonthill Excursion. A Paper read at the Seventeenth Annual Meeting of the Wiltshire Archæological and Natural History Society, at Wilton [14–16 Sept]*. Salisbury, Wilts: For private distribution, 1870. 25 pp. Notes for a proposed visit, with map, 15–24. Visit took place on 15 Sept 1870 when the Morrisons' porcelain and china at Fonthill Pavilion were seen.

REPORT. 'The Vale of Wardour Excursion.' *Wiltshire Archæological and Natural History Magazine* 13 (1872): 11, 21–22.

Olivier, Edith. *Wiltshire*. London: Robert Hale, 1951. Fonthill, 296–304.

Pevsner, Nikolaus. *Some Architectural Writers of the Nineteenth Century*. Oxford: Clarendon Press, 1972. Walpole & Fonthill, 9. SW view by Neale (1824), pl. 5.

Pythouse guide books. Kingdon, George. *A Guide to Pythouse and the Ben(n)etts of Pythouse*. 5th ed. N. p.: Privately printed, 1968. Benett bought part of Abbey estate, 26. Eyre, John. 'John Benett and Fonthill Abbey.' In *Pythouse and the Benetts*. 21–22. Banbury: Country Houses Association, 2002. Abbey estate bought by Benett in 1826 and sold by him to Earl Grosvenor in 1844. Buckler's litho of Abbey ruins (1825 [1826]) illus. Also 13, 23, 24.

Reader's Digest. 'The Folly of Riches.' In *Strange Stories. Amazing Facts*, 496–497 & SW view from Rutter (1823). London: Reader's Digest, 1975.

Rippon, Angela, foreword. *The Hidden Places of Gloucestershire & Wiltshire*. Plymouth: M & M Publishing, 1991. Fonthill Bishop & Fonthill Gifford, 51.

Robertson, Martin. *Exploring England's Heritage. Dorset to Gloucestershire*. London: HMSO, 1992. Remaining Abbey fragment, 59. Landscape still memorable, 60. Grottoes by Fonthill Lake, 61. Beckford's Tower, 65.

Sandell, Joseph. 'The Fonthill Collection.' In *Memoranda of Art and Artists, Anecdotal and Biographical*, 130–132. London: Simpkin, Marshall, 1871. A popular account of the Abbey.

Sebba, Anne. *The Exiled Collector: William Bankes and the Making of an English Country House*. London: John Murray, 2004. Bankes's fondness for the Gothic was influenced by Beckford, 31–32. Surreptitious visit to Fonthill in 1811, 47–48. For his letter describing this visit see William Bankes in 'Contemporary Accounts before 1822', above.

Simpson, Duncan, intro. *Gothick 1720–1840*. Brighton: Royal Pavilion, Art Gallery & Museums, 1975. Pp. 7, 8, 12, 15, 16 & pl. 19, 20. Exhibits: 'Fonthill Abbey': C92–101. Also A23, E1, 19, 58, 60, F32–34, K10, 15, 16.

Sproule, Anna. *Lost Houses of Britain*. Newton Abbot, Devon: David & Charles, 1982. Abbey was third of five lost Fonthills, 17. Beckford visited

Nelson in 1805, 203. Marble chimneypiece now at Clumber House, 101. Abbey compared to Deepdene, 104. Thomas Hope & William Atkinson's influence on Beckford's Bath buildings, 105–106. Hamilton Palace, 165–174. Also 10, 13, 71.

Steegman, John. 'Strawberry Hill and Fonthill.' In *The Rule of Taste from George I to George IV*, 71–92 at 79, 83–85 & S view from Rutter (1823). London: Macmillan, 1936. Beckford 'a product of the romantic movement'. Also 141.

Stratford, Joseph. *Wiltshire and Its Worthies*. Salisbury, Wilts: Brown, 1882. Beckford & his father, 76–77.

Street, Pamela. *The Illustrated Portrait of Wiltshire*. London: Hale, 1986. Fonthill Abbey, 78–79. Originally publ. in 1971 as *Portrait of Wiltshire*.

Tannahill, Reay. *Regency England: The Great Age of the Colour Print*. London: Folio Society, 1964. Havell's 1823 aquatint of Abbey from the south, pl. 12.

Temple, Gustav & Vic Darkwood. *The Chap Almanac: An Esoterick Yearbook for the Decadent Gentleman*. London: Fourth Estate, 2002. The Abbey ruins fulfilled Beckford's initial plan for a convent in the woods, 62–64.

Thompson F. M. L. *English Landed Society in the Nineteenth Century*. London: Routledge & Kegan Paul, 1963. Abbey may have cost £400,000, 88–89.

Thurley, Simon. 'Fonthill Abbey. Gothic Dream or Gothic Nightmare?' In *Lost Buildings of Britain*, 41–74 incl. 10 pl. London: Viking, 2004. Publ. to accompany a Channel 4 television series. Also colour pl. 2–5, Intro., xviii, xix and 'Further Reading', 210. Plan of the Principal Storey (detail), front endpaper. Other chapters on Whitehall Palace, Theatre Royal Drury Lane, Nottingham Castle, Millbank Penitentiary and Glastonbury Abbey. REVIEWS of Fonthill Abbey programme (shown on 16 Aug 2004 at 8 pm):

  Cork, Richard. 'Arts on TV: Culture Club.' *New Statesman*, 30 Aug, 30–32 at 31.

  Delingpole, James. 'The pity of war.' *Spectator*, 21 Aug, 42, 44.

  Woodward, Antony. 'Television.' *Country Life*, 19 Aug, 83.

Tibballs, Geoff. 'Fonthill Abbey – A Supreme Folly.' In *Business Blunders*, 52–53. London: Robinson, 1999. The successive falls of the central tower.

Timbs, John. *Abbeys, Castles and Ancient Halls of England and Wales*. 2nd ed. revised by A. Gunn. 3 vols. London: F. Warne, 1872. (1st ed. 1870.) Interesting account of Fonthill & Abbey, 2:8–11.

Watkin, Bruce. *A History of Wiltshire*. Chichester: Phillimore, 1989. Splendens, 80. 1764 map of Georgian houses, 89. Cuts of interior and exterior of Octagon, 84. 'Mock-Gothic' abbey, 90. Also 49.

Watson, Nicola J. 'Unit 31. The Royal Pavilion at Brighton.' In *From Enlightenment to Romanticism. c.1780–1830. Block 7: The Exotic and the Oriental*, 25, 27. Milton Keynes: Open University, 2004. Also *Vathek*, 17, 53.

Watts, Ken. *Exploring Historic Wiltshire. Volume 2: South*. East Knoyle, Wiltshire: Hobnob Press, 1998. Brief account of Beckford, with photos of Fonthill Arch, and Lake, 89.

White, T. H. *The Age of Scandal*. London: Jonathan Cape, 1950. 'Beckford's nightmare abbey', 157. Reprinted, Penguin Books, 1962, 137.

Whitelaw, Jeffery W. *Follies*. Aylesbury, Bucks: Shire, 1982. Photo of Tower, 4. Gazetteer: Tower, 19; Fonthill Gifford, 32.

Whitlock, Ralph. *Wiltshire*. London: Paul Elek, 1949. Two paragraphs on Beckford and the Abbey, 42. Vision of England Series.

Williamson, Barry. *Lord Arundell's Park at Wardour*. Bristol: The Author, 1997. In contrast to Fonthill, visitors were welcome at Wardour, 6. Grottoes, 22. Examples of the fashion for American Gardens at Wardour and Fonthill, 27.

Wilson, Margaret. *Touring Guide to Wiltshire Villages*. Rev. ed. Bradford-on-Avon: Ex Libris Press, 1991. (1st ed. 1987.) Abbey, 89. Area map, 90.

Winn, Christopher. 'Fonthill Abbey. He flew too high.' In *I Never Knew That About England*, 246–247. London: Ebury Press, 2005. Line drawing from SW.

Worth, R. N. *Tourist's Guide to Wiltshire*. London: Stanford, 1887. Pp. 48–49.

Ziolkowski, Theodore. *The View from the Tower: Origins of an Antimodernist Image*. Princeton: Princeton University Press, 1998. Fonthill's tower as an image of contemplation, 25 & 176 n28.

Articles

Alexander, Boyd. 'Fonthill, Wiltshire II – The Abbey and its Creator.' *Country Life*, 1 Dec 1966, 1430–1434. For Part I: Splendens, see Harris, above, and for Part III see Alexander in '8. The Collection'.

Ashworth, Katharine. 'Tisbury's Ancient Secrets.' *Country Life*, 4 Nov 1954, 1590, 1592. Beckford, 'that misguided genius'. Photo of Abbey remains.

Barnes, Max. 'a–z of West Ways. Fonthill Gifford.' *[Bristol] Evening Post*, 5 July 1971, 25. *a–z of West Ways* was reprinted as a booklet.

Barnes, Max. 'Follies. A dream in ruins.' *[Bristol] Evening Post*, 1 Aug 1978, 4.

Blake, Steven. 'William Beckford and Fonthill Abbey: A Victorian Showman's Account.' *Bath History* 9 (2002): 126–137. Ed. Brenda J. Buchanan. Cork model of Abbey made 1834–1836 and exhibited nationally with other models.

Blunt, Anthony. 'Fonthill Abbey.' *The Venture* No. 2 (Feb 1929): 75–81. Long quotation about the Abbey in an untraced work: Birlbeck, *Account of the Recent Architectural Embellishments of the Environs of Salisbury*,

1819. Noted in Jon Millington, 'Anthony Blunt's "Fonthill Abbey" ', *Beckford Tower Trust Newsletter*, Spring 1993, 16.

'Britton versus Rutter. A Battle of the Books. Unpublished letters of 1822–3.' *Wiltshire Gazette*, 24 Jan 1924, 3a–c. Letters in the library of Wiltshire Archæological and Natural History Society, Devizes, from Britton to Franchi, W. L. Bowles, Benjamin Hobhouse & Richard Colt Hoare. *Idem*, 31 Jan, 3c–d. Letters to Britton from W. Hatcher, John Broadley, Beckford (seven letters 1813–c.1840), Thomas Adams, Jr (a Shaftesbury printer intending to produce a priced cat. of the Abbey sale). Draft of letter from Britton to G. F. Beltz. Noted in *Wiltshire Archæological and Natural History Magazine* 42 (June 1924): 525.

'Building Fonthill Abbey.' *Bath and County Graphic* 8 no. 1 (May 1903): 11–12.

Butler, David B. 'Visitors to Fonthill.' *Country Life*, 3 Jan 1957, 25. Letter with illus. of entrance ticket and view of Abbey from Rutter's *New Guide* (1823).

Butterfield, Rev. C. E. 'The Fonthill Fever.' *The Times*, 24 Sept 1925, 8d. Letter quoting Hazlitt's unfavourable opinion of some lots in Phillips's sale of 1823.

Clarke, Stephen. 'Abbeys Real and Imagined: Northanger, Fonthill, and Aspects of the Gothic Revival.' *Persuasions* (Journal of the Jane Austen Society of North America) No. 20 (1998): 92–105 at 92, 93, 97–98, 102–105.

Clarke, Stephen. 'The Troubled Gestation of Britton's *Illustrations of Fonthill*.' *Beckford Journal* 6 (2000): 58–74. Britton's work compared with Rutter's.

Craft, Adrian. 'Subterranean Enlightenment at Fonthill.' *Beckford Journal* 3 (1997): 30–33. Beckford's fascination with the underworld.

'Curiosities of Early Art Sales.' *Chambers' Journal* 5th series 13 (26 Sept 1896): 621. Difficulty of finding accommodation while visiting the 1823 Fonthill sale. Reprinted in *Littell's Living Age* 211 (5 Dec 1896): 663.

Dobson, Roger. 'Living in a delusion of grandeur.' *Weekend Telegraph*, 1 April 1995, 13. Living in the Abbey today.

Esdaile, Edmund. 'Memento of Fonthill.' *Country Life*, 25 April 1968, 1050. Letter about entrance ticked to 1823 sale, with photo.

Excursion to Fonthill, Knoyle and Wardour. *Wiltshire Archæological and Natural History Magazine* 22 (1885): 142–145 at 143.

'The Fall of Fonthill Abbey Tower.' *Wiltshire Gazette*, 29 Nov 1923, 3a–b. Contemporary accounts. For 'Fonthill Abbey. The Estate, and the Successive Mansions' see above under 'General Accounts'. 'County Notes . . . Fonthill Abbey.' *Idem*, 8 Nov 1923, 5b. Notes heralding above two articles, prompted by a letter about the fall of the Tower from A. H. Wallace, 7f. (See also 'Fall of the Tower, 1825', above.)

Fisher, Michael. 'In the Shadow of Fonthill – Pugin's Early Years at Alton Towers.' *True Principles* (Pugin Society) 2 no. 1 (Winter 2000): 7–9. Resemblance between King Edward's Gallery at Fonthill and the Talbot Gallery at Alton.

Fitch, James Marston. 'Avant-Garde or Blind Alley?' *Horizon* 4 no. 4 (March 1962): 30–39 at 36. Gret Western Hall from Rutter (1823) illus.

'Fonthill Abbey.' *Scientific American*, 29 July 1893, 75. Half page on Beckford and building the Abbey, with John Martin's NW view from Rutter (1823).

'The Fonthill Abbey Sales of 100 Years Ago. William Beckford's extravagance and folly.' *Wiltshire Gazette*, 30 Aug, 3b–d; 6, 20, 27 Sept, 3c–e, 3a–c, 3a–b; 4, 11, 18, 25 Oct, 3a–b; 1 Nov 1923, 4a–b. Reprinted from the contemporary *Devizes Gazette*. 'The Great Fonthill Sale . . . Story to be Re-Told.' *Wiltshire Gazette*, 30 Aug 1923, 3a. Announcing the above articles. Noted in *Wiltshire Archæological and Natural History Magazine* 42 (June 1924): 523–524.

Fonthill Sales of 1822 and 1823. *Wiltshire Gazette*, 24 Sept 1925.

Gemmett, Robert J. 'The Critical Reception of William Beckford's Fonthill.' *English Miscellany* 19 (1968): 133–151 & S view from Neale (1824).

Gemmett, Robert J. "Fonthill and its Abbey: 'The Haunt of Eager Curiosity'." *Beckford Journal* 10 (2004): 30–45. Prominent visitors to 1823 sale.

Girard, Didier. 'William Beckford's Nostalgic Visions.' *Beckford Tower Trust Newsletter*, Spring 1988, 8–9. An extract from Girard's study of Beckford presented to the Beckford Tower Trust. One of seven copies of his typescript.

Godfrey, Alan. *Old Ordnance Survey Maps. Tisbury 1900*. Newcastle upon Tyne: Alan Godfrey, 1995. Includes southern part of Fonthill Lake and three-page account of Tisbury mentioning the Abbey, 'Beckford's Folly'.

Grigson, Geoffrey. 'The Demolishers at Work.' *Country Life*, 28 Jan 1960, 158–159 at 158. Paragraph on Fonthill Abbey with SW view from Britton (1823).

Hatchwell, Richard. 'The Life and Work of John Britton (1771–1857).' *Wiltshire Archaeological and Natural History Magazine* 85 (1992): 101–113 at 110. Britton's writings on Fonthill Splendens and the Abbey.

Hennessy, Alistair. 'Penrhyn Castle.' *History Today* 45 (Jan 1995): 40–45. Beckford fleeced by the Wildman Brothers, 41. 'Fonthill Abbey, the most daring imaginative and preposterous building of the Gothic Revival' & Danby's SW view, 42.

Herrick, George R. 'Fabulous Fonthill.' *College Art Journal* 12 (1953): 128–131. A general introductory article.

Jones, Margaret. 'Nelson at Fonthill.' *Country Life*, 28 Feb 1957, 389. Letter with illus. of Nelson's Arch from *Gentleman's Magazine* (April 1801).

Kite, Edward. *Devizes and Wiltshire Gazette*, 16, 23 April 1903.

Kite, Edward. 'Fonthill and the Beckfords.' *Wiltshire Advertiser*, 30 Sept, 7 Oct, 21 Oct 1909. Noted in *Wiltshire Archæological and Natural History Magazine* 36 (Dec 1909): 352.

"Lavish Feast of Fonthill 'Dream Palace'." *Bath & Wilts Chronicle & Herald*, 23 Dec 1949, 3b–d. Woodcut of 'Fonthill Abbey' from the SW heading Sul's 'Day by Day' diary, 5. Woodcut repeated 15 Sept 1950, 5.

'The Leverhulme Collection. "The Fonthill Fever.".' *The Times*, 22 Sept 1925, 12d. Collection withdrawn from sale in London for auction in New York compared with the cancelled Christie's sale of 1822.

Lewis, W. G. J. 'Follies at Fonthill.' *Country Life*, 14 March 1957, 485–486. Letter mentioning hermit's cave.

Longbourne, David. 'William Beckford and Fonthill Abbey.' *The Hatcher Review* (Salisbury) no. 7 (Spring / Summer 1979): 29–41. A general account.

Longford, Elizabeth. 'The Duke of Wellington's Search for a Palace.' *Horizon* 11 no. 2 (Spring 1969): 106–113 at 112, 113 & 106, SW view from Storer (1812).

Meehan, J. F. 'Famous Buildings of Bath and District. No. 31. Fonthill Abbey: the Wiltshire Residence of William Beckford.' *The Beacon* (Frome, Somerset) 3 no. 8 (Aug 1900): 127–128. Reprinted in his *Famous Houses of Bath and District*, Bath: B. & J. F. Meehan, 1901, 153–156 & pl. Noted in *Wiltshire Archæological and Natural History Magazine* 32 (June 1902): 250.

Norton, Rictor. 'A Visit to Fonthill.' *Gay News* 133 (Christmas 1977): 32–33. An illustrated article which includes a visit to Beckford's Tower.

'Picturesque Wiltshire. No. XXI. Fonthill.' *Wiltshire Times*, 15 May 1909, 12d–e. Popular account of Abbey and Beckford.

Rawlence, Guy. 'The Beckford Sale at Fonthill Abbey.' *The Field*, 5 Jan 1946, 15. Photo of frontis. of Phillips's 1823 catalogue.

Rushton, Andrée. 'The Fonthill Barrier.' *Beckford Journal* 4 (1998): 65–70. Includes a plan of Beckford's 4½ mile-long wall.

Scott, John. 'The Rise and Fall of Fonthill Abbey.' *British History Illustrated* (Gettysburg, PA) 2 no. 3 (Aug 1975): 2–11. Well-illus. general account.

Scott, T. G. 'Fonthill Buildings.' *Country Life*, 24 Jan 1957, 157. Letter with five illus. from Storer's account in *The Port-Folio* (1823).

Simpson-White, R. 'Visiting Fonthill.' *Country Life*, 10 Jan 1957, 67. Letter quoting John Timbs, *English Eccentrics and Eccentricities* (1875).

Skoggard, Carl. 'William Beckford, Fonthill Abbey.' *Nest* (New York) 4 (Spring 1999): 25–35. Captions and scholarly advice from Philip Hewat-Jaboor. Three watercolours by Margitta Zachert based on views from Rutter's *Delineations* (1823).

Southwick, Albert P. 'Alexander Dumas Pere.' *Galaxy* (New York) 10 (Nov

1870): 691–697 at 695–696. 'Dumas resolved, like the English Beckford, to erect a building which should be a realized romance'.

Spofford, Harriet P. 'Mediæval Furniture.' *Harper's New Monthly Magazine* 53 (Aug 1876): 809–829 at 809. '. . . it was only when Fonthill was thrown open to the public that a new departure was taken, profound study was given to Gothic art, and a flood of light thrown upon the dark places of mediæval life.'

Stamp, Gavin & André Goulancourt. *The English House 1860–1914.* London: Faber & Faber, 1986. Pp. 22, 23.

Strong, Roy, 'Collapsed. Fonthill: Beckford's Grand Folly.' *Sunday Times Magazine*, 19 Nov 1989, 70–72. Noted in Jon Millington, 'Sir Roy Strong's Fonthill', *Beckford Tower Trust Newsletter*, Spring 1990, 3. Revised reprint: 'The Fall of Fonthill', 188–201 & bibliography, 227–228, in his *Lost Treasures of Britain*, London: Viking, 1990. Endpapers: Buckler's lithograph of ruined Abbey (1825).

Tarbat, Alan. 'Shireways: Fonthill Bishop.' *Bristol Evening World*, 21 Feb 1947, 2. With sketch by Bas of remains of Abbey. Reprinted in Tarbat, *Shireways Number Four*, Bristol: Rankin Bros., [1948], 55–59.

Waser, Georges. 'Torheiten im Landschaftsgarten. «Follies» – eine Art von Grand Tour durch Grossbritannien.' *Neue Zürcher Zeitung*, 7–8 Jan 1995, 74–75.

Whitfield, Paul. 'Fonthill Abbey.' *Discovering Antiques* No. 48, 1971. 2 pp. & 5 illus. Publ. weekly by Purnell.

Wilson, Richard & Alan Mackley. " 'A Pleasure Not to be envied': The Building of the English Country House." *History Today* 51 (July 2001): 41–47 at 43. 'Fonthill Abbey, the Gothic extravaganza'.

ARCHITECTURAL STUDIES

Books

Aldrich, Megan. 'Romantic Gothic: Abbeys and Castles.' In *Gothic Revival*, 76–99 at 82–89 & 5 illus. London: Phaidon, 1994. Beckford said that Wyatt had long ago 'sunk from the plane of genius to the mire', 80. Abbey compared with remodelling of Windsor Castle interiors, 94. Eaton Hall interiors inspired by Abbey, 95–96. Plan of Palace of Westminster influenced by Abbey, 136, 137. Fonthill Abbey mentioned, 91, 109, 114, 133, 138.

Aldrich, Megan. 'William Beckford's Abbey at Fonthill: From the Picturesque to the Sublime.' In *William Beckford, 1760–1844: An Eye for the Magnificent*, ed. Derek E. Ostergard, 116–135. New Haven & London: Yale University Press for the Bard Graduate Center, 2001. Exhibition catalogue. Also discusses the interiors in the Abbey.

Andrews, Wayne. *American Gothic – Its Origins, Its Trials, Its Triumphs.* New York: Random House, 1975. Pp. 17–25 & 2 illus., 72, 90 & illus.

Bence-Jones, Mark. *The National Trust. Ancestral Houses*. Weidenfeld & Nicolson, 1984. Furniture bought at the 1823 Fonthill sale for Charlecote Park, 71. Beckford and Kitty Courtenay at Powderham Castle, 180–181.

Betjeman, John. *A Pictorial History of English Architecture*. London: John Murray, 1972. Collapse of Abbey's tower not easily forgotten, 75.

Blomfield, Reginald Theodore. *A Short History of Renaissance Architecture in England, 1500–1800*. London: Bell, 1900. P. 224.

Britton. Crook, J. Mordaunt. 'Britton, John (1771–1857).' In *Oxford Dictionary of National Biography*, ed. H. C. G. Matthew & Brian Harrison, 7:715. Oxford: Oxford University Press, 2004. Scathing quote by Beckford from *Life at Fonthill* (1957, 228–229).

Brooks, Chris. *The Gothic Revival*. London: Phaidon, 1999. Beckford & Fonthill, 155–157, 159, 223, 277, 415. Fonthill Abbey, pl. 83–84.

Brown, Roderick, ed. *The Architectural Outsiders*. London: Waterstone, 1985. Fonthill Arch, 75. Abbey, 126.

Clark, Kenneth. *The Gothic Revival*. London: Constable, 1928. Pp. 99, 104–111, pl. VI, VII & passim. 'The scenic effect for which Wyatt strove at Salisbury he achieved at Fonthill.', 104. No change to Fonthill pages in rev. eds.

Clarke, Basil F. L. *Church Builders of the Nineteenth Century. A Study of the Gothic Revival in England*. London: Society for Promoting Christian Knowledge, 1938. Abbey, 12, 13, 38. Church by T. H. Wyatt (1866), 264.

Cook, Olive. *The English Country House. An art and a way of life*. London: Thames & Hudson, 1974. Disappointment with Wyatt, 200. Description of Abbey, 211–212 & NW view of Abbey from Britton (1823), pl. 225.

Crook, J. Mordaunt. 'John Britton and the Genesis of the Gothic Revival.' In *Concerning Architecture*, ed. John Summerson, 98–119. London: Allen Lane: The Penguin Press, 1968. Fonthill, 98. Britton's condemnation of debauchery at Fonthill, 102 n5. Beckford's poor opinion of Britton, 103 & n4. Whittingham's superb printing of Britton's *Fonthill*, 113 n2. Beckford subscribed to Britton's *Bristol Cathedral* (1830), 114 n2. 7 out of 11 copper plates in Britton's *Fonthill* destroyed after publication, 116 & n2.

Curl, James Stevens. *Georgian Architecture*. Newton Abbot, Devon: David & Charles, 1993. Abbey & Moorish Teahouse in Bath, 70. Pugin overjoyed at collapse of tower in 1825, 110. Choragic Monument of Lysicrates, 78.

Davis, Terence. *The Gothick Taste*. Newton Abbot, Devon: David & Charles, 1974 [1975]. Fonthill Abbey, text (continuous): 100, 103, 106, 113, 117, 121, 122. Illus.: four on 108–112. Beckford, 14, 22, 48. Fonthill, 134.

Eastlake, Charles L. 'Fonthill Abbey.' In *A History of the Gothic Revival*, 61–65. London: Longmans, Green, 1872. A critical account, noting 'eccentricity of character, and bold adaptation of Gothic form'.

Germann, Georg. *Gothic Revival in Europe and Britain: Sources, Influences and Ideas*. Trans. from the German MS. by Gerald Onn. London: Lund

Humphries, 1972. Pugin 'objected to the abbey style in houses such as Fonthill Abbey', 71. View of Hall from Octagon (Britton, 1823), 198, fig. 15.

Glancey, Jonathan. *The Story of Architecture*. London: Dorling Kindersley, 2000. Abbey, 122–123 with distant SW view from Rutter (1823). *Vathek*, 42, 147.

Gloag, John. *The Englishman's Castle*. London: Eyre & Spottiswoode, 1944. Wyatt's role, 133.

Gloag, John. *Victorian Taste. Some Social Aspects of Architectural and Industrial Design, from 1820–1900*. London: Black, 1962. Abbey 'most extravagant example of Georgian Gothic', 11 & pl. 2 from Rutter's *Description* (1822).

Gloag, John. *The English Tradition in Architecture*. London: Black, 1963. The Abbey part of 'the taste for mediaeval fantasies', 214.

Gloag, John. *Architecture*. London: Cassell, 1963. Abbey mentioned, 171.

Goodhart-Rendel, H. S. *English Architecture since the Regency. An Interpretation*. London: Constable, 1953. Abbey (1786), 'romance had got the upper hand', 25–26. Wyatt, 35. Discomfort of Abbey, 37.

Harris, John. 'English Country House Guides 1740–1840.' In *Concerning Architecture*, ed. John Summerson, 68–69. London: Allen Lane: The Penguin Press, 1968. Storer (1812), Rutter (*Description*, 1822 & *Delineations*, 1823), Britton (1823) and Whittaker (1822, 'many more' than six eds.).

Harris, John. *The Design of the English Country House 1620–1920*. London: Trefoil, 1985. Account of Abbey, 192–193, incl. three Wyatt drawings. 'Ashridge is the only reminder of the huge scale of Beckford's abbey', 194.

Hughes, J. Quentin & Norbert Lynton. *Renaissance Architecture*. London: Longmans, 1962. Part Two by Norbert Lynton. Abbey, 393–394, with plan on 393. 'Fonthill completely satisfied the growing desire for the sublime and the terrible.' Simpson's History of Architectural Development Vol. IV. Expanded from a version publ. in 3 vols., 1905–1911.

Irwin, David. *English Neoclassical Art*. London: Faber & Faber, 1966. Beckford as critic of Benjamin West, 48 & n5. Admired 13th-century monument to Edmund Crouchback, 92. Monumental re-creation of a Gothic abbey, 95 & nn2–5. Abbey mentioned, 168. Bibliography, 178.

Irwin, David. *Neoclassicism*. London: Phaidon, 1997. Revelation chamber in the Abbey, 167.

Jordan, R. Furneaux. *Victorian Architecture*. Harmondsworth, Middlesex: Penguin Books, 1966. Fonthill Abbey, 71–72 with Octagon & NW view, 70, 81, 206, 209–210, 213. 'English eccentric', 42. 'Beckford's sham abbey at Fonthill', 45. A 'rich recluse', 79.

Macaulay, James. *The Gothic Revival 1745–1845*. Glasgow: Blackie, 1975. Abbey, 146–148. St. Michael's Gallery from Rutter, *Delineations* (1823), 147, pl. 80. Beckford chose the one architect who could realise his vision,

132. Walter Scott compared with Beckford, 223. Mentioned, 12, 29, 197, 209, 210, 228, 297–298, 302. Bibliography, 403–414.

Massey, James & Shirley Maxwell. *Gothic Revival*. New York: Abbeville Press, 1994. View of Abbey from SW, 70. Caption, 71.

McCarthy, Michael. *The Origins of the Gothic Revival*. New Haven: Yale University Press, 1987. Abbey mentioned, 2, 146.

Middleton, Robin & David Watkin. *Neoclassical and 19th Century Architecture*. New York: Abrams, 1980. Trans. of *Architettura Moderna*, Milan: Electa, 1977. Wyatt's 'astonishing' Abbey, 171. Claude-Nicolas Ledoux's involvement with Beckford, 190. St Peter's Church, Brighton, by Charles Barry reminiscent of Fonthill, 261. Ely source of 'staggering central tower', 318, 320. Views from Rutter's *Delineations*, 318–319, pl. 569–571. Owen Jones's interiors for Alfred Morrison, 405. List of Wyatt's works, 433.

Mignot, Claude. *Architecture of the Nineteenth Century in Europe*. New York: Rizzoli, 1984. Trans. from the French by D. Q. Stephenson. Fonthill Abbey "the most ambitious Romantic 'folly' in Europe", 50–51.

Parissien, Steven. *Regency Style*. London: Phaidon, 1992. 'Romantic extravagance' of 'Wyatt's notorious Fonthill Abbey', 59.

Pevsner, Nikolaus. 'Fonthill Gifford.' In *The Buildings of England. Wiltshire*, 219–221 & pl. 45b (Arch), 60a (Abbey). Very informative account with details of the grottoes. Harmondsworth, Middlesex: Penguin Books, 1963. Chimneypiece now at Bathampton House, Steeple Langford, 435 & pl. 60b. 2nd ed. rev. by Bridget Cherry, 1975, 246–249 & pl. 45b, 60a; 484 & pl. 60b.

Pilcher, Donald. *The Regency Style. 1800 to 1830*. London: Batsford, 1947. Habitable ruin, 9. Cobbett, 10, 40. Abbey plan, 11. Cottages as scenery, 89. Abbey, pl. 16, 18. Hadlow, pl. 17.

Prak, Niels Luning. *The Language of Architecture*. The Hague: Mouton, 1968. Pp. 47, 146.

Praz, Mario. *On Neoclassicism*. London: Thames & Hudson, 1969. Pseudo-Gothic Abbey, 242.

Raeburn, Michael. *Sacheverell Sitwell's England*. London: Orbis, 1986. Octagon in Abbey inspired by Fotheringhay Church, Northants, 72n. Also 194.

Richards, J. M. *The National Trust Book of English Architecture*. London: Weidenfeld & Nicolson, 1981. The 'ambitious and much publicised Fonthill Abbey, Wiltshire (1796–1812)', 157. Also 191.

Rutter. Hawkins, Desmond. 'Rutter, John (1796–1851).' In *Oxford Dictionary of National Biography*, ed. H. C. G. Matthew & Brian Harrison, 48:422. Oxford: Oxford University Press, 2004.

Rutter. Scott, C. Fell. 'Rutter, John (1796–1851).' In *Dictionary of National Biography*, ed. Sidney Lee, 50:32. London: Smith, Elder, 1897. Invited to Fonthill & wrote *Delineations* (1822 [1823]).

Summerson, John. *Architecture in Britain, 1530 to 1830*. Harmondsworth,
Middlesex: Penguin Books, 1953. 'As a composition, Fonthill was sheer
chaos', 283–284 & pl. 162A, 162B, 163 (SW view, plan, Octagon). Also
244, 290. New ed. (the 9th), New Haven: Yale University Press, 1993.

Summerson, John. *The Architecture of the Eighteenth Century*. London:
Thames & Hudson, 1986. (1st ed. 1969.) P. 94 & fig. 104 on p. 95.

Turnor, Reginald. *Nineteenth Century Architecture in Britain*. London: Batsford, 1950. Beckford & Abbey, 4, facing S view from Rutter (1823). Abbey
mentioned, 12. Rutter, 50–51. Also Beckford's Tower, 'a debased classical
effort suggesting the Choragic Monument of Lysicrates with almost every-
thing wrong with it', 40–41. Beckford's 'incredible' family tree, 54.

Watkin, David. *English Architecture. A Concise History*. London: Thames &
Hudson, 1979. Fonthill Abbey, with NW view from Britton (1823), 156.

Watkin, David. *The English Vision: The Picturesque in Architecture, Landscape and Garden Design*. London: John Murray, 1982. Abbey, 100,
102–107 incl. 3 illus., & 205 ch.5 nn22–29. Beckford's Tower, 108–109
& illus. Strawberry Hill 'a species of gothic mousetrap', 94 & 203 ch.5 n9.

Wilson, Richard & Alan Mackley. *Creating Paradise. The Building of the
English Country House 1660–1880*. London: Hambledon & London,
2000. Pp. 239, 241, 393 n12.

Wilton-Ely, John. 'A Model for Fonthill Abbey.' In *The Country Seat*, ed.
Howard Colvin & John Harris, 199–204 & 4 pl. London: Allen Lane,
1970. James Wyatt's model for the Abbey.

Wilton-Ely, John. 'Beckford the Builder [Fonthill].' In *William Beckford
Exhibition 1976*, [ed. Julian Berry], 34–57. Tisbury, Wilts: Compton
Press, 1976. See '6. Beckford's Tower and Bath. Architecture and History'
for 'Beckford the Builder [Lansdown]'.

Wilton-Ely, John. 'Beckford, Fonthill Abbey and the Picturesque.' In *The
Picturesque in late Georgian England*, ed. Dana Arnold, 35–44, 70–73 (2
appendices & nn1–54). London: The Georgian Group, 1994.

Wischermann, Heinfried. *Fonthill Abbey Studien zur Profanen Neugotik
Englands im 18. Jahrhundert*. Freiberg: Berichte, 1979.

Articles

Batey, Mavis & Catherine Cole. 'The Great Staircase Tower at Christ
Church.' *Oxoniensia* 53 (1988): 218 (Fig. 89) –220. Wyatt's transforma-
tion of the staircase, c.1801, compared with the Great Western Hall at
Fonthill.

Bell, E. Ingress. 'On some Pictorial Elements in English Secular Architecture.
– IV.' *The Magazine of Art* 3 (May 1880): 251–255 at 254. Comments on
'this strange caprice', with woodcut SW view by the author.

Brockman, H. A. N. 'Fonthill Abbey.' *Architectural Review* 95 (June 1944):
149–156 & 22 illus. Cover: black & white painting of the Abbey by John

Piper after John Martin, described on p. 141. Noted in *Wiltshire Archæological and Natural History Magazine* 51 (June 1945): 115.

Gemmett, Robert J. 'An Architect's View of Fonthill Abbey.' *Beckford Journal* 9 (2003): 19–26. On William Garbett, author of 'Candid Critique' of Abbey in *Gentleman's Magazine* 92 pt. 2 (Dec 1822): 491–494, entered above.

Glancey, Jonathan. 'Follies: Mad House.' *The Independent Magazine*, 23 Nov 1996. Fonthill Abbey, a folly built 'on a truly monumental scale'.

Honour, Hugh. 'A House of the Gothic Revival.' *Country Life*, 30 May 1952, 1665–1666 at 1666. Fonthill: 'fantastically grandiose' in article on Lee Priory.

Wilton-Ely, John. 'The Genesis and Evolution of Fonthill Abbey.' *Architectural History* 23 (1980): 40–51 & pl. 28a–36b (17 illus.).

Wilton-Ely, John. 'Beckford's Fonthill Abbey: A Theatre of the Arts.' In *The Beckford Society Annual Lectures 1996–1999*, ed. Jon Millington, 3–22. London: *The Beckford Society*, 2000. The first lecture, in 1996.

INTERIORS

Aldrich, Megan. 'William Beckford's Abbey at Fonthill: From the Picturesque to the Sublime.' In *William Beckford, 1760–1844: An Eye for the Magnificent*, ed. Derek E. Ostergard, 116–135 at 122–132, notes 133–135. New Haven & London: Yale University Press for the Bard Graduate Center, 2001. Exhibition catalogue. See also above, 'Architectural Studies'.

Banham, Joanna, Sally MacDonald & Julia Porter. *Victorian Interior Design*. London: Cassell, 1991. Gothic style, 54. St Michael's Gallery from Rutter (1823), pl. 54 on p. 55.

Bishop, Philippa. 'Beckford, William 1760–1844. British Antiquarian and Connoisseur.' In *Encyclopedia of Interior Design*, ed. Joanna Banham, 1:111–114. 2 vols. London: Fitzroy Dearborn, 1997. Interiors at Fonthill & Bath, with bibliography.

Bristow, Ian C. *Architectural Colour in British Interiors 1615–1840*. New Haven: Yale, for Paul Mellon Centre for Studies in British Art, 1996. Abbey, 123 & n200, 172, 182 & n185, 210–211 & n142, 215 & n187, 218 & n243, 219 & n251. Pl. 180, 181 from Britton (1823) on p. 173. Splendens, 163 & n31, 172 & n105, 198 & n60.

Cornforth, John. *English Interiors 1790–1848: The Quest for Comfort*. London: Barrie & Jenkins, 1978. 'Fonthill, Wiltshire', 114–115 & pl. 140–141. 'Lansdown Tower, Bath', 115 & pl. 142.

Dutton, Ralph. *The English Interior 1500–1900*. London: Batsford, 1948. Pp. 150–155. King Edward's Gallery from Rutter (1823), pl. 129.

Fowler, John & John Cornforth. *English Decoration in the 18th Century*.

London: Barrie & Jenkins, 1974. French furniture, 53. Lady Shelburne at Splendens in 1769, 63, 78. Curtains, 120 & n34. Abbey atypical, 208.

Jourdain, Margaret. *English Interior Decoration 1500 to 1830*. London: Batsford, 1950. Casali at Splendens, 50. Comments by Mrs Lybbe Powys, 70. Wyatt at Fonthill Abbey, 75.

Savage, George. *A Concise History of Interior Decoration*. London: Thames & Hudson, 1966. Chinese porcelain, 71. Beckford 'midwife' of Victorian revival, 187. Buyer at French sales, 208. Desire to surpass Walpole's 'Gothic mousetrap', 226. sw view from Rutter (1823), 227 (pl.179).

Thornton, Peter. *Authentic Décor. The Domestic Interior 1620–1920*. London: Weidenfeld & Nicolson, 1984. Britton's *Fonthill* (1823), 210.

Usick, Patricia. *Adventures in Egypt and Nubia: The Travels of William John Bankes (1786–1855)*. London: British Museum Press, 2002. Bankes decorated his rooms at Trinity, Cambridge, to emulate Fonthill, 15. Aged 26 he followed in the footsteps of Byron and Beckford to Spain and Portugal, 9.

Webb, George W. 'The Gothic Revival Revisited.' *Contemporary Review* 271 (Sept 1997): 143–150 at 144. General account with paragraph on 'fantastic' Fonthill Abbey, including the clerk of work's death-bed confession.

IMAGES OF THE ABBEY

J. M. W. Turner (1775–1851)

Full-length Study

Cundall, Edward George. *Fonthill Abbey. A Descriptive Account of Five Water-Colour Drawings by J. M. W. Turner, R.A.* Tarporley, Cheshire: Privately printed for Ralph Brocklebank, 1915. 15 pp. 16 pl. 29½ cm. Limited to 35 copies. The author was a salesman at Agnew's, Bond Street.
REVIEWS. *Times Literary Supplement*, 11 May 1916, 224.
'Turner's Fonthill Abbey drawings.' *Wiltshire Gazette*, 4 May 1916.
Wiltshire Archæological and Natural History Magazine 39 (June 1917): 511. Noted in *Idem* 39 (Dec 1916): 422.
ABRIDGEMENT. Cundall, Edward George. 'Turner Drawings of Fonthill Abbey', *Burlington Magazine* 29 (April 1916): 16, 21 & pl. I, II (5 views). Condensed from his *Fonthill Abbey* . . . at the editor's request.

Books

Bailey, Anthony. *Standing in the Sun. A Life of J. M. W. Turner*. London: Sinclair-Stevenson, 1997. Influences, 32. Invited to Fonthill in 1798, 46. One of Turner's earliest patrons, 49. Beckford bought 'The Fifth Plague', 60.

Butlin, Martin & Andrew Wilton. *Turner 1755–1851*. London: Tate Gallery, 1974. Exhibits: '37 Builders working on the Construction of Fonthill 1799', '38 View of Fonthill from a Stone Quarry 1799', '39 Fonthill from the North-East 1799–1800', 42. '70 The Fifth Plague of Egypt R.A. 1800', bought by Beckford, 48, 61. 'B25 John Robert Cozens. Sketchbook 1782', first of seven in Beckford's collection, 117. Beckford as patron, 9. Chronology, 195.

Finberg, Alexander J. *A Complete Inventory of the Drawings in the Turner Bequest*. London: Stationery Office, 1909. 'XLVII. – *"Fonthill"* Sketch Book.', 21 views, & 'XLVIII. – *"Smaller Fonthill"* Sketch Book.', 1 view, 120–124.

Finberg, A. J. *The Life of J. M. W. Turner, R.A.* 2nd ed. Oxford: Clarendon Press, 1961. (1st ed. 1939.) Cozens's seven sketchbooks, 38–39. Claude, 59ff. Exhibited five large views of Fonthill in 1800 Royal Academy exhibition, 67, 68, listed, 463–464. 'Fifth plague', 71. Engraving in *Anniversary* (1828), 305.

Gage, John. *Colour in Turner: Poetry and Truth*. London: Studio Vista, 1969. Claude, and Turner's visit to Fonthill, 31 & pl. 7, 8. Soane at Fonthill, 152 & 262 n110. Also 44, 45, 136 & 257 n40.

Gage, John. *J. M. W. Turner. 'A Wonderful Range of Mind'*. New Haven: Yale University Press, 1987. NW view (1798), 22 (fig 26), 23. East view at noon, 30 (fig 42). Turner's 'wealthiest patron', 30 & 245 n27. 'Altieri' Claudes, 108–109. Beckford bought 'Fifth Plague of Egypt' (Royal Academy, 1800) for 150 guineas, 170.

Herrmann, Luke. *Turner Prints. The Engraved Work of J. M. W. Turner*. Oxford: Phaidon, 1990. Splendens (1800) from Angus's *Seats*, 21 & nn29–30.

Herrmann, Luke. 'Turner, Joseph Mallord William (1775–1851).' In *Oxford Dictionary of National Biography*, ed. H. C. G. Matthew & Brian Harrison, 55:634, 635. Oxford: Oxford University Press, 2004. Invited to Fonthill for three weeks in Aug–Sept 1799.

Lindsay, Jack. *Turner*. London: Cory, Adams & Mackay, 1966. Invited to Fonthill in 1799, 42, 43. Mentioned, 73, 91, 229 n32.

Lindsay, Jack. *Turner. The Man and His Art*. London: Granada, 1985. At Fonthill in 1799, 21–22, 54. 'Fifth Plague' bought by Beckford, 32.

Lyles, Anne. *Young Turner: Early Work to 1800. Watercolours and Drawings from the Turner Bequest 1787–1800*. London: Tate Gallery, 1989. Three views: '44. Near View of Fonthill Abbey from the South-East 1799' & '45. View across a Valley towards the Tower of Fonthill Abbey c.1799–1800', 40; '46. View of Fonthill Abbey c.1800', 41. No. 45 again (in colour), 19. Abbey mentioned, 10. Exhibition catalogue (Jan–March 1988).

Meslay, Olivier. *J. M. W. Turner: The Man who set Painting on Fire*. London: Thames & Hudson, 2005. At Fonthill in 1779, 38, 39. East view, 39.

Trans. Ruth Sharman of *Turner: L'incendie de la peinture*, Paris: Gallimard, 2004.

Miller, Corinne, ed. *Watercolours from Leeds City Art Gallery*. Leeds, 1995. '41. View of Fonthill from a Stone Quarry', 72, described, 121. Also John Robert Cozens, nos. 23–26, described, 116–117. Beckford, 18. Exh. catalogue.

Monkhouse, Cosmo. 'Turner, Joseph Mallord William (1775–1851)' In *Dictionary of National Biography*, ed. Sidney Lee, 57:342. London: Smith, Elder, 1899.

Shanes, Eric. 'Dissent in Somerset House: Opposition to the Political *Status-quo* within the Royal Academy around 1800.' *Turner Studies: His Art & Epoch 1775–1851* 10 no. 2 (Winter 1990): 40–46 at 40, 46 n37. Five watercolours of Abbey exhibited at the Royal Academy in 1800. Other mentions, *Idem*: 2 no. 2 (Winter 1983): 2, 36; 3 no. 1 (Summer 1983): 46; 3 no. 2 (Winter 1984): 3; 6 no. 2 (Winter 1986): 24; 7 no. 1 (Summer 1987): 52; 9 no. 1 (Summer 1989): 58.

Smiles, Sam. *J. M. W. Turner*. London: Tate Publishing, 2000. Turner at Fonthill for three weeks in 1799, 16. Beckford bought his 'Fifth Plague of Egypt (1800), 25. British Artists Series.

Wilkinson, Gerald. *Turner's Early Sketchbooks (1789–1802)*. London: Barrie & Jenkins, 1972. Turner invited to Fonthill in 1799, 100–104 & 3 pl. from Sketchbook XLVII.

Other Images

Books

Abbey, John Roland. *Scenery of Great Britain in Aquatint and Lithography, 1770–1860*. London: Privately printed at the Curwen Press, 1952. No. 395. 'R. Havell. Noblemen's & Gentlemen's Seats 1814–1823', 257–258 with plate XXIII 'View from the South' facing 258. No. 418. 'J. Rutter. Delineations of Fonthill 1823', 276–277. For English's *Views* see '6. Beckford's Tower and Bath'.

Bell, W. Heward & Rev. E. H. Goddard. *Catalogue of the Collection of Drawings, Prints, and Maps, in the Library of the Wiltshire Archæological and Natural History Society at Devizes*. Devizes, 1898. 'Fonthill Abbey', forty-six entries, 44–47. 'Fonthill House', seven entries, 47–48.

Burnett, David. *A Wiltshire Portrait 1568–1856*. Wimborne, Dorset: Dovecote Press, 1983. Nelson's Arch from *Gentleman's Magazine* (1801), pl. 49. SW view from Rutter (1823), pl. 50. Ruins from Hoare's *Modern Wiltshire* (1829), pl. 51.

Coysh, A. W. *Blue-Printed Earthenware 1800–1850*. Newton Abbot, Devon: David & Charles, [1972]. Clews octagonal dish (1820s), 20.

Coysh, A. W. & Frank Stefano, Jr. *Collecting Ceramic Landscapes*. London: Lund Humphries, 1981. Wyatt & Fonthill, 19–21 & 2 pl. by Clews.

Coysh, A. W. & R. K. Henrywood. *The Dictionary of Blue and White Printed Pottery 1780–1880*. Woodbridge, Suffolk: Antique Collectors' Club, 1982. Five views, incl. two by James & Ralph Clews and two by Enoch Wood & Sons, 144. *Idem*, vol. 2, 1989. A sixth view under 'Fonthill Abbey'.

Harris, John. *Georgian country houses*. R.I.B.A. Drawings Series. Feltham, Middlesex: Country Life Books, 1968. James Wyatt, drawing of Abbey from NW with spire (*c*.1799), 45, illus., 54.

Hatchwell, Richard. *Art in Wiltshire*. Devizes: Wiltshire Archaeological and Natural History Society, 2005. Fonthill Gifford: "Fonthill Abbey. 'General View of the Ruins'.", lithograph, *c*.1830 [Spring 1826] & 'Fonthill House, north front', watercolour, 1806, both by John Buckler, 47, illus., 46.

Ingrams, Richard & John Piper. *Piper's Places. John Piper in England & Wales*. London: Chatto & Windus, 1983. 'Entrance to Fonthill, Wiltshire 1940', pl. 49 on p. 65. Oil painting of arch from north, 51 × 76 cm.

Lambourne, Lionel & Jean Hamilton. *British Watercolours in the Victoria and Albert Museum*. London: Sotheby Parke Bernet, 1980. Francia, 'Landscape with Angler. Fonthill Abbey in the Distance' (1804), 138. Sawrey Gilpin, 'Fonthill Abbey in the Process of Construction' (1797), 149. Charles Wild, NW view of the Abbey (*c*.1798), 415, illus., 416. Richard Westall, three illus. for *Vathek*, 411.

Lever, Jill, ed. *Catalogue of the Drawings Collection of the Royal Institute of British Architects. Vol. L–N*. Farnborough, Hants: Gregg, 1973. '[124] Drawings by J. M. Lockyer, (1846–7) and D. Mocatta', 89. Lists a drawing of the Abbey by David Mocatta (1806–1882).

Linstrum, Derek, ed. *Catalogue of the Drawings Collection of the Royal Institute of British Architects. The Wyatt Family*. Farnborough, Hants: Gregg, 1973. James Wyatt, '[8] Fonthill Abbey (Wilts)', three drawings: S & W elevations & perspective from SE [actually NW], 38. 'Drawings in other collections': Benjamin Dean Wyatt (1775–1850), 'elevation of a gate at Fonthill Abbey', 67. Thomas Henry Wyatt (1807–1880), 'Designs for Fonthill House [Pavilion] (Wilts)', 68. Both are in the Victoria and Albert Museum.

Neale, Gillian. *Miller's Collecting Blue & White Pottery*. London: Octopus, 2004. Soup tureen by Clews *c*.1815–1820 with a view of Abbey built by 'Beckworth' & active 'Beckworth society', 44. Abbey mentioned, 45, 49.

Parris, Leslie. *Landscape in Britain. c.1750–1850*. London: Tate Gallery, 1973. Fonthill, 85–86, incl. illus. of 2 pencil drawings & 4 watercolours of Abbey by J. M. W. Turner, c.1799, (cat. no. 193–198). 'Altieri' Claude, 16 (cat. no. 2). Beckford pupil of Alexander Cozens, 49. Turner's 'The

Fifth Plague of Egypt' bought by Beckford in 1800, 87 (cat. no. 200). Danby's 'Opening of the Sixth Seal' bought by Beckford in 1828, 117 (cat. no. 284).

Pointon, Marcia. *Bonington, Francia & Wyld*. London: Batsford, 1985. 'Landscape with an angler, Fonthill Abbey in the distance', watercolour by François Francia (1804), 102, illus., 103.

Prideaux, Sarah Treverbian. *Aquatint Engraving. A Chapter in the History of Book Illustration*. London: Duckworth, 1909. Beckford's patronage of J. R. Cozens, 86. Rutter's *Delineations* (1823), 351. (Havell's *Seats* (1823), 339.)

Priestman, Geoffrey H. *An Illustrated Guide to Minton Printed Pottery 1796–1836*. Sheffield: Endcliffe, 2002. Fonthill Abbey on one side of soup tureen, Canterbury Cathedral on the other, 169.

'Print exhibition sheds light on Wiltshire before photography.' *Blackmore Vale Magazine*, 7 Jan 2005, 27. Neale's (1824) SW view one of 30 prints on show.

Tucker, Ambrose. 'Fonthill Abbey.' In *A Catalogue of Some Portraits and Other Prints. Having to do with the County of Wilts. From the Collection of Ambrose Tucker*, 152–154. Salisbury: The Author, 1908. 31 entries. Also Alderman Beckford (1 entry), 61 & William Beckford (3 entries), 62.

Wedgwood, Alexandra. *Catalogue of the Drawings Collection of the Royal Institute of British Architects. The Pugin Family*. Farnborough, Hants: Teakfield, 1977. A. W. N. Pugin: '[20] Sketchbook . . . (1833–1834) . . . Observations on Fonthill Abbey . . . "the building is entirely misconceived and built in every part in the slightest manner" ', 48.

Whitton, Donald C. *The Grays of Salisbury*. San Francisco: ?Privately printed, 1976 & Wilton, Salisbury: Michael Russell, 1979. Abbey mentioned, 32. SW view from Neale (1824), 33, pl. 36. Very distant north view of Abbey, c.1840, by William John Gray (1817–1895), pl. 58 on p. 51.

Articles

Hughes, G. Bernard. 'Poor Man's Pottery Pictures.' *Country Life*, 11 Feb 1971, 297. Derby porcelain wall plaque, carefully 'framed'. In the V&A.

Inigo-Jones, Terry. 'Fonthill Abbey lives again.' *Bath and West Evening Chronicle*, 4 April 1981, 6. Michael Bishop's model of the Abbey.

Longbourne, David. 'A Painting of Fonthill Abbey Discovered.' *Beckford Journal* 3 (1997): 6–7. Watercolour from the SW by William Turner of Oxford, now in the Salisbury Museum and attributed to 'Warwick' Smith.

Mayhew, Edgar deN. 'A View of Fonthill Abbey.' *Register of the Museum of Art of the University of Kansas, Lawrence* [1] no. 9 (Dec 1957): 16–21. Reissued Spring 1965. Painting by Robert Gibb the elder

(1801–1837), copied from the distant SW view in Rutter's *Delineations* (1823), pl. 13.

Melikian, Souren. 'Turner: From Science to Art.' *International Herald Tribune*, 11–12 April 1998, 9. Watercolour from the NW by Wyatt (1798).

Millington, Jon. 'Francis Danby.' *Beckford Tower Trust Newsletter*, Spring 1985, 1, 3. Watercolour from the SW shown at the Christopher Wood gallery.

Millington, Jon. 'Engravings of Fonthill.' *Beckford Journal* 7 (2001): 47–59. Details of all known views, mostly of Splendens and the Abbey.

O'Donovan, Patrick. 'A land fit for artists.' *Observer Magazine*, 2 Dec 1973, 57. Distant view from the SW by Turner. Watercolour in the Tate Gallery.

Piper, John. 'The Colour of English Country Houses.' 8-page pamphlet publ. in *International Textiles* no. 8 (Aug 1944). 'Fonthill, Wiltshire', [1]. 'Vanished Fonthill, Wiltshire', lithograph by John Piper, 157 × 203 mm, [8]. See Orde Levinson, *John Piper. The Complete Graphic Works. A Catalogue Raisonné 1923–1983*, London: Faber, 1987, pp. 35, 37 (fig. 57).

Sales

Sotheby. London, 13 Nov 1997. Buckler watercolour of Abbey, lot 38.

'Turner watercolour for sale.' *Salisbury Property Journal*, 10 July 1997, 50. Sotheby's sale, 10 July, lot 84.

FONTHILL PAVILION (WEST WING OF SPLENDENS)
(*c*.1755–1768, ENLARGED 1846–1848,
MOSTLY DEMOLISHED 1921)

Books

Allibone, Jill. *George Devey, Architect, 1820–1886*. Cambridge: Lutterworth Press, 1991. Commissions from Alfred Morrison: cottage at Fonthill (*c*.1865), pl. 57; retaining walls at Fonthill Arch, (*c*.1877), pl. 58. Text, 82–84 & 64. List of works, 'Fonthill Estate (Wiltshire)', five commissions, 156.

Cooper, Jeremy. *Victorian and Edwardian Furniture and Interiors. From the Gothic Revival to Art Nouveau*. London: Thames & Hudson, 1987. Furniture for Alfred Morrison, 15. Mirror, pl. 57.

Gatty, Richard. 'Fonthill.' In *Portrait of a Merchant Prince. James Morrison 1789–1857*, 108–121. Northallerton, Yorks: Privately printed, [1977]. Life at Fonthill Pavilion from 1830 to 1866. Drawing (1829) facing 110. ?Witnessed Nelson's visit to Fonthill, 6. Britton's *Fonthill* (1823), 22–23. Also 55, 251.

Harris, John. *The Architect and the British Country House 1620–1920*. Washington: AIA Press, 1985. Two designs by Papworth, *c.*1835: porch and boudoir, 186–187. Three Wyatt drawings of Abbey *c.*1799, 192–193. Publ. in Britain as *The Design of the English Country House, 1620–1920*. London: Trefoil Books, 1985. Exhibition in Washington.

Jackson-Stops, Gervase, ed. *Basildon Park, Berkshire*. London: The National Trust, 1980. The Morrisons at Fonthill, 41, 42. Guide book.

McHardy, George. *Catalogue of the Drawings Collection of the Royal Institute of British Architects. Office of J. B. Papworth*. Farnborough, Hants: Teakfield, 1977. '[264] Fonthill (Wilts)', forty-four plans and elevations of Fonthill Pavilion and other buildings, *c.*1835, 115–117.

Middelboe, Penelope. *Edith Olivier from her Journals 1924–48*. London: Weidenfeld & Nicolson, 1989. Pp. 168–170.

Morrison, Alfred. Bell, Alan. 'Morrison, Alfred (1821–1897).' In *Oxford Dictionary of National Biography*, ed. H. C. G. Matthew & Brian Harrison, 39:329. Oxford: Oxford University Press, 2004. Inherited Splendens wing.

Morrison, James. Jones, Charles. 'Morrison, James (1789–1857).' In *Oxford Dictionary of National Biography*, ed. H. C. G. Matthew & Brian Harrison, 39:345. Oxford: Oxford University Press, 2004. Bought estate at Fonthill.

Morrison, Mabel. *The Quest of Joy*. London: Privately printed, *c.*1937. Fragments from the Manuscripts of Mabel Morrison, prefaced by 'Mabel Morrison: a character' by Edith Olivier. 94 pp. 14 illus. Fonthill, 28, 30, 35–41. 'Fonthill House with Mr. James Morrison's Additions', facing 35 & 'Fonthill House Shewing the Galleries added by Mr. Alfred Morrison', facing 36.

Olivier, Edith. *Without Knowing Mr. Walkley*. London: Faber & Faber, 1938. A sheep stealer at Bedford's [?Beckford's] Folly, near Salisbury, 96. Driving from Wilton Rectory to parties at Fonthill when a child in the 1880s, 186.

Walford, Edward. *The County Families of the United Kingdom*. London: Chatto & Windus, 1886. (26th annual publication.) Alfred Morrison, 745. Sir Michael Robert Shaw-Stewart (of Fonthill New Abbey), 978.

Articles

'County Notes . . . Breaking Up [&] A Country House.' *Wiltshire Gazette*, 21 July 1921, 3b. 'Fonthill House, which next week will be sold literally in pieces.' Splendens wing demolished and sale of building materials in 400 lots.

Darby, Michael. 'Fonthill House.' *Wiltshire Archaeological and Natural History Magazine* 94 (2001): 230–234. Furniture designed by Owen Jones.

Godfrey, Walter H. *Architectural Review* 21 (June 1907): 302 & 304.

Thatched lodges at Fonthill by George Devey & drawing of Fonthill Lodge.

Mirror of Literature 28 (15 Oct 1836): 249. James Morrison.

Wiltshire Archæological and Natural History Magazine 44 (Dec 1928): 254. Footnote: last part of Splendens recently demolished; now no trace. *Idem* 45 (June 1931): 381–382. Obituary of Hugh Morrison.

Sales

Robins Sale, 1829. 'Fonthill Park and Estate.' London, 29 Oct 1829. Catalogue with view of Fonthill Pavilion, and Plan.

'The Fonthill Estate.' 1829. *The Times*, 30 Oct 1829, 3b. Report of sale. 27 lines.

Phillips Sale, 1838. 'The Fonthill Abbey Estate.' London, 30 Oct 1838. 6 pp. & Plan.

Westminster, Marquess of. *The Times*, 12 June 1845, 5e. Bought Fonthill estate.

FONTHILL NEW ABBEY (1856–1859, DEMOLISHED 1955)

Books

Dorling, Rev. E. E. *Wilts and Dorset At the Opening of the Twentieth Century*. Brighton: Pike, 1906. Photos: 'Fonthill Abbey', 22 & 'Fonthill House', 56.

Hitchcock, Henry-Russell. *Early Victorian Architecture in Britain*. 2 vols. London: Architectural Press & New Haven: Yale University Press, 1954. Illus. VIII 30 & 31: 'Fonthill. South East View.' from R.I.B.A. drawings collection (see below) & photo from *Country Life*, 28 Dec 1901, 843. Beckford's buildings, 23–24, 29, 31, 41, 66, 84, 249, 439.

Jersey, Dowager Countess of, (Margaret Villiers). *Fifty-one Years of Victorian Life*. London: John Murray, 1922. The Shaw-Stewart family, peculiarity of New Abbey in that 'no room opened into another', Beckford's Abbey 'preserved as a sort of museum', 57–59.

Richardson, Margaret, ed. *Catalogue of the Drawings Collection of the Royal Institute of British Architects. Vol. B*. Farnborough, Hants: Gregg, 1972. Burn, W. Fonthill (Wilts): House. 41 drawings for the Marquess of Westminster, *c*.1846–1852. Nos. 1–18, designs; Nos. 19–40, working drawings; No. 41, 'Fonthill. South East View. 6 Stratton Street. 3 March 1852.' Pencil & grey wash (12 × 19¼). Pp. 128–129. No. 41 reproduced in Fig. 121.

Articles

'Fonthill Abbey, Wilts, a seat of Sir Michael Shaw-Stewart, Bart.' *Country Life*, 28 Dec 1901, 840–847. Fine photos of New Abbey & grounds, but text mainly about Beckford's Abbey.

Advert: 'Fonthill Abbey, Wilts.' *The Times*, 23 May 1925, 29e–f, to be sold
with 2062 acres by Rawlence and Squarey. 'The Estate Market . . .
Fonthill Abbey.' *Idem*, 25 May, 25d. Abbey among properties to be sold.
'The Estate Market . . . Fonthill Abbey.' *The Times*, 15 Aug 1925, 8e, Abbey
to be sold by Knight, Frank & Rutley. Their advert: 'Fonthill Abbey.'
Idem, 27 Aug, 20f, 'including Historic Remains of Fonthill Abbey'
'Fonthill Abbey Estate.' *The Times*, 13 July 1936, 26, advert by Jackson
Stops & Staff. 'The Estate Market . . . Fonthill.' *Idem*, 14 July, 28g, four
outlying farms to be sold by Mrs Walter Shaw Stewart. Estate once
belonged to Alderman Beckford, 24 lines. '. . . Fonthill Farms.' *Idem*, 28
July, 9g, sold for £11,557.
'The Estate Market. Around Fonthill.' *The Times*, 11 Nov 1939, 11f. Chick-
lade Rectory sold. Anecdotes about Fonthill Abbey, 20 lines.
'Sul'. 'Beckford's Abbey.' & 'His folly.' *Bath & Wilts Chronicle & Herald*,
*c.*1955. John Morrison, later Lord Margadale, to demolish part of New
Abbey. (Press cutting in Meredith Scrap Book, p. [9], Bath Central
Library.)
Hilliard, Elizabeth. 'Fonthill Redivivus.' *Beckford Tower Trust Newsletter*,
Spring 1989, 2–3. New Abbey bought by Bernard Nevill in 1975.

Fonthill Gifford Church

Church mentioned. *The Times*, 22 March 1864, 14d.
Consecration & notice. *The Times*, 2 June & 9 July 1866, 5f & 6c.
'New Church at Fonthill Gifford, near Salisbury.' *Illustrated London News*
44 (29 Sept 1866): 303 & woodcut, 305.

LITTLE RIDGE (1902–1904, ENLARGED 1914–1920, RENAMED FONTHILL HOUSE 1921, DEMOLISHED 1972)

Books

Drury, Michael. *Wandering Architects. In Pursuit of an Arts and Crafts
Ideal*. Stamford, Lincs: Shaun Tyas, 2000. Pp. 127–133, nn41–49 & pl.
72–76.
Ware, Dora. *A Short Dictionary of British Architects*. London: George Allen
& Unwin, 1967. Detmar Jellings Blow (1867–1939), architect of Fonthill
House, 42. Also Fonthill Abbey by Wyatt, 263.

Articles

Aaltonen, Gaynor, ed. 'Hourglass. The Eccentric: Mindblowing.' *National
Trust Magazine* No. 100 (Autumn 2003): 77. Portrait of Detmar Blow by
Augustus John.
Blow, Simon. 'Blow by Blow.' *Guardian Weekend*, 24 Feb 1979, 11. Impor-
tant article which also discusses the fate of the previous houses at Fonthill.

Jackson-Stops, Gervase. 'From Craft to Art. Detmar Blow's Wiltshire Houses.' *Country Life*, 3 July 1986, 18–23 at 20, 21–22.

Norman, Geraldine. 'Fonthill treasures sold for £89,118.' *The Times*, 3 Nov 1971, 4c–e. The sale included some items inherited from Alfred Morrison.

S., P. H. 'The Times Diary. How Fonthill missed the list.' *The Times*, 12 June 1972, 12d–e. Fonthill House demolished by Lord Margadale in spite of protests by the Victorian Society which were noted in their annual report.

[Weaver, Sir Lawrence.] 'Little Ridge, Wiltshire, a seat of Mr. Hugh Morrison.' *Country Life*, 26 Oct 1912, 566–574. Discussed in *Wiltshire Archæological and Natural History Magazine* 38 (June 1913): 127–128.

OTHER FONTHILLS

Charleville Castle, Ireland

Russell, Francis, ed. *Christie's Review of the Season*. London: Christie's, 1991. One of five views of Charleville painted in 1801 by William Ashford. It was designed by the owner, Charles William Bury, 1st Earl of Charleville, who based it on Strawberry Hill and Fonthill Abbey, 55.

Fonthill, Doylestown, Philadelphia

Dyke, Linda F. 'Henry Chapman Mercer: An Annotated Chronology.' *Mercer Mosaic* (Journal of the Bucks County Historical Society, Doylestown, PA) 6 no. 2–3 (Spring/Summer 1989): 35–65.

Jackson, Donald Dale. 'Henry Mercer makes more sense as time goes on.' *Smithsonian* 19 no. 7 (Oct 1988): 110–121, 207.

Poos, Thomas G. *Fonthill: The Home of Henry Chapman Mercer*. Manor House Publishing, 2000.

Fonthill Castle, Riverdale, New York

Lossing, Benson J. 'The Hudson, from the Wilderness to the Sea. Part XIX.' *Art Journal* n.s. 7 (1861). Text, 243, illus., 244.

Reynolds, Donald M., et al. *Fonthill Castle: Paradigm of Hudson-River Gothic*. Riverdale, New York: College of Mount Saint Vincent-on Hudson, 1976. Similarities to Fonthill Abbey's interior decoration, 13–15, 18.

Smith, Steven E. 'The Comedy, History, and Tragedy of Edwin Forrest and his Books.' *Book Collector* 49 no. 3 (Autumn 2000). The creator of Fonthill Castle, 367, 372. Also mentioned, 380. One illus.

Fonthill, Tasmania

Evans, K. Jane. 'The Fonthill Connection.' *Tabart of Fonthill: From England to Van Diemen's Land*, 64–65. Weston-super-Mare, Somerset: Privately printed, 1991. *Gloucester Journal* for 16 June & 13 Oct 1823 in bibliography.

Hadlow Castle, Kent

Dalleywater, Roger J. 'A Kentish Fonthill.' *Country Life*, 29 Dec 1966, 1748. Letter & photo of castle, built 1838–1840.

'Gothic fantasy: Hadlow Castle, Kent.' *Country Life*, 11 Sept 1975, 617. Photo of tower.

Ingham, Martin. *The Times*, 11 Feb 2002, 23. Letter about Hadlow being a copy of Fonthill, prompted by a Beckford Exhibition review on 6 Feb.

Ireland, Samuel. *England's Topographer. A New and Complete History of the County of Kent*. 4 vols. London: Virtue, 1828–1830. Hadlow, 3:346–350 & engraving facing 349.

Notes and Queries 3rd Series 5 (23 Jan 1864): 84. Hadlow compared with Fonthill.

Thirsk, Joan. *Hadlow Castle: A Short History*. Hadlow, Kent, 1985. Modelled on Fonthill Abbey, 15.

Highcliffe Castle, Hampshire

Hare, Augustus. *The Story of Two Noble Lives. Being memorials of Charlotte, Countess Canning, and Louisa, Marchioness of Waterford*. 3 vols. London: George Allen, 1893. Donthorn 'was ambitious of his own fame, [and] wanted to emulate Fonthill and Ashridge', 1:176.

O'Donnell, Roderick. "W. J. Donthorne (1799–1859): architecture with 'great hardness and decision in the edges'." *Architectural History* 21 (1978): 83–92 at 88. 'Massive porte cochère echoing Fonthill', illus. fig 30b.

Pevsner, Nikolaus & David Lloyd. *The Buildings of England. Hampshire and the Isle of Wight*. Harmondsworth, Middlesex: Penguin Books, 1967. 'Giant porch' and 'tremendous staircase hall' worthy of Fonthill, 292, & n: Louisa, Marchioness of Waterford's comment that Donthorn, the architect, had 'a silly desire to build a house that would emulate Fonthill or Ashridge'.

Vilalva Palace, Lisbon

Built by José Maria Eugénio de Almeida (1813–1872), created Conde de Vilalva. See Pires, *William Beckford e Portugal* (1987), 258–259.

6. Beckford's Tower and Bath

GENERAL ACCOUNTS

Books

English, Edmund. *Views of Lansdown Tower, Bath. The Favourite Edifice of the late William Beckford Esqr. From Drawings by Willes Maddox on stone by C. J. Richardson, F.S.A.* Bath: Edmund English Junr, & London: Thomas McLean, 1844. vi, 10 pp. 14 colour lithos. 6 sepia lithos. in text. 'Lithographed and printed at 70, St Martins Lane, London.' Publication intended for February 1844, but delayed.
  ADVERT. *Bath Chronicle*, 16 May 1844, 2g: English's *Views* to be publ. 'early in June'.

Millington, Jon. *Beckford's Tower, Lansdown, Bath.* Bath: L. T. Hilliard, 1973. 12 pp. 2nd ed. 1975. 12 pp. 2 pl. *Beckford's Tower, Bath.* 3rd–5th eds., 1978, 1983, 1986. 12 pp. 4 pl. 6th ed., Bath: Bath Preservation Trust, 1996. 16 pp. 20 colour illus. 7th ed., 2002. 24 pp. 28 colour illus. Guide book.

Albums in Bath Central Library

Gregory, William. Extra-illus. volume (location: B920 ALL) titled *Ralph Allen and Prior Park* [1886] which also contains his *The Beckford Family* ... (1887), Henry Venn Lansdown's *Recollections* ... (1893) and 'Beckford the Millionaire and Edgar Allan Poe. The American Poet. A Contrast. (From an American Review)', 12 pp., very similar to the article 'Beckford and Poe' (see Poe in '15. Literary Studies').

Hunt Collection, compiled by Rev. Ezra Hunt. Five folio vols. Press cuttings and illustrations relating to Beckford and the Tower in vol. 4, 164–197. Misc. cuttings, 164–169. Three lithographs: Tower from the NE after Goodridge, 169; 'Suggested Additions to Lansdown Tower, 1845', 170; 'Design for a Tower proposed to be erected by William Beckford, Fonthill Abbey, Wilts. Seat of W. Beckford Esq.' *c.*1823, 171. Text of Edmund English's *Views* (1844) with three lithos: Exterior View; Cabinets, etc; Sanctuary, 173–188. Cuttings from *Illustrated London News* 7 (22, 29 Nov, 6 Dec 1845) & obituary from *Gentleman's Magazine* n.s. 22 (Aug 1844), 189–195. Handlist: 'Lansdown Cemetery, Walcot, Bath. Table of Fees and Charges. Rev. Sidney Henry Widdrington. 1848' & small views of Tower, 197.

Huth Album (Location: SR/MSS Beckford), titled 'Fonthill Abbey'. Contains sale catalogues: Christie's, 1822, two eds: English & Fasana, 1841;

English & Son, 1845; English & Son, 1848. Two-page draft letter of 5 Sept 1837 from Beckford to unknown recipient about plans for the Duke of Hamilton to visit him. Numerous press cuttings.

Meredith Scrap Book (Location: B. B. Bec). Some forty press cuttings from the 1940s to the 1980s about Beckford, mainly from the *Bath Chronicle*.

POEMS

Chappelow, E. W. 'Beckford's Tomb and Tower.' *Somerset Year-Book* No. 34 (1935): 104. English sonnet. Reprinted in *Beckford Journal* 2 (1996): 68.

Harris, W. Gregory. 'Beckford's Tower (Lansdown, Bath).' *Bath & Wilts Chronicle & Herald*, 24 May 1933, 4. Twelve 4-line stanzas. Reprinted in his *Ballads of Bath And other West-country Verses*, 9–10. Bath: Mendip Press, 1943. 1000 copies printed.

R. [Reade, John Edmund.] 'Thoughts Suggested in Mr. Beckford's Park.' *Bath and Cheltenham Gazette*, 8 May 1844, 3c. Four stanzas: 6, 8, 6, 8 lines. Reprinted in Redding's *Memoirs* (1859), 2:289–290.

CONTEMPORARY BATH GUIDE BOOKS

Bath Directories. *Keenes' Bath Directory corrected to January, 1824*, 'Beckford, Mr. 20, Lansdown-crescent', 36. *Idem, 1826 & 1829*, 'Beckford, William, esq. 1 and 20 Lansdown crescent, West', 63 & 60. H. Silverthorne, *Bath Directory corrected to January, 1833*, 'Beckford, William, esq. 20 Lansdown Crescent', 23. All four, Bath: John & James Keene.

Gibbs, Samuel. *Gibb's Illustrated Bath Visitant*. Bath: Samuel Gibbs, [1845]. Abbey Cemetery consecrated 30 Jan 1844, Beckford's tomb 'hollowed from a single block of red granite' in front of Anglo-Norman chapel, 70–71. Tower, 74, 85. Beckford, 112–114. *Idem*, [1856]. 'Lansdown Cemetery', 87–89.

Meyler, publ. *Original Bath Guide*. Bath: Meyler, [1825]. 'Rides in the Vicinity of Bath', 109–110. Beckford 'occupies two large houses' separated by a bridge. *Idem*, [1829]. Brief account of Tower, 120–121. The same in [1830] ed. *Idem*, 1832. Similar account, with footnote about Beckford living at 20 Lansdown Crescent and 1 Lansdown Place West, 120. *Idem*, c.1847. Funeral & tomb at Abbey Cemetery, 86. 'Saxon Tower', 127–128. Fonthill, 151. Casali paintings from Fonthill in Theatre Royal ceiling, removed in 1839, 48.

Simms, publ. *The Improved Bath Guide*. Bath: S. Simms, [1824]. Lansdown-crescent: Beckford thinking of building a 'Saxon Tower', 18. Ceiling paintings by Casali from Fonthill in Theatre Royal, 133.

Tunstall, James. *Rambles about Bath, and its Neighbourhood*. London: Simpkin, Marshall, 1847. Tomb in Abbey Cemetery, 115–116. Tower,

222–223. Tower glimpsed from Weston, 192. *Idem*, 6th ed., rev. by R. E. Peach, 1876. 'Mr. Beckford', 316–324, with woodcut of Tower from Wright's *Historic Guide to Bath* (1864), 320. Tower from Prior Park, 132. Casali ceiling paintings, 121, 237. *Idem*, illus. ed., London: Isaac Pitman, 1889. Tower, 238–242, with woodcuts: 'Lansdown Cemetery', 238; from Wright (1864), 240. Tower from Prior Park Prior Park, 108. Casali paintings, 98, 188.

CONTEMPORARY ARTICLES, 1823–1844

Arrival at Lansdown Crescent this week. *Bath Herald*, 28 June 1823. Beckford bought land from there up to the summit of Lansdown Hill. Quoted in *Salisbury and Winchester Journal*, 30 June, 4b.

Arrival in Bath last week. *Bath and Cheltenham Gazette*, 1 July 1823, 3c. Also in *Bath Chronicle*, 3 July, 3b. 12 lines.

Plans for land behind Lansdown Crescent. *Bath Chronicle*, 3 July 1823, 3b. Beckford intending to buy land behind his house. Reprinted as '1823: Plans of Beckford', *Bath Weekly Chronicle*, 5 July 1975, 3.

Purchase of land from Capt. Gunning. *Bath Chronicle*, 28 Aug 1823, 3b. Quoted in *Salisbury and Winchester Journal*, 1 Sept, 3b. Also in *Bath and Cheltenham Gazette*, 2 Sept, 3b.

Notice to close footpaths & Public alarm over closure. *Bath and Cheltenham Gazette*, 16 Sept 1823, 2e & 3d. Also in *Bath Chronicle*, 18 Sept, 3c.

Saxon tower to be built on Lansdown. *The Courier*, 9 Oct 1823, 3. Similar account in *The Observer*, 13 Oct, which was reprinted over a century later in *Bath Chronicle*, 26 May 1938, 5b.

'Mr. Beckford – Bath, Oct 11.' *Devizes & Wiltshire Gazette*, 16 Oct 1823, 4c. Plans for Saxon tower and description of Lansdown Crescent. ¼ column.

Fisher, Archdeacon John. Letter to John Constable, 27 Jan 1825. Beckford 'playing with bricks & mortar'. See '5. Fonthill, 1822 and Christie's Sale.'

Beckford bought National School Garden behind his house in Lansdown Crescent. *Bath and Cheltenham Gazette*, 16 Aug 1825, 3b. Also in *Bath Chronicle*, 18 Aug, 3b. 4 lines. Reprinted as '1825: Buying the garden', *Bath Weekly Chronicle*, 21 Aug 1975, 3.

Construction of tower not to be delayed until the spring, as the 100 men employed would starve. *Bath and Cheltenham Gazette*, 3 Oct 1826, 3b–c. Similar account in *Bath Chronicle*, 5 Oct, 3c. 6 lines.

Theft at Tower. *Bath and Cheltenham Gazette*, 31 Oct 1826, 3e. 'On Tuesday night a copper boiler and the workmen's tools were stolen'. Also in *Bath Chronicle*, 2 Nov, 3c.

Masonry work completed. *Bath and Cheltenham Gazette*, 24 July 1827, 3d. 'These pillars will be gilt.' 25 lines. Also in *Bath Chronicle*, 26 July, 3c. 14 lines & 'Mr. Beckford's Tower', *Salisbury and Winchester Journal*, 30

July, 2a. 23 lines. Extract from *Gazette* in 'Domestic Occurrences. Intelligence from various parts of the country', *Gentleman's Magazine* 97 pt. 2 (Aug 1827): 171.

'Arrival of Her Royal Highness the Duchess of Kent in this City.' *Bath Journal*, 25 Oct 1830, 2e. Visit to the Tower on Saturday, 23 Oct, probably with Princess Victoria. Also in *Bath and Cheltenham Gazette*, 26 Oct, 3a and *Bath Chronicle*, 28 Oct, 3b. Visit noted in *Bath Weekly Chronicle and Herald*, 3 March 1934, 26, under 'Notes No. 40. Queen Victoria and Bath'.

Buys 19 Lansdown Crescent. *Bath Chronicle*. 15 Sept 1836, 3e. Also in *Bath and Cheltenham Gazette*, 20 Sept, 4e.

Saxon. [Elstob, Rev. William.] 'The Architecture of the Nineteenth Century.' *Gentleman's Magazine* n.s. 13 (April 1840): 409–411 at 410. Tower one of the earliest examples of the modern Italian style.

'A Walk over the Great Western Railway from Bath to Bristol.' *Bath Chronicle*. 28 May 1840, 3e. 'Mr. Beckford's tower is seen looking proudly down from its elevated site on Lansdown.'

'Visit of H. R. H. Prince Albert to Bath and Bristol, and Launch of the "Great Britain".' *Bath and Cheltenham Gazette*, 19 July 1843, 2a. Also in *Bath Chronicle*, 20 July, 3a: 'A glass of cut flowers, sent by W. Beckford, Esq.' on a circular table on the platform at Bath Station.

HENRY EDMUND GOODRIDGE (*bap.1797. d.1864*)

Exhibition

Blackmore, Sidney. Handlist to Exhibition: 'Henry Edmund Goodridge' at Beckford's Tower, Easter–October 1984.

    REVIEWS. Little, Bryan. 'Bath master of variety. An exhibition at Beckford's Tower, Lansdown, lovingly recalls the work of Bath architect Henry Edmund Goodridge.' *Bath & West Evening Chronicle*, 9 June 1984, 4.

    Rouse, Brenda. 'Exhibition after ten-year study.' *Bath & West Evening Chronicle*, 21 May 1984, 5.

Other works

Death announcements. *The Times*, 3 Nov 1864, 1a. 'In the 68th year of his age.' *Bath and Cheltenham Gazette*, 2 Nov, 5d. *Bath Chronicle*, 3 Nov, 5d.

G., A. S. [Goodridge, Alfred S.] 'Beckford's Tower.' *Bath and County Graphic* 6 no. 2 (June 1901): 26. A valuable account by Goodridge's son.

Goodridge, Alfred S. 'Brief Memoir of the late Henry Edmund Goodridge, of Bath, Fellow.' *R.I.B.A., Sessional Papers*, 1864–1865, extra pages 3–5.

Leach, Peter, rev. 'Goodridge, Henry Edmund (*bap.1797. d.1864*).' In *Oxford Dictionary of National Biography*, ed. H. C. G. Matthew & Brian Harrison, 22:809. Oxford: Oxford University Press, 2004. The Tower (1824–1827) his best-known work.

Lever, Jill, ed. *Catalogue of the Drawings Collection of the Royal Institute of British Architects. Vol. G–H.* Farnborough, Hants: Gregg, 1973. Henry Edmund Goodridge, '[1] Bath (Som): Lansdown Tower. Design for William Beckford, 1825–26', four drawings: elevation of entrance façade, elevation of rear façade showing access bridge, perspectives of entrance façade & interior of the library, 73.

Marriage on 10 July 1822. *Gentleman's Magazine* 92 pt. 2 (July 1822): 88.

Woodward, Christopher. 'Aerial Boudoirs of Bath.' *Country Life*, 4 Sept 1997, 68–71. Passim. Goodridge's work in Bath.

Woodward, Christopher. 'H. E. Goodridge in Bath: The End of the Terrace and the Rise of the Villa.' In *The Picturesque in late Georgian England*, ed. Dana Arnold, 57–66 & 74–75 (notes) at 62, 63, 66, 75. London: The Georgian Group, 1994. Beckford's influence on Goodridge and the 'un-Bathness' of the Tower.

SALE BY ENGLISH & FASANA, 21 JAN 1837 (CANCELLED)

Advert: '. . . in consequence of alterations now making at Lansdown Tower . . . Magnificent and Valuable Effects.' *Bath Chronicle*, 22 Dec 1836, 2e. Also in *Bath and Cheltenham Gazette*, 27 Dec, 3e.

'Sale Postponed.' *Bath and Cheltenham Gazette*, 10 Jan 1837, 3e.

SALE BY ENGLISH & FASANA, 4–5 JAN 1841

For the sale catalogues of 1841, 1845 and 1848 see '8. The Collection. Sales'

Adverts: 'Lansdown Tower.' *Bath and Cheltenham Gazette*, 15, 29 Dec 1840, 2g, 2f.

'Lansdowne Tower.' *The Times*, 28 Dec 1840, 7c. Repeated thefts prompted Beckford to sell all his articles of vertu. 6 lines. From *Bath Herald*.

'Lansdown Tower.' *Bath and Cheltenham Gazette*, 29 Dec 1840, 3d. Reprinted in *Bath Chronicle*, 31 Dec, 3d. Beckford to sell most of contents owing to thefts.

Bath Chronicle, 7 Jan 1841, 3d. Sale of paintings, 6 lines.

'Lansdown Tower. Sale of the effects.' *Bath and Cheltenham Gazette*, 12 Jan 1841, 3f. 39 lines. Also in *Bath Chronicle*, 14 Jan, 3c. 36 lines.

SALE BY ENGLISH & SON, 20–29 NOV 1845

Adverts: 'Lansdown Tower, Bath.' *Bath and Cheltenham Gazette*, 5 Nov 1845, 2g. 'Lansdown Tower. Splendid Effects.' *Idem*, 19 Nov, 3b. Sale to begin on Thursday, 20 Nov.

Sale of Lansdown Tower. *Pictorial Times* 6 (8 Nov 1845): 304 & woodcut of Tower from the north copied from English's sale catalogue.

Adverts: 8-day sale beginning on 20 Nov, *Bath Chronicle*, 13 Nov 1845, 3b. *Idem*, 'Sale commences this day', 20 Nov, 3g.

'Lansdown Tower.' *Bath and Cheltenham Gazette*, 19 Nov 1845, 3d. Background information on the Tower.

'Lansdown Tower.' *Bath Chronicle*, 20 Nov 1845, 3d. 49 lines about the quality of objects in the sale. Reprinted in *The Times*, 21 Nov, 6b.

'Lansdown Tower.' *Illustrated London News* 7 (22 Nov 1845): 324–325 & 6 illus. 'Sale of the Beckford Collection.' *Idem* (29 Nov, 6 Dec): 344–346 & 7 illus., 364–365 & 7 illus.

'Lansdowne Tower, "The delight of the eyes.".' *Pictorial Times* 6 (22 Nov 1845): 328–330. Woodcut of Tower from the SE, Embattled Gateway & five groups of 'Articles of vertu', all copied from English (1844).

'Sale of the Lansdown Tower Property.' *Bath and Cheltenham Gazette*, 26 Nov 1845, 3d–e. Reprinted in *The Times*, 28 Nov, 7c, and abridged in *Gentleman's Magazine* n.s. 25 (Jan 1846): 70–72.

'Sale of Lansdown Tower and its contents.' *Bath Chronicle*, 27 Nov 1845, 3d–e.

'Sale of Mr. Beckford's Tower and its Contents.' ?*Bath Journal*, c.29 Nov 1845.

'The Lansdown Tower Auction.' *Bath and Cheltenham Gazette*, 3 Dec 1845, 3d–e.

'Sale of the contents of Lansdown Tower.' *Bath Chronicle*, 4 Dec 1845, 4e. Reprinted as 'The Sale at Lansdown Tower', *The Times*, 5 Dec, 8f.

'Pottery and Porcelain.' *International Magazine of Literature, Art, and Science* 1 (1 Nov 1850): 596–599 at 599. Review of Joseph Marryat's book mentioning items sold at 'the late Mr. Beckford's sale, in November 1845'.

Advert. 'Sale of Miscellaneous Effects.' *Bath Chronicle*, 4 Dec 1845, 2f. Sale in garden of 20 Lansdown Crescent on 8 Dec of garden buildings.

SALE BY ENGLISH & SON, 24 JULY–2 AUG 1848

Adverts: '20 Lansdown Crescent: Mansion & Valuable and Costly Effects.' *Bath and Cheltenham Gazette*, 5, 12, 19 July 1848, 2e, 2f, 2d. Also in *Bath Chronicle*, 13, 20 July, 2e, 2e.

'Sale of the Valuable Effects of the Late W. Beckford Esq. in Lansdown Crescent.' *Bath and Cheltenham Gazette*, 2 Aug 1848, 4f, cont. on 3c. Also in *Bath Chronicle*, 27 July, 3 Aug, 3e, 3c.

OTHER ACCOUNTS, 1844–1848

[Redding, Cyrus.] 'The Tower of the Caliph.' *New Monthly Magazine* 71 (Aug 1844): 457–466. Signed 'Nerke'. Reprinted with alterations in his *Memoirs of William Beckford*, 1859, 2:261–279.

'Sale of Mr. Beckford's Tower.' *Illustrated London News* 10 (22 May 1847):

327b. Report from *Bath Gazette* saying Tower had been sold to publican for £1000 on Monday (17 May).

Tower sold to publican. *Gentleman's Magazine* n.s. 28 (Aug 1847): 195–196.

Duchess of Hamilton bought the Tower back. *Bath Chronicle*, 9 Sept 1847, 3c. 18 lines. Also *The Times*, 9 Sept, 5a, and 'The Beckford Tower', *Illustrated London News* 11 (11 Sept 1847): 167.

Beckford's Tower given to Walcot Parish by Duchess of Hamilton. *Gentleman's Magazine* n.s. 28 (Dec 1847): 628.

Lansdown Cemetery consecrated. *Bath and Cheltenham Gazette*, 3 May 1848, 1. 'Lansdown Cemetery.' *Bath Chronicle*, 4 May, 3d. ½ column. *Bristol Times and Bath Advocate*, 6 May, 4e.

THE CEMETERY QUESTION, 1858

Reports on ownership of Tower and cemetery. 'Burial in Walcot Parish.' *Bath and Cheltenham Gazette*, 3 Nov 1858, 3e–f. 'The General Cemetery Question.' *Idem*, 3 Nov, 6a. 'The Lansdown Cemetery.' *Idem*, 24 Nov, 3e–f. 'The Municipal Cemetery Question.' (letter from Joseph Dallaway) *Idem*, 1 Dec, 8b–c. 'The Lansdown Cemetery.' *Idem*, 8 Dec, 3c–d. Also in *Bath Chronicle*: 'The Parish of Walcot and the Lansdown Cemetery', 4 Nov, 2e–f & 3a. 'The Lansdown Cemetery.' *Idem*, 25 Nov, 2e–f & 3a. Letter from 'A Ratepayer of Walcot', 8c.

RESTORATION, 1898–1901

'Beckford Tower Repair Fund.' *Bath Chronicle*, 23, 30 June, 7 July 1898, 4d, 4e, 4f. Notices acknowledging donations. Half of the £250 required now received.

Walcot Parish Magazine. Rector's letter proposing to appeal for £250, June 1897. Contributions received, July 1897, 5, 7. Further contributions, Oct 1898. Tower in scaffolding (builders Hayward and Wooster) & £150 already subscribed, Rector's appeal for the balance, Nov 1898, 2 & 4–5. Contributions received, Dec 1898, 5; Jan, Feb, March, April 1899, 5, 9, 6–7, 5. Rector's letter thanking contributors, fund had reached £300, March 1899, 2.

'Bath and County Notes.' *Bath Chronicle*, 27 June 1901, 5b. Restoration fund insufficient to pay contractors. Appeal to parishioners of Walcot and others.

THE FIRE OF 1931 AND RESTORATION, 1931–1934

'Beckford's Tower Imperilled by Fire.' (Banner headline) 'Famous Bath Landmark. Lansdown Cemetery Chapel Ablaze. Scene of Desolation.' *Bath and Wilts Chronicle and Herald*, 27 Feb 1931, 1a–c. Photo of firemen on chapel roof. (Also in weekly ed., 28 Feb, 9.) Beginning & end of account quoted in *Bath and West Evening Chronicle*, 4 March 1981, 4.

'The Aftermath. Desolate Scene at Lansdown Cemetery. A Chapel's Fate. Rector & The Restoration of Beckford's Tower.' *Bath and Wilts Chronicle and Herald*, 28 Feb 1931, 1e. (Also briefly in weekly ed., 7 March, 8.) *Idem*, 5a. 'Sul', saying fire might revive interest in *Vathek*. *Idem*, 6. 'Beckford's Tower Fire.' Photo: 'The burnt-out interior of the chapel'.

'Bath and District. Fire Threatens Famous Landmark.' *Bristol Times and Mirror*, 28 Feb 1931, 11e, 13 (photo). *Idem*, 4 March, 5e, appeal by Rector of Walcot for complete renovation.

'Beckford's Tower. Part of Bath Landmark Burned.' *The Times*, 28 Feb 1931, 7f. The chapel gutted by fire on 27 Feb. *Idem*, 4 March, 10e, letter from Prebendary Francis E. Murphy launching restoration fund appeal.

'Beckford's Tower.' *Bath and Wilts Chronicle and Herald*, 16 March 1934, 7. (Also in weekly ed., 17 March, 5.) Beckford's Tower restoration finished and paid for.

'Historic God's Acre. Bishop of Taunton at Lansdown. Beckford's Tower.' *Bath and Wilts Chronicle and Herald*, 5 July 1934, 3b–c. (Also in weekly ed., 7 July, 20, & three photos, 28.) Dedication of fittings in restored chapel. *Idem*, 5b, the 'Sultan of Lansdown Tower.'

RESTORATION, 1954–1956

Beckford's Tower, Lansdown. Restoration. Bath: Walcot Parochial Church Council, 1954. 11 pp. Reprinted in 1956 with an appeal for more money, 10.

Waite, Vincent. 'Beckford's Tower.' *Somerset Countryman* 18 no. 3 (July–Sept 1954): 64–65. Photo of Tower, also in Pevsner, *North Somerset* (1958), pl. 69.

'Beckford's Tower Restoration. "Brilliant Amateur's Extravaganza".' *The Times*, 4 Aug 1954, 8d. Appeal launched today. Cost of repairs at least £1200.

'Sul'. 'Beckford's Tower', 'Literary spendthrift', 'Miniature Fonthill' & 'Last resting place'. *Bath & Wilts Chronicle & Herald*, 4 Aug 1954, 5. ¼ column. 'Appeal launched today'. (Also in weekly ed., 7 Aug, 16.)

'Sul'. 'Beckford's Tower.' *Bath & Wilts Chronicle & Herald*, 7 Aug 1954, 5. (Also in weekly ed., 14 Aug, 2.) Appeal launched last week but work began in May.

'Sul'. 'Beckford's tower.' *Bath & Wilts Chronicle & Herald*, 13 Sept 1954, 7. Article in St Stephen's Church parish magazine about supporting the appeal for the Tower as it was so close.

'Sul'. 'Beckford's Tower.' *Bath & Wilts Chronicle & Herald*, 30 Sept 1954,

5. Finance Committee recommended City Council to give £50 to Tower appeal.

'Sul'. 'Beckford's Tower.' *Bath & Wilts Chronicle & Herald*, 5 Oct 1954, 5. External repairs completed. £500 now needed for interior to make it safe enough for the public to be admitted.

'Sul'. 'Famous tower.' *Bath & Wilts Chronicle & Herald*, 15 Aug 1956, 5. (Also in weekly ed., 18 Aug, 16.) Exterior restored after appeal was launched two years ago. Rector needed more money to make interior safe for visitors.

OTHER ARTICLES, 1933–1969

'Beckford's Secret Passage.' Query No. 77, *Bath Weekly Chronicle and Herald*, 28 Oct 1933, 26, by S. W. Hayward of Parramatta, N.S.W., asking how Beckford got from Lansdown Crescent to the Tower. He remembered a 'Private Walk'. *Idem*, 4 Nov, 26, reply by 'M of Lansdown': it was a private walk, but he could find no confirmation of the legend that there were secret passages. Beckford was often seen in Bath. *Idem*, 11 Nov, 26. Reply by X. Y. Z. mentioning the short grotto tunnel by Hamilton House. *Idem*, 27 Jan 1934, 26, reply by S. W. Hayward: his father remembered arches under the roads between Lansdown Crescent and the Tower.

Beckford's Dwarf. Note No. 136. *Bath Weekly Chronicle and Herald*, 24 March 1934, 26. Report in *Bath Herald*, 25 Oct 1882, 16, about a ' "likeness of Beckford's dwarf," hanging in Mrs.— parlour. Pedro, the Spanish dwarf . . .'.

Tower history. Query No. 441. *Bath Weekly Chronicle and Herald*, 4 April 1936, 26. Reply by G.W.F.R.G., 11 April, 26 and another reply, 18 April, 26.

'Towers of Somerset – 2. Lansdown Tower. Beckford, Builder Without a Rest' *Bath Weekly Chronicle and Herald*, 2 Oct 1937, 8. With photo of the Tower.

'Beckford's Tower.' *Bath Preservation Trust Newsletter*, April 1942, [3]. Very brief history, with photo from the NE.

'Sul'. 'Link with Beckford', 'Wish Fulfilled' & 'Claimed Saxon Burial', *Bath & Wilts Chronicle & Herald*, 13 Feb 1943, 3. (Also in weekly ed., 20 Feb, 9.) Beckford originally buried at the Abbey Cemetery.

Anniversary of death. 'Sul'. Anecdotes (all p. 3): 'Beckford's Centenary', 'Son of Lord Mayor' & 'Commemoration Prospects' ('no project for the recognition of this forthcoming anniversary has been officially contemplated'), *Bath & Wilts Chronicle & Herald*, 25 Feb 1944 (also in weekly ed., 'William Beckford Centenary', 26 Feb, 12); 'Caliph of Fonthill', 'Sultan of Lansdown', 'Talented Eccentric', 'Perfumed Coal' & 'Beckford's Bath

Houses', *Idem*, 22 April; 'Beckford Myths Refuted', 'No Tunnel to Tower', 'An Old Portal' & 'Wedding Breakfast Myth', *Idem*, 24 April; 'A Beckford Memory', *Idem*, 28 April, the Duchess of Gordon's visit to Fonthill; 'Beckford's Tower. View from Lansdown to Fonthill', *Idem*, 6 May, Tower built to enable Beckford to see Fonthill Abbey from Lansdown.

'Sul'. 'From Beckford's Tower.' *Bath & Wilts Chronicle & Herald*, 14 May 1947, 3. (Also in weekly ed., 17 May 3.) Fonthill just visible from Tower.

'Sul'. 'Lansdown Cemetery.' *Bath & Wilts Chronicle & Herald*, 13 Oct 1947, 3. (Also in weekly ed., 18 Oct, 3.) Cemetery extension opened 'this month'.

Kelly, Felix. Painting, 'Beckford's Lansdown Tower', one of four views of Bath accompanying an unsigned article 'The Province of Pleasure.' *Lilliput* 21 no. 3 (Sept 1947): [202].

'Sul'. 'The advent of Beckford.' *Bath & Wilts Chronicle & Herald*, 17 Jan 1948, 3. (Also in weekly ed., 24 Jan, 12.) 125th anniversary of his settling in Bath.

'Sul'. Paragraphs on tunnels supposedly built by Beckford. *Bath & Wilts Chronicle & Herald*, 19, 24, 30 Jan 1948, 3: 'Mysterious tunnel' & 'Beckford legend'; "A Beckford 'burrow' ", " 'The Hermitage' " & 'Roman altar'; 'Beckford's hilly path', 'Beautified Lansdown' & "The 'spectre ship' ". (Also in weekly ed., 24 Jan, 9, and 31 Jan, 6 & 12.)

'Beckford and Lansdown.' Note no. 831. *Bath Weekly Chronicle and Herald*, 13 March 1948, 12. Vincent's gardening and Beckford's ride.

'Sul'. Woodcut of 'Beckford Tower, Lansdown' heading Sul's 'Day by Day' diary. *Bath & Wilts Chronicle & Herald*, 20 Jan 1950, 3. Some further occurrences: 13 Sept, 2 Nov 1950, 21 March, 27 April, 16 May 1951, 3. Also a different woodcut, 'Beckford's Tower, Bath', on 4 April 1936, 5.

Cottam, A. C. Stevenson. 'Hill-Top Towers.' *Somerset Countryman* 16 no. 10 (April–June 1950): 215–216 at 215. Tower 'built purely for spectacular effect'.

'The Tunnel remains, & so does the Mystery.' *Bath & Wilts Chronicle & Herald*, 15 Sept 1956, 4–5. Evidence that there was a tunnel on Lansdown.

Honour, Hugh. 'Adaptations from Athens.' *Country Life*, 22 May 1958, 1120–112 at 1121. Copies of the Choragic Monument of Lysicrates.

Ford, E. J. 'She saw Beckford.' *Bath & Wilts Chronicle & Herald*, 22 June 1966, 10. Letter about her grandmother, born 1815, who saw Beckford in Bath, 'followed closely by a black dwarf carrying a whip to drive off the boys . . .'

'Sul'. 'Black-magic birthday. Scandal stalked William Beckford, the Eccentric of Bath.' *Bath and Wilts Evening Chronicle*, 1 May 1969, 4. 'Tomorrow is the 125th anniversary of the death at Bath of William Beckford'.

SALE OF THE TOWER, 1969–1971

Some of the items in the *Bath and Wilts Evening Chronicle* also appeared in the *Bath Weekly Chronicle*, until it ceased publication in March 1980

'Rector wants to sell Beckford's Tower.' *Bath and Wilts Evening Chronicle*, 31 July 1969, 10.

Little, Bryan. 'It's too good to lose – but who would buy it?' *Bath and Wilts Evening Chronicle*, Thursday, 7 Aug 1969, 10. Whole-page article.

'Sorry, Rector – Our Tower stays.' *Bath and Wilts Evening Chronicle*, 12 Aug 1969, 4. Letter from 'Very Shocked'.

Jones, Gordon. 'Beckford's tower was just a plaything.' *Bath and Wilts Evening Chronicle*, 18 Aug 1969, 6. Letter from the Rector of Walcot.

Clifford, E. M. 'Long may it stand.' *Bath and Wilts Evening Chronicle*, 18 Aug 1969, 6. Letter defending the Tower.

'Sul'. 'The man who got a bird's-eye view of Bath's folly.' *Bath and Wilts Evening Chronicle*, 20 Aug 1969, 4. Photo of Percy Jackson astride the ball on top of the Tower in 1952 during renovation, with article about him.

Dodd, Edward W. 'Rector, you're a realist.' *Bath and Wilts Evening Chronicle*, 20 Aug 1969, 4. Letter defending the Rector's point of view.

Crallan, Hugh P. 'They took 'em to the tower by the busload.' *Bath and Wilts Evening Chronicle*, 21 Aug 1969, 4. Letter, also one from Tom Burnham, 'It's a gem'.

Orchard, E. 'Monument to an Eccentric.' *Country Life*, 2 Oct 1969, 813. Letter expressing the hope that the Tower would be rescued, with photo.

'For sale – tower (with views) in a cemetery.' *Bath and Wilts Evening Chronicle*, 13 April 1970, 8.

'Bath tower landmark for sale.' *The Times*, 18 April 1970, 3d. Planning application for a dwelling. 'Structurally it is in fair condition.'

'Landmark may be curio shop.' *Bath and Wilts Evening Chronicle*, 18 April 1970, 1. Planning Committee to meet on 23rd to consider two bids.

'Tower's future.' *Bath and Wilts Evening Chronicle*, 20 April 1970, 8.

'Bath landmark may be made into a house.' *Bath and Wilts Evening Chronicle*, 24 April 1970, 17.

Mr. West's Diary. 'Tower of red tape.' *Western Daily Press*, 28 May 1970, 4. Tower now the property of the parishioners of Walcot, Bath.

'A pagan tower of trouble for the rector.' *Western Daily Press*, 6 Oct 1970, 6. New rector, Rev. Philip Myatt, uncertain about Tower's future.

'Tower goes on the market.' *Bath and Wilts Evening Chronicle*, 2 Jan 1971, 8.

Riley, Brian. 'The truth about Beckford, grand old man of Bath.' *Bath and Wilts Evening Chronicle*, 4 Jan 1971, 4. Letter about Riley's plans for the Tower.

'Wanted at last: After years as a folly, the tower finds a friend.' *Western Daily Press*, 11 Jan 1971, 4. Brian Riley of Lansdown Crescent made an offer for the Tower, with photo of him there.

Goring, Edward. 'They are queueing to buy it.' *Bath and Wilts Evening Chronicle*, 26 Jan 1971, 4. Richard Stilgoe and Brian Riley among those wanting to buy the Tower.

Hanson, Michael. 'More land for private houses . . . Folly on Offer.' *Country Life*, 28 Jan 1971, 207. Offers for the Tower invited until 28 Feb.

Barnes, Max. 'Decision day for Beckford Tower.' *Bristol Evening Post*, 12 May 1971, 33. Church Commissioners likely to decide on a buyer on 15 May.

DR & MRS LESLIE HILLIARD, 1971–1977

In 1970 the Church authorities declared the Tower redundant and the Hilliards bought it the following year. They restored the Tower and opened it to the public in 1973. In 1977 they created the Beckford Tower Trust.

'Tower landmark is saved for Bath.' *Bath and Wilts Evening Chronicle*, 25 May 1971, 10. Bought by Dr and Mrs Hilliard of Batheaston House.

'Sold: One tower, minus all the sleazy stories.' *Western Daily Press*, 26 May 1971, 4. Tower to be restored by Dr and Mrs Hilliard.

'Life in Bath's tower.' *Bath and Wilts Evening Chronicle*, 16 Oct 1971, 8. Plans for two-storey house and caretaker's flat in Tower.

Lawrence, Hugh. 'Books: £600 the three.' *Bath and Wilts Evening Chronicle*, 27 March 1972, 4. One was English's *Views* (1844) at Bayntun's, Bath, for £100.

Goring, Edward. 'Working party.' *Bath and Wilts Evening Chronicle*, 6 June 1972, 4. Sherry party for helpers.

'A face-lift fund for Beckford's 'pagan' tower.' *Western Daily Press*, 19 June 1972, 4. Restoration well under way.

Hislop, Vivien. 'The house now standing at Platform One . . .' *Daily Mail*, 24 June 1972. A labour of love. Alterations will be 'quite formidable'.

'A <u>Sinister</u> tower? Piffle, say the Hilliards.' *Bath and Wilts Evening Chronicle*, 20 Jan 1973, 4. Nothing sinister about Tower, to be opened in time for Bath Festival. Photos of Elizabeth Hilliard and staircase.

'£2,500 grant for historic tower.' *Bath and Wilts Evening Chronicle*, 18 April 1973, 15. Governmnet grant towards part-conversion into a house and flat.

'Historic tower gets a face-lift grant.' *[Bristol] Evening Post*, 19 April 1973, 31. Photo of Dr Hilliard at the Tower.

'The Folly proves a wise buy.' *Western Daily Press*, 19 April 1973, 4.

Advert. 'Beckford's Tower . . . has been restored. *Bath and Wilts Evening Chronicle*, 25 May 1973, 2. Open from 30 May, admission 10p, children 5p.

Peterborough. 'Saved in Bath.' *Daily Telegraph*, 30 May 1973, 18. Tower, bought by the Hilliards for £5000, open for first time in nineteen years.

'Tower of orgies, or art?' *Western Daily Press*, 30 May 1973, 4. Tower open after 20 years.

Goring, Edward. 'In Beckford's footsteps.' *Bath and Wilts Evening Chronicle*, 6 June 1973, 4. Work at Tower shown to several hundred fellow members of Bath Preservation Trust.

Goring, Edward. 'It's £17 a week for a view of the tombs.' *Bath and Wilts Evening Chronicle*, 13 July 1973, 4. *Idem*, Adverts: two flats for rent and cottage for sale, 29.

Ely, Gerald. 'Watermills and windmills as homes.' *The Times*, 13 July 1973, 15d. Tower restored, including two flats for rent and cottage for sale.

'Around and about.' *Bath Chronicle*. 19 July 1973, 4. Benedict Blathwayt's photo of Tower staircase exhibited at Mignon Gallery, Abbey Green, Bath.

Parry, Tony, ed. 'Why the experts took a long look at Beckford's tower.' *Bath and West Evening Chronicle*, 14 May 1974, 4.

Aldous, Tony. 'Heights of success in preserving historic architecture.' *The Times*, 20 June 1974, 18c. Finalist for the Royal Institute of Chartered Surveyors / The Times Conservation Awards.

'Beckford's Tower wins award.' *Bath and West Evening Chronicle*, 11 July 1974, 18. Commended in national conservation contest.

Goring, Edward. 'No thanks, says the National Trust.' *Bath and West Evening Chronicle*, 27 Oct 1976, 4. The Hilliards' offer of the Tower declined.

BECKFORD TOWER TRUST, 1977–1992

Goring, Edward. 'Tower in trust.' *Bath and West Evening Chronicle*, 15 March 1977, 4. Formation of Beckford Tower Trust.

'Beckford's Tower opens to the public.' *Bath and West Evening Chronicle*, 31 March 1977, 15. Photo of the Hilliards with model of Tower.

Smith, Harry. 'Monumental gift. Tower goes into trust.' *Western Daily Press*, 31 March 1977, 3, & [Smith, Harry.] 'Ancient tower is given away.' *[Bristol] Evening Post*, 31 March 1977. Formation of Beckford Tower Trust, photo.

'Up the tower.' *Observer*, 3 April 1977. Tower now open for the season.

Peterborough. 'In search of a public.' *Daily Telegraph*, 12 April 1977. Tower reopened following creation of Beckford Tower Trust.

Adverts. 'Beckford's Tower and Museum.' *Bath and West Evening Chronicle*, 20 May 1977, 3 & 2 May 1985, 19; *Western Daily Press*, 16 April 1987, 4.

Blackmore, Sidney. *Times Literary Supplement*, 20 May 1977, 621. Letter announcing formation of Beckford Tower Trust in January 1977.

'Now we're all lottery winners.' *Bath and West Evening Chronicle*, 17 Feb 1979, 1. Tower Trust to receive £250 from Bath City Council lottery.

Blackmore, Sidney. 'Commentary.' *Beckford Tower Trust Newsletter*, Part 1, Spring 1980, 1–2. Formation of Beckford Tower Trust.

Hilliard, Leslie. 'Beckford Tower Trust Properties.' *Beckford Tower Trust Newsletter*, Part 1, Spring 1980, 2. Report on the state of the Tower.

Profit, Jasmine. 'Oh, publish and be damned says James', *Bath and West Evening Chronicle*, 3 Nov 1981, 4. Illus. of funeral procession leaving Lansdown Crescent, from *Pictorial Times*, 25 May 1844. Accompanying an article on James Lees-Milne to publicise his role in the forthcoming *Images of Bath*.

Millington, Jon. 'Postcards of Beckford's Tower.' *Beckford Tower Trust Newsletter*, Spring 1982, 6–7. Four early twentieth-century views discussed.

Hilliard, Elizabeth. 'Life at the Tower 1925–1948.' *Beckford Tower Trust Newsletter*, Spring 1983, 2–3. Memories of Tower caretaker, Joseph Bell.

Green, Roger. 'A folly facelift.' *Bath and West Evening Chronicle*, 11 Aug 1983, 5. Tower repainted. Photos of Hilliards and Tower.

Green, Roger. 'It's not a tall stor(e)y.' *Bath and West Evening Chronicle*, 18 Aug 1983, 3. Beckford Whisky.

Harwood, Carole. 'Tales of yore of whisky galore.' *Bath and West Evening Chronicle*, 23 Aug 1983, 4. Follow-up of Roger Green's article. Letter from R. G. Thorn on 25th linking whisky with the Dukes of Hamilton, 4.

Rouse, Brenda. 'A bit of a mystery up at old Bill's folly.' *Bath and West Evening Chronicle*, 25 April 1984, 4. Hatchment lent by the Duke of Hamilton.

Hilliard, Elizabeth. 'Wedgwood Etruscan Vases.' *Beckford Tower Trust Newsletter*, Spring 1984, 3. Two vases, possibly Beckford's, on display.

Millington, Jon. 'A Newly-discovered Water-colour of Beckford's Tower.' *Beckford Tower Trust Newsletter*, Spring 1984, 2–3. W. H. Bartlett's NW view of 1829 exhibited at Andrew Wyld's gallery in summer 1983.

Hansford, Christopher. 'Tower of treasures.' *Bath and West Evening Chronicle*, 28 Sept 1987, 13. Three oil paintings by Willes Maddox acquired from the Duke of Hamilton.

Mowl, Tim. 'A Taste for Towers.' *Country Life*, 1 Oct 1987, 152–155. Houses incorporating towers in and near Bath. Beckford's Tower, 153.

Profit, Jasmine. 'The doctor duo who saved a city's heritage.' *Bath and West Evening Chronicle*, 10 March 1988, 16. Leslie & Elizabeth Hilliard. Photo, also used in their obituaries in the *Beckford Journal* 3 (1997) & 8 (2002).

Bath Museums Service. *Bath Museums News* from 1988, bi-annually. Passim.

Lucy, Sue. 'It's breathtaking.' *Bath and West Evening Chronicle*, 22 April 1989, 6. The 1989 re-opening, photo of Casali's portrait on view.

Wilson, Arnold. 'Beckford's Tower.' *Bath City Life*, April 1990, 34–35. General account to promote the Tower.

BATH PRESERVATION TRUST, 1993–2005

*At the end of 1992 the Beckford Tower Trust merged with
Bath Preservation Trust, who became the Sole Trustee.*

Bath Preservation Trust Annual Reports. Publ. in Oct of the second year cited

Bishop, Philippa. 'Beckford's Tower.' (1991–92): 15–17. Brief account of the Tower and Beckford. Restoration by the Hilliards. Also 2.

Briggs, Michael. 'Beckford Tower Trust.' (1992–93): 23–24. Plans for survey. Encouraging number of group visits. Also 2.

Briggs, Michael. 'Beckford Tower Trust.' (1993–94): 6–7. 'Souvenirs of Fonthill' exhibition. Pair of ebonised chairs bought in 1993 and restored.

Sladen, Gillian. 'Gardens Committee.' (1993–94): 7–8. Survey of Beckford's Ride planned. W. H. Bartlett's watercolour (1829) of Tower illus.

Briggs, Michael. 'Beckford Tower Trust.' (1994–95): 7. Maintenance of the Grade 1 listed Tower over the past twelve months. Photo of spiral staircase.

Whittlesea, Adrian. "BPT Museums' Education Programme." (1994–95): 18–19 at 18. Key Stage 2 primary schools teachers' pack to promote the Tower.

Briggs, Michael. 'Beckford Tower Trust.' (1995–96): 9–10. Application to the National Heritage Lottery Board for repair funds. Photo of top of Tower.

Blackmore, Sidney. 'Second Cousins: Sir William Hamilton and William Beckford.' (1995–96): 12–13. Exhibition about these two great collectors.

Verdon-Smith, Jesca. 'Beckford Tower Trust.' (1996–97): 19–20. 'Builder of Towers' exhibition' in Bath and London. '[Exhibition] Events', 21.

Briggs, Michael. 'James Lees-Milne.' (1997–98): 5. Colour photo, 4.

Verdon-Smith, Jesca. 'Beckford Tower Trust.' (1997–98): 10–11. Fund-raising for restoration of Tower and bequests from James Lees-Milne. Also 2.

Williams, Theo. 'Beckford's Tower.' (1997–98): 12–14. Account of progress with restoration, including need to reconstruct lantern timberwork.

Verdon-Smith, Jesca. 'Beckford Tower Trust.' (1998–1999): 10–11. Completion of restoration. Cemetery tidied and Gateway repaired.

Williams, Theo. 'Beckford's Tower – Completion of the First Stage Repairs.' (1998–1999): 12–13. 'Vigilant programme' of maintenance needed in future.

Francis, Ela. 'Beckford Tower Trust.' (1999–2000): 10. Tower reopened to public on 1 July 2000. Photo of the 'newly restored golden lantern'.

Barrett, Constance. 'The Landmark Trust at Beckford's Tower.' (1999–2000): 11. Establishment of ground floor flat with re-creation of Scarlet Drawing Room.

Francis, Ela. 'Beckford's Tower & Museum.' (2000–2001): 7–8. Events in past year. Presentation of a Civic Trust Certificate of Commendation.

Bishop, Philippa. 'Doris Elizabeth Hilliard. Born 19th October 1903. Died 10 June 2001.' (2000–2001): 11–12. Obituary.

Millington, Jon & Jesca Verdon-Smith. 'Beckford Tower Trust.' (2001–2002): 10–11, 14. New guide book and acquisition of mahogany cabinet. Also 2, 3.

Frost, Amy. 'Beckford's Tower.' (2002–2003): 10–11. Colour photo of newly-acquired tripod, formerly in the Scarlet Drawing Room, 9.

Frost, Amy. 'Beckford's Tower.' (2003–2004): 9, 12. Colour photo of Siena marble table bought after successful appeal, 10. Also 3.

Frost, Amy. 'Beckford's Tower.' (2004–2005): 11, 13 (with illus.). Colour photo of Maddox lunette, one of four bought at auction, 12.

Bath Preservation Trust Newsletter. Publ. annually in April

Briggs, Michael. Chairman's note on acquisition of Tower. (1993): [1].

Bishop, Philippa. 'Beckford's Tower.' (1993): [2]. Pair of newly-restored ebonised chairs formerly in Crimson Drawing Room on show.

Briggs, Michael. 'Beckford Tower Trust.' (1994): [1–2]. 'Souvenirs of Fonthill Abbey' exhibition to open on 2 April. Illus. of some of the exhibits.

Lewis, Adrienne. 'Beckford Tower – Debois Landscape Survey.' (1994): [2–3]. Recommendations for historically appropriate replanting.

Whittlesea, Adrian. 'Bath Preservation Trust Education.' (1995): [2]. Teachers' pack of A3 information sheets being prepared.

Briggs, Michael. 'Beckford Tower Trust.' (1995): [12]. 'Beckford's Heraldry' exhibition in the Fonthill Room. 1823 Fonthill sale entrance ticket illus.

Millington, Jon. 'Beckford Society.' (1995): [12]. Plans for formation.

Briggs, Michael. 'Beckford Tower Trust.' (1996): [3]. Application to English Heritage for structural repairs grant. New guide book being printed.

Briggs, Michael. Chairman's report on grant to restore Tower. (1997): [1].

Scruton, Sophie. 'Beckford Tower Trust.' (1997): 10. Details on National Lottery funding for major restoration work. Death of Dr Hilliard in January.

Verdon-Smith, Jesca. 'Beckford Tower Trust.' (1998): 6. Exhibition at Christie's to promote Tower. Fund-raising for ongoing restoration. Lottery Fund, [1].

Williams, Theo. 'Beckford's Tower – Report on Construction Work.' (1998): 7. Protecting Tower from damage during repairs. Cast iron roof dismantled.

Briggs, Michael. Chairman's report on restoration and plans for Landmark Trust flat on ground floor. (1999): [1].

Williams, Theo. 'Beckford's Tower.' (1999): 3. Structural and external repairs now almost completed. Photos of officials on scaffolding at the top.

Verdon-Smith, Jesca. 'Beckford Tower Trust.' (1999): 4. Interiors to be refurbished. Funds still needed.

Millington, Jon. 'James Lees-Milne's Books from Beckford's Library.' (1999): 4–5. Twenty-one books among his bequests to the Beckford Tower Trust.

Barrett, Constance. 'Beckford's Tower and the Landmark Trust.' (1999): 5. Flat to be created subject to final negotiations.

Green, Stephen. 'The Beckford Ball.' (1999): 6. Account of event, with photos.

Hayward, Derek. 'Walcot Parish Burial Ground.' (1999): 7. Burial Ground closed in 1992. Generous restoration grant from Mrs Priscilla Fernando.

Briggs, Michael. Chairman's report on progress at the Tower. (2000): [cover].

Verdon-Smith, Jesca. 'Beckford Tower Trust.' (2000): 7. Reopening of Tower. Warm air heating to be installed. Replacement of missing railings. Also [1], 8.

Francis, Ela. 'Beckford Tower Trust.' (2001): 2. 2001 Civic Trust award. Bard & Dulwich Beckford Exhibition. Landmark flat officially opened in March.

Francis, Ela. 'Beckford's Jug Auctioned by Christie's.' (2001): 3. 13th-century Mamluk jug depicted by Willes Maddox sold for £3 million. With col. illus.

Briggs, Michael. Chairman's report hoping that New York & Dulwich Beckford Exhibition will result in more visitors to Tower. (2002): [cover].

Springthorpe, Helen. 'Beckford Tower Trust.' (2002): 4. Group visits prompted by Beckford Exhibition. Landmark Trust flat very popular.

Frost, Amy. 'Beckford's Tower and Museum.' (2003): 4. Mahogany cabinet on display. Bath Literature Festival. Recording cemetery memorials.

Frost, Amy. 'Beckford's Tower and Museum.' (2004): 5–6. TV programme on Fonthill. Recording graves in cemetery. Tripod update. Also Siena table, 13.

Frost, Amy. 'Beckford's Tower and Museum.' (2005): 7–8. Tomb trail in cemetery. Four lunettes by Willes Maddox on display at Tower from May.

REPORTS

Hughes, Pat. *Beckford Tower. Lansdown. Bath. Vol. I. A Report on the Documentary History of the Building.* Bath Preservation Trust: unpubl., 1999. Text: 67 pp. & 67 pp. appendices. Illus.: 126 on 85 pp. A4 size. Ch. 1, '1822–1830 – The Building of the Tower'. Ch. 2, 'The Interior of the Tower'. Ch. 3, '1830–1847 – Consolidation and Development'. Ch. 4, '1844–1848 – The Work of the Executors'. Ch. 5, '1848–1970 – The Cemetery Period'. Ch. 6, '1971–1996 – The Hilliards and the Restoration'.

Sampson, Jerry. *Beckford Tower. Lansdown. Bath. Vol. II. [Archaeological Survey].* Bath Preservation Trust: unpubl., 1999. 126 pp. 50 pp. of col. photos (1 folding). 5 col. drawings (2 folding). 9 black & white drawings (8 folding). A4 size. Ch. 1, 'Introduction'. Ch. 2, 'The central heating system . . .'. Ch. 3, 'The construction of the tower'. Ch. 4, 'The Repairs to the Fabric'. Two appendices. Bibliography.

INFORMATION PACK

[Whittlesea, Adrian.] *Beckford's Tower. Lansdown Bath.* A Resource for Schools. Bath Preservation Trust, 1995. Six A3 information sheets in folder, for Key Stage 2 (children aged 7–10).

ARTICLES, 1993–1999

Tyler, Jane. 'All-clear for history landmark's relaunch.' *[Bristol] Evening Post*, 10 Feb 1993, 11. Bath Preservation Trust's take-over of the Tower.

Stevens, Brian, photo. 'Delicate operation: tree surgeon . . .' *Bath Chronicle*, 19 Dec 1994, 4.

'Eccentric's tower tale.' *Bath Chronicle*, 25 Feb 1995, 19. Drawing of a tower, possibly by Beckford, to be sold in Bath by Phillips on 27th.

Millington, Jon. An unknown drawing of Beckford's Tower. *Beckford Journal* 1 (1995): 6–8, illus., 7. Sold for £130 at Phillips, Bath, on 27 Feb 1995.

Hansford, Christopher. 'Dark secrets of the tower.' *Bath Chronicle*, 22 June 1995, 14. Ghosts of Beckford and his dog.

Walsh, Julia. 'Leaning tower bid for Lottery money.' *Bath Chronicle*, 27 April 1996, 5, & '£1m lottery joy for landmarks.' *Idem*, 18 March 1997, 3.

'Share Beckford's view over Bath.' *Bath Chronicle Property*, 17 April 1997, 1. Sale of Beckford's Cottage.

'Moves to save city's landmark leaning tower.' *Bath Chronicle*, 26 May 1997, 12.

'New chance for Lansdown Tower.' *Country Life*, 18 Sept 1997, 89. Beckford Tower Appeal: a further £100,000 sought.

Williams, Peter. 'Bath in Art.' *Bath & West Country Life*, Jan & Feb 1998, 20. Painting of Tower from the east by Steffan Leyshon-Jones.

Cardy, Matt. 'Television tour of sights you'll recognise.' *Bath Chronicle 7 days*, 12 Dec 1998, 11. Slave trade mentioned in 'Travels with Pevsner' on BBC2 television.

Woodman, Mary. 'Beckford on slide.' *Bath Chronicle*, 16 Sept 1999, 24. Talk by Kirsten Elliott about the Tower and surrounding area.

FUNDRAISING, 1997–2000

'Editor's Desk.' *Wiltshire Life*, June 1997, 10. Inaugural meeting of Appeal Committee on 14 April: target £100,000.

'Heritage Lottery Round-up.' *Perspectives*, June/July 1997. £366,700 grant.

Kelly, Rachel. 'Towering folly needs £100,000. The eccentric William Beckford's last love is in danger of collapse.' *The Times*, 2 Feb 1998, 22c–f.

Brennan, Rosslyn. 'Tower ball to make thousands for folly.' *Bath Chronicle*, 12 June 1998, 18.

'Tickets to masked ball selling like hot cakes.' *Bath Chronicle*, 20 Aug 1998, 8.

'High hopes for tower's masked ball.' *Bath Chronicle*, 22 Aug 1998, 12.

Weston, Peter. 'The tower and the glory of a rich man.' *Western Daily Press*, 29 Aug 1998, 16.

'The Beckford Ball.' *Bath & West Country Life*, Summer 1998, 7.

Arkell, Harriet. 'Ball for tower appeal.' *Bath Chronicle*, 5 Sept 1998, 4. Watercolour of Tower by Tim Scott-Bolton.

'Ball in aid of tower restoration.' *Bath Chronicle*, 14 Sept 1998, 3.

'Face painting comes of age.' *Bath Chronicle Life & Soul*, 22 Sept 1998, IV–V.

'Cash from ball to help save tower.' *Bath Chronicle*, 24 Oct 1998, 8.

RESTORATION, 1997–2000

Wiltshire, Paul. 'Two year tower wait.' *Bath Chronicle*, 31 July 1997, 15. Tower will be closed to the public for nearly two years.

Walters, Sue. 'Work begins to save tower.' *Bath Chronicle*, 29 Oct 1997, 2.

McKim, Neil. 'Towers of Strength. Beckford's Tower, Blaine's Folly.' *[Bath, Bristol and Cheltenham] Folio* No. 39 (April 1998): 14.

Arkell, Harriet. 'Restored work nears completion.' *Bath Chronicle*, 4 Nov 1998, 11. A year of complex restoration coming to an end.

'Restorers iron out tower's problems.' *[Bristol] Evening Post*, 4 Nov 1998, 14.

'Gilding the landmark.' *Bath Chronicle*, 13 Nov 1998, 14. Photo of a cast iron column being gilded at Dorothea Restorations, Bristol.

'Down to earth work.' *Bath Chronicle*, 16 Dec 1998, 2. Lantern dismantled.

Chamberlain, Phil. 'The crowning glory to an historic tower.' *Bath Chronicle*, 16 Dec 1998, 9. 'Official unveiling of the golden crown' on 21 Dec.

Chamberlain, Phil. 'Green transport bid for revamped tower.' *Bath Chronicle*, 23 Dec 1998, 5. Possible cooperation with nearby Park and Ride scheme.

Arkell, Harriet. 'Plans to floodlight restored landmark.' *Bath Chronicle*, 5 Jan 1999, 9.

Granite vase from the staircase: whereabouts. Christopher Hansford. 'X marks the pot.' *Bath Chronicle. Bath Time*, 17 Feb 1999, 5. Jesca Verdon-Smith. 'Questions & Answers.' *Country Life*, 1 April 1999, 93. 'Beckford's lost vase.' *Bath & West Life*, Spring 1999, 5. 'Have you seen this vase?' *BBC Home & Antiques Magazine*, May 1999.

Chamberlain, Phil. 'New plan to revamp gilded tower interior.' *Bath Chronicle*, 10 April 1999, 5. Plans to re-create Crimson Drawing Room.

Brennan, Rosslyn. 'How we are saving Bath's wonderful oddities.' *Bath Chronicle*, 19 April 1999, 11.

'Towering moment.' *Bath Chronicle*, 13 August 1999, 5. Heritage Open Days on 11 & 12 Sept.

'Beckford's Tower.' *Heritage*, Aug/Sept 1999. Tower to re-open next year.

[Hansford, Christopher.] 'Down Memory Lane . . .' *Bath Chronicle*, 15 March 1999, 22. Photo taken at top of Tower in 1952, reprinted from 20 Aug 1969.

'Gilding the folly.' *Bath & West Life*, Winter 1999, 18. Dorothea Restorations.

Jones, Andrew. 'Guiding lights plea.' *Bath Chronicle*, 27 April 2000, 15. Call for volunteers at the Tower.

'Restored tower and path look as good as new.' *Bath Chronicle*, 2 May 2000, 12. Photo of volunteers.

Weston, Peter. 'The Beckford Tower at Bath.' *Mendip, Bath & Northern Somerset*, Summer 2000, 50–51.

Williams, Theo. 'The Restoration of Beckford's Tower.' *Beckford Journal* 6 (2000): 8–16. Comprehensive structural report.

Singmaster, Deborah. 'Towering Talent.' *The Architects' Journal*, 12 July 2001, 35–36, 38. Also covers Landmark Trust flat.

'Beckford's Tower, Bath. Lantern shines on.' *Ecclesiastical and Heritage World* 5 (2002): 39. Restoration and floodlighting.

LANDMARK TRUST FLAT, 1999–2005

Arkell, Harriet. 'Holiday homes plan at Beckford's Tower.' *Bath Chronicle*, 31 March 1999, 2.

Kelly, Rachel. 'How to make jolly in one man's great folly. Beckford's tower may be eccentric but it is beautiful.' *The Times*, 28 April 1999, 39a–d. The Landmark Trust's lease.

Blake, Daisy. 'Holiday cottage plans for tower.' *Bath Chronicle*, 7 August 1999, 12.

'Beckford's Tower beckons.' *Landmark Trust Autumn 2000 Newsletter*. Cover photo of floodlit Tower. Brief account of Scarlet Drawing Room.

McCready, Georgette. 'An Englishman's (holiday) home is his castle.' *Bath Chronicle Life & Soul*, 13 Feb 2001, III.

Blake, Daisy. 'Landmark that lies off the tourist trail.' *Bath Chronicle*, 15 March 2001, 15.

'Beckford's Tower.' *Landmark Trust Handbook*. 19th ed. Shottesbrooke, Maidenhead: Landmark Trust, 2001, p. 23. *Idem*, 20th ed., 2003, p. 26. *Idem*, 40th anniversary 1965–2005, 2005, p. 34.

'Rent a piece of history. Beckford's Tower, Bath, £425–£727 a week.' *Sunday Times*, 17 Feb 2002.

RECENT ARTICLES, 2000–2005

'Tower to reopen.' *The Bath Star*, 3 May 2000, 27. Due to open this month.

Charles, Fanny. 'Towering folly – Beckford at Bath.' *Blackmore Vale Magazine*, 12 May 2000.

Johnson, Andrew. 'Landmark tower set to reopen to public.' *Bath Chronicle*, 25 May 2000, 15. Tower to reopen on 1 July after 2¼ year restoration.

Garrett, Sophie. 'Tower re-opens after restoration.' *Bath Chronicle*, 30 June 2000, 12.

Brennan, Rosslyn. 'Landmark tower restored to former glory.' *Bath Chronicle*, 3 July 2000, 12. Reopening after three-year restoration.

Jenkins, Bob. 'Towering achievement.' *Bath Chronicle*, 15 July 2000, 3. Tower reopened after restoration.

Dunn, Charlotte. 'After-school activities.' *Bath Chronicle*, 22 July 2000, (insert w/e 26 July 2000). The Tower a good place for children to visit.

Brennan, Rosslyn. 'Our hidden treasures.' *Bath Chronicle*, 11 Sept 2000, 11. Tower open for Heritage Open Days.

Sparrow, Mark. 'A noble folly is back in fashion.' *Bath Chronicle*, 15 Sept 2000, 30. The National Lottery and Millennium Fund.

'The day the window cleaners dropped in on one of Bath's finest landmarks.' *Bath Chronicle*, 12 March 2001, 5. Reopening for 2001 season.

Kilby, Naomi. 'Towering glory.' *Western Daily Press*, 15 March 2001, 18, 31.

Woodward, Christopher. 'Beckford's Tower Bath.' *Country Life*, 15 March 2001, 78–83. Restoration & Landmark Trust flat. Fine colour photos.

'Tower wins national award.' *Bath Chronicle*, 23 March 2001, 18. Restoration commended by 2001 Civic Trust Awards scheme.

Eldridge, Keri. 'Tower re-opens at last.' *Bath Chronicle*, 16 April 2001, 4.

'Hidden Bath.' *Bath Chronicle*, 12 May 2001, 20. Photo of Tower staircase for readers to identify.

Dixon, Anne Campbell. 'Beckford's towering ambitions.' *[Daily] Telegraph Travel*. 26 May 2001, 15. General account of Tower and Landmark Trust flat.

Gorringe, Anne. 'Restoring Our Faith in the Best of English Eccentricity.' *Western Daily Press: West Country Life*, 26 May 2001, 8–11. Maddox's colour views from English (1844) and the Tower today. 'The History of the Tower', 11.

Rigby, Malcolm. 'Bath's tower of Babel: a curious monument to a strange man.' *Somerset Magazine* 11 no. 6 (June 2001): 40–41. Four colour photos.

Eldridge, Keri. 'Historic tower wins civic award.' *Bath Chronicle*, 17 Aug 2001, 20. Presentation of 2001 Civic Trust Commendation Certificate.

'Pick of the day.' *Bath Chronicle*, 18 Aug 2001, 22. Photo of Tower from west.

'Tower tour.' *Bath Chronicle*, 31 Aug 2001, 21. Heritage Open Days.

Jenkins, Bob. 'Hooray for our heritage.' *Bath Chronicle*, 8 Sept 2001, 3. Tower open for Heritage Open Days.

Coles, Lyn. 'Beckford the Collector.' *Bath Chronicle*, 2 Feb 2002, 4. Lecture by Sidney Blackmore on 7 Feb to University of the Third Age.

'Take a look inside the retreat of England's richest son.' *Bath Chronicle*, 30 March 2002.

'Easter crowds kick start tourist season.' *Bath Chronicle*, 1 April 2002, 17.

Burcher, Liz. 'Playing the tourist.' *Bath Chronicle*, 3 April 2002, 24.

Kelson, C. M. 'Is Beckford Tower slavery monument.' *Bath Chronicle*, 3 April 2002, 11. Letter.

Pentelow, Kylie. 'Another award for tower's revamp.' *Bath Chronicle*, 24 June 2002, 8, & [Anon.] 'Accolade to celebrate tower's transformation.' *The Bath Star*, 26 June 2002. Royal Fine Art Commission Trust: Building of the Year.

Spiers, Kate. 'One man and his towering obsession.' *The Countryman* 108 no. 7 (July 2002): 30–32. Account of Tower and, briefly, of Beckford.

'Chance to visit historical landmark for free.' *Bath Chronicle*, 7 Sept 2002, 16. English Heritage Open Days on 14, 15 Sept.

Jenkins, Bob. 'The freedom of the city.' *Bath Chronicle*, 13 Sept 2002, 12. Tower open for Heritage Open Days.

'In and around . . . Lansdown.' *Bath Life* (Property magazine) No. 2 (Sept 2002): 35, 37. Colour photos of Tower and Lansdown Crescent.

Gypps, Emma. 'Free entry to heritage sites.' *Bath Chronicle*, 21 Oct 2002, 17.

Hills, Sarah. 'TV crew shoots in Bath.' *Bath Chronicle*, 2 May 2003, 16. Filming at Lansdown Crescent and Tower for a *Blue Peter* television programme.

'Tower treat.' *Bath Chronicle*, 21 May 2003, 7. Behind the scenes tours of the Tower & Cemetery.

Briggs, Michael. 'Beckford's Tower: A Reflection on the Past Ten Years.' *Beckford Journal* 9 (2003): 6–9. By the Chairman, Bath Preservation Trust.

Jones, Darren. 'Rising of the Moon.' *Bath Chronicle 7Days*, 17 Jan 2004. Colour photo of Tower.

Maddox lunettes. 'Beckford's panels go up for auction.' *Bath Chronicle*, 10 Feb 2004, 13. To be sold by Duke's of Dorchester on 11 March 2004, lot 204.

'No folly: today's Bath view is of Beckford's Tower at Lansdown.' *Bath Chronicle*, 7 July 2004, 28.

Jenkins, Bob. 'Past, present and future.' *Bath Chronicle 7Days*, 17 Sept 2004, 6. Heritage Open Days, including Tower, with photo.

Child, Mark. 'A Georgian sense of persuasion.' *Somerset Life*, Sept 2004, 27. Colour photo of Tower from the SW on page of Bath attractions.

Sugden, Rachel. 'Buildings to be opened for Heritage Days.' *Bath Chronicle*, 3 Sept 2004, 18.

Pegg, Rachel. 'Tales of the Abbey's tombstones revealed.' *Bath Chronicle*, 14 Sept 2004, 16. Abbey Cemetery was the first home of Beckford's remains.

Lewins, David. 'See City's History – Free.' *Bath Chronicle*, 25 Oct 2004, 7. Interview with Amy Frost about visitors to the Tower, with photo of model.

Jackson, Colette. 'Row over an old ride.' *Bath Chronicle*, 6 Sept 2005, 17. Planning permission to demolish garages near Beckford's ride refused.

Jenkins, Bob. 'The Beckhams have nothing on Beckford.' *Bath Chronicle 7Days*, 24 Sept 2005, 6. General article publicising the Tower, with photos.

Rigby, Malcolm. 'Folly or Garden Shed.' *Somerset Life*, Oct 2005, 46–47. Popular account of Beckford and the Tower, with photo of staircase.

'Family Fright Night.' *Bath Chronicle*, 31 Oct 2005, 26. Silhouette of Tower to advertise 'tales of the ghosts of Beckford's pets'.

SIENA MARBLE TABLE FROM VESTIBULE

Bishop, Philippa. 'Beckford Items at No. 10 Circus, Bath.' *Beckford Tower Trust Newsletter*, Spring 1991, 4–6. Fire surround and ceiling also noted.

Frost, Amy. 'Bath, Beckford's Tower and Museum.' *2003 Review*, 50–51. The Annual Report of the National Art Collections Fund

'Mystery of Beckford's table valued at £220,000.' *Bath Chronicle*, 24 Feb 2004, 4. Photo of table.

'Three weeks to find £220,000 for museum-piece table.' *Bath Chronicle*, 30 March 2004, 4. Photos of Tower and staircase.

Wilson, Amy. '£7,000 already in pot to save Beckford's table for the nation.' *Bath Chronicle*, 14 April 2004, 5.

Alberge, Dalya. 'Trust appeals for cash to save Beckford table.' *The Times*, 15 April 2004, 37c.

Cooney, Emma. 'More time granted to put money on the table.' *Bath Chronicle*, 6 May 2004, 21. Photos of table and staircase.

Geddes-Brown, Leslie. 'Table which ran away to the Circus?' *Country Life*, 27 May 2004, 92. Appeal for contributions.

'News Review.' *Apollo* 159 (May 2004): 34.

Walker-Sowden, Samantha. 'Beckford's marble table saved after £220k raised.' *Bath Chronicle*, 10 July 2004, 4.

Museums Journal 104 no. 10 (Oct 2004): 51 (photo), 52.

Frost, Amy. 'Continuing the Art of Collecting at Beckford's Tower, Bath.' *Beckford Journal* 11 (2005): 30–36. Also discusses the Maddox lunettes.

BECKFORD'S TOMB AND RAILINGS
See also 'Contemporary Bath Guide Books', above

'Tomb of the late Mr. Beckford, at Bath.' *Illustrated London News* 9 (29 Aug 1846): 140, with woodcut.

Passingham, R. Beckford was buried on unconsecrated ground surrounded by a ditch. *Notes and Queries* 4th Series 10 (17 Aug 1872): 138. Corrections by R. W. F., (12 Oct): 301 & R. Passingham, 5th Series 1 (6 June 1874): 460.

Hake, Thomas Gordon. *Memoirs of Eighty Years*. London: Bentley, 1892. Tower had to be re-purchased and given to the church before Beckford could be buried there, 236–238.

Millington, Jon. In Editorial: Tomb restored and split columns repaired by David Odgers. *Beckford Tower Trust Newsletter*, Spring 1988, 1.

Brooks, Chris, et al. *Mortal Remains. The History and Present State of the Victorian and Edwardian Cemetery*. Exeter: Wheaton & Victorian Society, 1989. 'Lansdown Cemetery', 121–122.

Ellis, Andrew. 'N. The circle of grass.' In *Tombstone Trail. Bath Abbey*

Cemetery. Ralph Allen Drive, 9. Bath: The Widcombe Association, [2002]. Woodcut of tomb from *Illustrated London News* (29 Aug 1846), 10.

Birch, Karen. 'Tombs with a view.' *Bath Chronicle 7days*, 1–7 Nov 2003, 4–5. Colour photos of Lansdown & Abbey Cemeteries.

[Frost, Amy.] *Lansdown Cemetery Tomb Trail*. Bath: Beckford Tower Trust, 2005. Six-page leaflet listing 30 tombs, with a plan of the cemetery.

Railings, removed to Lansdown Cemetery, c.1847

'The Colebroke Dale Company's Railing for a Tomb.' *Illustrated London News* 18 (3 May 1851): 374, & woodcut showing six panels with the caption 'Railings for a Tomb. Coalbrook Dale.–By Cole' possibly suggesting that the railings were designed by Sir Henry Cole, 371.

Crystal Palace and its Contents. London: W. M. Clark, 1852. Railings for Beckford's tomb, with illus., 277. Gleaned from *Illustrated London News*.

'Sul'. 'Church Railings as Scrap.' & 'The railings around the old tombs in Walcot Cemetery and Lansdown Cemetery are to be removed for war scrap.' *Bath & Wilts Chronicle & Herald*, 15 Oct 1942, 3. Only to be removed if they are 'voluntarily relinquished'. Railings of 'historic interest' not to be removed.

'Requisition of Unnecessary Railings' to begin on 19 Oct. *Bath & Wilts Chronicle & Herald*, 17 Oct 1942, 5. *Idem*, 22 Oct, 2, 'Railings will be taken. "Without fear or favour".'

Crawford, Ernest. 'Beckford's Tomb Railings.' *Bath & Wilts Chronicle & Herald*, 21 Oct 1942, 3. Letter about note on gate at Lansdown Cemetery concerning the removal of graveside railings, and hoping this would not apply to those that 'top the wall near the entrance . . . [having] some historic interest'.

'When Beckford was re-buried. Torchlight conveyance.' *Bath & Wilts Chronicle & Herald*, 28 Oct 1942, 4. (Also in weekly ed., 31 Oct, 12.) Much interest had arisen over Ernest Crawford's plea that the railings should not be taken for scrap [which they were, probably in November, but there was no mention of this in the *Chronicle*]. Beckford's 'body was carried up to Lansdown at night by torchlight' in May 1848, after the consecration on 28 April.

Hobhouse, Christopher. *1851 and the Crystal Palace*. London: John Murray, 1937. 'Another contribution of the Coalbrookedale Company was a cast-iron altar-rail designed by Henry Cole for William Beckford.', 95 n1.

King, G. J. S. 'Shropshire played its part in the Great Exhibition of 1851.' *Shropshire Magazine*, April 1951, 19–20 at 20. Coalbrookdale cast iron railings for Beckford's tomb.

Millington, Jon. 'The Railings for Beckford's Tomb.' *Beckford Tower Trust Newsletter*, Part 2, Spring 1980, 1–3. Layout of tomb at the Abbey Cemetery.

Arkell, Harriet. 'New railings after 50 years' wait.' *Bath Chronicle*, 10 May 2000, 2. Cemetery railings copied by a Scottish iron founding company. Also in *Bath Preservation Trust Newsletter*, April 2000, 7, noted above.

ARCHITECTURE AND HISTORY

Books

Abbey, John Roland. *Scenery of Great Britain in Aquatint and Lithography, 1770–1860*. London: Privately printed at the Curwen Press, 1952. No. 420. 'W. Maddox. Views of Lansdown Tower, Bath 1844', 277–278. For No. 395, Havell, and No. 418, Rutter, see '5. Fonthill. Images of the Abbey'.

Aslet, Clive. *Landmarks of Britain: The Five Hundred Places that made Our History*. London: Hodder & Stoughton, 2005. 'Lansdown Tower', 7–8. Colour photo of staircase between 68 & 69.

Atkinson, J., et al. *A History of the Parish & Manor of Walcot*. Bath: Walcot/Larkhall Townswomen's Guild, 1987. P. 51 & two photos of Tower. *Idem, Book 2*. 1989. 'Notable Residents . . . Beckford', 5.

Barbeau, A. *Une Ville d'eaux anglaise au XVIIIᵉ siècle. La société élégante et littéraire à Bath sous la reine Anne et sous les Georges*. Paris: Picard, 1904. Beckford, 'le somptueux chatelain de Fonthill Abbey', 175. Also 303 n1, 315. Trans. as *Life & Letters at Bath in the xviijᵗʰ Century*, London: Heinemann, 1904. Beckford, 176. Also xviii, 303 n1.

Barton, Stuart. *Monumental Follies*. Worthing, Sussex: Lyle, 1972. Tower, 158.

Borsay, Peter. *The Image of Georgian Bath, 1700–2000*. Oxford: Oxford University Press, 2000. Beckford & the Tower, 132–134, 236. Bath 'does not please' Beckford, 68. 1966 exhibition, 237. Eccentric, 336.

Bowers, Felicity, compiler. *Greetings from Bath. A Collection of Postcards of Bath c.1900–1940*. Bath: Kingsmead Press, [1977]. No. 55: 'Lansdown Crescent, Bath', Grosvenor Series. No. 56: 'Beckford's Tower, Lansdown, Bath, 808', by Viner.

Bradford, Rev. John. *A Brief History and Survey of the Parish of Walcot St. Swithin, Bath*. Bath, Privately printed, 1963. Sidney Henry Widdrington (Rector, 1840–1858), 8.

Britton, John. *Bath and Bristol . . . from Original Drawings by Thos. H. Shepherd*. London: Jones, 1829 [1831]. 'Lansdown Tower', entirely about the Granville Monument (1720), 33, facing half-page engraving 'Lansdown Tower, Lansdown Hill, Near Bath'. 'Mr. Beckford has built a lofty and elegant Tower, with some splendid rooms attached', 15.

Calvert, Walter. *Anecdotes of Bath*. 1st Series. Bath, 1887. Beckford, 8–12.

Clarke, Benjamin. *The British Gazetteer, Political, Commercial, Ecclesiastical, and Historical . . .* 3 vols. London: H. G. Collins, 1849–1852. Engraving of Tower from the SE, showing Beckford's tomb, facing 1:198. Fonthill, 2:207.

Crathorne, James. *The Royal Crescent Book of Bath*. London: Collins & Brown, 1998. Colour photos of Maddox's Exterior & Belvidere, 144–146.

Crook, J. Mordaunt. *The Greek revival*. R.I.B.A. Drawings Series. Feltham, Middlesex: Country Life Books, 1968. Engraving of Choragic Monument of Lysicrates, 11. Drawing of Tower from the north by Goodridge, 32. Also 42.

Crook, J. Mordaunt. *The Greek Revival. Neo-Classical Attitudes in British Architecture 1760–1870*. London: John Murray, 1972. 'Beckford, that arch-Romantic', 66. Tower, 102–104 & photo from SE, pl. 143. Rev. ed., 1995.

Dixon, Reginald. '75. Beckford's Tower.' In *Cotswold Curiosities*, 108–109. Wimborne, Dorset: Dovecote Press, 1988. Goodridge's litho from N, 109.

Earle, John. *A Guide to the Knowledge of Bath. Ancient and Modern*. London: Longman, etc., 1864. 'Chronicle of Bath': death, 2 May 1844, 328; Tower sold by auction in May 1847 & Cemetery consecrated, 28 April 1848, 329.

Elliott, Kirsten. *A Window on Bath. Eight Walks in Bath*. Bath: Millstream Books, 1994. Beckford's estate, 59, 61–62. Drawing of Islamic Summer-house, 63.

Elliott, Kirsten & Neill Menneer. *Bath*. London: Frances Lincoln, 2004. Account of Tower with six colour photos, 194–199, 201. Goodridge's plans for Cleveland Place signed at Beckford's house, 162. Beckford may have pulled strings to get Goodridge a job, 178.

Ellison, Fred E. *Etchings of Bath*. Bristol: William George's Sons, 1888. Lansdown Tower, xviii & pl. XVIII. Limited to 250 copies.

English, Jane. *The History of The English Family in Bath 1770–1890*. Bath: The Author, 1995. Edmund Francis English arranged Beckford's funeral and the 1845 sale, 10–12, illus., 11 & 12.

Everitt, William, publ. *Everitt's Views of Bath and its Vicinity*. Bath: Everitt, [1850]. 'Beckford's Tower, Walcot Cemetery, Lansdown, Bath.' & 'The [Abbey] Cemetery, with distant view of Bath.' Beckford's tomb in the centre. Both views reissued by R. E. Peach in his *Graphic Views in Bath & Its Vicinity*. Bath: Peach, c.1876.

[Falkner, John Meade.] *Bath in History and Social Tradition*. London: John Murray, 1918. Brief biography, *Vathek*, Fonthill Abbey, Lansdown Crescent, burial of Beckford's dogs and poor state of Tower, 75–84.

Fitzgerald, Edward. *The Letters of Edward Fitzgerald*. Ed. A. M. & A. B. Terhune. 4 vols. Princeton: Princeton University Press, 1980. Vol. 2 (1851–1866). 'Old Vathek's Tower' in letter to Frederick Tennyson about a visit to Bath on 7 May 1854, 127, 129 n2.

Forsyth, Michael. 'Beckford's Tower and Lansdown Cemetery.' In *Bath*, 271–272 & photo, 270. London: Yale University Press, 2003. Plans of 19

& 20 Lansdown Crescent, 28. Tower, 34. Bath Abbey Altar rail bought by Beckford in 1833, 63. Siena marble fireplace in 10 Circus from the Tower, 145. Lansdown Crescent, 172–173. First Bath home, No. 66 Great Pulteney St, 182. Goodridge bought Italian paintings from Beckford, 198. Pevsner Architectural Guides.

Gordon, Archie. 'Lansdown Tower, Bath.' In *Towers*, 90–91. Newton Abbot, Devon: David & Charles, 1979. Text, 90. Goodridge drawing & photo, 91.

Granville, A. B. *The Spas of England and Principal Sea-bathing Places. Southern Spas.* London: Colburn, 1841. Tower, 371, 439.

Greenwood, Charles. 'Lansdown Crescent, and Lansdown Place West, including Beckford's Tower, Bath.' In *Famous Houses of the West Country*, 46–50. Bath: Kingsmead Press, 1977.

Haddon, John. *Portrait of Bath.* London: John Hale, 1982. Pp. 177–180.

Haggerty, George. 'Beckford in Bath.' In *William Beckford and the New Millennium*, ed. Kenneth W. Graham & Kevin Berland, 255–270 & 14 illus. New York: AMS Press, 2004 [2005].

Hatt, E. M. *Follies.* London: Chatto & Windus, 1963. Beckford's Tower, '. . . crammed with treasures from Fonthill and his Bath residences', 109.

Hinde, Thomas. [Sir Thomas Chitty, pseud.] 'Queen Victoria fails to return.' & 'Beckford and his tower.' In *Tales from the Pump Room*, 204 & 205–209. London: Gollancz, 1988. Princess Victoria's visit to the Tower in 1830.

Hudson, Kenneth. *Pleasures and People of Bath.* Folio Miniatures. London: Michael Joseph, 1977. Lansdown Cemetery, 22, 24. Watercolour by Samuel Poole of Beckford House in 1924, pl. [13].

Hunter, Rev. Joseph. *The Connection of Bath with the Literature and Science of England.* Bath: R. E. Peach, 1853. The 'eminent' author of *Vathek*, 95.

Hutton, Edward. *Highways and Byways in Somerset.* 1st pocket ed. London: Macmillan, 1923. (1st ed. 1912.) Beckford in Bath, 55. Houndstreet House, Shepton Mallet, built by Beckford, 60. Tower, 67–68. Witham Friary, 210.

Ison, Walter. *The Georgian Buildings of Bath.* London: Faber & Faber, 1948. Nos. 20 & 19 Lansdown Crescent, 109, 113 (plan, fig. 26) & pl. 94b. 'Beckford's Tower, Lansdown', 186 & pl. 109b (Shepherd, 1829 [1831]). Reprints: Bath: Kingsmead Reprints, 1969, revised, 1980; Bath: Bath Preservation Trust, 1996; Reading: Spire Books, 2004.

Jackson, Neil. 'Beckford's Walk.' In *Nineteenth Century Bath Architects and Architecture*, 89–95. Bath: Ashgrove Press, 1991. Also passim. Paperback reissue, 1998.

REVIEWS. Millington, Jon. *Beckford Tower Trust Newsletter*, Spring 1992, 15.

Stollar, Derek. 'Exposing the treasures of a forgotten century.' *[Bath] Evening Chronicle*, 1 July 1991, 6.

Jenkins, Simon. 'Beckford's Tower.' In *Britain's Thousand Best Houses*, 664–665. London: Allen Lane, 2003. Awarded one star (the 20 best received five). Reissued as 'Beckford's tower' in his *Discover Britain's Historic Houses. West Country*, 138–139 and photo of staircase, London: Reader's Digest, 2005. Also 10, 188.

Jones, Barbara. *Follies & Grottoes*. London: Constable, 1953. Tower, 224–225. Fonthill Abbey, 242. Enlarged ed., 1974. Tower, 283. Fonthill Abbey, 407.

Joyce, Maria & H. Mary Wills. *Bath in old picture postcards*. Zaltbommel, Netherlands: European Library, 1990. No. 126: 'Beckford's Tower, Lansdown, Bath', by Dafnis. No. 127: 'Lansdown Cemetery, Bath. 1046', York Publishing Co.

Knight, Charles, ed. *The Land We Live In*. 4 vols. London: Charles Knight, [1847–1850]. Brief account, 3 [1849]: 51–52, 55 & pl. '11.–Lansdowne Tower'. *Idem*, reissued *c*.1854 with 'Lansdowne Tower' beneath text on p. 352, all within border.

Knight, Charles. *Knight's Tourist Companion through the Land We Live In*. London: Natali & Bond, [1853]. No. 5 (of 20): 'Bath'. Beckford, 21–22 & small vignette of Tower with other views of Bath.

Laws, Peter. *Bristol, Bath and Wells. Then and Now*. London: Batsford, 1987. Account of Beckford and the Tower, 58.

Lees-Milne, James & David Ford. *Images of Bath*. Richmond, Surrey: Saint Helena Press, 1982. 'Narrative', 78–79 & passim. 'Gallery': 'Beckford's Tower', Nos. 421–442, captions, 305–306. 'Beckford's Tower, Interior', Nos. 443–451, captions, 306–307. 'Lansdown Crescent', Nos. 554–563, captions, 315–316. 'Abbey Cemetery', Nos. 800–805, captions, 335.
REVIEW. Millington, Jon. *Beckford Tower Trust Newsletter*, Spring 1983, 9.

Lever, Jill, ed. *Catalogue of the Drawings Collection of the Royal Institute of British Architects. Vol. T–Z*. Amersham, Bucks: Avebury Publ., 1984. Samuel Sanders Teulon (1812–1873). '[91] Album, *c*.1835–1851', pen drawing of top of Tower on p. 71 of Album, 25.

Little, Bryan. *The Building of Bath 47–1947. An Architectural and Social Study*. London: Collins, 1947. The Tower owed more to its patron than the nominal designer, 127.

Lowndes, William. 'Beckford, William (1759–1844).' In *They Came to Bath*, 16–17. Bristol: Redcliffe, 1982. General account. Portrait by Reynolds facing 17.

Mainwaring, Rowland. *Annals of Bath 1800–1834*. Bath: M. Meyler & Son, 1838. Under '1827': Saxon tower, 'when permission can be obtained, the stranger is amply repaid his walk to Lansdown . . .', 282–283.

Mais, S. P. B. *Walking in Somerset*. London: Chambers, 1938. Folly built on the top of Lansdown so that Beckford could see his house at Fonthill, 238, 240.

McLaughlin, David & Michael Gray. *Bath in Camera 1849–1861: Early Rare Photographs*. Calotypes by Rev. Francis Lockey. London: Dirk Nishen & Beckington, Bath: Monmouth Calotype, 1989. 'Plate 30. Lansdown Cemetery Gatehouse. 1853–9', sepia view from the south, 44. Beckford's tomb mentioned, 26.

Measom, George. *The Official Illustrated Guide to the Great Western Railway*. London: Richard Griffin, [1860.] Brief account of Tower, 788–789, with woodcut copy of Everitt's view [1850], 789.

Mee, Arthur. *Somerset*. New ed. London: Hodder & Stoughton, 1968. (1st ed. 1941.) One page on Beckford & Tower, 28. The King's England series.

Monkland, George. *Supplement to the Literature and Literati of Bath*. Bath: R. E. Peach, 1855. Willes Maddox 'made the drawings of Beckford's Tower', 59.

Morriss, Richard K. *The Buildings of Bath*. Stroud, Glos: Alan Sutton, 1993. Pp. 115 & photo of Tower, 117.

Mott, George & Sally Sample Aall. *Follies and Pleasure Pavilions*. London: Pavilion, 1989. Tower & Moorish Summerhouse, 33. Triumphal Arch at Fonthill, 60.

 REVIEW. Profit, Jasmine. 'Taking pleasure from acts of folly.' *Bath and West Evening Chronicle*, 28 June 1989, 17.

Murch, Jerom. 'Bath in its relation to Art, Science, Literature, and Education.' In *Handbook to Bath . . . Visit of the British Association, 1888*, ed. J. W. Morris, 99–136. Bath: Isaac Pitman, 1888. Maddox 'made good drawings' of the Tower, 106. Literary Institution Library 'bought at the celebrated Fonthill sale Mr. Beckford's fine set of the French "Transactions" . . . ceiling enriched with paintings from Fonthill', 124. Beckford's library at Lansdown Crescent, 125. Mentioned, 127–128. By other authors: Beckford's Tower, 96, 197, 259.

Murch, Jerom. 'Mr. Beckford. Parts I. & II.' In *Biographical Sketches of Bath Celebrities*, 288–297 & 298–308. London: Isaac Pitman, 1893. Part I is a vague general account, but Part II has interesting personal reminiscences of which pp. 300–303, 304–305 were reprinted in Gregory, *The Beckford Family* (2nd ed., 1898), 98–102. Quote from p. 299 of Murch in Robin Whalley, 'The Royal Victoria Park', *Bath History* 5 (1994): 155.

Norburn, A. E., ed. *The Book of Bath*. Bath: British Medical Association, 1925. 'Notable residents of the past', 242.

Norwich, John Julius. *The Architecture of Southern England*. London: Macmillan, 1985. Lansdown Tower, 17. Dodington: relief after Fonthill & staircase ironwork, 25 & 26. Ashridge chapel, 282. Hadlow Tower, 320. Regret that Fonthill could not be added to Wiltshire section, 655.

Peach, R. E. M. *Street-Lore of Bath*. London: Simpkin & Marshall, 1893. 'Lansdown Cemetery, Walcot', Tower built by John Vaughan, 43–44. Beckford unfavourably compared with Mr Tugwell of Crowe Hall, Widcombe, 61, noted in Maurice Scott, *Discovering Widcombe and Lyncombe, Bath*, rev. 2nd ed., Bath: Widcombe Association, 1993, 36.

Pennington, Jim. 'Lansdown, Beckford and Grenville Monuments.' In *Avon & Somerset. An Explorer's Guide*, 120–122. Castle Cary, Somerset: Castle Cary Press, 1989. Whole-page photo of Tower, 121.

Pevsner, Nikolaus. *The Buildings of England. North Somerset and Bristol*. Harmondsworth, Middlesex: Penguin Books, 1958. 'Lansdown Tower', 215–216 & pl. 69. Lansdown Crescent, 132,

Richardson, Albert Edward. *Monumental Classic Architecture in Great Britain and Ireland during the Eighteenth & Nineteenth Centuries*. London: Batsford, [1914.] Fine photo of Tower from the SE by E. Dockree, 'The Lansdown Tower, Bath', pl. XXX facing 64. Brief text, 64–65.

Robertson, Charles. 'Beckford's Tower.' In *Bath. An Architectural Guide*, 53–54. London: Faber & Faber, 1975. Also 20, 31, 57, 78, 127, 138.

Silvester, Rev. James. *The Parish Church of Walcot, Bath: Its History and Associations*. Bath: W. & F. Dawson, 1888. Cemetery & tomb, 22.

Sloman, Sue, intro. *Victoria Art Gallery, Bath: Concise Catalogue of Paintings and Drawings*. Bath: Bath Museums Service, 1991. Views of Beckford's Tower: British (19th century), 14; William Noble Hardwick, 50; Henry Venn Lansdown, 68; Willes Maddox, 73; Samuel Poole, 86–87; Thomas Hosmer Shepherd, 100.

Smith, Connie & Richard Harris. 'William Beckford's Tower.' In *Rural Rambles near Bristol and Bath*, 60. Newbury, Countryside Books, 2004. First publ. by Spurbooks, 1981, as *Walks in Avon*.

Smith, R. A. L. *Bath*. London: Batsford, 1944. Lansdown Crescent & Tower, 107–108. Maddox colour litho of Tower exterior (1844) facing 103. 2nd rev. ed. 1945.

Stuart, James & Nicholas Revett. 'Of the Choragic Monument of Lysicrates, commonly called the Lanthorn of Demosthenes.' In *The Antiquities of Athens*, 1:27–36 & 9 pl. London: Printed by J. Haberkorn, 1762. Source for the Tower's lantern.

Warren, Derrick. *Curious Somerset*. Stroud: Alan Sutton, 2005. Tower, 18–19.

Watkin, David. *Thomas Hope 1769–1831 and the Neo-Classical Idea*. London: John Murray, 1968. Beckford's Tower, 141, 142, 143 & pl. 45. Also passim.

Weston, Agnes. *My Life among the Bluejackets*. London: James Nisbet, 1910. Her father built a house in about 1860 near the Tower, prompting comments on Beckford, 42. Noted by 'Sul' in 'More about Beckford' & " 'Wonderful road' ", *Bath & Wilts Chronicle & Herald*, 21 Sept 1956, 5.

Wilton-Ely, John. 'Beckford the Builder [Lansdown].' In *William Beckford Exhibition 1976*, [ed. Julian Berry], 57–60. Tisbury, Wilts: Compton Press, 1976. See '5. Fonthill. Fonthill Abbey' for 'Beckford the Builder [Fonthill]'.

Wimhurst, Claude. *The Bombardment of Bath*. Bath: Bath & Wilts Chronicle, 1942. Beckford House in Lansdown Crescent damaged, [15].

Woodward, Christopher. 'Beckford's Tower in Bath.' In *William Beckford, 1760–1844: An Eye for the Magnificent*, ed. Derek E. Ostergard, 278–295. New Haven & London: Yale University Press for the Bard Graduate Center, 2001. Exhibition catalogue.

Young, David. *Bats in the Belfry*. Newton Abbot, Devon: David & Charles, 1987. Tower, 44, illus., 28 (colour) & 45. Tomb photo without columns, 96.

Articles

Bishop, Philippa. 'Beckford in Bath.' *Bath History* 2 (1988): 85–112. Important account of the last twenty-one years of Beckford's life. 8 illus.

Boyd, Judy. 'Centuries of worship in the city.' *Bath Chronicle*, 31 Jan 2005, 22. Kingswood School was built on part of Beckford's 218 acre estate.

C., T. S. 'The Historic Houses of Bath. William Beckford.' *Bath and County Graphic* 4 no. 2 (June 1899): 16. Photo of Beckford's house.

Crallan, Hugh. 'Beckford in Bath.' *Architectural Review* 143 (March 1968): 204–208. Valuable article incl. 13 photos & map of Beckford's ride.

Elliott, Kirsten. 'The Missing Islamic Summerhouse.' *Beckford Journal* 9 (2003): 15–18. Possibly not Beckford's, but *c*.1900.

Goring, Edward. 'The price of farewell.' *Bath and Wilts Evening Chronicle*, 15 June 1973, 4. Sale of 19 Lansdown Crescent by Lord Strathcona who had sold No. 20 two years previously.

Goring, Edward. 'The man who blackmailed Bath.' *Bath and West Evening Chronicle*, 31 Dec 1974, 4. Disputes with Bath Corporation about rights of way behind Lansdown Crescent.

Huddlestone, Linden. 'Beckford in Bath – Tradition and Innovation.' *Georgian Group in Gloucester and Avon Newsletter*, Spring 1986, 7–9.

[Kaye, John William.] 'Some Literary Ramblings about Bath. III.' *Cornhill Magazine* 28 (July 1873): 27–44 at 36–39, 40. Impressions of Beckford and his Tower in the third and last article about authors associated with Bath.

Lees-Milne, James. 'Beckford in Bath.' *Country Life*, 29 April 1976, 1106–1109. Article to promote the 1976 William Beckford exhibition.

Lees-Milne, James. 'William Beckford's Bath.' *Interiors*, June 1982, 132–137. How Beckford used his tower. Seven Maddox lithographs in colour.

McGarvie, Michael. 'William Beckford and the Perambulation of Walcot.' *Beckford Tower Trust Newsletter*, Spring 1985, 8. Embattled Gateway and walls at Tower divided the parishes of Walcot and those adjoining.

Meehan, J. F. 'Famous Buildings of Bath and District. No. 32. William Beckford's Bath Residence: 20, Lansdown Crescent.' *The Beacon* (Frome, Somerset) 3 no. 9 (Sept 1900): 131–132. Reprinted in his *Famous Houses of Bath and District*, Bath: B. & J. F. Meehan, 1901, 157–160 & pl.

Origo, Iris. 'The Pleasures of Bath in the Eighteenth Century.' *Horizon* 7 no. 1 (Winter 1965): 4–15 at 14. Beckford in Bath.

Spiers, Rowena. 'Luxury home for lovers of history.' *Bath Chronicle*, 27 April 2004, 38. Colour photo of first floor room over arch at 20 Lansdown Crescent.

Townsend, Patsy, Joan Hoffman & Margaret Sutherland. 'Beckford's Tower in Wartime.' *Beckford Tower Trust Newsletter*, Spring 1989, 3. Reminiscences by three volunteer lady firewatchers.

Warren, J. M. 'Abbey rails.' *Bath and West Evening Chronicle*, 9 Feb 2005, 11. Letter about communion rails from Bath Abbey removed by Beckford [in 1833], attached to his property at Lansdown Place West, and now returned.

'Where "Vathek" Was Written. Beckford's Library Destroyed by Raiders.' *Bath and Wilts Chronicle and Herald*, 27 May 1942, 5. (Also in weekly ed., 30 May, 10.) Library at No. 19 destroyed during air raids, 25–26 April.

Woodward, Christopher. 'William Beckford and Fonthill Splendens. Early works by Soane and Goodridge.' *Apollo* 147 (Feb 1998): 31–40 at 38–39, 40. Genesis of Beckford's Tower discussed. For pp. 31–38 see '5. Fonthill'.

LATER BATH GUIDE BOOKS

Baddeley, M. J. B. 'Wm. Beckford.' In *Bath and Bristol and Forty Miles Around*, 50–51. London: Dulau, 1902. Beckford House, 23, 43. Beckford's Tower mentioned, 44. Lansdown Cemetery & Beckford's Tower, 49. Fonthill [New] Abbey & Beckford's Abbey, 144–145. Thorough Guide Series.

Bullen, Annie. 'Beckford's Tower and Museum.' In *Bath . . . More than a Guide*, 38. Norwich: Jarrold, 2004. City-break Guides.

Chamberlain, V. C. *The City of Bath*. Bristol: Rankin Bros., 1951. 'Abbot of Fonthill', 65–66, 78. Photos of 20 Lansdown Crescent, 71, & Tower, 73.

Curtis, Frederick, publ. *Guide Through and Round Bath*. 4th ed., Bath: F. Curtis, [1873]. Tower, 16–17. *Idem.* 13th ed. Bath: Harding & Curtis, 1906. Beckford, 106, 108–110. Cemetery, 151–152.

Curtis, John. *Bath*. Norwich: Jarrold, 2001. 'William Beckford's House. Lansdown Crescent', 88. 'Beckford's Tomb. Lansdown Cemetery', 90. 'Beckford's Tower. Lansdown', 91. Fine colour photos.

Flash, Lesley. 'William Beckford.' In *Known at this Address*, 20. Bath: Bath City Council, 1982. Brief one-page account of Beckford in Bath.

Fraser, Maxwell. *Somerset*. London: Great Western Railway Company, 1934. 'On the summit of Lansdown hill is the tower' built by Beckford, 141.

Gibson, Neil, photographer. *Bath and its Surroundings*. Bradford-on-Avon: Moonraker Press, 1975. Whole-page photo of Tower with caption, 37.

Gorst, Thom. 'Beckford's Tower.' In *Bath*, 196–199. London: Ellipsis, 1997. Also 186, 188.

Green, Kim. 'William Beckford.' & 'The Lansdown Tower.' In *Bath: Valley of the Sacred Spring*, 103 & 104, photo. Bath: Second Nature Press, 2004.

Greenwood, Charles. *Walking In and Around Bath*. Bath: Kingsmead Press, 1975. Lansdown Crescent & Tower, 39–40.

Greenwood, Charles. *Walking in Bath*. Bath: Kingsmead Press, 1978. Tower, 61. Goodridge litho of Tower from the north (*c.*1827), 64.

Grigson, Geoffrey. *West Country*. London: Collins, for the Festival of Britain Office, 1951. Tower built to give a view of Fonthill, 65. About Britain No. 1.

Hallett, C. 'Cemetery, Lansdown (formerly Beckford's Tower).' & 'Beckford's Tower.' In *Objects of Interest in the City of Bath and Its Neighbourhood*, 10–11 & 27. 11th ed. Revised & enlarged. Bath: C. Hallett, 1887.

Hardy, Paul & William Lowndes. *Bath. Portrait of a City*. Bristol: Redcliffe Press, 1984. Lansdown Crescent (Tower's 'superlative view'), 51, illus., 50.

Jolly, publ. *The Handy Guide to Bath*. 43rd ed. Bath: Jolly & Son, *c.*1895. Woodcut, 'Lansdown Cemetery', from Tunstall's *Rambles about Bath* (1889 ed.), 57. Tower mentioned, 26, 52. New ed. *The Handy Guide to the City of Bath*. *c.*1902. Lansdown Crescent, 58.

Kibblewhite, Gideon. "William Beckford, 'The Fool of Fonthill' 1760–1844." In *The Naked Guide to Bath*, 64. Bath: Naked Guides, 2004. Also 103.

Knappett, Gill. *The Little Book of Bath*. Andover, Hants: Jarrold, 2003. 'Eccentric's edifice', [85]. Photo and brief account.

Lewis, Harold. *The Original Bath Guide*. Bath: William Lewis, 1906. 'Beckford House', 134–135, photo, 135. Tower, 140–141, photo from the SE, 140. Casali ceilings, 70. Conversation with Jerom Murch, 126.

Major, Samuel Dobell. *Notabilia of Bath*. London: Hodder & Stoughton, 1871. 'Beckford loaves. – A light kind of bread made from the finest flour,

mixed with milk, and fermented by German yeast', 9. 'Beckford William',
9. Lansdown Cemetery, 44. Rev. ed., Bath: E. R. Blackett, 1879.

Martin, Alfred Trice. *The Story of Bath*. London: Isaac Pitman for Bath
Education Committee, [1912]. An 'eminent man of letters', 265–266.

Mee, Arthur. *Bath*. London: St Hugh's Press, [1950]. Beckford Tower, 50,
52.

Michelin, publ. Tourist Guide. 'Beckford Tower and Museum.' In *England.
The West Country*, 32. London: Michelin Tyre Co., 1984.

Nelson, publ. 'Beckford's Tower and Lansdown Field.' In *Bath and Its
Neighbourhood*, 37–38. London: T. Nelson, c.1880. Lansdown Crescent,
15. Lansdown Cemetery, 35.

Newman, Paul. *Bath*. Newton Abbot, Devon: Pevensey, 1993. (1st ed.
1986.) Photo of Tower, 83. Text, 82. Photo of Beckford's Bridge, 76.

Peach, R. E. 'Beckford House, Lansdown Crescent.' In *Historic Houses in
Bath*, 1:104–108. 2 vols. London: Simpkin Marshall, 1883. Mostly a long
footnote reprinting Hazlitt's condemnation of paintings in Fonthill Abbey.

Peach, R. E. 'Lansdown Cemetery.' In *Bath Old and New. A Handy Guide
and a History*, 184–185. London: Simpkin Marshall, 1888. Casali ceilings from Fonthill in Theatre Royal & Royal Literary Institution,
173–174 & 181.

Salmon, Arthur L. *Bath and Wells*. London: Blackie, [1914]. One-page
account of Beckford and the Tower, 22–23.

Simmonds, Tricia. *Best of Bath*. Bath: Unichrome, 1994. Tower photos, 61,
62.

Spender, Constance & Edith Thompson. *Bath*. London: Society for Promoting Christian Knowledge, 1922. 'That curious character', 107.

Stannard, Dorothy. *Bath & Surroundings*. London: APA Publications, 2004.
(1st ed. 1996.) Tower & Museum, 26. An Insight Compact Guide.

Tompkins, John. *Portraits of Bath*. Bath: Kingsmead, 1976. Drawings by
Grace D. Bratton. Beckford's arch at Lansdown Crescent, 31, depicted,
30. Account of Beckford, 47.

Trewin, J. C. *The Story of Bath*. London: Staples Press, 1951. Beckford
mentioned, 24, 81–82, 89.

Ward, Lock. 'Beckford's Tower.' In *A New Popular and Descriptive Guide
to the City of Bath*, 75–76. London: Ward, Lock, 1897. Many later eds.

Wooller, M. P., photos. *The Historic City of Bath*. Bath: Spa Committee,
1959. '47. A Lansdown Crescent House'. Fine photo of Beckford's
house.

Wright, G. N. 'Lansdown Cemetery.' In *The Historic Guide to Bath*,
352–354. Bath: R. E. Peach, 1864. Woodcut of Tower & Cemetery
Entrance, 352. Casali paintings from Fonthill sale of 1801: in Theatre
Royal ceiling removed in 1839 & sold to Col. Blathwayt of Dyrham in
1845, 310; in library of the Royal Literary Institution, North Parade,

321–322. Beckford's set of *French Transactions* in library there, 322. 2nd ed., of the *Historic Guide*, 1883.

1966 BATH FESTIVAL, JUNE 15–26

For James Babb's lecture on June 16 see '1. Accounts of Beckford's Life'
For the 1966 Beckford Exhibition at the Holburne Museum
see '9. Exhibitions'

Arabian banquet. 'Beckford brings 40 hookahs to Assembly Rooms.' *Bath and Wilts Evening Chronicle: Bath Festival Supplement*, 14 June 1966, III. *Idem*, IV, Beckford exhibition and lectures by James Babb & Boyd Alexander.

Boardman, Maurice. 'Ugh . . . Those Sheep's Eyes.'–'Vathek mime at Arabian Banquet.' *Bath and Wilts Evening Chronicle*, 25 June 1966, 7–8. 'Turkish delight – or the night Bath went Arabian', *Idem*, 9, seven photos of participants. *Vathek* mime devised by Barbara Robertson and Veronica Crallan. (Also in *Bath Weekly Chronicle*, 2 July, 4 & 10, with 1 & 3 photos.)

'Glamour of Arabia lends colour to Festival fringe.' *Bath Weekly Chronicle*, 25 June 1966, 11. Five photos of rehearsal for the Arabian banquet.

'Sul'. 'Arabian Nights ended in Hell.' *Bath and Wilts Evening Chronicle*, 1 Feb 1966, 4. (Also in *Bath Weekly Chronicle*, 5 Feb, 2.) Plans for the fringe event, inspired by *Vathek*. *Idem*, 4 Feb, 9. Letter from a 'Mother of teenagers' asking 'Is this the real Beckford?'.

'Sul'. 'Beckford expert for Bath Festival.' *Bath and Wilts Evening Chronicle*, 22 Feb 1966, 4. (Also in *Bath Weekly Chronicle*, 26 Feb, 2.) James Babb to give a lecture on Beckford.

'Sul'. 'A preview of Arabian banquet.' *Bath and Wilts Evening Chronicle*, 4 June 1966, 4. Television programme on 13 June featuring some 12 cast members.

'Sul'. 'Descendants of William Beckford.' & 'Exotic guests at the Beckford banquet.' *Bath and Wilts Evening Chronicle*, 9 June 1966, 4.

W., P. W. 'Beckford: getting to know the real man.' *Bath and Wilts Evening Chronicle*, 24 June 1966, 8. Review of Boyd Alexander's lecture.

'William Beckford: An Eighteenth Century Eccentric.' & 'Events connected with William Beckford: Mr. Beckford's Arabian Banquet, William Beckford's Houses, Lectures on William Beckford, Beckford Exhibition.' In *Bath Festival 1966*, 9 & 11. Bath: Bath Festival Society, 1966.

7. Landscape Gardening

Books

Batey, Mavis & David Lambert. *The English Garden Tour. A View into the Past*. London: John Murray, 1990. Fonthill, 189. Beckford, 238.

Bettey, J. H. *The Landscape of Wessex*. Bradford-on-Avon: Moonraker Press, 1980. '. . . extravagant landscape remains [today]', 153. '. . . tree planting on a massive scale', 159. Very similar accounts in his *Wessex from AD 1000*, London: Longmans, 1986, 211, 213. Regional History of England series.

Bisgrove, Richard. *The National Trust Book of the English Garden*. London: Viking, 1990. Beckford & Fonthill, 123.

Bond, James. *Somerset Parks and Gardens. A Landscape History*. Tiverton, Devon: Somerset Books, 1998. Alderman Beckford at Witham, 70, 91. William Beckford, 91, 109, 125.

Brown, Jane. *The Pursuit of Paradise. A Social History of Gardens and Gardening*. London: HarperCollins, 1999. Fonthill, 116, 220.

Carritt, E. F. *A Calendar of British Taste. From 1600 to 1800*. London: Routledge & Kegan Paul, [1949]. 'Gardens', quotation from *Vathek*, 395. 'Manners and Tastes', quotation from *Modern Novel Writing*, 430.

Châtel, Laurent. 'Landscaping Utopias: Beckford's Gardens and the Politics of the Sublime.' In *William Beckford and the New Millennium*, ed. Kenneth W. Graham & Kevin Berland, 213–247 & 11 illus. New York: AMS Press, 2004 [2005].

Cotterell, T. Sturge. *Historic Map of Bath*. 5th ed. Bath: Spa Committee, [1939]. (1st ed. 1897.) 'The dell adjoining [the botanic garden] was planted with trees under the advice of William Beckford', 5. Beckford's house, no. 196 on map, noted, 26.

Cowell, Frank Richard. *The Garden as a Fine Art: From Antiquity to Modern Times*. London: Weidenfeld & Nicolson, 1978. Beckford lavished a fortune at Fonthill on house and grounds, 186.

Craft, Adrian. *Fonthill Revisited ~ Rediscovering William Beckford's Subterranean World*. Thesis for Bristol University, 1996. v, 43 pp.

Daniels, Stephen. *Humphry Repton. Landscape Gardening and the Geography of Georgian England*. New Haven: Yale University Press, 1999. Beckford's letter of 1799 declining Repton's offer of advice, 38 & 275 n79.

Debois Landscape Survey Group (John Phibbs). *Fonthill, Wiltshire. A Survey of the Landscape*. Privately printed reports commissioned by the owners of the Splendens site, 1991–1993.

Debois Landscape Survey Group. *Beckford's Tower. A Survey of the Landscape*. Privately printed reports commissioned by Bath Preservation Trust, Nov 1993. Revised March 1994.

    REVIEWS. Neal, James. 'Survey of the Beckford Ride. Summary of the Draft Report produced by the Debois Landscape Survey Group. December 1993.' *Beckford Tower Trust Newsletter*, Spring 1994, 9.

    Pook, Sally. 'Tower trust in garden project.' *Bath Chronicle*, 11 Oct 1994, 4.

Dutton, Ralph. *The English Garden*. 2nd rev. ed. London: Batsford, 1950. (1st ed. 1937.) Fonthill: Wyatt's 'ruin' of 1796, 115; 'Gothic extravagance', 116.

Elliott, Brent. *Victorian Gardens*. London: Batsford, 1986. Fonthill, 93.

Fearnley-Whittingstall, Jane. *The Garden. An English Love Affair. One Thousand Years of Gardening*. London: Weidenfeld & Nicolson, 2002. Beckford, 134, 223–224. Fonthill, 223.

Ferro, Maria Ines. *Queluz. The Palace and Gardens*. London: Scala Books, 1997. Beckford, 41, 62–63, 72, 86–87, 113, 115.

'Folly de Grandeur.' In *The Eccentric Gardener*, 42–46. Oxford: Past Times, 2005. Brief description of the garden at Fonthill in a general account.

Gemmett, Robert J. *William Beckford and the picturesque: a study of Fonthill*. Ann Arbor, Michigan: University Microfilms, 1967. viii, 307 pp. Bibliography. PhD thesis for the University of Syracuse, NY. *Dissertation Abstracts International* 28 no. 5 (Nov 1967): 1740A–1741A.

Gilding, R. *Historic Public Parks. Bath*. Bristol: Avon Gardens Trust, 1997. Beckford advised on the layout of the two dells in Victoria Park, 29, 30.

Grigson, Geoffrey. 'Caves of Verdure.' In *Gardenage*, 150–165. London: Routledge & Kegan Paul, 1952. Grottoes at Fonthill, passim.

Hadfield, Miles. *A History of British Gardening*. London: Spring Books, 1969. The Rockery, 296–297. Milne & Vincent, Beckford's gardeners. Originally titled *Gardening in Britain* (1960).

Hadfield, Miles & John. *Gardens of Delight*. London: Cassell, 1964. A paradise for the faithful in *Vathek*, 23–24.

Hadfield, Miles, Robert Harling & Leonie Highton. 'Beckford, William.' In *British Gardeners. A Biographical Dictionary*, 33. London: Zwemmer, 1980.

Harding, Stewart & David Lambert. 'Beckford's Ride.' In *Parks and Gardens of Avon*, 70–71, Bristol: Avon Gardens Trust, 1994. Embattled Gateway, fig. 64. Also 111, 122.

Hobhouse, Penelope. *The Story of Gardening*. London: Dorling Kindersley, 2002. Beckford & Fonthill, 200 & illus.

Hobhouse, Penelope & Patrick Taylor. *The Gardens of Europe*. London:

George Philip, 1990. Beckford, 46, 147–148. Queluz, 147. Monserrate, 148.

Honess, Keith A. 'Beckford, William.' & 'Fonthill Abbey.' In *The Oxford Companion to Gardens*, ed. Sir Geoffrey Jellicoe et al., 42 & 195. Oxford: Oxford University Press, 1986. Also 'American Gardens', 14–15, by Jean O'Neill, & 'Monserrate', 379, by Barbara Levinge.

Hoyles, Martin. *The Story of Gardening*. London: Journeyman Press, 1991. Fonthill, 47.

Hunt, John Dixon. *The Figure in the Landscape: Poetry, Painting and Gardening during the Eighteenth Century*. Baltimore: John Hopkins University Press, 1976. Loutherbourg at Fonthill in 1781, 216.

Hunt, John Dixon. *Gardens and the Picturesque*. Cambridge, MA: M.I.T. Press, 1992. Fonthill: genius loci, 229; shaping the environment, 237.

Hunt, John Dixon. *The Picturesque Garden in Europe*. London: Thames & Hudson, 2003. Gilpin visited Fonthill, 66. Fonthill estate dedicated to 'the qualities of roughness . . . sudden variations', 80–81.

Hunt, Peter, ed. *The Shell Gardens Book*. London: Phoenix House, 1964. Beckford & Fonthill, 223–224.

Hunt, Peter, ed. *The Garden Lover's Companion*. London: Eyre Methuen, 1974. Boboli Gardens, Florence: Beckford's letters of 1780, 241–244.

Hussey, Christopher. *The Picturesque*. London: Putnam, 1927. Volume of Beckford's pencil notes mentioning Repton, 162–163. Fonthill, 197, 199, 214. Cozens with Beckford in Italy, 264.

Huxley, Anthony. *An Illustrated History of Gardening*. London: Paddington Press, 1978. Beckford, 310.

Jacques, David. *Georgian Gardens. The Reign of Nature*. London: Batsford, 1983. Alderman Beckford's improvements after 1755 fire, 90. Abbey, 156–159, illus., 157. Loudon's praise of Fonthill, 167. 1822 sale, 174. Others wished to copy great spire at Fonthill, 179. Rutter's 1823 plan of Fonthill grounds, colour pl. X.

Jellicoe, Geoffrey & Susan. *The Landscape of Man*. London: Thames & Hudson, 1975. Whole-page illus. of Turner's distant view of Abbey from the south in 1799, 260 (pl. 450), caption, 261.

Joyce, David, ed. *Garden Styles. An Illustrated History of Design and Tradition*. London: Pyramid Books, 1989. Beckford & Fonthill, 77.

Keen, Mary. *The Glory of the English Garden*. London: Barrie & Jenkins, 1989. Beckford & Fonthill, 94.

Kluckert, Ehrenfried. 'William Beckford and Fonthill Abbey.' In *European Garden Design: From Classical Antiquity to the Present Day*, 398–399. Trans. from the German by Rolf Toman. Cologne: Könemann, 2000.

Laird, Mark. *The Flowering of the Landscape Garden. English Pleasure Grounds 1720–1800*. Philadelphia: University of Pennsylvania Press, 1999. 'American garden' at Fonthill, 97, 98.

Loudon, J. C. 'First-rate Residences . . . Fonthill Abbey.' In *Encyclopaedia of Gardening*, 1246. London: Longman, etc., 1822. Description of the grounds and planting in 1806.

Loudon, J. C. *Arboretum et Fruticetum Britannicum*. 8 vols. London: A. Spottiswoode for the Author, 1838. Visited Fonthill twice in 1806 & again for two days in 1833 when grounds were 'in a state of neglect'. 'The scenery of Fonthill has something of a Swiss character', 1:128.

Loudon, John Claudius. *In Search of English Gardens: The Travels of John Claudius Loudon and his wife Jane*. Ed. Priscilla Boniface. Wheathampstead, Herts: Lennard, 1987. Visit to Fonthill in 1833, 13, 144, 149–153, 221. Painting of Abbey from Old Wardour Castle, *c.*1825, by John Baverstock Knight, 145. Other illus., 149, 150, 151. Hamilton Palace, 212–215 & 3 illus.

Malins, Edward. *English Landscaping and Literature 1660–1840*. London: Oxford University Press, 1966. Pp. 166–168. View of Abbey from American Plantation from Storer (1812) facing 163.

Malins, Edward & The Knight of Glin. *Lost Demesnes. Irish Landscape Gardening, 1660–1845*. London: Barrie & Jenkins, 1976. Beckford dismissive of Richard Colt Hoare's *Journal of a Tour in Ireland* (1807), 82.

Marr, Alexander. 'William Beckford and the Landscape Garden.' In *William Beckford, 1760–1844: An Eye for the Magnificent*, ed. Derek E. Ostergard, 136–153. New Haven & London: Yale University Press for the Bard Graduate Center, 2001. Exhibition catalogue.

Mayoux, Jean-Jacques. *Richard Payne Knight et le pittoresque*. Paris: Les Presses modernes, 1932. P. 8.

Miller, Naomi. *Heavenly Caves. Reflections on the Garden Grotto*. London: George Allen & Unwin, 1982. P. 88.

Mosser, Monique & Georges Teyssot, eds. *The Architecture of Western Gardens*. Cambridge, MA: M.I.T. Press, 1991. Pp. 274, 276, 280 n. 29. Publ. simultaneously as *The History of Garden Design*, London: Thames & Hudson, 1991.

Mowl, Timothy. *Historic Gardens of Wiltshire*. Stroud, Glos: Tempus, 2004. Fonthill Splendens, 87–90. Fonthill Abbey, 119–121.

Pound, Christopher. *Genius of Bath. The City and its Landscape*. Bath: Millstream Books, 1986. Planting at Tower, 82–83 & n117, 86. Lithograph of Abbey Cemetery, *c.*1850, 86.

Quest-Ritson, Charles. *The English Garden Abroad*. London: Viking, 1992. Monserrate, 3, 9, 156–163 & two illus. Fonthill, viii, 160, 200. Also 175.

Sales, John. *West Country Gardens*. Gloucester: Alan Sutton, 1980. Fonthill Abbey 'still retains elements of the sublime', 13.

Sales, John. *West Country Houses*. Gloucester: Alan Sutton, 1980. Beckford & Fonthill, 80.

Sieveking, Albert Forbes. *The Praise of Gardens*. London: Dent, 1899. Six extracts about gardens from Beckford's *Italy* (1834), 223–228.

Strong, Roy. *A Celebration of Gardens*. London: HarperCollins, 1991. Loudon on Fonthill in 1833, 265. Henry Venn Lansdown on Beckford's garden at Bath in 1838, 295–297.

Strong, Roy. *Garden Party*. London: Frances Lincoln, 2000. Monserrate, 201–202.

Stuart, David C. *Georgian Gardens*. London: Robert Hale, 1979. Fonthill, 73, 81, 89, 107, 149, 221, illus., 218.

Summers, Peter. 'Notes on Beckford.' In *William Beckford. Some notes on his life in Bath 1822–1844 and a catalogue of the exhibition in the Holburne of Menstrie Museum*, ed. Peter Summers & Philippa Bishop, 6–15. Bath: Privately printed, 1966.

Taylor, Patrick. *Period Gardens*. London: Pavilion, 1991. Fonthill, 104.

Thacker, Christopher. 'England's Kubla Khan.' In *William Beckford Exhibition 1976*, [ed. Julian Berry], 63–76. Tisbury, Wilts: Compton Press, 1976.

Thacker, Christopher. *Masters of the Grotto. Joseph & Josiah Lane*. Tisbury, Wilts: Compton Press, 1976. Grottoes at Fonthill, 24–28, 29–31. Fonthill one of five different sites, 21. Grotto built in 1794, 23. Limited to 250 copies.

Thacker, Christopher. *The History of Gardens*. London: Croom Helm, 1979. Beckford, 7, 182, 184, 217, 221–224. Fonthill, 7, 17, 182, 197, 200, 221–224. Illus., xxxv, xxxviii, 147, 148.

Thacker, Christopher. *The Wildness Pleases*. London: Croom Helm, 1983. Pp. 45–46, 187–192, 197–198, 203, 210–212.

Thacker, Christopher. *England's Historic Gardens*. Dorking, Surrey: Templar, 1989. Fonthill 'the greatest of all Gothic follies . . . set within a walled and totally private forest paradise', 48.

Thacker, Christopher. *The Genius of Gardening. The History of Gardens in Britain and Ireland*. London: Weidenfeld & Nicolson, 1994. Alderman Beckford, 239. Beckford, 239–240. Fonthill, 181, 223, 239–240, 249.

Thacker, Christopher. *Building Towers, Forming Gardens. Landscaping by Hamilton, Hoare and Beckford*. London: St Barnabas Press, 2002. Ch. 3–6: 'Magna Charta in his Hand', Alderman Beckford & Fonthill Splendens, 49–61; 'We may Seek the Green Solitudes', William Beckford, 63–84; 'Building Towers, Forming Gardens', creation of the Abbey, 85–99; 'Twice Five Miles of Fertile Ground', life at the Abbey, 100–116. Also passim. With illus.

REVIEWS. Bond, James. *Transactions of the Ancient Monuments Society* 48 (2004): 120–121.

Bradley-Hole, Kathryn. *Country Life*, 7 Feb 2002, 80.

Marr, Alexander. 'Enchanting Paths of Paradise.' *Beckford Journal* 8 (2002): 10–15.

Mowl, Timothy. *Garden History* 30 no. 1 (Spring 2002): 101–102.

Woodbridge, Kenneth. *Landscape and Antiquity: Aspects of English Culture at Stourhead, 1718–1838*. Oxford: Clarendon Press, 1970. Beckford, 163–164. Fonthill, 52n, 163–164, 178, 194–195.

Woods, May. *Visions of Arcadia. European Gardens from Renaissance to Rococo*. London: Arum, 1996. Beckford, 129, 131, 208.

Articles

Blackmore, Sidney. 'Chambers, Beckford and Landscape: A Signpost.' *Beckford Tower Trust Newsletter*, Part 2, Spring 1980, [4]. Sir William Chambers's influence on Beckford's landscaping.

Châtel, Laurent. "The Mole, the Bat, and the Fairy or the Sublime Grottoes of 'Fonthill Splendens'." *Beckford Journal* 5 (1999): 53–74.

E., H. 'Fonthill and Wardour.' *Gardeners' Chronicle* 3rd series 13 (14 Jan 1893): 39–40. A brief account of the grounds.

E., H. 'Fonthill Abbey.' *Gardeners' Chronicle* 3rd series 14 (4 Nov 1893): 551–552. A fuller description than the one in January above.

Elliott, Charles. 'Death by rhododendron.' *The Independent*, 17 Feb 1996. American Plantation at Fonthill mentioned. American trees and shrubs.

Finlayson, Jean. 'Do keep calm, Mr B, only God can make a tree.' *Bath and West Evening Chronicle*, 10 Nov 1975, 4.

Gemmett, Robert J. 'Beckford's Fonthill: The Landscape as Art.' *Gazette des Beaux-Arts* 80 (Dec 1972): 335–356 incl. 19 illus.

Loudon, J. C. 'Horticultural Society and Garden.' *Gardener's Magazine* 1 (April 1826), 214. Comments on the luxuriant growth of American plants at Fonthill Abbey.

Loudon, J. C. 'Notes on Gardens and Country Seats, visited, from July 27. to September 16. 1833, during a Tour . . .' *Gardener's Magazine* 11 (Sept 1835): 441–449. '. . . scarcely any place of the same extent was ever formed that could be kept up at so little expense as Fonthill', 444–445. Important account dated 28 Aug, including first-hand description of the fall of the tower in 1825. Quoted in *Bath Chronicle*, 24 Sept 1835, 4e, *Bath and Cheltenham Gazette*, 29 Sept 1835, 1 and (p. 448) in *The Times*, 4 Sept 1835, 3b. Pp. 445–449 reprinted as 'Mr. Beckford and Fonthill Abbey', *Mirror of Literature* 26 (12 Sept 1835): 173–175. Entire account reprinted in Michael Charlesworth, ed. & intro, *The English Garden. Literary Sources and Documents*, 3 vols., Robertsbridge, Sussex: Helm, 1993, 3:213–216 (see also 3:211 & 1:33, 35, 46 (nn51, 52), 67, 69) and Gemmett, *Beckford's Fonthill* (2003), 362–371.

Loudon, J. C. *Gardener's Magazine* 12 (Sept 1836): 503–504, 505. Fonthill Pavilion and the grottoes.

McGarvie, Michael. 'Mr Beckford's vanished Arcadia. A retrospect on a Wessex dream of a wild and monastic paradise.' *The Field*, 20 May 1976, 912–914. Beckford's landscapes were influenced by his foreign travels.

McGarvie, Michael. 'Arcadia in Wessex: William Beckford and his gardens.' *Bath Evening Chronicle*, 5 June 1976, 7. Fine article on Beckford and gardens in England and Portugal.

McGarvie, Michael. 'William Beckford, Gardener, at Witham and Fonthill.' *Frome Society Yearbook* 7 (1997–1998): 112–121.

Miller, Norbert. 'William Beckfords Verwandlung von Fonthill / William Beckford's Metamorphosis of Fonthill.' *Daidalos. Berlin Architectural Journal* No. 4 (15 June 1982): 33–53. Beckford's vision of Fonthill as a landscaped paradise. 21 illus., incl. six Turner's watercolours in colour. Parallel German/English text.

Mowl, Tim. 'Inside Beckford's Landscape of the Mind.' *Country Life*, 7 Feb 2002, 60–63. Alderman Beckford's garden haunted his son.

Quest-Ritson, Charles. 'The Englishman's garden abroad.' *The English Garden* Issue 76 (Jan 2004) 50–53 at 51. Beckford's garden in the Sintra hills.

Rose, Graham. 'Portugal's Eden returns to the wilderness; Gardening.' *Sunday Times Style*, 21 July 1991, 3.8. Beckford's landscaping at Monserrate.

Sladen, Gillian. 'Beckford's Tower Garden.' *Beckford Journal* 1 (1995): 11. A report of recent work at the Garden.

Spaen van Biljoen, Baron Johan Frederik Willem van. 'A Dutchman's visits to some English Gardens in 1791: Extracts from the Unpublished Journal of Baron Johan Frederik Willem van Spaen van Biljoen, with a Biographical Introduction by Heimerick Tromp.' Trans. Evelyn Newby. *Journal of Garden History* 2 no. 1 (Jan–March 1982): 48–49.

Strong, Roy. 'A corner of a foreign field; Gardens in Europe.' *The Times Saturday Review*, 9 May 1992, 33. Beckford's landscaping at Monserrate.

Thacker, Christopher. 'The Volcano: Culmination of the Landscape Garden.' *Eighteenth-Century Life* 8 no. 2 (1983): 74–83 at 80–82 & 83 nn17–25. Beckford created the only garden volcano in England.

Vincent, James. *Gentleman's Magazine* n.s. 30 (July 1848): 108. Death at Fonthill Gifford, aged 80. Beckford's gardener at Fonthill and Lansdown.

W., W. H. 'Fonthill Abbey, Tisbury.' *Journal of Horticulture, Cottage Gardener, and Home Farmer* 3rd series 17 (26 July 1888): 69–70. A brief description of the grounds.

Sale

Guy, Mr. 'Specifications of 1300 Maiden Oak Trees.' Beckford Arms, Fonthill, 3–4 March 1841. 5pp. 180 lots.

8. The Collection

GENERAL ACCOUNTS

Books

Brodick Castle, Isle of Arran, guide books. Lady Jean Fforde. *Brodick Castle*. Brodick: The Author, 1956. Pp. 20–21. Colin McWilliam, *Brodick Castle & Garden*, Edinburgh: The National Trust for Scotland, 1964, pp. 7, 8, 11, 12. R. J. Prentice, *Brodick Castle & Gardens*, Edinburgh: The National Trust for Scotland, 1979, passim. Christopher Hartley et al., *Brodick Castle & Country Park*, Edinburgh: The National Trust for Scotland, 1987, passim.

Charlecote Park, Warwickshire, guide books. James Lees-Milne et al. *Charlecote Park. Warwickshire*. London: The National Trust, 1974, 1979 & 1985. Passim. Alice Fairfax-Lucy, *Charlecote and the Lucys*, Norwich: Jarrold, 1982. Fonthill sale of 1823, [20, 22, 25].

Davis, Frank. *Victorian Patrons of the Arts. Twelve Famous Collections and Their Owners*. London: Country Life, 1963. Quote from Beckford's letter of 1841 about selling paintings & two paintings from his collection in the Holford sale at Christie's, 1928, 14. Pair of coffers (Wallace Collection), 44.

Fedden, Robin. *Treasures of the National Trust*. London: Cape, 1976. Claudes at Anglesey Abbey, 46. Romney portrait at Upton, 49. Buying furniture in Paris, 116. Boulle commode at Petworth, 120. Porcelain at Charlecote, 169.

Fisher, Mark. *Britain's Best Museums and Galleries*. London: Allen Lane, 2004. Holburne at 1845 sale, 9. Romney portrait at Upton House, 200. With Cozens in Italy, 305, 313. Brodick Castle, 432. Paul Storr, 619.

Foss, Arthur. *Country House Treasures*. London: National Trust/Weidenfeld & Nicolson, 1980. Brodick Castle, 69–70. Charlecote Park, 95–96. Dodington House, 127. Dyrham Park, 133. Powderham Castle, 272.

Haskell, Francis. *Rediscoveries in Art: Some Aspects of Taste, Fashion and Collecting in England and France*. London: Phaidon, 1976. Beckford's 'love of the arts', 28, 29 n30.

Herrmann, Frank. 'The Beckford Collection Sold.' & 'Rogers on Fonthill Abbey.' In *The English as Collectors*, 210–217, pl. 22–23 & 218–219. London: Chatto & Windus, 1972. Also 4, 29, 66, 145, 151, 163, 165, 166, 244, 248, 269, 270, 348, 418, 421, 433.

Kingston Lacy, Dorset. London: The National Trust, 1994. Savonnerie carpet from the Grand Drawing Room at Fonthill Abbey, 64 & photo, 4. Also 29.

Lennoxlove, East Lothian, guide books. *The History and Treasures of Lennoxlove House. Home of the Duke of Hamilton, K.T.* London: Pitkin, *c.*1970. Casali's portrait of Beckford, 4–5. *Lennoxlove. Home of the Duke of Hamilton and Brandon.* New ed. Derby: Pilgrim Press, 1981. Susan Beckford, 1. Casali's portrait of Beckford, 4. Portrait of 10th Duke, 15. Family tree, 16–18. Rosalind Marshall. *Lennoxlove.* New Ed. Lennoxlove: Privately printed, *c.*1992. Family tree, 6–7. Portrait of Susan Beckford, 12.

Littlejohn, David. *The Fate of the English Country House.* New York: Oxford University Press, 1997. Sale of treasures in 1823, 133. Hamilton Palace sale, 133–134.

McLeod, Bet. 'A Celebrated Collector.' In *William Beckford, 1760–1844: An Eye for the Magnificent,* ed. Derek E. Ostergard, 154–175. New Haven & London: Yale University Press for the Bard Graduate Center, 2001. Exhibition catalogue.

Pearce, Susan M. *On Collecting: An Investigation into Collecting in the European Tradition.* London: Routledge, 1995. Beckford as collector, 131.

Redford, George. *Art Sales.* 2 vols. London: Publ. for the subscribers, 1888. Vol. 1, 'A History of Sales.' Hogarth's 'The Harlot's Progress' & 'The Rake's Progress', 33, 34, 35, 36. 'Sir William Hamilton's Collection' (1801), Leonardo's 'A Laughing Boy', 82. 'Mr. Day's Collection' (1800–1801), Raphael's 'St Catherine', 83. 'The Fonthill Collection' (1802), 86. 'The Beckford Collection' (1823), 121–123 & pl. Beckford at Earl of Mulgrave's sale (1832), 129. 'Mr. Gladstone's Collection' (1875), Bonifazio's 'The Virgin and Child with Saints', 203. 'The Novar Collection' (1878), Smirke's 'Seven Ages of Man', 271; Claude's 'Philip baptising the Eunuch', 273, 275; Jan Steen's 'The Effects of Intemperance', 276. 'The Bohn Collections' (1878), the King of Holland's Dresden service, 283. 'The Hamilton Palace Collection' (1882), 319–345 & plate. 'The Beckford Vandycks', 348. 'The Leigh Court Collection' (1884), 'Altieri' Claudes & Gaspar Poussin's 'The Calling of Abraham', 365. 'Death of Mr. H. G. Bohn' (1884), bought books for Beckford, 388. 'Mr. Beckett-Denison's Collection' (1885), bought from Beckford and Hamilton collections, 404; Ludovico Caracci's 'The Sibylla Lybica' & Marcello Venusti's 'The Adoration of the Magi', 406.

Reitlinger, Gerald. *The Economics of Taste.* 3 vols. London: Barry & Rockliff. Vol. 1, 1961, *The Rise and Fall of Picture Prices 1760–1960* & vol. 2, 1963, *The Rise and Fall of Objets d'Art Prices since 1750.* Both, passim.

Roberts, W. *Memorials of Christie's. A Record of Art Sales from 1766 to*

1896. 2 vols. London: Bell, 1897. 1817 sale realised £4339 9s 6d, 1:93. Fonthill, 1:101–103. Hamilton Palace, 2:1–45 & 24 pl.

Robinson, Frederick Sydney. 'A Connoisseur of Later Days.' In *The Connoisseur*, 123–134. London: George Redway, 1897. Fonthill sale (1822) & three paintings sold (1839), 88. Hamilton Palace sale, 90.

Wainwright, Clive. 'The Collector.' In *William Beckford Exhibition 1976*, [ed. Julian Berry], 77–90. Tisbury, Wilts: Compton Press, 1976.

Wainwright, Clive. *The Antiquarian Interior in Britain, 1780–1850.* 1987. PhD thesis for University College, London. *Aslib Index to Theses* 37 Pt. 1 (1988): 14.

Wainwright, Clive. 'Fonthill Abbey.' In *The Romantic Interior. The British Collector at Home 1750–1850*, 108–146, 302–303 nn1–145. New Haven & London: Yale University Press, 1989. Also 3–4, 25, 26, 43, 65, 73, 74, 174, 215–218, 230, 235–238, 262, 269, 280. Based on his PhD thesis.

Wainwright, Clive. 'Patronage and the Applied Arts in Early Nineteenth-century London.' In *London – World City 1800–1840*, ed. Celina Fox, 111–128 at 126–128. New Haven & London: Yale University Press, 1992. Catalogue of an exhibition at Villa Hügel, Essen. Entries: '298. Fonthill Abbey, 1821 [Buckler's drawing from SW]' by Lindsay Stainton, 395–396; '299. Cup and Cover [by James Aldridge], 1816' by Ann Eatwell, 396–397; '300. Cabinet [by Robert Hume], c.1820' by Clive Wainwright, 396–397. Beckford, a leader of taste, 382. Mentioned, 433. German ed., *Metropole London: Macht und Glanz einer Welstadt, 1800–1840*, ed. Jürgen Schultze, Recklinghausen: Bongers, 1992, pp. 126–128, 382, 395–397, 433 (as in English ed.).

Wainwright, Clive. 'William Beckford, his Collection and the Influence of his Excursion to Alcobaça and Batalha in 1794.' In *Portugal e o Reino Unido: A Aliança Revisitada*, ed. Angela Delaforce, 98–101. Lisbon: Fundação Calouste Gulbenkian, 1994. Exhibition catalogue.

Watkin, David. 'Beckford, Soane, and Hope: The Psychology of the Collector.' In *William Beckford, 1760–1844: An Eye for the Magnificent*, ed. Derek E. Ostergard, 32–48. New Haven & London: Yale University Press for the Bard Graduate Center, 2001. Exhibition catalogue.

Winch, Dinah. 'William Beckford, the Collector.' In *The British Galleries 1500–1900*, 43. London: V&A Publications, 2001. Agate cup with mounts by James Aldridge, 1815–1816, pl. 32.

Articles

Alexander, Boyd. 'Fonthill, Wiltshire III – William Beckford as Collector.' *Country Life*, 8 Dec 1966, 1572–1576. For Parts I & II see '5. Fonthill'.

Aslet, Clive. 'Lennoxlove, East Lothian– I.' *Country Life*, 8 Aug 1985, 366–370. Part II, 15 Aug, 446–449. Beckford's portrait by Thomas Bardwell [now attributed to Andrea Casali], 448.

Aslet, Clive & Christopher Hartley. 'Brodick Castle, Isle of Arran–I.' *Country Life*, 10 Feb 1983, 322–325. Part II, 17 Feb, 380–383. Portraits and objects: 'the largest single collection of Beckfordiana in existence'.

Brinton, Selwyn. 'The Hamilton Sale at Christie's.' *The American Magazine of Art* 11 no. 3 (Jan 1920).

Cave, Graham. 'Lennoxlove. Home of the Duke of Hamilton and Brandon.' *Beckford Tower Trust Newsletter*, Spring 1985, 5. Beckford's possessions.

Cornforth, John. 'Kingston Lacy Revisited–II.' *Country Life*, 24 April 1986, 1124, photo, 1125. Savonnerie carpet from Grand Drawing Room bought at 1823 sale and now in Saloon. Part III, 5 June, Clandestine visit to Fonthill, 1576; photo of carpet in Saloon, 1578.

Furst, Herbert. 'Two Famous Connoisseurs and Collectors – Beaumont and Beckford – I.' *Apollo* 35 (March 1942): 59–61, 75. Part II (April): 81–84. Sir George Beaumont (1753–1827) helped found the National Gallery.

Hall, Michael. 'Echoes of Fonthill.' *Country Life*, 7 Feb 2002, 68–71. Fonthill's influence on country house collections throughout the 19th century.

Hussey, Christopher. 'Charlecote Park, Warwickshire–II.' *Country Life*, 18 April 1952, 1164–1167 at 1164, 1165 (photo of Borghese table). Part III, 2 May, 1328–1331 at 1331. Treasures from the Fonthill Sale of 1822 [1823].

Jullian, Philippe. 'La fausse abbaye de Fonthill et les collections de l'extravagant William Beckford.' *Connaissance des Arts* 133 (March 1963): 95–103 & 32 illus. English précis, v–vi.

McLeod, Bet. 'Some further objects from William Beckford's collection in the Victoria and Albert Museum.' *Burlington Magazine* 143 (June 2001): 367–370 & figs 58–65.

McLeod, Bet. 'Treasures of England's Wealthiest Son.' *Country Life*, 7 Feb 2002, 40–45. Some of Beckford's objects unearthed by research for the William Beckford exhibition in New York and Dulwich.

Robertshaw, Ursula. 'Great Houses of Britain. 5. Brodick Castle: island fastness.' *Illustrated London News*, 6 Sept 1969, 13–14. Beckford's treasures.

Wainwright, Clive. 'William Beckford e La Sua Collezione. Parte I.' *Arte Illustrata* No. 37/38 (Jan/Feb 1971): 46–53, Fonthill Abbey. Part II, No. 39/40 (March/April): 52–60, Beckford's Tower. English text of both parts, 106–112.

Wainwright, Clive. 'Some objects from William Beckford's Collection now in the Victoria and Albert Museum.' *Burlington Magazine* 113 (May 1971): 254–264. Influential account, mainly of furniture and woodwork.

Wainwright, Clive. 'Charlecote Park, Warwickshire–I.' *Country Life*, 21 Feb 1985, 446–450 at 447. Part II, 28 Feb, 506–510. Valuable items bought at the Fonthill Sale of 1823.

Wainwright, Clive. 'The Romantic Interior in England.' *National Art-Collections Fund Review 1985*. Pp. 80–89 at 83–85, 89. Fonthill Abbey interiors. St Michael's Gallery from Britton (1823) illus., 80.

Wainwright, Clive. 'William Beckford and his collection.' *Christie's International Magazine,* Oct–Nov 1989, 2–5.

Wainwright, Clive. 'In Lucifer's Metropolis.' *Country Life,* 1 Oct 1992, 82–84. Beckford's acquisitions in Paris, mainly during the French Revolution.

Wainwright lecture. 'Spotlight falls on art treasures.' *Bath and West Evening Chronicle,* 11 August 1988, 11. Announcement of lecture by Clive Wainwright at the Holburne Museum, Bath, on Friday, 12 August.

White, Lisa. 'Sir William Holburne and William Beckford.' *Beckford Journal* 9 (2003): 70–74. The Holburne Museum, Bath, perpetuates his name.

BECKFORD'S LIBRARY

Full-length Study

Gemmett, Robert J., ed. *Sale Catalogues of Libraries of Eminent Persons. Volume 3. Poets and Men of Letters. William Beckford.* London: Mansell with Sotheby Parke-Bernet, 1972. vii, 465 pp. 24½ cm. Book sales of 1804, 1808, 1817 & entire 1823 catalogue, all with annotations. List of sales, 6–8. Partially reprinted from: 'The Beckford Book Sale of 1808', *Papers of the Bibliographical Society of America* 64 (Second Quarter 1970): 127–164; 'The Beckford Library Sale of 1817', *Library Chronicle* (University of Pennsylvania) 37 no. 1 (Winter 1971): 37–69; 'The Beckford Book Sale of 1804', *Bulletin of the New York Public Library* 77 (Winter 1974): 205–223.

REVIEWS. 'Beckford's Books.' *Times Literary Supplement,* 29 Sept 1972, 1175.

Osborne, Eric. 'Insatiable bibliophile.' *Books and Bookmen,* Jan 1973, 76–77.

Robinson, David. 'The book collector.' *Financial Times,* 2 Sept 1972.

Books

Bohn, Henry. Weedon, Alexis. 'Bohn, Henry George (1796–1884).' In *Oxford Dictionary of National Biography,* ed. H. C. G. Matthew & Brian Harrison, 6:438. Oxford: Oxford University Press, 2004. Bohn helped Beckford acquire his library.

British Museum. *List of Catalogues of English Book Sales 1676–1900 now in the British Museum.* London: Printed by order of the Trustees, 1915. Lists sales on 24 May 1804, 9 June 1808, 6 May 1817, 9 Sept 1823, 30 June & 11 Dec 1882, 2 July & 27 Nov 1883, 8 July 1884.

Brunet, Jacques-Charles. *Catalogue des livres rares et précieux de feu M. Jacques-Charles Brunet.* Biographical intro. A. J. V. Le Roux de Lincy. Paris: Potier, 1868. P. xxxiii.

Carter, John. *Taste & Technique in Book-Collecting.* Cambridge: Cambridge University Press, 1948. Collector, 14. Letters to George Clarke, 16 & n2.

Beckford Library Sale (1882–1883), 21, 74 & n1. Chapman Bibliography, 61. Connoisseur of bindings, 86. *Dreams* (1783), 168. *Vathek* (1786), 169.

Clarke, William, publ. *Repertorium Bibliographicum; or, Some Account of the most Celebrated British Libraries*. London: William Clarke, 1819. See '10. Beckford's Works. First Editions. Attributed Works' for Beckford's library.

Culot, Paul. *Jean-Claude Bozerian*. Brussels: Speeckaert, 1979. Beckford's copy of Casimir Freschot's *Etat ... des duchés de Florence ...* (1711) bound by Bozerian, 47–48 & pl. XXXII no. 6. (Library sale, 1883, pt. 4, no. 1015.)

Cundall, Joseph, ed. *On Bookbindings Ancient and Modern*. London: Bell, 1881. Kalthoeber and Charles Lewis 'bound most of the books in the collection of the late Mr. Beckford, of Fonthill', 106.

De Ricci, Seymour. 'Beckford and his Contemporaries.' In *English Collectors of Books & Manuscripts (1530–1930) and Their Marks of Ownership*, 84–87. Cambridge: Cambridge University Press, 1930. Also 159. Reprinted, 1960.

Fletcher, William Younger. *English Book Collectors*. London: Kegan Paul, 1902. Pp. 317–321.

Glaister, Geoffrey Ashall. *Glaister's Glossary of the Book*. 2nd ed. London: George Allen & Unwin, 1979. (1st ed. 1960.) Beckford's library, 32.

Hobson, A. R. A. 'William Beckford's Binders.' In *Festschrift Ernst Kyriss*, 375–381. Stuttgart: Max Hettler, 1961. Beckford's taste 'was fastidious but sober', 375. Drawing of Charles Lewis's bindery, 377. Extracts from George Clarke's letters (1830–1834), 378–380.

Keynes, Geoffrey. *The Gates of Memory*. Oxford: Clarendon Press, 1981. Volume of William Blake's watercolours which he executed to accompany pages of Thomas Gray's *Poems* (1790 ed.), from Beckford's library, 325–326.

Keynes, Geoffrey & Edwin Wolf. *William Blake's Illuminated Books. A Census*. New York: Grolier Club, 1953. Beckford an eager collector of Blake's books after his death, xviii. Beckford's copies of: *The Book of Thel*, 21; *Songs of Innocence and Experience*, 63; *Europe, a Prophecy*, 82; *Milton a Poem*, 103.

Millington, Jon. 'Bibliophile Extraordinary.' In *William Beckford Exhibition 1976*, [ed. Julian Berry], 91–94. Tisbury, Wilts: Compton Press, 1976.

Newton, A. Edward. *The Amenities of Book Collecting, and Kindred Affections*. Boston, MA: Atlantic Monthly, 1918. Presentation copy to Beckford of Disraeli's *Henrietta Temple*, 'with many pages of useless notes in Beckford's hand, he seems to have read the volumes with unnecessary care.'

Quaritch, Bernard. 'William Beckford 1759–1844.' In *Contributions Towards a Dictionary of English Book-collectors*, Part 4, May 1893, 7 pp & portrait (1797). 14 parts. London: Bernard Quaritch, 1892–1921. Account of Beckford by 'Editor', 1–3. 219 notable books from his library bought by Quaritch at the Beckford Library Sale (1882–1883), 3–7.

Roberts, W. *Rare Books and Their Prices*. London: Redway, 1895. Beckford Library Sale (1882–1883) of 9837 lots, 7, 8–9, 11, 17.

Weeks, Donald. ' "It's Yours, Sir" A Day at Sotheby's.' In *Pages: The World of Books, Writers, and Writing*. 1, ed. Matthew J. Bruccoli, 54–61. Detroit: Gale Research, 1976. Many references to Beckford's library and a two-page spread, 'William Beckford and Fonthill Abbey', 58–59 & 3 illus.

Articles

Beckford binding was Major Abbey's favourite. *Book Collector* 10 no. 1 (Spring 1961): 40.

Beckford's library unfavourably compared with Sunderland library. *Gentleman's Magazine* 253 (Sept 1882): 381.

'Boyd Alexander Bequest.' *Bodleian Library Record* 10 no. 5 (Aug 1981): 267. All his Beckford working papers & twenty books from Beckford's library.

Carter, John. 'Two Beckford Collections.' *The Colophon*. New Graphic Series No. 1 (March 1939): [67–74]. The libraries of Rowland Burdon-Muller & James T. Babb. Reprinted with passage on Mozart altered in Carter's *Books and Book-Collectors*, London: Hart-Davis, 1956, 22–31.

'Commentary.' *Book Collector* 13 no. 2 (Summer 1964): 145. Beckford's copy of Blake's *Urizen* (1794) bought by Houghton Library, Harvard.

Dearden, James S. 'John Ruskin and Bernard Quaritch: Some Additional Letters.' *Bodleian Library Record* 11 (1984): 264–269 at 267–268 & 269 n13. Ruskin to Quaritch, 1 June 1884, appealing for funds to buy for the nation the Hamilton and Beckford MS. (in Beckford Library Sale, 1882–1883).

'Extracts from Curious Books in the Fonthill Library.' *The Examiner*, 24, 31 Aug 1823, 550, 563–564.

Gemmett, Robert J. 'Beckford in the saleroom.' *Times Literary Supplement*, 17 Nov 1966, 1056. John Hodgkin's bequest to the Bodleian Library.

Hobson, Anthony. 'William Beckford's Library.' *Connoisseur* 191 (April 1976): 298–305. Fine essay, emphasising that the books were bought to read.

Hobson, Anthony & Thomas Woodcock. 'The Owners of the 'Carpe Diem' Armorial Binding Stamp.' *Book Collector* 54 (2005): 539–542. Beckford owned five volumes bearing this armorial stamp, probably that of John Webster, attorney (1751–1826).

Lamington, Lord (Alexander Baillie Cochrane). 'In the Days of the Dandies.' *Blackwood's Edinburgh Magazine* 147 (Feb 1890): 177. Beckford Library mentioned in article about Hamilton, 177–184. Reprinted in Lamington's *In the Days of the Dandies*, 65. Edinburgh: Blackwood, 1890. Hamilton, 64–85. Also reprinted in *Littell's Living Age* 184 (1 March 1890): 567.

Parreaux, André. 'Note sur la partie Portugaise de la Bibliothèque de William Beckford.' *Bulletin des Etudes Portugaises* 2 (1932): 87–93. Lists 20 works from Phillips (1823) cat. and 54 from Beckford Library Sale (1882–1883) cat.

Rosebery, Eva. 'Unfamiliar Libraries VII: Barnbougle Castle.' *Book Collector* 11 no. 2 (Spring 1962): 35–44 & 8 pl. Beckford, 37, 43, 44.

Rosebery, Eva. 'Books from Beckford's Library now at Barnbougle.' *Book Collector* 14 no. 3 (Autumn 1965): 324–334 & pl. 1–4. Altogether 533 works.

Smiley, P. O'R. 'Beckford's Library.' *Beckford Tower Trust Newsletter*, Spring 1982, 7. Bishop Percy's *Reliques of Ancient English Poetry* (1765).

Turner, John. 'William Beckford of Fonthill.' *Antiquarian Book Monthly Review* 7 no. 11 (Nov 1980): 524–525, 527. When Beckford's archive of Papers have been studied his life and work will be reassessed.

Beckford Library Sale, Sotheby's, 30 June 1882–30 Nov 1883

'The Beckford Library.' First Portion. *Athenæum*, 20 May 1882, 636. 'The Beckford Sale.' Second Portion. 23, 30 Dec, 849–850, 899. Third Portion, 2 June 1883, 701. Fourth Portion, 3 Nov, 1, 8 Dec, 566, 703, 739.

The Bibliographer 1 (Feb 1882): 85–87. *Idem* 2 (July & Aug): 25–27 & 60–62. *Idem* 3 (Jan & Feb 1883): 50 & 77–82. *Idem* 4 (July, Aug & Sept): 51, 83 & 111–115. *Idem* 5 (Jan 1884): 45–48. Hamilton Library Sale. *Idem* 6 (June): 13. Part of July 1882 article (pp. 25–27) quoted in Arthur Sherbo, 'The Bibliographer, Book-Lore, and the Bookworm', *Studies in Bibliography* 40 (1987): 208.

Bohn, Henry H. 'Hamilton Palace Library.' *The Times*, 19 Jan 1882, 5d. Letter about his experiences as Beckford's bookseller. ⅔ column.

The Scotsman. 'Sale of the Beckford Library.' 1, 3, 6, 7, ?10, 11, 13 July 1882 + more.

The Times. Leading articles, 6 Jan 1882, 7d–e; 6 July, 9e; 26 Dec, 7d; 30 June 1883, 11e. Sale reports: 6, 10, 13, 18 July 1882, 6a–b, 5d, 4e, 4c–d; 11, 14, 16, 19, 20, 21, 22, 23, 25 Dec 1882, 7d, 8b–c, 10a–b, 4c, 7e, 8a, 5b, 7b, 5e; 3, 11, 14, 16 July 1883, 8c, 5d, 6c–d, 7c; 27, 30 Nov, 10c, 8b; 4 Dec 3b.

Clements Sale, Sotheby's, 4–6 July & 31 Oct–1 Nov 1966

'News & Comment.' *Book Collector* 15 no. 4 (Winter 1966): 473–474. 329 lots of Beckford books.

'William Beckford in the saleroom.' *Times Literary Supplement*, 20 Oct 1966, 968.

Margadale Sale, Christie's, 2 April 1975

'News and Comment.' *Book Collector* 24 no. 2 (Summer 1975): 288–289.

Rosebery Sale, Sotheby's, 27–28 Oct 1975

'News and Comment.' *Book Collector* 25 no. 1 (Spring 1976): 84, 87.

Norman, Geraldine. 'Beckford interest raises price of Rosebery books.' & 'Outstanding prices in book sale.' *The Times*, 28 & 29 Oct 1975, 14d–e & 16c–e.

Wainwright, Clive, ed. A. R. A. Hobson. 'The last of Beckford's library.' *Times Literary Supplement*, 19 Dec 1975, 1525.

Bradley Martin Sale, Sotheby's N. Y., 30 April–1 May 1990

Checkland, Sarah Jane. 'Blake's first book fetches £74,000.' *The Times*, 2 May 1990, 4.

Watson, Peter, 'Unpublished poems to be sold in US auction of rare British literature.' *Observer*, 29 April 1990.

Gibbon's Library

Beer, Sir Gavin de. *Gibbon and his World*. London: Thames and Hudson, 1968. Hoppner portrait, 116. Also 117, 124–126.

Berry, Mary. *Extracts of the Journals and Correspondence of Miss Berry from the year 1783 to 1852*. Ed. Lady Theresa Lewis. 3 vols. London: Longman, 1865. Beckford bought Gibbon's library, 2:260–261.

Elton, Charles & Mary. *The Great Book-Collectors*. London: Kegan Paul, etc., 1893. Pp. 218–219.

Keynes, Geoffrey. *The Library of Edward Gibbon*. London: Jonathan Cape, 1940. Caustic note in *Decline and Fall* & library given to Dr Schöll, 28, 30.

Keynes, Geoffrey. 'Gibbon's Library Catalogue.' *Times Literary Supplement*, 22 Sept 1945, 456. Letter.

M., J. H. 'Was Gibbon's Library ever moved to Fonthill or Bath?' *Notes and Queries* 1st Series 7 (23 April 1853): 407. Replies by: James Dennistoun, (14 May 1853): 485; A. Holt White, (28 May 1853): 535; William Bates, 1st Series 8 (23 July 1853): 88, quote from Redding (1859); Edward D. Ingraham, (27 Aug 1853): 208.

Matthews, Henry (1789–1828). *Diary of an Invalid*. London: John Murray, 1820. Beckford owned Gibbon's library at Lausanne, 319.

Norwich, John Julius. *More Christmas Crackers*. London: Viking, 1990. Beckford's diatribe against Gibbon, 37.

Porter, Roy. *Edward Gibbon: Making History*. London: Weidenfeld & Nicolson, 1988. 'The rich and strange expatriate, William Beckford' and quote about Gibbon, 158. In index as 'Beckford, William (*d.*1799)'.

Read, John Meredith. *Historic Studies in Vaud, Berne, and Savoy from Roman Times to Voltaire, Rousseau, and Gibbon*. 2 vols. London: Chatto & Windus, 1897. Beckford bought Gibbon's library immediately after his death in 1794 and gave it to Dr Schöll in 1815 or 1816, 2:505.

S., H. P. 'Gibbon's Library.' *Notes and Queries* 3rd Series 11 (12 Jan 1867): 39–40.

Seylaz, Louis. 'La bibliothèque de Gibbon.' *Gazette de Lausanne*, 11 September 1932, 1–2.

Womersley, David. 'Gibbon, Edward (1737–1794).' In *Oxford Dictionary of National Biography*, ed. H. C. G. Matthew & Brian Harrison, 22:17. Oxford: Oxford University Press, 2004. Sold his library to Beckford for £950 against advice.

CERAMICS

Books

Craig, Sir Algernon Tudor. *Armorial Porcelain of the Eighteenth Century*. London: Century House, 1925. Illus. of Ch'ien-Lung bowl & plate, *c.*1760, made for Alderman Beckford, 32.

Dawson, Aileen. *A Catalogue of French Porcelain in the British Museum*. London: British Museum Press, 1994. Sèvres plate, 147.

Horvath, J. E. 'The Pedigree of Louis the Great's Ewer.' In *Louis the Great, King of Hungary and Poland*, ed. S. B. Vardy et al., 325–338. Boulder, Colorado: East European Monographs Series, 1986. A Yuan dynasty porcelain vase now in the National Museum of Ireland, Dublin.

Howard, David Sanctuary. *Chinese Armorial Porcelain*. London: Faber, 1974. Three Ch'ien-Lung plates: K5, Arms of 'Beckford of Jamaica and later of Fonthill Abbey', *c.*1745, round, 339; M3, Arms of 'Howard quarterly Earl of Effingham impaling Beckford', *c.*1750, round, 366; Q6, Arms of 'Beckford of Jamaica and Fonthill Abbey', *c.*1755, octagonal, 557.

Tait, Gerald Hugh. *Porcelain*. London: Spring Books, 1963. Gaignières-Fonthill ewer, 7–8. Watercolour of 1713 by Gaignières illus., 19.

Watson, Sir Francis. *Chinese Porcelains in European Mounts*. New York: China Institute of America, 1980. Gaignières ewer, 11–12.

Articles

'Chinese Armorial Plate.' *National Art Collections Fund Annual Report. Eighty sixth year* [for 1990, publ. 1991], 168. Bought by the Beckford Tower Trust with help from the NACF.

Hewat-Jaboor, Philip. 'An Early Nineteenth Century Dihl and Guerhard Porcelain Cup and Saucer made for William Beckford.' *Beckford Journal* 2 (1996): 7–8.

Lane, Arthur. 'The Gaignières-Fonthill Vase; A Chinese Porcelain of about 1300.' *Burlington Magazine* 103 (April 1961): 124–132 & 10 illus. Rediscovery (in 1959) of the vase in the National Museum of Ireland, Dublin.

McLeod, Bet. 'In Lucifer's Metropolis: William Beckford's Collection of French Porcelain.' *French Porcelain Society Journal* 16 (2001). Unpaginated.

Reitlinger, Gerald. 'Further adventures of the Gaignières-Fonthill Vase.' *Burlington Magazine* 104 (Jan 1962): 34. Letter pointing out that Beckford could not have acquired the vase before 1814.

White, Lisa. 'A collector of distinction: Sir William Holburne (1793–1874).' *Apollo* 158 (Sept 2003): 46–54 at 47 & n7, 48 & n22. Meissen cup and saucer from Beckford's collection illus., 52 (fig 15).

Whitehead, John. 'Some French Purchases by William Beckford.' *Beckford Journal* 2 (1996): 39–44. Savonnerie carpets and Sèvres porcelain.

FURNITURE

Books

Beurdeley, Michel. *Trois siècles de ventes publiques*. Paris: Tallandier, 1988. Beckford may have bought the Riesener roll-top desk (now in the Wallace Collection, No. F 102) directly in a private sale at the end of 1791, 63–70.

Hardy, John & Clive Wainwright. 'Elizabethan-Revival Charlecote Revived.' In *The National Trust Year Book 1976–77*, 12–19 at 14–16 London: Europa, 1976. Fonthill table illus., 14–15. 1823 sale: Ebony & pietre dure casket, 16.

Hughes, Peter. *The Wallace Collection Catalogue of Furniture*. 3 vols. London: Trustees of the Wallace Collection, 1996. Vol. 1: English Coffers, 56 (F 472–3, *c*.1815), 249–243. Vol. 2: French Desks & Secretaires, 191 (F 102, *c*.1770), 929–941

Leben, Ulrich, ed. *Bernard Molitor, 1755–1833: Ebeniste Parisien d'Origine Luxembourgeoise*. Luxemburg: Ville de Luxembourg, 1995. Desk commissioned by Beckford in autumn 1792, 87.

Mortimer, Martin. *The English Glass Chandelier*. Woodbridge, Suffolk: Antique Collectors Club, 2000. Grand chandelier by William Parker shipped to Beckford in Lisbon in 1791, 101.

Pradère, Alexandre. *Les Ebénistes Français de Louis XIV à la Révolution*. [Paris]: Chêne, 1989. 'Elephant' cabinet, 42. Also illus. in Thibaut Wolvesperges, *Le meuble français en laque au XVIIIe siècle*, Paris: Ed. de l'Amateur, 2000, Fig. 3.

Rogers, W[illiam] G[ibbs]. *A List of the Carvings and Other Works of Art Collected by W. G. Rogers*. London: Printed for the Proprietor by Bradbury & Evans, 1854. Priced catalogue of 624 lots for sale at his rooms in Soho. Note to lot 372: Franchi's demands for high standards of execution, 26.

Turpin, Adriana. 'Filling the Void: The Development of Beckford's Taste and the Market in Furniture.' In *William Beckford, 1760–1844: An Eye for the Magnificent*, ed. Derek E. Ostergard, 176–201. New Haven & London: Yale University Press for the Bard Graduate Center, 2001. Exhibition catalogue.

Watson, Francis J. B. *Wallace Collection Catalogues. Furniture*. London: Trustees of the Wallace Collection, 1956. 'F 102 Roll-top Desk (*Bureau à cylindre*) known as the *Bureau du Roi Stanislas*', 69–76 & pl. 72, 73. 'F 472 & 473 Pair of Coffers', 243 & pl. 63.

Wright, Lawrence. *Warm and Snug. The History of the Bed*. London: Routledge & Kegan Paul, 1962. 'Beckford's own bedroom was little more than an unheated monastic cell' at the Abbey, 152.

Articles

Beckfordiana at Brodick. *Book Collector* 9 no. 4 (Winter 1960): 392, 395–396. Guide book (1956) said Black Cabinet contained letters from Horace Walpole.

Bellaigue, Geoffrey de. 'Edward Holmes Baldock. Part I.' *Connoisseur* 189 (Aug 1975): 290–299 at 293, 295, 299 nn24, 28, 32. Baldock sold furniture and works of art to Beckford.

Bishop, Philippa. 'A Pair of Ebonised Chairs.' *Beckford Tower Trust Newsletter*, Spring 1993, 2. Very similar to chairs from the Scarlet and Crimson Drawing Rooms at the Tower.

Bishop, Philippa. 'Settees from Fonthill Splendens.' *Beckford Journal* 1 (1995): 15–17. Sold at Christie's on 17 Nov 1994, lot 107.

Bruxelles, Simon de. 'Churchgoers sat on £200,000 masterpieces.' *The Times*, 21 March 2003, 16. Forthcoming sale of the settees from Fonthill Splendens. Leading article, 'Folie de Grandeur', 23. *Idem*, 27 March, 'The Fool of Fonthill', letters from Malcolm Jack and Tom Hughes-Davies defending Beckford, 23.

Checkland, Sarah Jane. 'Commode sets new record.' *The Times*, 7 July 1989, 3b–d, and 'City's pot of gold', *Bath and West Evening Chronicle*, 7 July, 2. John Channon commode from Splendens sold for £1.1 million at Christie's.

Cornforth, John. 'Princely Pietra Dura.' *Country Life*, 1 Dec 1988, 162, 164. Charlecote table top from the Borghese Palace.

Davis, Frank. 'Talking about Salerooms.' *Country Life*, 20 Jan 1972, 151–152. Louis XVI secretaire by Riesener sold at Sotheby's for £72,000.

Fairfax-Lucy, Alice. 'The World's Largest Onyx.' *Country Life*, 9 Feb 1967, 292. Letter about the table at Charlecote from the Borghese Palace, with photo.

Fairfax-Lucy, Brian. 'Where, legend says, Shakespeare roamed . . .' *House & Garden*, Feb 1969, 26. Charlecote: table from the Borghese Palace, photo.

Frost, Amy. '[No.] 5196. Beckford's Tower and Museum, Bath. *Tripod pedestal.*' *2003 Review*, 62. The Annual Report of the National Art Collections Fund, with photo of tripod formerly in the Scarlet Drawing Room.

Hardy, John. 'A Beckford Bookcase.' *Beckford Journal* 2 (1996): 60–61. Probably designed by Beckford for the Oak Library at Fonthill Abbey.

Jaffer, Amin. *Luxury Goods from India: The Art of the Indian Cabinet-Maker*. London: V&A Publications, 2002. No. 16, chair, 46–47. No. 19, carved ivory box depicted in Willes Maddox's painting of 'Objects of Vertu', 52–53.

Jervis, Simon Swynfen. 'Splendentia recognita: furniture by Martin Foxhall for Fonthill.' *Burlington Magazine* 147 (June 2005): 376–382.

Levy, Martin. 'A Coffer from Lansdown Tower.' *Beckford Journal* 3 (1997): 25–29. One of four by Goodridge from the Scarlet Drawing Room.

Macaulay, David & Rachel Pegg. 'Export ban on Beckford coffer made.' *Bath Chronicle*, 20 Nov 2004, 2. By Goodridge, from Scarlet Drawing Room.

Mallalieu, Huon. 'Around the Salerooms.' *Country Life*, 16 Feb 1995, 49. Beckford's crest on pair of hall benches was not necessarily William's.

Mallalieu, Huon. 'Around the Salerooms.' *Country Life*, 8 May 2003, 136. Beckford's hall benches sold. *Idem*, 22 May, 88. 'Missing Beckford Benches.' Letter from Jeremy Capadose. *Idem*, 3 July, 64. 'Beckford's Bench.' Letter from Jesca Verdon-Smith concerning the whereabouts of third pair of benches.

Mallalieu, Huon. 'Review Salerooms.' *Country Life*, 11 Aug 2005, 62. Pair of benches sold at Christie's in 1994 sold again. Christie's also sold Louis XVI ormolu and ebony commode by Claude Charles Saunier, last sold in 1946, 63.

McLeod, Bet & Philip Hewat-Jaboor. 'Pietre Dure Cabinets for William Beckford: Gregorio Franchi's Role.' *Furniture History* 38 (2002): 135–143.

Mundt, Barbara. 'Tudor-Historismus.' *Weltkünst*, May 1999, 923. 17th C. Indo-Portuguese ebony chair in St Michael's Gallery at Fonthill Abbey.

Norman, Geraldine. 'Reversal of fortune.' *[Daily] Telegraph Magazine*, 3 July 1999, 24, 26. Riesener commode bought by Rothschilds from Hamilton Palace to be sold at Christie's on 8 July.

Payne, Christopher. 'Baldock, Beckford, Bridgens and Bullock.' *Antique Collecting* 23 no. 8 (Jan 1989): 17–20. Late Georgian furniture designers.

Colour photo of parcel-gilt oak cabinet from Lansdown Tower (*c*.1830), possibly designed by Beckford, sold at Sotheby's for £3630, 18.

Powley, Anna. 'Pair of Side Chairs.' *National Art Collections Fund Annual Review . . . 1993* [publ. 1994], 45. Bought by the Beckford Tower Trust with the help from the NACF.

'Recent acquisitions (1998–2004) of furniture and the decorative arts by British museums and galleries.' *Burlington Magazine* 147 (June 2005): 439. Photos of cabinet, Siena marble table and tripod now at Beckford's Tower.

Roberts, Hugh. 'Beckford, Vulliamy and Old Japan.' *Apollo* 124 (Oct 1986): 338–341. A pair of secretaires made for Beckford in 1803.

Smith, R. 'Benjamin Vulliamy's painted satinwood clocks and pedestals.' *Apollo* 141 (June 1995): 30 & 32 n32. Two cabinets for Beckford with elaborate mahogany doors made by Thomas Brownley in 1800.

Wainwright, Clive. 'William Beckford's Furniture.' *Connoisseur* 191 (April 1976): 290–297.

Wainwright, Clive. 'Only the True Black Blood.' *Furniture History Society* 21 (1985): 250–258 at 253–254, 256. Beckford's Indo-Portuguese 'Wolsey' furniture.

Watson, F. J. B. "The 'Tilsit' Table and the 'Stanislas' Bureau." *Burlington Magazine* 92 (June 1950): 166–167, 164 (pl. 17–18).

Watson, Francis J. B. 'Beckford, Mme de Pompadour, the Duc de Bouillon and the Taste for Japanese Lacquer in Eighteenth-Century France.' *Gazette des Beaux-Arts* 61 (Feb 1963): 101–127.

GOLD AND SILVER

Books

Bourne, Jonathan & Vanessa Brett. *Lighting in the Domestic Interior*. London: Sotheby, 1991. Candlesticks & spill vase, 182. Mentioned in Jon Millington, 'Beckford's Lighting', *Beckford Journal* 1 (1995): 56.

Clayton, Michael. *Christie's Pictorial History of English and American Silver*. Oxford: Phaidon, Christie's, 1985. Candlestick, 244–245, illus., 245.

Glanville, Philippa. *Silver*. London: Victoria & Albert Museum, 1996. Beckford, antiquarian collector, 52, 54, 58, 116. Woodcut, 'A Groupe of the Rarest Articles of Virtu', from Rutter's *Delineations* (1823), 54 & both endpapers.

Hayward, John. 'Introduction.' In Malcolm Baker, Timothy Schroder & E. Laird Clowes, *Beckford and Hamilton Silver from Brodick Castle*, [3–6]. London: Spink, 1980. Exhibition catalogue.

Hayward, John. 'Beckfordiana, une collection d'argenterie hors du commun.' In *Argenteries. Le Trésor du National Trust for Scotland*, 23–30. Brussels: National Trust for Scotland, 1992. Exhibition catalogue in French and Flemish. Pp. 7–10 in English trans.

Müller, Hannelore. *The Thyssen-Bornemisza Collection: European Silver*. Trans. P. S. Falla & Anna Somers Cocks. London: Philip Wilson for Sotheby's, 1986. Moringer cup, 136–139, cat. no. 36. Petzold cup, 194–199, cat. no. 58.

Schroder, Timothy B. *The Gilbert Collection of Gold & Silver*. Los Angeles: Los Angeles County Museum of Art, 1988. Basket by Paul Storr, 324–327. Ewer & basin by Henri Auguste, 617–621. Also 20, 109. Colour illus.

Schroder, Timothy. 'George Booth and William Beckford: A Study in Patronage.' *The International Silver & Jewellery Fair & Seminar*, April 1989, 21–28. A lecture delivered on 30 Jan during the 1988 Seminar to complement the loan exhibition of Beckford's silver from the Royal Museum of Scotland, Edinburgh. Noted in Jon Millington, 'Beckford's Silver', *Beckford Tower Trust Newsletter*, Spring 1990, 4.

Schroder, Timothy. 'L'argenterie continentale au chateau du Brodick.' In *Argenteries. Le Trésor du National Trust for Scotland*, 31–35. Brussels: National Trust for Scotland, 1992. Exhibition catalogue in French and Flemish. Pp. 11–12 in English trans.

Schroder, Timothy. 'An English silver-gilt and agate cup and cover *circa* 1820' In *Partridge Recent Acquisitions*, 18–21. London: Partridge, 1994. Cup in Christie's sale (1822, 8th day, lot 43), 19. Col. illus. 18. Followed by 'William Beckford (1760–1844)', on Beckford as a patron of goldsmiths, 20–21.

Schroder, Timothy B., ed. *Heritage Regained. Silver from the Gilbert Collection*. London: Heather Trust for the Arts, 1998. Basket by Paul Storr and Ewer & basin by Henri Auguste, 11, 50–51, 54, 55. Both illus. in colour, 54.

Snodin, Michael. 'William Beckford and Metalwork.' In *William Beckford, 1760–1844: An Eye for the Magnificent*, ed. Derek E. Ostergard, 202–215. New Haven & London: Yale University Press for the Bard Graduate Center, 2001. Exhibition catalogue.

Articles

Grimwade, A. G. 'A New List of Old English Gold Plate, Part III 1750–1830.' *Connoisseur* 128 (Oct 1951): 86–87. George III teapot and stand by Smith and Sharp (1785) now in the Barber Institute of Fine Arts, Birmingham University.

Hardy, John. 'Candlesticks from Fonthill Abbey.' *Beckford Journal* 2 (1996): 62–63. Probably made under Beckford's direction by Benjamin Vulliamy.

Hayward, J. F. 'Royal Plate at Fonthill.' *Burlington Magazine* 101 (April 1959): 145. Christie's 1822 sale: lot 814, silver-gilt salver with initials of William and Mary; lot 824, embossed dish formerly owned by Charles I.

Millington, Jon. 'Beckford's Silver.' *Beckford Tower Trust Newsletter*, Spring 1981, 3. Sotheby's sale at Lennoxlove, Spink exh. & articles in the *Burlington Magazine*.

Morison, Patricia. 'Silver freak.' *Daily Telegraph*, 30 Jan 1988. Loan exhibition at the Dorchester Hotel of Beckford's silver from the Royal Museum of Scotland, Edinburgh.

Norman, Geraldine. 'Nuremberg silver standing cup fetches £40,000.' *The Times*, 26 Oct 1973, 5a. Beckford's 17th century German and Dutch silver sold by the Duke of Hamilton.

Oman, Charles. 'Caddinets and a Forgotten Version of the Royal Arms.' *Burlington Magazine* 100 (Dec 1958): 431–435 at 435. Beckford's purchase of royal silver in 1808 from the royal goldsmiths.

Snodin, Michael & Malcolm Baker. 'William Beckford's Silver I.' *Burlington Magazine* 122 (Nov 1980): 734–748. Part II, (Dec): 820–831, 833–834 & cover illus. of Aldridge cup and cover. An exhaustive & fascinating study.

Tait, Hugh. 'Huguenot silver made in London (c.1690–1723). The Peter Wilding Bequest to the British Museum. Part I.' *Connoisseur* (Aug 1972): 267–277 at 270–274, figs 5–8 & nn6–16. Pair of silver-gilt vases with covers by David Willaume (1711).

PAINTINGS AND DRAWINGS

For portraits of Beckford see '2. Aspects of Beckford'

Books

Adams, Eric. *Francis Danby: Varieties of Poetic Landscape*. New Haven: Yale University Press, 1973. 'An Attempt to Illustrate the Opening of the Sixth Seal' (Exhibited at the Royal Academy 1828), 66, 68, 69, 154n, 175 & fig. 48. 'Subject from Revelations' (Exh. Royal Academy, 1829), 69, 176–177 & fig. 53.

Arnold, Bruce. *The Art Atlas of Britain and Ireland*. London: Viking, in association with the National Trust, 1991. Beckford & Horace Walpole important collectors, 35. Two of Beckford's paintings at Harewood House, 118. George Lucy of Charlecote Park at 1823 Fonthill Sale, 169, 409. 'Altieri' Claudes at Anglesey Abbey, 185. Beckford's collection at Brodick Castle, 296, 435. Casali ceilings from Splendens at Dyrham Park, 326.

Balston, Thomas. *John Martin 1789–1854. His Life and Works*. London: Duckworth, 1947. Made three drawings of Fonthill, 76. Quote from James G. Huneker, *Promenades of an Impressionist*, New York: Scribner, 1910: 'William Beckford's *Vathek*, that most oriental of tales, should have inspired Martin. Perhaps its mad fantasy did, for all we know', 253.

Bindman, David. 'The English Apocalypse.' In *The Apocalypse and the Shape of Things to Come*, ed. Frances Carey, 212, 213–214, 221, 229 nn26, 30, 31. London: British Museum Press, 1999. Benjamin West's paintings for Fonthill on Revelation subjects. Also Danby, 'Opening of the Sixth Seal' (1828), 269.

Brigstocke, Hugh. *William Buchanan and the 19th Century Art Trade: 100 Letters to his Agents in London and Italy*. [London]: Privately publ. typescript by The Paul Mellon Centre for Studies in British Art, 1982. Letters, mostly written between 1803 & 1805 to his agent in Italy (James Irvine) and in London (David Stewart), about selling paintings to Beckford, mentioning that the artist Henry Tresham acted as agent (as did Benjamin West, whom he hated) for Beckford, 4, 14–15, 17, 76, 89, 131, 148, 152, 172, 177, 191, 251, 254, 268, 315, 332, 358, 361, 363, 375, 382.

Buchanan, William. *Memoirs of Painting; with a chronological history of the importation of pictures by the great masters into England since the French Revolution*. 2 vols. London: Ackermann, 1824. Beckford bought Leonardo da Vinci's 'Laughing Boy' at Sir William Hamilton's sale at Christie's in 1801, and bought it back from Farquhar when he owned Fonthill Abbey, 1:78–79.

Chapel, Jeannie. 'William Beckford: Collector of Old Master Paintings, Drawings, and Prints.' In *William Beckford, 1760–1844: An Eye for the Magnificent*, ed. Derek E. Ostergard, 228–249. New Haven & London: Yale University Press for the Bard Graduate Center, 2001. Exh. catalogue.

Clark, Kenneth. *The Romantic Rebellion. Romantic versus Classical Art*. London: John Murray, 1973. Turner's 'The Tenth Plague of Egypt' commissioned by Beckford in 1796 but not painted until 1799, 228.

Croft-Murray, E. *Decorative Painting in England, 1537–1837. Vol. 2, Eighteenth and Early Nineteenth Centuries*. London: Country Life, 1970. P. 181.

Danby. Greenacre, Francis. *Francis Danby 1793–1861*. London: Tate Gallery & Bristol: City of Bristol Museum & Art Gallery, 1988. No. 24: 'An Attempt to Illustrate the Opening of the Sixth Seal' (1828), 99–100. No. 30, 'Subject from Revelations' (1829), 105–106. " 'Fonthill Abbey . . .', c.1813, watercolour," 168. Also 27, 28, 74, 107, 168. Exhibition catalogue.

REVIEW. Millington, Jon. *Beckford Tower Trust Newsletter*, Spring 1989, 1.

Danby. Greenacre, Francis. 'Danby, Francis (1793–1861).' In *Oxford Dictionary of National Biography*, ed. H. C. G. Matthew & Brian Harrison, 15:37. Oxford: Oxford University Press, 2004. Beckford bought his 'Attempt to Illustrate the Opening of the Sixth Seal' in 1828.

Davis, Frank. *Victorian Patrons of the Arts. Twelve Famous Collections and Their Owners*. London: Country Life, 1963. Quote from Beckford's letter of 1841 about selling paintings, 14. Satinwood coffers (Wallace Collection), 44.

Feaver, William. *The Art of John Martin*. Oxford: Clarendon Press, 1975. Pp. 60–62, 64, 76, 90, 221.

Fedden, Robin. *Anglesey Abbey*. London: The National Trust, 1970. 'Altieri' Claudes: 'The Father of Psyche sacrificing at the Temple of Apollo' (1663) & 'The Landing of Aeneas' (1675), 23, photo, facing 20. New ed., ed. Oliver Garnett, 2002. Colour photos of 'Altieri' Claudes, 28, 29. Guide books.

Hardie, Martin. *Water-colour Painting in Britain*. 3 vols. London: Batsford, 1968. 1:79–80, 83, 93, 134–135, 136. Alderman Beckford, 91. Brandoin, 166. Turner at Fonthill, 2:27

Ingamells, John. *The Wallace Collection Catalogue of Pictures*. 4 vols. London: Trustees of the Wallace Collection. Vol. 3, 1989, P 532: Corneille de Lyon (active 1533, d. 1575), 'Portrait of a young Man'. (Vol. 1, 1985, P 505: Studio of Canaletto, 'Venice: the Piazza S. Marco', pp. 246–247. Marked in 1870 inventory as Beckford's but not identifiable in any of the Beckford sales.)

Kitson, Michael. *The Art of Claude Lorrain*. Newcastle upon Tyne & then London: Arts Council, 1969. 'Altieri' Claudes, Nos. 21, 24 (London Nos. 32, 37) & pl. 25, 26. Bartholomeus Breenbergh, 'Landscape with Ruins', No. 78 (No 128) & pl. 3. John Robert Cozens, p. 52 (p. 73). Exhibition catalogues.

Levey, Michael. *National Gallery Catalogues. German School*. London: National Gallery, 1959. 'Elsheimer. Tobias and the Archangel Raphael', 40–42.

Middleton, Robin. 'Soane's Spaces and the Matter of Fragmentation.' In *John Soane: Architect Master of Space and Light*, ed. Margaret Richardson and MaryAnne Stevens, 35. London: Royal Academy of Arts, 1999. Hogarth's 'A Rake's Progress' formerly in Beckford's collection, 21.

Munby, A. N. L. *Connoisseurs and Medieval Miniatures 1750–1850*. Oxford: Clarendon Press, 1972. Miniatures in Beckford's MS. collection, 10, 77–78, 147.

Paley, Morton D. *The Apocalyptic Sublime*. New Haven: Yale University Press, 1986. Beckford's patronage of Benjamin West, passim. Danby's 'Opening of the Sixth Seal', 176 & pl. 79, and his 'Subject from Revelations', one of two unexecuted designs for overdoors in Lansdown Crescent, 177 & pl. 80.

Passavant, Johann David. 'Collection of pictures belonging to W. Beckford, Esq.' In *Tour of a German Artist in England, with Notices of Private Galleries, and Remarks on the State of Art*, 1:314–318. 2 vols. London: Saunders & Otley, 1836. Fonthill Abbey, 2:305. Reprinted, Wakefield: EP Publ., 1978. Abridged & revised trans. of *Kunstreise durch England und Belgien*. Frankfurt, 1833.

Rodgers, David. 'Beckford, William.' In *The Dictionary of Art*, ed. Jane Turner, 3:476–477. 34 vols. London: Macmillan, 1996. Also 'Casali, Andrea' by Olivier Michel, 5:907 & 'Hamilton, Alexander' by R. Windsor Liscombe, 14:107.

Turner, J. M. W. *Turner's Liber Studiorum*. 3 vols. London: Autotype Fine Art Co., 1872. Sepia autotypes. Vol. 2, 'Architectural and Historical Subjects': 'Fifth Plague of Egypt'. Etched by Turner and mezzotint by Charles Turner (no relation). Original etching titled: 'The 5th Plague of Egypt the Picture late in the possession of W. Beckford Esqr.' 'Publ. 10 June 1808. C. Turner, London.' Based on the painting bought by Beckford in 1800. J. M. W. Turner publ. 71 of 101 intended plates in *Liber Studiorum* between 1807 and 1819.

Waagen, G. F. *Works of Art and Artists in England*. 3 vols. London: John Murray, 1838. Important account of Beckford's pictures in Bath in Letter XXVI dated 4 Sept 1835, 3:111, 114–130. 'Altieri' Claudes at Leigh Court formerly owned by Beckford (he sold them in 1808), 3:139. He offered Angerstein £20,000 for Sebastian del Piombo's 'Raising of Lazarus', 1:191. Trans. by H. E. Lloyd of vols. 1 & 2 of *Kunstwerke und Künstler in England und Paris*, 3 vols., Berlin: Nicolaische, 1837–1838 (vols. 1 & 2, England), 1839 (vol. 3, Paris). Bath, 2:321, 324–338. Claudes, 2:349–350. *Works of Art and Artists in England* reprinted London: Cornmarket Press, 1970.

REVIEW. *Athenæum*, 3, 10 March 1838, 162–164, 181–183 at 182. Extracts from pp. 111, 114–115, 119–122 & 129.

Watson, F. J. B. *Wallace Collection Catalogues. Pictures and Drawings*. London: Trustees of the Wallace Collection, 1968. 'Corneille de Lyon . . . P532 The Earl of Hertford (?)', 70–71.

Whitley, William T. *Art in England. Volume 1. 1800–1820* [&] *Volume 2. 1821–1837*. 2 vols. New York: Hacker Art Books, 1973. (1st eds. 1928, 1930.) Vol. 1: Turner's watercolours of Fonthill (1800), 7. 'Altieri' Claudes (1800), 12. Fonthill Splendens sale (1807), 128–129. Vol. 2: Abbey sale & Topaz Cup (1823), 53–55. Sebastian del Piombo's 'Raising of Lazarus' (1824), 68, 73. Danby's 'Opening of the Sixth Seal' (1828), 148. Beckford viewed sale at Erlestoke Park, Devizes (1832), 240. Bought Gerard Dou's 'A Dutch girl gathering a pink' at Christie's (from *Morning Chronicle*, 14 April 1834), 272.

Articles

Alexander, Boyd. 'William Beckford as Patron.' *Apollo* 76 (July 1962): 360–364. Beckford's acquisition of landscapes and other paintings.

Beckford's Vandycks, prices at Hamilton sale. *The Times*, 14 July 1882, 10c.

Booker, John. 'What was the largest sum ever given for a picture?' *Notes and Queries* 2nd Series 3 (21 Feb 1857): 159. Beckford's refused offer of

£20,000 for 'Raising of Lazarus'. Reprinted in *Littell's Living Age* 54 (1 Aug 1857): 304.

Bruce, Donald. 'The Picture Galleries Outside London: The Bath and Bristol Galleries.' *Contemporary Review* 268 (May 1996): 240–247 at 240. Beckford "bought a replica of Danby's 'The Sixth Seal' for his collection at Fonthill".

Bruce, Donald. 'A Celebration at the Hayward Gallery: A Century of Rescued Art.' *Contemporary Review* 284 (Jan 2004): 43–48 at 46. The exhibition included Claude's 'St Philip Baptising an Ethopian' once owned by Beckford.

Claude. *The Times*, 10 May 1799, 3a. Pair of 'Altieri' Claudes bought by Beckford for 6000 guineas.

Davies, Damian Walford & Laurent Châtel. ' "A Mad Hornet". Beckford's Riposte To Hazlitt.' *European Romantic Review* 10 no. 4, 11 no. 1 (Fall 1999, Winter 2000): 452–479, 97–99.

Grassi, Marco. 'The Angelic Friar at the Met.' *New Criterion* 24 no. 4 (Dec 2005): 23–27 at 24. Beckford among the collectors of 'early art'.

Harris, Lucian. 'Archibald Swinton: a new source for albums of Indian miniatures in William Beckford's collection.' *Burlington Magazine* 143 (June 2001): 360–366 & figs 47–57.

Hauptman, William. "Beckford, Brandoin, and the 'Rajah'. Aspects of an eighteenth-century collection." *Apollo* 143 (May 1996): 30–39.

Hauptman, William. 'William Beckford as Connoisseur and Collector: Some Remarks from the Art Historical Perspective.' In *The Beckford Society Annual Lectures 1996–1999*, ed. Jon Millington, 35–54. London: *The Beckford Society*, 2000. The 1998 lecture.

[Hazlitt, William.] Pictures at Fonthill Abbey. *Morning Chronicle*, 5 Nov 1822. Also described the building and grounds.

[Hazlitt, William.] 'Fonthill Abbey.' *London Magazine* 6 (Nov 1822): 405–410. Reprinted in his *Criticisms on Art*, 284–299, London: Templeman, 1843.

[Hazlitt, William.] 'Pictures at Wilton, Stourhead, &c.' *London Magazine* 8 (Oct 1823): 357–360. Reprinted in his *Sketches of the Principal Picture-Galleries in England*, 127, 128, 134–137, 138, 139, London: Taylor & Hessey, 1824, & in his *Criticisms on Art*, 102, 103, 108–111, 112, London: Templeman, 1843.

[Hazlitt, William.] 'Notices of curious and highly finished cabinet pictures at Fonthill Abbey.' *Morning Chronicle*, 20, 22, 25 Aug, 1 Sept 1823, 3, 3, 3, 2. Reprinted in Gemmett, *Beckford's Fonthill* (2003), 313–321.

[Hazlitt, William.] 'The science of a connoisseur.' *Morning Chronicle*, 30 Sept 1823, 2. A satirical conversation on false taste between two friends. Reprinted in Gemmett, *Beckford's Fonthill* (2003), 322–325.

Holbein. Blair, C. 'Beckford: "Extracts from a Journal".' *Notes and Queries*

209 (Dec 1964): 477–478. Query about an album of Holbein drawings from 'Francfort' sold at Sotheby's in April 1863.

Jones, Stanley. 'The Fonthill Abbey Pictures: Two Additions to the Hazlitt Canon.' *Journal of the Warburg and Courtauld Institutes* 41 (1978): 278–296 & pl. 37, 38. Two articles in the *Morning Chronicle* in Aug & Sept 1823.

Millington, Jon. 'Beckford's Pictures now in the National Gallery.' *Beckford Journal* 1 (1995): 37–40. List of 19 paintings once owned by Beckford.

Nolan, J. C. M. ' "Ah Dear Comet . . .": Beckford and the Apocalyptic art of West and Danby.' *Beckford Journal* 3 (1997): 8–19.

[Patmore, Peter George.] 'British Galleries of Art. – No. IX. *Fonthill.*' *New Monthly Magazine* 8 (Nov 1823): 403–408. Reprinted as 'The Late Fonthill Gallery' in his *British Galleries of Art*, 119–141, London: Whittaker, 1824, and in Gemmett, *Beckford's Fonthill* (2003), 343–350.
ADVERT. *Literary Gazette* 8 (2 Oct 1824): 624.

Tuohy, Thomas. 'William Beckford's three picture collections: Idiosyncrasy and innovation.' *British Art Journal* 2 no. 1 (Autumn 2000): 49–53 & 7 illus. Collections: (1) Splendens, (2) Fonthill Abbey & (3) at Bath.

Cozens, Alexander (c.1717–1786) & John Robert (1752–1797)

Books

Binyon, Laurence. *English Water-Colours*. London: A. & C. Black, 1933. Pp. 39, 47, 51–52.

Clarke, Michael. *The Tempting Prospect*. London: British Museum Publications, 1981. Pp. 129–131.

Greaves, Margaret. *Sir George Beaumont*. London: Methuen, 1966. Beaumont met John Robert travelling with Beckford who had just finished *Vathek*.

Hawcroft, Francis W., intro. *Watercolours by John Robert Cozens*. Manchester: Whitworth Art Gallery and London: Victoria & Albert Museum, 1971. Beckford, aged 19, first met Cozens, 5, 6–7.

Lemaître, Henri. *Le Paysage anglais à l'aquarelle 1760–1851*. Paris: Bordas, [1955]. Alexander Cozens, 85–88, 93, 95, 432. John Robert Cozens, 103, 104n, 105, 106, 113n, 115, 117, 124, 130. Turner's six watercolours, 220n.

Monkhouse, Cosmo. 'Cozens, Alexander.' & 'Cozens, John Robert.' In *Dictionary of National Biography*, ed. Leslie Stephen, 12:425. London: Smith, Elder, 1887.

Oppé, A. P. *Catalogue of an Exhibition of Drawings & Paintings by Alexander Cozens*. Sheffield, Autumn 1946. Pp. 6, 12, 44, 52. Reprinted, London: The Tate Gallery, Dec 1946, 7–8, 17, 48, 55.

Oppé, A. P. *Alexander & John Robert Cozens*. London: A. & C. Black, 1952. Alexander taught Beckford, 30–37. With John Robert in Italy, 111–114 & passim.

Roget, John Lewis. *A History of the 'Old Water-Colour' Society, now the Royal Society of Painters in Water Colours*. 2 vols. London: Longmans, Green, 1891. Beckford and John (Robert) Cozens, 61–63.

Sloan, Kim. "Working for William Beckford. – 'The Shackles of Fantastic Folly and Caprice' 1780–4." In *Alexander and John Robert Cozens. The Poetry of Landscape*, 138–157 & notes, 176–177. London: Yale University Press, 1986. 'Beauty, Beckford, and the Sublime 1775–86', 73–79 & notes, 171–172. Also passim.

Sloan, Kim. *'A Noble Art'. Amateur Artists and Drawing Masters*. London: British Museum Press, 2000. Cozens, 155 (No. 108), 182 (No. 125), 207 (No. 150). Brandoin, 186 (No. 129). Dr Thomas Monro, 208 (No. 152).

Sloan, Kim. 'Cozens, John Robert (1752–1797).' In *Oxford Dictionary of National Biography*, ed. H. C. G. Matthew & Brian Harrison, 13:887–888, 889. Oxford: Oxford University Press, 2004. Beckford commissioned Italian paintings from Cozens whom he invited to join him on his visit to Italy from May–Nov 1782.

Upstone, Robert. *The Sketchbooks of the Romantics*. London: Tiger, 1993. John Robert Cozens, 145, 182. *Vathek*, 28.

Wilton, Andrew. *The Art of Alexander and John Robert Cozens*. New Haven: Yale Center for British Art, 1980. Passim.

Articles

Bell, C. F. & Thomas Girtin. *The Drawings and Sketches of John Robert Cozens*. Oxford: Walpole Society, 1935. passim. The Society's 23rd vol.

Davis, Frank. 'Talking about Salerooms.' *Country Life*, 31 Jan 1974, 179. Seven Cozens sketchbooks sold at Sotheby's for £135,000.

Dorment, Richard. 'Man of Mystery. Alexander Cozens at the V&A.' *Country Life*, 27 Nov 1986, 1703.

Hawcroft, Francis. 'J R Cozens (1752–97) *Six Landscapes in Italy*.' *National Art-Collections Fund Review*, 1985, 136–139 at 136. Bought by Whitworth Art Gallery, Manchester.

Markham, Rosemary. 'Thomas Jones: An Eighteenth-century Welsh Artist.' *Contemporary Review* 284 (Feb 2004): 85–90 at 88. When Beckford was in Italy in 1782, Jones called on him, 'but the outcome was unsatisfactory'.

Neve, Christopher. 'Two Journeys in Monochrome. John Robert Cozens at the Whitworth.' *Country Life*, 11 March 1971, 531. Journey with Beckford.

Peet, David. 'The Great Age of British Watercolours 1750–1880.' *Contemporary Review* 262 (June 1993): 306–? at 308. John Robert visited Italy with Beckford in 1782 and produced two exhibited paintings of the Great Temple of Pæstum.

Maddox, Willes (1813–1853)

Carter, Nicholas & Kathryn Turpin. 'Paintings for Beckford's Sanctuary.' *Apollo* 159 (May 2004): 64–67 & 6 illus. Four lunettes by Willes Maddox for the Tower sold at Duke's, Dorchester, on 11 March 2004, lot 204.

Cust, L. H., rev. Kenneth Bendiner. 'Maddox, Willis [Willes] (1813–1853).' In *Oxford Dictionary of National Biography*, ed. H. C. G. Matthew & Brian Harrison, 36:81. Oxford: Oxford University Press, 2004. Beckford his patron.

Hilliard, Elizabeth. 'Willes Maddox.' *Beckford Tower Trust Newsletter*, Spring 1987, 3. Brief account of his life.

Obituary. *Gentleman's Magazine* n.s. 41 (Jan 1854): 102.

Redgrave, Samuel. 'Maddox, Willes.' In *Dictionary of Artists of the English School . . .*, 283. New ed. London: George Bell, 1878. John Francis Moore won competition for Alderman Beckford's monument in Guildhall, 296.

West, Benjamin (1738–1820)

Alberts, Robert C. *Benjamin West. A Biography.* Boston, MA: Houghton Mifflin, 1978. West painted nine pictures for Beckford, 221. Beckford's failed attempt to buy land in America, 243–244. Commissions from Beckford, 244–245. Biographical sketch of Beckford, 247–249. West invited to Fonthill for Nelson's visit in Dec 1800, 255–257. Invited to Abbey in 1807, 337. Notes, 452–454. Mentioned, xvi, 59, 242, 261, 268, 330, 464. Illus. of West's drawing of Beckford's French dwarf, Pierre Colas de Grailly.

Cooke, George Alexander. *Topographical and Statistical Description of the County of Berks.* London: Sherwood, Neely & Jones, c.1820. Beckford's comments on the sketch of his by Benjamin West for 'Institution of the Most Noble Order of the Garter, April 23, 1349' at Windsor Castle, 154–155.

Dillenberger, John. 'Paintings for William Beckford and Fonthill Abbey: 1795–1810.' In *Benjamin West. The Context of His Life's Work with Particular Attention to Paintings with Religious subject Matter*, 106–209. San Antonio, Texas: Trinity University Press, [1977].

Evans, Dorinda. 'West, Benjamin (1738–1820).' In *Oxford Dictionary of National Biography*, ed. H. C. G. Matthew & Brian Harrison, 58:214. Oxford: Oxford University Press, 2004. Uncompleted commission in 1796 for scenes from Book of Revelations.

Hamilton-Phillips, Martha. 'Benjamin West and William Beckford: Some Projects for Fonthill.' *Metropolitan Museum Journal* 15 (1981):

157–174. Beckford's patronage of West, 'a national institution', with 20 illus.

Pressly, Nancy L. 'Visions of the Apocalypse – West at Fonthill Abbey.' In *Revealed Religion: Benjamin West's Commissions for Windsor Castle and Fonthill Abbey*, 56–73 incl. figs. 31–33, 36–38. San Antonio, Texas: San Antonio Museum of Art, 1983. Exhibition cat., 18 Sept–13 Nov.

Von Erffa, Helmut & Walter Staley. *The Paintings of Benjamin West*. New Haven: Yale, 1986. Passim.

SCULPTURE

Books

Baker, Malcolm. *Figured in Marble: the Making and Viewing of Eighteenth-century Sculpture*. London: Victoria & Albert Museum, 2001. Beckford's Giambologna group formerly in the Crimson Drawing Room at the Tower, 155–158. V&A Studies in the History of Design.

Busco, Marie. *Sir Richard Westmacott, Sculptor*. Cambridge: Cambridge University Press, 1994. 'Madonna della Gloria: a statue for Fonthill' exhibited at the Royal Academy in 1799 but not bought by Beckford, 12 & n51.

Gramaccini, Gisela. *Jean-Guillaume Moitte (1746–1810): Leben und Werke*. 2 vols. Berlin: Akademie Verlag, 1993. Beckford's patronage, 1:270 & passim.

Neale, John Preston. *Views of the Seats of Noblemen and Gentlemen*. 5 vols. 2nd series. London: Sherwood, Jones, 1824–1829. Statue of Bacchus mentioned in 'Pains Hill, Surrey', 1 (1824): [2].

Roberts, Jane, et al. *Wardour Castle*. Tisbury, Wiltshire: Cranborne Chase School, 1976. Statue of St Anthony by 'Theakstone', [13–14] & photo, [15]. Guide book.

Articles

Ivory Carvings at Fonthill. *Apollo Magazine* 1 (1823): 204–206. Reprinted in Gemmett, *Beckford's Fonthill* (2003), 360–361.

Kitz, Norman. 'The Hamilton Bacchus.' *Country Life*, 11 Jan 1990, 88. Enquiry as to its present whereabouts.

Kitz, Norman. 'The Search for a Lost 'Greek' Statue.' *Beckford Journal* 11 (2005): 14–19. Tracking down Bacchus.

Nares, Gordon. 'Painshill, Surrey – II.' *Country Life*, 9 Jan 1958, 65. Antique colossal statue of Bacchus bought by Beckford and removed to Fonthill.

Woodbridge, Kenneth. 'Henry Hoare's Paradise.' *The Art Bulletin* 47 (March 1965): 109 n233. Refers to *Country Life* article by Gordon Nares.

STAINED GLASS

Books

Barker, W. R. *St. Mark's; or, The Mayor's Chapel, Bristol.* Bristol: Hemmons, 1892. Glass from Fonthill Sale (1823) in nave, 99, 140–141. Thomas à Becket window in south aisle with new glass added in border, 155. Also mentioned in *St. Mark's. The Lord Mayor's Chapel, Bristol*, Bristol: Corporation of Bristol, 1939, 7, 17, and in rev. ed. by Elizabeth Ralph & Henley Evans, 1950, 8, 22.

Cowen, Painton. 'Bristol, St. Mark [The Lord Mayor's Chapel].' In *A Guide to Stained Glass in Britain*, 70–71. London: Michael Joseph, 1985. 'Much of the glass here came from the sale at Fonthill Abbey in 1823', 71.

Eginton. Harrison, W. Jerome. 'Eginton, Francis (1737–1805).' In *Dictionary of National Biography*, ed. Leslie Stephen, 17:164. London: Smith, Elder, 1889. Painted 32 figures of kings, etc., and many windows for Fonthill.

Eginton. Ellis, Martin. 'Eginton, Francis (1736/7–1805).' In *Oxford Dictionary of National Biography*, ed. H. C. G. Matthew & Brian Harrison, 17:1014. Oxford: Oxford University Press, 2004. Massive commission for painted glass in 1794.

Hamilton, William. Graves, R. E. rev. Deborah Graham-Vernon. 'Hamilton, William (1751–1801).' In *Oxford Dictionary of National Biography*, ed. H. C. G. Matthew & Brian Harrison, 24:927. Oxford: Oxford University Press, 2004. Paintings for gallery at Fonthill.

Lee, Lawrence, George Sedden & Francis Stephen. *Stained Glass*. London: Artists' House, 1982. 'Curiosities and Pastiches', Eginton, 145.

Morris, Stephen & Tim Mowl. *Open Doors. Bristol's hidden interiors*. Bristol: Redcliffe Press, 2002. 'St Mark's – The Lord Mayor's Chapel, College Green', No. 16. With fine colour photo of St Thomas à Becket window.

Williams, Cynthia. *The Stained Glass of Fonthill Abbey*. MA thesis, Cooper-Hewitt National Design Museum, New York, 1996.

Articles

Aitken, W. C. Francis Eginton. *Birmingham Daily Post*, 25 April 1871. Reprinted with corrections and additions as a pamphlet, Birmingham, 1871. 14 pp.

Baylis, Sarah. 'Knights in Painted Glass.' *Country Life*, 7 Feb 2002, 64–67. Sources for some of the stained glass in the Abbey. A by-product of her Cambridge PhD Thesis on the Revival of Stained Glass in Britain.

Pearson, James. *Gentleman's Magazine* 85 pt. 2 (July 1815): 28–29 at 28, 29. Letter about Beckford's patronage of modern English stained glass.

Rogers, Millard F., Jr. 'Benjamin West and the Caliph: two paintings for Fonthill Abbey.' *Apollo* 83 (June 1966): 420–425. St Thomas à Becket (1797) & St Michael and the Dragon (1797), both stained glass designs.

S., E. M. [Rev. James Dallaway.] 'Progress, &c. of Stained Glass in England.' *Gentleman's Magazine* 87 pt. 1 (April 1817): 309–315 at 315. Footnote on stained glass in Fonthill Abbey.

WORKS OF ART

Books

Alcouffe, Daniel, ed. 'La collection de Fonthill.' In *Les vases en pierres dures*. Paris: la Documentation française, Musée du Louvre, 2003.

Impey, Oliver & John Whitehead, 'Observations on Japanese Lacquer in the Collection of William Beckford.' In *William Beckford, 1760–1844: An Eye for the Magnificent*, ed. Derek E. Ostergard, 216–227. New Haven & London: Yale University Press for the Bard Graduate Center, 2001. Exh. catalogue.

Impey, Oliver & Christiaan Jörg. *Japanese Export Lacquer*. Amsterdam: Hotei Publishing, 2005. Passim.

Jarry, Madeleine. *Chinoiserie: Chinese Influence on European Decorative Art 17th and 18th Centuries*. New York: Vendome Press & London: Sotheby, [1981]. The van Diemen box, 212, 221, illus., plate 139.

Linsky, Jack & Belle. *The Jack and Belle Linsky Collection in the Metropolitan Museum*. New York: Metropolitan Museum of Art, 1984. 'Fonthill Ewer', 179–180.

Miller, James. *In the Public Eye. Treasures from the West of England*. Holburne Museum, Bath. Autumn 2002. '69 A magnificent Indian jade hookah, late 18th century'. Phillips sale, 1823, lot 1541. Sold for 209 guineas. [In Beckford exh, New York & London, 2001–2002, cat. no. 55.]

Wainwright, Clive. '19. Renaissance Revival cup and cover.' In *Fake? The Art of Deception*, ed. Mark Jones, 44–45. London: British Museum Publications, 1990. The agate cup mounted in silver gilt in 1815. Exh. catalogue. Noted in Jon Millington, 'Fake!', *Beckford Tower Trust Newsletter*, Spring 1991, 9.

Articles

Alsop, Joseph. 'The Faker's Art.' *New York Review of Books* 33 (23 Oct 1986): 28. Cellini cup in Linsky collection, Metropolitan Museum of Art.

'Beckford's fantastic legacy fires yet another bid battle.' *Antiques Trade Gazette*, 7 May 1994, 70. Sale of gilt-bronze candlesticks at Christie's.

Eisenberg, Jerome M. "The 'Rubens Vase' in Baltimore: An Oriental copy?" *Minerva* 8 no. 2 (March/April 1997): 20–25. 'Forgery and Ancient Art' series.

Gardner, J. Starkie. 'The Nautilus Shell as used by the Goldsmith.' *Connoisseur* 11 (March 1905): 178. Dutch nautilus cup, the shell engraved by C. Bellekin, with photo.

Impey, Oliver & John Whitehead, 'From Japanese box to French royal furniture.' *Apollo* 132 (Sept 1990): 161 & 164 n8. Van Diemen box (1636–1639).

Jaffé, Michael. 'William Beckford's Lapis-lazuli Cup.' In *National Art Collections Fund Review 1990*, 124–127. From Christie's, now in the Fitzwilliam Museum.

Leben, Ulrich. 'Le Nautile de la collection Beckford.' *Waddesdon Manor. Les collections exceptionnelles des Rothschild. L'objet d'art* No. 14 (Oct 2000): 54–55. Trans as: 'The Waddesdon Manor nautilus shell and triton: A masterpiece from the William Beckford Collection.' *The Magazine Antiques* (New York) 164 no. 4 (Oct 2003): 114–121 & 11 pl.

Mallalieu, Huon. 'Review Salerooms.' *Country Life*, 6 Oct 2005, 113–114. Louis XIV carved agate ewer & basin bought in Paris for Beckford, *c.*1801.

McLeod, Bet. 'Beckford's Cup of Rapture.' *Country Life*, 16 Aug 2001, 60. Agate cup mounted in silver gilt by James Aldridge (1815–1816).

Millington, Jon. 'A Lapis Lazuli Cup.' *Beckford Tower Trust Newsletter*, Spring 1990, 8. Sold at Christie's on 6 Dec 1989 to Fitzwilliam Museum, Cambridge.

Millington, Jon. 'The Barber Institute of Fine Arts, Birmingham University.' *Beckford Tower Trust Newsletter*, Spring 1994, 11–12. Bloodstone bowl with Paul Storr's silver-gilt mounts (1824) and a gold teapot (1785).

Moore, Susan. 'Batsheva's treasure chest.' *Evening Standard*, 18 Dec 2000. The Mamluk enamelled glass jug sold at Christie's for £3.3m.

Robinson, William. 'The Hamilton Jug.' *Christie's Magazine* 17 no. 7 (Dec 2000): 32–35. The Mamluk enamelled glass jug depicted in Willes Maddox's painting of 'Objects of Vertu No. 3' (*c.*1840).

Ross, Marvin Chauncey. 'The Rubens Vase. Its History and Date.' *Journal of the Walters Art Gallery* 6 (1943): 8–39.

Smith, H. Clifford. 'Van Diemen box.' *Burlington Magazine* 29 (Oct 1916): 299–303 & five illus., 301.

Stone, Richard E. 'A Noble Imposture: The Fonthill Ewer and Early-Nineteenth-Century Fakery.' *Metropolitan Museum Journal* 32 (1997): 175–206 & 60 figs. A detailed account.

Stone, Richard E. 'The Fonthill Ewer: Reconstructing the Renaissance.' *The Metropolitan Museum of Art Bulletin* (Winter 1997–98): 46–55, 56. 16 figs. Reprinted in *Appearance and Reality: Recent Studies in Conservation*, New York: Metropolitan Museum of Art, 1998. A much briefer version of the *Metropolitan Museum Journal* article, above.

Tilley, William. 'A Romantic Treasure House.' *Christie's International Magazine*, Oct/Nov 1992, 13. Chiddingstone Casket (1636–1639).

Vikan, Gary. 'A Voyage in Time . . .' *Walters Art Gallery Bulletin* 40 no. 1 (Feb 1987): 5. History of the agate Rubens Vase (*c.*400).

HAMILTON PALACE

'The Beckford Library at Hamilton Palace.' *The Times*, 13 May 1847, 6b. New library for Beckford's books designed by Goodridge. 45 lines. From *Globe*.

'The Beckford Vandyks.' *The Times*, 14 July 1882, 10c. Hamilton Palace sale.

Freyburger, Ronald. 'Eighteenth-Century French furniture from Hamilton Palace.' *Apollo* 114 (Dec 1981): 401–409 & nn1–78. Includes much of Beckford's furniture.

Gow, Ian. 'Treasures of the Country Life Library.' *Country Life*, 25 Sept 1997, 130–133. The lost glories of Hamilton Palace: photos taken in 1919.

Hamilton Palace Collection. Illustrated Priced Catalogue. Paris: Librairie de l'art & London: Remington, 1882. 244 pp. Buyers and prices at the Christie's sale, London, 17 June–20 July 1882.

'Hamilton Palace Sale.' *Illustrated London News* 80 (10 June 1882): 568, 569. (17 June): 591, 593. (24 June): 608, 609–610. *Idem* 81 (1 July): 6. (8 July): 31, 42. (15 July): 66, 69, 70, 72–73, 76. (22 July): 86. (30 Dec): 687.

Hamilton Palace Sale in *The Times*. Announcement of sale, 6 Feb 1882, 4a–b. Comments, 10 March, 3d. Letter, 5 June, 5b. Leading articles, 17 June, 11c–d (incl. Library, 11d); 21 June, 12a–b. Sale reports: 13, 15, 19, 20, 21, 26, 28 June, 5d, 4d, 7a–b, 10a, 7e, 10d–e, 10a–b; 3, 4, 5, 11, 12, 19, 21 July 1882, 6c–d, 10d, 10b–c (incl. Library), 11f, 8a–b, 5d–e, 4e.

Herrmann, Frank. *Sotheby's. Portrait of an Auction House.* London: Chatto & Windus, 1980. Hamilton Palace sale, 73–75, 78. Beckford Papers, 416.

Mitchell, Matt. *Strathclyde Country Park. Hamilton Mausoleum.* Hamilton: The Author, *c.*1985. Duplicated typescript. Intro., 12 pp. text, 2 pp. appendix of costs. 13 photos.

Royal Museum of Scotland. *French Connections. Scotland and the Arts of France.* Edinburgh: HMSO, 1985. Hamilton Palace, 71–93 & bibliography, 132–134.

Tait, A. A. 'The Duke of Hamilton's Palace.' *Burlington Magazine* 125 (July 1983): 394–402. The Duke 'had little interest in the Gothic Revival'.

Tipping, H. Avray. 'Hamilton Palace–I, Lanarkshire, a seat of the Duke of Hamilton & Brandon.' *Country Life*, 7 June 1919, 662–671. Part II, 14 June, 716–723. Part III, 21 June, 748–755.

Tipping, H. Avray. 'The Hamilton Palace Collection of Pictures.–I.' *Country Life*, 18 Oct 1919, 479–484. Part II, 25 Oct, 514–517. Eight family portraits. Part II discussed in 'Beckford Family Portraits', *Wiltshire Archæological and Natural History Magazine* 41 (June 1919): 86.

Tipping, H. Avray. 'The Hamilton Palace Collection of Silver.' *Country Life*, 1 Nov 1919, 558–561.

Walker, G. *Hamilton Palace. A photographic record.* 2nd ed. Hamilton: 1988. (1st ed. 1976.) Evocative interiors before demolition in 1921.

Ward, Humphry. 'Christie's.' *Scribner's Magazine* 8 (Dec 1890): 758–772 at 766–767. Hamilton Palace sale. Also Fonthill Sale, 764, 765.

SALES

19th Century

Phillips. *A Catalogue of Part of the Superlatively Elegant and Magnificent Household Furniture . . . the Genuine Property of William Beckford, Esq., of Fonthill . . .* London, 19–22 Aug 1801. Furniture, etc.

Christie's. *A Catalogue of a Most Superb, Capital, and Valuable Collection of Italian, French, Flemish and Dutch Pictures: the Property of a Gentleman . . . now brought from his Seat at Fonthill, in Wiltshire.* London, 27 Feb 1802.

Christie's. *A Catalogue of a Small Capital, Genuine, and Select Collection of Pictures lately consigned from Paris . . . the Property of a Gentleman, brought from his Seat at Fonthill, in Wilts.* London, 26–27 March 1802.

Leigh, Sotheby & Son. London, 24 & 26 May 1804. Books & prints.

Christie's. London, 10 April 1805. Drawings by Cozens.

Phillips. Fonthill, 17–22 & 24 Aug 1807. Pictures, furniture, etc.

Phillips. *Fonthill Mansion . . .* Fonthill, 16–19 Sept 1807. Building materials.

Leigh, Sotheby & Son. London, 9–11 June 1808. Books & prints.

Jeffrey's Gallery. *A Catalogue of a Valuable Collection of Paintings . . .* Salisbury, 1809. Twelve paintings from Fonthill, 28–29.

Leigh, Sotheby & Son. London, 6–8 May 1817. Books & drawings.

Christie's. *Catalogue of all the Elegant Furniture . . . of William Beckford, Esq., of Fonthill . . .* London, 9–10 & 12–13 May 1817. Pictures, drawings, etc.

Christie's. *Magnificent Effects at Fonthill Abbey, Wilts.* Fonthill, 17–27 Sept 1822. 95 pp. Pictures, furniture, etc. Two further issues: postponed to 1–11 Oct and again to 8–18 Oct. A ten-day sale was planned.

Phillips. *The Valuable Library of Books in Fonthill Abbey . . . The Unique and Splendid Effects of Fonthill Abbey . . . The Pictures and Miniatures at Fonthill Abbey.* London, 1823. Engraved frontis. based on the entrance ticket to the Abbey. 391 pp. (Also sold as three separate catalogues.) 37-day sale. Days 1–10: Books, [1]–113. Days 11–18: Unique Effects, [121]–175. Days 19–23: Books part 2, 291–342. Days 24–27: Pictures, [228]–278. Days 28–32: Unique Effects part 2, 176–222. Days 33–37: Books part 3, 343–391. On p. 391 of some copies additional text appears below 'End of the Thirty-seventh Day': 'See distinct Catalogue of useful Furniture, Wines, and Miscellanies. Printed by J. Davy, 15, Queen Street, Long Acre.' It was never publ.

Phillips. London, 1–4 March 1824. Drawings & prints.

Sotheby's. London, 19–20 March 1830 [attributed]. Drawings & prints.

English & Fasana. *Catalogue of Valuable Paintings, Magnificent Cabinets and Splendid Furniture, From Lansdown Tower.* Bath, 4–5 Jan 1841. 9 pp. Paintings, 4 Jan, 20 lots. Furniture, 5 Jan, 38 lots.

English & Son. *Catalogue of the Splendid Furniture, Cabinets, Paintings . . . the Property of the Late William Beckford, Esquire.* Bath, 20–29 Nov 1845. 37 pp. 8-day sale of 581 lots.

Roussel. Paris, 22–24 Feb 1847. Objects from China & Japan, etc.

English & Son. *Catalogue of the Valuable and Costly Effects at 20, Lansdown crescent, Bath, the property of the Late William Beckford, Esq.* Bath, 24 July–2 Aug 1848. 52 pp. 9-day sale of china, pictures, etc., 757 lots.

Christie's. *Catalogue of the Collection of Pictures, Works of Art, and Decorative Objects, the Property of His Grace the Duke of Hamilton, K.T.* London, 17 June–20 July 1882. 234 pp. 2213 lots. 78 photos. Hamilton Palace Collection.

Sotheby, Wilkinson & Hodge. *The Hamilton Palace Libraries. Catalogue . . . of The Beckford Library, removed from Hamilton Library.* London, 1882–1883. Four portions, 30 June 1882–30 Nov 1883. 9837 lots. Also, Books returned from four-part sale, 8 July 1884 & Manuscripts, 23 May 1889.

20th Century: A Selection

Christie's. *Catalogue of Family Portraits, Works by Old Masters and Modern Pictures. The Property of the Trustees of His Grace the late Duke of Hamilton.* London, 6–7 Nov 1919. Portraits from Hamilton Palace.

Sotheby's. *Catalogue of a Selected Portion of the Well-known Library from Killadoon.* London, 4–6 July 1966. Sale of first part of Clements Library. Books from Beckford's Library, 329 lots.

Sotheby's. *Catalogue of Printed Books from the Senhouse Collection.* London, 18–20 Oct 1971. Including part of Lytton Strachey's Library.

Sotheby's. *Catalogue of Valuable Printed Books.* London, 19 Nov 1973. Books from Beckford's Library, 37 lots.

Sotheby's. *Catalogue of Seven Sketch-Books by John Robert Cozens (Formerly in the Collection of William Beckford).* London, 29 Nov 1973.

Christie's. *Important Autograph Letter . . . The Property of Lord Margadale.* London, 2 April 1975. Books from Beckford's Library, 52 lots.

Sotheby's. *Catalogue of Valuable Printed Books Formerly in the Library of William Beckford.* London, 27–28 Oct 1975. Rosebery Library. 517 lots.

Sotheby's. *Catalogue of Valuable Autograph Letters, Literary Manuscripts, Historical Documents and Literary Relics and Portraits*. London, 6 July 1977. Lot 272: The Beckford Papers. Also issued as a separate offprint, *The Papers of William Beckford of Fonthill Abbey 1760–1844*, 16 pp.

Sotheby's Parke Bernet. *Livres Précieux . . . Major Adrian McLauchlin*. Monte Carlo, 7 Oct 1980. Books from Beckford's Library, 39 lots

Woolley & Wallis. Salisbury, Wilts, 11 Feb 1987. Beckford's works and books about him, lots 88–131 and 139–156.

Sotheby's. New York, 30 April 1990. Bradley Martin, lots 2596–2612.

Christie's. *Collection of the Late Baroness Batsheva de Rothschild*. 14 Dec 2000. Lot 15, 'A Mamluk Enamelled Glass and Gilded Clear Glass Jug', 58–65.

9. Exhibitions

Gotlieb, Howard B. *William Beckford of Fonthill. Writer, Traveller, Collector, Caliph. 1760–1844. A Brief Narrative and Catalogue of an Exhibition to Mark the Two Hundredth Anniversary of Beckford's Birth*. New Haven: Yale University Library, 1960. 100 pp. 10 pl. 22 cm.

James T. Babb, 'Preface', 9.

"Not an Animal Comprehends Me", 11–12. Brief biography and family tree.

Catalogue of 257 exhibits:

   1. 'William Beckford, Sr. (1709–1770)', 13–14. (7 exhibits.)
   2. 'The Life and Works of William Beckford', 15–47. (99 exhibits.)
   3. 'Books Attributed to William Beckford', 48–52. (21 exhibits.)
   4. 'The Caliph of Fonthill Abbey', 53–59. (35 exhibits.)
   5. 'Beckford the Collector', 60–78. (79 exhibits.)
   6. 'Books about William Beckford', 79–82. (16 exhibits.)

Appendices:

Boyd Alexander, 'The Authorship of Al Raoui', 83–85.

Boyd Alexander, ed., 'Beckford's 1794 Journal', previously unpubl., 86–100.

Reviews of the catalogue

H., J. [Hayward, John.] *Book Collector* 10 no. 1 (Spring 1961): 109–110.

M., F. M. [Moussa-Mahmoud, Fatma.] 'Catalogue of William Beckford Bicentenary Exhibition at Yale: A Review.' In *William Beckford of Fonthill, 1760–1844. Bicentenary Essays*, ed. Fatma Moussa-Mahmoud, 151–157. Suppl. to *Cairo Studies in English*, 1960.

M., R. F. [Metzdorf, Robert F.] & L. S. T. [Lawrence S. Thompson.] *Papers of the Bibliographical Society of America* 1st Quarter (1962): 131–135. A harsh review.

'William Beckford at Yale.' *Times Literary Supplement*, 28 Oct 1960, 699.

A typed 4-page handlist of 67 exhibits: 6 engravings of Fonthill, 12 watercolours & drawings by Turner, 13 lithographs of Lansdown Tower after

Maddox (1844), 8 portraits, 3 manuscripts, Limoges Triptych by Nardon Penicaud (*c.*1510), 11 of Beckford's Works, 8 books from his library, 5 books on Fonthill Abbey.

Review

'William Beckford Exhibition. Turner Drawings of Fonthill' *The Times*, 8 Dec 1960, 7c.

'WILLIAM BECKFORD'
HOLBURNE MUSEUM, BATH, 14 JUNE–3 JULY 1966

Summers, Peter & Philippa Bishop. *William Beckford. Some notes on his life in Bath 1822–1844 and a catalogue of the exhibition in the Holburne of Menstrie Museum.* Bath: Privately printed, 1966. 31 pp. & 9 pp. adverts. 4 drawings by John Newberry. 21¼ cm. Also a limited ed. of 150 numbered copies bound in red linson, gilt. 22 cm. 'The Notes on Beckford were written by Peter Summers / The Catalogue was compiled and written by Philippa Bishop'.
 'Foreword', 4.
 'Introduction', 5.
 'Notes on Beckford', 6–15.
 Catalogue of 110 exhibits:
  'Family Portraits', 17–19. (15 exhibits.)
  'Fonthill [House]', 19–20. (3 exhibits.)
  'Fonthill Abbey', 20–23. (28 exhibits.)
  'Lansdown Tower', 23–24. (10 exhibits.)
  'Beckford as Patron and Collector', 24–27. (23 exhibits.)
  'Books written by Beckford', 27–28. (7 exhibits.)
  'Letters and MSS', 28–30. (16 exhibits.)
  'Miscellaneous', 30. (8 exhibits.)
 Hugh Crallan, Map of Beckford's Ride on Lansdown, inside lower cover.

Previews

'Beckford exhibition on view.' *Bath and Wilts Evening Chronicle*, 13 June 1966, 9. Illus. by Romney's portrait. (Also as 'Beckfordiana', *Bath Weekly Chronicle*, 18 June, 10.)

Bishop, Philippa and Dorothy Hayes. 'He filled his houses with treasure.' *Bath and Wilts Evening Chronicle*, 4 May 1966, 4–5. Article to promote the exhibition, with a drawing of Fonthill Abbey ruins by Miriam Wells.

'Sul'. 'Beckford Exhibition for Festival.' *Bath and Wilts Evening Chronicle*, 8 Feb 1966, 4. (Also in *Bath Weekly Chronicle*, 12 Feb, 6.) Plans for an exhibition at the Holburne Museum.

Reviews

N., J. D. 'Elusive Genius of Beckford.' *Bath and Wilts Evening Chronicle*, 14
   June 1966, 5. (Also in *Bath Weekly Chronicle*, 18 June, 10.)
'Sul'. 'Festival guide to Beckford.' *Bath and Wilts Evening Chronicle*, 10
   June 1966, 4. Catalogue 'vastly more explanatory than the usual [one]'.
Sutton, Denys. 'The Lonely Tower.' *Financial Times*, 21 June 1966.

'WILLIAM BECKFORD EXHIBITION'
SALISBURY, 23 APRIL–15 MAY & BATH, 28 MAY–12 JUNE 1976

William Beckford Exhibition 1976. [Ed. Julian Berry.] Tisbury, Wilts:
Compton Press, 1976. 99 pp. & 22 pp. adverts. 21 cm.
   'Chronology', [4].
   Kenneth Clark, 'Foreword', [5].
   Catalogue of 244 exhibits:
      James Lees-Milne, 'Biographical Introduction', 7–10. (50 exhibits.)
      Jon Millington, 'Man of Letters', 22–27. (39 exhibits.)
      John Wilton-Ely, 'Beckford the Builder', 34–62. (65 exhibits).
      Christopher Thacker, 'England's Kubla Khan', 63–72. (27 exhibits.)
      Clive Wainwright, 'The Collector', 77–79. (52 exhibits.)
      Jon Millington, 'Bibliophile Extraordinary', 91–94. (11 exhibits.)
   [Jon Millington], 'Bibliography', 96–98.

Reviews

Alexander, Boyd. 'Shades of Beckford.' *Apollo* 104 (Aug 1976): 146–147.
   With a review of James Lees-Milne, *William Beckford* (1976).
'Art collector's bizarre hoard.' *Western Daily Press*, 22 April 1976, 4.
'Beckford – A monster but a Genius.' *Salisbury Journal*, 29 April 1976, 15.
   Photo of Kenneth Clark and Humphrey Stone looking at Wyatt's model.
Crombie, Theodore. 'Round the Galleries.' *Apollo* 103 (May 1976): 442.
Daily Telegraph, 8 May 1976.
Feaver, William. 'The sugar cane king.' *Observer Review*, 2 May 1976.
Goring, Edward. 'Beckford on exhibition.' *Bath and West Evening Chron-
   icle*, 22 April 1976, 4. Proposed film on Beckford by Clement Cave.
Goring, Edward. 'Bath stays unmoved by Beckford's spell.' *Bath and West
   Evening Chronicle*, 8 June 1976, 4.
Goring, Edward. 'Taken as red . . .' *Bath and West Evening Chronicle*, 18
   June 1976, 4. The exhibition lost money.
Johnson, Peter. 'Beckford, books and scandal.' *Art & Antiques Weekly* 23
   (24 April 1976): 22–25.
Lees-Milne, James. 'Beckford as Patron and Collector.' *Country Life*, 27
   May 1976, 1402–1403. Exh. to reopen in Bath. *Idem*, 29 July, 302–304.

Letter from Louis Robertson-Fullarton correcting statement that Duke of Hamilton was a descendant of Beckford, and J. L-M's acknowledgement of the error.

'Life and work of an 18th-century eccentric.' *Salisbury Journal*, 15 April 1976, 15. With Buckler's lithograph of Fonthill Abbey from the SW.

Meredith, Frederick D. 'The Beckford exhibition.' *Bath and West Evening Chronicle*, 19 June 1976, 7. Letter praising the setting, also mentioning C. F. Tayler's portrait, allegedly of Beckford.

Phelps, Edward. 'Towering Beckford.' *Bath and West Evening Chronicle*, 1 June 1976, 13.

Roberts, Keith. 'William Bed[ck]ford at Salisbury and Bath.' *Burlington Magazine* 118 (June 1976): 447 & 434, figs. 120, 122–124.

Stevenson, Alan. 'Bath Festival. Exhibitions.' *The Guardian*, 10 June 1976.

'William Beckford.' *Antique Collector*, May 1976.

'BECKFORD'S MOTIFS'
BECKFORD'S TOWER, EASTER–OCTOBER 1979

Millington, Jon. Exhibition handlist of 27 exhibits on Beckford's heraldic motifs, 2 pp. Exhibits: 17 photographs, 4 engravings, Coloured enlargement of Rutter's Achievement of 1823, 4 books from Beckford's library, Cornice and frieze in scagliola reputedly from Fonthill Splendens.

Review

Crocker, Horace. 'It's the Caliph's colourful coat of arms.' *Bath and West Evening Chronicle*, 5 June 1979, 4.

'ILLUSTRATIONS OF *VATHEK*'
BECKFORD'S TOWER, EASTER–OCTOBER 1980

Millington, Jon. Exhibition handlist of fifteen illustrated editions, 2 pp.

'BECKFORD AND HAMILTON SILVER FROM BRODICK CASTLE'
SPINK, LONDON, 4–28 NOV 1980

Baker, Malcolm, Timothy Schroder & E. Laird Clowes. *Beckford and Hamilton Silver from Brodick Castle*. London: Spink, 1980. 91 unnumbered pp. 24 cm.

Introduction by John Hayward, 4 pp.

Catalogue of 98 exhibits:

'Silver made for William Beckford', 1 p.

Beckford silver, 26 pp. (44 exhibits.)

'Hamilton Silver', 1 p.

Hamilton silver, 56 pp. (54 exhibits.)
'Bibliography', 1 p.

Reviews

Banister, Judith. 'Glimpses of Dark Splendour. Beckford and Hamilton Silver in London.' *Country Life*, 13 Nov 1980, 1760–1761.

Field, June. 'Gothic writer's legacy.' *Financial Times*, 25 Oct 1980.

Taylor, John Russell. 'Sparkling display of Renaissance court jewelry.' *The Times*, 28 Oct 1980, 11e–g. With a review of royal jewellery at the V&A and Horace Walpole.

'WILLIAM BECKFORD AS A COLLECTOR OF PAINTINGS'
BECKFORD'S TOWER, EASTER–OCTOBER 1981

Blackmore, Sidney. Exhibition handlist on Beckford's paintings, 2 pp.

'POSTCARDS OF BECKFORD'S TOWER'
BECKFORD'S TOWER, MAY–OCTOBER 1986

Millington, Jon. Exhibition handlist of 17 postcards and a carte-de-visite, 2 pp.

Review

Profit, Jasmine. 'Tower of cards.' *Bath and West Evening Chronicle*, 13 May 1986, 13.

'WILLIAM BECKFORD & PORTUGAL'
PALACE OF QUELUZ, NEAR LISBON, MAY–NOV 1987

Exposição. Exhibition. A Viagem de Uma Paixão. William Beckford & Portugal. An Impassioned Journey. 1787 1794 1798. Palácio de Queluz: Instituto Português do Património Cultural, 1987. In Portuguese and English. 198 pp. Landscape format, 22½ × 29 cm. Only the English titles are given below.

Simonetta Luz Alfonso, 'Introduction', 6–10.

'William Beckford' Chronology, 11.

Maria Laura Bettencourt Pires, 'William Beckford & Portugal', 12–17.

Jorge Borges de Macedo, 'William Beckford & Portugal', 18–29.

Ayres de Carvalho, 'Lisbon during the last quarter of the 18th C. as seen by William Beckford', 30–48.

Manuel Carlos de Brito, 'Music in Portugal in William Beckford's time', 50–61.

Duarte Ivo Cruz, 'The Theatre seen by William Beckford', 62–69.

João Castel-Branco Pereira, 'The Carriages of Lisbon', 70–79.

Luiz Alte da Veiga, 'Notes on Physics in Portugal in the 18th century', 80–83.

Maria Laura Bettencourt Pires, 'William Beckford Bibliography', 84–85.

Maria Laura Bettencourt Pires, 'William Beckford's Musical Compositions', 86.

Catalogue of 462 exhibits:

[I] 'Journeying: comforts and discomforts on the road in Portugal', 87–91. (20 exhibits.)

[II] 'The unfolding of a personality 1760–1836: from Fonthill to Bath – the evolution of a dream', 92–99. (57 exhibits.)

[III] 'The Capital of the Enchanted Kingdom. Lisbon: form, character and urban poetry', 100–119. (69 exhibits.)

[IV] 'The rituals of conviviality: a guest of Lusitanian hospitality', 120–146. (141 exhibits.)

[V] 'The rituals of connivance: fascination, grace and the spirit of Catholicism', 147–156. (56 exhibits.)

[VI] 'A Magical Place: *Sintra*', 157–167. (33 exhibits.)

[VII] 'Inroads through the Enchanted Kingdom: Mafra, Caldas, Alcobaça, Batalha', 168–180. (57 exhibits.)

[VIII] 'At the Court of the 'Great Mogul' . . . a world of its own at the end of an age: *Queluz*', 181–196. (29 exhibits.)

[Maria Laura Bettencourt Pires,] 'General Bibliography', 197–[198].

Reviews and Articles

Hilliard, Elizabeth. *Beckford Tower Trust Newsletter*, Spring 1988, 2–3.

Silva, Raquel Henriques da. 'William Beckford & Portugal. *A Viagem de uma Paixão*. 1787 | 1797 | 1798.' *O Estudo da História* No. 3–4, 2 série (April–June / July–Sept 1987): 48.

'UN CALIFE À LAUSANNE: WILLIAM BECKFORD ET "VATHEK" '
BIBLIOTHÈQUE CANTONALE ET UNIVERSITAIRE, LAUSANNE
10 DEC 1987–30 JAN 1988

Corsini, Silvio. *Un calife à Lausanne: William Beckford et "Vathek"*. Lausanne: Bibliothèque cantonale et universitaire, 1987. ii, 39 pp. 21 cm.

Introduction, 1–2.

Catalogue of 57 exhibits:

I. 'William Beckford 1760–1844: Le calife de Fonthill', 3–15. (20 exhibits.)

II. 'William Beckford sur les bords du Léman (Genève, La tour-de-Peilz, Lausanne)', 16–27. (19 exhibits.)

III. 'Vathek', 28–35. (14 exhibits.)

IV. 'Beckford et Gibbon', 36–39. (4 exhibits.)

'WILLIAM BECKFORD AS A COLLECTOR'
BECKFORD'S TOWER, EASTER–OCTOBER 1989

Bishop, Philippa. Exhibition handlist on Beckford as a collector, 2 pp.

Review

Profit, Jasmine. 'Treasures in the Tower.' *Bath and West Evening Chronicle*, 27 May 1989, 17. Exhibition, and objets de vertu painted by Willes Maddox.

'BECKFORD'S TRAVELS IN SPAIN AND PORTUGAL'
BECKFORD'S TOWER, MAY–OCTOBER 1990

Bishop, Philippa. Exhibition handlist of 18 exhibits on Beckford's travels, 4 pp.

Review

'Landmark with added attractions.' *?Western Daily Press*, May 1990, 5.

'BECKFORD AND HAMILTON SILVER FROM BRODICK CASTLE'
BANQUE BRUXELLES LAMBERT, BRUSSELS, 14 OCT–29 NOV 1992

Argenteries. Le Trésor du National Trust for Scotland / Schatten in Zilver. Topstukken van de National Trust for Scotland. Brussels: National Trust for Scotland, 1992. In French and Flemish. 192 pp. 29½ cm. Separate English trans., 25 pp. Only the French titles are given below.

 Christopher Hartley, 'Le Chateau de Brodick sur l'isle d'Arran', 12–15. English trans., 2–3.

 Jon Millington, 'William Beckford, une biographie sommaire', 16–22. English trans., 4–6.

 John Hayward, 'Beckfordiana, une collection d'argenterie hors du commun', 23–30. English trans., 7–10.

 Timothy Schroder, 'L'argenterie continentale au chateau du Brodick', 31–35. English trans., 11–12.

 Catalogue of 150 exhibits:

  'L'argenterie de William Beckford', 49–51. English trans., 13.

  Beckford silver, 52–95. English trans., 14–17. (50 exhibits.)

  'L'argenterie des Hamilton', 97–99. English trans., 18–19.

  Hamilton silver, 100–187. English trans., 20–25. (100 exhibits.)

 'Bibliography', 188–190.

Reviews

Mallalieu, Huon. 'Glories of the Isle.' *Country Life*, 12 Nov 1992, 40–41.

Millington, Jon. 'Beckford's Silver in Brussels.' *Beckford Tower Trust Newsletter*, Spring 1993, 15–16.

'SOUVENIRS OF FONTHILL ABBEY'
BECKFORD'S TOWER, 2 APRIL–30 OCT 1994

Millington, Jon. *Souvenirs of Fonthill Abbey. An exhibition to commemorate the 150th anniversary of the death of William Beckford.* Bath: Bath Preservation Trust, 1994. 24 pp. 24 cm.

'Introduction', 2.
'Chronology', 3.
'William Beckford', 4–6.
'Fonthill Abbey in 1822 and 1823', 7–8.
Catalogue of 58 exhibits:
   'Entrance Tickets', 9. (3 exhibits.)
   'Sale Catalogues', 10. (3 exhibits.)
   'Guide Books', 11–13. (9 exhibits.)
   'Ceramics', 14–15. (6 exhibits.)
   'Blue and White Plates', 16–18. (11 exhibits.)
   'Drawings and Watercolours', 19. (4 exhibits.)
   'Lithographs', 20–22. (12 exhibits.)
   'Magazines', 22. (5 exhibits.)
   'Books', 23. (4 exhibits.)
   'Replicas of Fonthill Abbey', 24. (1 exhibit.)
'Further Reading', lower cover.

Reviews

Bishop, Philippa. *Beckford Tower Trust Newsletter*, Spring 1994, 5.
Glancey, Jonathan. 'Fonthill: a house that haunts.' *The Independent II*, 6 April 1994, 20.
Hansford, Christopher. *Weekend [Bath] Chronicle*, 2 April 1994, II.
Hayward, Stephen. 'Tower view of history.' *Western Daily Press*, 24 March 1994, 24.
Yarham, Vicky. *Bath City Life*, Summer 1994, 21.

Articles

Country Life, 28 April 1994, 56. Announcement of exhibition.
Millington, Jon. "Research for the 'Souvenirs of Fonthill Abbey' Exhibition." *Beckford Tower Trust Newsletter*, Spring 1994, 9–10.

'BECKFORD'S HERALDRY'
BECKFORD'S TOWER, EASTER–OCTOBER 1995

Bishop, Philippa. Exhibition handlist.

'SECOND COUSINS. WILLIAM BECKFORD & SIR WILLIAM HAMILTON'
BECKFORD'S TOWER, JULY–OCTOBER 1996

Blackmore, Sidney. Exhibition handlist, 4 pp.

'BUILDER OF TOWERS: WILLIAM BECKFORD & LANSDOWN TOWER'
BUILDING OF BATH MUSEUM, 3 SEPTEMBER–30 NOVEMBER 1997
& CHRISTIE'S, LONDON, 15 JAN–3 FEB 1998

Blackmore, Sidney. Exhibition handlist of 25 exhibits, 6pp. Essays on 'Lansdown Tower' and 'Lansdown Tower Interiors'. 'Handlist of Loan Items': 2 family portraits, 5 architectural drawings, 4 of Beckford's precious objects, 3 silver pieces, oak coffer, porcelain, 1844 inventory of Beckford's library, 5 ceramics, 2 blue & white plates, Higham's pencil design for Fonthill Sale entrance ticket.

Reviews

'Beckford's life commemorated.' *Bath Chronicle*, 4 Sept 1997, 4. With photo of William Oxer, designer of the exhibition.
'Builder of Towers.' *Bath & West Country Life*, Nov & Dec 1997, 6.
Goodwin, Stephen. 'Bath rooms.' *Independent Saturday Magazine*, 10 Jan 1998, 31.
Guilding, Ruth. 'Wayward child of fortune.' *Spectator*, 31 Jan 1998, 46.
McKie, David. 'Tower Games.' *The Guardian – Arts*, 23 Jan 1998, 14–15.
'News and Comment.' *Book Collector* 47 no. 2 (Summer 1998): 238. James Lees-Milne's bequests to 'Beckford's folly, Lansdown Tower' also noted.
Powell, Kenneth. 'The gothic chief of patapoufs.' *Sunday Telegraph Review*, 11 Jan 1998, 10.
Taylor, John Russell. 'Around the Galleries.' *The Times*, 20 Jan 1998, 35g.
'William Beckford and Lansdown Tower.' *Christie's International Magazine*, Jan/Feb 1998, 17.
Windsor, John. 'Making history: in the best possible taste.' *The Independent – Eye*, 28 Jan 1998, 4–5.
Woodward, Christopher. 'Climb the Tower of Genius.' *Country Life*, 15 Jan 1998, 51. Henry Venn Lansdown's sepia drawing of *c*.1855 illus.

'WILLIAM BECKFORD, 1760–1844: AN EYE FOR THE MAGNIFICENT'
NEW YORK, 18 OCT 2001–6 JAN 2002. LONDON, 6 FEB–14 APRIL

Ostergard, Derek E. ed. *William Beckford, 1760–1844: An Eye for the Magnificent*. New Haven & London: Yale University Press for the Bard Graduate Center, 2001. 448 pp. 31¼ cm.

Jon Millington, 'Bibliography', 438–448.
Index of Chapters 1–16 was available on the Internet.

Dejardin, Ian. *William Beckford 1760–1844: An Eye for the Magnificent. A Companion to the Exhibition* . . . London: Dulwich Picture Gallery, 2002. 30 pp. in concertina form. 12 illus., incl. 3 double-page. 17 × 188 cm. Side 1: 'Biography', 'Beckford and Heraldry, a decorative obsession', 'William Beckford, in quotes'. Side 2: 'Two Encounters with Mr. Beckford', 'Credits'.

Previews

Anglo-Portuguese News, 18 Oct 2001 & 31 Jan 2002.
'Come along to a private view.' *Good Housekeeping*, March 2002.
Dixon, Anne Campbell. 'The days of big spenders.' *[Daily] Telegraph Travel*, 19 Jan 2002, 19.
'Event of the Month.' *Period Living & Traditional Homes*, Feb 2002, 18.
Flanders, Judith. 'Tall towers and taller tales.' *Sunday Telegraph Review*, 27 Jan 2002, 6.
Graham-Dixon, Andrew. 'In the picture. William Beckford (1781) by George Romney.' *Sunday Telegraph Magazine*, 3 Feb 2002, 82.
Hewat-Jaboor, Philip. 'Beckford Splendens.' *Christie's Magazine*, Sept/Oct 2001, 112–117. Excellent account, beautifully illus.
Kaufman, Jason Edward. 'Boys, buildings and baubles.' *The Art Newspaper* No. 118 (Oct 2001): 34.
'Round and About: February 2002.' *History Today* 52 (Feb 2002): 6.
Shawe-Taylor, Desmond. 'A favourite painting.' *The National Trust Magazine* No. 95, Spring 2002, 19.
Shilling, Jane. 'Beckford the Magnificent.' *The Times, Weekending*, 2 Feb 2002, 4.
Weldon, Susie, ed. 'The legacy of treasures.' *Western Daily Press*, 10 Jan 2002, 28–29.
Woodward, Christopher. 'Exhibition diary.' *World of Interiors*, Feb 2002, 108–109.

Reviews

'All aboard the Orient excess . . .' *Mail on Sunday*, 3 March 2002.
Bentkowska-Kafel, Anna. *The Art Book* (Blackwell) 9 no. 4, (Sept 2002): 16–19. Review of the catalogue and Ian Dejardin's *William Beckford* (see above).
Birbeck, Robert. 'Gothic survival.' *Building Design*, 22 Feb 2002, 17.
Blackmore, Sidney. *Bath Preservation Trust Newsletter*, April 2002, 5. Review of the exhibition and catalogue.

Bruce, Donald. 'William Beckford as Writer and Collector.' *Contemporary Review* 280 (April 2002): 227–233.

Charbonnier, Jean-Michel. 'La spirale de Beckford.' *Beaux-Arts* 215 (April 2002): 52. Photo of Beckford's Tower, 53.

Clarke, Stephen. *Eighteenth-Century Studies* 36 no. 1 (Fall 2002): 93–97.

Crook, J. Mordaunt. 'Oh my God, so many things!' *Times Literary Supplement*, 15 March 2002, 18–19.

Darwent, Charles. 'Renaissance man.' *The Lady*, 12 Feb 2002, 38–39.

Farquhar, Eugene. *The Chap* Issue 13 (Spring 2002): 16–19.

Feay, Suzi. 'The Spoils of Fonthill.' *Independent on Sunday*, 3 Feb 2002, *Life*, 6.

'Gothic Survival.' *Building Design*, 22 February 2002, 17.

Hales, Linda. 'Scandalous Obsession with Beauty. William Beckford Was Rich, Notorious – A Prodigious Collector.' *Washington Post*, 27 Oct 2001, C2.

Jervis, Simon. 'New York and London. William Beckford.' *Burlington Magazine* 144 (March 2002): 186–187.

Leates, Louise. 'An eye for the magnificent.' NADFAS *Review*, Spring / Summer 2002, 24–27. National Association of Decorative & Fine Arts Societies.

Lethbridge, Lucy. *The Tablet*, 23 Feb 2002.

'News and Comment.' *Book Collector* 52 no. 1 (Spring 2003): 73–74. Mainly a review of the catalogue.

Nicholson, Kathleen. *Albion* (Appalachian State University) 35 part 2 (Summer 2003): 318–319. A review of the catalogue.

'Objects of a strange desire.' *Daily Telegraph*, 7 Feb 2002.

Perl, Jed. 'Making Taste.' *The New Republic*, 4 Feb 2002, 25–33.

Rankin, Carol. *Anglo-Portuguese News*, 21 March 2002.

Richardson, Margaret. 'Oh My God, So Many Things.' *Architectural Review* 211 (May 2002): 96–97. ¼ page review of the catalogue.

Russell, Francis. *Apollo* 155 (May 2002): 55–56.

Sawyer, Jean. *Journal of the Society of Architectural Historians* 61 no. 2 (June 2002): 214–215.

'The Sensualist.' *Fable*, Feb 2002.

Singmaster, Deborah. 'Shop till you drop.' *The Architects' Journal*, 21 Feb 2002, 43.

Thicknesse, Robert. 'The arch goth.' *The Times* 2, 6 Feb 2002, 25.

Tuohy, Thomas. 'Beckford at Dulwich.' *The British Art Journal* 3 no. 2 (Spring 2002): 81–82. With a review of Christopher Thacker, *Building Towers, Forming Gardens* (2002).

Walsh, John. 'Outrageous fortune.' *The Independent Weekend Review*, 23 February 2002, 9.

The Week, 23 February 2002, 23.

Wilson, Arnold. 'The William Beckford Exhibition at Dulwich.' *Beckford Journal* 8 (2002): 36–40.

Wilton-Ely, John. *Beckford Journal* 8 (2002): 25–35. Review of the catalogue.

Winkfield, Trevor. 'Money Well Spent.' *Modern Painters* 15 (Spring 2002): 68–71.

Wise, Sarah. 'The man who had too much.' *Guardian Saturday Review*, 9 Feb 2002, 5.

Retrospect

Hewat-Jaboor, Philip. 'Creating a Beckford Exhibition.' *Beckford Journal* 8 (2002): 15–24. Extensive research needed to achieve exhibition's purpose.

PART TWO
LITERATURE

10. Beckford's Works: First Editions

*Most of these entries also appear, together with later editions
and related articles, in the succeeding sections*

PROSE

Biographical Memoirs of Extraordinary Painters. London: J. Robson, New-
Bond-Street, 1780. iv, 158 pp. 18½ cm. The chapters are 'Aldrovandus
Magnus', 'Andrew Guelph, and Og of Basan, Disciples of Aldrovandus
Magnus', 'Sucrewasser of Vienna', 'Blunderbussiana' and 'Watersouchy'.
Chapman, *Bibliography* (1930), 1(i).

*Dreams, Waking Thoughts and Incidents; in a Series of Letters, from Various
Parts of Europe*. London: J. Johnson, St. Paul's Church Yard, 1783. xv, 334
pp. 30 cm. Large paper, 31½ cm. Suppressed on eve of publication, except
for six copies. Beckford later publ. it in revised form as vol. 1 of *Italy* . . .
(1834). Chapman, *Bibliography* (1930), 2(i).

*An Arabian Tale, from an Unpublished Manuscript: with Notes Critical and
Explanatory. [Vathek]*. London: J. Johnson, St. Paul's Church-yard, 1786.
viii, 334 pp. 20½ cm. Also a limited ed. of 50 copies on large paper. Chapman, *Bibliography* (1930), 3A(i).

*Modern Novel Writing, or the Elegant Enthusiast; and Interesting Emotions
of Arabella Bloomville. A Rhapsodical Romance; interspersed with Poetry*.
'By the Right Hon. Lady Harriet Marlow.' 2 vols. London: G. G. & J.
Robinson, 1796 [?1795]. viii, 243 pp. & vi, 232 pp. 18½ cm. Chapman,
Bibliography (1930), 4(i) & 4(i, a).

*Azemia: A Descriptive and Sentimental Novel. Interspersed with Pieces of
Poetry*. 'By Jacquetta Agneta Mariana Jenks.' 2 vols. London: Sampson Low,
1797. xii, 254 pp. & iv, 253 pp. 19½ cm. Chapman, *Bibliography* (1930), 5(i).

Italy; with Sketches of Spain and Portugal. 2 vols. London: Richard Bentley,
1834. xvi, 371 pp. & xv, 381 pp. 22½ cm. Chapman, *Bibliography*
(1930), 8(i).

Recollections of an Excursion to the Monasteries of Alcobaça and Batalha.
London: Richard Bentley, 1835. xi, 228 pp. Frontis., portrait after
Reynolds. 23½ cm. Chapman, *Bibliography* (1930), 9(i).

POETRY

'Mr. Beckford, Fonthill, at the Grand Chartreuse.' *The Western County
Magazine* 3 (Dec 1789): 381–382. Revised version of the 'Ode' from

Dreams (1783), 'To orisons, the midnight bell', with the last four lines of
the original 50-line poem being replaced by two new lines here, and other
minor changes. Noted in Jon Millington, "Beckford's 'Ode' ", *Beckford
Tower Trust Newsletter*, Spring 1987, 5.

Four untitled stanzas. *Literary Gazette* 6 (9 Nov 1822): 714. Sixteen lines.
Later known as 'A Prayer'. Chapman, *Bibliography* (1930), pp. 105–106.

'Original Poetical Varieties.' *Literary Gazette* 7 (8 March 1823): 155–156.
Six poems by *Viator*. *Idem* (5 April): 221–222, five further 'Epitaphs'.
These eleven, with twelve others, were publ. as *Epitaphs, some of which
have appeared in the Literary Gazette of March and April, 1823*. N. p.: Privately printed, [1825]. 49 pp. 20¼ cm. Chapman, *Bibliography* (1930), 7(i).

'The Last Day.' In John Britton, *Fonthill Abbey* (1823), 60. Ten lines. Also
known as 'Dies Iræ'. Chapman, *Bibliography* (1930), p. 106. 'A Prayer'
from the *Literary Gazette* also appeared on page 60 of Britton.

POSTHUMOUS WORKS

[*The Episodes of Vathek*]. 'Histoire de la Princesse Zulkaïs et du Prince
Kalilah.' & 'Histoire du Prince Alasi et de la Princesse Firouzkah.' *The
English Review* 4 (Dec 1909): 163–184 & 6 (Aug, Sept 1910): 137–147,
309–322. In French.

The Episodes of Vathek. Trans. Sir Frank Marzials. London: Stephen Swift,
1912. Frontis., xxxi, 207 pp. (in English) & 127 pp. (in French). 23½ cm.
Intro. Lewis Melville. Includes the third Episode, 'The Story of Prince
Barkiarokh'. Chapman, *Bibliography* (1930), 10(i).

The Vision and *Liber Veritatis*. Ed. Guy Chapman. London: Constable,
1930. xxix, 166 pp. 4 pl. 23 cm. *The Vision* (*c.*1777), 3–88. *Liber Veritatis* (1830s): 'Female Nobility', 93–110; 'Record of Some of the Less Brilliant Alliances . . .', 111–118; 'Further Records', 119–138. Limited to 750
copies. Chapman, *Bibliography* (1930), 11.

The Journal of William Beckford in Portugal and Spain 1787–1788. Ed.
Boyd Alexander. London: Hart-Davis, 1954. 340 pp. 10 pl. 22 cm. Beckford's revision of this *Journal* was publ. as vol. 2 of *Italy . . .* (1834).

Beckford's 1794 Journal. Ed. Boyd Alexander. In Howard B. Gotlieb,
William Beckford of Fonthill (1960), 90–100. New Haven: Yale University Library, 1960. 22 cm. Exhibition catalogue. A revised version of the
1794 Journal became *Recollections of an Excursion to the Monasteries of
Alcobaça and Batalha* (1835).

'Fragments of a Romance.' *Beckford Tower Trust Newsletter*, Spring 1992,
2–7. Bodleian Library, MS. Beckford c.48, transcribed by Didier Girard.

Suite de contes arabes. Trans. Didier Girard. Paris: José Corti, 1992. 339 pp.
16 cm. From Bodleian Library, MSS. Beckford c.47, 48 & d.12, 23, 26.
Six illus. by Hélène Varchavsky. Collection romantique, No. 34.

Histoire du Prince Ahmed. Ed. Didier Girard. Paris: José Corti, 1993. 213 pp. 16 cm. From Bodleian Library, MS. Beckford d.24 (1780). Five illus. by Kevin Pearsh. Collection romantique, No. 37. Chapman, *Bibliography* (1930), p. 100.

REVIEW. Braudeau, Michel. 'Quelques entrées dans le décor.' *Le Monde*, 12 March 1993, 24. With a review of Didier Girard, *William Beckford: Terroriste au Palais de la Raison* (1993).

'*The State of Innosense.*' *Beckford Journal* 1 (1995): 50–51. Bodleian Library, MS. Beckford e.3 (*c.*1774), transcribed by Didier Girard.

The Transport of Pleasure. Ed. Dick Claésson. Gothenburg: Göteborgs universitet, 1996. 75 pp. 21 cm. From Bodleian Library, MS. Beckford d.10 (*c.*1777–1778). Entitled 'Fonthill Foreshadowed' by Boyd Alexander.

'*Fragments of an English Tour.*' *Beckford Journal* 5 (1999): 14–32. Bodleian Library, MS. Beckford d.3 (1779), transcribed by Dick Claésson.

L'esplendente et autres contes inédits. Ed. Didier Girard. Paris: José Corti, 2003. 265 pp. 21¼ cm. All from Bodleian Library, MS. Beckford: (1) 'Le transport de plaisir' (French trans.), d.10; (2) 'Les royaumes du jour éternel', c.48; (3) 'Le génie du lieu', c.47; (4) 'Histoire de Kebal, roi de Damas', d.26 & Chapman, *Bibliography* (1930), p. 101; (5) 'Les montagnes de la lune', c.48; (6) 'Histoire de Mazin', d.25 & Chapman, p. 100; (7) 'L'esplendente', d.11 (1780) & Chapman, pp. 95–96. Domaine romantique.

REVIEW. Delon, Michel. 'Vathek au complet.' *La Quinzaine littéraire*, No. 852, 16 April 2003. With a review of Girard, ed., *Vathek et ses épisodes*.

" 'A Day at Tojal' including 'The Idyllium of Hylas'." *Bodleian Library Record* 18 no. 1 (April 2003): 39–42. Bodleian Library, MS. Beckford d.9 fols. 44–46 (*c.*1778, revised 1835), transcribed by Jerry Nolan and preceded by his notes, 31–38. Chapman, *Bibliography* (1930), p. 99.

LETTERS

Books & Pamphlets

Beckford, William. *A Letter from William Beckford to Sir William Hamilton. Containing a description of his household.* New Haven: Bibliographical Press, 1952. 8 pp. Three-page letter (owned by James T. Babb) from Evian, 7 Sept 1792.

Beckford, William. *Life at Fonthill 1807–1822. With Interludes in Paris and London.* Trans. from the Italian & ed. Boyd Alexander. London: Hart-Davis, 1957. 352 pp. 10 pl. 22 cm. Letters, mostly to Franchi.

Beckford, William. *Christmas at Fonthill 1781.* Inro. Timothy d'Arch Smith. London: Privately printed, 1962. 8 pp. Limited to 150 copies for his friends. Being a note Beckford appended in 1838 to a letter to Louisa written in spring 1782 and reprinted in Oliver's *Life of William Beckford* (1932), 89–91. Beckford wrote the original slightly different draft on the fly leaves of Waagen's *Works of Art and Artists in England* (1838). This draft was reprinted in Chapman's *Beckford* (1937), 104–106.

Beckford, William. *The Consummate Collector: William Beckford's Letters to His Bookseller.* Ed. Robert J. Gemmett. Wilby, Norfolk: Michael Russell, 2000. 336 pp. Frontis. & 14 illus. 24 cm. Over 350 letters to George Clarke between 1830 and 1834. Limited to 450 copies.

Morrison, Alfred. *The Collection of Autograph Letters and Historical Documents formed by Alfred Morrison.* 2nd Series, vol. 1 (A–B). Compiled by A. W. Thibaudeau. [London]: Privately printed, 1893. 49 letters, all but two to Henley, 'A Fragment [of a letter to Alexander Cozens?]' & letter from Lettice to Henley, 182–200. Also 1st Series, vol. A–C, 1883, twelve Alderman Beckford letters 61–62, five William Beckford letters, 62–63. See also 'The Hamilton & Nelson Papers', 2 vols., 1893–1894. Vol. 1, 1765–1797, letters 153, 157, 165, 169, 170, 183, 212, 213, 215, 216, 218, 219, 227, 228. Vol. 2, 1798–1815, letters 78, 193, 194.

Norton, Rictor. 'Dearest Impresario.' In *My Dear Boy: Gay Love Letters through the Centuries,* 109–113. San Francisco: Leyland, 1998. A selection of Beckford's letters.

Articles

'Beckford's letter from Geneva to Lord Thurlow, 22 May 1778.' *Beckford Journal* 7 (2001): 20–29. Preceded by Dick Claésson, "Introduction to 'Beckford's letter . . .'.", 18–19.

'A Letter to Emma Hamilton from Beckford in 1805.' *Beckford Journal* 1 (1995): 17–22. Asking her to arrange a meeting with Lord Nelson.

[Mayer, Mrs Gertrude Townshend.] 'The Sultan of Lansdown Tower.' *Temple Bar* 120 (June 1900): 182–212, including brief extracts from Beckford's letters to George Clarke from 1830 to 1834, 194–211. Noted in *Wiltshire Archæological and Natural History Magazine* 31 (Dec 1900): 266, 'a gossiping article'.

Melville, Lewis. [Lewis S. Benjamin, pseud.] 'William Beckford's Adventure in Diplomacy. An Unpublished Correspondence.' *Nineteenth Century* 65 (May 1909): 783–799. Letters mostly to and from Nicholas Williams, Beckford's agent in Paris. Noted in *Wiltshire Archæological and Natural History Magazine* 36 (Dec 1909): 349.

ANNOTATIONS

B., G. *Notes and Queries* 5th Series 2 (7 Nov 1874): 364 & 5th Series 6 (22 July 1876): 65. Transcripts of Beckford's notes in his copy of Robert

Southey's *A Vision of Judgement* (1821) & Rob Mignan's *Travels in Chaldea* (1829).

'Mr. Beckford's Critiques and Commentaries.' *County Literary Chronicle and Weekly Review*, 20 Sept 1823, 602. Beckford's notes in B. C. Walpole's *Recollections of the Life of Rt. Hon. Charles James Fox* (1806) and Sir Walter Scott's *Minstrelsy of the Scottish Border* (1802–1803). Notes in Walpole's *Recollections* also in *Courier* (Daily evening paper), 11 Sept 1823, 2.

Besterman, Theodore, ed. 'William Beckford's notes on a life of Voltaire.' *Studies on Voltaire and the Eighteenth Century* 163 (1976): 53–55. Transcription of notes in Frank Hall Standish's *The Life of Voltaire* (1821).

Colbert, Benjamin. *Shelley's Eye. Travel Writing and Aesthetic Vision.* Aldershot, Hants: Ashgate, 2005. Beckford's comments in his copy of Mary Shelley's *History of a Six Weeks' Tour through . . . France . . .* (1817), 83, 87.

Elfenbein, Andrew. *Byron and the Victorians.* Cambridge: Cambridge University Press, 1995. Beckford's marginalia in his copy of Moore's *Life of Byron*, 224, 243.

Janzen, Gerlof. 'Beckford's Manuscript Notes in Two Travel Books from his Own Library.' *Beckford Journal* 2 (1996): 9–16. William Dorset Fellowes, *Visit to the Monastery of La Trappe* (1818) and Louis Simond, *Journal of a Tour and Residence in Great Britain . . .* (1817).

Memoirs of Mary Queen of Scots by Elizabeth Benger (Longman, 1823) with five pages of notes by Beckford. *Wiltshire Notes and Queries* 6 (Dec 1909): 380. 'I wish, dear Miss Benger, that your style was a *little* less ornate, and your information a *little* less inaccurate'.

Millington, Jon. 'Beckford's Marginalia.' *Beckford Journal* 5 (1999): 48–52. Beckford's notes in the Hon. Richard Boyle Bernard's *A Tour through some parts of France, Switzerland . . .* (1815).

Nolan, Jerry. 'The Myriad-Minded Book Collector.' *Beckford Journal* 11 (2005): 2–13. A study of Beckford's reading-notes.

'Notes on Buchanan's Memoirs, by the late Mr. Beckford.' *Mirror of Literature* n.s. 5 (1 June 1844): 341–343. David Irving's *Memoirs of George Buchanan* (1817).

Sherbo, Arthur. 'From the *Gentleman's Magazine* . . . VII. William Beckford's Copy of William Beloe's *Sexagenarian* in the Cambridge University Library.' *Studies in Bibliography* 35 (1982): 285–305 at 303–305.

MUSIC

Ouverture du Ballet de Phaeton. 'Composée par Monsieur de Beckfort, Amateur pour L'Académie Royale de Musique. Gravée par Mle Crahay'. Paris: Privately printed, *c.*1781. 18 pp. Chapman, *Bibliography* (1930), pp. 109–110.

ATTRIBUTED WORKS

Popular Tales of the Germans. 2 vols. London: J. Murray, 1791. xi, 264 pp. & iv, 284 pp. 18½ cm. Trans. from Johann Carl August Musæus, *Volksmährchen der Deutschen,* 5 vols., (1782). Formerly attributed to Beckford but now known to be by Dr Thomas Beddoes. See '14. Beckford's Other Works. Attributed Works' for details. Chapman, *Bibliography* (1930), Attrib. 1.

The Story of Al Raoui, A Tale from the Arabic. London: C. Geisweiler, Pall Mall, 1799. vii, 59 pp. 19½ cm. English text, 9–24. German text, 33–44. Three poems: 'Verses', 47; 'Conjugal Love', 48–52; 'Written, in the close of Winter, to A Friend, just leaving a favourite retirement, previous to settling abroad', 53–59. Chapman, *Bibliography* (1930), 6(i).

'William Beckford, Esq. Fonthill Abbey, Wilts.' In *Repertorium Bibliographicum; or, Some Account of the most Celebrated British Libraries,* 203–230. London: William Clarke, 1819. Limited to 350 copies, 25½ cm. Also large paper limited to 50 copies, 28 cm. Libraries at the Abbey followed by 25-page catalogue. Engraving, 'Francis 1', facing 214. 146 entries including 8 incunabulae, 19 MSS. & 10 drawings or prints. Chapman, *Bibliography* (1930), Attrib. 2.

ADVERT. *Gentleman's Magazine* 84 pt. 1 (June 1814): 560, 'Speedily will be published'.

REVIEW. *Idem* 89 pt. 1 (May 1819): 434–435.

A Dialogue in the Shades, Between William Caxton, Fodius, a Bibliomaniac, and William Wynken, Clerk . . . and *Rare Doings at Roxburghe-Hall.* [1819.] Two burlesques, each of eight unnumbered pages, sometimes bound with *Repertorium Bibliographicum.* Engraving depicting Beckford with Caxton and 'William Wynken' on the first page. Chapman, *Bibliography* (1930), Attrib. 3. 2nd ed., with *The Diary of Roger Payne* appended. London: William Clarke, 1821. 36 pp. Chapman, *Bibliography* (1930), Attrib. 3(ii). Also small paper, Attrib. 3(ii, a).

'Lines Written under Denon's Lithographic Print of Samuel Rogers, Esq. By William Beckford, Esq. Late of Fonthill.' *Fraser's Magazine* 7 (March 1833): 368. A caustic six-line epigram on Rogers. According to 'Our Weekly gossip on Literature and Art', *Athenæum,* 2, 9 March 1833, 138, 154, it was a paraphrase of the original by Byron in the *Courier* fifteen years previously.

Histoire d'Aladdin roi de l'Yemen. Clichy, Paris: Jasmin, 1998. 109 pp. 19 cm. Illus. by Natacha de Molènes. Contes d'Orient et d'Occident No. 1. Chapman, *Bibliography* (1930), p. 100.

11. *Vathek* and *The Episodes*: Editions

Seven versions of Vathek *were published in Beckford's lifetime. There were four in English, 1786, 1816, 1816 2nd issue & 1823, and three in French, Lausanne 1787 [1786], Paris 1787 & Londres 1815. From 1815 the 11,000 steps in the thirteenth paragraph were reduced to 1500.*

ENGLISH

An Arabian Tale, from an Unpublished Manuscript: with Notes Critical and Explanatory. [*Vathek*]. With notes by Samuel Henley. London: J. Johnson, St. Paul's Church-yard, 1786. viii, 334 pp. 20 cm. Also a limited ed. of 50 copies on large paper. Chapman, *Bibliography* (1930), 3A(i).

An Arabian Tale, from An Unpublished Manuscript: with Notes Critical and Explanatory. A New Edition. London: Printed for W. Clarke, New Bond Street, 1809. viii, 334 pp. 20 cm. A reissue of the 1786 ed. with a cancel title page. Chapman, *Bibliography* (1930), 3A(ii).

Vathek. Third Edition. London: Printed for W. Clarke, New Bond Street, 1816. iv, 284 pp. 19½ cm. Frontis. About half of Henley's Notes. Chapman, *Bibliography* (1930), 3A(iii).

Vathek. Third Edition. London: Printed for W. Clarke, New Bond Street, 1816. iv, 284 pp. 19½ cm. Frontis. Altered passage on p. 220 (names of princes omitted). About half of Henley's Notes. Chapman, *Bibliography* (1930), 3A(iii,a). Also occurs with 'Sold also by Taylor & Hessey, Fleet Street.' Chapman, *Bibliography* (1930), 3A(iii, b).

Vathek. From the Third London Edition, Revised and Corrected. Philadelphia: M. Carey, 1816. 234 pp. 14¼ cm. The first American edition. Chapman, *Bibliography* (1930), 3C, from 3A(iii, a).

Vathek. Fourth Edition. London: Printed for W. Clarke, New Bond Street, 1823. iv, 284 pp. 20 cm. Frontis. About half of Henley's Notes. Chapman, *Bibliography* (1930), 3A(iv).

Vathek. Fifth edition. London: George Clarke, Mount Street, Berkeley Square, 1832. ii, 284 pp. 20 cm. Identical to the fourth edition except for the title page & both lines of verse on p. 249 now in smaller type. Probably the 1823 edition with a cancel title page. About half of Henley's Notes. Not in Chapman's *Bibliography*.

Vathek; An Arabian Tale. London: Richard Bentley, etc., 1834. iv, 128 + 22 pp. 17½ cm. Frontis. 1823 version. Henley's Notes with Beckford's additions. With Horace Walpole, *The Castle of Otranto* and *The Bravo of*

Venice trans. by M. G. Lewis. Bentley's Standard Novels, No. 41. Chapman, *Bibliography* (1930), 3A(v).

Vathek. Philadelphia: Carey, Lee & Blanchard, 1834. 206 pp. 17½ cm. 2nd American edition.

Vathek. Baltimore: Joseph Robinson, 1834. 233 pp. Trans. from the French.

Vathek: An Arabian Tale. Paris: Baudry's European Library, 1834. 127 pp. 22 cm. 1823 version. Henley's Notes with Beckford's additions. Appended to *Italy, with Sketches of Spain and Portugal*. Collection of Ancient and Modern British Novels and Romances, vol. 59. Chapman, *Bibliography* (1930), 3A(vi), but listed under *Italy*, 8(ii).

Vathek; An Arabian Tale. London: Richard Bentley, etc., 1836. iv, 150 pp. 17½ cm. Frontis. 1823 version. Henley's Notes with Beckford's additions. With Horace Walpole, *The Castle of Otranto* and *The Bravo of Venice* trans. by M. G. Lewis. Reprint of the 1834 edition with corrected pagination. Bentley's Standard Novels, No. 41. Chapman, *Bibliography* (1930), 3A(v, a).

Vathek: An Oriental Romance. New York: Morris, Willis & Fuller, 1845. 50 pp. in two columns. 26½ cm. Brief biography of Beckford by Cyrus Redding. The Mirror Library.

Vathek; An Arabian Tale. London: Richard Bentley, etc., 1849. iv, 150 pp. 17½ cm. Frontis. 1823 version. Henley's Notes with Beckford's additions. With Horace Walpole, *The Castle of Otranto* and *The Bravo of Venice*, trans. M. G. Lewis. Reprint of the 1836 edition. Bentley's Standard Novels, No. 41.

Vathek; An Arabian Tale. Memoir by William North. London: George Slater, 1849. xv, vi, pp. & pp. [7]–160. 14 cm. 1786 version. Only 26 of Henley's Notes. Slater's Shilling Series. Reprinted, 1850.

Vathek; An Arabian Tale. Memoir by William North. New York, 1849.

Vathek; An Arabian Tale. Memoir by William North. London: H. G. Bohn, 1852. xvi pp. & pp. [7]–160. 14 cm. 1786 version. Only 26 of Henley's Notes. Reprint of Slater (1849). With *The Amber Witch*, ed. W. Meinhold.

Vathek; An Arabian Tale. Memoir by William North. Philadelphia: Henry Carey Baird, 1854. 180 pp. 19 cm. Some notes. Sometimes publ. with *The Amber Witch*, ed. W. Meinhold.

Vathek; An Arabian Tale. London: Ward & Lock, 1856. 150 pp. ?1823 version.

Vathek. In *The Arabian Nights' Entertainments*, 541–580. London: Charles Griffin, 1866.

Vathek; An Arabian Tale. Memoir by R. S. London: William Tegg, 1868. xxii, 184 pp. 16½ cm. Frontis., title page vignette & ten illus. 1823 version. Henley's Notes with Beckford's additions, from Bentley (1834), but missing those on the last leaf (pp. *117–*118). The first illus. edition.

Vathek: An Arabian Tale. Memoir by William North. New York: James Miller,

647 Broadway, 1868. 207 pp. 18 cm. 1786 version. Some footnotes. Also *Idem*, 779 Broadway, undated. Reprinted, [1872]. 207 pp. 19 cm.

The History of the Caliph Vathek. 'Printed verbatim from the First Edition, with the Original Prefaces and Notes by Henley.' London: Sampson, Low etc., 1868. x, 189 pp. 15½ cm. 2nd ed., 1869. 3rd ed., 1873. 4th ed., 1875. 5th ed., 1878. 6th ed., 1881. 6th [7th] ed., 1885. 7th [8th] ed., 1888. 9th ed., 1892. 10th ed., 1893. Unsigned 'Preface' stating that Beckford married twice, p. vi.

The History of the Caliph Vathek. 'Printed verbatim from the First Edition, with the Original Preface and Notes by Henley.' 2nd ed. New York: Scribner, Welford & Co., 1869. 189 pp. 15 cm.

Vathek. In *A Library of Famous Fiction Embracing the Nine Standard Masterpieces of Imaginative Literature*, 847–897 in two columns. New York: J. B. Ford, 1873. Intro. to *Vathek* by Harriet Beecher Stowe, 843–844. Author's preface, 845. Two illus.: 'The Indian, the Caliph, the Court, and the People' by Harley, 856, & 'The Hall of Eblis' by J[ohn] Karst, 894. 24½ cm. 1786 version.

Vathek: An Arabian Tale. Nashville, Tennessee: A. Setliff, 1880. 57 pp.

The History of the Caliph Vathek. London: Nimmo & Bain, 1883. xxi pp. & pp. [17]–218. Portrait frontis. of Beckford & two etchings for *Vathek* by A. H. Tourrier. 1786 version. Henley's Notes. With Samuel Johnson, *Rasselas*. Limited to 1000 copies, 20 cm. Also large octavo edition on laid paper limited to 150 numbered copies, 24 cm.

The History of the Caliph Vathek. Memoir by William North (16 pp). New York: Thomas R. Knox, [1886]. Pp. 19–207. With Samuel Johnson, *Rasselas*.

The History of the Caliph Vathek. Intro. Henry Morley. Cassell's National Library, No. 97 [?96]. New York: Cassell, 1886. 192 pp. 14 cm.

The History of the Caliph Vathek. Intro. Henry Morley. Cassell's National Library, No. 96. London: Cassell, 1887. 192 pp. 15½ cm. 1786 version. No Notes. Issued in pink cloth (stapled) and paperback (sewn), Perhaps the first paperback edition. Reissued 1892 & 1893 in blue cloth and again in 1901–1903.

The History of the Caliph Vathek. Intro. Henry Morley. New York: F. M. Lupton, n.d. 192 pp. 15 cm.

Vathek. An Arabian Tale. Memoir by William North. New York: John B. Alden, 1887. 136 pp. 19 cm. 1786 version. Only 26 of Henley's Notes as in Slater (1849), but as footnotes here. Elzevir Library 291.

Vathek. An Arabian Tale. Memoir by William North. New York: Hurst, n.d. 136 pp. 19 cm. Some notes. Arlington Edition.

The History of the Caliph Vathek. 'Printed verbatim from the First Edition, with the Original Preface and Notes by Henley.' 8th ed. New York: Scribner, Welford & Co., 1889.

The History of the Caliph Vathek. 'Printed verbatim from the First Edition, with the Original Preface and Notes by Henley.' 8th ed. Philadelphia: Porter & Coates, 1889. 189 pp. 15½ cm.

The History of the Caliph Vathek. 'Printed verbatim from the First Edition, with the Original Preface and Notes by Henley.' 8th ed. New York: William L Allison, *c.*1889. 199 pp. 19 cm. Arundel Series.

The History of the Caliph Vathek. Memoir by William North. New York: Pollard & Moss, [1889]. 207 pp. 19 cm. Selected Notes, as in Alden (1887).

The History of the Caliph Vathek. 'Printed verbatim from the First Edition, with the Original Preface and Notes by Henley.' 8th ed. New York: J. W. Lovell, ?1889.

The History of the Caliph Vathek; and European Travels. Intro. G. T. Bettany, London: Ward, Lock, 1891. xxiv, 549 pp. 18 cm. Frontis. & 8 pl. *Vathek,* 1–92. 1786 version. No Notes. With *Dreams, Waking Thoughts, and Incidents* & *Alcobaça and Batalha.* Minerva Library of Famous Books, No. 24.

Vathek: An Arabian Tale. Intro. Richard Garnett. London: Lawrence & Bullen, 1893. xxx, 253 pp. 23 cm. Eight etchings by Herbert Nye. 1823 version (not 1816, as stated on p. xvi). Henley's Notes with Beckford's additions, from Bentley (1834). Limited to 600 numbered copies and a further 70 numbered copies on Japanese vellum, with an extra etching.

The History of the Caliph Vathek. 'Editorial Note' by C. S. C. London: Newnes, [1897]. 33 pp. in two columns. 21 cm. 1786 version. No Notes. With C. F. Vandervelde, *The Anabaptist: A Tale of the Sixteenth Century.* The Penny Library of Famous Books, No. 94.

The History of the Caliph Vathek. In *Famous Tales of the Orient,* ed. Frederick B. De Berard, 9–124. New York: International Book and Publishing Co., 1899. 18½ cm. 1786 version. With 'Aladdin', 'The Forty Thieves' and 'The Three Calenders' from the *Arabian Nights,* and Maria Edgeworth, *Murad the Unlucky.*

Vathek: An Arabian Tale. Intro. Richard Garnett. London: Gibbins, 1900. xl, 266 pp. 19½ cm. Six etchings by Herbert Nye. 1823 version (not 1816, as stated on p. xxiv). Henley's Notes with Beckford's additions, from Bentley (1834). Reprint of Garnett's 1893 ed. in smaller format. Limited to 1500 copies.

Vathek: An Arabian Tale. Intro. Richard Garnett. London: Privately printed for members of the Society of English Bibliophilists, *c.*1900. xl, 266 pp. 19½ cm. Six etchings by Herbert Nye. 1823 version (not 1816, as stated on p. xxiv). Henley's Notes with Beckford's additions, from Bentley (1834). Reissue of Garnett's 1900 ed. Half calf. Limited to 100 copies.

The History of the Caliph Vathek. An Eastern Romance. Intro. Justin Hannaford. London: Greening, 1900. 272 pp. 19 cm. Nine illus. by W. S. Rogers. 1786 version. About half of Henley's Notes.

The History of the Caliph Vathek. 'Printed verbatim from First Edition, with the Original Prefaces and Notes by Henley.' New York: James Pott, 1900. 271 pp. 16 cm. Portrait frontis. Preface and text from Sampson, Low edition, 1868. Title page in red and black. Gem Classics.

The History of the Caliph Vathek. Intro. E. Denison Ross. London: Methuen, 1901. xxxi, 149 pp. 15½ cm. Portrait frontis. 1786 version. The Little Library. Also publ., London: Selfridge, n.d. 15½ cm. Crimson suede, Yapp edges.

Vathek. Intro. Justin Hannaford. London: Greening, 1905. 272 pp. 18 cm. Eight illus. by W. S. Rogers. List of illus. is a cancel in some copies. 1786 version. About half of Henley's Notes. Reprint of Greening (1900).

Vathek. Intro. Justin Hannaford. London: Greening, [1905]. 272 pp. 18 cm. Eight illus. by W. S. Rogers. 1786 version. About half of Henley's Notes. Reprint of Greening (1900). Reissued with new title page, London: Greening / New York: Brentano's, n.d. The Lotus Library. Upper cover no longer gilt.

Vathek. Intro. Justin Hannaford. London: Collins, n.d. 272 pp. 18 cm. No illus. 1786 version. About half of Henley's Notes. Reprint of Greening (1900). The Lotus Library.

[*The Episodes of Vathek*]. 'Histoire de la Princesse Zulkaïs et du Prince Kalilah' & 'Histoire du Prince Alasi et de la Princesse Firouzkah' *The English Review* 4 (Dec 1909): 163–184 & 6 (Aug, Sept 1910): 137–147, 309–322. In French.

The Episodes of Vathek. Trans. Sir Frank Marzials. London: Stephen Swift, 1912. 23½ cm. Frontis. xxxi, 207 pp. (in English) & 127 pp. (in French). Includes the third Episode, 'The Story of Prince Barkiarokh'.

Vathek: An Arabian Tale. Intro. Richard Garnett. London: Stephen Swift, 1912. xl, 266 pp. 19½ cm. Portrait frontis. & two etchings by Herbert Nye (the two omitted from Garnett's 1900 ed). 1823 version (not 1816, as stated on p. xxiv). Henley's Notes with Beckford's additions, from Bentley (1834). Reissue of Garnett's 1900 ed.

Vathek. An Arabian Tale. Memoir by R. S. London: Routledge, [1912]. xxix, 179 pp. 14 cm. Five colour illus. by W. B. Handforth. 1823 version. Henley's Notes with Beckford's additions, from Bentley (1834), but missing those on the last leaf (pp. *117–*118), as in Tegg (1868). Bound either in 'leather-velvet' or French Roan with gilt edges. Reissued in paper boards with one of the colour illus. pasted on to upper cover.

Vathek. Intro. Justin Hannaford. New York: Brentano's, 1921. 272 pp.

Vathek. Intro. Reginald Brimley Johnson. London: Chapman & Dodd, [1922]. xx, 219 pp. 18 cm. Ornamented by Martin Travers. 1786 version. About half of Henley's Notes, as in Greening (1900). Also London: Simpkin, n.d. (but with Chapman & Dodd on the title page) and Boston, MA: Small, Maynard, n.d. Abbey Classics, No. 2.

The Episodes of Vathek. Trans. Sir Frank Marzials. Intro. Lewis Melville. London: Chapman & Dodd, [1922]. xxiv, 227 pp. 18 cm. Ornamented by Martin Travers. Abbey Classics, No. 3.

Vathek. Intro. J[ohn]. G[abriel]. L[ockhart]. London: Philip Allan, [1923]. xv, 212 pp. 24½ cm. Eight colour illus. (by Violet Dale). 1786 version. About half of Henley's Notes. (Limited to 1000 copies.) Blue/grey cloth, bevelled boards. Remainder binding: dark blue cloth, unbevelled boards.

Vathek: An Arabian Tale. Intro. Richard Garnett. London: William Glaisher, 1924. xl, 266 pp. 18 cm. Reprint of Gibbins, 1900, but without the etchings. 1823 version (not 1816, as stated on p. xxiv). Henley's Notes with Beckford's additions, from Bentley (1834).

Vathek. Intro. Ben Ray Redman. New York: John Day, 1928. xx, 229 pp. 24 cm. Illus. Mahlon Blaine. 1786 version. About half of Henley's Notes, as in Philip Allan [1923]. Green cloth. Slipcase. Remainder binding: light grey-green with device on upper cover printed in black only.

Vathek. Trans. & intro. Herbert B. Grimsditch. London: Nonesuch Press, 1929. 172 pp. 23½ cm. Ten colour lithographs by Marion V. Dorn (see Christine Boydell, *The Architect of Floors*, London: Schoeser, 1996, 6 (pl. 4), 13, 24, 37, 126). Trans. of the Londres 1815 edition. Limited to 1550 numbered copies, 1050 for England and 500 for the United States. Chapman, *Bibliography* (1930), p. 78.

Vathek. In *Shorter Novels. Eighteenth Century*, intro. Philip Henderson, 193–306. London: Dent, 1930–1953. 17½ cm. 1823 version. About half of Henley's Notes with Beckford's additions, from Bentley (1834). With Samuel Johnson, *The History of Rasselas* and Horace Walpole, *The Castle of Otranto*. Reissued as *Shorter Novels of the Eighteenth Century* with new intro. by Philip Henderson, 1953 and later. 18½ cm. *Vathek*, 193–278. No Notes. Everyman's Library, No. 856.

Vathek. In *Three Eighteenth Century Romances*, 125–243. Intro. Harrison R. Steeves (*Vathek*, xix–xxiii). New York: Scribner, 1931. 1823 version. With Horace Walpole, *The Castle of Otranto* and Ann Radcliffe, *The Romance of the Forest*. Reprinted 1959 & subsequently.

[*The Episodes of Vathek*] 'The Story of the Princess Zulkais and the Prince Kalilah.' *Leaves* (Leavenworth, Kansas) 1st issue (Summer 1937): 1–20. The Third Episode of *Vathek* completed by Clark Ashton Smith. (See '16. Works influenced by Beckford. Works influenced by *Vathek*'.)

Vathek: an Arabian Tale. Trans. Herbert B. Grimsditch. New York: Limited Editions Club, 1945. xi, 135 pp. 16 cm. Eight colour plates and other decorations by Valenti Angelo, and limited to 1500 numbered copies signed by him. Trans. of the Londres 1815 edition. Issued in millboard folder and/or slipcase.

Vathek. London: The Bodley Head, 1953. 126 pp. Black cloth. 20½ cm. Trans., intro. & notes by Herbert B. Grimsditch. Eight illus. by Charles

W. Stewart. Trans. of the Londres 1815 edition. Remainder binding, orange linson, 21 cm.

Vathek. London: The Folio Society, 1958. 128 pp. 22 cm. Trans., new intro. & notes by Herbert B. Grimsditch. Eight colour lithographs by Edward Bawden. Trans. of the Londres 1815 edition. Slipcase.

Vathek. In *Three Gothic Novels*, 107–253. New York: Dover, 1966. 21½ cm. Ed. & intro. E. F. Bleiler, 'William Beckford and *Vathek*', pp. xix–xxx. 1823 version. Henley's Notes with Beckford's additions, from Bentley (1834). With Horace Walpole, *The Castle of Otranto*, John Polidori, *The Vampyre* and Lord Byron, *Fragment of a Novel*. Later reprints.

Vathek. An Arabian Tale. London: New English Library, 1966. 123 pp. 18 cm. 1786 version. Only 26 of Henley's Notes (appearing as footnotes here), as in Slater (1849). Four Square Books.

Vathek. In *Three Gothic Novels*, ed. Peter Fairclough with intro. by Mario Praz, 149–255. Harmondsworth, Middlesex: Penguin, 1968 and later. 18 cm. 1823 version. No Notes. With Horace Walpole, *The Castle of Otranto* and Mary Shelley, *Frankenstein*. Penguin English Library, No. EL 36. Reissued 1986 and subsequently. 18 cm, then 20 cm. Penguin Classics.

Vathek. Ed. Roger Lonsdale. Oxford: Oxford University Press, 1970. xliii, 187 pp. 21 cm. Frontis. Mostly 1816 2nd issue version. About half of Henley's Notes, as in that ed. Also paperback with cover illus. by Edward Bawden but no frontis. 20½ cm. Reissued with new cover in World's Classics, 1983, 1989, 1991. xliii, 170 pp. 18½ cm. Reissued in Oxford World's Classics, 1998. 19½ cm.

Vathek. Menston, Yorkshire: Scholar Press, 1971. vii, 334 pp. 21 cm. Facsimile reprint of Henley's 1786 ed. with one page intro. Henley's Notes. Hardback & paperback editions.

The History of the Caliph Vathek, including The Episodes of Vathek. New York: Ballantine, 1971. xiii, 305 pp. 18 cm. Intro. Lin Carter. *Episodes* trans. Sir Frank Marzials. Decorations from Chapman & Dodd [1922]. 1786 version. About half of Henley's Notes, as in Philip Allan [1923].

Vathek. Facsimile reprints of the Henley (1786), Lausanne (1787 [1786]) and Paris (1787) eds. Intro. Robert J. Gemmett. Delmar, NY: Scholars' Facsimiles & Reprints, 1972. xx, vii, 334, iv, 204, 190 pp. 22 cm.

The Episodes of Vathek. Intro. Robert J. Gemmett. Rutherford, NJ: Fairleigh Dickinson University Press, 1975. L, 211 pp. 21¼ cm. Facsimile reprint of 1912 trans. by Sir Frank Marzials.

Vathek. In *The Oxford Library of Short Novels*, chosen & intro. John Wain, 1:109–205. 3 vols. Oxford: Clarendon Press, 1990. 22½ cm. 1786 version. Vol. 1, 'Goethe to Stevenson', also contains Goethe, *The Sorrows of Young Werther* (1774); Edgeworth, *Castle Rackrent, an Hibernian Tale* (1800); Gaskell, *Mrs Harrison's Confessions* (1851); Tolstoy, *The Death of Ivan Ilych* (1886) and Stevenson, *The Strange Case of Dr Jekyll and Mr Hyde* (1886). Also issued by Guild Publishing, London, 1990.

Vathek. In *Vathek and Other Stories – A William Beckford Reader*, ed. Malcolm Jack, 27–121. London: Pickering & Chatto, 1993. xxxviii, 314 pp. 22½ cm. Mostly 1816 2nd issue version. About half of Henley's Notes, as in that ed. Also contains extracts from *The Vision, Biographical Memoirs of Extraordinary Painters, Modern Novel Writing, Azemia, Dreams . . ., The Journal . . . in Portugal and Spain 1787–88, Italy; with Sketches . . ., Recollections of an Excursion to the Monasteries of Alcobaça and Batalha*. Reprinted Harmondsworth, Middlesex: Penguin Books, 1995. 20 cm.

The Episodes of Vathek. Trans. Sir Frank Marzials. Ed. Malcolm Jack. Sawtry, Cambs: Dedalus, 1994. 207 pp. 20 cm.

Vathek. In *Four Gothic Novels*, 81–154. Oxford: Oxford University Press, 1994. 19½ cm. With Horace Walpole, *The Castle of Otranto*, M. G. Lewis, *The Monk* and Mary Shelley, *Frankenstein*.

Vathek. Intro. Jeremy Reed. London: Creation Books, 2000. 123 pp. 21½ cm. Intro. Eight illus. by Odilon Redon. 1816 2nd issue version. No Notes.

Vathek with The Episodes of Vathek. Ed. Kenneth W. Graham. Peterborough, Ontario: Broadview, 2001. 397 pp. 21½ cm. Mostly 1816 version. Trans. of *Episodes* by Sir Frank Marzials and Kenneth W. Graham.

Vathek. In *Three Oriental Tales*, 79–179. Ed. Alan Richardson. Boston, MA: Houghton Mifflin, 2002. 1816 version. With Frances Sheridan, *The History of Nourjahad*; Lord Byron, *The Giaour*; and Adam Potkay, 'Beckford's Heaven of Boys', reprinted from *Raritan* (Rutgers University) 13 no. 1 (Summer 1993). See also viii, 1, 2, 8–10, 14, 15, 18, 247. New Riverside ed.

Vathek. Stroud, Glos: Nonsuch, 2005. 160 pp. 17 cm. 1816 2nd issue version.

FRENCH

Vathek. Lausanne: Isaac Hignou, 1787 [1786]. iv, 204 pp. 20 cm. Chapman, *Bibliography* (1930), 3B(i).

Vathek, Conte Arabe. Paris: Poinçot, 1787. [5], 4–190, [2] pp. 21½ cm. With Notes. Chapman, *Bibliography* (1930), 3B(ii). Two further issues with slight changes appeared in that year. Chapman, *Bibliography* (1930), 3B(ii, a & b).

Les Caprices et les Malheurs du Calife Vathek. Traduit de l'Arabe. Londres, 1791. iv, 204 pp. 19½ cm. Lausanne ed. with cancel title. Not in Chapman.

Vathek. Londres: Clarke, New Bond Street, 1815. iv within iv, 218 pp. 18½ cm. Frontis. & title page vignette. Only 35 of Henley's Notes. Also a limited ed. of 25 copies on large paper, 24½ cm. Chapman, *Bibliography* (1930), 3B(iii).

Histoire du Calife Vathek. 2 vols. Paris: Anthᵉ Boucher, 1819. vii, 160 pp. & iv, 134 pp. 18½ cm. Re-trans. of 1786 version. With Notes. Chapman, *Bibliography* (1930), 3C, and noted in 3B(iii, b).

Vathek. Londres: Clarke, Mount Street, Berkeley Square, c.1828. iv within iv, 218 pp. 18½ cm. Frontis. & title page vignette. A reissue of the 1815 ed. Only 35 of Henley's Notes. Chapman, *Bibliography* (1930), 3B(iii, a).

Vathek. With Notes. Nouvelle Edition. Londres: Richard Bentley, 1834. 218 pp. 18 cm. Frontis. Londres 1815 version. Only 35 of Henley's Notes. Chapman, *Bibliography* (1930), 3B(iv).

Vathek. Lyon & Paris: Cormon & Blanc, 1835.

Vathek. 'Réimprimé sur l'original français.' Preface by Stéphane Mallarmé. Paris: Adolphe Labitte, 1876. xl, 192 pp. 20½ cm. Paris 1787 version. Limited to 220 copies initialled by the editor. Mallarmé also issued his *Préface* separately, limited to 95 copies 'hors commerce' signed & numbered by him.

Vathek. 'Réimprimé sur l'original français.' Preface by Stéphane Mallarmé, shortened by him. Paris: Perrin, 1893. xlvii, 208 pp. 19 cm. Paris 1787 version. Also a limited ed. of 15 copies on Hollande Van Gelder paper.

Vathek, conte arabe. Foreword, 'Beckford, ou le Démon des fables', & trans. by G. Jean-Aubry. Paris: Les Exemplaires, 1928. xxxvi, 341 pp. 27 cm. Limited to 99 numbered copies.

Vathek with The Episodes of Vathek. Ed. Guy Chapman. 2 vols. Cambridge: Printed at the University Press for Constable, 1929. xxv, 176 pp. & vii, 162 pp. 22½ cm. Eight illus. Paris 1787 version of *Vathek*. Limited to 1000 copies. Chapman, *Bibliography* (1930), pp. 77–78.

Vathek: Conte Arabe. Foreword by Eugène Bressy. Paris: José Corti, 1946 [1947]. 128 pp. 16 cm. Paris 1787 version. Also a limited ed. of 11 copies on Fil Lafuma vellum numbered 1 to 10 and one 'hors commerce', and 50 copies on Vergé Blanc numbered 11 to 60. Collection romantique, No. 5.

Vathek et Les Episodes. Intro. J. B. Brunius with Preface (shortened) by Stéphane Mallarmé. Paris: Editions Stock, 1948. 381 pp. 19 cm. Ten illus. by Edmond Maurice Pérot. Paris 1787 version. Limited to 2200 numbered copies, plus 100 'hors commerce'. Voyages Imaginaires.

Vathek et Les Episodes. Intro. Ernest Giddey. Lausanne: Editions Rencontre, 1962. 319 pp. Paris 1787 version.

Vathek: conte arabe. 'Beckford' by Stéphane Mallarmé. Paris: Le club français du livre, 1962. xvi, 132 pp. 21½ cm. Ten illus. by Paul Elie. Paris 1787 version. 'Note biographique', 123–132. Limited to 7000 numbered copies and 26 copies marked A to Z and 100 copies numbered I to C.

Vathek. Preface by Marc Chadourne. Paris: Cercle du livre précieux, 1962. 151 pp. 20 cm. Twenty illus. by Edouard Goerg. Limited to 500 numbered copies on Lana vellum. Portfolio in slipcase. Cercle des amateurs de livres et d'art typographique No. 2.

Vathek: Conte Arabe. Foreword by Eugène Bressy and Preface by Stéphane Mallarmé. 2nd ed. Paris: José Corti, 1965. 225 pp. 16 cm. Paris 1787 version. Also 3rd ed., 1970. 4th ed., 1973. 5th ed., 1978. 6th ed., 1984. 7th ed., 1992. Collection romantique, No. 5 (as is the 1st ed., above).

Vathek. Preface by Stéphane Mallarmé. Grenoble: Roissard, 1971. xxx, 124 pp. 22 cm. Eight illus. by Van Hamme. Issued in two-fold wallet and slipcase. Limited to 842 numbered copies and 132 copies numbered I to CXXX and 26 copies marked A to Z of which 8 contain an original illus. Cercle des professeurs bibliophiles de France.

Vathek, conte arabe. Paris: Editions de l'Erable, François Beauval, 1971. Includes Adelbert von Chamisso, *L'homme qui a vendu son ombre ou La merveilleuse histoire de Pierre Schemihl.* 267 pp. Illus. Les chefs-d'oeuvre du mystère et du fantastique.

Vathek. Histoire du Prince Alasi. Histoire du Prince Barkiarokh. Preface by Maurice Lévy. Paris: Flammarion, 1981. 315 pp. 18 cm. Paris 1787 version. Garnier-Flammarion No. 375.

Vathek. Preface by Jean Raimond. Geneva & Paris: Editions Slatkine, 1997. 197 pp. 17½ cm. Fleuron series.

Vathek et ses épisodes. Ed. & postface Didier Girard. Preface by Stéphane Mallarmé. Paris: José Corti, 2003. 458 pp. 21½ cm. Lausanne version with changes for Paris (1787) and Londres (1815) noted. Domaine romantique.

GERMAN

Der Thurm von Samarah . . . Aus dem Arabischen, Trans. of Lausanne ed. by Georg Schatz. Leipzig: Dykischen Buchhandlung, 1788. 253 pp. 17½ cm.

Vathek, eine arabische Erzählung. Trans. of Paris ed. Vienna, 1788.

Vathek, eine arabische Erzählung. Trans. from the French by Georg Christian Römer. Mannheim, 1788. Chapman, *Bibliography* (1930), 3C.

Vathek, eine arabische Erzählung. Trans. from the English by Otto Mohnike. Leipzig: Cnobloch, 1842. 256 pp.

Vathek. Trans. & intro. Franz Blei. Leipzig: Julius Zeitler, 1907. iv, 139 pp. 19 cm. By 'John Beckford'.

Vathek. Trans. & intro. Karl Toth. Zurich: Amalthea, 1921. 144 pp. 15 cm. Ten colour illus. by K. A. Wilke. Also an ed. on Japanese art paper limited to 250 copies numbered and signed by the artist, nos. I–L bound in silk and 51–250 bound in leather. ?1786 version.

Vathek. Eine arabische Erzählung. Trans. Hans Schiebelhuth. Ten etchings by Fritz Heubner. Berlin: Fritz Gurlitt, 1924. 99 pp.

Kalif Vathek. Eine orientalische Erzählung. Trans. Albert Hess. Menziken: Kolumbus Verlag, c.1947. 173 pp. 19 cm.

Vathek. Eine arabische Erzählung. Afterword by Siegfried Schmitz. Trans. Hans Schiebelhuth. Munich: Winkler, 1964. 119 pp. 19½ cm.

Vathek mit der Episoden. Preface by Stéphane Mallarmé (trans. Max Hölzer). Afterword by Reinhold Grimm. *Vathek* trans. from the French by Franz Blei, revised by Robert Picht. *Episodes* trans. Ronald Weber. Frankfurt: Insel, 1964. 345 pp. Sometimes with 14 lithographs by Wilfred Blecher.

Die Geschichte vom Kalifen Vathek: mit der Episoden. Afterword by Stephan Hermlin. *Vathek* trans. Franz Blei, revised by Robert Picht. *Episodes* trans. Ronald Weber. Leipzig: Insel, 1974. 314 pp. 20 cm.

Die Geschichte des Kalifen Vathek. Commentary by Gisela Dischner. Wagenbachs Taschenbücherei No. WAT 10. Berlin: Wagenbach, 1975. 191 pp.

Vathek. Preface by Stéphane Mallarmé. Foreword by Reinhold Grimm. Trans. Franz Blei. Leipzig: Insel, 1976. 346 pp.

Vathek. Ed. & intro. Jorge Luis Borges. Trans. Hans Schiebelhuth. Stuttgart: Edition Weitbrecht, 1983. 158 pp. Die Bibliothek von Babel 3.

Vathek, Eine orientalische Erzählung. Trans. & afterword by Wolfram Benda. Bayreuth: Bear Press, 1985. 194 pp. 29 cm. Eleven etchings by Gottfried Helnwein. ?Paris 1787 version. Limited to 170 hand-bound copies signed by the artist. Also a limited edition of 25 copies and further 5 copies numbered I to V. New ed., Munich: Winkler, 1987. 194 pp. 25 cm. Eleven colour illus. by Gottfried Helnwein.

Vathek. Eine orientalische Erzählung. Trans. & afterword Wolfram Benda. Munich: Deutscher Taschenbuch Verlag, 1988. 194 pp. 18 cm. Eleven illus. by Gottfried Helnwein.

Vathek. Preface by Stéphane Mallarmé. Trans. from the French by Franz Blei. Includes the *Episodes*, trans. ?Ronald Weber. Frankfurt: Insel Taschenbuch, 1989. (1st ed. 1964.) 345 pp. 18 cm.

Vathek. Preface by Stéphane Mallarmé. Trans. from the French by Franz Blei. Frankfurt: Suhrkamp, 1999. 337 pp.

ITALIAN

Vathek. Trans. Giaime Pintor. Turin: Einaudi, 1946. xxi, 117 pp. 19 cm. Universale Einaudi 64.

Vathek: racconto arabo. Ed. Giovanni Paoletti. Intro. Francesco Orlando. Venice: Marsilio, 1966. 258 pp. 19 cm.

Vathek e gli episodi. Preface by Salvatore Rosati. Trans. Aldo Camerino (*Vathek*) & Ruggero Savinio (*Episodes*). Milan: Bompiani, 1966. xiv, 309 pp. 20½ cm.

Vathek. Intro. Alberto Moravia. Trans. Giaime Pintor. Turin: Einaudi, 1973. xv, 122 pp. 20 cm.

Vathek. Trans. Aldo Camerino & Ruggero Savinio. Milan: Club degli editori, 1974. xii, 235 pp. 23 cm.

Vathek. Ed. & intro. Jorge Luis Borges. Trans. Aldo Camerino. Milan: Franco Maria Ricci, 1978. 148 pp. 22½ cm. ?Paris 1787 version. La Biblioteca di Babele 10.

Vathek. Afterword by Malcolm Skey. Trans. Giaime Pintor. Turin: Einaudi, 1989. 135 pp. 19 cm. Scrittori tradotti da scrittori 30.

Racconti orientali, ‹three tales from the *Episodes*›. Ed. G. Servadio. Trans. L. Romito. Soveria Mannelli: Rubbettino (Il colibrì), 1989. 228 pp. 21 cm.

Vathek. Ed. & intro. Jorge Luis Borges. Trans. Aldo Camerino. Milan: Arnoldo Mondadori. 1990. 168 pp. 19 cm. ?Paris 1787 version. La Biblioteca di Babele 18.

Vathek e gli episodi. Preface by Salvatore Rosati. Trans. Aldo Camerino (*Vathek*) and Ruggero Savinio (*Episodes*). Milan: Fabbri-Bompiani-Sonzogno-Etas, 1991. xii, 257 pp. 18½ cm. Tascabili Bompiani 547. 2nd ed., Milan: Tascabili Bompiani, 2003. 20 cm. Tascabili Bompiani 875.

Storia del principe Alasi e della principessa Firuzkah. Trans. & ed. Giandonato Crico. Palermo: Sellerio, 1992. 107 pp. 15½ cm. Il divano, No. 42.

Vathek. Ed. & intro. Jorge Luis Borges. Trans. Aldo Camerino. Milan: Franco Maria Ricci, 1992. 141 pp. 26 cm. ?Paris 1787 version. La Biblioteca di Babele 10.

PORTUGUESE

Vathek o Califa Maldito. Trans. from the French by Max da Costa Santos. Rio de Janeiro: Civilização Brasileira, 1971. xv, 139 pp. 21 cm. Sempr viva. obras celebres da literature universal 9.

Wathek. Lisbon: Amigos do Livro, 1976. Includes Adelbert von Chamisso, *O homem que vendeu a própria sombra*. 114 pp. Illus. 18 cm.

Vathek. Trans. Manuel João Gomes. Lisbon: Estampa, 1978. 143 pp. 18½ cm. With footnotes. Limited to 3200 copies. Printed on pale green paper. ?Londres 1815 version. Series: Livro B 34.

História do Califa Vathek. Intro. Michael Gordon Lloyd. Trans. Mário Cláudio. Porto: Edições Afrontamento, 1982. 191 pp. 21 cm. Five illus. by Manuela Bacelar. With notes. Fixões 3.

Vathek. Trans. Henrique de Araújo Mesquita. Porto Alegre: L & PM Pocket, 1986. 136 pp. 21 cm. Series: biblioteca fantastica.

Vathek. Trans. Henrique de Araújo Mesquita. Porto Alegre & São Paulo: L & PM Pocket, 1997. 139 pp. 17 cm. L & PM Pocket vol. 26.

Vathek – Conto Árabe. Trans. Albert Demazière. Lisbon: Os Amigos do Livro, n.d.

RUSSIAN

Khalif Vatek. Arabskaya skazka (Caliph Vathek. An Arabian Tale). Trans. from the French. St Petersburg: St Petersburg Mining Institute, 1792. 206 pp.

Vatek. Arabskaya skazka (Vathek. An Arabian Tale). Introductory essay 'Beckford – Author of *Vathek*' by P. Muratov. Trans. Boris Zaitsev. Moscow: K. F. Nekrasova, 1912. 181 pp. Portrait of Beckford & illus. of Fonthill Abbey. Paris 1787 version. 2nd ed., 1916.

Vatek (Vathek). Trans. M. & E. Ramm. *News on Foreign Literature* (St Petersburg), 1913. 72 pp.

Vatek (Vathek). Trans. Boris Zaitsev. In *Fantasticheskie Povesti* (Fantasy Stories), ed. V. M. Zhirmunsky & N. A. Sigal, 163–228. Leningrad: Nauka, 1967. Intro. to *Vathek*, 272–284. Bibliography & Notes, 287–290. 22 cm. Portrait & illus. of Fonthill Abbey. Paris 1787 version. With Horace Walpole, *The Castle of Otranto* and Jacques Cazotte, *Le Diable Amoureux*. Academy of Sciences of the USSR: Literary Masterpieces.

Vatek. Arabskaya skazka (Vathek. An Arabian Tale). Trans. Boris Zaitsev. Moscow: Moscow State University, 1992–1993. Paris 1787 version.

SPANISH

Vathek; cuento árabe. Preface by Stéphane Mallarmé. Trans. Guillermo Carnero. Barcelona: Editorial Seix Barral, 1969. 164 pp. 18 cm. Biblioteca Breve de Bolsillolibros de Enlace 48.

Vampiros y otros monstruos. Selected & trans. by Enrique Luis Revol. Buenos Aires: R. Alonso, 1969 and 1972. Includes *Vathek* and tales by Mary Shelley, John Polidori and Lord Byron.

Vathek, cuento árabe. Preface by Stéphane Mallarmé. Trans. Manuel Serrat Crespo. Barcelona: Bruguera., 1982. 156 pp. 18 cm. Libro Amigo 940.

Vathek. Ed. & intro. Jorge Luis Borges. Trans. Guillermo Carnero. Madrid: Siruela, 1984. 155 pp. 23 cm. La Biblioteca de Babel 10.

Vathek. Ed. & intro. Jorge Luis Borges. Preface by Stéphane Mallarmé. Trans. Manuel Serrat Crespo. Madrid & Buenos Aires: Hyspamérica, 1985. 159 pp. 20 cm. Biblioteca personal 47.

Vathek. Trans. Manuel Serrat Crespo. Madrid: Hyspamérica, 1987. 159 pp. 20 cm. Biblioteca personal 53.

Los Episodios de Vathek. Trans. Claudia Monfils. Madrid: Valdemar, 1991. Contains 'The Story of Prince Alasi and the Princess Firouzkah' and 'Story of Prince Barkiarokh'.

Vathek, cuento árabe (Con sus tres Episodios). Trans. Javier Martín

Lalanda. Madrid: Alianza, 1993. 384 pp. 18 cm. Paris 1787 version. El libro de bolsillo 1650.

Vathek. Buenos Aires: Nuevo Siglo, 1995. 124 pp.

Historia de la Princesa Zulkais y el Principe Kalilah (El tercer episodio de Vatek). Trans. José María Nebreda. Madrid: Valdemar, 1999. 'El Club Diógenes' series.

Vathek, cuento árabe. Preface by Stéphane Mallarmé. Trans. Manuel Serrat Crespo. Palma de Mallorca: Olañeta, 2001. 135 pp. 21 cm. Torre de viento 20.

OTHER LANGUAGES

Catalan. *Vathek: un conte àrab.* Trans. Carles Urritz. Barcelona: Laertes, 1995. 123 pp. 20 cm. ?1786 version. Series: L'arcà 68.

Chinese. *Vathek.* 1890s. Noted in Herbert A. Giles, *A History of Chinese Literature*, London: Heinemann, 1901, 429.

Croatian. *Vatek.* Zagrab: Binoza, 1939. 275 pp. 19 cm. Includes *The Episodes.* Svjetski pisci 54.

Croatian. *Vathek Williama Beckforda.* Ed. & intro. Jorge Luis Borges. Trans. Filip M. Dominiković & Gordana Tintor. Zagrab: Grafički zavod Hrvatske, 1982. 132 pp. 23 cm. Babilonska biblioteka 4.

Czech. *Vathek.* Preface by Adela Príhodová. Trans. from the English. Bratislava: Slovenský spisovatel', 1978. 219 pp. 20 cm. *Vathek*, pp. 125–215. Includes Horace Walpole, *The Castle of Otranto.*

Czech. *Vathek.* In *Anglický gotický roman*, ed. Jaroslav Hornát. Prague: Odeon, 1970. 721 pp. With works by Horace Walpole, Clara Reeve & Ann Radcliffe.

Dutch. *Vathek: Eene Arabische Vertelling.* Trans. from the French by E. J. Potgieter. Amsterdam: J. H. en G. van Heteren, 1837. vi, 160 pp. 24 cm.

Dutch. *Vathek.* Trans. Max Schuchart. Utrecht/Antwerp: Uitgeverij het Spectrum, 1982. 367 pp. 22 cm. Includes Horace Walpole, *The Castle of Otranto* and Mary Shelley, *Frankenstein.* Prisma klassieken, vol. 60.

Hungarian. *Vathek kalifa története.* Trans. Júlia Képes. Budapest: Holnap, 1991. 155 pp. 19 cm.

Japanese. *Vathek.* 1980. 173 pp. 22 cm.

Japanese. *Vathek.* Trans. from mainly French versions by Yasuhiko Kisaichi. 2 vols. Tokyo: Kokusho Kankokai, 1990.

Korean. *Vathek.* 2003. 162 pp. 20 cm.

Polish. *Wathek: opowieść arabska.* Preface by Zofia Sinko. Trans. from the French by Anna Jasińska. Illus. by Bronisław Kurdziel. Crakow: Wydaw. Literackie, 1976. 107 pp. 20 cm.

Romanian. *Vathek.* Preface with chronological table by Dan Grigorescu.

Trans. Raluca Dana Cotruţă. Bucharest: Minerva, 1987. xli, 293 pp.
Includes Clara Reeve, *The Old English Baron* (1777). Biblioteca pentru
toţi 1275.

Slovenian. *Vathek: arabska zgodba*. Trans. Tomo Rebolj. Ljubljana: Dolenc,
1998. 96 pp. 21 cm.

Swedish. *Vathek eller Kalifen på Resa*. Intro. Reginald Brimley Johnson.
Trans. Ragnhild Haglund. Stockholm: Wahlström & Widstrand, 1927.
229 pp. 19½ cm. ?1786 version.

Turkish. *Vathek*. Trans. from the French by Ýsmail Yerguz. Ankara: Dost
Kitabevi, 1998. 2nd ed., 2000.

Turkish. *Vathek: Gotik Roman*. Trans. Pýnar Gürcan. Istanbul: Bordo Siyah
Klasik Yayýnlar, 2004. 160 pp.

ABRIDGEMENTS OF *VATHEK*

Benét, William Rose. *The Reader's Encyclopedia*. New York: Crowell, 1948.
Two paragraphs (in vol. 4, S–Z), 1166. 2nd rev. ed., London: Black, 1965.
'Beckford, William', 88. 'Vathek', 1050. 'Gothic Novel', 413.

Hammerton, J. A. & Arthur Mee, eds. 'History of the Caliph Vathek.'
Harmsworth Fortnightly. The World's Great Books No. 4 (1909):
406–411 & five illus. by W. S. Rogers. Publ. by Amalgamated Press,
London, who also issued it in book form, in Vol. 1 (*c*.1910). Reissued as
'Vathek' without illus. in Part 21 (24 Aug 1926), ed. J. A. Hammerton,
pp. 1978–1983. American ed., *The World's Greatest Books*. [New York]:
S. S. McClure, 1910. (20 vols.) Ed. Lord Northcliffe (Alfred Harmsworth
& S. S. McClure. Reprinted, [New York]: McKinlay, Stone & Mackenzie, 1913, (20 vols.), 1:244–254. Condensed version, 'to allow the original author to tell his own story over again in his own language, but in the
shortest possible space'.

Haydn, Hiram & Edmund Fuller. *Thesaurus of Book Digests*. New York:
Crown, 1949. Fifteen lines, 776.

Johnson, Rossiter, ed. *Authors Digest. The World's Great Stories in Brief*. 20
vols. [New York:] Author's Press, [1908]. Précis of *Vathek*, 2 (Aus–Beh):
382–293. Biography of Beckford, 19:40–42. Vol. 20, 'Dictionary of
Famous Names in Fiction . . .': Carathis, 78; Gulchenrouz, 200; Nouronihar, 313; Vathek, 398.

Magill, Frank, ed. *Masterpieces of World Literature in Digest Form. Second
Series*. New York: Harper, 1951. Pp. 1094–1096. One of 500 two-page
summaries. Formerly publ. as *Masterplots*.

Peck, Harry. T. *Masterpieces of the World's Literature Ancient and Modern
. . .* 20 vols. New York: American Literary Society, 1898. 2:1090–1098.

Tracy, Ann B. 'William Beckford.' In *The Gothic Novel 1790–1830: Plot*

Summaries and Index to Motifs, 18–19. Lexington, KY: University Press of Kentucky, 1981.

EXTRACTS FROM *VATHEK*

See also Chadourne in '1. Accounts of Beckford's Life.
Full-length Studies'

Carter, Lin, ed. *Imaginary Worlds: Great Short Novels of Adult Fantasy*. New York: Ballantine, 1973. 3 pp.

Carter, Lin, ed. 'The Palace of Subterranean Fire.' In *Kingdoms of Sorcery*, 17–25. Garden City, New York: Doubleday, 1976. Intro. on Beckford, 15–16.

Chambers, Robert, ed. *Cyclopaedia of English Literature*. 2 vols. Edinburgh: W. & R. Chambers, 1844. Beckford, 2:539–540. *Vathek* extracts: 'Description of the Caliph Vathek and his Magnificent Palaces', 541–542 & 'The Hall of Eblis', 542–545. 'Morning in Venice' from *Italy*, 673–674. *Chambers's idem.* 4th ed. 2 vols. 1881. Ed. Robert Carruthers. 2:243–245, 245–246, 246–247 (shorter Eblis), 402–403. *Idem.* New ed. 3 vols. 1901–1903. Ed. David Patrick. Vol. 2 (1902): 620–622, 622–623, 623–624. No extract from *Italy*.

Cohen, J. M. & M. J., eds. *The Penguin Dictionary of Quotations*. Harmondsworth, Middlesex: Penguin, 1960. Two quotations from *Vathek*, 26.

Cunliffe, John W. & Ashley H. Thorndyke. *The Warner Library*. 30 vols. New York: Warner, 1917. Selections from Beckford's works & biography in vol. 3.

Garnett, Richard, ed. *International Library of Famous Literature*. 20 vols. London: The Standard, 1900. 10:4461–4483. Also publ. London: Edward Lloyd, n.d.

Garnett, Richard, et al., eds. *Universal Anthology, A Collection of the Best Literature, Ancient, Medieval and Modern, with Biographical and Explanatory Notes*. 33 vols. London: The Clarke Co., 1899. Vol. 19.

Gibbon, Charles, ed. 'The Hall of Eblis.' In *The Casquet of Literature*, 6:218–223. 6 vols. London: Blackie, 1884. *Idem*, new ed. 1896. 6:238–243 & illus. by G. P. Jacomb-Hood, 'Here the Giaour awaited them with the key in his hand.'

Haining, Peter, ed. *The Craft of Terror. Extracts from the Rare and Infamous Gothic 'Horror' Novels*. London: New English Library, 1966. Intro, 61–62. Text, 62–75 (from 1st ed. (1786), 37–67). Biography, 76. Reprinted, London: Mews Books, 1976.

Hill, Brian, compiler. 'Atrocious meals . . . Desert Fare.' In *The Greedy Book*, 214. London: Hart-Davis, 1966. '. . . so savage a repast', 87–88 in the 1786 ed.

Knight, Charles, ed. '283 – The Hall of Eblis.' In *Half-hours with the Best Authors*, 4:117–124. 4 vols. London: Charles Knight, 1847–1848. Intro. by Knight. *Idem*, 4th ed. London: Routledge et al., c.1860. 4:45–50. *Idem*, 3 vols. Philadelphia: Porter & Coates, 1885. 3:313–319.

Lachman, Gary, ed. *The Dedalus Occult Reader: The Garden of Hermetic Dreams*. Sawtry, Cambs: Dedalus, 2004. Beginning, 17–31 & child sacrifice at the chasm, 31–35.

Mackay, Charles, ed. 'The Hall of Eblis.' In *A Thousand and One Gems of English Prose*, 264–267. London: Routledge, [1890]. First publ. 1872.

McGowan, Ian, ed. *Macmillan Anthologies of English Literature. The Restoration and Eighteenth Century*. Basingstoke: Macmillan, 1989. 'From Vathek. [Sacrifice to the Giaour]', 559–563. *Vathek*, Lonsdale ed. (1970, 30–36).

Nimmo, publ. 'The Hall of Eblis.' In *Episodes of Fiction; or, Choice Stories from the Great Novelists*, 151–157. Edinburgh: Nimmo, 1870 [1869]. Intro. on William Beckford, 149–150.

Nimmo, publ. 'The Hall of Eblis.' In *The Treasury of Literature and Art*, 97–103. Edinburgh: Nimmo, 1872. Intro. on William Beckford, 149–150.

North, W., intro. 'The Reward of Eblis' Votaries.' *Literature. An Illustrated Weekly Magazine* (Alden, Publ., New York) 2 no. 45 (29 Dec 1888): 53–55. Reprinted in *Literary Portraits*, 2 vols., New York: Alden, 1888–1889, 2:53–55.

Norton, Rictor, ed. *Gothic readings: the first wave, 1764–1840*. London: Leicester University Press, 2000. *Vathek*, 17–22 (1823 ed., 57–72). *Azemia*, 261–263 (2nd ed. (1798), 2:89–93, 236, 240).

Noyes, Russell M., ed. *English Romantic Poetry and Prose*. New York: Oxford University Press, 1956. Chronology, 104. Intro., 104–105. *Vathek*, 105–114 (1786 ed., 1–21, 181–211). Author Bibliographies, 1296.

Oxford Dictionary of Quotations. London: Oxford University Press, 1941. Three quotations from *Vathek*, 23b (Garnett ed., 1893, pp. 1, 2, 134).

Schreck, Nikolas, ed. *Flowers from Hell. A Satanic Reader*. New York: Creation Books, 2001. Pp. 75–84.

Valentine, Mrs L., compiler. 'The Hall of Eblis.' In *Cameos of Literature from Standard Authors*, 11:61–70 (from 1st ed. (1786), 187–202). 12 vols. London: Warne, 1894. Rev. ed. of *Half Hours with the Best Authors*. Reissued, London: Library Press, 1924. 'Eblis' in vol. 8.

Warner, Charles Dudley, ed. 'Introduction' and two extracts, 'The Incantation and the Sacrifice' & 'Vathek and Nouronihar in the Halls of Eblis'. In *Library of the World's Best Literature Ancient and Modern*, 3:1699–1712. 31 vols. New York: The International Society, 1896. There was also an offprint.

Willsher, James, ed. *The Dedalus Book of English Decadence: Vile Emperors and Elegant Degenerates*. Sawtry, Cambs: Dedalus, 2004. *Vathek*, 42–49. *Episodes*, 57–62.

Woods, George Benjamin, ed. 'From The History of the Caliph Vathek.' In *English Poetry and Prose of the Romantic Movement*, 134–145. Chicago: Scott, Foresman, 1916. Reprinted 1929 & 1950. Brief note on Beckford, followed by the first 27 and last 26 pages of the 1786 ed. 'William Beckford; Editions; Biography; Criticism; Bibliography; Critical Notes', 1203–1204.

12. *Vathek* and *The Episodes*: Criticism

REVIEWS, ANNOUNCEMENTS & ADVERTISEMENTS

An Arabian Tale [Vathek]. London, 1786
  Critical Review 62 (July 1786): 37–42.
  English Review 8 (Sept 1786): 180–184.
  European Magazine 10 (Aug 1786): 102–104.
  Gentleman's Magazine 56 pt. 2 (July 1786): 593–594.
  Monthly Review 76 (May 1787): 450.
  New Review 9 (June 1786): 410–412 & 10 (July 1786): 33–39.
  Town & Country Magazine 18 (1786): 400.

Vathek. Lausanne. 1787 [1786]
  Journal de Lausanne 1 (2 Dec 1786): 1–2.

Vathek. Londres. 1815
  Augustan Review 1 (Dec 1815): 843–844.

Vathek. London. 1816
  Dublin Examiner 1 (Sept 1816): 338–350.

Vathek. Philadelphia. 1816
  Clark, Lewis Gaylord. 'Editor's Table.' *The Knickerbocker Magazine; or New York Monthly Magazine* 15 (Feb 1840): 163–164.
  Philadelphia Democrat Press, 27 Nov 1816, 1.

Vathek. London. 1823
  Edinburgh Review 38 (May 1823): 523. Announcement.
  Literary Gazette 7 (17, 31 May 1823): 320, 351. Advert.
  London Review and Weekly Journal of Literature and the Fine Arts No. 2 (16 June 1827): 24–25. With a review of *Memoirs of Painters* (1824).

Vathek. London. 1834
  Bath Chronicle, 14 May 1835, 4e. 'Warm admiration'. Also advert, 2c.
  Morning Chronicle, 10 July 1834.
  Redding, Cyrus. *Bath Herald*, 3 Oct 1835. Reprinted in his *Memoirs of William Beckford* (1859), 1:258–269.
  Spectator, 12 July 1834, 663–664.

Vathek. Philadelphia. 1834
  'Current Literature.' *New York Mirror*, 5 Sept 1835, 79.

Fra Diavolo. [pseud.] *Richmond [Virginia] Compiler*, 6 April 1835.

Hall, James. 'Vathek. An Oriental Tale.' *Western Monthly Magazine and Literary Journal* 2 (Feb 1835): 110–111.

[Heath, James E.] *Southern Literary Messenger* 1 (Dec 1834): 188–189. Dismissive review. *Idem* (Feb 1835): 270. *Vathek* condemned by *Western Monthly Magazine*.

Heath, James E. *Southern Literary Messenger* 1 (March 1835): 386. Condemnation of *Vathek*.

Vathek: An Oriental Romance. New York. 1845
 Broadway Journal 14 (June 1845): 379.
 New York Herald, 14 July 1845, 2.
 New York Saturday Emporium, 12 July 1845, 2.
 New York Weekly Mirror, 18 Oct 1845, 23. Also in *American Whig Review* 2 (Oct 1845): 434–435.

Vathek. Philadelphia. 1854
 'Literary Notices.' *Harper's New Monthly Magazine* 8 (May 1854): 857–858.
 Quericus. [William Gilmore Simms.] *Southern Quarterly Review* (Charleston) 26 (July 1854): 252–253.
 [Simms, William Gilmore.] *Charleston Evening News*, 14 Dec 1854, 2.

Vathek. London: Sampson Low. 1868
 Illustrated Times review partly quoted in advert in *Notes and Queries* 4th Series 2 (15 Aug 1868): title page.
 'Vathek.' *Saturday Review* 26 (4 July 1868): 28–29. Reprinted in *Littell's Living Age* 98 (19 Sept 1868): 756–758.

Vathek. Preface by Stéphane Mallarmé. Paris. 1876
 Knight, Joseph. *Sunday Times*, 25 June 1876.
 O'Shaughnessy, Arthur. *Morning Post*, 6 June 1876.
 'Le Vathek de Beckford.' *Athenæum*, 3 June 1876, 758–759.

Vathek: An Arabian Tale. Intro. Richard Garnett. 1893
 'A Decadent.' *The Speaker*, 3 Feb 1893, 143–144.
 'Holiday Publications.' *Dial*, 1 Dec 1893, 344.
 'The Literary World.' *St James's Gazette*, 4 Nov 1893, 12. *Idem*, 21 May 1898, 12, reprinted in *San Francisco Chronicle*, 26 June 1898, 4.
 O'Brien, Desmond. 'Letters on Books.' *Truth*, 30 Nov 1893, 1176–1177.

The History of the Caliph Vathek. London: Greening. 1900
 'Books and Their Writers.' *Sunday Times*, 4 March 1900, 2.
 'Books of the Day.' *Lady's Pictorial*, 31 March 1900, 533.
 'Reviews.' *Publishers' Circle*, 24 March 1900, 321.
 St. Barbe. [Douglas Sladen.] 'Dinner Out.' *The Queen, the Lady's Newspaper and Court Chronicle*, 15 Dec 1900, 964.

The Episodes of Vathek. Trans. Sir Frank Marzials. 1912
  Athenæum, 14 Sept 1912, 265–266.
  English Review 13 (Jan 1913): 329.
  'The Episodes of *Vathek.*' *Blackwood's Edinburgh Magazine* 192 (Nov
    1912): 699–701.
  'The Rest of Vathek.' *Times Literary Supplement*, 3 Oct 1912, 400.

Vathek and *The Episodes of Vathek.* Chapman & Dodd. [1922]
  New Statesman 20 (6 Jan 1923), 413–414. Seven Abbey Classics vols.
    noted.
  Times Literary Supplement, 16 Nov 1922, 737.

Vathek. Philip Allan. [1923]
  Times Literary Supplement, 29 Nov 1923, 817.
  Wiltshire Gazette, 7 Feb 1924, 3c–b.

Vathek with *The Episodes of Vathek.* Ed. Guy Chapman. 1929
  King, William. *The Criterion* 8 no. 33 (July 1929): 745–748, reprinted
    1967. With a review of *The Travel-Diaries of William Beckford of
    Fonthill* (1928).
  Nation and Athenæum 45 (21 Sept 1929): 804, 806.
  'Vathek.' *Times Literary Supplement*, 18 July 1929, 572.
  Welby, T. Earle. *Saturday Review*, 23 Feb 1929, 249.

Vathek. Nonesuch Press. 1929
  G., D. 'Prospectus of books for the Summer, Autumn and Winter of 1929.
    Vathek'. In *Bodkin Permitting. Being the Prospectus and Retrospectus for
    1929 of The Nonesuch Press*, 10–11. London: Nonesuch Press, *c.*1929.
  Times Literary Supplement, 21 Nov 1929, 953. Publication announced at
    17/6d, 3 Oct, 771. Letters from: John Hodgkin, 26 Dec, 1097; Guy
    Chapman, 2 Jan 1930, 12; Herbert B. Grimsditch, 9 Jan, 28; Hodgkin,
    9 Jan, 28; Chapman, 16 Jan, 44; Hodgkin, 23 Jan, 60; Grimsditch, 20
    Feb, 142.

Vathek: an Arabian Tale. Limited Editions Club. 1945
  'What the Eblis!' *The Monthly Letter of The Limited Editions Club* No.
    176, Dec 1944. 4 pp.

Vathek et Les Episodes. Lausanne. 1962
  Boudry, Denise. *Etudes de Lettres* 2nd Ser. 5 (1963): 277–278.

Vathek. In *Three Gothic Novels.* Ed. E. F. Bleiler. 1966
  Mizelle, Athena. 'Vathek: an Arabian Tale.' *Southern Dancer* (Florida) 4
    no. 4 (Jan 1983): 33–36.

The Episodes of Vathek. Ed. Robert J. Gemmett. 1975
  Graham, Kenneth W. *The Eighteenth Century: A Current Bibliography*

n.s. 1 for 1975 (1978): 247–248. Also briefly noted: Brian Fothergill, 'William Beckford, Prince of Amateurs', *Essays by Divers Hands* n.s. 38 (1975): 33–47; Kenneth W. Graham, 'Beckford's Adaptation of the Oriental Tale in *Vathek*', *Enlightenment Essays* 5 no. 1 (Spring 1974): 24–33; Kenneth W. Graham, '*Vathek* in English and French', *Studies in Bibliography* 28 (1975): 153–166.

Graham, Kenneth W. 'Beckford's Design for *The Episodes*: A History and a Review.' *Papers of the Bibliographical Society of America* 71 (Third Quarter 1977): 336–343.

Steeves, Harrison R. *Studies in Burke and His Time (1750–1800)* 19 (Spring 1978): 163–166.

Vathek and Other Stories. A William Beckford Reader. Ed. M. Jack. 1993
Clarke, Roger. 'Reviews of the classics.' *Sunday Times Books*, 20 April 1997, 8.7. (Penguin edition.)

Cormack, P. *The House Magazine* (Houses of Parliament), 25 July 1994, 12.

Hall, Michael. *Country Life*, 29 Sept 1994, 120.

Millington, Jon. *Beckford Tower Trust Newsletter*, Spring 1994, 3.

The Episodes of Vathek. Ed. Malcolm Jack. 1994
Botting, Fred. *British Journal for Eighteenth-Century Studies* 20 no. 1 (Spring 1997): 95–98. With reviews of two other works.

Cope, Kevin L. 'Editor's Choice. Underapplauded Books.' *1650–1850: Ideas, Aesthetics, and Inquiries in the Early Modern Era* 3 (May 1997): 431–434.

Vathek with The Episodes of Vathek. Ed. Kenneth Graham. 2001
Graham, Kenneth W. 'An Introduction to the Broadview edition of *Vathek with the Episodes of Vathek*.' *Beckford Journal* 7 (2001): 11–18.

Jack, Malcolm. 'Deconstructing the Caliph.' *Beckford Journal* 8 (2002): 41–43.

Jack, Malcolm. *Eighteenth-Century Fiction* 15 no. 1 (Oct 2002): 157–160. With a review of Sophia Lee, *The Recess; or, A Tale of Other Times* (1785).

Vathek et ses épisodes. Ed. & postface Didier Girard. 2003
Delon, Michel. 'Vathek au complet.' *La Quinzaine littéraire*, no. 852, 16 April 2003. With a review of Girard, ed., *L'esplendente et autres contes inédits* (2003).

Shaffer, Elinor. 'Composing and decomposing the corpus of William Beckford: French and English Beckford.' *Comparative Criticism* 25 (2003): 255–265. With reviews of Graham, ed., *Vathek* (2001), Mowl, *William Beckford* (1998) & Ostergard, ed., *William*

Beckford 1760–1844: An Eye for the Magnificent (exhibition catalogue, 2001).

Full-length Studies
See also 'Full-length Studies' in Sections 1 and 15

Benrahhal-Serghini, El-Habib. *The Road to Istakhar: A Critical Study of the Text and Context of William Beckford's "Vathek" and the "Episodes" 1760–1844*. Ann Arbor, Michigan: University Microfilms, 1995. 354 pp. PhD thesis for Universitaire Instelling Antwerpen. *Dissertation Abstracts International* 55 no. 9 (March 1995): 2839A.

Graham, Kenneth W., ed. *Vathek & The Escape from Time. Bicentenary Revaluations*. New York: AMS Press, 1990. xiv, 277 pp. 2 pl. 23½ cm. 13 essays on aspects of *Vathek*, celebrating the bicentenary of publication. See below under Baridon, Craig, Fothergill, Frank, Gill, Graham, Hyland, Klein, Maynard, Pires, Svilpis, Varma, and see '17. Bibliographies' under Frank.

REVIEW. Botting, Fred. *British Journal for Eighteenth-Century Studies* 14 no. 2 (Autumn 1991): 205–207 at 205–206. With a review of Manuel Aguirre, *The Closed Space: Horror Literature and Western Symbolism* (1990).

COMMENTARIES ON *VATHEK*

For Lord Byron see '4. Contemporaries'

Books
Allen, Walter. *The English Novel*. London: Phoenix House, 1954. Pp. 85, 86–87.
Arnold, Thomas W. *The Caliphate*. Oxford: Clarendon Press, 1924. Caliph Wāthiq bi'llāhi Ibrāhīm, 99–100.
Baker, Ernest A. 'The Oriental Story from *Rasselas* to *Vathek*.' In *The History of the English Novel * * * * * The Novel of Sentiment and the Gothic Romance*: 5 (1934): 55–76 at 60, 70–76. 10 vols. London: Witherby, 1924–1939. Also 60, 153, 225, 232 and 'Select Reading', 258, 259.
Baldensperger, Philippe Jules Fernand. *Orientations étrangères chez Honoré de Balzac*. Paris: Honoré Champion, 1927. P. 29.
Ballaster, Rosalind. *Fabulous Orients: Fictions of the East in England 1662–1785*. Oxford: Oxford University Press, 2005. *Vathek*, 24, 46, 74, 99, 229, 364, 365–370.
Balzac, Honoré de. *Pensées, sujets, fragmens*. Original ed. with preface and notes by Jacques Crépet. Paris: Blaizot, 1910. P. 26.

Baridon, Michel. *Edward Gibbon et le Mythe de Rome*. Paris: Champion, 1977. *Vathek*, 817 & n3. Alderman Beckford, 500.

Baridon, Michel. 'Vathek – Megalomaniac Caliph or Pundit of the Avant-Garde?' In *Vathek & The Escape from Time. Bicentenary Revaluations*, ed. Kenneth W. Graham, 73–95. New York: AMS Press, 1990.

Baugh, Albert, ed. *A Literary History of England*. London: Routledge & Kegan Paul, 1948. Book III. *The Restoration and Eighteenth Century (1660–1789)* by George Sherburn. Love of luxury stressed in *Vathek*, 975. Also 1030 (& n16)–1031. Book IV. *The Nineteenth Century and After (1789–1939)* by Samuel C. Chew. Elements of *Vathek* in Byron's *Manfred*, 1223. Eblis, 1124. Also 1155 n23.

Beaumarchais, Marie-Alice. 'Beckford William (1760–1844).' In *Dictionnaire des littératures de langue française*, ed. Jean-Pierre de Beaumarchais, Daniel Couty & Alain Rey, 1:223–224. 4 vols. Paris: Bordas, 1984.

Beer, Dorothee. 'Beckford, William.' In *Der Romanführer*, ed. Johannes Beer, 7 (1956): 8–9. 15 vols. Stuttgart: Hiersemann, 1950–1971.

Beers, Henry A. *A History of English Romanticism in the Eighteenth Century*. London: Kegan Paul, 1899. *Vathek* 'morbid and fantastic', 403 & 405n.

Belloc, Hilaire. 'On Vathek.' In *A Conversation with an Angel*, 86–93. London: Jonathan Cape, 1928. 'At any rate, one may call *Vathek* one of the most profoundly moral books of the world.', 92.

Benedict, Barbara M. *Curiosity. A Cultural History of Early Modern Inquiry*. Chicago: University of Chicago Press, 2001. 'Connoisseurship in the Mental Cabinet', 175–177. Also 21, 162.

Bennett, Arnold. *The Journal of Arnold Bennett*. New York: Garden City Publ., 1933. On 8 Nov 1904, *Vathek*: superb imagination, irony and style, 195.

Benrahhal-Serghini, El-Habib. 'William Beckford's Symbolic Appropriation of the Oriental Context.' In *Oriental Prospects: Western Literature and the Lure of the East*, ed. C. C. Barfoot & Theo D'haen, 43–64. Amsterdam: Rodopi, 1998. Also 66, 67. DQR Studies in Literature 22.

Birkhead, Edith. 'The Oriental Tale of Terror. Beckford.' In *The Tale of Terror. A Study of the Gothic Romance*, 94–99. London: Constable, 1921. Also 118, 215–216.

Blackstone, Bernard. *The Lost Travellers. A Romantic Theme with Variations*. London: Longmans, 1962. Vathek, 'earthly paradise', x. Shelley imitated Johnson & Beckford, 228. Also 21, 39, 40.

Bleiler, E. F. 'William Beckford.' In *The Penguin Encyclopedia of Horror and the Supernatural*, ed. Jack Sullivan. New York: Viking, 1986.

Bloom, Harold, ed. 'William Beckford.' In *Classic Fantasy Writers*, 14–26. New York: Chelsea House, 1994. Introduction; extracts about *Vathek* from Byron (1812), Redding (1844), Lafcadio Hearn (1927), Lovecraft

(1927), Borges (1943), Boyd Alexander (1960), Kenneth Graham (1972), Robert Gemmett (1975), R. D. Stock (1982), R. B. Gill (1990); List of Beckford's works.

Borges, Jorge Luis. 'About William Beckford's *Vathek.*' (Buenos Aires, 1943.) In *Other Inquisitions 1937–1952*, 137–140. Trans. Ruth L. C. Simms. Austin: University of Texas, 1964. Beckford's fame rests 'on the final ten pages' of *Vathek*, 138. Also in *Selected Non-Fictions*, New York: Viking, 1999 & *The Total Library: Non-Fiction 1922–1986*, London: Allen Lane, 2000, pp. 266–269. Both ed. Eliot Weinberger.

Borges, Jorge Luis. 'William Beckford: Vathek.' In *Biblioteca personal*, 106–108. Madrid: Alianza, 1988. His foreword to *Vathek*.

Botting, Fred. *Gothic*. London & New York: Routledge, 1966. Also paperback.

Bousquet, Jacques. *Les Thèmes du Rêve dans la Littérature Romantique (France, Angleterre, Allemagne)*. Paris: Didier, 1964. Pp. 269–270.

Brown, Marshall. *The Gothic Text*. Stanford, CA: Stanford University Press, 2005. *Vathek* mentioned, 2, 96.

Butler, Marilyn. *Romantics, Rebels and Reactionaries. English Literature and its Background 1760–1830*. Oxford: Oxford University Press, 1981. *Vathek*, 27, 28, 29, 175.

Cannon, Peter. 'The Influence of *Vathek* on H. P. Lovecraft's *The Dream-Quest of Unknown Kadath.*' In *H. P. Lovecraft: Four Decades of Criticism*, ed. S. T. Joshi, 153–157. Athens, Ohio: Ohio University Press, 1980.

Carnochan, W. B. 'Which Way I Fly.' In *Confinement and Flight: An essay on English Literature of the Eighteenth Century*, 102–146 at 135–142. Berkeley: University of California Press, 1977. Christmas 1781 house party the inspiration for the Hall of Eblis. Eblis mentioned, 21, 103, 119. Also 18.

Cavaliero, Glen. *The Supernatural and English Fiction*. Oxford: Oxford University Press, 1995. Reasons for excluding *Vathek*, vii. 'Gusty relish for the macabre' in *Vathek*, 46.

Cawthorn, James & Michael Moorcock, eds. 'William Beckford Vathek.' In *Fantasy: The 100 Best Books*, 15–16. London: Xanadu, 1988. Summary of *Vathek* with comments justifying its inclusion.

Cazamian, Madeleine L. *Le Roman et les Idées en Angleterre*. 3 vols. Paris: Société d'éditions. Les belles lettres, 1923–1955. 3:75.

Church, Richard. *The Growth of the English Novel*. London: Methuen, 1951. *Vathek* dismissed, 107–109. Also 31.

Claésson, Dick. 'Paul-Henri Mallet and the critical reception of William Beckford's *Vathek* (1786).' In *Gudar på jorden. Festskrift till Lars Lönnroth*, ed. Stina Hansson & Mats Malm, 241–250. Brutus Östlings Bokförlag Symposion: Stockholm/Stehag, 2000. Swiss historian Mallet's 'verses on *Vathek* may well be the earliest critical commentary on William Beckford's (1760–1844) short Oriental tale.', 241.

Clarac, Pierre, ed. *Dictionnaire universel des lettres.* Laffont-Bompiani. Paris: Société d'édition de dictionnaires et encyclopédies, 1961. 'Beckford', 73. 'Vathek', 895.

Colvin, Sidney. *John Keats: His Life and Poetry. His Friends, Critics and After-fame.* London: Macmillan, 1917. *Vathek* among Keats's familiar reading, 184.

Conant, Martha Pike. *The Oriental Tale in England in the Eighteenth Century.* New York: Columbia University Press, 1908. *Vathek* as a dream, 61–71. *Mogul Tales*, 37–41 Also xv, xvii, xxvi, 43n, 229–230, 248, 251–252, 288–289. Reprinted, New York: Octagon Books, 1966.

Conrad, Joseph. *The Collected Letters of Joseph Conrad.* 7 vols. Cambridge: Cambridge University Press, 1983–2005. Ed. Frederick R. Karl & Laurence Davies. To R. B. Cunninghame Graham on 26 Feb 1899, 'I've read Vathek at once. C'est très bien. What an infernal imagination!', 2 (1986): 171–172 & nn2, 1. To Valéry Larbaud on 2 Dec 1913 in which Larbaud's 'diary', *A. O. Barnabooth* (1913), makes Conrad think of Beckford, 5 (1996): 309 & n3.

Cornwell, Neil. *The Literary Fantastic: From Gothic to Postmodernism.* New York: Harvester Wheatsheaf, 1990. *Vathek* belongs to literature of exotica, 49. Beckford influenced Mary Shelley, 65.

Coyle, Martin, et al., eds. *Encyclopedia of Literature and Criticism.* London: Routledge, 1990. 'Asian gothic *Vathek*', 1048.

Cross, Wilbur L. *The Development of the English Novel.* New York: Macmillan, 1899. Beckford: 'grander whims than Walpole', 103–104.

Daiches, David. *A Critical History of English Literature.* 4 vols. London: Secker & Warburg, 1960. 3:741.

Dawson, William James. *The Makers of English Fiction.* (Vol. 3 of *Makers of Modern English*). London: Hodder & Stoughton, 1905. Ch. III. 'From Fielding to Jane Austen.' *Vathek*, 26–28. It 'is intellectually impressive'.

Dédéyan, Charles. 'Beckford et son *Vathek*.' In *Le thème de Faust dans la littérature européenne*, vol. 2 (1955), *Le Préromanticisme*, 2:211–234. 4 vols. Paris: Lettres Modernes, 1954–1961.

Demata, Massimiliano. 'Discovering Eastern Horrors: Beckford, Maturin, and the Discourse of Travel Literature. In *Empire and the Gothic: The Politics of Genre*, ed. Andrew Smith & William Hughes, 13–24 & 31–33 nn1–23. Basingstoke: Palgrave Macmillan, 2003. Also 3, 6, 220–221, 222, 224.

Dendy, Walter Cooper. *The Philosophy of Mystery.* London: Longmans, etc, 1841. 'What a treasury of secrets . . . from the tales of Arabia to *Vatheck*', 5.

De Ricci, Seymour. *The Book Collector's Guide.* Philadelphia: Rosenbach, 1921. Prices for *Vathek* (1786), 41.

DeVoto, Bernard. 'Witchcraft in Mississippi.' *Saturday Review of Literature*

15 (31 Oct 1936): 14. William Faulkner's *Absalom, Absalom!* 'has link-ages with Eblis'.

Digeon, Aurelien. *Le roman anglais au dix-huitième siècle*. Paris: Henri Didier, [1940]. P. 75.

Douglass, Paul. *Lady Caroline Lamb. A Biography*. New York: Palgrave Macmillan, 2004. *Ada Reis* a weak imitation of *Vathek*, 252. Also 106.

Drabble, Margaret, ed. *The Oxford Companion to English Literature*. 6th ed. Oxford: Oxford University Press, 2000. (1st ed. 1932.) 'Beckford, William', 79. 'Gothic Revival', 421. 'Oriental Novel', 745. '*Vathek*', 1054. Abridged as *The Concise Oxford Companion to English Literature*, ed. Margaret Drabble & Jenny Stringer, Oxford: Oxford University Press, 1987. 'Beckford, William', 44. 'Gothic Novel', 232. 'Gothic Revival', 233.

Duffy, Maureen. *The Erotic World of Faery*. London: Sphere, 1989. (1st ed. 1972.) 'The Magic Carpet', 246–248.

Dufrenoy, Marie-Louise. *L'Orient Romanesque en France, 1704–1789*. 2 vols. Montreal: Beauchemin, 1946–1947. 1:55, 153, 322. 2:225–226. Vol. 3. Amsterdam: Rodopi, 1975. 3:259–266.

Dunlap, William. *Diary of William Dunlap*. Ed. Dorothy C. Barck. New York: Blom, 1969. (1st ed. 1930.) Read *Vathek* on 2 Feb 1833 and admired it, 653.

Duperray, Max. 'Héros gothique et figure grotesque: Beckford et son Calife.' In *Le Roman noir anglais dit gothique*, ed. Max Duperray, 139–145. Paris: Ellipses, 2000.

Elton, Oliver. *A Survey of English Literature 1780–1830*. 2 Vols. London: Edward Arnold, 1912. 'The Novel of Suspense', 1:202–226 at 206–209, 435–436nn. Also 1:4, 11, 17, 172, 173, 175, 185, 221, 419, 456n & 2:274, 367.

Ernle, Lord Rowland Edmund Prothero. *The Light Reading of Our Ances-tors: Chapters in the Growth of the English Novel*. London: Hutchinson, [1927]. *Vathek* 'the most famous Oriental tale in the English language', 292–293. *The Elegant Enthusiast* (i.e. *Modern Novel Writing*, 1796 [?1795]), 253 and Arabella Bloomville, 271.

Fairchild, Hoxie Neale. *The Romantic Quest*. New York: Russell, 1965. (1st ed. 1931.) *Vathek* transported the novel of terror to an oriental setting, 268.

Feldman, Paula & Diana Scott-Kilvert. *The Journals of Mary Shelley*. Oxford: Clarendon Press, 1987. Caliph *Vathek* in 'Reading List. 1815', 90 & n2.

Filteau, Claude. *Le Statut Narratif de la Transgression. Essais sur Hamilton* [author of *Memoirs of Count of Grammont*] *et Beckford*. Quebec: Naaman, 1981. 'Le pacte faustien et la production de l'effet-sujet', 149ff. 'L'occultisme dans *Vathek* et l'effet de fantastique', 189ff.

Fisher, Benjamin F. ' "To Distinguish Between One That Translates and One That Invents": Some Recondite Beckford Legacies.' In *Fictions of Unease: The Gothic from Otranto to The X-Files*, ed. Andrew Smith et al., 43–57. Bath: Sulis Press, 2002. Beckford's critical reception in the nineteenth and early twentieth centuries.

Flaubert, Gustave. *Correspondance*. New ed. 7th series (1873–1876). Paris: Conard, 1930. Told his niece Caroline on 17 June 1876 that he had been given Mallarmé's edition of *Vathek*, 302. To Turgenev on 25 June 1876, remarking of *Vathek*, "c'est drôle", 313.

Fletcher, Robert Pearson. *The Convention of the Double-Self in Nineteenth-Century English Fiction*. PhD thesis for University of Delaware, 1976. *Dissertation Abstracts International* 37 no. 4 (Oct 1976): 2195A. Idea of doppelganger used as vehicle for character portrayal.

Foster, James R. *History of the Pre-Romantic Novel in England*. New York: Modern Languages Association of America, 1949. 'William Beckford's Faust-like pseudo-oriental romance', 190. Monograph Series No. 17.

Fothergill, Brian. 'The Influence of Landscape and Architecture on the Composition of *Vathek*.' In *Vathek & The Escape from Time. Bicentenary Revaluations*, ed. Kenneth W. Graham, 33–47. New York: AMS Press, 1990.

Fox, Henry Edward. *The Journal of the Hon. Henry Edward Fox (afterwards fourth and last Lord Holland) 1818–1830*. Ed. the Earl of Ilchester. London: Thornton Butterworth, 1923. Entry for 12 Nov 1827 doubting that Beckford could write in French, 240.

Frank, Frederick S. 'William Beckford's *Vathek: An Arabian Tale*.' In *Survey of Modern Fantasy Literature*, ed Frank N. Magill, 2023–2027. 5 vols. Englewood Cliffs, NJ: Salem Press, 1983.

Frank, Frederick S. 'The Gothic *Vathek*: The Problem of Genre Resolved.' In *Vathek & The Escape from Time. Bicentenary Revaluations*, ed. Kenneth W. Graham, 157–172. New York: AMS Press, 1990.

Franklin, Michael. 'Beckford, William (1760–1844).' In *The Handbook to Gothic Literature*, ed. Marie Mulvey-Roberts, 20–23. Basingstoke: Macmillan, 1998. Also Vathek, 42–43. Gothic Revival, Fonthill, 91, 93–94. Graveyard School, 107. Imagination, 134. Madness, 153. Orientalism, 170. Edgar Allan Poe, 173. Ann Radcliffe, 183. Mary Shelley, 214.

Garber, Frederick. 'Meaning and Mode in Gothic Fiction.' In *Racism in the Eighteenth Century*, ed. Harold E. Pagliaro, 155–170 at 162, 164–166. Cleveland & London: Case Western Reserve University Press, 1973. Studies in Eighteenth-Century Culture, vol. 3.

Garnett, Richard. 'Beckford's "Vathek".' In *Essays of An Ex-Librarian*, 163–193. London: Heinemann, 1901. Reprint of the preface to his 1893 ed. of *Vathek*. One of twelve essays.

Garzanti, publ. 'Beckford, William.' In *Encyclopédie de la littérature*, 137.

Paris: Société d'edition de dictionnaires et encyclopédies, 2003. 'Gothique (roman)', 626. 'Roman', 1381. Trans. from the Italian ed., 1997.

Giddey, Ernest. 'La Vision créatrice de *Vathek* de Beckford.' In *Mélanges offerts à Monsieur Georges Bonnard*, 43–56. Geneva: Droz, 1966. Université de Lausanne, Publications de la Faculté des Lettres, XVIII.

Giles, Herbert A. *A History of Chinese Literature*. London: Heinemann, 1901. Recent publication of *Vathek* in Chinese, 429.

Gilfillan, George. *Gallery of Literary Portraits*. 1st series. Edinburgh: William Tait, 1845. 'William Godwin', wants 'the oriental gusto and gorgeousness of Beckford', 20. 'Robert Southey', Beckford among authors drawn to the East, 425. Essays reprinted from the *Dumfries Herald*.

Gill, R. B. 'The Enlightened Occultist: Beckford's Presence in *Vathek*.' In *Vathek & The Escape from Time. Bicentenary Revaluations*, ed. Kenneth W. Graham, 131–143. New York: AMS Press, 1990.

Girard, Didier. 'Exposure and Repentance in William Beckford's French Manuscripts.' In *William Beckford and the New Millennium*, ed. Kenneth W. Graham & Kevin Berland, 95–118. New York: AMS Press, 2004 [2005].

Gittings, Robert. 'Most Enormous Caf.' In *The Mask of Keats*, 100–107. London: Heinemann, 1956. Keats's *Hyperion* partly inspired by *Vathek*.

Gittings, Robert. *John Keats*. London: Heinemann, 1968. Keats's borrowings from 'Beckford's popular oriental tale, *Vathek*', 255–256.

Gordon, Lyndall. *Mary Wollstonecraft. A New Genus*. London: Little, Brown, 2005. *Vathek*, a 'private cult for same-sex lovers', 125. Also 387.

Graham, Kenneth W. *The Fiction of William Thomas Beckford of Fonthill*. 1967. M.Phil thesis for University College, London. *Aslib Index to Theses* 17 (1966–1967): 18.

Graham, Kenneth W. *William Beckford's 'Vathek': a critical edition*. 1971. PhD thesis for University College, London. *Aslib Index to Theses* 21 (1970–1971): 16.

Graham, Kenneth W. 'Perverse Interactions of the Gothic, Enlightened, and Oriental: William Beckford's *Vathek with The Episodes of Vathek*.' In *William Beckford and the New Millennium*, ed. Kenneth W. Graham & Kevin Berland, 119–130. New York: AMS Press, 2004 [2005].

Griffin, Gilderoy Wells. 'Vathek.' In *Studies in Literature*, 39–46. Baltimore: Turnbull, 1870. Beckford's life and *Vathek* outlined.

Haußler, Karl. 'William Beckford. Vathek.' In *Kindlers Neues Literatur Lexikon*, 2 (1989): 389–390. 22 vols. Munich: Kindler, 1988–1998.

Hennessy, Brendan. 'William Beckford: Vathek.' In *British Writers*, ed. Ian Scott-Kilvert, 3:327–329. New York: Scribner, 1980. Vol. 3, 'Daniel Defoe to the Gothic novel'. British Council, 7 vols., 1979–1984.

Henriot, Emile. "Beckford et 'Vathek'." In *XVIIIe siècle*, 2:217–224. 2 vols. Paris: La Renaissance du Livre, 1945.

Heppenstall, Rayner. 'The Palace of Subterranean Fire.' In *The Fourfold Tradition*, 78–89. London: Barrie & Rockliff, 1961. *Vathek* a small classic in English literature.

Herbelot, Barthélémy d'. *Bibliothèque Orientale, ou Dictionnarie Universel contenant généralement tout ce qui regarde la connoissance des peuples de l'Orient*. Paris, 1697. Sources for *Vathek*, 911–912.

Hopwood, Derek. *Sexual Encounters in the Middle East: the British, the French and the Arabs*. Reading: Ithaca Press, 1999. Beckford and *Vathek*, 21–22.

Hume, Robert D. 'Exuberant Gloom, Existential Agony, and Heroic Despair: Three Varieties of Negative Romanticism.' In *The Gothic Imagination: Essays in Dark Romanticism*, ed. G. R. Thompson, 109–127 at 113–117. Pullman: Washington State University Press, 1974. '*Vathek* is a distinctly puzzling work.' Also 109, 111, 112, 122, 124.

Irwin, Robert. *The Arabian Nights, A Companion*. London: Allen Lane, 1994. *Vathek* 'the first oriental tale to have any real and lasting literary worth', 245–255 & 323 nn10–11. Beckford drew heavily on Herbelot's *Bibliothèque Orientale*, 15. Also 264, 265, 277, 287.

Jacobs, Robert D. 'Poe in Richmond: The Double Image.' In *Southern Writers: Appraisals in Our Time*, ed. R. C. Simonini, Jr., 19–49 at 39 & n34, 41. Charlottesville: University of Virginia Press, 1964. Harsh review of *Vathek* in *Southern Literary Messenger*, although Byron admired it.

Jaloux, Edmond. *Johann-Heinrich Füssli*. Geneva: Cailler (pasted over Montreux: L'Aigle), 1942. *Vathek* compared to *Mille et Une Nuits* in chapter on Fuseli's depiction of Obéron, 144.

Jones, Frederick L., ed. *Mary Shelley's Journal*. 2 vols. Norman: University of Oklahoma Press, 1947. In 1815 the Shelleys read *Vathek*, 48, 219, 228.

Jones, Frederick L., ed. *The Letters of Percy Bysshe Shelley*. 2 vols. Oxford: Clarendon Press, 1965. 'Shelley's Reading', 1815, including *Vathek*, 469.

Jordan, John E., ed. *De Quincey as Critic*. London: Routledge & Kegan Paul, 1973. '*Vathek* is a monstrous chaos of absurdities', 29.

Joshi, S. T. *A Subtler Magick*. San Bernadino, CA: Borgo Press, 1996. Affirms the influence of Beckford and *Vathek* on the style and plot of Lovecraft's *The Dream Quest of Unknown Kadath*, 113.

Joshi, S. T. *H. P. Lovecraft: A Life*. West Warwick, RI: Necronomicon Press, 1996. *Vathek* cited in a list of Gothic novels in a background summary of supernatural literature prior to Lovecraft's career, 28; Beckford and the influence of *Vathek* on Lovecraft's fictional grimoire, *The Necronomicon*, and their influence on an unfinished project by Lovecraft, *Azathoth*, 285–286.

Jusserand, J. J. *Histoire abrégé de la littérature anglaise*. 3rd ed. Paris: Delagrave, 1921. 'Histoires orientales, merveilleuses et terribles comme celle du "Caliph Vathek" ', 209.

Keats, John. *The Letters of John Keats 1814–1821*. Ed. Hyder Edward Rollins. 2 vols. Cambridge: Cambridge University Press, 1958. To J. H. Reynolds: on 25 March 1818 about santons, who also appear in *Vathek*, 1:261 (& n1: Santon, 'A kind of dervish or priest, regarded as a saint'); on 13 July 1818, wanting to 'employ Caliph Vatheck' to kick a man at Burns's cottage, 1:324 & n4.

Keymer, Thomas & John Mee. *The Cambridge Companion to English Literature 1740–1830*. Cambridge: Cambridge University Press, 2004. *Vathek* 'signalled a momentous shift', 65. *Modern Novel Writing*, 126.

Kiely, Robert. 'Vathek.' In *The Romantic Novel in England*, 43–64 & 261–262 nn1–26. Cambridge, MA: Harvard University Press, 1972. Also 2, 22, 81, 100, 104, 147, 155, 172, 188, 191, 253.

Kilgour, Maggie. *The Rise of the Gothic Novel*. London: Routledge, 1995. *Vathek* 'a big baby, absorbed in his own voracious appetites', 33. '['Monk'] Lewis had inherited Beckford's position', 165. Also 41.

Klein, Jürgen. 'William Beckford (1760–1844): >Vathek<.' In *Der gotische Roman und die Ästhetik des Bösen*, 277–301 & nn19–122. Darmstadt: Wissenschaftliche Buchgesellschaft, 1975. Adapted as '*Vathek* and Decadence' in *Vathek & The Escape from Time. Bicentenary Revaluations*, ed. Kenneth W. Graham, 173–199. New York: AMS Press, 1990.

Knipp, Charles C. *Types of Orientalism in Eighteenth-Century England*. Ann Arbor, Michigan: University Microfilms, 1974. 346 pp. PhD thesis for University of California, Berkeley. *Dissertation Abstracts International* 35 no. 5 (Nov 1974): 2944A–2945A. *Vathek* 'an amoral Faustian tale full of romantic portents'.

Kroeber, Karl & William Walling, eds. *Images of Romanticism. Verbal and Visual Affinities*. New Haven: Yale University Press, 1978. Beckford's influence on John Martin, 222 & n21.

Lachman, Gary. *The Dedalus Book of the Occult: A Dark Muse*. Sawtry, Cambs: Dedalus, 2003. Beckford's life, *Vathek*, and his encounter with the French occultist Claude-Nicolas Ledoux, 35–39.

Larbaud, Valéry. *Ce vice impuni, la lecture. Domaine anglais*. Paris: 1925. Reprint of three articles. New ed., Paris: Gallimard, 1998.

Larbaud, Valéry & G. Jean-Aubry. *Correspondance 1920–1935*. Paris: Gallimard, 1971. With intro. and notes by Frida Weissman. Beckford & *Vathek*, passim.

Leask, Nigel. " 'Wandering through Eblis'; absorption and containment in romantic exoticism." In *Romanticism and Colonialism: Writing and Empire, 1780–1830*, ed. Tim Fulford & Peter J. Kitson, 165–188. Cambridge: Cambridge University Press, 1998. Title 'refers to Halls of Eblis' in *Vathek*, 165 n1. Loutherbourg's 'Egyptian Hall', 170–171 & nn15–16. Byron's praise for *Vathek* & Henley's notes, 180–181 & nn47–48. William Beckford of Somerley, 'the cousin of the author of

Vathek, was a historian who had lived in Jamaica for thirteen years',
96–98.

Leavis, Q. D. *Fiction and the Reading Public*. London: Chatto & Windus,
1932. *Vathek* one of the few of the 1300 or so novels reviewed by
Monthly Review and *Critical Review* between 1770 and 1800 to have
survived, 145.

Legouis, Emile. *A Short History of English Literature*. Trans. V. F. Boyson &
J. Coulson. Oxford: Clarendon Press, 1934. Beckford & *Vathek*, 267.

Legouis, Emile & Louis Cazamian. *A History of English Literature*. Rev. ed.
London: Dent, 1957. Influence on Moore's *Lalla Rookh*, 1067. Also 922
& n3, 939 n1.

Lévy, Maurice. *Le Roman "Gothique" Anglais 1764–1824*. Toulouse: Asso-
ciation des Publications de la faculté des lettres et sciences humaines de
Toulouse, 1968. *Vathek*, 167 n116, 251–252 & n189. *Modern Novel
Writing*, 484 & nn16–17. Fonthill, 119, 147. Also 500.

Le Yaouanc, Collette. 'Le thème sexuel dans *Vathek*.' In *Linguistique,
Civilisation, Littérature . . .*, ed. André Bordeaux, 257–264. Paris: Didier,
1980.

Lovecraft, H. P. *Supernatural Horror in Literature*. Foreword by August
Derleth. New York: Ben Abramson, 1945. Reprinted with new intro. by
E. F. Bleiler, New York: Dover, 1973. *Vathek* and the *Episodes* amongst
the material Lovecraft re-read in 1926 as research for *Supernatural
Horror in Literature* in his *Selected Letters, Vol. 2*, ed. August Derleth &
Donald Wandrei, Sauk City, WI: Arkham House, 1968. P. 36.

Lovecraft, H. P. 'Supernatural Horror in Literature.' In *Dagon and Other
Macabre Tales*, 141–221. London: Panther Books, 1969. *Vathek*
discussed and summarised in Ch. 5, 'The Aftermath of Gothic Fiction',
161–162.

Lowes, John Livingston. *The Road to Xanadu. A Study in the Ways of the
Imagination*. London: Constable, 1927. Coleridge may have read *Vathek*,
398–399. Also 252, 590.

Maggs, Barbara W. 'Asia.' In *Encyclopedia of the Enlightenment*, ed. Alan
Charles Kors, 1:85–90 at 86. 4 vols. Oxford: Oxford University Press,
2003. *Vathek* among a new genre, the Oriental tale. Also Barbara C.
Morden, 'Gothic', 2:141, Fonthill Abbey mentioned.

Magill, Frank N. *Cyclopedia of Literary Characters*. 2 vols. Englewood
Cliffs, NJ: Salem Press, 1963. 'Vathek', 2:1194. Outlines of Vathek,
Nouronihar, Carathis, the Giaour, Gulchenrouz & Emir Fakreddin. Rev.
ed. with similar outlines: A. J. Sobczak. 'Vathek: An Arabian Tale.' In
Cyclopedia of Literary Characters, 5:2051. 5 vols. Pasadena, CA: Salem
Press, 1998.

Makdisi, Saree. *Romantic Imperialism: Universal Empire and the Culture
of Modernity*. Cambridge: Cambridge University Press, 1998. The

'Orients of Beckford's *Vathek*', 147. *Vathek*, 'enormous weight of the notes', 206 n39.

Mallarmé, Stéphane. *Pages*. Brussels: Deman, 1891. Fragment of his preface to *Vathek*, 'Morceau pour résumer *Vathek*.'

Mallarmé, Stéphane. *Vers et prose. Morceaux chosis*. Paris: Librarie académique Didier Perrin, 1893.

Mallarmé, Stéphane. 'Morceau pour résumer *Vathek*.' & 'Beckford [Préface à *Vathek*].' in *Divagations* (Digressions), 61–63, 95–109. Paris: Bibliothèque Charpentier, 1922. (1st ed. 1897.)

Mallarmé, Stéphane. 'Préface à *Vathek*.' In *Œuvres completes*, ed. with notes by Henri Mondor & G. Jean-Aubry, 549–565. Paris: N. R. F. Bibliothèque de la Pléiade, 1945. Bibliographie, *Vathek*, 1327–1328 (in 1876 ed.), 1337–1338 (in 1893 ed.). Notes et Variantes. Préface à *Vathek* (1865), 1589–1595.

Mallarmé, Stéphane. *Correspondance*. 5 vols. Paris: Gallimard, 1959–1981. Vol. 2 (1965), letters mainly from 1875–1876 about his *Préface* to: Alponse Lemerre, 61 n2; Arthur O'Shaughnessy, 74 & n1, 79, 85 & n1, 96 & n1, 113, 117–119, 117 n3, 118 nn1–6, 120–121, 120 n3, 124–125, 124 nn1–2, 125 n1; Algernon Charles Swinburne, 99 & n2, 121; Marius Roux, 117 n2; Léon Valade, 126 n4; Mrs Sarah Helen Whitman, 144, 149; John Payne, 232 n1; Léo d'Orfer, 265 n2.

Maynard, Temple J. 'The Movement Underground and the Escape from Time in Beckford's Fiction.' In *Vathek & The Escape from Time. Bicentenary Revaluations*, ed. Kenneth W. Graham, 9–31. New York: AMS Press, 1990.

McCullogh, Bruce. *Representative English Novelists. Defoe to Conrad*. New York: Harper & Row, 1946. *Vathek* in Selected Reading List, 349.

Meester, Marie E. de. '*Vathek* and its Influence.' In *Oriental Influences in the English Literature of the Nineteenth Century*, 19–22. Heidelberg: Carl Winters, 1915. Also 2, 24, 34, 35.

Melville, Herman. *The Melville Log. A Documentary Life of Herman Melville 1819–1891*. 2 vols. New York: Harcourt Brace, 1951. On 20 Dec 1849 he bought Bentley's ed. of *Vathek* in London, 1:351.

Mérimée, Prosper. *Portraits historiques et littéraires*. Paris: Lécy frères, 1874. Vathek mentioned in article on Pushkin, 310.

Miles, Robert. *Gothic Writing 1750–1820*. London: Routledge, 1993. P. 44.

Moran, Leslie J. 'Law and the Gothic Imagination.' In *The Gothic*, ed. Fred Botting, 87–109 at 87 & n2. Cambridge: Brewer, 2001. Beckford's choice of 'Caliph'. Essays and Studies, n.s. 54, for the English Association.

Morley, Edith J., ed. *Henry Crabb Robinson on Books and their Writers*. 3 vols. London: Dent, 1938. 3–5 & 10 March 1816, read *Vathek*, 1:180 & n2–181. 10 June 1834, Read 'very interesting account of Beckford's travels in Italy' in *Quarterly Review . . . Vathek* to me one of the most odious books I ever laid eyes on', 1:443. 17 Sept 1836, 'I read Beckford's *Italy*.

This is a very pleasing volume', 2:504. 5 April 1837, 'To relieve the ennui of a very dull drive I read this afternoon Beckford's *Vathek* with renewed disgust' during an Italian tour with Wordsworth, 2:517–518. Robinson (1775–1867) kept a diary from 1811. Also *The Diary of Henry Crabb Robinson. An Abridgement*. Ed. & intro. Derek Hudson. London: Oxford University Press, 1967. All the above entries (except 17 Sept 1836), 43, 134, 167. (No references to Beckford when extracts from Robinson's diary were first publ. in 3 vols., 1869.)

Moussa-Mahmoud, Fatma. 'The Oriental Tale in England in the Early Nineteenth Century (1786–1824).' PhD thesis for London University, Westfield College, 1957. *Aslib Index to Theses* 8 (1957–1958): 11.

Muir, William. *The Caliphate. Its Rise, Decline and Fall*. London: Religious Tract Society, 1891. Motassim succeeded by his son Wâthic in AH 227 (842 AD), 515–518. Reprinted, London: Routledge, 2000.

Murray, James A. H., ed. *A New English Dictionary on Historical Principles . . . [The Oxford English Dictionary*.] 10 vols. Oxford: Clarendon Press, 1888–1928. Vol. 8 Part 2 (1914), ed. Henry Bradley: 'Sarsar' from the Arabic, a cold wind, first appeared in English in *Vathek* (1786, 207) as 'Sansar', 113. *Idem, Introduction, Supplement, and Bibliography*, 1933: 'A List of Books quoted in the Oxford English Dictionary', *Dreams* (1783), *Vathek* (1786), *Popular Tales of the Germans* (1791), *Italy* (1834) & *Recollections* (1835), 7.

Neill, S. Diana. *A Short History of the English Novel*. London: Jarrolds, [1951]. Pp. 85–89, 106.

Oliphant, Mrs [Margaret]. *The Literary History of England in the end of the Eighteenth Century and beginning of the Nineteenth Century*. London: Macmillan, 1882. Beckford and *Vathek*, 2:364–372.

Oliver, John W. Passages chosen from the 1782 MS. translation of *Vathek*, Henley's translation of June, 1786, the Lausanne edition of December 1786 and the Paris edition of July, 1787, to illustrate his lecture to the Edinburgh Bibliographical Society on 'The problems of Beckford's Vathek'. Edinburgh, 1957. Typescript in National Library of Scotland, Shelfmark 6.727.

Oueijan, Naji B. *Progress of an Image. The East in English Literature*. New York: Peter Lang, 1996. *Vathek* contributed to the popular awareness of the East; it exhibits both 'a visionary world and a concrete one', 52–58 & nn81–124. American University Studies. Series IV. English Language and Literature. Vol. 181.

Ousby, Ian. 'Beckford, William.' & 'Vathek.' In *The Cambridge Guide to Literature in English*, 74 & 1027. Cambridge: Cambridge University Press, 1988. *Vathek* mentioned in 'Gothic fiction', 405. New ed., 1993.

Paris: Bibliothèque Nationale. *Le Livre anglais. Trésor des collections anglaises*. Paris: Bibliothèque Nationale, 1951. P. 107.

Patterson, John Brown. *Discourses by the late Rev. John B. Patterson; to which is prefixed a memoir of his life and select literary and religious remains.* 2 vols. Edinburgh: Oliver & Boyd, 1837. Portrait frontis. Diary entry for 4 June 1823 giving his impressions on reading *Vathek*, 'a work of considerable genius . . . but destitute of any permanent sentiment of utility or comfort', 1:92.

    REVIEWS quoting this diary entry. [Johnstone, Christian.] *Tait's Edinburgh Magazine* n.s. 1 no. 4 (Feb 1837): 89–94 at 90.

    Gentleman's Magazine 7 n.s. (June 1837): 601–604 at 601, with a footnote by the editor defending *Vathek*, 'a work of Imagination'.

Phelps, Gilbert. 'Varieties of English Gothic.' In *From Blake to Byron*, ed. Boris Ford, 110–127 at 111 & 126. Harmondsworth, Middlesex, Penguin Books, 1982. *Vathek* 'in part an oriental tale' & has 'a cult following'. New Pelican Guide to English Literature, vol. 5. Not in 1st ed., 1957.

Piranesi. Focillon, Henri. *Giovanni-Battista Piranesi, 1720–1778.* Paris: Librarie Renouard, 1963. (1st ed. 1918.) Eblis, 301–302.

Pires, Maria Laura Bettencourt. '*Vathek* and Portugal.' In *Vathek & The Escape from Time. Bicentenary Revaluations*, ed. Kenneth W. Graham, 225–246. New York: AMS Press, 1990.

Pirie, David B. *The Penguin History of Literature. The Romantic Period.* London: Penguin, 1994. *Vathek* in bibliography, 488, & in table of dates, 496. *The Elegant Enthusiast* (i.e. *Modern Novel Writing*, 1796 [?1795]) mentioned, 96.

Poe, Edgar Allan. *Collected Works of Edgar Allan Poe.* Ed Thomas Ollive Mabbott. 3 vols. Cambridge, MA: Belknap Press of Harvard Univ. Press, 1968–1978. Vols. 2 & 3. Possible debt of Poe's infernal palace to *Vathek*, 32. *Vathek* was the name of a real caliph, 95 n12. Characters inscribed on cliff, 116 n15, 200 n10. H. B. Wallace's *Stanley* (1838) influenced by *Vathek*, 972, 1342 n14. Mrs. Gore's *Cecil* (1841) cribbed from Beckford, 1060 n10. Mentioned, 1266, 1284 n19.

Pope-Hennessy, Una. *Edgar Allan Poe 1809–1849. A Critical Biography.* London: Macmillan, 1934. Poe impressed by *Vathek*, 171.

Praz, Mario. *La Carne, La Morte e Il Diavolo. Nella Letteratura Romantica.* Milan: La Cultura, 1930. Eblis in *Vathek*, 83 n17, 191. *Dreams* & *Vathek*, 200. English trans. by Angus Davidson, *The Romantic Agony*, London: Oxford University Press, 1933, pp. 84 n24, 193, 201. 2nd rev. ed., 1951, pp. 86 n24, 211, 284 n16b (a new footnote about Beckford's exoticism, 14 lines).

Prickett, Stephen. 'Romantic Literature.' In *The Romantics*, ed. Stephen Prickett. 202–261 at 204, 205, 207. London: Methuen, 1981. Beckford wrote gothic novels & lived in a gothic palace. Context of English Literature Series.

Pringle, David, ed. 'Vathek.' In *The Ultimate Encyclopedia of Fantasy*, 218. London: Carlton, 1998. 'Caliph who sells his soul to Eblis (the Devil)'. Also 27.

Punter, David. *The Literature of Terror: A History of Gothic Fictions from 1765 to the present day*. London: Longman, 1980. *Vathek*, 50. Eblis, 98 n14, 232. Mary Shelley read work by Beckford, 121. *Nymph of the Fountain*, 163, 187 n4. Poe knew Beckford's works, 197. Fonthill Abbey, 8, 380.

Punter, David, ed. *A Companion to the Gothic*. Oxford: Blackwell, 2000. Pp. 5, 29, 45, 54 n4, 55 n8, 67 n7.

Punter, David & Glennis Byron. 'William Beckford (1760–1844).' & 'William Beckford. *Vathek* (1786).' In *The Gothic*, 87–88 & 181–184. Malden, MA: Blackwell, 2004. Herman Melville's *The Bell Tower* (1855) reminiscent of tower in *Vathek*, 151. Fonthill Abbey, 10.

Queneau, Raymond, ed. *Histoire des littératures*. 3 vols. Paris: Gallimard, 1955–1968. Vol. 2 (1968), *Littératures occidentals*. Pp. 440–441, 451. Vol. 3 (1958), *Littératures françaises, connexes et marginales*. P. 865.

Railo, Eino. *The Haunted Castle: A Study of the Elements of English Romanticism*. London: Routledge & Kegan Paul, 1927. *Vathek* aimed to evoke terror, 27–28 & 334–335 n38. Oriental tyrant, 37–38. Also passim. Reprinted, New York: Humanities Press, 1964.

Raleigh, Walter. *The English Novel*. London: John Murray, 1895. Pp. 250–251.

Reddin, Chitra Pershad. *Forms of Evil in the Gothic Novel*. New York: Arno Press, 1980. Beckford and *Vathek*, passim.

Reilly, Donald T. *The Interplay of Natural and Unnatural: A Definition of Gothic Romance*. Ann Arbor, Michigan: University Microfilms, 1970. 210 pp. Analyses of the Gothic novels of six authors, including Beckford. PhD thesis for University of Pittsburgh. *Dissertation Abstracts International* 31 no. 5 (Nov 1970): 2353A.

Revauger, Marie-Cécile. 'L'Unique et le multiple dans le *Vathek* de William Beckford: Folie du mimétisme.' In *Folie, Folies, Folly dans le Monde Anglo-Américaine aux XVIIe et XVIIIe Siècles*, 71–80. Aix-en-Provence: Université de Provence, 1984.

Ríos-Cordero, Hugo J. *Charting the Route: From Gothic to Magic Realism*. MA thesis for University of Puerto Rico, 2003. Walpole's *Castle of Otranto* compared to later Gothic novels, including *Vathek*. Elements of the supernatural reign supreme, 33, 63. 'Hyperbolic *Vathek*', 38–39. 'Labyrinthine halls of hell', 45–46. Borges considered *Vathek* the first uncanny story ever written, 108. Vathek portrayed as evil villain, 116, 125.

Robinson, Frank M. et al. *Art of Imagination: 20th Century Visions of Science Fiction, Horror, and Fantasy*. Portland, OR: Collectors Press, 2003.

Rudé, George. *Europe in the Eighteenth Century*. London: Weidenfeld & Nicolson, 1972. *Vathek* originally publ. in French, 144.

Sage, Victor, ed. *The Gothick Novel: A Casebook*. Basingstoke: Macmillan, 1990. Beckford and his works, 11, 14–15, 16, 17, 18, 21, 49–50.

Saglia, Diego. 'Orientalism.' In *A Companion to English Romanticism*, ed. Michael Ferber, 467–485 at 475. Malden, MA: Blackwell, 2005. *Vathek* 'one of the great intercultural texts of European Romantic Orientalism'.

Saintsbury, George. *The English Novel*. London: Dent, 1913. Pp. 158–159.

Saintsbury, George. *The Peace of the Augustans*. London: Bell, 1916. Pp. 171–172.

Saunders, Frederick. *The Story of some Famous Books*. London: Elliot Stock, 1887. Brief background to Beckford and *Vathek*, 124–125. H. B. Wheatley's 'The Book-Lover's Library'.

Sedgwick, Eve Kosofsky. *The Coherence of Gothic Conventions*. Rev. ed. New York: Arno Press, 1980. *Vathek* 'an Oriental tale with some strong Gothic influences', 19–20 & n110. Also 47, 154. Gothic Studies & Dissertations.

Shaffer, E. S. *'Kubla Khan' and The Fall of Jerusalem. The Mythological School in Biblical Criticism and Secular Literature 1770–1880*. Cambridge: Cambridge University Press, 1975. *Vathek's* Mohammedan and Hindu settings, 115–116, 330 nn50–55. '. . . in *Vathek* the familiar motifs are printed in the negative'.

Shaffer, E. S. 'Milton's Hell: William Beckford's place in the graphic and literary tradition.' In *Milton, the Metaphysicals and Romanticism*, ed. Lisa Low & Anthony John Harding, 65–83. Cambridge: Cambridge University Press, 1994.

Sharafuddin, Mohammed. 'Beckford's *Vathek*.' In *Islam and Romantic Orientalism: Literary Encounters with the Orient*, xxxi–xxxiv. London: I. B. Tauris, 1994. Also viii, xviii, 16, 22, 45, 49, 62, 67, 71, 132, 133, 134, 194, 197, 202, 216, 222.

REVIEW. Jack, Malcolm. 'Arabian tales.' *Times Literary Supplement*, 3 Feb 1995, 11.

Skilton, David. *Defoe to the Victorians*. Harmondsworth, Middlesex: Penguin Books, 1977. Pp. 66, 70.

Smeed, J. W. *Faust in Literature*. London: Oxford University Press, 1975. *Vathek* linked with the Faust legend, 225.

Smith, Warren Hunting. *Architecture in English Fiction*. New Haven: Yale University Press, 1934. '*Vathek* was suggested by the Egyptian hall of Beckford's paternal mansion', 42–47, 157–158. Also 3, 9, 18, 22, 23, 28, 31, 163, 189, 214. Two linocuts based on NW view & Hall in Rutter's *Delineations* (1823), frontis. & facing 44. Yale Studies in English, vol. 83.

Spark, Muriel. *Child of Light: A Reassessment of Mary Wollstonecraft Shelley*. Hadleigh, Essex: Tower Bridge Publ., 1951. By contrast with *Vathek*, 'Mary Shelley's narrative style reads like a scientific treatise . . .', 141.

Spector, Robert Donald. 'The Gothic.' In *Encyclopedia of Literature and Criticism*, ed. Martin Coyle et al., 1044–1054 at 1048. London: Routledge, 1990. Beckford's 'Asian gothic *Vathek*'.

Stableford, Brian. 'Beckford, William.' In *St. James Guide to Horror, Gothic, & Ghost Writers*, ed. David Pringle, 39–40. Detroit: St. James Press, 1998.

Stapleton, Michael. 'Beckford, William.' & '*Vathek. An Arabian Tale.*' In *The Cambridge Guide to English Literature*, 60 & 915. Cambridge: Cambridge University Press, 1983.

Steeves, Harrison R. 'Oriental Romance (Johnson and Beckford).' In *Before Jane Austen: The Shaping of the English Novel in the Eighteenth Century*, 226–242 at 233–242. New York: Holt, Rinehart & Winston, 1965. '*Vathek* must be seen, then, as the product of an unquiet mind under strong mental and emotional stimulation.', 234.

Stevenson, Lionel. *The English Novel*. Boston, MA: Houghton Mifflin, 1960. Survey of Gothic fiction, 156–157, 166, 177, 207, 343, 503, 521.

Stock, R. D. 'Spiritual Horror in the Novel: Richardson, Radcliffe, Beckford, Lewis.' In *The Holy and Daemonic from Sir Thomas Browne to William Blake*, 259–313 at 291–300. Princeton: Princeton University Press, 1982. Also 261, 262, 263, 305.

Sultana, Donald. *Benjamin Disraeli in Spain, Malta and Albania 1830–32*. London: Tamesis Books, 1976. *Vathek*, 4, 6, 54, 56. Portugal, 20.

Sutherland, John. 'The Novel.' In *A Companion to Romanticism*, ed. Duncan Wu, 333–344 at 335. Malden, MA: Blackwell, 1998. Exotic setting of *Vathek*.

Svilpis, J. E. 'Orientalism, Fantasy, and *Vathek*.' In *Vathek & The Escape from Time. Bicentenary Revaluations*, ed. Kenneth W. Graham, 49–72. New York: AMS Press, 1990.

Swinburne, Algernon Charles. *The Swinburne Letters*. Ed. Cecil Y. Lang. 6 vols. New Haven: Yale University Press, 1959–1962. To Stéphane Mallarmé on 9 June 1876, thanking him for sending his ed. of *Vathek*, 6:276–277.

Swoyer, Ardeth Grace. *Matthew Gregory Lewis and His Contributions to the Gothic Novel*. MA thesis for University of Virginia, 1944. More sensation and horror in Lewis than in the writings of Walpole, Beckford, Mrs. Radcliffe.

Tinkler-Villani, Valeria, et al., eds. *Exhibited by Candlelight: Sources and Developments in the Gothic Tradition*. Amsterdam: Atlanta, 1995. Reasons why *Vathek*, 'successful as a "wild tale" ', was omitted from the studies, 1–2. Studies in Literature 16.

Todorov, Tzvetan. *Introduction à la littérature fantastique*. Paris: Éditions du Seuil, 1970. Supernatural, 82–83, 88. Homosexuality, 138–139, 140. Trans. as *The Fantastic: A Structural Approach to a Literary Genre*. Ithaca, NY: Cornell University Press, 1975. Pp. 77–79, 83, 131, 132–133.

Tomasi di Lampedusa, Giuseppe. *Letteratura Inglese*. Vol. 2. *L'Ottocento e il Novecento*. Milan: Arnoldo Mondadori, 1991. *Vathek*: Byron, 70; shorter novels, 117–118; novel of terror, 468.

Tuckerman, Bayard. *A History of English Prose Fiction from Sir Thomas Malory to George Eliot*. New York: G. P. Putnam's Sons, 1882. 'The descriptions of the Caliph and of the Hall of Eblis are full of power', 807.

Varma, Devendra P. *The Gothic Flame. Being a History of the Gothic Novel in England: Its Origins, Efflorescence, Disintegration, and Residuary Influences*. London: Arthur Barker, 1957. '*Vathek* not only a pseudo-Oriental tale', 132–135. It survives as a 'classic', vii. 'Pseudo-gothic style', 24. 'Wild fantasy', 37. 'Extravagant incidents and luxuriant descriptions', 52. 'Morbid and fantastic creations', 131. 'Keats knew *Vathek*', 196. 'Oriental and exotic horror', 206. 'Eblis, ruler of the realm of despair', 216. Bibliography, 245–259. Reissued with 'Acknowledgements' (unavailable for 1st ed.), [v–vi]: New York: Russell & Russell, 1966, & Metuchen, NJ: Scarecrow Press, 1987.

Varma, Devendra P. 'William Beckford.' In *Supernatural Fiction Writers. Fantasy and Horror*, ed. E. F. Bleiler, 1:139–144. 2 vols. New York: Scribner, 1985.

Varma, Devendra P. 'Beckford Treasures Rediscovered; Mystic Glow of Persian Sufism in *Vathek*.' In *Vathek & The Escape from Time. Bicentenary Revaluations*, ed. Kenneth W. Graham, 97–111. New York: AMS Press, 1990.

Verona, Elisabetta. *Vathek di William Beckford: un analisi*. Thesis for Instituto Universitario di Lingue Moderne, Milan, 1991.

Viatte, Auguste. *Les sources occultes du romantisme: illuminisme-théosophie, 1770–1820*. 2 vols. Vol. 1, Le préromanticisme. Paris: Librarie ancienne Honoré Champion, 1928. P. 42 & n5

Voller, Jack. 'William Beckford.' In *Gothic Writers: A Critical and Bibliographical Guide*, ed. Douglass H. Thomson, Jack G. Voller & Frederick S. Frank, 53–59. Westport, CT: Greenwood Press, 2002.

Wagenknecht, Edward Charles. '*Vathek* and the Oriental Tale.' In *Cavalcade of the English Novel. From Elizabeth to George VI*. New York: Henry Holt, 1943. Outline of Gothic currents, 110–133.

Ward, Aileen. *John Keats: The Making of a Poet*. London: Secker & Warburg, 1963. Keats read *Vathek*, one of the 'thrillers popular with schoolboys', 18.

Weber, Henry W. *Tales of the East.* 3 vols. Edinburgh, John Ballantyne et al., 1812. The 'sublime tale of the Caliph Vathek, which could not be inserted without invading the rights of literary property', 1:lxii.

Weiss, Frederic Norman. *Satirical Elements in Early Gothic Novels.* PhD thesis for the University of Pennsylvania, 1975. *Dissertation Abstracts International* 36 no. 5 (Nov 1975): 2860A–2861A. *Vathek* example of a popular genre.

Wheeler, William A. *A Dictionary of Noted Names of Fiction.* New ed. London: George Bell, 1889. (1st ed. 1852.) Carathis, 67. Eblis, 112. Vathek, 379. Bohn's Reference Library.

White, Newman Ivey. *Shelley.* 2 vols. New York: Knopf, 1940. *Caliph Vathek* in 'List of books read in 1815' by Shelley as well as Mary, 2:541.

Widdowson, Peter. *The Palgrave Guide to English Literature and its Contexts, 1500–2000.* Basingstoke: Palgrave Macmillan, 2004. Under 1786: *Vathek,* 'Gothic fantasy; unauthorised Eng. edtn', 82.

Winter, William. *The Wallet of Time.* 2 vols. New York: Moffat, Yard, 1913. *The Darling of the Gods* (1902), play compared with *Vathek,* 2:252. *Vathek* one of the 'great representative novels of the English language', 2:270.

Wittmann, Anna M. 'Gothic *Trivialliteratur*: From Popular Gothicism to Romanticism.' In *European Romanticism. Literary Cross-Currents, Modes, and Models,* ed. Gerhart Hoffmeister, 59–75 at 65, 73, 74 n21. Detroit: Wayne State University Press, 1990. *Vathek* a 'bizarrely original work'.

Womersley, David, ed. *A Companion to Literature from Milton to Blake.* Oxford: Blackwell, 2000. *Vathek* & *Castle of Otranto,* 557.

Woolf, Virginia. *Virginia Woolf & Lytton Strachey. Letters.* Ed. Leonard Woolf & James Strachey. London: Hogarth Press & Chatto & Windus, 1956. Lytton Strachey to Virginia Woolf on 24 Aug 1908: he had been reading *Vathek,* 16. Also on 23 Aug 1921, asking if she had read *Memoirs of Painters,* 93.

Wright, Walter Francis. 'Beckford's "Vathek".' In *Sensibility in English Prose Fiction 1760–1814. A Reinterpretation,* 115–117 & nn1–3. Urbana: University of Illinois, 1937. A general outline of *Vathek.* Also 123–124, 150, 153. Illinois Studies in Language and Literature, vol. 22, nos. 3–4.

Wynne-Davies, Marion, ed. *Bloomsbury Guide to English Literature.* London: Bloomsbury, 1989. 'Beckford, William', 346. 'Gothic Novel', *Vathek,* 567. Publ. in America as *Prentice Hall Guide to English Literature,* New York: Prentice Hall, 1990.

Zeidler, Karl. *Beckford, Hope und Morier als Vertreter des orientalishcen Romans.* Königsee I, Thür: Selmar v. Ende, 1908. 77 pp. *Vathek,* 2–29. Inaugural dissertation for his doctorate at Leipzig University.

Articles

Adams, Percy G. 'The Anti-Hero in Eighteenth-Century Fiction.' *Studies in the Literary Imagination* 9 (Spring 1976): 29–51 at 38–39. Male protagonists 'who end in hell, as in Beckford's Vathek (1787)'.

Alamoudi, Carmen. 'Un Sourire déchiré: l'ironie dans le *Vathek* de Beckford.' (A lacerating smile.) *Eighteenth-Century Fiction* 8 (April 1996): 401–414.

Alamoudi, Carmen Fernandez. '*Vathek*: le choix d'une écriture cursive et piquante.' *Eighteenth-Century Fiction* 15 no. 1 (Oct 2002): 1–17.

Baker, Kenneth. 'True confessions.' *Daily Telegraph – Arts & Books*, 16 April 1994, 10. Reproduced in *Beckford Journal* 1 (1995): 4. He had not read *Vathek*, but thought that Beckford was 'possibly more interesting'.

Baridon, Michel. 'La Modernité de Beckford.' In *Cahiers Charles V. 9. Le Passé Présent*, 19–40. Paris: Centre National des Lettres: 1988.

Baxter, Kenneth. 'A terrible eye for evil.' *The Independent*, 9 Oct 1993, 29.

Bloom, Margaret. 'William Beckford's *Vathek*.' *University of California Chronicle* 33 (Oct 1931): 424–431.

Bonner, Sherwood. *Memphis Daily Avalanche*, 26 Dec 1875, 2; 26 March 1876, 1. Letters from Massachusetts & Europe about Beckford and *Vathek*.

Brown, Wallace Cable. 'Thomas Moore and English Travel Books about the Near East.' *Studies in Philology* 34 (Oct 1937): 576–588 at 588. Moore identified himself with the group of English writers beginning with Beckford.

Brown, Wallace Cable. 'Prose Fiction and English Interest in the Near East, 1775–1825.' *Publications of the Modern Language Association of America* 53 (Sept 1938): 827–836 at 828–829. '*Vathek* (1786), generally recognised as the best English imitation of a genuine eastern tale'.

Bruneau, Jean. 'Madame de Genlis, William Beckford, et *Vathek*.' *Nineteenth-Century French Studies* 5 (1976–1977): 34–38.

Carter, John. 'The Lausanne Edition of Beckford's *Vathek*.' *The Library* 4th Series 17 no. 4 (March 1937): 369–394. Discusses the publishing history of *Vathek* and the relative dates of the Lausanne and Paris editions.

Carter, John. 'Beckford and *Vathek*; Ged and Stereotype.' *The Library* 5th Series 18 no. 4 (Dec 1963): 308–309 at 308. Letter, partly about the Lausanne *Vathek*.

Cé, Camille. 'Vathek, conte oriental.' *Figaro*, 23 April 1932.

Châtel, Laurent. 'Back Where it Belongs or *Vathek's* French Womb.' *Beckford Journal* 2 (1996): 16–25. The use of French a perfect match to the contents.

Châtel, Laurent. "Enlightening the 'powers of darkness': Beckford's *avant-gardiste* nature laboratory." *Studies on Voltaire and the Eighteenth Century* 346 (1996): 440–442.

Cope, Kevin. 'Moral Travel and the Pursuit of Nothing: *Vathek* and *Siris* as Philosophical Monologue.' *Studies in Eighteenth-Century Culture* 18 (1988): 167–186, especially at 167–169, 175–182 & nn1–8, 19–25 on 183–186. *Vathek* compared with George Berkeley's *Siris* (1744).

Cope, Kevin L. 'William Beckford's *Vathek* as philosophical monologue.' *Studies on Voltaire and the Eighteenth Century* 265 (1989): 1673–1676. *Vathek* and Berkeley's *Siris* (1744). Delivered at Beckford Round Table, Budapest, 1987.

Coykendall, Frederick. "Lewis's *Monk*." *Bibliographical Notes and Queries* 1 (Feb & March 1935): 4 & 1.

Craig, Randall. 'Beckford's Inversion of Romance in *Vathek*.' *Orbis Litterarum* (Copenhagen) 39 (1984): 95–106. Reprinted as '*Vathek*: The Inversion of Romance' in *Vathek & The Escape from Time. Bicentenary Revaluations*, ed. Kenneth W. Graham, 113–129, New York: AMS Press, 1990.

D., P. [Dukas, Paul.] 'William Beckford et son Vathek.' *La Liberté*, 9 Sept 1893, 3.

Darton, Eric. 'William Beckford's Most Popular Literary Work: *Vathek*.' *Beckford Journal* 1 (1995): 30–37.

De Graaf, D. A. 'Potgieter en Vathek.' *Revue des Langues Vivantes* 24 (1958): 469–475. Influence of *Vathek* on the nineteenth-century Flemish writer.

Delattre, Floris. 'L'orientalisme dans la littérature anglaise.' *Le Beffroi*, Aug 1912. Reprinted in his *De Byron à Francis Thompson*, 38–51, Paris: Payot, 1913.

De Quincey, Thomas. Review of *Blackwood's Edinburgh Magazine* for September 1827 in *Edinburgh Saturday Post*, 8 Sept 1827, 142. Dismissive remarks on *Vathek* at the end, in an analysis of Moore's *Epicurean*. Reprinted in *The Works of Thomas De Quincey*, ed. David Groves, 21 vols., London: Pickering & Chatto, 2000–2003. Vol. 5 (2000), 'Articles from the *Edinburgh Saturday Post* 1827–1828', 60 & 341 nn40–42.

Dickens, Charles, conductor. 'Béranger. [P. J. de, songwriter]' *Household Words* 16 (22 Aug 1857): 185–191 at 187. 'Beckford has, by *Vathek* alone, gained for himself no fleeting reputation as a romancist.' Reprinted in *Littell's Living Age* 55 (7 Nov 1857): 340.

Didier, B. 'L'Exotisme et la mise en question du système familial et moral dans le roman, à la fin du XVIIIème siècle: Beckford, Sade, Potocki.' *Studies on Voltaire and the Eighteenth Century* 152 (1976): 571–586 at 572–574, 582, 585–586. All three authors shared a love of the bizarre.

Edwards, Steve. 'Factory and Fantasy in Andrew Ure.' *Journal of Design History* 14 no. 1 (2001): 17–33 at 29. 'Ure's utopia is one side of a dialectical image . . . writers of gothic . . . fiction' including Beckford grasped the other.

Einstein, Carl. 'Vathek.' *Hyperion* (Munich) 11/12 (1910): 125–128.

Reprinted in *Der Demokrat* 26 (1910), *Die Aktion* (Berlin) 3 (1913): 298–301 & *Anmerkungen* (Notes), Berlin: Die Aktion, 1916. Also reprinted in *Werke. Carl Einstein*, ed. Rolf-Peter Baacke & Jens Kwasny, 1:28–31. 3 vols. Berlin: Medusa, 1980–1985.

Einstein, Carl. Kiefer, Klaus H. *Diskurswandel im Werk Carl Einsteins. Ein Beitrag zur Theorie und Geschichte der europäische Avantgarde*. Tübingen: Max Niemeyer, 1994. *Vathek*, 53–54, 110, 148–149. Communicatio vol. 7.

Eliot, George [Marian Evans.] 'Arts and Belles Lettres.' *Westminster Review* 65 (April 1856): 625–650 at 638. George Meredith's *Shagpat* recalls *Vathek*. Noted in W. Robertson Nicoll, *A Bookman's Letters*, London: Hodder & Stoughton, 1913, p. 3.

'Extracts from the Portfolio of a Man of the World.' *Gentleman's Magazine* n.s. 28 (Oct 1847): 357–360 at 357. The author's impressions of a new ed. of *Vathek* in May 1823 which he thought 'sublime'. 7 lines.

Fiske, Christabel Forsythe. 'The Tales of Terror.' *The Book-Lover* 4 (Summer 1900): 401–416. History of Gothic novels.

Folsom, James K. "Beckford's 'Vathek' and the Tradition of Oriental Satire." *Criticism* 6 (Winter 1964): 53–69. *Vathek* a satire on the Oriental tale.

Fuseli. 'From Vision to Sentiment.' *Times Literary Supplement*, 4 May 1973, 500. Fuseli's Romanticism and *Vathek*.

Garrett, John. 'Ending in Infinity: William Beckford's Arabian Tale.' *Eighteenth-Century Fiction* 5 no. 1 (Oct 1992): 15–34. Beckford's use of Occident-Orient tensions.

Garrett, John. 'Beckford's amorality: deconstructing the house of faith.' *Studies on Voltaire and the Eighteenth Century* 346 (1996): 455–458.

Gelli, Frank Julian. 'Borges on Beckford's Hell.' *Beckford Journal* 6 (2000): 46–50. Jorge Luis Borges and his essay, 'About William Beckford's *Vathek*'.

Gemmett, Robert J. 'The Caliph Vathek from England and the Continent to America.' *American Book Collector* 18 no. 9 (May 1968): 12–19.

Gide, André, et al. 'Le Dossier Vathek.' *Nouvelle Revue Française* 9 (1913): 1044–1050.

Gifford, Stephanie. 'Genesis of a Caliph.' *John O'London's* 5 (24 August 1961): 221. *Vathek* autobiographical, like most first novels.

Gill, R. B. 'The Author in the Novel: Creating Beckford in *Vathek*.' *Eighteenth-Century Fiction* 15 no. 2 (Jan 2003): 241–254. Searching for the inner Beckford.

Gosse, Edmund. 'Stéphane Mallarmé.' *Saturday Review* 86 (17 Sept 1898): 372–373 at 372. Mallarmé 'braved opinion' by offering 'a reprint of Beckford's "Vathek," with a preface'. Reprinted in *Littell's Living Age* 219 (22 Oct 1898): 261.

Graham, Kenneth W. 'Beckford's *Vathek*: A Study in Ironic Dissonance.' *Criticism* 14 (Summer 1972), 243–253. Reprinted in *Nineteenth-Century Literature Criticism*, Detroit: Gale, 1988, 248–252.

Graham, Kenneth W. 'Who Revised the 1823 *Vathek*?' *Papers of the Bibliographical Society of America* 67 (Third Quarter 1973): 315–322. Probably Beckford himself. Lists five substantial variant readings and sixty-two 'accidental' ones between 1816 and 1823 editions.

Graham, Kenneth W. 'Beckford's Adaptation of the Oriental Tale in *Vathek*.' *Enlightenment Essays* 5 no. 1 (Spring 1974): 24–33.

Graham, Kenneth W. '*Vathek* in English and French.' *Studies in Bibliography* 28 (1975): 153–166. The reading experience depends on the language.

Graham, Kenneth W. 'Implications of the Grotesque: Beckford's *Vathek* and the Boundaries of Fictional Reality.' *Tennessee Studies in Literature* 23 (1978): 61–74.

Graham, Kenneth W. ' "*Inconnue dans les annales de la terre*": Beckford's Benign and Demonic Influence on Poe.' *Sphinx* #16 (University of Regina) 4 no. 4 (1985): 226–240. Revised reprint in *Vathek & The Escape from Time. Bicentenary Revaluations*, ed. Kenneth W. Graham, 201–223, New York: AMS Press, 1990.

Graham, Kenneth W. "Vathek with the Episodes of Vathek: The Role of the Suppressed 'Story of Alasi and Firouz'." *East-Central Intelligencer* n.s. 14 no. 3 (Sept 2000): 10–12.

Graham, Kenneth W. 'Beckford, Godwin, Austen and the Divisive 1790s.' *Persuasions* (Journal of the Jane Austen Society of North America) 24 (2002): 33–46.

Graham, Kenneth W. 'Between Restriction and Ostracism: William Beckford's Rebellious *Episodes of Vathek*.' In *The Beckford Society Annual Lectures 2000–2003*, ed. Jon Millington, 51–66. London: The Beckford Society, 2004. The 2002 lecture.

Green, Andrew J. 'Essays in Miniature: *Vathek*.' *College English* 3 (May 1942): 723–724. *Vathek* 'a potpourri of the absurd and the unforgettable'.

Green, Thomas. 'Diary of a Lover of Literature.' *Gentleman's Magazine* n.s. 7 (April 1837): 353–358 at 358 & n.s. 15 (Jan 1841): 14–18 at 15. Entries about reading *History of the Caliph Vathek* (both with editorial footnotes): 20 Jan 1812, 'a strange mixture of wit, voluptuousness, and horror', & 7 Sept 1817, 'displaying wonderful powers of imagination'. *Idem* n.s. 19 (March 1843): 243–248 at 245. 1 Oct 1823, Fonthill cat. prompted remarks on Veronese.

Grimm, Reinhold. '*Vathek* in Deutschland: Zwei Zwischenfälle ohne Folgen?' *Revue de Littérature Comparée* 38 (1964): 127–135.

Hallays, André. 'Vathek.' *Journal des Débats*, 27 Aug 1893, 1.

Hanford, James Holly. 'Open Sesame: Notes on the *Arabian Nights* in English.' *Princeton University Library Chronicle* 26 (Autumn 1964): 48–56 at 55. '. . . the oriental tale, reaching its height in Beckford's *Vathek*'.

Hazlitt, William. 'Mr. Beckford's Vathek.' *Morning Chronicle*, 10 Oct 1823. *Vathek*'s merits 'are not only considerable but first-rate'.

Henley, Samuel. 'Conjectures concerning The History of *Vathek* obviated.' *Gentleman's Magazine* 57 pt. 1 (Feb 1787): 120. Letter signed S. H., who was Samuel Henley according to Melville (1910), p. 140. See also W., S. [Weston, Stephen] below.

Hodgkin, John. " 'Vathek': the Henley Letters." *Athenæum*, 25 Dec 1909, 789–790. Refutation of some points in Melville's two articles. Subsequent replies to Melville, 26 March 1910, 368–369 & 16 April, 460–461.

Hollingsworth, Keith. ' "Vathek" and the "Ode to a Nightingale".' *Times Literary Supplement*, 27 Oct 1961, 771. Keats was acquainted with *Vathek* when writing the *Ode*.

'How Great Men Work.' *Cassell's Magazine*. 'Beckford's celebrated "Vathek" was composed by the uninterrupted exertion of three whole days and two whole nights, during which time the ecstatic author supported himself by copious draughts of wine.' Reprinted in *Littell's Living Age* 137 (6 April 1878): 59–62 at 61.

Hunter, A. O. 'Le *Vathek* de William Beckford: historique des éditions françaises.' *Revue de Littérature Comparée* 15 (1935): 119–126.

Hussain, Imdad. 'Beckford, Wainewright, De Quincey, and Oriental Exoticism.' *Venture* (Karachi University) 1 (Sept 1960): 234–248. Article mostly about Beckford, 'the first real exoticist in English literature'.

Hyland, Peter. '*Vathek*, Heaven and Hell.' *Research Studies* 50 no. 2 (1982): 99–105. Revised reprint in *Vathek & The Escape from Time. Bicentenary Revaluations*, ed. Kenneth W. Graham, 145–155, New York: AMS Press, 1990.

Jack, Malcolm. 'William Beckford: the poor Arabian story-teller.' *Studies on Voltaire and the Eighteenth Century* 346 (1996): 451–454. Delivered at the 1995 Beckford Round Table.

Jack, Malcolm. "A Response to '*Vathek* and *The Episodes of Vathek* — separately, but not together' by Elinor Shaffer." *Beckford Journal* 2 (1996): 45–46. Argues against publishing the *Episodes* with *Vathek*.

Jantzen, Hermann. 'Quellenuntersuchungen zu Dichtungen Barry Cornwalls (Bryan Waller Proctors). III. The Hall of Eblis.' *Archiv für das Studium der neueren Sprachen und Literaturen* 108 (1902): 318–323. Discloses the passages in *Vathek* which inspired Cornwall in his poem 'The Hall of Eblis'. (See also Cornwall in '16. Works influenced by Beckford'.)

Janzen, Gerlof. 'Errors in the first edition of *Vathek*.' *Beckford Journal* 1 (1995): 8. Page 48 misprinted as 84.

Jean-Aubry, G. 'Autour du «Vathek» de William Beckford.' *Revue de Littérature Comparée* 16 (July 1936): 549–552. Comments on A. O. Hunter's article in *Idem* 15 (1935): 119–126.

Johns, Derek. 'Faithful translation.' *Times Literary Supplement*, 2 Jan 2004, 15. Letter alleging that Beckford lived in France for many years and noting that Borges admired the English trans.

Keegan, P. Q. 'Gleanings from Anglo-Oriental Literature: *Vathek – Anastatius – Hajji Baba*.' *New Monthly Magazine* n.s. 11 (Dec 1877): 674–687. Includes a plot summary of *Vathek*, which stands 'unrivalled'.

Kidwai, A. R. & Vincent Newey. "The Burning Heart in Poe's 'Al Aaraaf': Another Possible Source." *Notes and Queries* 242 no. 3 (Sept 1997): 365–366. *Vathek* identified as a source for the Burning Heart.

Knox-Shaw, Peter. 'The West Indian *Vathek*. A Novel by William Beckford.' *Essays in Criticism* 43 no. 4 (Oct 1993): 284–307.

Knox-Shaw, Peter. "*Vathek* and 'The Seven Fountains' by Sir William Jones." *Notes and Queries* 240 no. 1 (March 1995): 75–76. Beckford's debt to Jones's poem, publ. in 1772.

Lange, Bernd-Peter. 'Orientierungsarbeit: Radikale Fantasie in William Beckfords *Vathek*.' *Zeitschrift für Anglistik und Amerikanistik* (Würtzburg) 33 (1985): 33–43.

Larbaud, Valéry. 'The Episodes of Vathek.' *Nouvelle Revue Française* 9 (1913): 143–148.

Lavault, Lucien. 'Qui a écrit *Vathek*?' *Nouvelle Revue Française* 9 (1913): 687–698. Reply by Valéry Larbaud, " 'Qui a écrit *Vathek*?' Réponse à M. Lucien Lavault", *Idem* 9 (1913): 868–873.

Liu, Alan. 'Towards a Theory of Common Sense: Beckford's *Vathek* and Johnson's *Rasselas*.' *Texas Studies in Literature and Language* 24 no. 2 (1984): 183–217. Draws on Lacan's notion of the mirror stage to explain Vathek's 'infantile dread of the symbolic'.

[Macnish, Robert.] 'The Book of Aphorisms, by an Oriental Author.' *Fraser's Magazine* 6 (Dec 1832): 727–728. Aphorism CXLI, 'The most splendid piece of modern prose composition is, perhaps, the description of the hall of Eblis'. Footnote by Sir Morgan O'Doherty, Bart. on marriage of Lord Lincoln to Beckford's granddaughter.

Magnier, Mireille. '*Vathek* Hommage à Voltaire ou Avatar de Faust?' *Mythes, Croyances et Religions dans le Monde Anglo-Saxon* 4 (1986): 98–108.

Mahmoud, Fatma Moussa. See Moussa-Mahmoud, Fatma.

Manzalaoui, Mahmoud. 'Pseudo-Orientalism In Transition: The Age of *Vathek*.' In *William Beckford of Fonthill, 1760–1844. Bicentenary Essays*, ed. Fatma Moussa-Mahmoud, 123–150. Suppl. to *Cairo Studies in English*, 1960.

Marshall, Julian. "Beckford's 'Vathek'." Query about Lausanne & Paris eds. of *Vathek*. *Notes and Queries* 7th Series 1 (23 Jan 1886): 69. Replies by W. E. Buckley & G. F. R. B., *Idem* (20 Feb): 154. Thanks from Julian Marshall, *Idem* (13 March): 217. Julian Marshall, 7th Series 7 (20 April 1889): 312–313, query about the Chavannes copy of *Vathek*, partly answered by H. S. Ashbee, *Idem* (25 May): 413.

Maturin, Charles. 'Melmoth the Wanderer.' *Athenæum*, 30 April 1892, 560. *Melmoth* & *Vathek* better known in France and '*Vathek* mostly forgotten in England'.

Maynard, Temple J. 'The Landscape of *Vathek*.' *Transactions of the Samuel Johnson Society of the Northwest* 7 (1974): 79–98. With a reply by David McCracken, 99–103.

Maynard, Temple J. 'Depictions of Persepolis and William Beckford's Istakar.' *Eighteenth-Century Life* 3 (June 1977): 119–122.

Maynard, Temple J. 'Eschewing present pleasure for an eternity of bliss: the irreligious motivation of Beckford's protagonists in *Vathek*.' *Studies on Voltaire and the Eighteenth Century* 265 (1989): 1676–1679. Protagonists in *Vathek* are deluded. Delivered at Beckford Round Table, Budapest, 1987.

Melville, Herman. Sealts, Merton M., Jr. 'Melville's Reading: A Checklist of Books Owned and Borrowed.' *Harvard Library Bulletin* 2 no. 3 (Autumn 1948): 378–392 at 387. In the list, #54: *Vathek*, Bentley (1849).

Melville, Lewis. [Lewis S. Benjamin, pseud.] " 'Vathek.' I." *Athenæum*, 27 Nov 1909, 658. " 'Vathek.' II." 4 Dec, 696. Replies to Hodgkin, 12 Feb 1910, 186–187 & 9 April, 428–429.

Meredith, George. 'Belles Lettres and Art.' *Westminster Review* 69 (Jan 1858): 291–304 at 292. *Vathek* superior to *Lalla Rookh*.

Millington, Jon. 'William Beckford's Vathek.' *Bath Preservation Trust Annual Report* 1992–93 (Oct 1993): 25–26. Brief publishing history, illus. by eye from *Vathek* (1815).

Millington, Jon. 'Dramatisations of *Vathek*: Genlis and After.' *Beckford Journal* 7 (2001): 34–38. Also discusses George Yeilding MacMahon's *Vathek, a Dramatic Poem* (1859). See also '16. Works influenced by Beckford'.

Mochi, Giovanna. 'L'inferno rassicurante di *Vathek*.' *Paragone Letteratura* (Florence) 30 no. 350 (April 1979): 64–102.

Moore, Steve. 'Completing the Episode: Clark Ashton Smith and *The Story of the Princess Zulkaïs and the Prince Kalilah*.' *Beckford Journal* 10 (2004): 54–60.

Mouret, François J. L. "Le 'Vathek' de William Beckford et le 'Voyage d'Urien' d'André Gide." *Modern Language Review* 64 (1969): 774–776.

Moussa-Mahmoud, Fatma. '*Rasselas* and *Vathek*.' In *Bicentenary Essays on 'Rasselas'*, ed. Magdi Wahba, 51–57. Suppl. to *Cairo Studies in English*, 1959. 'Like *Rasselas*, *Vathek* owes much to the *Persian Tales*', 54.

Moussa-Mahmoud, Fatma. 'Beckford, *Vathek* and The Oriental Tale.' In *William Beckford of Fonthill, 1760–1844. Bicentenary Essays*, ed. Fatma Moussa-Mahmoud, 63–121. Suppl. to *Cairo Studies in English*, 1960.

Moussa-Mahmoud, Fatma. 'Orientals in Picaresque: A Chapter in the History of the Oriental Tale.' *Cairo Studies in English*, 1961–1962, 145–188.

Mowl, Timothy. 'The English Caliph who never made it.' *The Independent*, 11 June 1998. The involvement of others in *Vathek*.

Nevins, Jess. *The Encyclopedia of Fantastic Victoriana*. Austin, Texas: MonkeyBrain Books, 2005. Synopsis of *Vathek* with quotations and brief biography of Beckford, 896–899.

'Noctes Ambrosianæ No. VIII.' *Blackwood's Edinburgh Magazine* 13 (May 1823): 609. Dialogue between Odoherty and Tickler comparing Caroline Lamb's novel *Ada Reis* unfavourably with *Vathek. Idem* 14 (Aug 1823): 138. Eblis mentioned in article by Procurante.

Nolan, Jerry. 'Fatma Moussa-Mahmoud: Brief Encounter with an Egyptian Beckfordian.' *Beckford Journal* 9 (2003): 52–61. An in-depth interview.

Osborne, Edna. 'Oriental Diction and Theme in English Verse, 1740–1840.' *Bulletin of the University of Kansas. Humanistic Studies* 2 no. 1 (May 1916): 52. *Vathek* compared with Joanna Baillie's play *Constantine Paleologus* (1804).

Oueijan, Naji B. 'Orientalism: The Romantics' Added Dimension.' *Romanticism in its Modern Aspects* (Wilmington) ns. 1 (1998): 37–50 at 40, 43–44 & 50 nn22–23. '*Vathek* was ahead of its time' and extensively used Eastern material.

Pailler, A. 'L'originalité du *Vathek* de William Beckford.' *La Licorne. Revue de langue et de littérature française* (University of Poitiers) No. 2: XVIIIe Siècle (1978): 73–84.

Parreaux, André. 'Le Tombeau de Beckford par Stéphane Mallarmé.' *Revue d'Histoire littéraire de la France* 55 (1955): 329–338.

Parreaux, André. 'Un *Vathek* ignoré.' *Bulletin du Bibliophile et du Bibliothécaire* No. 5 (1957): 176–179.

Parreaux, André. "Note 99. Beckford's *Vathek*, '*Londres 1791*'." *The Book Collector* 7 no. 3 (Autumn 1958): 297–299. *Idem*, 11 no. 2 (Summer 1962): 211, note by Harriet Marlow about a third copy of this ed. Also 293, 'Commentary', another copy sold at Sotheby's on 2 July for £170.

[Paul, Charles Kegan.] 'Tennyson's Poems.' *British Quarterly Review* 72 (Oct 1880): 273–291 at 283–284. Tennyson borrowed from *Vathek*. Reprinted in *Littell's Living Age* 147 (25 Dec 1880): 791–792.

Piranesi. Anderson, Jorgen. 'Giant Dreams. Piranesi's Influence in England.' *English Miscellany* 3 (1952): 49–60 at 53–60. Also Walpole's *Otranto*, 50–53.

Poston, M. L. 'Contemporary Collectors XXXIV. Bibliotheca Medici.' *Book Collector* 12 no. 1 (Spring 1963): 51–52. *Vathek* (1786) in the library.

Q., P. *Bath Herald*, 18 May 1844, 3e. Letter disputing the greatness of *Vathek*.

Quennell, Peter. 'The Moon Stood Still on Strawberry Hill.' *Horizon* 11 no. 3 (Summer 1969): 114, 115, 117.

'Rapid and Slow Authorship.' *Penny Magazine* 14 (25 Oct 1845): 410–412 at 412. Cyrus Redding's assertion that Beckford "wrote 'Vathek' at one sitting."

Rieger, James H. 'Au Pied de la Lettre: Stylistic Uncertainty in Vathek.' *Criticism* 4 (Fall 1962): 302–312.

Roberts, Adam & Eric Robertson. 'The Giaour's Sabre: A Reading of Beckford's *Vathek*.' *Studies in Romanticism* 35 no. 2 (Summer 1996): 199–211.

Roth, Georges. 'Sur la sincérité de Stéphane Mallarmé: A propos de la préface de *Vathek*.' *Revue de Littérature Comparée* 4 (1924): 335–336.

Sena, John F. 'Drawing from Blots: The Landscapes of *Vathek* and the Paintings of Alexander Cozens.' *Études Anglaises* 26 no. 2 (April–June 1973): 212–215. Foreboding scenes in *Vathek* inspired by Cozens' work.

'Sensation Artists and Sensation Daubers.' *London Review* 14 (25 May 1867): 589–590 at 589. Horrors 'conjured up by *Vathek*'.

Serstevens, A. T'. "Le 'Vathek' de Beckford." *Revue Palladienne* No. 19–20 (1952): 304–309.

Shaffer, Elinor. '*Vathek* and *The Episodes of Vathek* — separately, but not together.' *Beckford Journal* 1 (1995): 23–29. Regrets separate publication. For a reply by Malcolm Jack, see above.

Solomon, Stanley J. 'Subverting Propriety as a Pattern of Irony in Three Eighteenth-Century Novels: *The Castle of Otranto*, *Vathek*, and *Fanny Hill*.' *Erasmus Review* 1 (Nov 1971): 107–116. Excessive imagination in *Vathek*.

Thompson, Karl F. 'Henley's Share in Beckford's *Vathek*.' *Philological Quarterly* 31 no. 1 (Jan 1952): 75–80.

Tintner, Adeline. 'Fire of the Heart in "Al Aaraaf": Beckford and Byron as Source.' *Poe Studies* 22 (1989): 47–48.

Tunison, J. S. 'The Coming Literary Revival. II.' *Atlantic Monthly* 80 (Dec 1897): 797–806 at 797–798. Trans. of the *Arabian Nights* 'culminated in the excessive popularity of Moore's Lalla Rookh and Beckford's Vathek'.

Ure, Peter. "Beckford's Dwarf and 'Don Juan,' V, lxxxvii–xciv." *Notes and Queries* 196 (31 March 1951): 143–144. Byron inspired by Piero.

'Varieties.' *Literary Gazette* 7 (4 Oct 1823): 638. *Vathek* may be trans. into Persian.

W., S. [Weston, Stephen.] 'Conjectural Criticism on a famous Passage in Virgil.' *Gentleman's Magazine* 57 pt. 1 (Jan 1787): 55–56 at 55. Letter about verses by Virgil quoted in *Vathek*. See also Henley, above.

[Warburton, Bartholomew Elliott.] 'Eōthen.' *Quarterly Review* 75 (Dec

1844): 54–76 at 76. '. . . in his gorgeous descriptions and power of sarcasm [Kinglake] rivals Vathek'. Reprinted in *Littell's Living Age* 4 (22 Feb 1845): 477.

Watson, William. 'Fiction – Plethoric and Anæmic.' *National Review* 14 (Oct 1889): 167–183. Beckford wrote *Vathek* at one sitting, although its intrinsic value was not enhanced by that fact. Reprinted in *Littell's Living Age* 183 (23 Nov 1889): 490–499 at 490.

Weitzman, Arthur J. 'The Oriental tale in the eighteenth century: a reconsideration.' *Studies on Voltaire and the Eighteenth Century* 58 (1967): 1839–1855 at 1839, 1850, 1855.

[Wilson, John.] 'Some Remarks of the Use of the Preternatural in Works of Fiction.' *Blackwood's Edinburgh Magazine* 3 (Sept 1818): 648–650 at 648–649. *Vathek* 'has never been very popular in this country'.

13. Travel

Dreams, Waking Thoughts and Incidents *(1783)*,
became Italy; with Sketches of Spain and Portugal, *vol. 1 (1834)*

Dreams, Waking Thoughts and Incidents. London: J. Johnson, St. Paul's Church
  Yard, 1783. xv, 334 pp. 30 cm. Large paper, 31½ cm. Suppressed on eve of
  publication, except for six copies. Chapman, *Bibliography* (1930), 2(i).
Dreams, Waking Thoughts and Incidents. Ed. Robert J. Gemmett. Ruther-
  ford, NJ: Fairleigh Dickinson University Press, 1971. 328 pp. 24 cm.
Voyage d'un rêveur éveillé de Londres à Venise. Trans. Roger Kann of first
  half of *Dreams.* Paris: José Corti, 1988. 151 pp. 16 cm. 2nd ed. 1990.
  Collection romantique, No. 17.
Voyage d'un rêveur éveillé de Venise à Naples. Trans. Roger Kann of second
  half of *Dreams.* Paris: José Corti, 1989. 299 pp. 16 cm. Collection romantique, No. 18.
Een dromer op reis; een Grand Tour (A Dreamer on His Travels). Amsterdam: Uitgeverij Contact, 1991. 279 pp. 23½ cm. Map of Beckford's
  Grand Tour. Robert J. Gemmett's 1971 ed. of *Dreams* trans. into Dutch
  & intro. by Gerlof Janzen.

Articles and Reviews

Billi, Mirella. '*Dreams, Waking Thoughts, and Incidents:* Beckford's Grand
  Tour as personal and cultural rite of passage.' *Beckford Journal* 8 (2002):
  6–10.
Chapman, Guy. 'Vathek's Grand Tour.' *Times Literary Supplement*, 10 May
  1928, 358. Letter about *Dreams.*
Garnett, Richard. "Beckford's 'Dreams'." *Universal Review* 8 (Sept 1890):
  112–126. Hoping that *Dreams* would be 'reprinted, as it must one day be'.
Parreaux, André. *Études Anglaises* 26 no. 2 (April–June 1973): 232–233.
  Review of Robert J. Gemmett's ed. (1971).

Extracts

Benda, Wolfram, trans. *Venedig.* Bayreuth: Bear Press, 1997. 84 pp. 18
  lithographs by Rolf Escher. Limited to 150 copies. The Venice chapters
  from *Dreams* (1783).
Foss, Michael, ed. *On Tour. British Travellers in Europe.* London: O'Mara,
  1989. *Dreams* (1783), 22–23, 43–44, 87, 141, 185–186, 197–199, 210.

'The Grand Chartreuse.' In *Historic Buildings. As Seen and Described by Famous Writers*, ed. Esther Singleton, 40–53. New York: Dodd, Mead, 1903.

The Grand Tour of William Beckford. Compiled & ed. Elizabeth Mavor. Harmondsworth, Middlesex: Penguin Books, 1986. 161 pp. 20 cm. Selections, with a map.

'The Hills of Rome.' In *The Grand Tour*, ed. Sheila Pickles, 86–87. London: Pavilion, 1991. From *Dreams, Waking Thoughts and Incidents* (Gemmett, 1971, 190–191). Also Intro, 10.

'In the Apennines.' In *The Pelican Book of English Prose: Prose of the Romantic Period 1780–1830*, ed Raymond Wright, 4:149–150. 5 vols. Harmondsworth, Middlesex: Penguin Books, 1956. From *Dreams, Waking Thoughts and Incidents* (Gemmett, 1971, 153–154).

MacDonogh, Katharine. *Reigning Cats and Dogs*. London: Fourth Estate, 1999. Quotes from *Dreams* about pets. Lap-dogs in Bologna, 68. Pugs in Utrecht, 93. Skeleton of Petrarch's cat, 187.

Maugham, H. Neville. *The Book of Italian Travel (1580–1900)*. London: Grant Richards, 1903. Pp. 111–114, 120–129, 182–185, 245–247, 297–298, 447–450. Beckford, 477.

Rheinreise. A fragment from *Dreams* trans. into German by Wolfram Benda, with an etching by Klaus Böttger. Bayreuth: Bear Press, 1990. A single leaf (No. XVIII) limited to 120 copies.

The Journal of William Beckford in Portugal and Spain 1787–1788, *became* Italy; with Sketches of Spain and Portugal, *vol. 2 (1834)*

The Journal of William Beckford in Portugal and Spain 1787–1788. Ed. Boyd Alexander. London: Hart-Davis, 1954 & New York: John Day, 1955. 340 pp. 10 pl. 22 cm. Transcript, mostly from Bodleian Library, MS. Beckford c.43.

Diário de William Beckford em Portugal e Espanha. Trans. into Portuguese and preface by João Gaspar Simões of *The Journal of William Beckford in Portugal and Spain 1787–1788*, ed. Boyd Alexander (1954). Lisbon: Emprensa Nacionade Publicidade, 1957. 315 pp. 2nd ed. rev. Lisbon: Biblioteca Nacional, 1983. 233 pp. 25 cm. Portugal e os estrangeiros series. 3rd ed. Lisbon: Biblioteca Nacional, 1988. 233 pp. 25 cm.

EXTRACTS. Augusto, António Carlos. 'Beckford.' *Ramalhão. O Tempo e as Gentes*, 30–31. Sintra: Associação de Professores de Sintra, 1997.

Gouveia, António Camões. 'O Diário de William Beckford em Portugal.' *O Estudo da História* No. 3–4, 2 série (April–June / July–Sept 1987): 31–41.

Santos, Piedade Braga et al. *Lisboa Setecentista Vista por Estrangeiros*. Lisbon: Livros Horizonte, 1987. Beckford, 13–14, 96–97.

Journal Intime au Portugal et en Espagne 1787–1788. Paris: José Corti, 1986.

335 pp. 7 pl. incl. map of Lisbon in 1833. 21½ cm. Trans. into French, intro. and notes by Roger Kann from Bodleian Library, MS. Beckford c.43.

Lettres d'Espagne et de Portugal. 1787–1788. Intro. G. Jean-Aubry. Trans. Madeleine Clemenceau-Jacquemaire. Paris: Eugène Figuière, [1936] & Corroa, 1937. 269 pp. 19 cm.

Menuetten met de markies. Portugees dagboek 1787 (Minuets with the Marquis). Amsterdam: Uitgeverij Contact, 1992. 271 pp. 23½ cm. Trans. into Dutch & intro. by Gerlof Janzen of *The Journal of William Beckford in Portugal and Spain. 1787–1788*, ed. Boyd Alexander (1954).

Reviews

'Beckford's Diary.' *Times Literary Supplement,* 2 July 1954, 427.

Connolly, Cyril. 'Beckford's Fandango.' *Sunday Times,* 20 June 1954. Reprinted in his *Previous Convictions,* 150–152. London: Hamish Hamilton, 1963.

Macaulay, Rose. 'Beckford's Journal.' *Observer,* 20 June 1954.

Mayoux, Jean-Jacques. 'Beckford au Portugal.' *La Quinzaine littéraire,* No. 470, 16 Sept 1986. Review of *Journal Intime au Portugal et en Espagne.*

Parreaux, André. 'Le «Journal» de Beckford.' *Études Anglaises* 7 no. 4 (Oct–Dec 1954): 362–379.

Parreaux, André. *Les Langues Modernes* ?49 no. 4 (?1955): 351–352 (67–68).

Pritchett, V. S. 'Beckford's Portugal.' *New Statesman and Nation,* 26 June 1954, 836.

'Recent Books. Beckford Abroad. An Eccentric Journal.' *The Times,* 19 June 1954, 8f.

Sandeman, Philip. 'Beckford's Travels.' *Spectator,* 18 June 1954, 744–746.

Spring, Howard. 'The Eccentric of Fonthill.' *Country Life,* 1 July 1954, 57.

Beckford's 1794 Journal, *became* Recollections of an Excursion
to the Monasteries of Alcobaça and Batalha *(1835)*

'Beckford's 1794 Journal.' Ed. Boyd Alexander. In Howard B. Gotlieb. *William Beckford of Fonthill,* 90–100. New Haven: Yale University Library, 1960. 22 cm. Exhibition catalogue. From Bodleian Library, MS. Beckford d.7. Also an unpaginated offprint which included 'The Authorship of Al Raoui'.

Italy; with Sketches of Spain and Portugal *(1834)*

Italy; with Sketches of Spain and Portugal. 2 vols. London: Richard Bentley, 1834. xvi, 371 pp. & xv, 381 pp. 22½ cm. Chapman, *Bibliography* (1930), 8(i).

Italy; with Sketches of Spain and Portugal. 2nd ed. 2 vols. London: Richard
 Bentley, 1834. xvi, 371 pp. & xv, 381 pp. 22½ cm. Poem in Portuguese
 added, 2:205. Chapman, *Bibliography* (1930), 8(i, b). 3rd ed., 1835.
Italy, with Sketches of Spain and Portugal. Paris: Baudry's European Library,
 1834. vi, 338 pp. 22 cm. With *Vathek: An Arabian Tale*, 127 pp., appended.
 Collection of Ancient and Modern British Novels and Romances, vol. 59.
 Chapman, *Bibliography* (1930), 8(ii). See also *Vathek*, 3A(vi).
Italy, with Sketches of Spain and Portugal. 2 vols. Philadelphia: Key &
 Biddle, 1834. First American ed. Chapman, *Bibliography* (1930), p. 66.

Reviews of the first ed., London, 1834

Athenæum, 14, 21, 28 June 1834, 447–449, 465–468, 487–489.
Bath Chronicle, 19 June 1834, 3c, Travels about to be published. *Idem*, 10 July,
 4d, quote from *Quarterly Review* (June 1834), 19 lines. *Idem*, 16 Oct, 4e.
 Under 'Literature in 1834', *Italy* characterised by Talleyrand as '*The Book
 of the Century*'. *Idem*, 9 May 1844, 2f. Advert by Simms for 'best edition'.
Bath Herald, 4 July 1834.
Literary Gazette, 16 Aug 1834, 558–560.
[Lockhart, John Gibson.] *Quarterly Review* 51 (June 1834): 426–456.
 Enthusiastic review composed mainly of extracts from *Italy*. Reprinted in
 The Museum of Foreign Literature, Science and Art (Philadelphia) 25
 (July–Dec 1834). Reprinted as 'The Author of Vathek' in *Famous
 Reviews*, ed. Reginald Brimley Johnson, 185–189. London: Pitman, 1914.
[Mitford, John.] *Gentleman's Magazine* n.s. 2 (Aug, Sept 1834): 115–121,
 234–241.
Monthly Review n.s. 3 no. 1 (Sept 1834): 23–41.
Morning Chronicle, 19 Sept 1834. Reprinted from *Leeds Mercury*.
Morning Post, 3 Dec 1834. Reprinted from a Wiesbaden newspaper.
[Redding, Cyrus.] *Bath Guardian* 1 no. 24 (12 July 1834): 4a–b. Partly
 reprinted in his *Memoirs of William Beckford* (1859), 2:396–402.

Other Reviews

Atkinson's Casket (Philadelphia) 9 (Dec 1834): 555–558. Reprinted from
 the *Philadelphia Gazette*.
'Beckford's Italy.' *New York Mirror*, 18 Oct 1835, 127.
New York Weekly News, 22 Aug 1846, 127. New York ed., 1845.
Parreaux, André. 'Beckford en Italie. Rêve et Voyage au XVIIIe siècle.' *Revue
 de Littérature Comparée* 33 no. 3 (1959): 321–347.
[Tuckerman, Henry T.] *North American Review* 40 (April 1835): 417–447.

Extracts

Battilana, Marilla, compiler. *English Writers and Venice, 1350–1950: An
 Anthology of Texts in the Original Language.* Parallel trans. into Italian

by Dario Calimani as *Scrittori inglesi e Venezia*. Venice: La stamperia di Venezia editrice, 1981. Part of 2, 3 Aug 1780, 111–112. From *Italy* (1834, 1:102–104).

Blythe, Ronald, ed. 'A Dinner Invitation in Portugal.' In *Pleasures of Diaries. Four Centuries of Private Writing*, 318–322. New York: Pantheon Books, 1989. Letter 28 of 12 Sept 1787 (Cintra) from *Italy* (1834, 2:169–178).

Un califfo a Venezia. Trans. into Italian & ed. Paolo Pepe. Naples: Alfredo Guida Editore, 1994. 101 pp. Letters I–VII from *Italy* (1834, 1:89–148).

A Côrte da Rainha D. Maria I. Most of the letters on Portugal from *Italy*, trans. Zacarias d'Aça, 2:23–275. Lisbon: Tavares Cardoso & Irmâo, 1901. 191 pp. 21½ cm. Reprinted, Lisbon: Frenesi, 2003.

'An Evening walk in Lisbon.' & 'Visit to the Escurial.' *Mirror of Literature* 24 (5 July, 27 Sept 1834): 11–12, 217–219.

Un Inglés en la España de Godoy (An Englishman in Godoy's Spain). Trans., selection & intro. Jesús Pardo. Madrid: Taurus, 1966. 155 pp. 19 cm. Anecdotes about Beckford in Portugal and trans. of eighteen of Beckford's Spanish letters from 1787–1795. Temas de España 45.

'Itali, com Descrições de Espanha e Portugal.' In Maria Laura Bettencourt Pires. *Portugal visto pelos Ingleses*, 27–33. Lisbon: Instituto Nacional de Investigação Cientifica, 1981. Portuguese letters 7, 8, 22 (Mafra) & 31 from *Italy* (1834, 2:23–33, 127–142, 212–228). Textos de literatura-9.

Italy, Sketches. Paris: Cormon & Blanc, 1835. 118 pp. Letters I–VII only. Chapman, *Bibliography* (1930), p. 66.

Italy. In Mrs Jameson, *Sketches of Italy*, 1–202. Frankfort: Charles Jugel, 1841.

'Lettres de Venise.' *Revue de Paris* 44 (1 Aug 1937): 520–548. Intro. G. Jean-Aubry. Trans. Madeleine Clemenceau-Jacquemaire. Six letters from *Italy* (1834, 1:99–144).

Da Trieste alla laguna veneta con scrittori del passato. Trans. Franca Piazza. Florence: Barbèra, 1968. 90 pp. 32 colour plates. Extracts from William Beckford, Chateaubriand, William Howells and Stendhal. Also issued in English, French and German.

Von Venedig zu den Dolomiten mit William Beckford. Intro. Franca Piazza. Trans. Dora Mitzky. Florence: Barbèra, 1963 & Munich: Reich, [1967]. 122 pp. 32 pl. 30 cm.

Da Venezia alle Dolomiti con William Beckford. Trans. Franca Piazza. Florence: Barbèra, 1963. 99 pp. Illus.

From Venice to the Dolomites with William Beckford. Intro. & choice of texts by Franca Piazza. Florence: Barbèra, 1963. Reissued with intro. & trans. John Garrett, 1968. 100 pp. 32 colour pl. with captions in Italian, French, English and German. 'The Italy of Today Seen Though the Eyes of Yesterday.' Text also publ. in Italian, French and German.

De Venise aux Dolomites avec William Beckford. Trans. François Pitti Ferrandi. Florence: Barbèra, 1963. 99 pp. 21 pl. 26 cm.

'Viagens de Beckford a Portugal. Cartas Escriptas em 1777.' (Trans. of *Sketches* with study by Luís Augusto Rebelo da Silva). In *O Panorama* 12–14 (1855–1857).

Recollections of an Excursion to the Monasteries of Alcobaça and Batalha *(1835)*

Recollections of an Excursion to the Monasteries of Alcobaça and Batalha. London: Richard Bentley, 1835. xi, 228 pp. Frontis., portrait after Reynolds (three states are known). 23½ cm. Chapman, *Bibliography* (1930), 9(i).

Recollections of an Excursion to the Monasteries of Alcobaça and Batalha. Philadelphia: Carey, Lea and Blanchard, 1835. 188 pp. First American ed. Chapman, *Bibliography* (1930), p. 69.

Erinnerungen von einem Ausfluge nach den Klöstern Alcobaça und Batalha. Trans. S. H. Spiker. Berlin: Duncker & Humblot, 1835.

Alcobaça e Batalha (Recordações de uma excursão). Trans. into Portuguese by Joaquim Lúcio Lobo & M. Vieira Natividade. Alcobaça: A. M. de Oliveira, 1914. 98 pp. 16 cm.

Excursion à Alcobaça et Batalha. Preface by Guy Chapman. Trans. André Parreaux. Paris: Société d'Editions 'Les Belles Lettres', 1956. lii, 299 pp. Portrait frontis. & 22 illus. 22 cm. Parallel English & French Texts.

REVIEWS. Parreaux, André. 'A propos de l'excursion à Alcobaça et Batalha de William Beckford.' *Bulletin des Etudes Portugaises* n.s. 20 (1957 [1958]): 233–239.

Saunal, Damien. *Revue de Littérature Comparée* 31 (1957): 291–293.

Recollections of an Excursion to the Monasteries of Alcobaça and Batalha. Intro. Boyd Alexander. Fontwell, Susssex: Centaur Press, 1972. xlix, 228 pp. Frontis. & 3 pl. 22 cm. Intro., xiii–xxxvi. 'Beckford's 1794 Journal', xxxvii–xlix. Facsimile reprint of the first ed. (1835).

REVIEWS. 'Banquet of sense.' *Times Literary Supplement*, 22 June 1973, 724.

Sewell, Gordon. 'An excursion with William Beckford.' *Bournemouth Evening Echo*, 29 Dec 1972, 32.

Recollections of an Excursion to the Monasteries of Alcobaça and Batalha. Watchung, NJ: Saifer, [1972].

Recollections of an Excursion to the Monasteries of Alcobaça and Batalha. Folcroft, PA: Folcroft Library Editions, 1974.

Recollections of an Excursion to the Monasteries of Alcobaça and Batalha. Norwood, PA: Norwood Editions, 1978.

Alcobaça e Batalha; Recordações de Viagem. Trans. into Portuguese with notes by Iva Delgado & Frederico Rosa. Almeirim: Vega, 1983.

Excursión a Alcobaça y Batalha. Trans. into Spanish & intro. Luis Antonio de Villena. Barcelona: Laertes, 1983. 128 pp. 20 cm. Series: Nan Shan 5.

Souvenirs d'Alcobaça et Batalha. Preface by Didier Girard. Trans. André Parreaux. Paris: José Corti, 1989. 245 pp. 16 cm. 2nd ed. 1992. Collection romantique, No. 19.

Ricordi di viaggio al monasteri di Alcobaca e Batalha. Intro. Gaetano D'Elia. Trans. into Italian by Domenico Cosmai. Bari: Ladisa, 1994. 93 pp.

Alcobaça e Batalha; Recordações de Viagem. Trans. into Portuguese by Iva Delgado & Frederico Rosa. Lisbon: Vega, 1994. Reprinted 1997. 126 pp. 12 pp. illus. 23 cm.

Contemporary Reviews

Athenæum, 27 June & 4 July 1835, 486–487 & 509.

Bath Herald, 4 July 1835, 4a–b.

'Beckford's Recollections.' *Spectator* 8 (27 June 1835): 610–611.

'Mr. Beckford's Recollections of Alcobaça and Batalha.' *The Times*, 11 July 1835, 3c. 29 lines.

Leigh Hunt's London Journal 2 (11 July 1835): 223–224.

Mirror of Literature 26 (18, 25 July 1835): 36–39, 57–60. Mainly extracts from Days One to Six & Days Seven to Twelve.

[Mitford, John.] *Gentleman's Magazine* n.s. 4 (Sept, Dec 1835): 273–276, 591–594.

[Poe, Edgar Allan.] *Southern Literary Messenger* 1 no. 12 (Aug 1835): 714. Poe, having disliked 'tumid' *Vathek*, dismissed *Recollections* unread.

Quarterly Review 54 (July 1835): 230.

[Redding, Cyrus.] *Bath Guardian* 2 no. 76 (11 July 1835): 4a–c.

The Times, 11 July 1835, 3c.

Extracts

See also Chadourne in '1. Accounts of Beckford's Life. Full-length Studies'

Harrison, William Henry. *The Tourist in Portugal.* London: Robert Jennings, 1839. Extracts on Batalha, 226–230, 234–235. From *Recollections* (1835, 71–78, 133–135). Jennings's Landscape Annual for 1839.

'A Mausoleum in Portugal.' In *The New Oxford Book of English Prose*, ed. John Gross, 301–302. Oxford: Oxford University Press, 1998. From *Recollections of an Excursion . . . Alcobaça and Batalha* (1835, 135–139).

ANTHOLOGIES

Italy, Spain, and Portugal, with an Excursion to the Monasteries of Alcobaça and Batalha. London: Richard Bentley, 1840. xxiv, 440 pp. 17 cm. Frontis., portrait after Reynolds. *Italy* (1834), 1–351. *Excursion* (1835), 352–440. Chapman, *Bibliography* (1930), 8(iii) & 9(ii).

Italy, Spain, and Portugal, with an Excursion to the Monasteries of Alcobaça and Batalha. 2 vols. in 1. New York: Wiley & Putnam, 1845.

REVIEW. 'New Publications Received.' *North American Review* 63 (Oct 1846): 514.

The History of the Caliph Vathek; and European Travels. Intro. by G. T. Bettany. London: Ward, Lock, 1891. xxiv, 549 pp. 18 cm. Frontis. & 8 pl. *Vathek,* 1–92. *Dreams, Waking Thoughts, and Incidents,* 93–300. *Portugal,* 303–412. *Spain,* 413–465. *Alcobaça and Batalha,* 466–549. Minerva Library of Famous Books, No. 24.

The Travel-Diaries of William Beckford of Fonthill. Ed. Guy Chapman. 2 vols. London: Constable, 1928. lxii, 347 pp. 6 pl. & xvii, 374 pp. 5 pl. 23 cm. Limited to 1000 copies. Vol. 1: *Memoir of William Beckford,* xiii–lxii. *Dreams, Waking Thoughts and Incidents,* 1–347. Vol. 2: *Sketches of Spain & Portugal,* 1–249. *Recollections of an Excursion to the Monasteries of Alcobaça and Batalha,* 251–374. Reprinted, 2 vols. in 1, New York: Kraus Reprint, 1972 & again, 2 vols., Temecula, CA: Reprint Services Corp, 1992.

REVIEWS. King, William. *The Criterion* 8 no. 33 (July 1929): 745–748, reprinted 1967. With a review of *Vathek* with *The Episodes of Vathek* (1929).

McBride, Henry. 'Genius in England.' *The Dial* 86 (May 1929): 385–388.

Times Literary Supplement, 3 May 1928, 331 & letter, 10 May, 358.

'Travellers' Tales.' *Saturday Review,* 19 May 1928, 634–635.

Extracts

Bloomfield, Paul & Millicent, compilers. *The Traveller's Companion. A Travel Anthology.* London: Bell, 1931. *Dreams* (1783), 32, 35, 191, 206, 211, 219, 228. *Italy* (1834), 59, 272, 273. All from Minerva ed. (1891).

Brilli, Attilio. *English and American Travellers in Siena.* Siena: Monte Dei Paschi Di Siena, 1987. Beckford in Siena, 26–27 Oct 1780, 94.

David, Elizabeth. *A Book of Mediterranean Food.* Harmondsworth, Middlesex, Penguin, 1955. (1st ed. 1950.) 'A Portuguese Supper Party', 97, & 'Alcobaca', 113. Both from Guy Chapman's *Travel-Diaries* (1928).

Garnett, W. J. 'William Beckford.' In *English Prose Selections: Eighteenth Century,* ed. Henry Craik, 4 (1894): 571–572. 5 vols. London: Macmillan, 1893–1896. 'A Dream in Kent' from *Dreams, Waking Thoughts and Incidents,* (Minerva ed., 1891, 95–96) 4:573–574. 'The Court of the Queen of Portugal' from *Italy; with Sketches of Spain and Portugal,* vol. 2, Portugal, Letter 27 (Minerva ed., 1891, 372–375), 4:574–576. W. J. Garnett was Richard Garnett's brother.

Grigson, Geoffrey. *The Romantics. An Anthology.* London: Routledge,

1942. 'Entrance to Italy', 72–74 & 338 n92. 'Watersouchy', 82–83 & 339 n106. *Vathek*, 'The Flaming Heart', 84–85, 340 n109 & 350 n282. 'Via Coeli: The Entrance to the Grande Chartreuse', 90–93. 'The Escurial', 107–109. 'Sarsar is the icy wind of death [in De Quincey's *Autobiographic Sketches*], first used by Beckford in "Vathek," according to the O.E.D.', 350 n282.

Jack, Malcolm, compiler & ed. *Vathek and Other Stories – A William Beckford Reader*. London: Pickering & Chatto, 1993. Extracts from *Dreams . . ., The Journal . . . in Portugal and Spain 1787–88, Italy . . ., Recollections of an Excursion to the Monasteries of Alcobaça and Batalha*. Reprinted, Harmondsworth, Middlesex: Penguin Books, 1995. For a fuller entry see '11. *Vathek* and *The Episodes*: Editions'.

Newby, Eric. *A Book of Travellers' Tales*. London: Pan, 1986. (1st ed. 1985.) 'A feather from the wings of the Archangel Gabriel in the Escorial, near Madrid, 1787', 139.

GENERAL COMMENTARIES

Books

Anderson, Patrick. 'The Enchanted Garden: William Beckford in Italy and Portugal.' In *Over the Alps*, 73–144. London: Hart-Davis, 1969. Also passim.

REVIEW. Sewell, Gordon. 'William Beckford on the Grand Tour.' *Bournemouth Evening Echo*, 18 July 1969, 13.

Times Literary Supplement, 5 June 1969, 607.

Appleton, William W. *A Cycle of Cathay. The Chinese Vogue in England during the Seventeenth and Eighteenth Centuries*. New York: Columbia University Press, 1951. Beckford 'constantly dreamed of more distant scenes' in the course of his European travels, 155–156 & nn50–52.

Black, Jeremy. *The Grand Tour in the Eighteenth Century*. Stroud, Glos: Alan Sutton, 1992. Beckford left England over scandal, 201. With J. R. Cozens, 262. Bought 'Altieri' Claudes, 264. Liked wild, primitive scenery, 277.

Burgess, Anthony & Francis Haskell. 'City of Petrified People.' In *The Age of the Grand Tour . . .*, 51. London: Paul Elek, & New York: Crown, 1967. Beckford's opinion of Antwerp in a letter from Ostend (*Italy*, 1834, 1:10), 51. 'Grand Fair at Munich' (*Italy*, 64–66), 87–88. William & Peter Beckford in 'Notes on Authors and Artists', 132. Also extracts from Peter Beckford's *Familiar Letters from Italy* (Letters IX & XXV), 101–102 & 112–113.

Butt, John. *The Mid-Eighteenth Century*, ed. & completed by Geoffrey Carnall. Oxford: Clarendon Press, 1979. Travels, 261–263. *Vathek*, 492–494. Also 245, 495. Oxford History of English Literature.

Delaforce, Patrick. *The Grand Tour*. London: Robertson McCarta, 1990.

Beckford, 9. Naples opera, 115. Bologna, 151. Verona, 156. Antwerp, 172–173, Brussels, 173. Dutch neatness, 187. Geneva, 199–200.

Hibbert, Christopher. *The Grand Tour*. London: Weidenfeld & Nicolson, 1969. Passim. A well-illustrated popular account.
REVIEW. Sewell, Gordon. 'Wessex Notebook.' *Bournemouth Evening Echo*, 7 Nov 1969, 23.

Hood, Edwin Paxton, compiler. *The World of Anecdote*. London: Hodder & Stoughton, 1870. Beckford's Travels: 'Beckford and the Feather of the Archangel Gabriel', 535.

Hudson, Roger, ed. *The Grand Tour, 1592–1796*. London: Folio Society, 1993.

Immerwahr, Raymond. " 'Romantic' and Its Cognates in England, Germany, and France before 1790." In *'Romantic' and Its Cognates / The European History of a Word*, ed. Hans Eichner, 17–97 at 46–48 & 94 nn118–125. Manchester: Manchester University Press, 1972. Beckford's 'erotic imagination' in his travel writing. Also 52, 75.

Lambert, R. S., ed. *Grand Tour. A Journey in the Tracks of the Age of Aristocracy*. London: Faber & Faber, 1935. Passim. Articles from *The Listener*.

Plumb, J. H. *Men and Places*. London: Cresset Press, 1963. Beckford and Cozens on the Grand Tour, 59.

Sitwell, Osbert. *Winters of Content, and Other Discursions on Mediterranean Art and Travel*. London: Duckworth, 1950. Quotations from *Italy* (1834): Venice, 40, 54–55, 58–59; Lucca, 227–228; Royal Palace, Madrid, 249–250.

Sitwell, Sacheverell. *Southern Baroque Art. A Study of Painting, Architecture and Music in Italy and Spain in the 17th and 18th Centuries*. 2nd ed. London: Duckworth, 1927. (1st ed. 1924.) Beckford's description of rooms in Charles III's palace on visit to Madrid in 1787 and his visit to the Palace of Aranjuez in 1795, 62. Mafra's 'nearly Gothic gloom' appealed to Beckford, 188.

Tuckerman, Henry T. 'The Traveller. Beckford.' In *Characteristics of Literature, illustrated by the Genius of Distinguished Writers*, 179–215 at 210–215. 2nd series. Philadelphia: Lindsay & Blakiston, 1851. An essay on travel literature in general, perhaps based on his article, below.
REVIEW. 'Literary Notices.' *Harper's New Monthly Magazine* 3 (June 1851): 138–140 at 140.

Viviès, Jean. *English Travel Narratives in the Eighteenth Century*. Trans. Claire Davidson. Aldershot, Hants: Ashgate, 2002. Portugal & Spain, 24, 30 n7, 102, 118. Studies in Early Modern English Literature.

Whistler, Laurence. *The Laughter and the Urn. The Life of Rex Whistler*. Weidenfeld & Nicolson, 1985. Beckford, Cozens, and the discomfort of travelling on the Grand Tour, 144, 145, 146.

Articles

Curley, Thomas M. 'William Beckford and the Romantic tradition of travel literature.' *Studies on Voltaire and the Eighteenth Century* 305 (1992): 1819–1823. Delivered at the 1991 Beckford Round Table.

Elliott, Kirsten. 'The British Abroad.' *The Bath Magazine* No. 10 (July 2003): 21. Beckford's love of Venice, with photo of his tower at Bath.

Fontainas, A. 'Le Fantasque Beckford et ses voyages.' *Figaro*, 14 May 1932.

Oliver, John W. 'The Caliph of Fonthill.' *Times Literary Supplement*, 17 Nov 1932, 859. Letter about Beckford not being an ideal traveller.

Scott, James J. *Notes and Queries* 1st Series 10 (28 Oct 1854): 344. Query about Beckford's works mentioned in Moore's *Life of Byron*, 1832.

Tuckerman, H. T. 'William Beckford and the Literature of Travel.' *Southern Literary Messenger* 16 (Jan 1850): 7–14 at 7, 10, 12–14. Despite the title, mainly about travel literature in general.

ENGLAND

Books

Jenkin, A. K. Hamilton. *The Mines and Miners of Cornwall. 6 Around Gwennap*. Truro: Truro Bookshop, 1963. Beckford's visit to a Cornish mine in 1787, 5–6.

Rowse, A. L. 'William Beckford at Falmouth.' & 'The Mines of Gwennap.' In *A Cornish Anthology*, 153–154 & 168–169. London: Macmillan, 1968. Falmouth, 6 & 7 March 1787. From Guy Chapman, ed., *The Travel-Diaries of William Beckford of Fonthill* (1928): 2:5–8.

Articles

Claésson, Dick. " 'Sinking Apace into the Bosom of Delusions'. William Beckford's Earliest Narrative of Travel. An introduction to *Fragments of an English Tour*." *Beckford Journal* 5 (1999): 6–13.

Falmouth. *The Times*, 30 June 1796, 3d. Beckford's arrival from Lisbon.

FRANCE

Books

Alger, John Goldworth. *Napoleon's British Visitors and Captives: 1801–1815*. London: Constable, 1904. Beckford's visits to Paris in 1782 & 1791–1793, 111–112. Also 46.

Arnault, Antoine Vincent, et al. *Biographie Nouvelle des Contemporains*. 20 vols. Paris: Librarie historique, 1821. 2:295–296. Beckford: 'étranger que Paris voit partir avec regret'. Also noted in [Pierre Louis Pascal de Jullian, ed.,] *Galerie Historique des Contemporains, ou Nouvelle Biographie*. 8 vols. Brussels: Wahlen, 1817–1820. 1:420–421.

Eschapasse, Anne. 'William Beckford in Paris, 1788–1814: "*Le Faste Solitaire*".' In *William Beckford, 1760–1844: An Eye for the Magnificent*, ed. Derek E. Ostergard, 98–115. New Haven & London: Yale University Press for the Bard Graduate Center, 2001. Exhibition catalogue.

Paris: Musée Galliera, 1948. *Huit siècles de vie britannique à Paris*. Exhibition catalogue. No. 230, p. 82.

Pinkerton, John. *Literary Correspondence of John Pinkerton, Esq.* 2 vols. London: Colburn & Bentley, 1830. From Joseph Mawe in Paris on 18 April 1802, saying that Beckford was out when he called & that he had seen him in a procession of consuls going to Notre Dame, 2:215 & 217.

[Roussel, Pierre-Joseph-Alexandre, d' Epinal.] *Le château des Tuileries . . . avec des particularités sur la visit que le Lord Bedfort y a faite après le 10 Août 1792 . . .* 2 vols. Paris: Lerouge, 1802. Opinions on revolutionary events, almost certainly by Beckford.

Staël-Holstein, Anna Louise Germaine de, Baroness. *Correspondance générale. Vol. 1. Lettres de jeunesse*. Ed. Béatrice W. Jasinski. 6 vols. Paris: Pauvert, 1960. Contact with the Necker family in Paris in 1784, 1:19–20

Whaley, Buck. *Buck Whaley's Memoirs . . . Written by Himself in 1797*. Ed. Sir Edward Sullivan. London: Moring, 1906. Whaley visited Beckford: at Evian, summer 1792, 294–297, 298; at Lausanne, 304–305. Appendix, 344–345. Also xix, 292. Portrait after Reynolds facing 294.

Articles

Girard, Didier. 'Beckford in Paris, 1792: Unconcerned but not Indifferent (Man Ray's Epitaph).' *Beckford Tower Trust Newsletter*, Spring 1993, 5–9.

Morgulis, Grégoire. 'Un Épisode de la vie de Beckford.' *Revue de Littérature Comparée* 14 (Oct 1934): 690–694. Beckford in Paris in 1793.

Nolan, J. C. M. 'Beckford's Excursion to the Grande Chartreuse Revised.' *Beckford Journal* 5 (1999): 33–42. Revisions in 1834 of his 1783 account.

Paris visits in *The Times*. Living at Hôtel de Boulogne, 21 March 1791, 2d. Visited a theatre, referred to as the Duc de Betford, 27 June 1801, 3a. Recently arrived, renting a Hôtel, 17 Oct 1801, 2b.

HOLLAND

Articles

Browne, Junius Henri. 'Holland and the Hollanders.' *Harper's New Monthly Magazine* 63 (Aug 1881): 349–364 at 364. WB's low opinion of Holland.

Janzen, Gerlof. 'Strange Bedfellows or The Ambivalent Feelings and Attitudes of William Beckford toward Holland and the Dutch.' *Beckford Journal* 6 (2000): 17–28.

ITALY

Books

Black, Jeremy. *Italy and the Grand Tour*. New Haven: Yale University Press, 2003. Beckford admired primitive scenery, 16. With Cozens in 1782, 56, 187.

Bullen, J. B. *Continental Crosscurrents: British Criticism and European Art 1810–1910*. Oxford: Oxford University Press, 2005. Beckford's reaction to the Campo Santo, Pisa, in Oct 1780, 14 &n18.

Chaney, Edward. *The Evolution of the Grand Tour: Anglo-Italian Cultural Relations since the Renaissance*. London: Frank Cass, 1998. Visit to Vallombrosa, 285–291. Mentioned, xviii, 114, 129, 303 n3, 305 n20, 307 n32, 308 n35, 310 n43, 311 n46, 323.

Chaney, Edward. 'The Italianate Evolution of English Collecting.' In *The Evolution of English Collecting*, ed. Edward Chaney, 20, 78 & n499. New Haven: Yale University Press, 2003.

Churchill, Kenneth. *Italy and English Literature*. London: Macmillan, 1980. Travel diaries, 13–15, & bibliography, 213. Piranesian feel of Venice, 28.

Hawcroft, Francis W. *Travels in Italy 1776–1783: Based on the 'Memoirs' of Thomas Jones*. Manchester: Whitworth Art Gallery, 1988. Catalogue entry, 87–88.

Hopkins, Keith & Mary Beard. *The Colosseum*. London: Profile Books. 2005. Beckford had no time for the 'few lazy abbots' in the arena, 169. From *Dreams* (1783), see Gemmett's ed. (1971, p. 194).

Hyatt, Alfred H., ed. *The Charm of Venice. An Anthology*. London: Chatto & Windus, 1908. 'Venice seen in the distance', 72–74. 'An island visit', 214–218. 'The Grand Canal', 228–230.

Ingamells, John, ed. *A Dictionary of British and Irish Travellers in Italy 1701–1800*. New Haven: Yale University Press for Paul Mellon Centre for Studies in British Art, 1997. Peter Beckford, 70b–71a. William Beckford of Somerley, 71a–71b. William Beckford, 71b–73a.

Lees-Milne, James. *Venetian Evenings*. London: Collins, 1988. Some references to Beckford and quotations from *Dreams* (1783): Torcello, 26–27; St Mark's, 47; San Giorgio Maggiore, 131.

Littlewood, Ian. *Venice. A Literary Companion*. London: John Murray, 1991. Pp. 115, 119, 124, 128, 129, 189–191, 236.

Macaulay, Rose. *Pleasure of Ruins*. London: Weidenfeld & Nicolson, 1953. Beckford in Rome in 1780, from *Dreams* (1783), 189–191. Fonthill Abbey in 1796, 'a sort of habitable ruin', 33.

Marqusee, Michael, compiler. *Venice. An Illustrated Anthology*. London: Conran Octopus, 1988. Pp. 15, 34, 39, 60–61, 82, 111–112.

Morton, H. V. *In Search of Italy*. London: Methuen, 1964. Seeing "Venus de' Medici' in a gallery", 435.

Norwich, John Julius, ed. *Venice. A Traveller's Companion*. London: Constable, 1990. Pp. 130–2, 158–9, 212–214, 287–289, 319, 322–323, 351.

Pfister, Manfred. *The Fatal Gift of Beauty: The Italies of British Travellers*. Amsterdam: Rodopi, 1996. Pp. 469–470. Internationale Forschungen zur allgemeinen und vergleichenden literaturwissenschaft, No. 15.

Praz, Mario. *Il Mondo che ho Visto*. Milan: Adelphi, 1982. Pp. 15, 18, 19. Biblioteca Adelphi 123.

Prindl, Andreas. *A Companion to Lucca*. Lucca: Maria Pacini Fazzi, 2000. Letter from Lucca, 25 Sept 1780, about the city and Pacchierotti, 256–257.

Redford, Bruce. *Venice and the Grand Tour*. New Haven: Yale University Press, 1996. What might have transpired had Beckford met Byron, and Beckford's response to Venice in *Dreams* (1783), 105–115.

Ross, Nicholas. *Canaletto*. London: Studio Editions, 1993. Beckford in Venice (on Canaletto), 5.

Shaffer, E. S. " 'To Remind us of China' – William Beckford, Mental Traveller on the Grand Tour: The Construction of Significance in Landscape." In *Transports, Travel, Pleasure, and Imaginative Geography 1600–1830*, ed. Chloe Chard & Helen Langdon, 207–242. New Haven: Yale University Press, 1996. Also 20, 50–51, 65.

Shaffer, Elinor. 'William Beckford in Venice, Liminal City: The Pavilion and Indeterminal Staircase.' In *Venetian Views, Venetian Blinds. English Fantasies of Venice*, ed. Manfred Pfister & Barbara Schaff, 73–88. Amsterdam: Rodopi, 1999. Internationale Forschungen zur allgemeinen und vergleichenden literaturwissenschaft, No. 34.

Sully, James. *Italian Travel Sketches*. London: Constable, 1912. Beckford struck by the loveliness of the scenery, 49–50, 52 & 182–183. Reprinted from 'Development of Travel in Italy', *Edinburgh Review* 212 (July 1910): 26–27 & 'Terracina', *Quarterly Review* 215 (Oct 1911): 383.

Wilton, Andrew & Ilaria Bignamini. *Grand Tour. The Lure of Italy in the Eighteenth Century*. London: Tate Gallery Publishing, 1996. Nos. 104, 116, 122, 147, 259. Catalogue of exhibition in London and Rome.

Woodward, Christopher. *In Ruins*. London: Chatto & Windus, 2001. Rome, 13–16. Also 31, 41, 181, 192.

Articles

Chaney, Edward. 'Gibbon, Beckford and the Interpretation of *Dreams, Waking Thoughts, and Incidents*.' In *The Beckford Society Annual*

Lectures 2000–2003, ed. Jon Millington, 25–50. London: The Beckford Society, 2004. The 2001 lecture.

'Editor's Easy Chair.' *Harper's New Monthly Magazine* 22 (May 1861): 845–849 at 849. Beckford's description of the Campagna admired.

Ford, Brinsley. 'The Grand Tour.' *Apollo* 114 (Dec 1981): 390–400 at 393, 400. Beckford at the Leone Bianco in Venice in Aug 1781.

[Hayward, Abraham.] 'The Republic of Venice: Its Rise, Decline and Fall.' *Quarterly Review* 137 (Oct 1874): 416–458 at 431. Quote from *Italy* (1834, 1:113) 'by the author of "Vathek" ' about Henry III leaving Poland. Reprinted in *Littell's Living Age* 124 (30 Jan 1875): 267.

Jones, Thomas. *Memoirs*. Ed. A. P. Oppé. London: Walpole Society, 1951. Beckford in Italy in summer 1782, iii, 112–114. The Society's 32nd vol.

S., C. What other writers did Beckford have in mind in his preface to *Italy*? *Notes and Queries* 2nd Series 3 (20 June 1857): 487. Reply by W. L. N. that he was plagiarised by Moore, Samuel Rogers and Byron, 2nd Series 4 (4 July 1857): 14–15.

'Venice.' *North American Review* 86 (Jan 1858): 83–120 at 83. Beckford's *Travels in Italy, Spain and Portugal* one of eight works in review article.

PORTUGAL

Full-length Studies

Jack, Malcolm. *William Beckford. An English Fidalgo*. New York: AMS Press, 1996 [Jan 1997]. xv, 170 pp. 23½ cm. An in-depth exploration of Beckford's Portuguese years. Revised reprint, 1996 [July 1997].

REVIEWS. Berland, Kevin. *Eighteenth-Century Studies* 33 no. 3 (2000): 457–460. With a review of Timothy Mowl, *William Beckford: Composing for Mozart* (1998).

Cope, Kevin L. *1650–1850: Ideas, Aesthetics, and Inquiries in the Early Modern Era* 8 (2003): 392–396.

Drake, Robert. 'An English Fidalgo.' *Beckford Journal* 5 (1999): 4–5.

Flor, João de Almeida. 'William Beckford: A Portuguese Milord.' *Beckford Journal* 4 (1998): 18–22.

Hall, Michael. *Country Life*, 19 Feb 1998, 79.

Year's Work in English Studies for 1996 vol. 77 (1999): 406–407.

Kingsbury, Ida. *Castles, Caliphs and Christians: a Landscape with Figures. Monserrate*. Lisbon: British Historical Society of Portugal & Associação Amigos de Monserrate, 1994. 68 pp. 11 illus. 23 cm. Sponsored by Grupo Espírito Santo, p. [5]. Also discusses Sir Francis Cook, 'The second Caliph'. Reprinted 1995 with new p. [5] giving the Lisbon address of the Associação.

Parreaux, André. *Le Portugal dans l'œuvre de William Beckford*. Paris:

Société d'Editions «Les Belles Lettres», 1935. xxiii, 199 pp. Portrait frontis. 21½ cm.

Pires, Maria Laura Bettencourt. *William Beckford e Portugal: Uma visão diferente do Homem e do Escritor*. Lisbon: Edições 70, 1987. 292 pp. 8 pl. Bibliography, 271–283. 22½ cm. A revised version of her doctoral dissertation for the Universidade Nova, Lisbon, 1985. 948 pp. 30 cm.

REVIEWS. Boxer, C. R. 'Maria Laura Bettencourt Pires. *William Beckford e Portugal*.' 9 Dec 1988. (Source untraced.)

Jack, Malcolm. 'Beckford and Portugal: a Review Essay.' *Beckford Tower Trust Newsletter*, Spring 1990, 2–3.

Books

Alfonso, Simonetta Luz. 'Introduction.' In *Exposição. Exhibition. A Viagem de Uma Paixão. William Beckford & Portugal. An Impassioned Journey. 1787 1794 1798*, 6–10. Palácio de Queluz: Instituto Português do Património Cultural, 1987. Exhibition catalogue in Portuguese and English.

Bombelles, Marc de. *Journal d'un Ambassadeur de France au Portugal, 1786–1788*. Ed. Roger Kann. Paris: Presses Universitaires de France, 1979. Beckford's arrival in Lisbon, 117.

Branco, Fernando Castelo. 'Autores Estrangeiros.' In *Breve História da Olispografia* (Brief History of Writings on Lisbon), 85, 86, 88. Lisbon: Instituto de Cultura Portuguesa, 1980. Beckford one of the overseas writers. There is a longer reference to Beckford's publications on 103 n142.

Bridges, Ann & Susan Lowndes. *The Selective Traveller in Portugal*. London: Evans, 1949. Cintra, 61, 65–66. Alcobaça, 140.

Bullough, Geoffrey. "Beckford's Early Travels and His 'Dream of Delusion'." In *William Beckford of Fonthill, 1760–1844. Bicentenary Essays*, ed. Fatma Moussa-Mahmoud, 31–50. Suppl. to *Cairo Studies in English*, 1960.

[Carrére, J. B. F.] *Voyage au Portugal, et particulièrement à Lisbon . . .* Paris: Deterville, 1798. Pp. 119–127.

Cartledge, H. A. *William Beckford*. Coimbra, 1945. 18 pp. 24 cm. ?Manuscript.

Carvalho, Ayres de. 'Lisbon during the last quarter of the 18th C. as seen by William Beckford.' In *Exposição. Exhibition. A Viagem de Uma Paixão. William Beckford & Portugal. An Impassioned Journey. 1787 1794 1798*, 30–48. Palácio de Queluz: Instituto Português do Património Cultural, 1987. Exhibition catalogue in Portuguese and English.

Carvalho, João Pinto de. *Lisboa de outrora*. 3 vols. Lisbon: Ediçâo do Grupo Amigos de Lisboa, 1938. 1:99–112.

Costa, Francisco. *Beckford em Sintra no Verão de 1787. Narrativa literária seguida de – História da Quinta e Palácio do Ramalhão*. Sintra: Câmara Municipal de Sintra, 1982. Passim.

Costa, Francisco. *História da Quinta e Palácio de Monserrate*. Sintra: Câmara Municipal de Sintra, 1985. Passim.

Cruz, Duarte Ivo, 'The Theatre seen by William Beckford.' In *Exposição. Exhibition. A Viagem de Uma Paixão. William Beckford & Portugal. An Impassioned Journey. 1787 1794 1798*, 62–69. Palácio de Queluz: Instituto Português do Património Cultural, 1987. Exhibition catalogue in Portuguese and English.

Delaforce, Angela. *Art and Patronage in Eighteenth-Century Portugal*. Cambridge: Cambridge University Press, 2001. Passim.
    REVIEW: Jack, Malcolm. 'Magnificence in Eighteenth-Century Portugal.' *Beckford Journal* 10 (2004): 46–49.

Evans, Arthur Benoni. *The Phylactery*. A Poem. London: Longmans et al., 1836. Note about a passage in *Alcobaça and Batalha* illustrating some 'awful regrets' in the poem, 100–101.

Flor, João de Almeida. *Sintra na literatura romântica inglesa*. Sintra: Câmara Municipal de Sintra, 1978.

Freitas, João Sande de & Raul Constâncio. *rvores de Monserrate*. Texts, Emma Andersen Gilbert et al. Monserrate [Lisbon]: INAPA / Associação Amigos de Monserrate, 1997. Trans. Peter Ingham: *Trees of Monserrate*. Publ. and date as above. Pp. 2–4, 15, 18, 28, 48, 102, 117.

Gladstone. *The Gladstone Diaries*. Ed. M. R. D. Foot & H. C. G. Matthew. 14 vols. Oxford: Clarendon Press, 1968–1994. Vol. 3 (1974), 1840–1847: On 11 Aug 1846, Gladstone 'Read Beckford's Book on Alcobaca & Batalha' (1840 ed.), 565 & n4. Vol. 2 (1968), 1833–1839: Dined at the Duke of Hamilton's, son-in-law of Beckford, 25 & n9.

Gordon, Pryse Lockhart. *Personal Memoirs; or Reminiscences of Men and Manners . . .* 2 vols. London: Colburn & Bentley, 1830. Cintra in 1806, 'a villa erected by Fonthill Beckford in 1796, of which splendid house not a vestige remains except the walls', 2:3–4. Beckford's Claudes, 2:15.

Graham, Kenneth W. 'Narrative self-projection in Beckford's Portuguese writings.' In *Romantismo: Imagens de Portugal na Europa Romântica*, 108–112. Sintra: Instituto de Sintra, 1998.

Herbert, Henry John George, Earl of Carnarvon. *Portugal and Galicia*. 3rd ed. London: John Murray, 1848. (1st ed. 1836.) Villa at Monserrate, 11.

Hogg, Anthony. 'William Beckford (1760–1844).' In *Travellers' Portuguese*, 15. Chichester: Solo Mio, 1983. Beckford, former British Traveller. Also 176, 217.

Hogg, Garry. *Portuguese Journey*. London: Travel Book Club, n.d. 'That strange traveller and recluse, William Beckford' at Alcobaça, 130.

Hume, Martin. *Through Portugal*. London: Grant Richards, 1907. Batalha, 170, 172–173, 175, 177, 180, 181, 182. Aljubarrota, 187. Alcobaça, 188–189, 190–192, 194, 195, 196–197. Cintra, 215–216, 220.

Inchbold, A. C. *Lisbon & Cintra*. London: Chatto & Windus, 1907. Passim. Monserrate, 156–158. Ramalhão, 174–177.

Jack, Malcolm. 'The World of Beckford's Portuguese Palaces.' In *William Beckford, 1760–1844: An Eye for the Magnificent*, ed. Derek E. Ostergard, 88–97. New Haven & London: Yale University Press for the Bard Graduate Center, 2001. Exhibition catalogue.

Jack, Malcolm. *Sintra. A Glorious Eden*. Manchester: Carcanet, 2002. Pp. 157–168. Also 119–120, 123–127 & passim.

    REVIEW. Blackmore, Sidney. '*Sintra: A Glorious Eden*. A Review.' *Beckford Journal* 9 (2003): 2–5.

Jackson, Lady Catherine Charlotte. *Fair Lusitania*. London: Richard Bentley, 1874. Beckford's description of Cintra, 180.

Jacobson, Dawn. *Chinoiserie*. London: Phaidon, 1993. Beckford's description of Pillement's pavilion at Cintra, 75. Fonthill boundary wall 'like that of the emperor's palace at Yuan-ming-yuan', 184.

Kelly, Marie Noële. *This Delicious Land. Portugal*. London: Hutchinson, 1956. Monserrate, 73.

Kinsey, Rev. William Morgan. *Portugal Illustrated*. London: Treuttel, Würtz & Richter, 1828. Cintra, 133.

Kühl, Paulo Mugayar. '*Vendica i torti miei*: Beckford, Opera, and Portuguese Society.' In *William Beckford and the New Millennium*, ed. Kenneth W. Graham & Kevin Berland, 165–179. New York: AMS Press, 2004 [2005].

Latouche, John. *Travels in Portugal*. 2nd ed. London: Ward, Lock and Tyler, c.1875. (1st ed. 1875.) Cintra 'greatly overpraised', 188–189. Originally publ. as 'Notes of Travel in Portugal' in *The New Quarterly Magazine*.

Macaulay, Rose. 'Aesthete. William Beckford.' In *They Went to Portugal*, 108–142. London: Jonathan Cape, 1946. Sympathetic account of Beckford's three visits in 1787, 1795–1796 & 1798–1799.

Macedo, Jorge Borges de. 'William Beckford & Portugal.' In *Exposição. Exhibition. A Viagem de Uma Paixão. William Beckford & Portugal. An Impassioned Journey. 1787 1794 1798*, 18–29. Palácio de Queluz: Instituto Português do Património Cultural, 1987. Portuguese society in Beckford's time. Exhibition catalogue in Portuguese and English.

Malta, Eduardo. *Estrangeiros sôbre Portugal: retratos*. N.p., n.d. (?1948). Nine portraits, including Beckford, Robert Southey and James Murphy.

Metcalf, Priscilla. 'Cook's Villa at Cintra.' In *James Knowles: Victorian Editor and Architect*, 43–50, passim & pl. 8. Oxford: Clarendon Press, 1980.

Nunes, João Manuel de Sousa. *A obra de William Beckford perante a mentalidade e a cultura do tempo*. Lisbon: J. S. Nunes, 1990. 20 pp.

Pereira, João Castel-Branco. 'The Carriages of Lisbon.' In *Exposição. Exhibition. A Viagem de Uma Paixão. William Beckford & Portugal. An*

Impassioned Journey. 1787 1794 1798, 70–79. Palácio de Queluz: Instituto Português do Património Cultural, 1987. Exhibition catalogue in Portuguese and English.

Pires, Maria Laura Bettencourt. 'William Beckford & Portugal: A different perspective on the man and the writer.' In *Exposição. Exhibition. A Viagem de Uma Paixão. William Beckford & Portugal. An Impassioned Journey. 1787 1794 1798*, 12–17. Palácio de Queluz: Instituto Português do Património Cultural, 1987. Exhibition catalogue in Portuguese and English.

Pires, Maria Laura Bettencourt. 'Imagens de Alcobaça e Batalha na Obra de William Beckford.' In *Ensaios-Notas Reflexões*, 157–171. Lisbon: Universidade Aberta, 2000.

Pires, Maria Laura Bettencourt. 'William Beckford and Portugal: A Case of Mutual Attraction.' In *William Beckford and the New Millennium*, ed. Kenneth W. Graham & Kevin Berland, 131–163. New York: AMS Press, 2004 [2005].

Quillinan [neé Wordsworth], Dorothy. *Journal of a Few Months' Residence in Portugal, and Glimpses of the South of Spain.* 2 vols. London: Moxon, 1847. 2:56–57.

Robertson, Ian. *Portugal. A Traveller's Guide.* London: John Murray, 1992. Passim.

[Sherer, Moyle.] *Recollections of the Peninsula.* 5th ed. London: Longman, etc., 1827. (1st ed. 1823.) Beckford's house at Monserrate 'in a state of desolation and ruin . . . this costly temple of pleasure', 39–40.

Shore, H. N. *Three Pleasant Springs in Portugal.* London: Sampson Low, 1899. Lisbon aqueduct, 41. Caldas, 54–55. Alcobaça, 60–61, 62–65, 67, 68, 69, 71, 72, 73, 80, 117. Batalha, 85, 86–87, 88, 89, 90–92, 93. Fonthill, 278. Also 3, 4, 127, 256.

Silva, José Cornélio da & G. Luckhurst. *Sintra. A Landscape with Villas.* Lisbon: Edições Inapa, 1989. Passim.

Sitwell, Sacheverell. *Portugal and Madeira.* London: Batsford, 1954. Quotations from Travels, 114–116 & passim. Fine photos of monasteries.

Soares d'Azevedo Barbosa de Pinho Leal, Augusto. *Portugal antigo e moderno.* 12 vols. Lisbon, 1875. Monserrate, 5:436–438.

Tennyson, Alfred, Lord. *The Letters of Alfred Lord Tennyson.* Ed. Cecil Y. Lang & Edgar F. Shannon, Jr. 3 vols. Oxford: Clarendon Press, 1982–1990. Vol. 2 (1987), 1851–1870. To the Duke of Argyll on 3 Oct 1859, mentioning Beckford at Cintra, 244 & n3.

Veiga, Luiz Alte da. 'Notes on Physics in Portugal in the 18th century.' In *Exposição. Exhibition. A Viagem de Uma Paixão. William Beckford & Portugal. An Impassioned Journey. 1787 1794 1798*, 80–83. Palácio de Queluz: Instituto Português do Património Cultural, 1987. Exhibition catalogue in Portuguese and English.

Wahba, Magdi. 'Beckford, Portugal and "Childish Error".' In *William Beckford of Fonthill, 1760–1844. Bicentenary Essays*, ed. Fatma Moussa-Mahmoud, 51–62. Suppl. to *Cairo Studies in English*, 1960.

Walter, Felix. *La littérature portugaise en Angleterre à l'époque romantique.* Paris: Honoré Champion, 1927. P. 29.

Watson, Walter Crum. *Portuguese Architecture.* London: Archibald Constable, 1908. Beckford's 'memorable visit' to Alcobaça, 59.

Articles

Alexander, Boyd, 'The Marquis of Marialva's Friendship with Beckford.' *British Historical Society of Portugal. Second Annual Report and Review* (Lisbon, 1975): 11–22. Includes quotations from the Beckford Papers.

Alexander, Boyd, 'Beckford's Debt to Portugal.' *British Historical Society of Portugal. Fifth Annual Report and Review* (Lisbon, 1978): 21–36.

'Beckford, William por ocasião de um bicentenário 1787–1987.' *O Estudo da História* No. 3–4, 2 série (April–June / July–Sept 1987): 31–33. Striking portrait by E[duardo] Malta, 1948, (? from his *Estrangeiros sôbre Portugal: retratos*) based on Dean's engraving (1835) of Reynolds's portrait, 31.

Benjamin, S. G. W. 'Portugal and the Portuguese.' *Atlantic Monthly* 40 (Dec 1877): 659–669 at 666, 667. Beckford's works made Cintra & Mafra famous.

Bernhardt, Paul. 'In Beckford's Footsteps. A Literary Journey through Estremadura.' *Essential Algarve* No. 19 (June–July 2003): 50–54. In English and German. Colour photos of Alcobaça and Batalha.

Borenius, Tancred. 'A Footnote to Beckford.' *Burlington Magazine* 78 (June 1941): 201–202. Portrait of St Thomas à Becket at Alcobaça mentioned by Beckford in *Recollections* (1835), 45.

Brittain-Catlin, Timothy. 'View from Lisbon . . .' *Architectural Review* 214 (July 2003): 22–23 at 23. '. . . beautiful landscape . . . that once attracted Beckford'.

Castro, D. Luis de. 'Beckford em Cintra.' *Ilustração Portugueza* Nos. 36, 37, 38 (1906): 411–416, 425–431, 46?–472.

Champney, Lillie W. 'A Neglected Corner of Europe.' *Harper's New Monthly Magazine* 63 (June 1881): 36–51 at 38. Hanging gardens at Belem 'reminded the eccentric Beckford of places of interment'. *Idem* (Aug 1881): 339–415 at 399, 400–401, 413–414. Monserrate ('Beckford's hermitage') and Alcobaça.

Davey, R. 'Inez de Castro.' *Galaxy* (New York) 24 (Sept 1877): 305–313 at 312. 'Alcobaça, so exquisitely described by Beckford'.

Dewey, Clive. 'Monserrate, Sintra, Portugal.' *Country Life*, 1 Nov 1990, 88, 89, 91.

Elliott, Kirsten. 'Finding Beckford in Portugal.' *The Bath Magazine*, June 2004, 11. Retracing Beckford's footsteps in Sintra and Monserrate.

Falmouth. *Salisbury and Winchester Journal,* 22 Oct 1798, 4c. Beckford embarked from Falmouth to visit the Prince of Brazil (heir to the Portuguese throne). Abbey building to continue.

Flor, João de Almeida. 'How the Portuguese experience influenced Beckford.' *Anglo-Portuguese News,* 8 Jan 1998, 8, 13.

Gihon, A. L. 'A Look at Lisbon.' *Harper's New Monthly Magazine* 33 (July 1866): 170–183 at 181. 'Monserrat, the gorgeous residence of Beckford'.

Gracias, J. A. Ismael. 'Bocage na India.' *Oriente Português* 14 (1917): 29ff.

Gregory, Isabella Augusta. 'Through Portugal.' *Fortnightly Review* n.s. 34 (1 Oct 1883): 571–580 at 574. At Alcobaça, 'visited the convent where Beckford lived.' Reprinted in *Littell's Living Age* 159 (10 Nov 1883): 361.

Guerra, Oliva. 'Sintra e Lord Beckford.' *Coloquio* 46 (1967): 14–16.

Hall, Fitzedward. 'Shall We Say "Is Being Built"?' *Scribner's Monthly* 3 (April 1872): 700–707 at 702. Beckford on Lisbon's fortune tellers in 1787.

Hancock, Matthew. 'In search of . . . William Beckford in Sintra.' *The Independent,* 17 March 2002.

Hilliard, Elizabeth. 'Dr and Mrs Hilliard's Visit to Portugal.' *Beckford Tower Trust Newsletter,* Spring 1986, 7–8. Ramalhão, Alcobaça and Batalha.

Jack, Malcolm. 'William Beckford: traveller, artist, escapist.' *Studies on Voltaire and the Eighteenth Century* 305 (1992): 1823–1824. Beckford's Portuguese works. Delivered at the 1991 Beckford Round Table.

Jack, Malcolm. 'Ramalhão: Beckford's First Sintra House.' *Beckford Journal* 3 (1997): 20–24.

Jack, Malcolm. 'Monserrate: Beckford's Second Sintra House.' *Beckford Journal* 4 (1998): 48–51.

Jack, Malcolm. Beckford Society Portuguese tour. *Anglo-Portuguese News,* 24 June 1999. The Society's visit, May 29–June 4.

Jack, Malcolm. 'Portuguese Pilgrims and Irish Seminarians.' *Beckford Journal* 6 (2000): 5–6. Beckford Society visit (and 1999 Round Table in Dublin).

Kingsbury, Ida. 'Post Script to the Excursion. In Beckford's Footsteps to Alcobaça and Batalha.' *British Historical Society of Portugal. Seventh Annual Report and Review* (Lisbon, 1980): 23–40.

Lisbon. *Salisbury and Winchester Journal,* 11 June 1787, 3b. Beckford's stormy voyage to Jamaica. Ship made for Lisbon where he remained.

Mayoux, Jean-Jacques. 'Note sur l'Excursion à Alcobaça et Batalha.' *Critique* 13 (Oct 1957): 905–907.

Parreaux, André. 'Précisions sur les séjours de William Beckford au Portugal.' *Bulletin des Etudes Portugaises* 6 (1939): 45–49.

Parreaux, André. 'Beckford et le Portugal. Du Nouveau sur Quelques Problèmes.' *Bulletin des Etudes Portugaises* n.s. 18 (1955): 93–130. Also publ. as an offprint, Paris, 1955, 42 pp.

Parreaux, André. 'Beckford et le Portugal.' *Bulletin des Etudes Portugaises* n.s. 21 (1958): 97–155. Also publ. as an offprint, Paris, 1958, 63 pp.

Pires, Maria Laura Bettencourt. 'A Re-examination of William Beckford's Life and Accomplishments in Portugal.' *Beckford Tower Trust Newsletter*, Spring 1986, 2–6.

Pires, Maria Laura Bettencourt. 'Imagens de Beckford em Portugal.' *Diário de Notícias*, 3 Nov 1987, 6.

Pires, Maria Laura Bettencourt. 'Sintra-Cidade de Conto de Fadas.' *Jornal de Sintra*, Página Cultural, No. 11, 1987, 1.

Pires, Maria Laura Bettencourt. 'William Beckford et le Portugal.' *Bulletin des Études Portugaises et Brésiliennes* 46–47 (1986), 299–303.

'Portugal's Glory and Decay.' *North American Review* 83 (Oct 1856): 456–476 at 467. Review of books in Portuguese. 'Mafra, said to be the largest building in the world, and best known by the description in Beckford's Vathek'.

Silva, Raquel Henriques da. 'Lisboa, 1787 em imagens de William Beckford.' *O Estudo da História* No. 3–4, 2 série (April–June / July–Sept 1987): 42–47.

'Smith's *Tour in Portugal*.' *Edinburgh Review* 131 (April 1870): 450–469 at 453, 461, 465. Beckford 'inspired us long ago with an extreme desire to visit' Alcobaça & Batalha – he was 'regally entertained' at Alcobaça' and 'galloped in the freshness of the morning' at Aljubarrota – his 'deserted abode at Montserrat'.

Soares, J. E. F. 'Recordando o segundo centenario de William Beckford.' *Boletim da Academia Portuguesa de Ex-Libris* 18 (1961): 25–29.

Villiers, G. H. 'Mr. Beckford in Portugal.' *National Review* 74 (Feb 1920): 808–816. Beckford's excursion to Alcobaça and Batalha in 1794.

SPAIN

Books

Ford, Richard. *A Hand-Book for Travellers in Spain.* 2 parts. London: John Murray, 1845. Beckford congratulates himself on 'his happiness in sleeping through the journey' from Badajoz to Madrid, pt. 1, 528. Writing (*Italy*, 1834, 2:325) about a 'quill from Gabriel's wing' in the Escorial, pt. 2, 817.

Articles

[Ford, Richard.] 'Cloister Life of Charles V.' *Quarterly Review* 92 (Dec 1852): 107–136 at 135. In Madrid in 1780, Beckford asked to see the face of Charles V. Reprinted in *Littell's Living Age* 36 (12 March 1853): 492.

Notes and Queries 3rd Series 3 (16, 23 May 1863): 382–383, 401. Beckford's visit to the Escorial in 1787.

Pennell, Elizabeth Robins. 'In Spain. Light and Shadows of the Alhambra.' *Century* (New York) 52 (June 1896): 198–215 at 213.

Spanish cookery. 'Thoughts upon Dinners.' *Blackwood's Edinburgh Magazine* 71 (June 1852): 734–749 at 748. No one since Beckford has 'spoken in praise of Spanish cookery' when he described a 'monastic banquet of rare excellence'.

'The Spirit of Eighteenth-Century Madrid.' *Times Literary Supplement*, 30 Dec 1955, 795. Review of *La Condesa – Duquesa de Benavente* mentioning Beckford dancing the bolero.

SWITZERLAND

Books

Gauthier, Madame. *Voyage d'une française* ... 2 vols.: Imprints: 1 'en Suisse', 2 'Londres', 1790. In 1789 a company of musicians from Geneva had been imported for the season, by 'un Anglois nommé Becfort', 2:64–65.

Hauptman, William. 'Clinging Fast "To My Tutelary Mountains": Beckford in Helvetia.' In *William Beckford, 1760–1844: An Eye for the Magnificent*, ed. Derek E. Ostergard, 72–87. New Haven & London: Yale University Press for the Bard Graduate Center, 2001. Exhibition catalogue.

Lawless, Valentine Browne, Baron Cloncurry. *Personal Recollections of the Life and Times, with Extracts from the Correspondence, of Valentine, Lord Cloncurry.* Dublin: McGlashan, 1849. Beckford at Neufchatel, Oct 1792, 11.

McCormack, W. J. *Sheridan Le Fanu and Victorian Ireland.* Oxford: Clarendon Press, 1980. Lord Cloncurry, landowner, had met Beckford, 25.

Whaley, Buck. *Buck Whaley's Memoirs* ...1797. See above, under 'France'.

Articles

Beer, Gavin R. De. 'Anglais au pays de Vaud. v. William Beckford.' *Revue historique vaudoise* 59 (December 1951): 165–180.

Hauptman, William. 'Beckford, Brandoin, and the Gessner Monument in Zurich.' *Beckford Journal* 9 (2003): 27–36.

Jaloux, Edmond. 'Beckford.' & 'Lettres de Beckford.' *Gazette de Lausanne*, 24 Nov & 8 Dec 1945, 1 & 1.

Perrochon, Henri. 'Un ami de Gibbon.' *Gazette de Lausanne*, 1 May 1932, 1.

14. Beckford's Other Works

Biographical Memoirs of Extraordinary Painters *(1780)*

Biographical Memoirs of Extraordinary Painters. London: J. Robson, New-Bond-Street, 1780. iv, 158 pp. 18½ cm. Chapman, *Bibliography* (1930), 1(i).

Biographical Memoirs of Extraordinary Painters. 2nd ed. London: J. Robson, New Bond Street, 1780. iv, 158 pp. 18½ cm. A reissue of the first edition with a cancel title page. Chapman, *Bibliography* (1930), 1(ii).

Biographical Memoirs of Extraordinary Painters. London: William Clarke, New Bond Street, 1824. iv, 150 pp. 19 cm. Frontis., lithograph by 'Og of Basan' of St Denis bearing his own head in his hand. Chapman, *Bibliography* (1930), 1(iii).

Biographical Memoirs of Extraordinary Painters. London: Richard Bentley, 1834. iv, 150 pp. 19 cm. Frontis., lithograph by 'Og of Basan'. Identical to the 1824 ed, except for the prelims and printer's imprint on p. 150. Chapman, *Bibliography* (1930), 1(iv).

Biographical Memoirs of Extraordinary Painters. Ed. Robert J. Gemmett. Rutherford, NJ: Fairleigh Dickinson University Press, 1969. 111 pp. 21¼ cm. Reprinted 1975.

Biographical Memoirs of Extraordinary Painters (1780). Intro. Philip Ward. Cambridge: Oleander Press, 1977. xiv, iv, 158 pp. 21 cm. Facsimile reprint of the first edition.

Memórias Biográficas de Pintores Extraordinários. Intro. Vincente Molina Foix. Trans. into Spanish by Jorge Mara. Madrid: Alfaguara Nostromo, 1978.

Vies authentiques de peintres imaginaires. Trans. Roger Kann. Paris: José Corti, 1990. 123 pp. 16 cm. Collection romantique, No. 24.

Vite immaginarie di pittori straordinari. Intro. Violetta Candiani. Trans. into Italian by Mariapaola Dèttore. Rome: Biblioteca del Vascello, 1994. 139 pp. 14 cm. I vascelli No. 24.

Memorie biografiche di pittori straordinari. Essay by G. Fossi. Trans. into Italian by Mirella Billi. Florence: Giunti, 1995.

Memórias Biográficas de Pintores Extraordinários. Trans. into Spanish & notes by Paulo Mugayar Kühl. Coria, 2001. 106 pp. 20 cm.

Contemporary Reviews and Advertisements

Athenæum, 23 Aug 1834, 626. A paragraph on the 1834 reissue.

Critical Review 49 (June 1780): 478–480.

Gentleman's Magazine 50 (June 1780): 290.

Literary Gazette 8 (29 May, 11 Sept 1824): 349, 352, 592. Advert.

London Review and Weekly Journal of Literature and the Fine Arts No. 2 (16 June 1827): 24–25. With review of *Vathek* (1823).

Monthly Review 63 (Dec 1780): 469.

Retrospective Review 10 pt. 1 (Aug 1824): 172–179.

Later Reviews and Articles

Adams, Eric. 'Five fake masters.' *Times Literary Supplement*, 18 March 1977, 314. Oleander Press ed. (1977). *Idem*, Letter from Robert J. Gemmett mentioning his 1969 ed., 29 April, 523.

Barolsky, Paul. 'Leonardo, Satan, and the Mystery of Modern Art.' *Virginia Quarterly Review* 74 no. 3 (Summer 1998): 393–414 at 393. Beckford carried the fable of art to the pitch of high farce and fantasy.

Chard, Chloe. *Pleasure and guilt on the Grand Tour. Travel writing and imaginative geography 1600–1830*. Manchester: Manchester University Press, 1999. Og of Basan, 135, 141–143, 173–175, 182–183, 224 & n40, 230 n59. *Dreams* (1783), 7 n22, 45, 201 & n74, 247–248.

Darton, Eric. 'William Beckford's First Published Work: Biographical Memoirs of Extraordinary Painters.' *Beckford Tower Trust Newsletter*, Spring 1994, 6–8.

Delon, Michel. 'Beckford le rêveur éveillé.' *La Quinzaine littéraire*, No. 569, 1 Jan 1991. With a review of *La Vision*, Trans. Didier Girard (1990).

Fitzhopkins. 'Beckford's "Lives of the Painters".' *Notes and Queries* 3rd Series 8 (7 Oct 1865): 287. Explanation by J. H. Burn, (2 Dec 1865): 463.

Gemmett, Robert J. 'The Composition of William Beckford's *Biographical Memoirs of Extraordinary Painters*.' *Philological Quarterly* 47 no. 1 (Jan 1968): 139–141. Discusses when the work was written.

Hilliard, Elizabeth. 'Watersouchy of Amsterdam.' *Beckford Tower Trust Newsletter*, Spring 1987, 8. Her discovery of a recipe for water souchy in Eliza Acton's *Modern Cookery, for Private Families . . .* (1845).

Junod, Karen. "Artists' Lives in Eighteenth-Century Britain: The Strange Case of William Beckford." *The Age of Johnson* (Rutgers University) 16 (2005): 237–257. Analyses the contemporary reception of *Memoirs* and re-establishes its importance in the Beckford canon.

Lipking, Lawrence. 'Horace Walpole's *Anecdotes*. 9. Walpole, Beckford and New Directions.' In *The Ordering of the Arts in Eighteenth-Century England*, 159–163. Princeton: Princeton University Press, 1970.

Mattick, Paul. 'Bookend. Imagining Imaginary Artists.' *The New York Times*, 14 June 1998. Mainly about *Nat Tate: An American Artist, 1928–1960* by William Boyd.

Modern Novel Writing *(1796 [?1795])*

Modern Novel Writing, or the Elegant Enthusiast; and Interesting Emotions of Arabella Bloomville. A Rhapsodical Romance; interspersed with Poetry. 'By the Right Hon. Lady Harriet Marlow.' 2 vols. London: G. G. & J. Robinson, 1796 [?1795]. v, 243 pp. & iii, 232 pp. 18½ cm. First issue, [?1795], not in Chapman's *Bibliography* (1930). Second issue, 1796, in Chapman, 4(i), and also 4(i, a) with no dedication in vol. 2.

Miss Arabella Bloomville. Ein Rhapsodisticher Roman von Lady Harriet Marlow. Weissenfels: Severin, 1798.

Modern Novel Writing (1796) and Azemia (1797). Facsimile reprints introduced by Herman Mittle Levy, Jr. 4 vols. in 1 (with 4 pages to a page). Gainesville, Florida: Scholars' Facsimiles & Reprints, 1970. 265 pp. Reprinted 1999.

Modern Novel Writing. Intro. Gina Luria. 2 vols. New York: Garland, 1974. The Feminist Controversy in England, 1788–1810 Series.

Contemporary Reviews

British Critic 9 (Jan 1797): 75–76.
Critical Review n.s. 18 (Dec 1796): 472–474.
Monthly Mirror 2 (Sept 1796): 286.
Monthly Review n.s. 20 (Dec 1796): 477.

Books

Griebel, Deborah Joanne. *A Critical Edition of William Beckford's 'Modern Novel Writing' and 'Azemia'.* PhD thesis for University of Toronto. *Dissertation Abstracts International* 48 no. 11 (May 1988): 2879-A.

Parreaux, André. 'The Caliph and The Swinish Multitude.' In *William Beckford of Fonthill, 1760–1844. Bicentenary Essays,* ed. Fatma Moussa-Mahmoud, 1–15. Suppl. to *Cairo Studies in English,* 1960. Discusses *Modern Novel Writing* and *Azemia.*

Articles

Darton, Eric. 'The Satirical Novels of William Beckford: 1. Modern Novel Writing (1796).' *Beckford Tower Trust Newsletter,* Spring 1990, 5–7.

Freeman, Arthur. "William Beckford's *Modern Novel Writing,* 1795–6: Two issues, 'Three States'." *Book Collector* 41 no. 1 (Spring 1992): 69–73. Argues that *Modern Novel Writing* was first publ. in 1795, not 1796.

Gemmett, Robert J. 'William Beckford's Authorship of *Modern Novel Writing* and *Azemia.' Papers of the Bibliographical Society of America* 98 no. 3 (Sept 2004): 313–325. Evidence to support claim that Beckford wrote both works.

Azemia *(1797)*

Azemia: A Descriptive and Sentimental Novel. Interspersed with Pieces of Poetry. 'By Jacquetta Agneta Mariana Jenks.' 2 vols. London: Sampson Low, 1797. xii, 254 pp. & iv, 253 pp. 19½ cm. Chapman, *Bibliography* (1930), 5(i).

Azemia, A Novel: Containing Imitations of the Manner, both in Prose and Verse, of Many of the Authors of the Present Day; with Political Strictures. 'By J. A. M. Jenks.' 2nd ed. 2 vols. London: Sampson Low, 1798. xii, xxx, 254 pp. & iv, 253 pp. 18½ cm. Contains the 27-page story 'Edward and Ellen' after the prelims in Vol. 1. Chapman, *Bibliography* (1930), 5(ii).

Arnold et la Belle Musulmane. 'Par J. A. M. Jenks. Traduit de l'Anglais par F. Soulès.' 2 vols. Paris: Frechet, 1808. iv, 251 pp. & iv, 251 pp. 18½ cm. Chapman, *Bibliography* (1930), 5(iii).

Azemia. Intro. Gina Luria. 2 vols. New York: Garland, 1974. The Feminist Controversy in England, 1788–1810 series.

Azemia. Editor's intro. & Most of first four chapters from vol. 1:1–50. In *Parodies of the Romantic Age*, ed. John Strachan, 3:69–72 & 73–93, 355–356 nn1–3. 5 vols. London: Pickering & Chatto, 1999. '*Azemia* probably the finest blend of sentiment and parody ever written', 3:72. Also Cyrus Redding, 4:131n; Fonthill 1823 sale, 4:139n; Fonthill collection, 5:xi.

Azemia. Extracts from vol. 1:39–41, 50–54. In *Gothic documents. A sourcebook 1700–1820*, eds. E. J. Clery & Robert Miles, 202–204 Manchester: Manchester University Press, 2000. Also 2.

Contemporary Reviews

British Critic 10 (Oct 1797): 433–434.
Critical Review n.s. 20 (Aug 1797): 470.
Monthly Mirror 4 (July 1797): 95–97.
Monthly Review n.s. 24 (Nov 1797): 338.
Monthly Visitor and Entertaining Pocket Companion 2 (July 1797): 85–87.

Books

London, April. *Women and Property in the Eighteenth-Century English Novel.* Cambridge: Cambridge University Press, 1999. Beckford's mockery, 170–171, 194.

Norton, Rictor. *Mistress of Udolpho: the life of Ann Radcliffe.* London: Leicester University Press, 1999. Identifies Beckford's allusions to her work, 164–165.

Articles

Darton, Eric. 'The Satirical Novels of William Beckford: 2. Azemia (1797).' *Beckford Tower Trust Newsletter*, Spring 1991, 7–9.

Nolan, Jerry. 'William, Elizabeth & William or Female Impersonation and Radical Satire.' *Beckford Journal* 6 (2000): 35–45. Elizabeth Hervey and William Pitt the Younger's influence on *Azemia* & *Modern Novel Writing*.

Paradise, Nathaniel. 'The Novel and Female Accomplishment.' *Philological Quarterly* 74 (1995): 57–76 at 73, 74 & 76 nn30,31. 'Beckford in his parodies insistently links bad sentimental poetry with the novel', 73.

POETRY

'A Prayer' (1822)

Literary Gazette 6 (9 Nov 1822): 714. Four untitled stanzas later known as 'A Prayer'. Chapman, *Bibliography* (1930), pp. 105–106.

Britton, John. *Fonthill Abbey* (1823), p. 60. With 'The Last Day' on same page.

County Literary Chronicle and Weekly Review, 13 Sept 1823, 578. With 'The Last Day'.

Gentleman's Magazine 93 pt. 2 (Sept 1823): 262. With 'The Last Day'.

Ladies' Monthly Museum 18 (Oct 1823): 216. With 'The Last Day'.

Watts, Alaric, ed. *The Poetical Album; and Register of Modern Fugitive Poetry*. London: Hurst Robinson, 1828 [but privately printed 1824]. P. 151.

The Sacred Muse. London: Thos Allman, 1840. P. 193. With 'The Last Day'.

Bath Herald, 18 May 1844, 3e. In a letter from 'G', also noting Beckford's praise for William Jay's *The Christian Contemplated* (1826). Same letter in *Bath and Cheltenham Gazette*, 22 May 1844, 2c.

Mirror of Literature n.s. 5 (8 June 1844): 363.

'Lines, by Mr. Beckford.' *Littell's Living Age* 2 (17 Aug 1844): 115.

'The Last Day' (1823). Also known as 'Dies Iræ'

Britton, John. *Fonthill Abbey* (1823), p. 60. With 'A Prayer' on the same page. Chapman, *Bibliography* (1930), p. 106.

Literary Gazette 7 (30 Aug 1823): 555.

County Literary Chronicle and Weekly Review, 13 Sept 1823, 578. With 'A Prayer'.

Gentleman's Magazine 93 pt. 2 (Sept 1823): 262. With 'A Prayer'.

Ladies' Monthly Museum 18 (Oct 1823): 217. With 'A Prayer'.

Watts, Alaric, ed. *The Poetical Album; and Register of Modern Fugitive Poetry*. London: Hurst Robinson, 1828 [but privately printed 1824]. P. 35.

The Talisman. Ed. Z. M. Watts. London: Whittaker, etc, 1831. P. 146.

The Sacred Muse. London: Thos Allman, 1840. P. 193. With 'A Prayer'.

The Transient Gleam: A Bouquet of Beckford's Poesy.
Ed. Devendra P. Varma. (1991)

The Transient Gleam: A Bouquet of Beckford's Poesy. Presented with intro.
by Devendra P. Varma. Upton, Wirral: Aylesford Press, 1991. 101 pp. 5
pl. Foreword by Brocard Sewell. 'Lyrical Poems', 28–55. 'Sonnets',
58–61. 'Elegies', 65–69. 'Epitaphs', 72–81. 'Fonthill and Lansdown
Poems', 84–99 and 100–101. Limited to 300 numbered copies.

REVIEW. Roberts, Marie Mulvey. *British Journal for Eighteenth Century
Studies* 16 no. 2 (Autumn 1993): 253. Much verse 'interesting rather
than inspiring'.

POSTHUMOUS WORKS

The Visio*n and* Liber Veritatis. *1930*

The Vision and *Liber Veritatis.* Ed. Guy Chapman. London: Constable,
1930. xxix, 166 pp. 4 pl. Limited to 750 copies. Chapman, *Bibliography*
(1930), 11.

REVIEWS. 'Beckford trifles.' *Times Literary Supplement,* 14 Aug 1930, 650.

H., J. [Hayward, John.] *Life and Letters* 5 no. 31 (Dec 1930): 449–451.
With a review of Chapman's *Bibliography* (1930), 451–452.

King, William. *The Criterion* 10 no. 39 (Jan 1931): 369–371, reprinted 1967.
With a review of *Bibliography of William Beckford of Fonthill* (1930).

ARTICLES. Darton, Eric. 'William Beckford's First Literary Work – The
Vision.' *Beckford Tower Trust Newsletter,* Spring 1992, 10–13.

Nolan, Jerry. '*Liber Veritatis* or Why has the Child been so Abused?'
Beckford Journal 7 (2001): 2–10.

La Vision. Trans. by Didier Girard of Guy Chapman's 1930 ed. Paris: José
Corti, 1990. 159 pp. Five illus. by Olivier Darry. Collection romantique,
No. 25.

REVIEW. 'Delon, Michel. 'Beckford le rêveur éveillé.' *La Quinzaine
littéraire,* No. 569, 1 Jan 1991. With a review of *Vies authentiques de
peintres imaginaires.*

The Vision. Intro. Darrell Schweitzer. New York: Wildside Press (Judson
Rosebush), 2004. 108 pp.

LETTERS

Life at Fonthill 1807–1822. With Interludes
in Paris and London. *1957*

*Life at Fonthill 1807–1822. With Interludes in Paris and London. From the
Correspondence of Willim Beckford.* Trans. from the Italian & ed. Boyd

Alexander. London: Hart-Davis, 1957. 352 pp. 10 pl. Letters, mostly to Franchi.
REVIEWS. 'Beckford behind the barrier.' *The Times*, 28 Feb 1957, 11d–e.
Heppenstall, Rayner. 'Fed-up at Fonthill.' *New Statesman and Nation*, 23 Feb 1957, 249–250.
'Letters of an eccentric.' *Times Literary Supplement*, 8 March 1957, 142.
Plumb, J. H. 'Beckford's Folly.' *Spectator*, 22 Feb 1957, 257.
Raymond, John. 'The madman of Fonthill.' ?, Sunday, 17 Feb 1957.
Spring, Howard. 'Beckford's Obsessions.' *Country Life*, 28 March 1957, 623.

The Consummate Collector: William Beckford's Letters to His Bookseller. *2000*

The Consummate Collector: William Beckford's Letters to His Bookseller. Ed. Robert J. Gemmett. Wilby, Norfolk: Michael Russell, 2000. 336 pp. Frontis. & 14 illus. Annotated transcriptions of over 350 letters to George Clarke between 1830 & 1834.
REVIEWS. Clarke, Stephen. 'No More Green Cloth Boardings: The Fastidious Book Collecting of William Beckford.' *Beckford Journal* 7 (2001): 39–45.
Hobson, Anthony. 'Nothing second-rate enters here.' *Times Literary Supplement*, 20 July 2001, 36. The title comes from a draft letter to Bohn, 18 June 1842.
Hunt, Arnold. *Book Collector* 51 no. 1 (Spring 2002): 134–141. Highly critical.

Articles

[Carter, John.] 'Beckford's Letters to George Clarke.' *Times Literary Supplement*, 16 Feb 1962, 112. Bought privately by a bookseller after the sale at Richard Bentley's house, The Mere, Upton, Berks, on 3–4 Oct 1961.
Girard, Didier. 'The Beckford-Clarke Correspondence. 1830–1834.' *Beckford Tower Trust Newsletter*, Spring 1991, 10.
Millington, Jon. 'Beckford's Letters to Clarke.' *Beckford Tower Trust Newsletter*, Spring 1990, 7. Bradley Martin sale, Sotheby's NY, 30 April 1990, lot 2612.

OTHER WORKS

Alexander, Boyd. 'An Unpublished Beckford Novel as Autobiography.' *Cairo Studies in English* 32 (1978): 59–75. A study of *L'Esplendente*, 1777–1780, 135 quarto pages. *Idem*, 'The Dome of the Setting Sun', 76–78.

Beckford's letters. *Monthly Magazine; or, British Register* 54 (1 Nov 1822): 348. Volume of letters 'from the pen of Mr. Beckford' to be publ. 'in the ensuing winter'.

Claésson, Dick. 'A Survey of William Beckford's unpublished romance *L'Esplendente.' Studies on Voltaire and the Eighteenth Century* 358 (1998): 189–201.

Cope, Kevin L. 'Beckford and the emerging consciousness: projective collecting and the aesthetic dynamics of acquisition.' *Studies on Voltaire and the Eighteenth Century* 305 (1992): 1815–1819. A study of Beckford's early works. Delivered at the 1991 Beckford Round Table.

Girard, Didier. 'Beckford's "Juvenilia"?' *Beckford Tower Trust Newsletter*, Spring 1992, 2. Some early MSS., including *Suite de contes arabes*.

Grimsditch, Herbert B. 'William Beckford's Minor Works.' *London Mercury* 14 (Oct 1926): 599–605. Includes a brief survey of Beckford's life.

MUSIC

Full-length Study

Steer, Maxwell. *The Beckford Edition.* 6 vols. Tisbury, Wiltshire: Steer, 1999. '1. Instrumental', '2. Arcadian Pastoral (1782)', '3. Voice(s) & Instruments', '4. Solo Voice & Continuo', '5. Piano', '6. Miscellanea'.

Books

Brito, Manuel Carlos de. 'Music in Portugal in William Beckford's time.' In *Exposição. Exhibition. A Viagem de Uma Paixão. William Beckford & Portugal. An Impassioned Journey. 1787 1794 1798*, 50–61. Palácio de Queluz: Instituto Português do Património Cultural, 1987. Exhibition catalogue in Portuguese and English.

Jenkins, John. *Mozart and the English Connection.* London: Cygnus Arts, 1998. Beckford mentioned, 64–68, 75.

Matcham, M. Eyre. *The Nelsons of Burnham Thorpe*, London: John Lane, 1911. Extract from George Matcham's journal, 11 Sept 1805: 'This day Mr. Beckford dined here. Talkative. Praised his own composition. Play'd extempore on the Harpsichord. Sung. I thought it a very horrible noise', 231. Quoted in Tom Pocock, *Nelson's Women*, London: Deutsch, 1999, 214. Also: Emma Hamilton's 'attitudes' at Fonthill, 150–151 & 260 nn15–16; Beckford lent 22 Grosvenor Square to the Hamiltons, 147 & 265 n48.

[Pires, Maria Laura Bettencourt.] 'William Beckford's Musical Compositions.' In *Exposição. Exhibition. A Viagem de Uma Paixão. William Beckford & Portugal. An Impassioned Journey. 1787 1794 1798*, 86. Palácio de Queluz: Instituto Português do Património Cultural, 1987. Exhibition catalogue in Portuguese and English. Lists eleven works from 1780 to 1839.

Rosenfeld, Sybil. *Temples of Thespis*. London: Society for Theatre Research, 1978. 'Arcadian Pastoral', 55–57. Beckford's ballad opera performed in 1782.

Schott, Howard. *Catalogue of Musical Instruments in the Victoria and Albert Museum. Part 1, Keyboard Instruments.* London: Victoria & Albert Museum Publications, 1998. P. 83, no. 28, illus., fig. 28a.

Troost, Linda. 'Beckford, William.' In *The New Grove Dictionary of Music and Musicians*, ed. Stanley Sadie, 3:53. 2nd ed. 29 vols. London: Macmillan, 2001.

Wilson, Michael. *The English Chamber Organ*. Oxford: Cassirer, 1968. Note 1, pp. 18 & 19.

Wilson, Michael I. *The Chamber-Organ in Britain, 1600–1830*. London: Ashgate Publishing, 2001.

Articles

Anderson, Emily. 'Beckford and Mozart.' *Notes and Queries* 166 (24 March 1934): 206. Asking whether Beckford really was Mozart's pupil. Helpful but inconclusive replies by H. J. B. Clements & B. J. Maslen, (7 April): 246.

'Beckford and Music.' *Bath Weekly Chronicle*, 6 May 1944, 12. Notes – No. 605. An article on Beckford's musical activities to mark the centenary of his death.

Botting, Meg Crang. 'A Tuneful Family History. Crang and Hancock, Organbuilders.' *Country Life*, 6 Nov 1980, 1660.

Cave, Graham. 'William Beckford (1760–1844) and Fonthill Abbey.' *Notes and Queries* 217 (June 1972): 229. Asking for details about the organ in the octagon and whether Farquhar added a new case. No reply was forthcoming.

Cave, Graham. 'The Beckford Organ.' *Beckford Tower Trust Newsletter*, Spring 1981, 5. Organ from late 1760s formerly at Splendens & now in the V&A.

Charles, Fanny. 'Gothic horrors and an Arcadian Pastoral.' *Blackmore Vale Magazine*, 9 July 1999, 57. Brief account of Beckford's life and Maxwell Steer's work on his music.

Darton, Eric. 'William Beckford and Music.' *Beckford Tower Trust Newsletter*, Spring 1983, 4–8. Beckford was a talented musician.

Darton, Eric. 'William Beckford and Music. 2. His teachers?' *Beckford Tower Trust Newsletter*, Spring 1984, 4–5. John Nares & Sir William Parsons.

Darton, Eric. 'William Beckford and Music. 3. The Organ.' *Beckford Tower Trust Newsletter*, Spring 1985, 6–8. The organ previously noted by Cave, above.

Darton, Eric. 'William Beckford and Music. 4. The Harpsichord and Pianoforte.' *Beckford Tower Trust Newsletter*, Spring 1988, 5–7.

Darton, Eric. 'William Beckford and Music: 5. The Fonthill Abbey Organ?' *Beckford Journal* 2 (1996): 35–38. Doubts that there was one in the Abbey.

Darton, Eric. 'William Beckford and Music. 6. Beckford and Mozart.' *Beckford Journal* 3 (1997): 40–44. Lessons from Mozart in doubt.

Darton, Eric. 'William Beckford and Music. 7. The Singers.' *Beckford Journal* 5 (1999): 43–48. Farinelli, Pacchierotti, Tenducci and Rauzzini.

Darton, Eric. 'William Beckford and Music. 8. Publication and Performance of His Own Works.' *Beckford Journal* 6 (2000): 29–34.

Darton, Eric. 'William Beckford and Music. 9. Music in Portugal – 1787.' *Beckford Journal* 9 (2003): 10–15.

Freeman, Andrew. 'The Beckford (Fonthill) Organ at Towcester Parish Church.' *Musical Opinion*, June 1937, 818–819. Discusses the organ case.

Huxley, Aldous. *Westminster Gazette*, 4 Nov 1922. Asking, 'Can these strange Brazilian melodies [described in Beckford's *Letters from Portugal*] have been the ancestor to the Tango?'

Jean-Aubry, G. 'Beckford et la musique.' *The Chesterian*, 1 Nov 1931 and *Revue Musicale* 14 (Feb 1934): 103–122.

Maslen, B. J. 'Celebrities and Music. 11. William Beckford.' *Musical Opinion*, May 1933, 691–692. 'Music destroys me, – and what is worse, I love being destroyed.'

Miller, T. 'The Restoration of the Fonthill Organ.' *The Conservator* No 12 (1988): 38–43 with 11 figs.

Oldman, C. B. 'Beckford and Mozart.' *Music and Letters* 47 (April 1966): 110–115. Evidence of lessons from Mozart is inconclusive.

Reading Mercury, 22 April 1782. 'Arcadian Pastoral' performed at Queensberry House on 17 April.

Skinner, Raymond J. 'Seeds of Romanticism: Muzio Clementi and the Beckfords.' *The Hatcher Review* (Salisbury) 4 no. 31 (Spring 1991): 3–11.

Steer, Maxwell. 'The love that ruined a genius.' *Wiltshire Life* 4 no. 12 (June 1999): 12–15. Beautiful colour photos of Fonthill.

White, E. W. 'Two Eighteenth Century Composers of Opera.' *The Listener*, 10 Feb 1955, 265.

Williams, Peter Lloyd. 'Caught speeding.' *Bath Chronicle*, 18 Oct 1999, 13. Concert by Bath Baroque on 16 Oct, including music by Beckford.

Young, William H. 'Finished Symphonies: Clementi's Neglected Orchestral Music is Far Better than his Present Reputation Suggests.' *Atlantic Monthly* 277 no. 3 (May 1996): 104–108 at 105. William Beckford's cousin Peter's patronage of Muzio Clementi.

THE BECKFORD PAPERS

This large archive passed by descent from Beckford's daughter, Susan,
to successive Dukes of Hamilton. The 15th Duke sold the Papers at
Sotheby's in 1977 and they were bought by Blackwell's of Oxford.
In 1984 they donated them to the Bodleian Library, Oxford,
where they may be consulted.

Books

Rogers, Timothy D. *Catalogue of the papers of William Beckford*
(1760–1844). Oxford: Bodleian Library, 1987. 146 pp. Unpubl. typescript, but an indispensable work with an annotated index, 87–146.

Smith, Margaret M. 'William Beckford.' In *Index of English Literary Manu-*
scripts, vol. 3, 1700–1800, part 1, Addison–Fielding, 21–31. London:
Mansell, 1986. Essay, 21–23. List of 88 MSS. (of which 81 are in the
Bodleian Library, but were not then catalogued): verse (Nos. 1–16),
25–26; prose (Nos. 17–67), 26–29; prose fragments (Nos. 68–72), 29–30;
translations (No. 73), 30; dramatic works (No. 74), 30; diaries & notebooks (Nos. 75–82), 30–31; miscellaneous (Nos. 83–88), 31.

Sotheby's, London, 6 July 1977. Lot 272: 'The Beckford Papers', 143–150.
Also issued as a separate offprint, 16 pp incl. eight whole-page illus.

Articles

Alexander, Boyd. 'The sale of the Beckford Papers.' *Times Literary Supple-*
ment, 8 July 1977, 833.

[Dickinson, Gillian.] 'Headlines and Footnotes. Rape of the Muniment
Rooms.' *British Book News*, Aug 1977, 580–581. Hoping that the
Papers, bought by Blackwell's, can be kept together.

Ford, Brinsley, Chairman, NACF. 'The Beckford Papers.' *The Times*, 10 June
1977, 17b.

'Hair under the hammer.' *Times Literary Supplement*, 1 July 1977, 802.
Speculation about the destination of the Papers.

Moussa-Mahmoud, Fatma. 'A Manuscript Translation of the *Arabian*
Nights in the Beckford Papers.' *Journal of Arabic Literature* (Leiden) 7
(1976): 7–23. The Wortley Montagu MS. of the *Arabian Nights*.

Moussa-Mahmoud, Fatma. 'The Beckford Papers.' *Times Literary Supple-*
ment, 22 July 1977, 895. *Suite to Al Raoui* not by Beckford but trans.
from an Arabic MS. of the *Arabian Nights*.

'News and Comment.' *Book Collector* 26 no. 3 (Autumn 1977): 400.
Beckford Papers bought by Blackwell's, with H. P. Kraus the under-
bidder.

Norman, Geraldine. "Manuscripts of 'England's Kubla Khan' for sale." *The*
Times, 4 June 1977, 1h.

Norman, Geraldine. 'British Library buys early writings of Jane Austen.' *The Times*, 7 July 1977, 4d–e at d. Beckford Papers sold to Blackwell's.

Rogers, Timothy D. 'Western Manuscripts.' *Bodleian Library Record* 12 no. 1 (Oct 1985): 73–75. Blackwell's gift of the Beckford Papers in July 1984.

'£120,000 for Beckford manuscripts.' *Bath and West Evening Chronicle*, 7 July 1977, 8.

OTHER BECKFORD PAPERS IN THE BODLEIAN LIBRARY

Alexander. Papers of Boyd Alexander (1913–1980) relating to Beckford. Shelfmarks (46 in all): MSS. Eng. lett. c. 687–695; Eng. misc. c. 888–893, d. 1288–1298, e. 1446–1458, f. 857–858; Facs. d. 291; Film 1766; Photogr. c. 5, d. 2; Top. gen. a. 23, fols. 1–2. The papers contain working notes, mainly relating to his published works on Beckford; drafts of his unpublished works on Beckford, with related notes; and correspondence, press cuttings, prints, photocopies, articles, lectures, and printed items.

Clapinson, Mary & T. D. Rogers. *A Summary Catalogue of Post-Medieval Western Manuscripts in the Bodleian Library Oxford which have not hitherto been catalogued in the Quarto series.* 3 vols. Oxford: Clarendon Press, 1991. 'Essays, notes and transcripts by John Hodgkin relating to bibliographical and other work on William Beckford . . . (43584–90)', 497–498. Nos. 43587–8, MS. Eng. lett. c.11, d.36. The rest, MS. Eng. misc. d.224, d.225, e.198, d.222, d.223.

Madan, Falconer, et al. *A Summary Catalogue of Western Manuscripts in the Bodleian Library at Oxford which have not hitherto been catalogued in the Quarto series.* 7 vols. Oxford: Clarendon Press, 1895–1953. Vol. 4 (1897): 'List of portraits at Mr Beckford's house in Bath' (MS. Pigott e.1 fol. 15), 683. Letter of 19 March 1844 to Miss Piggot (MS. Pigott d.8 fol. 78), 688. Vol. 5 (1905): Letter of 29 Nov 1796 to Ozias Humphreys (MS. Montagu d.6 fol. 122), 122. Vol. 6 (1924): Autographed note (MS. Autogr. b.4, 118b), 365.

ATTRIBUTED WORKS
Popular Tales of the Germans *(1791)*

Translation formerly attributed to Beckford but now known to be by Dr Thomas Beddoes (See William Zachs, *The First John Murray [1737–1793] . . . With a Checklist of his Publications*, Oxford: Oxford University Press, 1998, p. 378, no. 842.)

Popular Tales of the Germans. 2 vols. London: J. Murray, 1791. xi, 264 pp. & iv, 284 pp. 18¼ cm. Trans. from Johann Carl August Musæus, *Volksmährchen der Deutschen*, 5 vols., (1782).

'The Magic Mirror.' *The Talisman*. Ed. Z. M. Watts. London: Whittaker, etc, 1831. Pp. 251–288. 'Richilda' from *Popular Tales*, 1:1–73. ' "The Magic Mirror," . . . attributed, pretty confidently, to the pen of the author of the "Memoirs of the Caliph Vathek." ', viii–ix.

Select Popular Tales of the German of Musaeus. Trans. attributed to Beckford. London, 1845. Six wood engravings. Burns Fireside Library.

Lemon, Mark, compiler. *Legends of Number Nip [Tales selected from the works of J. C. A. Musaeus]*. London: Macmillan, 1864. Illus. Charles Keene. From *Popular Tales*, 2:1–195.

'The Nymph of the Fountain' In *Great British Tales of Terror. Gothic stories of horror & romance 1765–1840*, ed. Peter Haining, 117–150. London: Gollancz, 1972. From *Popular Tales*, 2:196–284. Reprinted by Penguin Books, 1973, pp. 138–175. Also in *Gothic Tales of Terror. Classic Horror Stories from Great Britain, Europe and the United States 1765–1840*, ed. Peter Haining, New York: Taplinger, 1972.

La Ninfa della Sorgente (The Nymph of the Fountain). Trans. into Italian & ed. Lucia Perri. Rome: Theoria, 1984. 90 pp. 15 cm. Riflessi No. 14.

La Ninfa de la Font (The Nymph of the Fountain). Trans. into Catalan by Roser Berdagué. Barcelona: Laertes, 2001. 83 pp. 23 cm. Series: L'arcà 80.

Contemporary Reviews

Analytical Review 10 (1791): 217–220.
Critical Review n.s. 3 (Sept 1791): 56–57.
English Review 19 (1792): 248–255.
European Magazine 19 (1791): 350–352.
General Magazine 5 (1791): 244–246.
[Gough, Richard.] *Gentleman's Magazine* 61 pt. 2 (Dec 1791): 1126.
Monthly Review n.s. 5 (1791): 467.

Later Reviews and Articles

Axon, William E. A. 'William Beckford.' *Notes and Queries* 9th Series 1 (21 May 1898): 404. Observations on the compilation of *The Talisman* (1831).

Carlyle, Thomas. *The Collected Letters of Thomas and Jane Welsh Carlyle*. Ed. Charles Richard Sanders. 12 vols. Durham, NC: Duke University Press, 1970–1984. Vol. 3, 1824–1825 (1970): to Jane on 12 Aug 1824, Crabb Robinson told him that 'Number Nip' had been printed in English, 133 & n2. Number Nip is the first tale in vol. 2.

Jerdan, William, ed. 'German Stories. Selected by R. P. Gillies.' *Literary Gazette* 10 (11 Nov 1826): 710. Review ending with: 'Since 1791, when Mr. Beckford (we believe) published, anonymously, his Tales from the German . . .'

Millington, Jon. '*Popular Tales of the Germans*.' *Beckford Journal* 1 (1995): 52–55. Discusses Beckford's alleged involvement as translator of the work.

Stockley, Violet. *German Literature as Known in England, 1750–1830*. London: Routledge, 1929. Beckford may have trans. *Popular Tales*, 247n.

Al Raoui. *1799*

The Story of Al Raoui, A Tale from the Arabic. London: C. Geisweiler, Pall Mall, 1799. vii, 59 pp. English text, 9–24. German text, 33–44. Three poems: 'Verses', 47; 'Conjugal Love', 48–52; 'Written, in the close of Winter, to A Friend, just leaving a favourite retirement, previous to settling abroad', 53–59. 19½ cm. Chapman, *Bibliography* (1930), 6(i). 2nd ed. in the same year, 6(ii).

Articles

Alexander, Boyd. 'The Authorship of Al Raoui.' In Howard B. Gotlieb. *William Beckford of Fonthill . . . 1760–1844*, 83–85. New Haven: Yale University Library, 1960. Exhibition catalogue. Attributes authorship to Beckford. Also an unpaginated offprint which included 'Beckford's 1794 Journal'.

Chapman, Guy. 'Beckford & "Al Raoui".' & 'The Story of Al Raoui.' *Times Literary Supplement*, 31 Oct 1936 & 25 Nov 1960, 887 & 759. Letters explaining his reasons for believing that the story is by Samuel Henley and not Beckford.

A Dialogue in the Shades. Rare Doings at Roxburghe-Hall. *1819*

A Dialogue in the Shades, Between William Caxton, Fodius, a Bibliomaniac, and William Wynken, Clerk . . . and Rare Doings at Roxburghe-Hall. [1819.] Two burlesques, each of eight unnumbered pages, sometimes bound with *Repertorium Bibliographicum*. Engraving depicting Beckford with Caxton and 'William Wynken' on the first page. Chapman, *Bibliography* (1930), Attrib. 3. 2nd ed., with *The Diary of Roger Payne* appended. London: William Clarke, 1821. 36 pp. Chapman, *Bibliography* (1930), Attrib. 3(ii). Also small paper, Attrib. 3(ii, a).

A Dialogue in the Shades and *Rare Doings at Roxburghe-Hall*. Ipswich: Claude Cox, 1985. 27 pp. Facsimile reprint of 1819 ed., ed. & intro. Claude Cox. Limited to 250 numbered copies.

Contemporary Reviews & Advertisement

Gentleman's Magazine 89 pt. 1 (Suppl. 1819): 631–632. Review of *Dialogue*. Idem 91 pt. 1 (Aug 1821): 140–141. Review of *Dialogue* & *Rare Doings*.

Literary Gazette 5 (9 June 1821): 368. Advert.

Book

Vaulbert de Chantilly, Marc, ed. *The Bibliomania by John Ferriar. Bibliography by Thomas Frognall Dibdin. Two Poems.* London: Vanity Press of Bethnal Green, 2001. *A Dialogue in the Shades* and Beckford, 19–20 & notes.

Article

Rabaiotti, Renato. 'Beckford's *A Dialogue in the Shades* and Dibdin's *The Lincolne Nosegay.*' *Book Collector* 38 no. 2 (Summer 1989): 210–228. Beckford's satire was directed against Dibdin's *Nosegay* (1814).

15. Literary Studies

Full-length Studies
See also 'Full-length Studies' in Sections 1 and 2

Claésson, Dick. *The narratives of the biographical legend. The early works of William Beckford.* Gothenburg: The Author, 2001. iv, 369 pp. 21 cm. PhD thesis for Gothenburg University. Limited to 150 copies. 2nd ed., Gothenburg: Göteborgs universitet, 2002. Frontis. iv, 221 pp. 24 cm. Skrifter utgivna av Litteraturvetenskapliga institutionen vid Göteborgs universitet No. 41.
REVIEW. Allen, Richard. 'So who is this William . . . ?' *Beckford Journal* 10 (2004): 2–10.

Farrell, John T. *A Reinterpretation of the Major Literary Works of William Beckford.* Ann Arbor, Michigan: University Microfilms, 1984. 200 pp. Bibliography. PhD thesis for University of Delaware. *Dissertation Abstracts International* 45 no. 6 (Dec 1984): 1758A.
REVIEW. Lees-Milne, James. 'A Reinterpretation of the Major Literary Works of William Beckford. PhD Thesis by John T. Farrell. 1984.' *Beckford Tower Trust Newsletter*, Spring 1985, 4.

Gemmett, Robert J. *William Beckford.* Boston, MA: Twayne, 1977. 189 pp. Frontis. 21 cm. Discusses Beckford's minor works as well as examining *Vathek* and the *Episodes.*
REVIEW. Graham, Kenneth W. *Studies in Burke and His Time (1750–1800)* 19 (Autumn 1978): 238–241. A critical review.

Books

Adams, Walter Davenport. *Dictionary of English Literature.* London: Cassell Petter & Galpin, 1878. 'Beckford, William', 65. 'Cecil, or the Adventures of a Coxcomb', Beckford's help with, 123. 'Extraordinary Painters, Memoirs of', 212. 'Vathek', 662.

Allibone, S. Austin. *A Critical Dictionary of English Literature.* 3 vols. Philadelphia: Lippincott, 1859. 1:152–154.

Astaldi, Maria. 'William Beckford (1759–1844).' In *Tre Inglesi Pazzi*, ed. Mario Praz, 209–318. Milan: Rizzoli, 1974. Jonathan Swift and Samuel Johnson were the other two.

Barbour, Judith. 'Beckford, William (1760–1844).' In *An Oxford Companion to the Romantic Age: British Culture 1776–1832*, ed. Iain McCalman,

418–419. Oxford: Oxford University Press, 1999. Also Fonthill Abbey, 239. Beckford, 'rich connoisseur', 240. 'Gothic Novel', *Vathek*, 528. 'West, Benjamin', Beckford's patronage, 757. 'Wyatt, James', at Fonthill, 774.

Billi, Mirella. 'Beckford's Visionary Landscapes: A Contemporary Reading.' In *William Beckford and the New Millennium*, ed. Kenneth W. Graham & Kevin Berland, 37–51. New York: AMS Press, 2004 [2005].

Cellini, Benvenuto. 'Beckford, William.' In *Dizionario Letterario Bompiani degli Autori*, 1 (1956): 203–204. 3 vols. Milan: Bompiani, 1956–1957. New ed. 4 vols., 1987, 1:208. Also *Idem, degli Opere*. 7 vols., 1947–1949. Aldo Camerino, 'Sogni, pensieri del risveglio e incidenti' (*Dreams*, 1783), 6 (1948): 815 & Mario Praz, 'Vathek, racconto arabo', 7 (1949): 654–655.

Châtel, Laurent. 'Grottes et grotesques dans l'écriture de William Beckford (1760–1844): *Genius of the Place* ou *Genius of the Face*? Quelques remarques sur le portrait dans ses rapports avec l'art du paysage.' In *Le Portrait*, ed. Pierre Arnaud, 61–86. Paris: Presses de l'Université de Paris-Sorbonne, 1999. Collection Sillages critiques.

Claésson, Dick. ' "Lost in Dreams and Magic Slumbers": An Outline of Beckford's Aesthetic Dichotomy of Fancy and Reason.' In *William Beckford and the New Millennium*, ed. Kenneth W. Graham & Kevin Berland, 53–72. New York: AMS Press, 2004 [2005].

Clery, E. J. *The Rise of Supernatural Fiction 1762–1800*. Cambridge: Cambridge University Press, 1995. *Modern Novel Writing* and *Azemia*, 146, 202 n45. *Vathek*, 89–90.

De Bruyn, Frans. 'William Beckford.' In *British Novelists 1660–1800*, ed. Martin Battestin, 31–48. Detroit: Gale Research, 1985. *Dictionary of Literary Biography*, vol. 39.

Dyson, H. V. D. & John Butt. *Augustans and Romantics 1689–1830*. Rev. ed. London: Cresset Press, 1950. (1st ed. 1940.) 'William Beckford's Oriental tale, *Vathek*, is more luxurious than "horrid" ', 237. Also 36, 135.

Eagle, Dorothy & Hilary Carnell. *The Oxford Literary Guide to the British Isles*. Oxford: Oxford University Press, 1977. Bath, 17. Fonthill, 112. Born at 22 Soho Square, London, 217.

Emerson. *The Journals and Miscellaneous Notebooks of Ralph Waldo Emerson*. Various eds. 16 vols. Boston, MA: Harvard University Press, 1960–1982. Journal U (1843), 'Superiority of "Vathek" over [Disraeli's] "Vivian Grey" ', 9 (1971): 15. Journal V (1844 or 1845), 'Beckford's Italy & Spain is the book of a Sybarite', 9 (1971): 97–98. Journal RS (1848), Beckford one of three rich men, 11 (1975): 63 & n213. Mentioned, 12 (1976): 554. In 1853, 'Fonthill of Beckford a freak', 13 (1977): 150 & 227.

Franci, Giovanna. 'William Beckford.' In *La Messa in Scena del Terrore. Il Romanzo Gotico inglese*, 67–96. Ravenna: Longo Editore, 1982. Also, Walpole, 'Monk' Lewis, etc.

Fuller, Margaret. *The Letters of Margaret Fuller*. Ed. Robert N. Hudspeth. 3 vols. Ithaca, New York: Cornell University Press, 1983–1984. To Caroline Sturgis on 16 Aug 1837, praising Beckford's writing, 297, 298 n6.

Fumaroli, Marc. 'William Beckford, l'auteur de Vathek.' & 'Goya, la marquise de Santa-Cruz et Beckford.' In *Quand L'Europe parlait français*, 289–304 & 305–321. Paris: Editions de Fallois, 2001.

Garrett, John. 'Uncouth Characters: Tonal Instability in Beckford's Men Without Qualities.' In *William Beckford and the New Millennium*, ed. Kenneth W. Graham & Kevin Berland, 73–94. New York: AMS Press, 2004 [2005].

Gosse, Edmund. *English Literature. An Illustrated Record*. 4 vols. London: Heinemann, 1903. Pp. 86–88.

Gourmont, Remy de. *Esthétique de la langue française*. Paris: Mercure de France, 1955. (1st ed. 1899.) P. 201.

Grieve, Ann. 'Beckford, William.' In *Le nouveau dictionnaire des auteurs: de tous les temps et tous les pays*, 1:284–285. 3 vols. Laffont-Bompiani. N.p.: Editions Robert Laffont, 1994. *Idem, des œuvres*. 7 vols. 'Vathek, conte oriental', 6:7403. Ann Grieve, 'Voyage d'un rêveur éveillé', 6:7613.

Grimsditch, Herbert B. 'William Beckford.' In *British Authors of the Nineteenth Century*, ed. Stanley J. Kunitz, 42–44. New York: H. W. Wilson, 1960. (1st ed. 1936.) Engraved portrait of Beckford from Smeeton's *Unique* (1823), 43.

Haggerty, George E. 'The Gothic Novel, 1764–1824.' In *The Columbia History of the British Novel*, ed. John Richetti, 220–246. New York: Columbia University Press, 1994. *Vathek*, 232–234, 239. *Azemia* & *Modern Novel Writing*, 257–258. *Vathek*, 565. Brief biography, 991.

Hardwick, Michael. *A Literary Atlas & Gazetteer of the British Isles*. Newton Abbot, Devon: David & Charles, 1973. Somerset, 18. Wiltshire, 26.

Hardy, Barbara. 'Beckford, William.' In *Cassell's Encyclopaedia of Literature*, ed. S. H. Steinberg, 1:663. 2 vols. London: Cassell, 1953. Entry rev. by M. Butler in *Cassell's Encyclopaedia of World Literature*, ed. J. Buchanan-Brown, 2:130–131. 3 vols. London: Cassell, 1973.

Kirkpatrick, D. L., ed. *Reference Guide to English Literature*. 2nd ed. 3 vols. Chicago: St. James Press, 1991. 'Beckford, William', 1:234–235. 'Vathek' by William Ruddick, 3:1921.

Kitchin, George. *A Survey of Burlesque and Parody in English*. Edinburgh: Oliver & Boyd, 1931. Pp. 173–175.

Krahé, Peter. *Literarische Seestücke: Darstellungen von Meer und Seefahrt in der englischen Literatur des 18. bis 20. Jahrhunderts*. Hamburg: Kabel, 1992. William Beckford, 102, 139.

Lacroix, Jean. "William Beckford, voyageur-voyeur: La Réalité et son 'double'; Scritti in memoria di Lynn Salkin Sbiroli." In *Il Senso del nonsenso*, ed. Monique Streiff Moretti et al., 73–92. Naples: Edizioni Scientifiche Italiane, 1994.

Lunetta, Mario. *Le dimore di Narciso*. Rome: Rai-Eri, 1997. Studies of fifteen writers, including Beckford, Byron, Walpole, Apollinaire & Ezra Pound.

McCracken, David. 'Beckford, William.' In *Great Writers of the English Language: Novelists and Prose Writers*, ed. James Vinson, 98–99. London: Macmillan, 1979. Includes a list of Beckford's principal works.

Mérimée, Prosper. *Correspondance générale*, ed. Maurice Parturier. 2nd series. 9 vols. Toulouse: Privat, 1953–1961. Letters to Turgenev, 10 December 1860, vol. 4 (1956): 112.

Mézières, Louis. *Histoire critique de la littérature anglaise depuis Bacon jusqu'au commencement du dix-neuvième siècle*. 2nd ed. 3 vols. Paris: Allouard, 1841. (1st ed. 1834.) 3:412–447.

Millington, Jon. 'Man of Letters.' In *William Beckford Exhibition 1976*, [ed. Julian Berry], 22–27. Tisbury, Wilts: Compton Press, 1976. A survey of Beckford's role as an author.

Myers, Robin, compiler. 'Beckford, William.' In *A Dictionary of Literature in the English Language from Chaucer to 1940*, 1:57–58. 2 vols. Oxford: Pergamon, 1970.

Napier, Elizabeth R. *The Failure of Gothic: Problems of Disjunction in an Eighteenth-Century Literary Form*. Oxford: Clarendon Press, 1987. Beckford, 17, 37, 40, 65, 68. *Azemia* & *Modern Novel Writing*, 68. *Vathek*, 53, 64–68.

Newman, Donald J. '*Azemia* (56), *Biographical Memoirs of Extraordinary Painters* (33), *Modern Novel Writing* (69), *Vathek* (21).' In *Dictionary of British Literary Characters: 18th- and 19th-Century Novels*, ed. John R. Greenfield. New York: Facts on File, 1993. In brackets are the number of entries which are scattered throughout the work. Index, 571–572.

Poulet, Georges. *Trois essais de mythologie romantique*. Paris: Corti, 1966. Piranesi & *Dreams* (1783), 156–157, 158. *Vathek*, 158–159.

Praz, Mario. *The Flaming Heart*. New York: Doubleday, 1958. Beckford confessed to a partiality for Ludovico Ariosto's *Orlando Furioso*, 305.

Raimond, Jean & J. R. Watson, eds. *A Handbook to English Romanticism*. Basingstoke: Macmillan Press, 1992. Wyatt, 13–14. Chatterton, 60. Piranesi in *Dreams* (1783), 104. *Vathek*, 193.

Ross, Angus. 'Beckford, William (1759–1844).' In *The Penguin Companion to Literature: Britain and the Commonwealth*, ed. David Daiches, 40. London: Allen Lane The Penguin Press, 1971.

Rousseau, George. 'Beckford, William.' In *The Continuum Encyclopedia of British Literature*, ed. Steven R. Serafin & Valerie Grosvenor Myer, 73–74. New York & London: Continuum, 2003. Gay male literature, 392.

Said, Edward W., ed. *Orientalism. Western Concepts of the Orient*. London: Penguin Books, 1985. (1st ed. 1978.) Beckford mentioned, 22, 101, 118.

Simms, William Gilmore. *The Letters of William Gilmore Simms*. Ed. Mary C. Simms Oliphant et al. Columbia: University of South Carolina Press: 1952–1982. 2:65–69, 157–158. 3:287–289. 6:156–157. Simms reviewed some of Beckford's works and admired his style.

Surkov, A. A., ed. 'Bekford (Beckford), Uil'yam.' In *Kratkaya Literaturnaya Entsiklopediya* (Concise Literary Encyclopaedia), 1:501. 9 vols. Moscow: State Academic Publishing House, 1962–1978.

Tieghem, Philippe van, ed. 'Beckford (William).' In *Dictionnaire des Littératures*, 1:388. 3 vols. Paris: Presses Universitaires de France, 1968.

Varey, Simon. *Space and the Eighteenth-Century English Novel*. Cambridge: Cambridge University Press, 1990. Quote from Rutter's *Delineations* (1823, p. 8) about showing visitors the architectural features of Fonthill Abbey gradually, 39 n165.

Voller, Jack G. 'Beckford, William (1760–1844).' In *Encyclopedia of Romanticism: Culture in Britain, 1780s–1830s*, ed. Laura Dabundo, 30–31. London: Routledge, 1992. Also 241, 416–417, 427, 457, 587.

Ward, A. W. & A. R. Waller, eds. *Cambridge History of English Literature*. 15 vols. Cambridge: Cambridge University Press, 1907–1927. Vol. 10 (1913), lists eight of Beckford's works & Melville's *Life of Beckford* (1910), 423. Vol. 11 (1914), Beckford's works, 289–292. *Vathek*, 161, 304, 306, 307, 459.

Ward, Geoffrey, ed. *A Guide to Romantic Literature*. London: Bloomsbury, 1993. Beckford, 81. Elizabeth Hervey, 141.

[Watkins, John & Frederick Shoberl.] 'Beckford, William, Esq. F.A.S. of Fonthill.' & 'Beckford, William, Esq. cousin to the preceding.' In *A Biographical Dictionary of the Living Authors of Great Britain and Ireland . . .*, 19. London: Colburn, 1816. 'Beckford, Peter, Esq', 413.

Wilson, Edmund. 'Firbank and Beckford.' In *The Shores of Light. A Literary Chronicle of the Twenties and Thirties*, 264–266. London: W. H. Allen, 1952. 'They both had luxurious tastes and eccentric curiosities', 266.

Woodcox, Cole. 'William Beckford (1760–1844) British Novelist and Travel Writer.' In *Literature of Travel and Exploration. An Encyclopedia*, ed. Jennifer Speake, 1:79–81. 3 vols. New York: Fitzroy Dearborn, 2003. Mentioned, 2:692, 977.

Articles

Billi, Mirella. 'The Impact of Italy on Beckford's Taste, Aesthetics and Literary Style.' In *The Beckford Society Annual Lectures 2000–2003*, ed. Jon Millington, 67–88. London: The Beckford Society, 2004. The 2003 lecture.

Buck, Gerhard. 'Neue Beckford-Literatur.' *Beiblatt zur Anglia* 44 (1933): 373–378. A general essay on recent Beckford publications, mentioning Chapman's eds. of *Travel Diaries* (1928), *Vathek* (1929), *The Vision & Liber Veritatis* (1930), *Bibliography* (1930), Sitwell's *Beckford and Beckfordism* (1930) and Oliver's *Life of Beckford* (1932).

Carnero, Guillermo. 'William Beckford (1760–1844) o el erotismo de fina estampa.' *Insula* (Madrid) 24 (Oct–Nov 1969): 18–19 & Romney's portrait.

Châtel, Laurent. 'Kaleidoscopic Senses: Landscape Writing and the Art of Chiaroscuro in William Beckford (1760–1844).' *Images* 9 (1996): 107–128. Excursion to the Grande Chartreuse, *The Long Story* and *Dreams*.

Châtel, Laurent. 'Grottoes and Grotesques: The Art of Portraiture in Beckford's Writing.' *Beckford Journal* 4 (1998): 51–63.

Châtel, Laurent. "Orientalist Translations, Grafts and Outgrowths: New Perspectives on Beckford's 'Complete Works'." *Beckford Journal* 11 (2005): 39–49.

Claésson, Dick. "A Brief Note on Beckford's 'Queen of Delusions'." *Notes and Queries* 242 no. 2 (June 1997): 214. Beckford's reveries.

Claésson, Dick. 'At a Crossroads: Assessing and Redefining the Beckford Agenda.' *Beckford Journal* 4 (1998): 22–33. A wide-ranging study.

Claésson, Dick. 'The Scenario of Letters; Beckford and the Epistolary Narrative.' *Orbis Litterarum* (Copenhagen) 54 no. 3 (1999): 161–173.

'Current Literature.' *Galaxy* (New York) 11 (May 1871): 744–750 at 745. Reviewer of Hans Christian Anderson's *The Story of My Life* thought that English biographies including Byron's and Beckford's are narrow in range, even if the subjects travel abroad.

De Graaf, Daniel A. 'William Beckford (1760–1844).' *Revue des langues vivantes* 29 (1963): 581–584. In Flemish.

Flor, João de Almeida. 'Portuguese Tears and Treasures: On Beckford's Literary Fortune.' In *The Beckford Society Annual Lectures 1996–1999*, ed. Jon Millington, 23–34. London: The Beckford Society, 2000. The 1997 lecture.

Girard, Didier. 'Literary Curiosities.' *Beckford Tower Trust Newsletter*, Spring 1989, 4–7. Beckford in French and Italian literature.

Hoerr, Wilmer R. 'The Case of Sundry Sources.' *Baker Street Journal* (New York) 22 no. 4 (Dec 1972): 215–218 at 216. Conan Doyle's. *The Hound of the Baskervilles* owes a debt to Beckford among others.

Jack, Malcolm. 'The Visual and the Literary in William Beckford.' *Beckford Tower Trust Newsletter*, Spring 1993, 10–11. Images in Beckford's works.

Junius's Letters. Bates, William. 'Hannah Lightfoot.' *Notes and Queries* 1st Ser. 10 (16 Sept, 21 Oct 1854): 228, 328. Beckford said that the letters were by Dr Wilmot [Rev. James Wilmot (1726–1807)]. Also H. B., (28 Oct 1854): 349.

'Laurence Sterne.' *North American Review* 81 (Oct 1855): 361–389 at 377. In contrast to Sterne's opinion that 'to write a book is for all the world like humming a song', Beckford 'revelled in the luxuries of art and climate'.

'Literary Intelligence.' *New York Weekly News*, 17 Sept 1844, 3.

'Literature.' *Leeds Mercury*, 25 Feb 1901, 3.

Millington, Jon. 'French Editions of Beckford's Works.' *Beckford Tower Trust Newsletter*, Spring 1990, 4. Publications by José Corti, Paris.

Murawska, Katarzyna. 'An image of mysterious wisdom won by toil: the tower as symbol of thoughtful isolation in English art and literature from Milton to Yeats.' *Artibus et historiae* 3 (1982): 141–162. Fonthill Abbey and prospect towers in landscape parks.

Poe. 'Beckford and Poe.' *The Broadway, A London Magazine* n.s. 2 (June 1869): 317–322. Reprinted with alterations in Gregory, *The Beckford Family* (2nd ed., 1898), 124–137, 'By an American author'. Wrongly attributed to Gregory by Benjamin F. Fisher in *Fictions of Unease: The Gothic from Otranto to The X-Files*, ed. Andrew Smith et al. (Bath: Sulis Press, 2002), 51.

Poe. Fisher, Benjamin F. 'Poe and the 1890s: Bibliographical Gleanings.' *American Renaissance Literary Report: An Annual* 8 (1994): 163–164. Discusses chapter on Poe in Gregory, *The Beckford Family* (2nd ed., 1898).

Poe. Stedman, Edmund Clarence. 'Edgar Allan Poe.' *Scribner's Monthly* 20 (May 1880): 107–124 at 117, 121. Not Beckford's pupil. If Poe had been wealthy he would have outvied Beckford in 'barbaric extravagance of architecture'.

Poe. Wilson, Edmund. 'Beckford & Poe.' *New Republic* (New York), 8 Sept 1926.

Saglia, Diego. 'Looking at the Other: Cultural Differences and the Traveller's Gaze in *The Italian*.' *Studies in the Novel* 28 (1996): 12–37. Beckford mentioned in study of Ann Radcliffe's *The Italian* (1797).

Saglia, Diego. "William Beckford's 'Sparks of orientalism' and the material-discursive orient of British Romanticism." *Textual Practice* (Sussex) 16 no. 1 (Spring 2002): 75–92.

Thiébaut, Marcel. 'De Romain Gary à William Beckford.' *Revue de Paris* 63 (Dec 1956): 159–163.

'Ugo Foscolo.' *North American Review* 91 (July 1860): 213–258 at 245. Beckford and Walpole, when alive, were better known for their unique dwellings than for their writings.

Vigil, Julián Josué. 'A Nightmare in Literary Criticism.' *New Mexico Highlands University Journal* 1 (1979): 48–50.

16. Works influenced by Beckford

BECKFORD IN FICTION

Principal Novels

Kyle, Elizabeth. [Agnes Dunlop, pseud.] *The Pleasure Dome*. London: Peter
Davies, 1943. 242 pp. Hamilton Palace in the 19th century. Beckford at
Palace for 1820s rebuilding, 1–30. 10th Duke visits Beckford at Bath,
71–72. 12th Duke in the Beckford Library at Hamilton Palace before
1882 sale, 212–213. 2nd ed., 1944. Reprinted, Bath: Chivers, 1965.
    REVIEW. 'Two Nations.' *Times Literary Supplement*, 16 Oct 1943, 497.
Menen, Aubrey. *Fonthill. A Comedy*. New York: Putnam, 1974. 223 pp.
Dust jacket: Edward Gorey. London: Hamish Hamilton, 1975. 188 pp.
Dust jacket: John Lawrence. Beckford and Farquhar involved in scan-
dalous goings-on.
    REVIEWS. *Daily Telegraph*, 5 June 1975, 13.
    Norton, Rictor. 'Joyous gay romp.' *Gay News* 72 (1975): 19.
    Observer, 1 June 1975.
    Times Literary Supplement, 4 July 1975, 713.
    Tinniswood, Peter. *The Times*, 29 May 1975, 12g–h.
Sadleir [Sadler], Michael. *Privilege*. London: Constable, 1921. 270 pp.
Dedicated to ' . . . the gracious memory of William Beckford'. The setting
is Whern, a Gothic abbey based on Fonthill.
    REVIEW. *Times Literary Supplement*, 27 Jan 1921, 57.
Sarasin, J. G. [Geraldine Gordon Salmon, pseud.] *The Court of Dusty Feet*.
London: Hutchinson, [1942]. Much of the action takes place in and
around Fonthill Abbey while under construction during the Napoleonic
wars. 'The author is indebted to Mrs. Walter Shaw Stewart for advice
upon this story and permission to visit the scenes of William Beckford's
life at Fonthill.' The dust jacket depicts Fonthill Abbey framed by
portraits of Beckford and the two leading characters.
Sichère, Bernard. *Je, William Beckford*. Paris: Denoël, 1984. 364 pp. Historical novel vividly evoking a number of episodes in Beckford's life.
    REVIEWS. Hilliard, Elizabeth. *Beckford Tower Trust Newsletter*, Spring
    1989, 8–9.
    Jordis, Christine. 'William Beckford, personage de roman.' *La Quinzaine
    littéraire*, No. 428, 16 Nov 1984.
Silva, Luís Augusto Rebelo da. *Lágrimas e Tesouros* (Tears and Treasures) –

Fragmento de uma História Verdadeira. Porto: Typographia do Comércio, 1863. A historical novel inspired by Beckford's life.

ARTICLE. Parreaux, André. 'Etudes Portugaises sur William Beckford.' *Bulletin des Etudes Portugaises* 2 (1932): 177–184.

Sontag, Susan. *The Volcano Lover: A Romance.* New York: Farrer Straus Giroux, 1992. Relationship with Catherine, Sir William Hamilton's first wife, 86–105. Nelson's visit to Fonthill, 332–344. Also 244, 378.

Stacton, David. *Sir William or A Lesson in Love.* London: Faber & Faber, 1963. Hamilton's move to Beckford's house in Grosvenor Square, 266. Nelson's visit to Fonthill & Beckford's hoped-for peerage, 272–278. Beckford likening a house to 'the Halls of Eblis, *cottage orné* style', 302.

[Townsend, Frederic.] 'Hortensius – Beckford.' In *Ghostly Colloquies*, 69–89. New York: Appleton, 1856. An imaginary conversation with Hortensius (114–50 BC), orator and consul of Rome.

REVIEW. 'Editorial Notes – Literature.' *Putnam's Monthly Magazine of American Literature, Science and Art* 6 (Dec 1855): 650–663 at 655.

White, T. H. 'No Gratuities.' In *The Maharajah and Other Stories*, 75–84. London: Macdonald, 1981. Anecdotes of Beckford in fictional form.

Article

Millington, Jon. 'Three Novelists' Debt to Beckford.' *Beckford Tower Trust Newsletter*, Spring 1981, 5–6. Michael Sadleir's *Privilege*, Elizabeth Kyle's *The Pleasure Dome* and Aubrey Menen's *Fonthill*.

Other Fiction, Poems and Sketches

See also '5. Fonthill. Contemporary Poems' and
'6. Beckford's Tower and Bath. Poems'

Books

Berners, Lord Gerald Hugh Tyrwhitt-Wilson. *Collected Tales and Fantasies of Lord Berners.* New York: Turtle Point Press, 1999. In 'Percy Wallingford' (1914), the Villa Rosebery evokes the Italy of Beckford, 29. In 'Mr. Pidger' (1939), 'an edition of Gibbon with Beckford's disapproving comments on the margins', 145.

Dias, Carlos Malheiro. *O Grande Cagliostro – Novela Romântica.* Lisbon: Livraria Bertrand, 1905. Serialised in *A Ilustração Portuguesa* (1904–1906). Also publ. as a play, *O Grande Cagliostro – Comédia em cinco actos.* Porto: Magalhães e Moniz, 1905.

Disraeli, Benjamin. *Contarini Fleming. A Psychological Auto-biography.* 4 vols. London: John Murray, 1832. 'At last I opened the door, and the stranger of the Abbey entered.', 1:207 (at end of Ch. 17). Modelled on Beckford, this was Peter Winter, an artist, who acts as a surrogate father to Contarini Fleming. See also '4. Contemporaries' and 'Works influenced by *Vathek*' below.

Donatone, Guido. *William Hamilton. Diario segreto napoletano (1764–1789)*. Naples: Grimaldi, 2000. Fictional papers ('by' Hamilton and others) supposedly found in an old bookcase in Naples. Beckford, 103–104, 107. Much about Lady Catherine Hamilton. Biblioteca napoletana 14.

Edwards, Amelia Blandford. *My Brother's Wife*. London: Routledge, 1855. Thoughts of Beckford and the wealth needed to collect books and works of art, 193.

[Egan, Pierce.] *Real Life in London*. 2 vols. London: Jones, 1822. Conversation between the Hon. Tom Dashall, his cousin Squire Bob Tallyho and their friend Sparkle about Farquhar and Christie's sale at Fonthill Abbey, 2:640–648. Alderman Beckford's monument in Guildhall, 2:328.

Gilchrist, R. Murray. 'A Night on the Moor.' In *Lords and Ladies. Stories*, 247–267. London: Hurst & Blackett, 1903. 'Dost remember at my aunt's ball, the Bath Assembly Rooms the place, after young Mr. Beckford had led me through the minuet, you fumed and fretted (foolish boy!) and swore that you would spit him on your rapier.', 262. Reprinted in *The Basilisk and Other Tales of Dread*, 163–171. Ashcroft, BC: Ash Tree Press, 2003.

Gore, Mrs. *Cecil, or the Adventures of a Coxcomb*. 3 vols. London: Bentley, 1841. Reputedly written with Beckford's help. See also '4. Contemporaries'.

Gore, Mrs. *Agathonia*. London: Moxon, 1844. Beckford was possibly responsible for information on London clubs. See also '4. Contemporaries'.

Gosse, Edmund. 'The Sultan of My Books.' In *Ballads of Books*, ed. James Brander Matthews, 62. New York: Coombes, 1887. Poem in ten verses in which Gosse regretted that he would never 'Be Beckford or Locker'. *Ballads* was dedicated to Frederick Locker-Lampson (1821–1895), poet and bibliophile. Reprinted from *Century* (New York) 31 (Dec 1885): 319–320 at 320.

Jullian, Philippe. *Mémoires d'une bergère*. Paris: Plon, 1959. In the chapter 'Intermède Gothique' an armchair from the Royal *garde meuble* reaches Fonthill and witnesses Nelson's visit, illus. with sketches by the author. English ed.: Violet Trefusis (trans.) & Philippe Jullian, *Memoirs of an Armchair*, London: Hutchinson, 1960. 'Gothic Interlude', 40–44.

Hamilton-Paterson, James. 'Frank's Fate.' In *The Music: Stories*. London: Jonathan Cape, 1995. *Vathek*, and 'that brilliant voluptuary William Beckford' involved in a Black Mass in 1781, 77–78.

Hardy, Thomas. *Jude the Obscure*. Oxford: Oxford University Press, 1996. (1st ed. 1896.) 'Part Third. At Melchester.' When Jude's proposal to visit some ruins was rejected, he suggested a trip to Wardour Castle and 'then we can do Fonthill if we like – all in the same afternoon.', 141.

Hartmann, Theodore. *Charity Green, or, The Varieties of Love*. New York: Norton, 1859. 'How Beckford might have wooed, with a touched heart, amidst the splendors of Fonthill.' In Ch. 24, 'Marie Devereux', 304.

Harwood, John Berwick. *Lady Flavia*. 3 vols. London: Richard Bentley, 1865. The heroine recollected 'tortured beasts that roam in the Halls of Eblis – I read of such things in a strange book – *Vathek* – was it not . . .', 1:192.

Hollinghurst, Alan. *The Swimming Pool Library*. London: Penguin, 1988. The narrator was helping to compile a crackpot dictionary of architecture, 'an Escorial that turned into a Fonthill the longer we worked on it', 3.

Huxley, Aldous. *Antic Hay*. London: Chatto & Windus, 1932. (1st ed. 1923.) Gumbril searches in vain for a copy of [Melville's] *Life of Beckford* in the London Library, 241.

Huxley, Aldous. *Crome Yellow*. Harmondsworth, Middlesex: Penguin Books, 1955. (1st ed. 1921.) Mr. Scogan on the eccentricity of English aristocrats: 'Beckford builds towers', 57–58.

Invisible Sam. [Reuben Vose, pseud.] *Despotism; or The Last Days of the American Republic*. New York: Hall & Willson, 1856. Ch. 5, 'The Chaplets'. Among the guests at a levee were 'Beckford, the richest commoner in England, and his son-in-law Earl of Hamilton', 135.

Kirkland, Caroline [under pseud. Mrs. Mary Clavers, an actual settler]. *A New Home – Who'll Follow? Or Glimpses of Western Life*. New York: C. S. Francis, 1839. A room as 'dark as the Hall of Eblis', 18.

    REVIEW. 'Art VIII.– *A New Home, Who'll Follow? . . .*', *North American Review* 50 (Jan 1840): 206–223 at 210. Hall of Eblis passage quoted.

Kirkland, Caroline Matilda. *A Book for the Home Circle, or, Familiar Thoughts on Various Topics, Literary, Moral and Social*. New York: Scribner, 1853. Mention of Beckford's 'accounts of the groaning tables of Alcobaça' in chapter titled 'Fashionable and Unfashionable', 120.

Kirkland, Caroline Matilda. *The Evening Book, or, Fireside Talk on Morals and Manners, with Sketches of Western Life*. New York: Scribner, 1852. 'Beckford, of Fonthill, demanded that life should be thrice winnowed for his use, but what was his life?, 124. In chapter titled 'Fastidiousness'.

The Knickerbocker Gallery. A Testimonial to the Editor of the Knickerbocker Magazine. New York: Hueston, 1855. 'Robert Browning's poem of "My Last Duchess" and Beckford's tale of the old woman near Naples [*Italy* (1834), 1:263–279] are simple studies from life.' In an article, 'The Shrouded Portrait', 343.

Lovric, M. R. *Carnevale*. London: Virago, 2001. Novel mixing fiction with reality and set in late 18th century Venice where the heroine paints Beckford's portrait, 161–174. Married but disgraced, 228–229. Mozart, 238. Sir William Hamilton marries Emma, 244. Byron & *Vathek*, 307–308, 310–311 & further scattered references.

Melville, Herman. *White Jacket; or, The World in a Man-of-war*. New York:

Russell, 1963. (1st ed. 1850, soon after buying a copy of *Vathek*.) The sailors' sleeping decks are compared to the Hall of Eblis, 384. The Works of Herman Melville. Standard ed., vol. 6.

Pamuk, Orhan. *The Black Book*. London: Faber & Faber, 1996. (1st ed. 1994.) Trans. Guneli Gun. The author worked up a piece on a cyclops who assumes the shape of a Negress in *Vathek*, a novel 'which I really love', 97.

A Pedestrian. [Nicholas Cowen, pseud.] *A Tour in search of Chalk through Parts of South Wiltshire in 1807* . . . East Knoyle, Wiltshire: Hobnob Press, 2005. A modern account cast in the form of letters written in 1807. Wager to visit Fonthill Abbey and climb the central tower without invitation, 86–87. The visit, 91–123. Beckford, 49, 195. Fonthill mentioned, 134, 139, 145–146, 166. Sketch of Abbey facing 156.

Psmith, Levenston. 'A Pastoral Id Ill.' In *Lords of the Chase: Tales from the Shires and Beyond*. London: Woodpecker, 1995. Eight 5-line stanzas, including one where Louisa seeks solace with William Beckford, with vignettes of him in profile and Fonthill Abbey, 172–173 at 172. Brief account of William Beckford under 'Beckford, Peter', 226–227 at 227. See '3. Family. Peter Beckford (1740–1811), cousin'.

Reade, Charles. *Hard Cash. A Matter-of-fact romance*. 3 vols. London: Sampson Low, Son & Marston, 1863. Thoughts of the Hall of Eblis while in prison, 3:123.

Rita. [Eliza Humphreys, pseud.] *A Grey Life. A romance of modern Bath*. London: Stanley Paul, 1913. Beckford's Tower, 116–117. *A Grey Life* because Bath's streets were grey. Quoted in Charles Whitby, ed., *The Bath Anthology Of Prose and Verse*, London: Folk Press, 1928. P. 141.

A Southern Lady. [Catherine Ann Warfield, pseud.] *The Household of Bouverie, or, The Elixir of Gold*. 2 vols. New York: Derby & Jackson, 1860. 'Mr. Beckford's strange book', *Vathek*, among those deemed objectionable and locked away by the narrator's teacher. In Vol. 1, Book 2 (of 5), Ch. 10, 173.

Stretton, Hesba. [Sarah Smith, pseud.] *Hester Morley's Promise*. 3 vols. London: Henry S. King, 1873. Boys reading about the hall of Eblis, 1:198.

Unsworth, Barry. *Losing Nelson*. London: Hamish Hamilton, 1999. Penguin ed., 2000. Charles Cleasby painstakingly re-enacts the great sea battles of his hero, Nelson. Visit to Fonthill, 184–187. Also 110.

Vance, Louis Joseph. *The Bronze Bell*. London: Grant Richards, 1909. 'In darkness as of the Hall of Eblis', 309. In Ch. 18, 'The Hooded Death'.

Veilletet, Pierre. *Mari-Barbola*. Paris: Arléa, 1988. Novel with many episodes. Beckford and his dwarf appear in Lisbon without being named, 164ff.

[Warren, Nathan Boughton.] *The Lady of Lawford and Other Christmas Stories*. Troy, New York: Nims, c.1874. In the fourth story, *Hidden Treasure; or, The Good St. Nicholas*: 'But the most interesting of these curious works was "Elfin Freaks, or the Seven Legends of Number Nip," translated from the German by Beckford.', 217. 'Number Nip' also mentioned, 215, 219.

Webber, Charles Wilkins. *"Sam:" or, The History of Mystery*. Cincinnati: Rulison, 1855. Alderman Beckford denouncing a bill of 1765 for collecting a stamp tax in America, 283. In Ch. 31.

Whyte-Melville, George John. 'The Interpreter.' *Fraser's Magazine* 55 (March 1857): 265–281. A mason 'is employed repairing Beckford's Tower; by the way, he has heard of *Vathek*'. Reprinted in *Littell's Living Age* 53 (20 June 1857): 738–753 at 742.

Wilde, Oscar. *The Picture of Dorian Gray*. Ed. Isobel Murray. London: Oxford University Press, 1974. (1st ed. 1891.) Gray was offered a picture frame 'admirably suited for a religious subject' from the Fonthill sale, 120 & 243n. Expanded from *Lippincott's Monthly Magazine* 46 (July 1890): 61.

Zangwill, Israel. *The Big Bow Mystery*. London: Henry & Co., 1892. Feeling like a farthing rushlight in the Hall of Eblis, 29.

Articles

Bulwer-Lytton, Edward. 'The Caxtons.' *Blackwood's Edinburgh Magazine* 65 (March 1849): 298. Eblis 'a great awful space'. Publ. in book form as *The Caxtons. A Family Picture*, London: Routledge, 1874 (1st ed. 1849), 291.

[Colmache, Georgina A.] 'The Last Ball at the Tuileries.' *New Monthly Magazine* 76 (April 1846): 409–420. Dancers 'were compelled, like the damned souls in the "Hall of Eblis", to wander up and down'. Reprinted in *Littell's Living Age* 9 (30 May 1846): 402–407 at 402.

De Forest, J. W. 'Overland.' *Galaxy* (New York) 11 (Feb 1871): 205–219 at 208. Although the hero of the novel 'had only heard of "Vathek," he thought of the Hall of Eblis.' Publ. in book form, New York: Sheldon, [1872].

'The Drift-Wood Fire.' *Harper's New Monthly Magazine* 61 (Nov 1880): 888–893 at 888. A face reminded the author 'of the princess in the halls of Eblis'.

Hartley, Gilfrid W. 'Sir Simon's Courtship.' *Macmillan's Magazine* 70 (Aug 1894): 241–255 at 242. Mr. Kemp suggested that Sir Simon became a book collector, 'a second Beckford'. Reprinted in *Littell's Living Age* 202 (1 Sept 1894): 532.

Irwin, Robert. 'An Incident at the Monastery of Alcobaça.' *Interzone* (Brighton) No. 58 (April 1992): 21–24. Fantasy account of an interview with Beckford in 1839 about the plurality of worlds. Shortened version printed in *Beckford Journal* 9 (2003): 37–44.

[Lawless, Emily.] 'A Millionaire's Cousin.' *Macmillan's Magazine* 51 (Jan 1885): 215–230 at 220. The narrator dreams of 'wandering about through the halls of Eblis'. Reprinted in *Littell's Living Age* 164 (7 Feb 1885): 333. Publ. in book form, London: Macmillan, 1885.

Le Fanu, J. Sheridan. 'The Drunkard's Dream.' ('being a fourth extract from the legacy of the late F. Purcell, P. P. of Drumcoolagh'.) *Dublin University Magazine* 12 (Aug 1838): 151–157 at 155. A vision is compared to 'Vatheck and the "Hall of Ebles" '. Publ. in book form in his *The Watcher and Other Weird Stories*, London: Downey, [1894], which was reviewed in *Athenæum*, 16 Feb 1895, 214, where " 'The Dream' reminds us perhaps of 'Vathek,'."

[Lindsay, Margaret.] 'The Story of a Railway Journey [Pt. 1].' *Temple Bar* 63 (Sept 1881): 209–236. Groups of dark figures 'looking like lost souls wandering in the hall of Eblis.' Reprinted in *Littell's Living Age* 151 (17 Dec 1881): 656–671 at 667.

MacDonald, George. 'The Flight of the Shadow.' *Sunday Magazine*. Ch. 34: 'We were filled with such blind and oblivious passion as was fitter to wander the halls of Eblis, than the palaces of God.' Reprinted in *Littell's Living Age* 189 (11 April 1891): 76–95 at 87. Publ. in book form, London: Kegan Paul, 1891.

Pike, Albert. 'Disunion.' *The Knickerbocker; or New York Monthly Magazine* 35 (March 1850): 241–241 at 241. Poem about human folly which "will be like the fable of Eblis' fall". Reprinted in *Littell's Living Age* 24 (30 March 1850): 590.

Poe, Edgar Allan. 'The Domain of Arnheim.' *Columbian Lady's and Gentleman's Magazine* 7 (March 1847): 123–129. Reprinted in *The Fall of the House of Usher, and other Tales and Prose Writings of Edgar Poe*, ed. Ernest Rhys, 93–109. London: Walter Scott, *c.*1901. Beckford influenced other Poe stories including: 'Ligeia' which described a remote abbey possibly modelled on Fonthill, 30–31; 'Landor's Cottage', where the French ed. of *Vathek* was quoted, 117; and 'Thou Art the Man'. 'The Domain of Arnheim', an expanded version of 'The Landscape Garden' (1842), was also reprinted in *The Collected Works of Edgar Allan Poe*, ed. Thomas Ollive Mabbott, 3:1266–1288, 3 vols., Cambridge, MA: Belknap Press, 1968–1978.

'Recollections and Reflections of Gideon Shaddoe, Esq. No. 3.' *Hood's Magazine* 1 (9 May 1844): 425. The 'fearful crowd in the halls of Eblis, hurrying on in anguish, seeking rest and finding none*'. Footnote: '*Vathek.' Reprinted in *Littell's Living Age* 4 (15 Feb 1845): 415.

Rushton, Andrée. 'The Ballad of Fonthill Abbey.' *Beckford Journal* 11 (2005): 36–38. Original poem of 16 four-line stanzas. (See '5. Fonthill. Later Accounts – General'.)

Simões, João Gaspar. 'Herói de um romance histórico.' *O Estado de Sao Paulo, Supplemento Literário*, 28 Jan 1967, 1. Rebelo da Silva used Beckford as a model for a character in *Rausso por homizio*.

Spiffkins. 'The Oyster-Supper Critic.' *Punchinello* (New York) 2 (24 Dec
  1870): 196. Poem about a drama critic who is "Like Vathek lost in Eblis'
  hall".

Waite, Arthur Edward. 'Touchstone.' *The Occult Review* 48 no. 1 (July
  1928). A prince who 'sorrowed with Vathek and Solomon in the Hall of
  Eblis'.

Wells, H. G. 'Tono-Bungay [1st part].' *English Review* 1 (Dec 1908):
  81–154 at 97 & 100. ' "Vathek" was glorious stuff' & 'I won his [a
  friend's] heart by a version of "Vathek" '. Publ. in book form, London:
  Macmillan, 1909.

Williams, Ella. 'Very Narrow Indeed.' *Galaxy* (New York) 13 (April 1872):
  533–541 at 537. A character observes: "In 'Vathek,' which, by the way, is
  one of the finest books in the world, the prince of Eblis is of noble stature
  and presence, but his face seems to be tarnished with malignant vapors."

Essays

Dickens, Charles, conductor. 'Fairyland in 'Fifty-Four.' *Household Words* 8
  (3 Dec 1853): 313–317 at 314. Crystal Palace 'immeasurably beyond' the
  palaces in *Aladdin* & *Vathek*. Reprinted in *Littell's Living Age* 40 (14 Jan
  1854): 141.

Dickens, Charles, conductor. 'Case of Real Distress.' *Household Words* 8
  (14 Jan 1854): 457–460 at 458. 'The Eastern Queen Mab could show you
  Halls of Eblis'. Reprinted in *Littell's Living Age* 40 (4 March 1854): 452.

'The Doom of the Slaver.' *Harper's New Monthly Magazine* 1 (Nov 1850):
  846–847 at 847. In *Vathek*, a whole city's population is described as
  'following in the chase of a black genie, who rolled himself up into a ball.'

F. 'My Boots.' *New-England Magazine* 6 (Feb 1834): 154–155 at 155. 'I had
  a fire within me, like that of the poor victim of Kehama's curse, or Caliph
  Vathek.'

Holmes, Oliver Wendell. 'The Autocrat of the Breakfast-Table.' *Atlantic
  Monthly* 2 (Aug 1858): 360–370 at 369. Recollections of the Hall of Eblis
  in 'Extract from my private journal. (To be burned unread.)'. Publ. in
  book form, Boston, MA: Phillips, Sampson, 1858.

Holmes, Oliver Wendell. 'The Poet at the Breakfast-Table.' *Atlantic
  Monthly* 29 (Jan 1872): 90–105 at 98. The heart of a tree is set on fire by
  a thunderbolt 'like those of the lost souls in the Hall of Eblis.' Publ. in
  book form, Boston, MA: Osgood, 1872.

'Proverbs.' *Blackwood's Edinburgh Magazine* 88 (Oct 1860): 472–484 at
  477, 479. Fables such as *Vathek* where 'men are the actors as well as the
  scholars'.

[Thackeray, William Makepeace.] 'A Roundabout Journey: Notes of a
  Week's Holiday.' *Cornhill Magazine* 2 (Nov 1860): 623–640 at 639.
  Marble hall in palace in Amsterdam as frightening as any in *Vathek*.

'Roundabout Papers (No. XVI): On Two Roundabout Papers which I Intended to Write.' *Cornhill Magazine* 4 (Sept 1861): 377–384 at 377. The 'dusky realms of Eblis'.

Dramatisations & Events

Beckford. Stylites Film Group, Kingswood School, Bath. ½ hour. 1967
  Bayne, Jo. 'Boys make a film on a writer whose wild parties shocked Bath.' *Bath & Wilts Evening Chronicle*, 8 Nov 1967, 6.
  'Beckford.' Cast: William Beckford – Mark Goodridge; Script and Research – Alan Charles Scott; Direction – Andrew Barnett. *Kingswood School Magazine*, Jan 1968, 25.
  Greeves, Adrian. 'Beckford's 8mm ID.' *Kingswood School Magazine*, Jan 1968, 25–26. Impressions of making the film. Photo of Mark Goodridge as William Beckford, 27.

The Caliph of Fonthill. Radio play, 1940 & 1944
  Constanduros, Denis. *The Caliph of Fonthill*. BBC Home Service, 10.15–10.45 pm, 9 Sept 1940. With Robert Farquharson. Produced by Francis Dillon. *Radio Times*, 6 Sept 1940, 11. Woodcut of Fonthill Abbey by Eric Fraser.
  Play repeated 10.45–11.15 pm, 2 May 1944. With Dennis Arundell. Produced by Peter Watts. *Radio Times*, 28 April 1944, 10. Reduced & cropped version of Eric Fraser's woodcut. Also paragraph in Editorial, 1.

The Romantic Sickness. Radio play, 1978
  Constanduros, Denis. *The Romantic Sickness*. BBC Radio 4, 8.45–9.30 pm, 30 May 1978. With David Collings.

William Beckford. Radio play, France 1991
  Estebe, Françoise. *William Beckford*. France Culture, 9 & 12 Dec 1991. With Bernard Sichère, Gerard Julien Salvy & Didier Girard. 2 hours.

Waking Thoughts. Play first staged by Tagus Theatre at the Teatro Taborda, Lisbon, 4 & 5 Aug 1998, and at the Rondo Theatre, Bath, 31 March & 1 April 2000. About the Anglo-Portuguese friendship between Beckford & Gregorio Franchi.
  Hanson, Christopher. 'The tower of love.' The story behind the play. *Bath Chronicle. Bath Time*, 29 March 2000, 8.
  Saffell, Michael. 'Towering success.' Review. *Bath Chronicle*, 3 April 2000, 13.
  Weightman, Jonathan. 'Staging Beckford: *The Theatre of Place and the Theatre of Self*.' *Beckford Journal* 6 (2000): 50–57.
  Wiltshire, Paul. 'Toupee or not toupee.' *Bath Chronicle*, 3 April 2000, 17. Wigs for *Waking Thoughts*.

Pageant of Beckford's life at Fonthill. 15 June 1986
> William Beckford. A Pageant of his life at Fonthill. Sunday 15 June at
> Fonthill Old Abbey. Programme. Fonthill, 1986. 8 pp. The pageant, in
> aid of Salisbury Cathedral Spire Appeal, was written and directed by
> Norah Sheard.
>
> REVIEW. Girard, Didier. ' "Delineations" on the Fonthill Pageant',
> *Beckford Tower Trust Newsletter*, Spring 1987, 2–3.

Reviews of 'The Slavery Business: Sugar Dynasty', transmitted on Channel 4
television, 10 Aug 2005, 9–10 pm.
> Delingpole, James. 'Crash landing.' *Spectator*, 13 Aug 2005, 44.
>
> Hanks, Robert. 'Not such a sweet story.' *The Independent*, 11 Aug 2005,
> 48.
>
> Johns, Ian. 'How long will you be able to stay Lost? *The Times T2*, 11
> Aug 2005, 27.
>
> Woodward, Antony. 'Treats among the repeats.' *Country Life*, 11 Aug
> 2005, 71.
>
> Woolgar, Gabi. 'From slaves to fortune.' *Bath Chronicle 7 days*, 6 Aug 2005,
> 4–5. General account prompted by Channel 4 television programme.

See also '6. Beckford's Tower and Bath. 1966 Bath Festival, June 15–26'

WORKS INFLUENCED BY *VATHEK*
Prose Fiction, Poetry and Drama

Brulart de Genlis, Stéphanie Félicité. Marchioness de Sillery. '*Vathek,
Comédie en deux actes.*' In *Théâtre à l'usage des jeunes personnes.* (Also
known as *Théâtre d'éducation.*) 4 vols. Paris: Panckoucke, 1779–1780.
Reprinted, 4 vols., Paris: Lambert & Baudouin, 1781, 3:91–149. 'Le
Théâtre représente l'intérieur d'une des salles du Palais.', 95. English
trans. by Thomas Holcroft, *Theatre of Education,* 4 vols, London: T.
Cadell & P. Elmsly; T. Durham, 1781. Reissued in *The Beauties of Genlis,*
151–190. Perth: Morison, 1787. German & Italian trans. of *Théâtre* in
1780, and Dutch in 1786–1788. (See Millington in '12. *Vathek* and *The
Episodes*: Criticism'.)
Byron, Lord George Gordon. *Manfred* (1817), etc. (See '4. Contem-
poraries'.)
Corelli, Marie. *Ardath. The Story of a Dead Self.* 3 vols. London: Richard
Bentley, 1889.
Cornwall, Barry. [Bryan Waller Procter, pseud.] 'The Hall of Eblis.' In *The
Poetical Works of Milman, Bowles, Wilson, and Barry Cornwall*, part 4,
167–168. 4 parts in one. Paris: Galignani, 1829. 130-line poem. Also
Bowles's poem on Fonthill, part 2, 180. (See Jantzen in '12. *Vathek* and
The Episodes: Criticism'.)

Disraeli, Benjamin. *The Wondrous Tale of Alroy*. 3 vols. London: Saunders & Otley, 1833. Also *Contarini Fleming* (1832). (See '4. Contemporaries' and 'Other Fiction, Poems and Sketches' above.)

Doyle, Sir Arthur Conan. *The Hound of the Baskervilles* (1902). (See Hoerr in '15. Literary Studies. Articles'.)

Faulkner, William. *Absalom, Absalom!* (1936). (See DeVoto in '12. *Vathek* and *The Episodes*: Criticism'.)

Genlis, Madame de. See Brulart de Genlis above.

Gide, André. *Le voyage d'Urien* (1893). (See Mouret in '12. *Vathek* and *The Episodes*: Criticism'.)

Hawthorne, Nathaniel. *The Scarlet Letter* (1850) and *Fanshawe* (1826) (See Luedtke in '4. Contemporaries. Southey'.)

Keats, John. *Hyperion* (1820), etc. (See Gittings, Keats, Varma in '12. *Vathek* and *The Episodes*: Criticism. Books' and Hollingsworth in '12. *Vathek* and *The Episodes*: Criticism. Articles'.)

Knight, Charles [under pseud. Pendragon]. 'An Unpublished Episode of Vathek.' *Knight's Quarterly Magazine* 1 no. 2 (Oct 1823); 309–314. A parody of *Vathek* at the time of the 1823 Fonthill sale. Reprinted with minor alterations in his *Once Upon a Time*, 2 vols., London: John Murray, 1854, 2:220–230. Also in *Weekly Entertainer; and West of England Miscellany* n.s. 9 (23 Feb 1824): 108–112 and Gemmett, *Beckford's Fonthill* (2003), 294–301. (See Knight in '5. Fonthill. 1823 and Phillips's Sale'.)

ADVERT. List of contents in *Literary Gazette* 7 (4 Oct 1823): 640.

Lamb, Lady Caroline. *Ada Reis* (1823). (See Douglass in '12. *Vathek* and *The Episodes*: Criticism. Books' and 'Noctes Ambrosianæ No. VIII' in '12. *Vathek* and *The Episodes*: Criticism. Articles'.)

Lovecraft, H. P *The Dream-Quest of Unknown Kadath* (completed 1927), etc. (See Cannon, Joshi in '12. *Vathek* and *The Episodes*: Criticism'.)

MacMahon, George Yeilding. 'Vathek.' In *Vathek, A Dramatic Poem; The Dream of the Captive City, and Other Poems*, 1–97. London: J. F. Hope, 1859. 'The following poem is founded on the "Vathek" of Beckford; but the incidents of that tale have been made use of, or rejected, as suited the purpose of the author. In particular, the catastrophe in the third Act will be found to present an entirely different scene from the "Hall of Eblis."' Act 1, 'Neighbourhood of Samarah – Palace of Vathek', 1–18. Act 2, 'Neighbourhood of Samarah – Then Samarah', 19–46. Act 3, 'Persia, Vale of Fakreddin – Istakar – Infinite space', 47–97. (See Millington in '12. *Vathek* and *The Episodes*: Criticism'.)

Melville, Herman. 'The Bell Tower' (1855). (See Punter in '12. *Vathek* and *The Episodes*: Criticism'.)

Meredith, George. *The Shaving of Shagpat*. Intro. Lin Carter. New York: Ballantine Books, 1970. (1st ed. 1855.) Successor to *Vathek*, vii–x. (See Eliot in '12. *Vathek* and *The Episodes*: Criticism'.)

Moore, Thomas. *Lalla Rookh* (1817). (See '4. Contemporaries'. See also Legouis & Cazamian in '12. *Vathek* and *The Episodes*: Criticism. Books' and Brown in '12. *Vathek* and *The Episodes*: Criticism. Articles'.)

Poe, Edgar Allan. *Al Aaraaf* (1829), etc. (See Poe in '12. *Vathek* and *The Episodes*: Criticism. Books'. See also Kidwai & Newey, Tinter in '12. *Vathek* and *The Episodes*: Criticism. Articles' and Poe in '15. Literary Studies'.)

Smith, Clark Ashton. 'The Story of the Princess Zulkais and the Prince Kalilah.' *Leaves* (Leavenworth, Kansas) 1st issue (Summer 1937): 1–20. Reprinted in *The Abominations of Yondo*, Sauk City, WI: Arkhàm House, 1960, 177–222. Also London: Neville Spearman, 1972, 177–222 & London: Panther, 1974, 188–235. The Third Episode of *Vathek* by William Beckford & Clark Ashton Smith (1893–1961). Also reprinted in Lin Carter, ed., *New Worlds for Old*, New York: Ballantine, 1971, as 'Zulkais and Kalilah' ['by William Beckford (translated by Clark Ashton Smith)'], 3–57. Trans. as 'Historia de la Princesa Zulkaïs y el Príncipe Kalilah' by José María Nebreda, Madrid: Valdemar, 1999. Smith added about 4000 words to end the tale. See also *Selected Letters of Clark Ashton Smith*, ed. David E. Schultz & Scott Connors, Sauk City, WI: Arkham House, 2003. In 1932 H. P. Lovecraft lent Smith the *Episodes* and suggested he conclude the third; his pleasure in doing so, and his submission of the completed work to Farnsworth Wright, editor of *Weird Tales*, who declined to publish it, 188–191, 195, 199. Smith read *Vathek* at age 15 (1908) and its influence on his juvenile writing, xvi, 249, 359, 371. (See Moore in '12. *Vathek* and *The Episodes*: Criticism'.)

Southey, Robert. *Thalaba the Destroyer* (1801) and *The Curse of Kehama* (1810). (See '4. Contemporaries'.)

V., A. [Richard Gough.] 'The Palace of Istaker.' *Gentleman's Magazine* 60 pt. 1 (Jan, Feb, March 1790): 69–70, 163–165, 258–259. The latter part of *Vathek* in verse, 4¾ pp. Reprinted in Robert J. Gemmett, *William Beckford* (1977), 149–158.

[Wallace, Horace Binney.] *Stanley; or the Recollections of a Man of the World.* 2 vols. Philadelphia: Lea & Blanchard, 1838. Byron's spirit was 'like the form of Eblis, in Beckford's marvellous creation', 1:123. (See Poe in '12. *Vathek* and *The Episodes*: Criticism'.)

Visual and Performance Arts
(See also '8. The Collection. Paintings and Drawings')

Branco, Luís de Freitas. *Vathek.* 1913. Symphonic poem first performed in Lisbon in 1950.

Cork, Richard. 'Rip it up and start again.' *New Statesman*, 25 July 2005, 42–43 at 43. Review of 'Big Bang', an exhibition at the Pompidou Centre, including Cristina Inglésias's *Passage II*, inspired by an extract from Vathek, with Beckford's words stencilled on raffia mats.

Downes, William Howes. *John S. Sargent. His Life and Work*. London: Thornton Butterworth, 1926. 'Princess Nouronihar', oil on canvas, 22¼ × 28 inches, *c*.1910, 236. Depicting three women wrapped in identical cashmere shawls, asleep on a flower-dotted, mountain-ringed plateau, it was probably executed in the Simplon Pass. He and his companions were great enthusiasts of *Vathek* which they read on their Alpine holidays. Also noted in Richard Ormond, *John Singer Sargent: Paintings, drawings, watercolours*, London: Phaidon, 1970, p. 75.

Einstein, Carl. 'Nuronihar. Eine Pantomime für Frau Napierkowska.' *Die Aktion* (Berlin) 3 (1913): columns 1006–1017. (Trans. in *La Phalange*, Sept 1913.) Reprinted in *Werke. Carl Einstein*, ed. Rolf-Peter Baacke & Jens Kwasny, 1:173–183. 3 vols. Berlin: Medusa, 1980–1985. Dance pantomime in three scenes based on Nouronihar.

Millington, Jon. 'Suppressed Illustrations for Vathek.' *Beckford Tower Trust Newsletter*, Spring 1992, 14. Two etchings in Richard Garnett's ed., (1893) were omitted from the 1900 reissue and may have been suppressed.

'Music.' *Atlantic Monthly* 1 (Nov 1857): 125–128 at 126. 'The lovers of opera have something to look forward to in Boston . . . Our townsman, Mr. L. H. Southard, the composer of "The Scarlet Letter," has also written an Italian opera, on an oriental subject, with the title "Omano," the libretto by Signor Manetta, founded on Beckford's "Vathek." ' *Idem* (March 1858): 634–636 at 635–636. One-page review of performance of selections with piano accompaniment.

Parker, Horatio. *Vathek: Symphonic Poem*. Op. 56 (1903). 14 min 54 sec. Recorded in 'Music of America' series on Bridge Records (New Rochelle, NY) in 2003, with programme notes by Malcolm MacDowell

Pyke, Elizabeth. 'Carathis. Illustration to "Vathek".' In *The Chap Book. A Miscellany*. No. 40, ed. Harold Munro, 85. London: Jonathan Cape, 1925. Black and white linocut.

'A Scene from Vatheck. (Realized).' A caricature on the Corn Laws depicting politicians in Eastern dress kicking a ball. Lithograph, 24 × 36 cm. Signed ?HB. Publ. 22 Dec 1845 by Thos McLean, 26 Haymarket, London.

Ward, Alfred Charles. *Illustrated History of English Literature*. 3 vols. London: Longmans, 1953–1955. Richard Westall produced several illus. for *Vathek*, *c*.1795, and one of the three in the V&A is reproduce, 3:32.

INCIDENTAL REFERENCES TO *VATHEK* OR THE HALL OF EBLIS

Broderip, W. J. 'Leaves from the Note-Book of a Naturalist. Part VI.' *Fraser's Magazine* 41 (June 1850): 654–666. Reference to Carathis and Vathek in remarks on camels. 'Leaves . . . Part VII.' *Idem* 42 (July 1850): 25–38. A huge crack in the ground which 'was not quite so big as the gulf into which Vathek tumbled the fair boys whom he offered to the insatiate Giaour'. Both reprinted in *Littell's Living Age* 26 (17 Aug & 21 Sept 1850): 307–315 at 311 & 548–557 at 549. Reprinted in book form, London: Parker, 1858.

[Bryce, James.] 'The Polish Alps.' *Cornhill Magazine* 39 (Feb 1879): 213–230 at 218. Thoughts of 'the Hall of Eblis in "Vathek," '. Reprinted in *Littell's Living Age* 140 (8 March 1879): 606.

A Chess-player. [George Walker, pseud.] 'The Café de la Régence.' *Fraser's Magazine* 22 (Dec 1840): 669–683 at 676. Chess amateurs wandering about the metropolis, like the condemned in Vathek's Hall of Eblis.

Cobbe, Francis Power. 'The Little Health of Ladies.' *Contemporary Review* 31 (Jan 1878): 276–296 at 292–293. The 'follies of luxury and fashion have gone on in a sort of *crescendo* like the descent of Vathek into the Hall of Eblis'. Reprinted in *Littell's Living Age* 136 (2 Feb 1878): 312.

Edwards, Matilda Barbara Betham. *The Roof of France; or, the Causses of the Lozère*. London: Bentley, 1889. 'Soon straight before us . . . rises the Causse Noir—dark, formidable, portentous as the rock of Istakhar keeping sentinel over the dread Hall of Ebliss', 71.

Fowler, Frank. *Southern Lights and Shadows. Being Brief Notes of Three Years' Experience of Social, Literary, and Political Life*. London: Sampson Low, 1859. Dreaming 'of the *Inferno* or Beckford's Hall of Eblis', 43.

Furniss, Louise E. 'What's in a Name?' *Harper's New Monthly Magazine* 28 (Dec 1863): 95–101 at 98. Bran the Blessed, who 'like Carathis in the palace of Eblis, . . . revolves in a whirl of the wildest fiction'.

Galton, Francis. *Inquiries into Human Faculty and Its Development*. London: Dent, 1907. (1st ed. 1883.) Inmates at Hanwell Asylum conjured up 'a scene like that fabled in Vathek's hall of Eblis', 46. Everyman edition.

'Ghosts of the Old and New School.' *National Review* (London). Reviewer of three new books mentioned a Glasgow rake 'condemned to the more orthodox hell . . . apparently fresh from the perusal of *Vathek*'. Reprinted in *Littell's Living Age* 58 (14 Aug 1857): 483–506 at 501.

Gilfillan, George. 'James Montgomery.' *Tait's Edinburgh Magazine* n.s. 13 (Sept 1846): 545–548. A 'supper in Eblis'. Reprinted in *Littell's Living Age* 11 (10 Oct 1846): 57–60 at 59, and in his *A Second Gallery of Literary Portraits*, Edinburgh: William Tait, 1850.

Kipling, Rudyard. *The Giridih Coal-Fields*. In *From Sea to Sea and Other Sketches. Letters of Travel*, 2:315, 317. 2 vols. London: Macmillan, 1904. (1st ed. 1900.) A coal mine in eastern India is reminiscent of 'a great Hall of Eblis' in Ch. 2, 'In The Depths'.

Lee, Vernon. 'An English Writer's Note Book on England.' *Atlantic Monthly* 84 (Jan 1872): 90–105 at 103. 'In the blue darkness stands out the great ribbed huge hall-of-Eblis palace [the Crystal Palace], made of beams of moonlight'.

'The Mauvaises Terres of Nebraska.' *National Era* (Washington D.C.). 'The grim background of the Black Mountains – a scene to remind one of the ruinous stony halls of Istakar, through the portals of which the mad Caliph in Vathek sought the presence of the infernal deities.' Reprinted in *Littell's Living Age* 39 (8 Oct 1853): 110–111 at 110.

Meyers, Francis. 'The Jenolan Caves.' In *Picturesque Atlas of Australasia*, ed. Andrew Garran. Sydney: Picturesque Atlas Publ. Co., [1886]. One of the five caves, the Grand Arch, likened to the Hall of Eblis, 149–154 at 150. In 'Descriptive Sketch of New South Wales'.

Noel, Roden. 'Sark and its Caves.' *Gentleman's Magazine* 243 (Sept 1878): 273–287 at 280. '. . . a long grand granite staircase suggesting the "Arabian Nights" or "Vathek,".' Reprinted in *Littell's Living Age* 139 (12 Oct 1878): 120.

[Pollock, W. Frederick.] 'Buckle's History of Civilization in England.' *Quarterly Review* 104 (July 1858): 38–74 at 69. Individuals carrying awful secrets 'as the multitude in Vathek's Hall of Eblis did their own hearts.' Reprinted in *Littell's Living Age* 58 (28 Aug 1858): 685.

[Reeve, Henry.] 'Count Beugnot's Memoirs.' *Edinburgh Review* 125 (April 1867): 303–331 at 314. Madame Roland pictured 'in that hall of Eblis'. Reprinted in *Littell's Living Age* 93 (25 May 1867): 488.

Tennyson. 'Alfred Tennyson.' *Portrait Gallery* (not traced). 'You are scanning with the wonder of Vathek the thousand-throned hall of Eblis'. Reprinted in *Littell's Living Age* 62 (23 July 1859): 195–201 at 196.

Turner, Frederick J. 'The Problem of the West.' *Atlantic Monthly* 78 (Sept 1896): 289–297 at 292. 'The West of our own day reminds Mr. Bryce "of the crowd which Vathek found in the hall of Eblis, each darting hither and thither".'

17. Bibliographies

Full-length Study

Chapman, Guy, with John Hodgkin. *A Bibliography of William Beckford of Fonthill*. Ed. Michael Sadleir [Sadler]. London: Constable, 1930. xxii, 128 pp. 16 pl. Publ. books, 3–78. Attributed works, 81–89. Unpubl. prose writings, 93–101. Verses, 105–106. Music, 109–111. Portraits, 115–119. Appendix: Vathek, 121–128. Limited to 500 copies. Bibliographia No. 2. An indispensable and wholly admirable bibliography covering works publ. in Beckford's lifetime, with full collations and collotype facsimiles of the principal title pages. Reprinted, Folcroft, PA: Folcroft Library Editions, 1974 & Mansfield Centre, CT: Martino Publishing, 2001.

REVIEWS. *Dublin Magazine* 6 (Jan–March 1931): 47.

Gathorne-Hardy, R. E. 'The Books of Beckford.' *The Book-Collector's Quarterly* No. 1 (Dec 1930–Feb 1931): 59–63.

H., J. [Hayward, John.] *Life and Letters* 5 no. 31 (Dec 1930): 451–452. With a review of *The Vision & Liber Veritatis* (1930), 449–451.

Jean-Aubry, G. 'Beckford ou l'ermite de Fonthill.' *Revue de Paris*, 15 Sept 1931, 348–371.

King, William. *The Criterion* 10 no. 39 (Jan 1931): 369–371, reprinted 1967. With a review of *The Vision & Liber Veritatis* (1930).

P[ollard], A. W. *The Library* 4th Series 11 (1930): 386–387.

Times Literary Supplement, 4 Dec 1930, 1034.

Wiltshire Archæological and Natural History Magazine 47 (June 1935): 153–154.

Books (some entries have already appeared in the relevant sections)

Anderson, John. *The Book of British Topography*. London: Satchell, 1881. Fonthill Abbey (7 entries), 300. Bath, 252–254.

Bath. *A Select list of books on Bath*. Bath Municipal Libraries, 1971. 16 pp. Under 'Biographies': Brockman (1956) & Lansdown (1893).

Bath Architecture and Planning. Books and Articles 1900–1972. Rev. ed. Bath Municipal Libraries, 1972. [12] pp. *Idem, 1900–1974*. Bath: Avon County Library, *c*.1974. [15] pp. Both list Hugh Crallan's 'Beckford in Bath', *Architectural Review* 143 (March 1968): 204–208.

Bath Guides, Directories and Newspapers. Bath Municipal Libraries, 1969. [23] pp. 2nd ed., 1973. Helpful list of guides to Bath.

'Bibliographie Sommaire.' In *Argenteries. Le Trésor du National Trust for Scotland / Shatten in Zilver. Topstukken van de National Trust for Scotland*, 188–190. Brussels: National Trust for Scotland, 1992. Exhibition catalogue.

Block, Andrew. *The English Novel 1740–1850. A Catalogue* . . . London: Grafton, 1939. *Vathek, Azemia, Modern Novel Writing, The Story of Al Raoui*, 18–19. Entry unchanged in new rev. ed., London: Dawsons, 1961, p. 18.

British Library General Catalogue of Printed Books to 1975. London: Saur, 1984. Peter Beckford (21 entries), 512. Alderman Beckford (5 entries), 512. William Beckford of Somerley (4 entries), 513. William Beckford (108 entries), 513–516. Fonthill Abbey (8 entries), 155.

Conlon, Pierre M. *Le Siècle des Lumières. Bibliographie chronologique. Tome XXII. 1786–1787*. Geneva: Droz, 2003. *Vathek*, Lausanne (1787) & Paris (1791), 345 (Entry no. 87: 1397).

Cox, Michael, ed. 'Beckford, William.' In *A Dictionary of Writers and their Works*, 29. Oxford: Oxford University Press, 2001. *Dreams, Vathek, Modern Novel Writing, Azemia, Al Raoui, Italy & Recollections*. Also *Vathek*, 593.

Crane, Ronald S. et al. *English Literature 1660–1800. A Bibliography of Modern Studies compiled for Philological Quarterly*. Princeton: Princeton University Press. Vol. 1, 1926–1938 (1950): 61, 145, 187, 239, 326, 363, 443, 467, 544. Vol. 2, 1939–1950 (1952): 612, 683, 841, 937. Vol. 3, 1951–1956 (1962): 181, 208, 290, 389, 506. Vol. 4, 1957–1960 (1962): 627, 756, 859, 976, 1006. Vol. 5, 1961–1965 (1972): 46, 171, 294, 410, 523. Vol. 6, 1966–1970 (1972): 621, 730, 850, 994. Notes from the *Philological Quarterly* on new works and reviews of them. Page numbers refer to those at the foot of the page.

Desmond, Ray. *Bibliography of British Gardeners*. Winchester: St. Paul's Bibliographies, 1984. Fonthill Abbey, 126–127. Fonthill House, 127. Beckford's Tower, 283.

Dobell, Bertram. *Catalogue of Books Printed for Private Circulation*. London: The Author, 1906. Henry Venn Lansdown's *Recollections* (1893), 8. 'I know of no work which give so vivid a picture of William Beckford, and of the wonderful contents of his two residences, as the present small book.'

Elkins, A. C., Jr. & L. J. Forstner. *The Romantic Movement Bibliography 1936–1970. A Master Cumulation from English Literary History, Philological Quarterly and English Language Notes*. 7 vols. Ann Arbor, Michigan: Pierian Press, 1973. *English Literary History*, 1:44. *Philological Quarterly*, 2:666, 3:1004, 3:1091, 4:1494, 4:1583. *English Language Notes*, 4:1771, 5:1920, 5:2054, 5:2081, 5:2307, 6:2506.

Farrell, John T. *A Reinterpretation of the Major Literary Works of William*

Beckford. Ann Arbor, Michigan: University Microfilms, 1984. Pp. 185–200.

Fisher, Benjamin Franklin. 'Beckford, William (1760–1844): British.' In *The Gothic's Gothic: Study Aids to the Tradition of the Tale of Terror*, 9–16 (items 41–85). New York: Garland, 1988. Further mentions: Beckford, 38 items; *Azemia*, 1 item; *Vathek*, 32 items.

Forster, Antonia. *Index to Book Reviews in England 1775–1800*. London: British Library, 1997. *Vathek* (1786), *Popular Tales of the Germans* (1791), *Modern Novel Writing* (1796 [?1795]) & *Azemia* (1797), pp. 27–28 (Nos. 258–261).

Frank, Frederick S. 'William Beckford.' In *Guide to the Gothic: An Annotated Bibliography of Criticism*, 50–65. Metuchen, NJ: Scarecrow Press, 1984.

Frank, Frederick S. *The First Gothics: A Critical Guide to the English Gothic Novel*. New York: Garland, 1987. Pp. 23–27.

Frank, Frederick S. 'William Beckford.' In *Gothic Fiction: A Master List of Twentieth Century Criticism and Research*, 18–25. Westport, CT: Meckler, 1988.

Frank, Frederick S. 'A Checklist of *Vathek* Criticism.' In *Vathek & The Escape from Time. Bicentenary Revaluations*, ed. Kenneth W. Graham, 247–268. New York: AMS Press, 1990. 159 entries.

Gemmett, Robert J. *William Beckford and the picturesque: a study of Fonthill*. Ann Arbor, Michigan: University Microfilms, 1967. Beckford's gardening books, 252–256. Beckford's works, 265–280. Books, 281–291. Manuscripts, 291–293. Articles, 293–301. Other works consulted, 302–306.

Goddard, Rev. E. H. 'Fonthill Gifford.' In *A Wiltshire Bibliography*, 117–119. [Salisbury, Wilts]: Wilts Education Committee, 1929. Fonthill Abbey, 22 entries. Fonthill House, 9 entries. Biography and Genealogy, 16 entries. Copies of Goddard's typescript updated with more recent entries are in the libraries of the Society of Antiquaries, London, and the Wiltshire Archaeological and Natural History Society, Devizes.

Green, David Bonnell & Edwin Graves Wilson. *Keats, Shelley, Byron, Hunt, and Their Circles: A Bibliography* [of the *Keats-Shelley Journal*]. Lincoln: University of Nebraska. Vols. 1–12, July 1, 1950–June 30, 1962, (1964). 5:107, 11:184, 12:168, 169, 187 & 281. Vols. 13–25, July 1, 1962–June 30, 1974, (1978). 14:95, 17:251, 18:242 & 400, 20:193.

Green, Emanuel. *Bibliotheca Somersetensis*. 3 vols. Taunton, Somerset: Barnicott & Pearce, 1902. Vol. 1 (Bath books). Britton (1823), English's Sale cat. (1845) & Redding's *Memoirs* (1859) listed, 62.

Green, Rosemary. *A Bibliography of Printed Works Relating to Wiltshire 1920–1960*. Trowbridge, Wilts: Wiltshire . . . Library & Museum Service, 1975. Fonthill Bishop, two entries, 93–94; Fonthill Gifford, three entries, 94.

Grimsditch, Herbert B. 'William Beckford.' In *Cambridge Bibliography of English Literature*, ed. F. W. Bateson, 2:528–529. 4 vols. Cambridge: Cambridge University Press, 1940. *Idem. Supplement*, ed. George Watson, Publ. 1957. Seven entries, 455.

Gulbenkian Foundation. *Biblioteca Geral VI. Catálogos. Fundo British Council*. Lisbon: Fundação Calouste Gulbenkian, 1984. Nine of Beckford's works, 42.

Halkett, Samuel & John Laing. *A Dictionary of the Anonymous and Pseudonymous Literature of Great Britain*. 4 vols. Edinburgh: William Paterson, 1882–1886. Numbers refer to columns. Vol. 1 (1882): *Arabian Tale*, 166; *Azemia*, 206; *Biographical Memoirs*, 236; *Dreams*, 706; *Epitaphs*, 787. Vol. 2 (1883): *Italy*, 1257; *Modern Novel Writing*, 1642. Vol. 3 (1885): *Popular Tales*, 1975; *Recollections*, 2099; *Story of Al Raoui*, 2498. All these also in James Kennedy et al., eds. Rev. ed. 7 vols. Edinburgh: Oliver & Boyd, 1934. Beckford one of nine 'Viators', 7:570.

Harris, John. *A Country House Index*. Shalfleet Manor, Isle of Wight: Pinhorns, 1971. Works depicting Fonthill House (2) & Abbey (2), 12. List of eight guide books to the Abbey: Storer (1812), Rutter *Description* (1822) & *New Descriptive Guide* (1823), Weale *Fonthill Abbey* (1822) [not traced], Whittaker *New Guide* (1822), Rutter *Delineations* (1823), Britton (1823) & Nichols (1836), 38. 2nd ed., 1979.

Hoare. *Catalogue of the Hoare Library at Stourhead, Co. Wilts*. Privately printed, 1840. Lists several Fonthill sales catalogues and the main 1822–1823 guide books on the Abbey.

Holmes, Michael. *The Country House Described. An index to the Country Houses of Great Britain and Ireland*. Winchester: St Paul's Bibliographies in association with the Victoria and Albert Museum, 1986. 'Fonthill Abbey', 14 entries & 'Fonthill House', 4 entries, 104. 'Lansdown Tower', 3 entries, 157. Guide to works in the National Art Library at the V&A.

Howard-Hill, T. H. *Bibliography of British Literary Bibliographies*. Oxford: Clarendon Press, 1969. Five entries: Chapman & Hodgkin (1930); Parreaux (*The Monk*, 1960); Gotlieb (1960); Bishop (1966), 355; Gemmett (Checklist, 1967). 2nd ed., 1987. Gemmett (Addenda, 1967) added & Parreaux removed.

Humphreys, Arthur L. *A Handbook to County Bibliography*. London: 187 Piccadilly, 1917. Bath, 233–235. Wiltshire, 277–286.

Laidler, John. *Lisbon*. Oxford: Clio Press, 1997. Items 6, 233, 375, 381 on pp. 2, 63, 104, 105. Sintra, Items 90, 93 on pp. 24, 25. World Bibliographical Series, vol. 199.

Lowndes, William Thomas. 'Beckford, William (of Fonthill).' In *The Bibliographer's Manual of English Literature*, 1:142. New ed. 6 vols. London: Bell, 1890. (1st ed. 1834.) Lists, with comments and sale prices, *Biographical Memoirs* (1780) and *Vathek* (1786). *Italy* (1834) and *Recollections*

(1835) were also noted. (Identical to entry in Bohn's 1857 ed.) Fonthill guide books: Britton (1823), 1:278; Neale (1824), 3:1656; Nichols (1836), 3:1686; Rutter, *Descriptive Guide* (1823) & *Delineations* (1823), 4:2159; Storer (1812), 5:2522 (also under Fonthill, 2:815).

Mazzeno, Laurence W. *The British Novel 1680–1832: An Annotated Bibliography*. Lanham, MD: The Scarecrow Press, Inc. & Salem Press, 1997. 'General studies', five entries & *Vathek*, five entries, 55–57. Magill Bibliographies.

McNutt, Dan J. *The Eighteenth Century Gothic Novel: An Annotated Bibliography of Criticism and Selected Texts*. Folkestone, Kent: Dawson (Garland Publishing), 1975. Selected works, 265–270. Bibliographies, 270–271. Full-length studies, 271–276. Articles in English, 276–301. Books, 301–304. Early reviews, 304–310. Foreign language articles, 314–315.

[Millington, Jon.] 'Bibliography.' In *William Beckford Exhibition 1976*, [ed. Julian Berry], 96–98. Tisbury, Wilts: Compton Press, 1976.

Millington, Jon. 'Bibliography.' In *William Beckford, 1760–1844: An Eye for the Magnificent*, ed. Derek E. Ostergard, 438–448. New Haven & London: Yale University Press for the Bard Graduate Center, 2001. Exhibition catalogue. The present bibliography is a greatly revised and expanded version of this.

National Union Catalog. Pre-1956 Imprints. London: Mansell, 1969. Peter Beckford, 42:477–478. Alderman Beckford, 42:478. William Beckford, 42:478–485. William Beckford of Somerley, 42:485–486. *Idem*, (1971). Fonthill Abbey, 177:222. *Idem, Supplement*, (1980). Beckford, 696:332–333. Fonthill, 724:517. *Idem, 1956–1967*, Totowa, NJ: Rowman & Littlefield, 1970. Beckford, 10:10–6 (the page number).

Nineteenth Century Short Title Catalogue. Series I Phase I. 1801–1815. 6 vols. Newcastle-upon-Tyne: Avero, 1984–1986. 4 entries, 1:123. *Idem. Series II Phase I. 1816–1870*. 56 vols. 1986–1995. 'Alcobaça', 1 entry, 1:272. 'Beckford, William Thomas', 22 entries, 3:292–293. 'Fonthill Abbey', 6 entries, 14:533. 'Italy', 1 entry, 21:305. 'Memoirs [of Painters]', 1 entry, 27:404. 'Vathek', 3 entries, 41:261.

Palau y Dulcet, Antonio. *Manual del Librero Hispano-americano Bibliografía General* . . . 2nd ed. 28 vols. Barcelona: Librería Anticuaria de A. Palau, 1948–1977. Five entries, 2 (1949): 132.

Parreaux, André. *William Beckford, Auteur de Vathek*. Paris: Nizet, 1960. 'Bibliographie Sommaire', 543–563. Part 1. Beckford's Works: Printed works, 543–549; Manuscripts, 551–552. Part 2. Works relating to Beckford: Printed works, 553–561; Manuscripts, 561; Articles, 561–563.

Parreaux, André. 'William Beckford.' In *The New Cambridge Bibliography of English Literature, Vol. 2, 1660–1800*, ed. George Watson, columns 973–976. 5 vols. Cambridge: Cambridge University Press, 1969–1977.

Vol. 2 (1971): Bibliographies, 973; Works, 973–974; Biographies, etc, 974–976. *Vathek*: in French, 145; in German, 182. Works on Italy, 195. Continental travels, 1426. Vol. 3 (1969), 1800–1900: Three entries, 92. *Italy* (1834), 1679.

Pires, Maria Laura Bettencourt. *William Beckford e Portugal*. Lisbon: Edições 70, 1987. 'Bibliografia Seleccionada', 271–283.

Pires, Maria Laura Bettencourt. 'William Beckford Bibliography.' In *Exposição. Exhibition. A Viagem de Uma Paixão. William Beckford & Portugal. An Impassioned Journey. 1787 1794 1798*. 'Manuscripts (Beckford Archive)', 84. 'Published Works', 84–85. Palácio de Queluz: Instituto Português do Património Cultural, 1987. Exhibition catalogue. [Pires, Maria Laura Bettencourt.] 'General Bibliography.' *Idem*, 197–198.

Quérard, Joseph-Marie. *La France littéraire, ou dictionnaire bibliographique des savants, historiens et gens de letters de la France aussi que des littérateurs étrangers qui ont écrit en Français, plus particulièrement pendant les XVIIIe et XIXe siècles*. 12 vols. Paris: Firmin Didot, etc, 1827–1839. 'Beckford (W).' 1:250, *Vathek*, 1786, 1791, 1819 eds. 'Ouvrage fort estimé en Angleterre, et très peu connu en France'. Continued as *La littérature française contemporaine*. 6 vols. Paris: Daguin, 1827–1840. *Italy*, Baudry (1834) & *Vathek* (1835), 1:232.

Schimmelman, Janice G. *American Imprints on Art through 1865. An Annotated Bibliography*. Boston, MA: G. K. Hall, 1990.

Schlobin, Roger C. *The Literature of Fantasy*. New York: Garland, 1979. Items 82–85: *Vathek* (1786); Chapman, *Bibliography* (1930); Gemmett, 'Checklist', *PBSA* (1967); Graham, '*Vathek* in English and French', *Studies in Bibliography* (1975), 17–18.

Shum, Frederick. 'Beckford, William.' In *A Catalogue of Bath Books*, 25–27. Bath: S. W. Simms, 1913. 32 entries.

Spector, Robert Donald. *The English Gothic. A Bibliographic Guide to Writers from Horace Walpole to Mary Shelley*. Westport, CT: Greenwood Press, 1984. Literary biography, 170–194. Bibliography, 197–203.

Summers, Montague. *A Gothic Bibliography*. London: Fortune Press, 1940. Beckford, 20 entries, 8–9. *Vathek*, 41 entries, 544–545.

Tobin, James E. *Eighteenth Century English Literature and its Cultural Background*. New York: Fordham University Press, 1939. Nine entries, 71.

Unwin, P. T. H. *Portugal*. Oxford: Clio Press, 1987. Items 65–67 & 73–74 on pp. 17–18 & 19. World Bibliographical Series, vol. 71.

Upcott, William. *A Bibliographical Account of the Principal Works Relating to English Topography*. 3 vols. London: R. & A. Taylor, 1818. Storer's *Fonthill* (1812), 3:1312–1313.

Ward, William S. *Literary Reviews in British Periodicals 1798–1820. A Bibliography*. 2 vols. New York: Garland, 1972. Two reviews of *Vathek*, from *Augustan Review* (1815) & *Dublin Examiner* (1816), 1:151.

Articles

Finley, William K. *William Beckford Collection.* GEN MSS *102*. New Haven: Yale, 1991. 21 pp. Yale University Library, available on the Internet.

Gemmett, Robert J. 'An Annotated Checklist of the Works of William Beckford.' *Papers of the Bibliographical Society of America* 61 (Third Quarter 1967): 243–258. Comprehensive listing of all known editions of Beckford's works.

Gemmett, Robert J. 'William Beckford: Bibliographical Addenda.' *Bulletin of Bibliography* 25 no. 3 (1967): 62–64. Additions to Parreaux (1960).

Millington, Jon. 'Boyd Alexander's Works on Beckford.' *Beckford Tower Trust Newsletter*, Spring 1981, 6. Lists nineteen works. Also 'Boyd Alexander.' *Idem*, Spring 1987, 8. Three further works noted.

Millington, Jon. 'The Beckford Tower Trust Newsletter: Contents 1980–1994.' *Beckford Journal* 2 (1996): 64–67.

Millington, Jon. 'Editions of William Beckford's Works Published since 1967.' *Beckford Journal* 3 (1997): 45–52. Lists 74 works.

Parreaux, André. 'Beckford: bibliographie selective et critique.' *Bulletin de la Société d'Etudes Anglo-Américaines des* XVIIe *et* XVIIIe *Siècles* 3 (1976): 45–55.

Index

Rosati, Salvatore, 267, 268
Rose, Graham, 203
Rosebery, Archibald, 5th Earl of, 97
Rosebery, Lady Eva, 211
Rosenfeld, Sybil, 338
Ross, Angus, 348
Ross, E. Denison, 261
Ross, Marvin Chauncey, 230
Ross, Nicholas, 320
Rossington, Michael, 52
Roth, Georges, 305
Rothschild family, 216
Rouse, Brenda, 164, 174
Rousseau, André-Michel, 48, 50
Rousseau, George S., 59, 348
Roussel, Pierre-Joseph-Alexandre, d' Epinal, 318
Roux, Marius, 289
Rowse, Alfred Leslie, 317
Royal Institute of Chartered Surveyors / The Times Conservation Award, 173
Ruddick, William, 347
Rudé, George, 293
Rule, John, 69
Rushton, Andrée, 143, 358
Ruskin, John, 210
Russell, Constance, 69
Russell, Francis, 159, 246
Russell, Lord John, 91, 92
Russell, Lord William, later 1st Duke of Bedford, 78
Russell, William Clark, 38
Rutter, John, 41, 42, 92, 95, 108, 109, 110, 111, 118, 121, 123, 125, 135, 136, 138, 139, 141, 142, 143, 146, 147, 148, 149, 150, 152, 154, 155, 186, 199, 217, 238, 293, 349, 370, 371
Ryskamp, Charles, 68

S., C., 321
S., E. M. See Dallaway, Rev. James
S., H. P., 213
S., J., 23
S., L., 69
S., P. H., 159
S., R., 258, 261
S., W. H., 113
Sade, Marquis de, 53, 298
Sadie, Stanley, 338
Sadleir [Sadler], Michael, 52, 72, 352, 353, 367
Saffell, Michael, 360
Sage, Lorna, 60
Sage, Victor, 293
Saglia, Diego, 293, 351
Said, Edward W., 349
Saintsbury, George, 293

Salaman, Malcolm C., 52
Sales
  1801, Phillips, London, 106, 195, 232
  1802 Feb, Christie's, London, 106, 232
  1802 March, Christie's, London, 106, 232
  1804, Books & prints, Leigh, Sotheby, London, 208, 232
  1805, Christie's, London, 232
  1807, Building materials, Phillips, Fonthill, 107, 232
  1807, Phillips, Fonthill, 47, 85, 102, 107, 232
  1808, Books & prints, Leigh, Sotheby, London, 107, 208, 232
  1809, Paintings, Jeffrey's, Salisbury, 232
  1817, Books & drawings, Leigh, Sotheby, London, 107, 208, 232
  1817, Christie's, London, 232
  1822, Christie's, Fonthill, 17, 82, 108, 111, 116–122, 143, 161, 163, 218, 232, 354
  1823, Phillips, Fonthill, 17, 91, 116, 124–131, 141, 142, 143, 145, 204, 208, 211, 222, 229, 232, 243, 300, 357, 362
  1824, Phillips, London, 233
  1830, Drawings & prints, Sotheby's, London, 233
  1841, English & Fasana, Bath, 161, 165, 233
  1845, English & Son, Bath, 162, 165, 187, 204, 233, 369
  1847, Objects, Roussel, Paris, 233
  1848, English & Son, Bath, 162, 166, 233
  1882, Hamilton Palace Collection, Christie's, London, 78, 96, 205, 206, 207, 216, 222, 231, 232, 233
  1882–1883, Hamilton Palace, Beckford Library, Sotheby's, London, 66, 97, 208, 209, 211, 233
  1919, Portraits from Hamilton Palace, Christie's, London, 231, 233
  1919, Silver from Hamilton Palace, Christie's, London, 232
  1966, Clements library, Sotheby's, London, 40, 211, 233
  1971, Senhouse library, Sotheby's, London, 233
  1973, Beckford's library, Sotheby's, London, 233
  1973, Cozens sketch-books, Sotheby's, London, 225, 233
  1975, Lord Margadale, Christie's, London, 97, 212, 233
  1975, Rosebery library, Sotheby's, London, 212, 233

Index to Beckford's Writings

(including attributed and posthumous works)

List of Subscribers

Richard Allen and Edward Pope
Miles Bartley
Bath Central Library
Edward Bayntun-Coward
Beckford Tower Trust
Mrs A. L. Biddle
Michael and Philippa Bishop
Sidney Blackmore and David Wiltshire
Geoffrey Blum
Robert Borsje
S. Brinded
Jean-Daniel Candaux
Charles Cator
Graham Cave
Dr Laurent Châtel
Stephen Clarke
Mr A. W. Coombes
Michael G. Cousins
Dr Angela Delaforce
Lorna Darlington
Carlos Enrich
Andrew Fletcher
Miss Elanor Beckford Fraser
Robert J. Gemmett
Professor Dr Didier Girard
C. J. Glaser
Kenneth W. Graham
Paul Grinke
Luis Fernando Webb Henriques
Philip Hewat-Jaboor
James Hine
Keith A. Honess
Malcolm Jack
Simon Swynfen Jervis
David Laws

The Lewis Walpole Library, Yale University
Martin P. Levy
Dr Stephen Lloyd
Dr Alexander Marr
Diana Matthews-Duncan
Paul Mellon Centre for Studies in British Art
Valerie Merritt
Pat Millington
Steve Moore
Jerry Nolan
Pickering & Chatto Rare Books
Mrs Susan Rainbow
Dr E. V. R. Ratcliff
Peter Sabor
Salisbury and South Wiltshire Museum
Rose Sanguinetti
Adrian Sassoon
Roger & Susan Southgate
Judith E. Stanton
Peter-Ayers Tarantino
Veronica Watts
Arnold D. P. Wilson
Trevor Winkfield
Wiltshire Archaeological and Natural History Society
Min Wood